T0183502

Communications in Computer and Information Science   1612

Editorial Board Members

Joaquim Filipe ⓘ
Polytechnic Institute of Setúbal, Setúbal, Portugal

Ashish Ghosh
Indian Statistical Institute, Kolkata, India

Raquel Oliveira Prates ⓘ
Federal University of Minas Gerais (UFMG), Belo Horizonte, Brazil

Lizhu Zhou
Tsinghua University, Beijing, China

More information about this series at https://www.springer.com/bookseries/7899

...thias Jarke · Markus Helfert ·
Oleg Gusikhin (Eds.)

Smart Cities, Green Technologies, and Intelligent Transport Systems

10th International Conference, SMARTGREENS 2021
and 7th International Conference, VEHITS 2021
Virtual Event, April 28–30, 2021
Revised Selected Papers

 Springer

Editors
Cornel Klein
Siemens
Munich, Germany

Matthias Jarke
RWTH Aachen
Aachen, Germany

Markus Helfert
Maynooth University
Maynooth, Kildare, Ireland

Karsten Berns
Universität Kaiserslautern
Kaiserslautern, Germany

Oleg Gusikhin
Ford Research and Advanced Engineering
Dearborn, MI, USA

ISSN 1865-0929   ISSN 1865-0937 (electronic)
Communications in Computer and Information Science
ISBN 978-3-031-17097-3   ISBN 978-3-031-17098-0 (eBook)
https://doi.org/10.1007/978-3-031-17098-0

© Springer Nature Switzerland AG 2022
This work is subject to copyright. All rights are reserved by the Publisher, whether the whole or part of the material is concerned, specifically the rights of translation, reprinting, reuse of illustrations, recitation, broadcasting, reproduction on microfilms or in any other physical way, and transmission or information storage and retrieval, electronic adaptation, computer software, or by similar or dissimilar methodology now known or hereafter developed.
The use of general descriptive names, registered names, trademarks, service marks, etc. in this publication does not imply, even in the absence of a specific statement, that such names are exempt from the relevant protective laws and regulations and therefore free for general use.
The publisher, the authors, and the editors are safe to assume that the advice and information in this book are believed to be true and accurate at the date of publication. Neither the publisher nor the authors or the editors give a warranty, expressed or implied, with respect to the material contained herein or for any errors or omissions that may have been made. The publisher remains neutral with regard to jurisdictional claims in published maps and institutional affiliations.

This Springer imprint is published by the registered company Springer Nature Switzerland AG
The registered company address is: Gewerbestrasse 11, 6330 Cham, Switzerland

Preface

This book includes extended and revised versions of a set of selected papers from the 10th International Conference on Smart Cities and Green ICT Systems (SMARTGREENS 2021) and the 7th International Conference on Vehicle Technology and Intelligent Transport Systems (VEHITS 2021), held during April 28–30, 2021, as web-based events, due to the COVID-19 pandemic.

SMARTGREENS 2021 received 32 paper submissions from 14 countries, of which 28% were included in this book.

VEHITS 2021 received 108 paper submissions from 34 countries, of which 11% were included in this book.

The papers were selected by the event chairs and their selection was based on a number of criteria that included the classifications and comments provided by the Program Committee members, the session chairs' assessment, and also the program chairs' global view of all papers included in the technical program. The authors of selected papers were then invited to submit a revised and extended version of their papers having at least 30% innovative material.

The purpose of the 10th International Conference on Smart Cities and Green ICT Systems (SMARTGREENS 2021) was to bring together researchers, designers, developers, and practitioners interested in the advances and applications in this field of smart cities, green information and communication technologies, sustainability, and energy aware systems and technologies.

The purpose of the 7th International Conference on Vehicle Technology and Intelligent Transport Systems (VEHITS) was to bring together engineers, researchers, and practitioners interested in the advances and applications in this field. VEHITS focuses on innovative applications, tools, and platforms in all technology areas, such as signal processing, wireless communications, informatics, and electronics, related to different kinds of vehicles, including cars, off-road vehicles, trains, ships, underwater vehicles, or flying machines, and the intelligent transportation systems that connect and manage large numbers of vehicles, not only in the context of smart cities but also in many other application domains.

The papers selected to be included in this book contribute to the understanding of relevant trends of current research on smart cities, green ICT systems, vehicle technology, and intelligent transport systems including

- frameworks and services for energy-efficient smart cities and smart buildings under different climatic conditions and hazards such as strong rainfall or public safety threats, and
- intelligent and connected vehicles in combination with data analytics involving deep learning technologies, communication technologies, and others.

We would like to thank all the authors for their contributions and all the reviewers who have helped ensure the quality of this publication.

April 2021   Cornel Klein
                                                                    Matthias Jarke
                                                                    Markus Helfert
                                                                    Karsten Berns
                                                                    Oleg Gusikhin

Organization

SMARTGREENS Co-chairs

Matthias Jarke	RWTH Aachen, Germany
Markus Helfert	Maynooth University, Ireland

VEHITS Chair

Oleg Gusikhin	Ford Motor Company, USA

SMARTGREENS Program Chair

Cornel Klein	Siemens AG, Germany

VEHITS Program Co-chairs

Karsten Berns	University of Kaiserslautern, Germany
Markus Helfert	Maynooth University, Ireland

SMARTGREENS Program Committee

Javier M. Aguiar	Universidad de Valladolid, Spain
Laura Alcaide Muñoz	University of Granada, Spain
Mahmoud Amin	Manhattan College, USA
Carlos Antunes	University of Coimbra/INESC Coimbra, Portugal
Blanca Caminero	Universidad de Castilla-La Mancha, Spain
Ken Christensen	University of South Florida, USA
Chia-chi Chu	National Tsing Hua University, Taiwan, China
Georges Da Costa	IRIT, Paul Sabatier University, France
Wanyang Dai	Nanjing University, China
Cléver Ricardo de Farias	University of São Paulo, Brazil
Venizelos Efthymiou	University of Cyprus, Cyprus
Tullio Facchinetti	University of Pavia, Italy
Javier Faulin	Public University of Navarre, Spain
Ana Fernández Vilas	University of Vigo, Spain
Panos Fitsilis	University of Thessaly, Greece
Adrian Florea	Lucian Blaga University of Sibiu, Romania
Yoshikazu Fukuyama	Meiji University, Japan

Andre Gradvohl	State University of Campinas, Brazil
Adriana Grigorescu	National University of Political Studies and Public Administration, Romania
Kerry Hinton	University of Melbourne, Australia
Hartmut Hinz	Frankfurt University of Applied Sciences, Germany
Bo Jørgensen	University of Southern Denmark, Denmark
Jai Kang	Rochester Institute of Technology, USA
Stamatis Karnouskos	SAP, Germany
Nicos Komninos	Aristotle University of Thessaloniki, Greece
Mani Krishna	University of Massachusetts Amherst, USA
Zheng Ma	University of Southern Denmark, Denmark
Annapaola Marconi	Fondazione Bruno Kessler, Italy
Giaoutzi Maria	National Technical University of Athens, Greece
Majid Moazzami	Islamic Azad University, Najafabad Branch, Iran
Hazlie Mokhlis	University of Malaya, Malaysia
Fabio Mottola	University of Naples Federico II, Italy
Ali Nabavi	University of Toronto, Canada
Elsa Negre	Paris Dauphine University - PSL, France
Vitor Pires	Instituto Politécnico de Setúbal, Portugal
Philip Pong	New Jersey Institute of Technology, USA
Ana Carolina Riekstin	Kaloom, Canada
Eva González Romera	University of Extremadura, Spain
Huasong Shan	JD.com American Technologies Corporation, USA
Hussain Shareef	United Arab Emirates University, UAE
Gerard Smit	University of Twente, The Netherlands
Nirmal Srivastava	Dr. B. R. Ambedkar National Institute of Technology Jalandhar, India
Norvald Stol	Norwegian University of Science and Technology, Norway
Thomas Strasser	AIT Austrian Institute of Technology, Austria
Afshin Tafazzoli	Siemens Gamesa Renewable Energy, Spain
Alexandr Vasenev	ESI (TNO), The Netherlands
Silvano Vergura	Polytechnic University of Bari, Italy
Ramin Yahyapour	University of Göttingen, Germany
Sotirios Ziavras	New Jersey Institute of Technology, USA
Ahmed Zobaa	Brunel University London, UK

VEHITS Program Committee

Felix Albu	Valahia University of Targoviste, Romania
Paolo Barsocchi	National Research Council (CNR), Italy

Neila Bhouri	IFSTTAR, France
Gergely Biczók	Budapest University of Technology and Economics, Hungary
Nebojša Bojovic	University of Belgrade, Serbia
Jean-Marie Bonnin	IMT Atlantique, France
Paolo Bosetti	University of Trento, Italy
Christine Buisson	Université de Lyon, France
Carlos Calafate	Polytechnic University of Valencia, Spain
Roberto Caldelli	National Inter-University Consortium for Telecommunications (CNIT), Italy
Pedro Cardoso	Universidade do Algarve, Portugal
Rodrigo Carlson	Federal University of Santa Catarina, Brazil
Graziana Cavone	Polytechnic University of Bari, Italy
Abdelghani Chahmi	Université des Sciences et de la Technologie d'Oran, Algeria
Gihwan Cho	Jeonbuk National University, South Korea
Adam Cohen	University of California, Berkeley, USA
Michele Colajanni	University of Modena and Reggio Emilia, Italy
Baldomero Coll-Perales	Universidad Miguel Hernandez de Elche, Spain
Gonçalo Correia	TU Delft, The Netherlands
Noelia Correia	University of Algarve, Portugal
Antonio de la Oliva	Universidad Carlos III de Madrid, Spain
Danny De Vleeschauwer	NOKIA, Belgium
Rui Dinis	Universidade Nova de Lisboa, Portugal
Sabeur Elkosantini	University of Carthage, Tunisia
Oscar Esparza	Universitat Politècnica de Catalunya, Spain
Christian Esposito	University of Salerno, Italy
Peppino Fazio	University of Calabria, Italy
Attilio Fiandrotti	Télécom Paris, France
Dieter Fiems	Ghent University, Belgium
Lino Figueiredo	Instituto Superior de Engenharia do Porto, Portugal
Péter Gáspár	MTA SZTAKI, Hungary
Yi Guo	University of Texas at Dallas, USA
Levent Guvenc	Ohio State University, USA
Sonia Heemstra de Groot	Eindhoven Technical University, The Netherlands
Sin C. Ho	Chinese University of Hong Kong, Hong Kong
Tamás Holczer	Budapest University of Technology and Economics, Hungary
Yoichi Hori	University of Tokyo, Japan
Zechun Hu	Tsinghua University, China
Govand Kadir	University of Kurdistan Hewlêr, Iraq

Markus Kampmann	Koblenz University of Applied Sciences, Germany
Athanasios Kanatas	University of Piraeus, Greece
Tetsuya Kawanishi	Waseda University, Japan
Lisimachos Kondi	University of Ioannina, Greece
Anastasios Kouvelas	ETH Zurich, Switzerland
Zdzislaw Kowalczuk	Gdansk University of Technology, Poland
Francine Krief	University of Bordeaux, France
Yong-Hong Kuo	University of Hong Kong, Hong Kong
Deok Lee	Kunsan National University, South Korea
Salim M. Zaki	Dijlah University College, Iraq
Michael Mackay	Liverpool John Moores University, UK
Zoubir Mammeri	IRIT, Paul Sabatier University, France
Barbara Masini	Italian National Research Council (CNR), Italy
José Manuel Menéndez	Universidad Politécnica de Madrid, Spain
Lyudmila Mihaylova	University of Sheffield, UK
Aleksandar Milosavljevic	University of Niš, Serbia
Wrya Monnet	University of Kurdistan Hewlêr, Iraq
Jânio Monteiro	Universidade do Algarve, Portugal
Pedro Moura	University of Coimbra, Portugal
Mirco Nanni	Italian National Research Council (CNR), Italy
Daniela Nechoska	St. Kliment Ohridski University, Bitola, North Macedonia
Marialisa Nigro	Roma Tre University, Italy
Manuel Ocaña Miguel	University of Alcala, Spain
Dario Pacciarelli	Roma Tre University, Italy
Brian Park	University of Virginia, USA
Cecilia Pasquale	Università degli Studi di Genova, Italy
Paulo Pereirinha	Polytechnic Institute of Coimbra, Portugal
Fernando Pereñiguez	University Centre of Defence, Spanish Air Force Academy, Spain
Joshue Pérez Rastelli	Tecnalia, Spain
Valerio Persico	Network Measurement and Monitoring (NM2) and University of Naples "Federico II", Italy
Hesham Rakha	Virginia Tech, USA
Gianfranco Rizzo	University of Salerno, Italy
Enrique Romero-Cadaval	University of Extremadura, Spain
Adel Sadek	University at Buffalo, USA
Jose Santa	Technical University of Cartagena, Spain
Oleg Saprykin	Propzmedia and Samara State Aerospace University, Russia
Uwe Stilla	Technische Universitaet Muenchen, Germany

Todor Stoilov	Bulgarian Academy of Sciences, Bulgaria
Wai Yuen Szeto	University of Hong Kong, Hong Kong
Costin Untaroiu	Virginia Tech, USA
Ottorino Veneri	Institute of Sciences and Technologies for Sustainable Energy and Mobility (STEMS), Italy
Jorge Villagra	Automation Robotics Center, Spain
Francesco Viti	University of Luxembourg, Luxembourg
Shaw Voon Wong	University of Putra Malaysia, Malaysia
Chung-Hsing Yeh	Monash University, Australia

VEHITS Additional Reviewers

Christian Albrecht	Technical University of Munich, Germany
Péter Bauer	Széchenyi István University, Hungary
Tamás Bécsi	Budapest University of Technology and Economics, Hungary
Mate Fazekas	Institute for Computer Science and Control, Hungary
Andras Gazdag	Budapest University of Technology and Economics, Hungary
Michail Makridis	ETH Zurich, Switzerland
Héctor Masip	Universitat Politècnica de Catalunya, Spain
András Mihály	Institute for Computer Science and Control, Hungary
Balazs Nemeth	Institute for Computer Science and Control, Hungary
Sleiman Safaoui	University of Texas at Dallas, USA
Dario Stabili	University of Modena and Reggio Emilia, Italy
Tomasz Stefanski	Gdansk University of Technology, Poland
Aradi Szilard	Budapest University of Technoloigy and Economics, Hungary
Tamás Tettamanti	Budapest University of Technology and Economics, Hungary
Yu Yan	University of Michigan, USA
Lu Zhan	University of Minnesota, USA

Invited Speakers

Markus Eisenhauer	Luxemburg Institute for Science and Technology, Luxembourg
Bart van Arem	TU Delft, The Netherlands
Hesham Rakha	Virginia Tech, USA

Contents

Vehicle Technology and Intelligent Transport Systems

Smart Cities and Green ICT Systems

Designing Air Quality Monitoring Systems in Smart Cities

Andrea Marini[1]([📧]), Patrizia Mariani[2], Massimiliano Proietti[1], Alberto Garinei[1,2], Stefania Proietti[2], Paolo Sdringola[3], Lorenzo Menculini[1], and Marcello Marconi[1,2]

[1] Idea-Re S.R.L., Perugia, Italy
amarini@idea-re.eu
[2] Department of Engineering Sciences, Guglielmo Marconi University, Rome, Italy
[3] ENEA Italian National Agency for New Technologies, Energy and Sustainable Economic Development, Rome, Italy

Abstract. Handling pollution issues is one of the main challenges that cities have to face nowadays. The reason is twofold. On the one hand the urban areas are the main sources of emission of pollutants, which indeed are mainly related with anthropogenic factors. On the other hand, cities, being the areas with higher densities of inhabitants, are the areas where the impact of pollution on human health is more important. The main effects of high values of pollutants on human health regard respiratory apparatus, cardiovascular system and neurological system. Evidence shows that there are connections between the spread of viruses and environmental pollution. Thus, urban monitoring of pollutants is crucial, since it is the preliminary and necessary step to elaborate and then perform actions aimed at reducing pollution in order to safeguard citizens' health.

This study proposes a method to design a low-cost urban air quality monitoring system that can be implemented in any small-to-medium-sized smart city. We focus on the monitoring of atmospheric particulate matter (PM10 and PM2.5) since this is one of the main sources of pollution and it is the one with strongest impact on human health. The proposed method uses a combination of the AHP multi-criteria decision-making technique and of a cellular automaton model for the identification of the most suitable positions for the monitoring sensors. Furthermore, the data infrastructure architecture of the monitoring system is defined.

Keywords: Air quality · Urban monitoring · LoRaWAN · Sensors · AHP · Cellular automata · ODL · Smart city

1 Introduction

The improvement of economic, industrial and demographic conditions has led to better quality of life for human beings. However, such a development has also had some major drawbacks on the environment, most notably a deterioration of air quality. The latter is deeply affected by anthropogenic factors: traffic, industrial processes and domestic heating are among the main sources of air pollution [1].

© Springer Nature Switzerland AG 2022
C. Klein et al. (Eds.): SMARTGREENS 2021/ VEHITS 2021, CCIS 1612, pp. 3–20, 2022.
https://doi.org/10.1007/978-3-031-17098-0_1

Four factors can be identified as the main air pollutants, as stated by the World Health Organization (WHO). They are particulate matter (PM10 or PM2.5), sulfur dioxide (SO2), nitrogen dioxide (NO2) and ozone (O3). When the concentration of these pollutants reaches high values, human health is put at risk and the emergence of clinical problems, such as respiratory, cardiovascular or neurological pathologies can be witnessed [2]. Moreover, the balance of ecosystems is at stake [3].

In 2016, the WHO has reported that 91% of the global population was living in places with air quality levels below the minimum threshold indicated in the guidelines. Moreover, 4.2 million people died worldwide in the same year due to air pollution. It has been argued that reducing particulate matter from 70 to 20 μg per cubic meter can cause a 15% reduction in mortality, together with a lower incidence of diseases [4].

The effects of pollution on the respiratory system were investigated in [5]: the findings indicated that ozone and particulate matter play an important role in the onset of cardiopulmonary diseases, with children being the most sensitive to such pollution-induced effects. Indeed, a greater amount of respiratory tract dysfunctions was found in children with long-term exposure to high pollution in a study conducted in India, comparing 265 children from two cities [6]. Moreover, the role of pollutants – especially particulate matter - in contributing to the spread of viruses has been established. For example, during days of Asian dust storms a higher concentration of the Avian Influenza Virus was found in the air; it is known that in such periods the concentrations of PM10 and PM2.5 are also increased. Thus, dust storms play an important role in transporting viruses at long-range [7].

In the wake of the SARS-CoV-2 virus spreading – which caused the Covid-19 pandemic – a number of studies evaluated the contribution of high levels of pollution in spreading the disease, together with their consequences on the degree of severity of the disease and on its mortality rate. Covid-19, which is in many respects similar to the severe acute respiratory syndrome (SARS) of 2002, had its outbreak in Wuhan, China in December 2019 and subsequently spread throughout the world. Italy recorded its first cases of infections in February 2020 in the Lombardy and Veneto regions, in the northern part of the country.

A correlation was hypothesized in March between air pollution and the spread of the SARS-Cov-2 virus, with an important position paper written by experts of the Italian Society of Environmental Medicine (SIMA) and other researchers from Italian universities [8]. By analyzing daily concentrations of PM10 and daily recorded cases of Covid-19 in each Italian province, the authors found a significant relationship between high concentrations of PM10 exceeding the thresholds, in the period February 10th - February 29th 2020, and the number of COVID-19 cases up to March 3rd, taking into consideration a typical latency time of 14 days for the diagnosis of the disease. Shortly afterwards, SIMA also claimed to have found SARS-CoV-2 in particulate matter by having extracted its RNA [9]. This was the outcome of three weeks of data collection (February 21st–March 13th 2020), resulting in 34 samples of PM10.

Samples were collected in industrial sites in the Bergamo province. A confirmation of the results came from 12 samples for the three genes E, N, RdRP used as molecular markers. As stated by the European Public Health Alliance, people living in cities having high concentrations of pollutants turn out to be more exposed to Covid-19 and associated risks. This was first hypothesized according to statements made by the European Respiratory Society (ERS), asserting that chronic lung and heart diseases caused by long-term exposure to low quality of air reduce the ability to fight lung infections, including also Covid-19.

A study on SARS data also supported this hypothesis [10]. According to this study, people living in areas with moderately high pollution index show an 84% higher chance of dying as compared to people living in regions with a lower index. Differences as small as one microgram in the PM2.5 average concentration have been proved to be able to increase the mortality rate of Covid-19 by 11% in the long term [11, 12]. Such conclusion was reached by comparing the level of particulate matter in 3089 American counties and deaths due to Covid-19 up to June 18th, 2020, examining several variables, among which: weather, population size, hospital beds, socioeconomic and behavioral conditions. Moreover, an Italian study [13] addressed the role of chronic exposure to air pollutants: by considering the values of NO_2, PM2.5 and PM10 recorded in Italy in the last four years, northern Italy was seen to have been continuously exposed to high levels of atmospheric pollution, and a correlation was found between pollution data and Covid-19 cases for 71 provinces.

It appears therefore evident how the monitoring of air pollution plays a fundamental role in improving wellness and human health. In order to assess levels of pollution and, when appropriate, propose solutions to avoid a negative impact on the environment and human health, it is often crucial to monitor air quality through data collection [14]. The measurement points should be chosen so that the area's air quality is well represented. To this end, it is also crucial to identify source points such as industrial sites [15].

In [16] it was spelled out how to find the locations of two air quality monitoring stations in urban and rural areas by employing two techniques. These are the Analytic Hierarchy Process (AHP) and Elimination Et Choix Traduisant la Realité III (ELECTRE III). Seven criteria were considered to make this possible: pollution levels, security, availability of electricity, collaborations, staff support, easy access, distance. Remarkably, both the AHP and ELECTRE III method have identified the same positions.

In [17] the area under investigation was split into a grid, where each cell corresponds to a possible location for the air quality monitoring network sensor. Following the AHP method, a pairwise comparison fuzzy matrix was filled in and a score was then assigned to each location with respect to the following criteria: air quality, location sensitivity, cost, population sensitivity and population density. The optimal sensor locations were defined through the values derived from the Fuzzy Analytical Hierarchy Process (FAHP), in addition to considering the representativeness of the given area. The FAHP method was also employed to assess the atmospheric environmental quality in five different cities in China [18]. The results obtained with an index system turned out to be better than using the standard air pollution index.

A mathematical model able to simulate environmental phenomena varying over space and time is given by the Cellular Automaton. In [19], the pollution flow was modelled and simulated using a Cellular Automaton over an area of 3x3 km. They considered a variable number of sensors, and the status of each cell was updated by considering pollution levels and wind action. In [20] the propagation of air pollution was modelled with Cellular Automata and considering three factors: gravity, diffusion and wind transport.

Another interesting direction was taken in [21] where Cellular Automata were combined with Artificial Neural Networks to assess the methane atmospheric dispersion in 2D. More in detail, Cellular Automata were employed to make space-time simulations, while Neural Networks for making predictions.

In this work, following our previous research [22], we define the design of an urban monitoring system for air quality that can be adopted in smart cities. To do this we focus on two points: 1) engage the typical stakeholders of a smart city as government, suppliers, experts, scientists, entrepreneurs and citizens; 2) develop a data infrastructure architecture that can interconnect, manage sensing and control systems such air-quality monitoring [23].

The goal is to improve the assessment of atmospheric pollution levels, enabling those who are in charge of ensuring good air quality to take suitable actions and thus limit the spread of Covid-19 and other diseases. Our methodology considers the main anthropogenic sources of air pollution and can be applied to a smart city by taking into account its specific urban structure; moreover, the method benefits from the direct involvement of citizens, who participate in the process by answering specific questions that help identifying the most relevant sources of air pollution. The system takes into account the needs of a smart city about leveraging information from control and monitoring infrastructures [24].

2   Theoretical Background

In this section, we briefly review the main technical tools employed in this paper to locate sensors for monitoring the smart city air quality. More in detail, we introduce first the Analytic Hierarchy Process (AHP), then Cellular Automata (CA) and Opera-tional Data Layers, which are crucial for preparing the ground for a smart city.

The AHP is a technique useful when dealing with complex decision processes, developed by T. L. Saaty in the 1970's. See [25] or [26] for reviews of the AHP method. In this paper, AHP is employed to define the initial positions of the sensors. As we will see in the following, we aim at creating a LoRaWAN network where six sensors are placed in six different positions, chosen among twelve different possibilities by means of AHP. The initial configuration for the sensors is then refined using Cellular Autom-ata (CA), defining a probability of transition to a different position given the level of pollution in the neighbourhood of the sensors.

The operational Data Layer (ODL) based on NoSQL databases provides a flexible and scalable solution for high volume unstructured data collected by smart city monitoring and control systems.

2.1   Analytic Hierarchy Process

As we said before, AHP is a multi-criteria decision-making technique. Its strength relies on the fact that most decision problems can be broken down in smaller components which, in turn, can be analyzed independently.

In particular, in AHP every decision problem can be modelled as a hierarchy, made of three levels:

- the goal, that is the objective driving the decision problem;
- the alternatives, namely the different options available for the final decision;
- the criteria, namely the standards by which the alternatives are evaluated with respect to the goal.

For some problems it might be necessary to define also sub-criteria, adding layers of complexity. The basic structure of the AHP method is, of course, unchanged. The three levels above (or more, if we define sub-criteria associated with each criterion) define the hierarchy of any AHP problem. Let us now show why such a structured framework is useful when analyzing decision problems.

We define a set of pairwise comparison matrices for the criteria (and sub-criteria, if present) and alternatives. Specifically, assume that we have n alternatives for a given goal. We define the matrix of pairwise comparison among the alternatives with respect to a given criterion as

$$A = \{a_{ij}\}, \tag{1}$$

where $i, j = 1, \ldots, n$. Here, a_{ij} tells us how the i-th object (alternative in this case) compares to the j-th object according to a given criterion. For example, if the i-th alternative is as important as the j-th alternative for a given criterion we will have $a_{ij} = 1$, while if the i-th alternative is more important than the j-th alternative we will have $a_{ij} > 1$. The same procedure is carried out at the level of criteria. This means that in AHP we should fill in a pairwise comparison matrix for the criteria as well. The dimension of such a matrix is, of course, equal to the total number of criteria.

To have consistent judgments, the following rule, known as multiplicative consistency, should be respected when filling in a pairwise comparison matrix:

$$a_{ik} = a_{ij} \, a_{jk}, \tag{2}$$

for any $i, j, k = 1, ..n$. The last equation, in turn, implies that $a_{ij} = 1/a_{ji}$ for any $i, j = 1, 2, ..n$. This last condition is simply telling us that any pairwise comparison matrix should be reciprocal, as we would expect when making comparisons between pairs.

So far, we have not said anything about what scale we should adopt to make pairwise comparisons. In other words, one obvious question is: what values can the a_{ij}'s take on? The first and most widely used scale is the Saaty's $1 - 9$ scale, see Table 1.

Once a pairwise comparison matrix is given, according to the AHP method we should compute the priority vector, i.e. the vector whose components are the priorities associated with the different alternatives. The priority (or weight) vector, which we call w, is found by solving the following eigenvalue equation,

$$A \bullet w = \lambda_{max} w \tag{3}$$

where λ_{max} is the largest of the eigenvalues of A. In fact, it can be shown that if the matrix A is consistent, it has only one non-zero eigenvalue which is equal to n, the dimension of A.

Table 1. The fundamental scale for pairwise comparison (from [22]).

Intensity of importance	Definition
1	Equal importance
2	Weak importance
3	Moderate importance
4	Moderate plus importance
5	Strong importance
6	Strong plus importance
7	Very strong importance
8	Very, very strong importance
9	Extreme importance

Given that it is, in general, very hard to have consistent matrices, various indices assessing consistency have been proposed. For instance, the Consistency Index ($C.I.$), defined as

$$C.I. = \frac{\lambda_{max} - n}{n - 1}, \tag{4}$$

measures how much λ_{max} differs from n. It is somewhat accepted that if the $C.I.$ is less than 10% of the Random Inconsistency ($R.I.$) for a random matrix of the same dimension (), the original pairwise comparison matrix is considered sufficiently consistent (Table 2).

Table 2. Random Inconsistency index for matrices of different dimensions (from [22]).

n	$R.I.$	n	$R.I.$
1	0.00	6	1.24
2	0.00	7	1.32
3	0.58	8	1.41
4	0.90	9	1.45
5	1.12	10	1.49

How do we compute the weights in Eq. (3)? We can, of course, apply standard methods in linear algebra. However, any standard procedure is not free of inconsistency in AHP (for instance a right-eigenvector is not a left-eigenvector). In the literature, several other (equivalent, in the case of consistent matrices) methods have been proposed. One of the most widely used methods relies on the fact that, for nearly consistent matrices, the discrepancy from a fully consistent matrix is log-normal distributed. In that case, the weights are computed from the pairwise comparison matrix in the following manner,

$$w_i = \left(\prod_j a_{ij} \right)^{1/n}. \tag{5}$$

Finally, from local priorities we should compute the global priorities, taking into account the weights of all criteria [27]. If we denote by l_{ij} the local priority (weight) of the alternative i with respect to the alternative j and by w_j the weight of the j-th criterion, we find that the global priority for the i-th alternative is

$$p_i = \Sigma_{j=1}^n w_j l_{ij} \tag{6}$$

It is possible to normalize the p_i such that $\Sigma_{i=1}^n p_i = 1$.

We now move on to describing some basic features of cellular automata.

2.2 Cellular Automata

A cellular automaton [28] is a discrete model of computation firstly introduced by J. von Neumann in 1947 and then further sharpened by others, most notably by J. H. Conway in his "Game of Life" in 1968.

In brief, Cellular Automata (CA) consist of a regular grid of cells, each initialized in some state, such as on and off. The grid can be of any dimension. In other words, we can think of a cellular automaton as a d-dimensional lattice of bits (or even a more general finite set of variables). An initial state (say at time $t = 0$) is given by assigning a state to each cell. The state is then updated (say advancing t by 1) according to some fixed rules which determine a new state for the system. More precisely, the update of a given cell state is obtained by considering the state of the neighboring cells. It is customary to have the same rules for each of the cells, and these rules stay the same over time.

The neighborhood of a cell consists of the set of its adjacent cells. The two most common types of neighborhoods are the von Neumann and Moore ones. The former is made of the four orthogonally adjacent cells, for a total of five cells including the original one, while the latter includes the von Neuman plus the diagonally adjacent cells, for a total of nine cells including the original cell. In this paper, we will focus on the Moore neighborhood, as we explain in Sect. 3.

One of the reasons for which CA are fascinating systems and have found applications in areas like physics or biology is that they often provide a fertile framework where highly complex behaviors emerge from very simple systems.

Jumping a little ahead (see Sect. 3), we use CA to better refine the initial position assigned to each sensor. The rule for updating whether a cell should contain a sensor or not is given in terms of transition probabilities, determined starting from the level of pollution of the Moore-neighboring cell. We give a thorough explanation on how to carry this out in the next section.

2.3 Operational Data Layers

The data generated by smart city services are produced continuously, in large quantities and unstructured formats. Databases are often inadequate to store these data due to the model connection, slow processing speed and costs of storage expansion [29].

The term NoSQL (Not Just SQL) refers to database technologies that are not bound to obey stringent relational model constraints. NoSQL databases are highly scalable, essentially because they do not display the typical properties of the relational models, such as ACID transactions.

There exist different types of NoSQL databases: key-value, column-oriented, graph, document:

- Key-Values Stores: these databases store data in pairs (key, value) within simple and independent tables. Only the keys represent a searchable parameter within a database.
- Documents Database: they store and manage data through documents, generally in standard data exchange formats such as JSON, BSON, XML. The number and type of attributes can change from line to line within a document. Both keys and values are searchable parameters within a database.
- Column Stores: data is stored in columns where each row identifies a specific record.
- Graph Databases: in this framework, relational tables are replaced by graph structures where the nodes represent specific entities, and the edges are the relations between the nodes. Properties are generally expressed by pairs (key, value). The peculiarity of these databases relies on the connections between entities.

A solution based on Operational Data Layer (ODL) is studied in this paper. An ODL is an architectural scheme that integrates and organizes data of an organization residing in different systems. It also makes the data available to applications for data analytics, artificial intelligence, visualization, and so on. The ODL provides Data-As-Service by collecting data from different organization sources and organizing them in one place so that they can be used, through API for example, without the need for changes every time a new feature has to be added.

3   Results

3.1   Sensor Positioning Through AHP and Cellular Automata

We apply our considerations to the town of Santa Maria degli Angeli (43°03′32″N 12°34′41″E), a part of the Municipality of Assisi (Italy), which has 8470 inhabitants. It represents one of the most visited destinations in the region, especially because of the presence of many important religious sites. The area has undergone important urban developments in recent years. It is now equipped with the services needed for residential settlement and, moreover, with industrial activities. Industrial activities are located in the south-west region, while a foundry is located in a populated area. Industrial activities, along with traffic and home heating, are the main sources of pollution, see Fig. 1.

The initial configuration of the sensor network for monitoring the air quality is found by means of the AHP method. The goal, namely the objective, of the AHP corresponds to finding the most appropriate locations for the sensors. The criteria for determining the positions are home heating, road traffic and presence of industrial activities. The alternatives, namely the potential sensor positions, are shown Fig. 2. See also Fig. 3 for the full AHP problem structure. The positions for the sensors are twelve in total, and

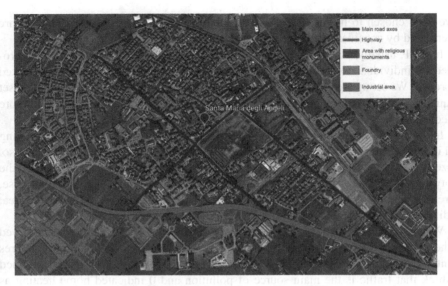

Fig. 1. View of the study area (from [22]).

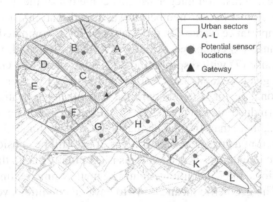

Fig. 2. Potential positions of the air quality monitoring sensors in the study area (from [22]).

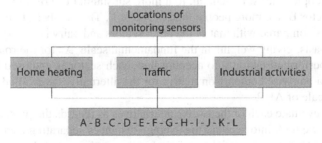

Fig. 3. AHP hierarchy for the selection of sensor positions for the case study (from [22]).

have been chosen to lie on the barycentric points of the urban sectors. The latter are determined by considering the road network structure of the given area, see Fig. 2.

In AHP, usually, pairwise comparison matrices and the resulting priorities are provided by individuals or group of people. In the present study, we opted for a mixed approach. We set up a participatory process, where citizens were engaged through a set of questionnaires in order to determine the relative weights of criteria, along with more objective methods to evaluate the optimal sensor positions.

In the questionnaire, we asked citizens to indicate what, among traffic, home heating and industrial activities, would be the main source of pollution in the given area. Also, citizens were asked to fill in pairwise comparison matrices among criteria using the Saaty's 1–9 to scale, according to standard AHP method. The questionnaires, of course, were kept anonymous and distributed to a heterogeneous set of people, living in the area, of different age and gender.

We collected 38 questionnaires, 19 from males and 19 from females who had lived in the area for more than 10 years. Eventually, we found that 25 of the 38 questionnaires pointed out industrial activities as the main source of pollution, 13 were more inclined to think that traffic is the main source of pollution and 0 indicated home heating as the main cause for pollution. We then used the geometric mean to aggregate the results of the questionnaires. When non integer weights come out of the geometric mean, we approximate to the closest integer number. It was found that industrial activities have very, very strong importance (value 8 in the Saaty's scale) as compared to home heating and strong importance (5) compared to traffic. On the other hand, road traffic has a very strong importance (7) with respect to home heating (Table 3). Given the pairwise comparison matrix given in Table 3, the corresponding priority eigenvector is found to be a three-dimensional vector with components: 0.0544 (home heating), 0.2331 (road traffic) and 0.7125 (industrial activities). The C.I. (Consistency Index defined above) is computed to be 0.12, more than 10% larger than the corresponding R.I. index. However, given that it comes from a group decision process, it can still be considered acceptable, and no review of the judgements is needed. This is essentially due to the fact that, in the case of group decisions, three conditions should be met: symmetry, linear homogeneity and concordance. The geometric mean allows to have all conditions verified.

The comparison among the twelve alternatives, as for the home heating criterion, was carried out by considering the number of people living in a given area (alternative): having more people results, in general, to a more substantial use of home heating. For example, in sector B live more people than in sector L. The number of people living in each sector was compared with that of the other sectors and pairwise comparisons were made on this basis, giving weights in the fundamental scale. As for the road traffic, the analysis was performed taking into account how each sector is enclosed by the main roads. Again, a pairwise comparison matrix for the alternatives was filled in using the fundamental scale of AHP.

In order to evaluate each of the twelve alternatives as regards the presence of industrial activities, we took into account the average distances separating each sector from the foundry and from the industrial area found in the south-west of the town. As for the two previously considered criteria, the values to be included in the matrix were defined objectively. Then, we calculated the eigenvector of each matrix and obtained weights

Table 3. Matrix of pairwise comparisons of the criteria (from [22]).

	Home heating	Traffic	Industrial activities
Home heating	1	1/7	1/8
Traffic	7	1	1/5
Industrial activities	8	5	1

for each alternative, connected to each criterion, with ensuing normalization. The consistency of the matrices was checked, and all matrices turned out to be consistent; in particular, the Consistency Indices (C.I.) were 0.1071, 0.099 and 0.1028, all below the 10% threshold for the Random Inconsistency (R.I.) value.

As the last step of the AHP method, hierarchical reconstruction was performed. For each of the twelve alternatives, the products of local weights and weights of relative criteria (see Table 4) were added. The six alternatives with the highest global weights were dubbed F, G, H, J, K and L, and they specify the initial configuration of the LoRaWAN network.

Table 4. Results of AHP for the localization of monitoring sensors (from [22]).

Sector	Home heating (0.0544)	Traffic (0.2331)	Industrial activities (0.7125)	Global weights
A	0.1710	0.0214	0.0141	0.0244
B	0.3174	0.0149	0.0114	0.0288
C	0.1315	0.0546	0.0434	0.0508
D	0.0364	0.0434	0.0114	0.0202
E	0.0251	0.0159	0.0411	0.0344
F	0.0800	0.0346	0.1290	0.1043
G	0.1034	0.2832	0.2008	0.2147
H	0.0156	0.0271	0.1515	0.1151
I	0.0482	0.0546	0.0674	0.0634
J	0.0431	0.0689	0.2008	0.1614
K	0.0156	0.1685	0.1017	0.1126
L	0.0127	0.2128	0.0275	0.0698

The present work is characterized by the use of cellular automata to establish the actual position of the sensors for air quality monitoring. The automata are employed to optimize the configuration produced by the AHP method, in view of finding refined configurations that maximize the coverage of polluted areas. In order to do so, one first defines the grid that should be superimposed to the study area, by specifying the dimensions of the grid cells. For the case study under examination, we chose an 11×8

grid with cells measuring 200×200 m. Each cell is accompanied by twofold information: the two variables record the presence or absence of a sensor and the level of pollution in the given cell, respectively. The first variable is determined from the outputs of the AHP method, while the second from the citizens' answers in the questionnaires. The initial state of the cellular automaton is specified by such information (Fig. 4). Then, transition rules are assigned, employing Moore's neighborhood (which included eight cells plus one); these rules guide the system dynamics. The configuration at a certain step gives the set of positions of the sensors in the grid, and at each iteration a sensor can either move to one of the cells in its neighborhood or remain in its current position. The procedure for determining whether and how the sensor moves is of stochastic nature and follows these rules:

1. For the current sensor position and for all the other possible configurations at the following step (that is, the eight cells in the neighborhood), calculate the coefficient k of polluted areas coverage: this coefficient is given by the weighted sum of polluted cells falling in the Moore neighborhood of the considered cell, with weights chosen so that they decrease exponentially with distance from the central cell (that is, the actual position of the sensor). The matrix of weights is:

$$\begin{bmatrix} 0.24 & 0.37 & 0.24 \\ 0.37 & 1 & 0.37 \\ 0.24 & 0.37 & 0.24 \end{bmatrix} \tag{7}$$

2. Using the previously calculated coefficients of polluted areas coverage, and denoting them as k_i for a certain displacement i of a given sensor, a corresponding probability p_i is assigned to the displacement through the formula:

$$p_i = \frac{e^{k_i}}{\sum_i e^{k_i}} \tag{8}$$

3. Then, one determines the future position of the sensor by extracting it randomly among the nine possibilities, each having a probability p_i of being selected.

The new sensor configuration determined in this way must then be compared to the previous one, so that it can be established whether the associated overall coverage of polluted areas has improved. The overall coverage is computed by taking the sum of the polluted areas coverage coefficients associated to each sensor, with the addition of negative penalties whenever a pair of sensors lie in adjacent cells or in the same cell. The rule for accepting a new configuration is that the global coverage must increase, otherwise the configuration is rejected. In the case under study, the final positions of the sensors determined by following this rule turned out to be different from the ones in the initial state; the resulting configuration, ensuring a wider coverage of polluted areas, is shown in Fig. 4.

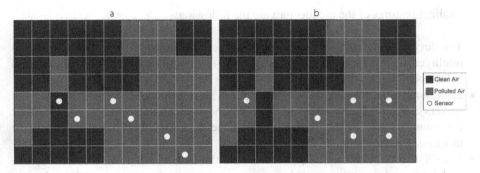

Fig. 4. Evolution of sensor positions from the initial state (a) to the final configuration (b) through the cellular automaton (from [22]).

3.2 Smart City Monitoring System and Control Architecture

In smart cities, monitoring and control systems must be interconnected and should generate databases so that the information extracted from them can be used to manage infrastructures and services efficiently and in real-time. In this respect, also personal devices should be part of the same sensing system: this is crucial to improve interactions between services and citizens.

The design of a monitoring system for a smart city must include the development of a data infrastructure that can integrate the various types of sensors and actuators, and which can add new monitoring systems as they become available.

The architecture designed and developed for the collection, management and analysis of data generated by monitoring and control systems of a smart city is shown in Fig. 5.

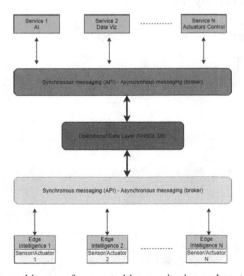

Fig. 5. Data architecture for smart cities monitoring and control systems.

Salient features of the architecture are the following:

- The devices that contain the sensors and/or actuators require the presence of edge-intelligence units for data processing (such as the execution of inference algorithms) before being sent to the database.
- Communication between devices equipped with sensors/actuators and data storage servers can take place both in synchronous and asynchronous mode. Asynchronous communication is, in fact, preferable given the heterogeneity of the devices and the tasks assigned to them.
- The ODL is based on a NoSQL database (in this case MongoDB). It has the speed, scalability and flexibility suitable for managing monitoring systems and the devices connected to them.
- The ODL communicates (both synchronously and asynchronously) with the various data processing services (such as AI algorithms and data visualization dashboards). This approach allows for more flexibility, scalability and resilience of the infrastructure.

As already mentioned, in a smart city, citizens can be integral part of monitoring systems thanks to the use of their devices. Data infrastructures of a smart city must know how to handle the possibility that a device is part of multiple monitoring systems. To meet this need, we developed a model where the measurements made by a sensor at a certain time (or changes of state of an actuator) are recorded in the database as an event. The time series of measurements of a monitoring system is made up of a set of events. The same event can belong to multiple projects.

An event pool contains the events produced by the various systems, which are recorded within a database collection (event collection). In Fig. 6 we show how the logic just described works (Fig. 7).

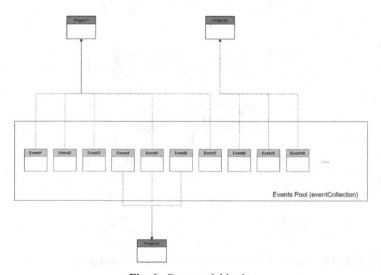

Fig. 6. Data model logic.

See the following diagram representing part of the model just described.

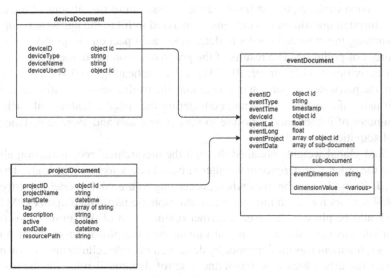

Fig. 7. Part of database schema.

This diagram describes essentially three documents:

- *projectDocument:* this document describes the project (i.e. the monitoring or control system) and contains the information associated with it.
- *deviceDocument:* it describes the sensor or actuator employed (deviceType)
- *eventDocument:* it describes an event interpreted as a sensor reading or an actuator status' change (eventType). Data (readings/status) are stored in the eventData sub-document. The information on the projects (eventProject) and the device that generated it (deviceId) are linked to projectDocument and deviceDocument, respectively.

4 Conclusions

The focus of this paper has been the definition of a design method for an air quality urban monitoring system allowing the assessment of pollution levels deriving from different sources. We aimed at solving the following issues:

- identification of the most suitable positions for the monitoring sensors within the study area;
- definition of the data infrastructure architecture.

The first point has been tackled by using a combination of the AHP multi-criteria decision-making technique and of a cellular automaton model. The choice of using the AHP as a first step is related to the nature of the problem, which involves different alternatives, namely the possible positions for the sensors, to be assessed with respect to multiple criteria, i.e. the various sources of pollution.

The decision-making process involved the assessment of the citizens of the considered area: through questionnaires citizens were asked to fill in the pairwise comparison matrices among the criteria, in order to determine the impact on air quality of the three main sources of pollution. The results of the group decision led to the following scale: industrial activities (0.7125), traffic (0.2331) and home heating (0.0544). Then, for each criterium, the pairwise comparison matrix among the twelve sensor position alternatives was built using the available data and considering the specific features of each urban sector: number of inhabitants, exposure to very busy roads and average distance from industrial activities.

The final global weights obtained through the hierarchical reconstruction allow to determine the order of preference of the alternatives. The six sectors with highest weights (F, G, H, J, K and L) are the ones where, according to the AHP model employed, the LoRaWAN sensors for urban monitoring of atmospheric particulate matter (PM10 and PM2.5) should be placed. However, a further optimization of the sensors' positioning configuration was carried out, aiming at maximizing the global coverage of polluted areas. This refinement was implemented by defining a suitable cellular automaton model. A grid over the urban area was drawn and a set of dynamical rules for the evolution of the state (presence/absence of sensor) of the cells were defined. After letting the system evolve according to this model, the positions of the sensors initialized in the configuration determined by the AHP method were corrected ensuring a greater coverage of the polluted area. The final configuration achieved in this way is shown in Fig. 4b.

Finally, we provided a method for designing data architectures based on NoSQL database (like MongoDB). This architecture can manage data collected from different types of devices, including citizens smartphones. The logic behind the architecture allows to gather, store, and analyze data that can be used in different projects at the same time.

Acknowledgements. We would like to thank the Municipality of Assisi for their collaboration. The study presented in this paper is part of the PLANET project financed to Idea-re S.r.l. by Regione Veneto (IT) POR FESR 2014–2020 Asse I Azione 1.1.1.

References

1. Samad, A., Vogt, U.: Investigation of urban air quality by performing mobile measurements using a bicycle (MOBAIR). Urban Clim. **33**, 100650 (2020)
2. Ghorani-Azam, A., Riahi-Zanjani, B., Balali-Mood, M.: Effects of air pollution on human health and practical measures for prevention in Iran. J. Res. Med. Sci. **21**(1), 65 (2016)
3. De Marco, A., et al.: Impacts of air pollution on human and ecosystem health, and implications for the national emission ceilings directive: insights from Italy. Environ. Int. **125**, 320–333 (2019)
4. WHO website. https://www.who.int/news-room/fact-sheets/detail/ambient-(outdoor)-air-qua lity-and-health. Accessed 15 Sept 2021
5. Kurt, O.K., Zhang, J., Pinkerton, K.E.: Pulmonary health effects of air pollution. Curr. Opin. Pulm. Med. **22**(2), 138 (2016)

6. De, S.: Long-term ambient air pollution exposure and respiratory impedance in children: a cross-sectional study. Respir. Med. **170**, 105795 (2020)
7. Chen, P.S., et al.: Ambient influenza and avian influenza virus during dust storm days and background days. Environ. Health Perspect. **118**(9), 1211–1216 (2010)
8. Setti, L., et al.: Position Paper: Relazione circa l'effetto dell'inquinamento da particolato atmosferico e la diffusione di virus nella popolazione (2020). SIMA website. https://www.simaonlus.it/wpsima/wp-content/uploads/2020/03/COVID19_Position-Paper_Relazione-circa-l%E2%80%99effetto-dell%E2%80%99inquinamento-da-particolato-atmosferico-e-la-diffusione-di-virus-nella-popolazione.pdf. Accessed 15 Sept 2021
9. Setti, L., et al.: SARS-Cov-2RNA found on particulate matter of Bergamo in Northern Italy: first evidence. Environ. Re., 109754 (2020)
10. Cui, Y., et al.: Air pollution and case fatality of SARS in the People's Republic of China: an ecologic study. Environ. Health **2**(1), 1–5 (2003)
11. Wu, X., Nethery, R. C., Sabath, M.B., Braun, D., Dominici, F.: Air pollution and COVID-19 mortality in the United States: strengths and limitations of an ecological regression analysis. Sci. Adv **6**(45), eabd4049 (2020)
12. Wu, X., Nethery, R.C., Sabath, B.M., Braun, D., Dominici, F.: Exposure to air pollution and COVID-19 mortality in the United States. MedRxiv (2020)
13. Fattorini, D., Regoli, F.: Role of the chronic air pollution levels in the Covid-19 outbreak risk in Italy. Environ. Pollut., 114732 (2020)
14. Kainuma, Y., Shiozawa, K., Okamoto, S.I.: Study of the optimal allocation of ambient air monitoring stations. Atmos. Environ. Part B. Urban Atmos. **24**(3), 395–406 (1990)
15. Kibble, A., Harrison, R.: Point sources of air pollution. Occup. Med. **55**(6), 425–431 (2005)
16. Hacıoğlu, H., et al.: A new approach for site selection of air quality monitoring stations: multi-criteria decision-making. Aerosol Air Qual. Res. **16**(6), 1390–1402 (2016)
17. Mofarrah, A., Husain, T., Alharbi, B.H.: Design of urban air quality monitoring network: fuzzy based multi-criteria decision making approach. Air Qual. Monit. Assess. Manag. **11**, 25–39 (2011)
18. Lv, W., Ji, S.: Atmospheric environmental quality assessment method based on analytic hierarchy process. Disc. Contin. Dyn. Syst.-S **12**(4–5), 941–955 (2019)
19. Benjavanich, S., Ursani, Z., Corne, D.: Forecasting the flow of urban pollution with cellular automata. In: 2017 Sustainable Internet and ICT for Sustainability (SustainIT), pp. 1–6. IEEE (2017)
20. Marín, M., Rauch, V., Rojas-Molina, A., López-Cajún, C.S., Herrera, A., Castaño, V.M.: Cellular automata simulation of dispersion of pollutants. Computational Mater. Sci. **18**(2), 132–140 (2000)
21. Lauret, P., Heymes, F., Aprin, L., Johannet, A.: Atmospheric dispersion modeling using Artificial Neural Network based cellular automata. Environ. Model. Softw. **85**, 56–69 (2016)
22. Marini, A., et al.: Design of an urban monitoring system for air quality in smart cities. In: Proceedings of the 10th International Conference on Smart Cities and Green ICT Systems (SMARTGREENS 2021), pp. 94–101. SCITEPRESS – Science and Technology Publications (2021)
23. Jayasena, N.S., Mallawaarachchi, H., Waidyasekara, K.G.A.S.: Stakeholder analysis for smart city development project: an extensive literature review. In: MATEC Web of Conferences, vol. 266, p. 06012. EDP Sciences (2019)
24. Khan, Z., Kiani, S.L.: A cloud-based architecture for citizen services in smart cities. In 2012 IEEE Fifth International Conference on Utility and Cloud Computing, pp. 315–320. IEEE (2012)
25. Saaty, T.L.: Mathematical principles of decision making (Principia mathematica decernendi), RWS Publications (2010)

26. Ishizaka, A., Labib, A.: Review of the main developments in the analytic hierarchy process. Expert Syst. Appl. **38**(11), 14336–14345 (2011)
27. Latora, A., Trapani, N., Nicosia, G.: Una metodologia di Multi Criteria Decision Making a supporto dei processi di Public Management. Rivista italiana di Public Management **1**(2) (2018
28. Mitchell, M., Gramss, I.T., Bornholdt, S., Gross, M., Pellizzari, T.: Computation in cellular automata: a selected review. Non-standard Comput. (2005)
29. Kang, Y., Park, I., Rhee, J., Lee, Y.: MongoDB-based repository design for IoT-generated RFID/sensor big data. IEEE Sensors J. **16**(2), 485–497 (2016). https://doi.org/10.1109/JSEN.2015.2483499

Identifying Requirements to Model a Data Lifecycle in Smart City Frameworks

Claudia Roessing[✉] and Markus Helfert[✉]

Lero, the Science Foundation Ireland Research Centre for Software, Innovation Value Institute,
Maynooth University, Maynooth, Ireland
{claudia.rocha,markus.helfert}@lero.ie

Abstract. The population in cities has increased, which causes problems when offering services to their citizens. As a way to overcome these issues, information and technology are used to transform a city into smarter. Thousands of gigabytes are created every day and much of this data is used to create products and services. Hence with a vastly amount of data available, a framework is needed to assist organizations in order to understand the flow of data necessary to provide services and products to citizens. Data lifecycles are used for this purpose. However, the literature points out some limitations in the modelling of this framework, and in previous work, these authors started to identify necessary requirements to improve modelling of a data lifecycle [1]. In this work, the authors will provide some insights on data lifecycle modelling limitations, and detail how modelling requirements were identified with aid of a data taxonomy. Furthermore, five smart city frameworks will be analyzed using requirements identified in this study as a reference, as well as a new illustrative use case that uses sensitive information will be presented.

Keywords: Data lifecycle · Data lifecycle requirements · Data lifecycle modelling · Smart city framework

1 Introduction

According to a UN report, the world population will reach 9.7 billion by the year 2050 [2]. It is also stated that by 2050, the percentage of the population living in urban areas will be 68%, which will bring about more challenges to managing cities [3]. In addition to population growth, it has been observed the migration of people from rural areas to cities with the aim of improving their living standards [4]. Several authors have identified factors that lead to rural migration as climate variation, better access to basic services, better infrastructure, and an opportunity to find a better livelihood [5, 6].

The overpopulation in cities has been causing serious problems in infrastructure, transport, pollution, housing, health system [6–8].

Information and communication technology have begun to be used with intention of overcoming these problems, thus the concept of a smart city has appeared, therefore the objective of smart cities is to use technology to improve citizens' lives using resources wisely [9–11].

© Springer Nature Switzerland AG 2022
C. Klein et al. (Eds.): SMARTGREENS 2021/ VEHITS 2021, CCIS 1612, pp. 21–33, 2022.
https://doi.org/10.1007/978-3-031-17098-0_2

However, the advance of technology is bringing other challenges to the cities. Data management is considered one of the biggest challenges, and this occurs at all stages of a lifecycle [12–14]. Big data and IoT make smart cities possible, however, they also bring more difficulties to manage data, as data is collected from various sources (sensors, smart meters, smartphones, CCTV cameras, etc.), which increases complexity when integrating and managing data [12, 13, 15, 16].

Due to the type of data that is collected to make a city smart, other important issues are being raised, for instance, quality, privacy, and security of data [12, 14, 17–23]. On the other hand, privacy and security are factors that concern not only cities but also their citizens, as they have their data collected, processed, and stored. These are relevant factors that make usage of a data lifecycle essential in order to provide better management of data in a smart city as a data lifecycle is used to guarantee the collection of data for a specific use likewise preparing data for relevant users meeting the requirements for quality and security [24].

2 Objectives of this Paper

This work aims to analyze data lifecycles, focusing on their modeling, identifying their limitations, and thus identifying points of improvement through the identification of requirements. Subsequently, five smart city frameworks are analyzed according to identified requirements. An illustrative use case is presented to show the use and importance of requirements in modeling a data lifecycle.

3 Issues of Data Lifecycle Modelling

The advance of technology has led to the emergence of new devices like smartphones, smart meters, sensors and with the Internet of Things (IoT) and Big Data, the evolvement in data management has happened in order to adapt to requirements in this new scenario [12–14]. Therefore, it is paramount that there are enhancements in the way data lifecycles are modelled too [25].

As mentioned previously, a data lifecycle is used to guarantee the collection and processing of data necessary for a specific use, however, available lifecycles are modeled from a high abstraction point of view, and they do not represent the reality of data management available nowadays [14, 26]. Therefore, some studies have stressed a requirement for the evolution of the modeling framework [25].

There are several issues in data lifecycles modeling identified in the literature [26–28]. Data lifecycles consist of blocks of phases/activities linked to each other and several authors state that this type of representation is not sufficient to demonstrate data processing that occurs nowadays, as these models do not show the transformation of data during its collection, processing, and deletion. Another problem identified is the lack of involvement of stakeholders during data processing. Furthermore, most data lifecycles indicate in their models that data collection only occurs at beginning of a process [26–29].

A smart city is a complex ecosystem, therefore an improvement in data lifecycle modeling is a necessary advance to assist to understand this ecosystem, assist with stakeholder communication, and also to assist to maintain necessary alignment between objectives and services [25, 30]. Table 1 shows issues identified in the literature.

Table 1. Data lifecycle limitations [1].

References	Lack of necessary phases	Lack of flexibility to adapt	Lack of user feedback	Do not consider data quality	Lack of reality representation	Do not consider data privacy	Need to contribute to politic, social and economic values
El Arass et al. 2017	X	X					
Pouchard, L. 2015					X		
Plale, B., & Kouper, I. 2017					X		
Cox et al. 2018					X		
Ball, A. 2012					X		
Carlson, J. 2014	X				X		
van Veenstra et al. 2015	X				X		
Sinaeepourfard, A. et al. 2015	X			X			
Elmekki, H. et al. 2019			X	X			X
Faundeen, J. et al. 2017	X						
Sinaeepourfard,A. et al. 2016	X						
Paskaleva, K. et al. 2017						X	
Bohli,J. et al. 2015						X	
Liu, X. et al 2017						X	
Alshammari, M. et al. 2018						X	
Attard, J. et al. 2016							X

4 Data Lifecycle Modelling Requirements

In this session, the requirements that authors identified in a previous work [1] during a literature review (see Appendix A) will be revised. The lack of a formal specification in the modeling of this framework was also identified and problems caused by this are presented by Cox and Tam (2018). The intention of using these requirements is to improve how data is modeled thus targeting researchers and practitioners' needs. The requirements are presented below.

1. Phase - it is the steps used and necessary to transform data into a specific outcome.

2. Activities - they are the processes that make up the phases to prepare data.
3. Data input - data that will be used in a phase or activity.
4. Data output - data produced at end of each phase or activity.
5. Role - actors responsible for conducting phases and/or activities.
6. Pre and post requirement (phase quality) - these requirements are used to control the quality of data, that is, to check if outcomes of phases and activities were carried out successfully, or if they need to be processed again.
7. Relationship between phases – data life is composed of phases and activities, so it is necessary to know the relationship between them and thus process data in the correct order of phases or activities.
8. Variation driver - this requirement is composed of important components related to data such as regulations, lifespan, category, and sensitivity. There is a need to process data differently, so it is essential to know the category and sensitivity of data in order to process it properly and in compliance with regulations.

5 Development of a Taxonomy

To show how data influences activities of a lifecycle and to identify modelling requirements, this study thought it was paramount to understand different categories of data, therefore a data taxonomy (Fig. 1) was developed. The development of taxonomy followed the methodology suggested by Nickerson [31]. The identification of new objects was done with the assistance of literature (see Appendix B) using coding and categorization of data using the inductive approach proposed by Thomas [32].

Data is being considered the most valuable asset in an organization, therefore it is necessary to protect it accordingly, as some type of data is protected by law, regulation, e.g. protected health Information (PHI), personal cardholder information (PCI), personal identifiable information (PII) or intellectual property (IP) and failure of doing so can have significant consequences to business, loss of customer trust, damage to organization's reputation, financial penalties, just to mention a few [33–40]. To improve the modelling of a lifecycle, it is necessary to understand the necessity of models variations and the reasons for that. The need for life cycle variation was identified in order to respect processing requirements of different types of data, however, this is not considered by several studies and data life cycles. Due to the need to treat data as an asset, it is necessary to process it taking into account particularities of the types of data.

Up to date specifications identified are: data principles were identified as influencing variation drivers, which determine variations in phases and activities of a data lifecycle. Data principles are principles that guide the usage of data, and in this case specifically, smart cities [41–44]. Some of the principles used by cities are listed as transparency, trust, responsibility, privacy, reusability, governance. The principles influence variation drivers, which in turn are composed of:

*   Data category - Based on data taxonomy presented previously.
*   Data sensitivity - Based on data taxonomy presented previously.
*   Regulations - These are regulations that must be obeyed to process data, failure to comply with them may result in fines to organizations. The general data protection regulation is an example of regulation [45].

And the variation driver determines necessary variations in models.

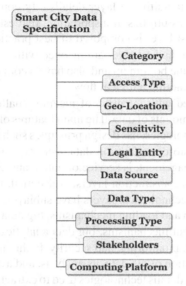

Fig. 1. Smart city data specification taxonomy.

6 Analysis of Smart Cities Frameworks

Enterprise Architecture (EA) is a blueprint that shows the business and IT and their relationships in an organization. It is used to reduce organizational complexity and to assist communication between stakeholders [46]. Several models of enterprise architectures can be found in the literature, and these models can be specific or generic [47]. This blueprint is also used to model smart cities.

In this section, we will analyze five frameworks based on requirements identified in the previous section and using concept centric approach proposed by Webster and Watson [48]. The selected frameworks are: smart city framework, big data architecture for smart cities (BASIS), Barcelona smart city IT architecture, Rotterdam Smart city architecture, and the smart city platform. The frameworks are presented and analyzed below.

The Smart City Framework [49] was developed by Cisco and aims to provide a process to assist key stakeholders and city/community participants to identify the objectives of a city and stakeholders' roles. Moreover, to acknowledge how a city operates and understand the role of ICT in the operation of a city. Using this framework, cities can follow a standard "catalog" system that facilitates activities necessary for the easy implementation and management of a smart city. The framework has four layers, city objectives, city indicators, city components, and city content. City Objectives is the first layer and is located at the bottom of the framework. The purpose of this layer is to provide a link between the city's goals and its projects and initiatives in order to improve the social, environmental, and economic pillars of a city. The second layer contains city indicators, which are used to measure and benchmark a city according to objectives defined in the previous layer. The penultimate layer details city components, where physical components of a city such as utilities, transportation, real estate, and city services are detailed. The fourth and last layer is composed of best practices and policy examples, where objectives defined in the first layer are mapped with best practices and policies. The layers are linked from the bottom up and also have a connection between layer four and the first layer, thus promoting a logical flow.

BASIS [50] was created with intention of meeting challenges found to integrate, process, and analyze vast amounts of data. The main features of the framework are: focus on the use of Big Data technologies, has design principles such as open data, has multiple abstraction layers, takes into consideration data security, privacy, and trust concerns, includes data lifecycle management, is service oriented, and client independent.

The framework has three abstraction layers, conceptual, technological, and infrastructural. Conceptual and technological layers have sublayers such as high volume and variety data, data extraction and loading mechanisms, big data storage, background jobs for big data flow, data output mechanisms, big data analytics, data services and applications, and administration, monitoring, and security. In the first layer, components that are necessary for the extraction of big data, its analysis, and availability are represented.

The technological layer details technologies used to extract, process, and make use of big data. Infrastructural layer presents technological infrastructure, that is, the hardware part of a solution, which describes storage clusters, job executive nodes, web servers, and development machines.

Barcelona Smart City Architecture [22] was developed by Barcelona City Council and Municipal Institute of Informatics with the purpose of defining an architecture with basic principles to define strategies and policies. The architecture has three layers, information sources, middleware, and smart city applications.

The information sources layer is located at bottom of the architecture and shows different sources from which data is collected. The middleware layer defines processes, analytics, and semantics required to transform raw data collected from the information layer and send it to the smart city applications layer. The applications that provide services to the city are found in this layer.

Rotterdam Smart city architecture [51] is composed of 7 layers: users, applications, intelligence, data, communication, sensors, and objects. The aim of this architecture is to align the physical city and at the same time, project it into the digital world. Using this platform, it is also possible to see the origin of demand for information, as well as where data comes from. Furthermore, architecture shows the flow of data, communication, and governance, ownership, and security in both directions (bottom and up) passing through all layers. The Intelligence layer is where services used in the data marketplace are found, which is in the layer below. The services are sharing, fusion, import, export, interpretation, and statistics. A standardized connection is being developed in conjunction with EU-Project Espresso in order to facilitate data in and out of datahub.

The Smart City Platform [51] was developed by the Technical Committee for the Normalization on Intelligent cities in the standard UNE 178104 as a reference. The platform has five layers, support, intelligent services, interoperability, knowledge, and acquisition/interconnection layers.

The objective of this standard is to define components, capabilities, and requirements necessary for a city's comprehensive platform, thus aiming to facilitate services to citizens, and also to increase efficiency and integration in the environment. The platform's goal is to provide a comprehensive view of a city. The standard describes the functional and technological views and metrics of a comprehensive platform. The support layer, as the name states, aims to support other features such as auditing, monitoring, security, and so on. In the knowledge layer, data is received from acquisition and interoperability layers to support data processing.

Table 2. Analysis of smart city frameworks.

Frameworks	Phase	Activity	Input	Output	Role	Pre/Post Requirement	Phases Relationship
Barcelona smart city IT architecture	x	x	x	x			
Rotterdam smart city architecture	x	x			x		
Smart city platform			x			x	
Smart city framework					x		
BASIS	x	x	x	x	x		

7 Illustrative Use Case

Several kinds of researches in the medical field use patient data to develop medications and also to understand certain factors. However, these data are sensitive, so they need to be handed in an appropriate way, that is, they must be collected, used, anonymized, and deleted according to existing regulations. Data need to be anonymized before sending to be used in research to make it impossible to identify patients. Data lifecycle requirements applied to this use case can be seen below (Table 3).

Table 3. Use case data lifecycle requirements.

Phases	Activities	Input	Output
Plan	Specification	Service description	Processing plan Access specification Definition of roles
Collect	Collection	Set of data values	Collected data values (Patient name, age, gender, address, medical records)
Storage	Storage Archive Backup	Storage plan Data values	Storage data
Use	Use Manipulation Access system	Retrieved data values	Reports (csv, pdf)
Anonymize	Use Manipulation	Retrieved data values	Remove identifiable data
Share	Preparation Presentation	Retrieved data values	Disclosed data (age, gender, medical records)
Delete	Destruction	Processing plan to destroy data	Set of destroyed data

Variation driver:

– regulations: as personal data is collected, there are specific regulations that an organization needs to be in compliance with.
– lifespan: an organization has decided to keep data for 20 years.
– category and sensitivity: data collected in this service is classified as sensitive.
– Relationship between phases: Phases are conducted in sequential order (Plan, Collect, Storage, Use, Anonymize, Share, Delete).
– Pre and Post requirements: Inputs and outputs are verified before and after each phase and activity in order to check if quality requirements have been met
– Role: doctors, researchers, system users.

8 Discussion

As mentioned earlier, there are variations in modeling smart cities frameworks and this can be seen in the analysis of frameworks in the previous section, as they have a wide variety in their modeling.

Table 2 shows that none of the frameworks has all the data lifecycle requirements identified in this study.

The smart city platform and BASIS identify different types of data processing as real time processing, batch processing, low or high velocity.

Smart cities collect data from various sources and are composed of several stakeholders, however not all frameworks analyzed presented stakeholders involved.

Security is taken into account by Barcelona, Rotterdam, and Smart city platform, however, this aspect is more detailed in BASIS, wherein administration, monitoring, and security sublayer mentioned access control, permissions, privacy preservation, and so on.

Most frameworks distinguish open data from other types.

Based on the principle of offering better services to citizens and enhancing citizens' lives, there must be an alignment between services offered with business, policies, regulations, and technical approaches [30].

Cisco framework was the only one that has city objectives as a start point, which links the city's objectives with projects, policies, and initiatives in order to improve social, environmental, and economic pillars, however, the framework is represented in a very high-level way.

Regulations, sensitivity, and category were taken into account to some extent in a few of the frameworks analyzed, but none of them took into account data lifespan.

9 Conclusion

Due to the increase in population, cities have faced problems in transport, health system, housing, among others. The use of technology and communication has helped cities to become smart, but several challenges are faced in order to transform a city into smart.

In a multi-stakeholder ecosystem like smart cities, services from different domains are offered to citizens, which collect data from different sources with different formats that need to be in compliance with regulations, privacy, and security requirements.

One way to assist data management in smart cities is to use data lifecycles, however, literature states a necessity to improve data lifecycle modeling. The aim to leverage modeling of lifecycles in smart city architectures is to take into account novelty in the data management process in smart city scenario and provide better modeling of data flow.

The implementation of a smart city requires an alignment between services, policies, and security requirements, therefore it is necessary that frameworks reflect this requirement.

This work presented an application of data lifecycle requirements identified in an illustrative use case, in which sensitive data was used. The use case has shown the importance of using identified requirements in a data lifecycle, especially when sensitive data is used. Improved lifecycle modeling can assist stakeholders to align services, regulations, and security requirements.

Future work includes conducting case studies to validate findings and integrate identified requirements with smart city frameworks.

Acknowledgements. This work was supported by the Science Foundation Ireland grant "13/RC/2094" and co-funded under the European Regional Development Fund through the Southern & Eastern Regional Operational Programme to Lero, the Science Foundation Ireland Research Centre for Software (www.lero.ie) and Innovation Value Institute, Maynooth University, Maynooth, Ireland (https://www.maynoothuniversity.ie/innovation-value-institute-ivi).

References

1. Roessing, C., Helfert, M.: A comparative analysis of smart cities frameworks based on data lifecycle requirements. In: Proceedings of the 10th International Conference on Smart Cities and Green ICT Systems - SMARTGREENS, pp. 212–219 (2021). https://doi.org/10.5220/0010479302120219. ISBN 978-989-758-512-8. ISSN 2184-4968
2. United Nations: Growing at a slower pace, world population is expected to reach 9.7 billion in 2050 and could peak at nearly 11 billion around 2100 | UN DESA | United Nations Department of Economic and Social Affairs. UN DESA | United Nations Department of Economic and Social Affairs. https://www.un.org/development/desa/en/news/population/world-population-prospects-2019.html. Accessed 18 Aug 2021
3. United Nations: 68% of the World Population Projected to Live in Urban Areas by 2050, Says UN | UN DESA | United Nations Department of Economic and Social Affairs. United Nations Department of Economic and Social Affairs. https://www.un.org/development/desa/en/news/population/2018-revision-of-world-urbanization-prospects.html. Accessed 18 Aug 2021
4. Albino, V., Berardi, U., Dangelico, R.: Smart cities: definitions, dimensions, performance, and initiatives. J. Urban Technol. 22(1), 3–21 (2015). https://doi.org/10.1080/10630732.2014.942092
5. Lyu, H., Dong, Z., Roobavannan, M., et al.: Rural unemployment pushes migrants to urban areas in Jiangsu Province China. Palgrave Commun. 5, 92 (2019)
6. Manzi, L.: Migration from rural areas to cities: challenges and opportunities | Regional Office for Central America, North America and the Caribbean (2016). https://rosanjose.iom.int/SITE/en/blog/migration-rural-areas-cities-challenges-and-opportunities. Accessed 18 Aug 2021
7. Fernandez-Anez, V., Fernández-Güell, J., Giffinger, R.: Smart city implementation and discourses: an integrated conceptual model. The case of Vienna. Cities 78, 4–16 (2018). https://doi.org/10.1016/j.cities.2017.12.004
8. Rahman, M., Hassan, M., Bahauddin, K., Khondoker, A., Hossain, M.: Exploring the impact of rural–urban migration on urban land use and land cover: a case of Dhaka city Bangladesh. Palgrave Commun. 7(2), 222–239 (2019). https://doi.org/10.1057/s41599-019-0302-1
9. Lim, C., Kim, K., Maglio, P.: Smart cities with big data: reference models, challenges, and considerations. Cities 82, 86–99 (2018). https://doi.org/10.1016/j.cities.2018.04.011
10. Pérez-Delhoyo, R., García-Mayor, C., Mora-Mora, H., Gilart-Iglesias, V., Andújar-Montoya, M.: Making smart and accessible cities: an urban model based on the design of intelligent environments. In: Proceedings of the 5th International Conference on Smart Cities and Green ICT Systems, SMARTGREENS 2016 (Smartgreens), pp. 63–70 (2016). https://doi.org/10.5220/0005798100630070
11. Rabelo, A., Oliveira, I., Lisboa-Filho, J.: An architectural model for intelligent cities using collaborative spatial data infrastructures. In: Proceedings of the 6th International Conference on Smart Cities and Green ICT Systems, SMARTGREENS 2017 (Smartgreens), pp. 242–249 (2017). https://doi.org/10.5220/0006306102420249
12. Chen, J., et al.: Big data challenge: a data management perspective. Front. Comput. Sci. 7 (2013). https://doi.org/10.1007/s11704-013-3903-7
13. Chen, M., Mao, S., Liu, Y.: Big data: a survey. Mob. Netw. Appl. 19(2), 171–209 (2014). https://doi.org/10.1007/s11036-013-0489-0
14. Gharaibeh, A., et al.: Smart cities: a survey on data management, security, and enabling technologies. IEEE Commun. Surv. Tutor. 19(4), 2456–2501 (2017). https://doi.org/10.1109/COMST.2017.2736886
15. EMC Education Services: Data Science and Big Data Analytics: Discovering, Analyzing, Visualizing and Presenting Data. Wiley (2015)

16. Siddiqa, A., et al.: A survey of big data management: taxonomy and state-of-the-art. J. Netw. Comput. Appl. **71**, 151–166 (2016). https://doi.org/10.1016/j.jnca.2016.04.008
17. Barnaghi, P., Bermúdez-Edo, M., Tönjes, R.: Challenges for quality of data in smart cities. J. Data Inf. Qual. **6**, 1–4 (2015). https://doi.org/10.1145/2747881
18. Bohli, J., Skarmeta, A., Moreno, V., García, D., Langendörfer, P.: SMARTIE project: secure IoT data management for smart cities. In: International Conference on Recent Advances in Internet of Things (RIoT), Singapore, pp. 1–6 (2015). https://doi.org/10.1109/RIOT.2015.710 4906
19. Kshetri, N.: Big data's impact on privacy, security and consumer welfare. Telecommun. Policy **38** (2014). https://doi.org/10.1016/j.telpol.2014.10.002
20. Rubinstein, I.: Big data: the end of privacy or a new beginning? Int. Data Priv. Law **3**(2), 74–87 (2013). https://doi.org/10.1093/idpl/ips036
21. Sinaeepourfard, A., Garcia, J., Masip-Bruin, X., Marín-Tordera, E.: A comprehensive scenario agnostic Data LifeCycle model for an efficient data complexity management. In: Proceedings of the 2016 IEEE 12th International Conference on E-Science, e-Science 2016, pp. 276–281 (2016). https://doi.org/10.1109/eScience.2016.7870909
22. Sinaeepourfard, A., et al.: Estimating smart city sensors data generation. In: 2016 Mediterranean Ad Hoc Networking Workshop, Med-Hoc-Net 2016 - 15th IFIP MEDHOCNET 2016 (2016). https://doi.org/10.1109/MedHocNet.2016.7528424
23. Tene, O., Polonetsky, J.: Big data for all: privacy and user control in the age of analytics. Northwestern J. Technol. Intellect. Property **11** (2012)
24. Sinaeepourfard, A., Masip-Bruin, X., Garcia, J, Marín-Tordera, E.: A Survey on Data Lifecycle Models: Discussions toward the 6Vs Challenges. Technical Report (UPC-DAC-RR-2015–18) (2015)
25. Plale, B., Kouper, I.: The centrality of data: data lifecycle and data pipelines. In: Data Analytics for Intelligent Transportation Systems, pp. 91–111 (2017). https://doi.org/10.1016/B978-0-12-809715-1.00004-3
26. Carlson, J.: The use of life cycle models in developing and supporting data services. In: Research Data Management: Practical Strategies for Information Professionals, pp. 63–86. Purdue University Press (2014)
27. Cox, A., Tam, W.: A critical analysis of lifecycle models of the research process and research data management. Aslib J. Inf. Manag. **70**(2), 142–157 (2018). https://doi.org/10.1108/AJIM-11-2017-0251
28. Pouchard, L.: Revisiting the data lifecycle with big data curation. Int. J. Digit. Curation **10**(2), 176–192 (2015). https://doi.org/10.2218/ijdc.v10i2.342
29. Ball, A.: Review of Data Management Lifecycle Models (2012). University of Bath http://opus.bath.ac.uk/28587/1/redm1rep120110ab10.pdf
30. National Institute of Standards and Technology: Framework for improving critical infrastructure cybersecurity. In: Proceedings of the Annual ISA Analysis Division Symposium, vol. 535, pp. 9–25 (2018)
31. Nickerson, R., Varshney, U., Muntermann, J.: Eur. J. Inf. Syst. **22**, 336 (2013). https://doi.org/10.1057/ejis.2012.26
32. Thomas, D.: A general inductive approach for analyzing qualitative evaluation data. Am. J. Eval. **27**(2), 237–246 (2006). https://doi.org/10.1177/1098214005283748
33. British Standard, BS 10010:2017, Information classification, marking and handling (2017)
34. Cabinet Office, Government Security Classifications
35. Cabinet Office, International Classified Exchanges
36. Carnegie Mellon University: Information Security Office. https://www.cmu.edu/iso/governance/guidelines/data-classification.html. Assessed 18 Aug 2021
37. Digital Guardian: The Definitive Guide to Data Classification (n.d.a)

38. ISO: ISO/IEC 27001:2005 - Information technology – Security techniques – Information security management systems – Requirements (n.d.a). https://www.iso.org/standard/42103.html
39. ISO: ISO/IEC 27005:2008 - Information technology – Security techniques – Information security risk management (n.d.a)
40. NIST FIPS PUB 199: 'Standards for Security Categorization of Federal Information and Information Systems' (2004). https://doi.org/10.6028/NIST.FIPS.199
41. Barcelona. Barcelona City Council Digital Plan (2018). https://ajuntament.barcelona.cat/digital/sites/default/files/2018_mesuradegovern_en.pdf
42. Eurocities. Data people cities, Eurocities citizen data, principles in action (2019). http://nws.eurocities.eu/MediaShell/media/Data_people_cities_-_EUROCITIES_citizen_data_principles_in_action.pdf
43. Finland. Finland's Presidency of the Council of the European Union, EU2019.FI: Principles for a human-centric, thriving and balanced data economy (2019). https://api.hankeikkuna.fi/asiakirjat/2d0f4123-e651-4874-960d-5cc3fac319b6/1f6b3855-fc1d-4ea6-8636-0b8d4a1d6519/RAPORTTI_20191123084411.pdf
44. Ireland. Department of Public Expenditure and Reform: Public Service Data Strategy 2019–2023 (2018). https://www.gov.ie/en/publication/1d6bc7-public-service-data-strategy-2019-2023/
45. Voigt, P., Bussche, A.: The EU General Data Protection Regulation (GDPR): A Practical Guide (2017). https://doi.org/10.1007/978-3-319-57959-7
46. Lankhorst, M.: Enterprise Architecture at Work: Modelling, Communication and Analysis. In Enterprise Engineering Series, 4th edn. (2017)
47. Urbaczewski, L., Mrdalj, S.: A comparison of enterprise architecture frameworks. Issues Inf. Syst. 7(2), 18–23 (2006)
48. Webster, J., Watson, R.: Analyzing the past to prepare for the future: writing a literature review. MIS Q. 26(2) (2002)
49. Falconer, G., Mitchell, S.: 'Smart City Framework: A Systematic Process for Enabling Smart+Connected Communities', … /web/about/ac79/docs/ps/motm/Smart-City-Framework (2012). http://scholar.google.com/scholar?hl=en&btnG=Search&q=intitle:Smart+City+Framework+A+Systematic+Process+for+Enabling+Smart+++Connected+Communities#2
50. Costa, C., Santos, M.: BASIS: a big data architecture for smart cities. In: SAI Computing Conference (SAI), pp. 1247–1256 (2016). https://doi.org/10.1109/SAI.2016.7556139
51. Cox, A., et al.: Definition of Smart City Reference Architecture (2016). http://espresso.espresso-project.eu/wp-content/uploads/2017/03/D4-17579.2-Smart-City-reference-architecture-report.pdf

Appendix A

52. Ali, I.M., et al.: Measuring the performance of big data analytics process. J. Theor. Appl. Inf. Technol. 97(14), 3796–3808 (2019)
53. Alshammari, M., Simpson, A.: Personal data management: an abstract personal data lifecycle model. In: Teniente, E., Weidlich, M. (eds.) BPM 2017. LNBIP, vol. 308, pp. 685–697. Springer, Cham (2018). https://doi.org/10.1007/978-3-319-74030-0_55
54. Attard, J., Orlandi, F., Auer, S.: Data driven governments: creating value through open government data. In: Hameurlain, A., et al. (eds.) Transactions on Large-Scale Data- and Knowledge-Centered Systems XXVII. LNCS, vol. 9860, pp. 84–110. Springer, Heidelberg (2016). https://doi.org/10.1007/978-3-662-53416-8_6
55. Coleman, S.: Measuring Data Quality for Ongoing Improvement. A Data Quality Assessment Framework. MK Series on Business Intelligence. Morgan Kaufmann (2013)

56. DAMA International: The DAMA Guide to the Data Management Body of Knowledge – DAMA-DMBOK. Technics Publications (2017)
57. Elmekki, H., Chiadmi, D., Lamharhar, H.: Open government data: towards a comparison of data lifecycle models. In: Proceedings of the ArabWIC 6th Annual International Conference Research Track (ArabWIC 2019), Article 15, p. 6. ACM, New York (2019). https://doi.org/10.1145/3333165.3333180
58. El Arass, M., Tikito, I., Souissi, N.: Data lifecycles analysis: towards intelligent cycle. In: Intelligent Systems and Computer Vision (ISCV), Fez, pp. 1–8 (2017)
59. El Arass, M., Tikito, I., Souissi, N.: An audit framework for data lifecycles in a big data context (2018). https://doi.org/10.1109/MoWNet.2018.8428883
60. Erl, T., Khattak, W., Buhler, P.: Big Data Fundamentals: Concepts, Drivers & Techniques, 1st edn. Prentice Hall (2016)
61. Faundeen, J., Hutchison, V.: The evolution, approval and implementation of the U.S. geological survey science data lifecycle model. J. eScience Librarianship 6. e1117 (2017). https://doi.org/10.7191/jeslib.2017.1117
62. Higgins, S.: The DCC curation lifecycle model. Int. J. Digit. Curation 3, 453 (2008). https://doi.org/10.1145/1378889.1378998
63. Inter-university Consortium for Political and Social Research (ICPSR): Guide to Social Science Data Preparation and Archiving: Best Practice Throughout the Data Life Cycle, 5th edn. Ann Arbor, MI (2012)
64. Levitin, A., Redman, T.: Data as a resource: properties, implications, and prescriptions. MIT Sloan Manag. Rev. 40(1), 89 (1998)
65. Möller, K.: Lifecycle models of data-centric systems and domains: the abstract data lifecycle model. Semant. Web 4, 67–88 (2013). https://doi.org/10.3233/SW-2012-0060
66. Sutherland, M., Cook, M.: Data-driven smart cities: a closer look at organizational, technical and data complexities, pp. 471–476 (2017). https://doi.org/10.1145/3085228.3085239
67. Urbinati, A., Bogers, M., Chiesa, V., Frattini, F.: Creating and capturing value from big data: a multiple-case study analysis of provider companies. Technovation (2018, forthcoming). https://doi.org/10.1016/j.technovation.2018.07.004
68. van Veenstra, A.F., van den Broek, T.: A Community-driven open data lifecycle model based on literature and practice. In: Boughzala, I., Janssen, M., Assar, S. (eds.) Case Studies in e-Government 2.0, pp. 183–198. Springer, Cham (2015). https://doi.org/10.1007/978-3-319-08081-9_11

Appendix B

69. Chauhan, S., Agarwal, N., Kar, A.: Addressing big data challenges in smart cities: a systematic literature review. Info (2016)
70. Deren, L., Yuan, Y., Zhenfeng, S.: Big data in smart city. Geomatics Inf. Sci. Wuhan Univ. 39(6), 631–640 (2014)
71. Liu, X., Heller, A., Nielsen, P.S.: CITIESData: a smart city data management framework. Knowl. Inf. Syst. 53(3), 699–722 (2017). https://doi.org/10.1007/s10115-017-1051-3
72. Lněnička, M., Komárková, J.: Developing a government enterprise architecture framework to support the requirements of big and open linked data with the use of cloud computing. Int. J. Inf. Manag. 46, 124–141 (2019). https://doi.org/10.1016/j.ijinfomgt.2018.12.003
73. Lyko, K., Nitzschke, M., Ngonga Ngomo, A.-C.: Big data acquisition. In: Cavanillas, J.M., Curry, E., Wahlster, W. (eds.) New Horizons for a Data-Driven Economy, pp. 39–61. Springer, Cham (2016). https://doi.org/10.1007/978-3-319-21569-3_4

A Spatial-Temporal Comparison of EV Charging Station Clusters Leveraging Multiple Validity Indices

René Richard[1]([✉]) [iD], Hung Cao[1] [iD], and Monica Wachowicz[1,2] [iD]

[1] University of New Brunswick, Fredericton, Canada
{rene.richard,hcao3}@unb.ca
[2] RMIT University, Melbourne, Australia
monica.wachowicz@rmit.edu.au

Abstract. Decoupling vehicles from the immediate consumption of fossil fuels introduces new opportunities in supporting sustainable mobility. Fostering a shift from vehicles with internal combustion engines to Electric Vehicles (EV) often involves using publicly funded subsidies. Given early EV adoption challenges, some charging stations may be under-utilized, others will serve a disproportionate number of users. An understanding of EV charging patterns is crucial for optimizing charging infrastructure placement and managing costs. Clustering has been used in the energy domain to ensure service continuity and consistency. However, clustering presents challenges in terms of algorithm and hyperparameter selection in addition to pattern discovery validation. The lack of ground truth information, which could objectively validate results, is not present in clustering problems. Therefore, it is difficult to judge the effectiveness of different modelling decisions since there is no external validity measure available for comparison. This work proposes a clustering process that allows for the creation of relative rankings of similar clustering results that will assist practitioners in the smart grid sector. The approach supports practitioners by allowing them to compare a clustering result of interest against other similar groupings over multiple temporal granularities. The efficacy of this analytical process is demonstrated with a case study using real-world EV charging event data from charging station operators in Atlantic Canada.

Keywords: Agglomerative hierarchical clustering · EV adoption · Charging infrastructure usage patterns · Clustering process · Cluster validity indices

1 Introduction

The trend of vehicle electrification is happening rapidly in many countries around the world. In spite of the pandemic-related worldwide downturn in car sales, new electric car registrations increased by 41% alongside $120 billion in consumer expenditures on electric vehicles (EV) in 2020 [9]. The International Energy Agency predicts that global EV stock will reach 145 million vehicles by 2030 in the Stated Policies Scenario and global EV fleet will reach 230 million vehicles by 2030 in the Sustainable Development

© Springer Nature Switzerland AG 2022
C. Klein et al. (Eds.): SMARTGREENS 2021/ VEHITS 2021, CCIS 1612, pp. 34–57, 2022.
https://doi.org/10.1007/978-3-031-17098-0_3

Scenario [9]. The futuristic vision of advanced and modern urbanization is a core concept of a smart city, in which cutting-edge infrastructure is able to offer a high quality of life for citizens and the sustainable management of natural resources. Adopting the usage of EVs is expected to improve air quality, provide sustainable mobility, mitigate greenhouse gas emissions, reduce urban noise pollution, and therefore contributes to this vision.

Building public charging infrastructure brings about high capital costs in addition to the usage of public funds to accelerate the transition to EVs. This necessitates smart decision-making at all stages of the adoption life-cycle. Given the challenges of early EV adoption, some charging stations may be under-utilized, others will serve a disproportionate number of users. Moreover, uncontrolled EV charging behaviors may cause numerous problems for existing power grids such as high load peaks, increased operational costs, degraded power quality, increased energy consumption, and the potential risk of power outages [3,31]. Therefore, reliable control of the EV charging behavior will be paramount for a successful mass market penetration. Clustering stations together based on usage patterns is an important and useful planning tool for operators. In addition, as the number of EVs increases, so does the demand for electricity and the possible strain on electrical grids. Utilities and other power generators need to prepare for increased demand. Accurate load forecasting is a tool that can help operators ensure service continuity and consistency.

Clustering is an unsupervised machine learning technique that assists practitioners in revealing hidden patterns and insights from a given dataset. In smart grid applications, this method has been used by practitioners to group similar consumers, categorize related energy consumption reports, forecast future demand, and grow EV adoption. Statistical and probabilistic models, built with data from EV charging stations having similar charging patterns, will reportedly have increased accuracy [29]. As a result, energy load projecting methods might perform better when applied to homogeneous clusters of EV stations as opposed to all stations. Hidden patterns in energy usage behavior are the key to improving services provided by utility companies, which are responsible for managing peaks and imbalances in EV charging infrastructure usage patterns [12].

Although clustering algorithms have been applied in many knowledge domains and applications, practitioners face the challenge of selecting the proper clustering algorithm with hyperparameter combination for their specific application. An additional concern includes evaluating the quality of clustering results. Moreover, it tends to require specialists to be able to assess and make sense of the clustering results due to the subjectivity found in deep expert knowledge. This is one of the main reasons why existing automated machine learning frameworks tend to focus on supervised learning tasks that require labeled data as input rather than unsupervised learning tasks that deal with unlabeled data [22]. Because the identification of the most similar clusters can be subjective, it usually requires different approaches to automate this process [23]. In addition, one of the challenges in clustering is finding the results that align with a practitioner's needs. In practice, there are several plausible clusters in complex datasets. What's more, practitioners may have different priorities and preferences. An unsupervised clustering algorithm has no way to intrinsically infer which clusters exhibit these desired priorities and preferences [5].

In spatial-temporal datasets (e.g. EV charging event datasets), evaluating the structure consistency of discovered clusters over different temporal granularities is normally an arduous, manual and time-consuming activity. Several examples of metrics can be utilized to determine the structure consistency of the clusters such as inter-cluster homogeneity, inter-cluster separation, density, and uniform cluster sizes. Nevertheless, the question of how to select a particular clustering result that is more meaningful than another based on practitioner priorities and preferences, still heavily depends on the practitioner's expert knowledge. Doing this for multiple results on data that has been sliced by weekly, monthly or seasonal partitions prior to applying the clustering algorithm would be very time consuming. Towards this challenge, this study explores whether, given the prospect of a clustering result of interest, a process of objectively highlighting and recommending similar clustering results can be automated in order to support practitioners in evaluating how clustering patterns persist over multiple temporal granularities, allowing practitioners to find meaningful clusters according to their preferences and priorities. This work aims to assist practitioners in identifying multiple clustering results of interest for different temporal partitions of the same data. Providing the practitioner with an initial ranked list of clustering results and a mechanism to determine clustering similarities can assist practitioners in downstream analytical tasks such as improving regression or classification model performance.

Consequently, a clustering process in which internal cluster validity indices are utilized to enable the identification of similar clustering results across various temporal slices of data is proposed. The main focus of this study is to support practitioners in identifying similar clustering results by using a reference result of interest and comparing this reference result with other results where all results are obtained from a-priori selected temporal partitions of the input data (i.e. weekly, monthly and seasonal partitions). To demonstrate the proposed approach, a case study using real-world charging event data from EV station operators in Atlantic Canada is utilized to evaluate our clustering process in identifying similar clusters of charging stations according to their usage patterns (e.g. high vs low utilization). This work is part of a larger ongoing research project. It continues the activities documented in [25] which examined charging events from EV charging stations exclusively. This paper extends this work by providing additional spatial context to the interpretation of the weekly clustering results. In addition to these enhanced results, supplementary background and clustering process details have been added.

The rest of the paper is organized as follows. In Sect. 2, previous research work is described. Section 3 describes the background of this work. Section 4 describes the proposed clustering process underpinning our work. Section 5 provides a detailed description of the real-world EV charging event data and the end-to-end automated implementation of our proposed clustering process. In Sect. 6, we discuss the results. Finally, Sect. 7 concludes and indicates future research work.

2   Related Work

Clustering techniques have played a significant role in finding new value and insights in many smart grid applications [26]. They are an essential tool in the pattern analysis process to discover energy usage behavior (i.e. the EV charging demand) in the energy domain [3]. For example, Straka and Buzna [29] carried out a comparison of the clustering results from the k-means, hierarchical, and DBScan algorithms aiming to explore usage patterns related to segments of charging stations. This experiment is based on a dataset of 1700 charging stations distributed across the Netherlands with about 1 million charging transactions collected during a 4-year period. The clustering algorithms successfully identified four groups of EV charging stations characterized by distinct usage patterns. In [8], the authors analyzed a dataset of seven public smart charging stations located across the City of Rochester, US. These stations recorded the charging activities of vehicles during a period of 2-years. By applying the k-means clustering algorithm, they were able to identify different clustering patterns and their behaviors with respect to charging activity, parking without charging activity, and parking durations. Another example of using clustering algorithms to reveal the charging patterns from EV stations can be found in [31]. In this study, the k-means clustering technique is used to categorized EV user behavior into different groups and label them for further prediction purposes. This work is developed based on a dataset collected from more than 200 EV charging stations installed in public parking structures in many locations in Los Angeles, US.

The aforementioned research [8,29,31] had a common point that the clustering results are mainly analysed based on the time series and the temporal characteristics of the datasets. Indeed, Xiong et al. [31] mainly used the arrival and departure schedule that are fixed at certain timestamps with little variance to label the groups, while [8,29] mainly used timestamps of charging events and utilization or energy consumed (kWh) to compute the clusters.

Very few research works exploit the spatial component of EV-related datasets to enhance knowledge discovery [20]. Recent work by Kang et al. [14] used location-based service data to identify spatial-patterns of EV usage behavior in urban areas to characterize the distribution of home and charging station clusters as well as user charging preferences. From the literature, few attempts [11,13] have conducted spatial-temporal clustering to improve the integration of an EV fleet with power management and operations.

A common issue in clustering is how to objectively and quantitatively assess and analyse the results. From this, some important research questions emerge such as (Q1) How to use the spatial-temporal information from a given dataset to assist practitioners in understanding hidden patterns revealed in the clustering results? (Q2) How to interpret and make sense of the clustering results yielded from a large quantity of grouped data points? and (Q3) How to automatically identify similar patterns across multiple temporal granularities without manually inspecting the results one by one?

Cluster validation is an essential task in the clustering process since it aims is to compare clustering results and solve the question of optimal cluster count. Many internal validity indices have been proposed in the literature to evaluate the "success" level that a clustering algorithm can achieve in discovering the natural groupings in data without any class label information [18,24]. Currently, the majority of studies validating cluster results have been focused on the computation of individual cluster validity indices (CVI), which are normally selected to specify the relative performance of clustering results. For example, Arbelaitz et al. [4] perform a comparison of 30 CVIs using an experimental setup on multiple datasets with ground truth information to propose the "best" partitioning. The optimal suggested number of partitions is defined as the one that is the most similar to the correct one measured by partition similarity measures. The authors found that noise and cluster overlap had the greatest impact on CVI performance. Some indices performed well with high dimensionality data sets and in cases where homogeneity of the cluster densities disappeared. The conclusion in this work suggests using several CVI to obtain robust results.

Sun et al. [30] proposed a time series clustering method using a modified Euclidean distance to group the similar charging tails from ACN-Data collected from smart EV charging stations. In this work, they evaluated their clustering results with Dynamic Time Warping distance (DTW) and Euclidean distance method using the silhouette coefficient. In [32], the Davies-Bouldin index is used to determine the best value for the cluster count parameter using the k-means algorithm.

All in all, the CVIs have been traditionally used for validation purposes. However, utilizing multiple CVIs together in combination with a proximity measure such as Euclidean distance has a strong potential to offer a new pairwise similarity measure that can enhance the comparison of clustering results by practitioners. This is also the key to answering the research questions (Q1), (Q2), (Q3) that we mention above. Certainly, this is not a common practice in data science as well as in the energy domain.

3 Background

Partitioning data into groups based on internal and a-priori unknown schemes inherit in the data is a main concern of clustering. In this unsupervised learning approach, algorithms are presented with data instances having features describing each object but no information, or label, is given as to how instances should be grouped in terms of their similarity. Clustering plays an important role in discovering hidden patterns in a dataset. It has been utilized in the energy domain to group similar consumers and help predict future demand. Clustering can serve as a pre-processing step for other algorithms. For example, statistical models built with data from charging stations having similar charging patterns will reportedly have superior accuracy [29].

Many clustering algorithms have been developed. These have been broadly categorized into a handful of groupings in the literature based on aspects of the approach such as the partitioning criteria, clustering space, procedures used for measuring the similarity and whether samples belong strictly to one cluster or can belong to more clusters in differing degrees. A common grouping of clustering algorithms is *partitioning*, *density*, *grid* and *hierarchical* methods [2, 10, 19, 21].

3.1 Partitioning Methods

Partitioning-based methods split data points into k partitions, where each partition represents a cluster. The data is split to optimize a certain, often distance-based, criterion function. Examples of commonly known partition-based methods include k-means and k-medoids [19]. The k-means clustering algorithm is easy to implement and is appropriate for large datasets. However, it has the disadvantage of being inappropriate for clusters of different densities and being dependent on initial centroid values. Additionally, noisy data and outliers are problematic for this algorithm. Centroids can be tugged by outliers, or outliers might get their own cluster instead of being ignored. Similarly, the k-Medoids algorithm is easy to implement. The advantage of this algorithm is that it converges quickly and is less sensitive to outliers. However, it is also dependent on the initial set of medoids and can produce different clusterings on iterative runs [2]. Partitioning methods have the drawback of whenever a point is close to the center of another cluster; poor results are obtained due to overlapping.

3.2 Density Methods

Density-based methods group neighboring objects into clusters based on local density conditions instead of distance-based criterion. Groups are formed either according to the density of neighborhood objects or a density function. This class of methods interprets clusters as dense regions that are separated by low density noisy regions. Examples of commonly known density-based methods include DBSCAN, and OPTICS. This class of methods can handle noisy data and can discover arbitrarily shaped clusters. Outliers are not problematic with this class of methods. However, density-based techniques have difficulty with data of varying densities. Together with hierarchical and partitioning-based methods, density-based methods have difficulties working with high dimensional data. As dimensionality increases, the feature space increases and objects appear to be sparse and dissimilar which affects clustering tendency [28].

3.3 Grid Methods

Grid-based methods form a grid structure from a finite number of cells quantized using the original data space. This class of methods denotes a fast processing time. Density-based methods require the practitioner to specify a grid size and a density threshold. However, this can be done automatically by using adaptive grids. Examples of commonly known grid-based methods include STING and CLIQUE. These methods are typically not effective for working with high dimensional data [19].

3.4 Hierarchical Methods

Hierarchical-based methods create a hierarchical decomposition for a given set of data points (i.e. divide similar instances by constructing a hierarchy of clusters). The family of methods can take an agglomerative (bottom-up) or divisive (top-down) approach. This class of methods can easily work with many forms of similarity or distance measures and are applicable to many attribute types. These methods suffer from a vagueness in termination criteria and also have difficulties in handling outliers or noisy data [19]. However, hierarchical clustering has the added advantage in that clustering results can be easily visualized and interpreted using a tree-based representation called a dendrogram (See Fig. 1).

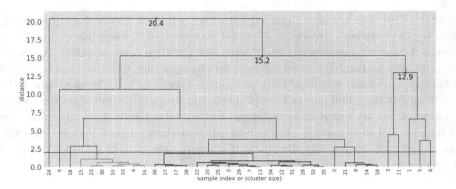

Fig. 1. Example dendrogram.

One example of a hierarchical clustering method is the Hierarchical Agglomerative Clustering (HAC) algorithm. The HAC algorithm needs to determine the distance between samples in order to form similar groupings of data points. There are many options available to practitioners when selecting a distance measure. Among popular metrics are the Euclidean and Manhattan distance metrics. Proximity measures can affect the shape of clusters. Different similarity measures can produce valid clusterings but they will have different meanings. Often, the importance of the clustering depends on whether the clustering criterion is associated with the phenomenon under study. Euclidean distance is a preferred distance measure by researchers in the field of clustering. This distance metric measures the root of square differences between co-ordinates of pairs of objects [27] and is defined as [7]:

$$D(x,y) = \sqrt{\sum_{i=1}^{d}(x_i - y_i)^2} \tag{1}$$

The Manhattan distance computes the absolute differences between coordinate of pairs of objects and is defined as [27]:

$$Dist_{XY} = |X_{ik} - X_{jk}| \tag{2}$$

Kapil and Chawla [15] found that clustering using Euclidean distance outperformed clustering using Manhattan distance in terms of the number of iteration, sum squared errors and time taken to build the model. Manhattan distance is usually preferred over the more common Euclidean distance when there is high dimensionality in the data [1].

HAC also requires a measure of distance between the clusters when deciding how to group the data at each iteration. This measure of cluster distances is done with a linkage function that captures the distance between clusters. Common measures of distance in this context include Ward and complete. Ward minimizes the variance of the clusters being merged. When making a merge decision with the Ward approach, two clusters will be merged if the new partitioning minimizes the increase in the overall intra-cluster variance. Complete uses the maximum distances between all observations of the two sets. When making a merge decision with the complete approach, two clusters will be merged if the new partitioning maximizes the distance between their two most remote elements. Even though the algorithm does not require pre-specifying the number of clusters prior to its usage, in order to get the best possible partitioning of the data, a decision on exactly where to cut the tree must be made.

4 Methodology

4.1 Clustering Algorithm Selection

Selecting an appropriate algorithm in clustering is critical since its performance may vary according to the distribution and encoding of data. For instance, the application of the HAC algorithm is usually limited to small datasets because of it's quadratic computational complexity. Additionally, hierarchical methods are not always successful in separating overlapping clusters and the clusters are static in the sense that a point previously assigned to a cluster cannot be moved to another cluster once allocated [17,33].

Essential to the practice of clustering is that different clustering techniques will work best for different types of data. There is no clustering algorithm that can be universally used to solve all problems. In fact, practitioners have become interested in recent years in combining several algorithms (e.g. clustering ensemble methods) to process datasets [16].

The clustering method selected for use in this work is the HAC algorithm. The input data is of low dimensionality and the number of instances is small. A single and simple algorithm was selected in order to simplify the workflow execution and experimental setup. The case study is focused on how the proposed solution facilitates the comparison of clustering results and reduces the cognitive demand on practitioners in identifying, understanding and comparing similar clustering results.

4.2 The Proposed Analytical Workflow

Figure 2 provides a conceptual overview of the main tasks of our proposed workflow. The numbered items in the figure link back to individual Python scripts described in detail in the implementation section. At the end of the process, a database is used to persist all clustering results and a RESTful Application Programming Interface (API) facilitates querying these results by different practitioners.

Data Preprocessing and Fusion. The data preprocessing and fusion task uses raw data from the public EV charging stations. Preprocessing consists of data cleaning and consolidation steps. Data cleaning, ensures good data quality and produces a set of cleaned files by eliminating errors, inconsistencies, duplicated and redundant data rows, and handling missing data. Data consolidation combines data from various data files into a single dataset. A variety of files from the cleaned dataset are used as the input for this operation. The output of these steps is a unique file that merges all attributes into one big table.

Moreover, data fusion consists of combining multiple data sources followed by a reduction or replacement for the purpose of better inference. In our proposed clustering process, consolidated station location information and charging event data files are combined to produce more consistent, accurate, and useful data files.

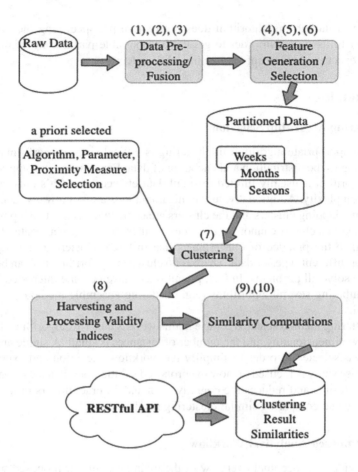

Fig. 2. Our proposed analytical workflow [25].

Feature Generation and Selection. The aim of the feature generation and selection task is to enrich pre-processed and fused data files by adding new attributes to each data row according to a specific context. This task is defined by a contextualization function that can produce a set of new data rows using contextualization parameters to add new attributes to the fused data rows. Transformed data is then partitioned using multiple temporal granularities (e.g. weekly, monthly or seasonally).

Clustering. The aim of the clustering task is to find the patterns from transformed input data using a hierarchical agglomerative clustering algorithm. The algorithm seeks to build a hierarchy of clusters by merging current pairs of mutual closest input data points until all the data points have been used in the computation. The measure of inter-cluster similarity is updated after each step using Ward linkage. This a priori selected algorithm is utilized to fit the various temporal granularities of the input data, producing multiple clustering results. Internal cluster validity indices are recorded during each application of the clustering algorithm.

Harvesting and Processing Validity Indices. Each application of the clustering algorithm generates a record consisting of the cluster count parameter value, the various cluster validity index values and the input data used to generate the clusters. Processing the validity indices involves selecting and normalizing the index values in preparation for Euclidean distance computations. This task utilizes the combination of eight cluster validity indices which are thoroughly described in [25] and listed in Table 3.

Similarity Computations. Our work uses a proximity measure in the clustering task and in the computation of the results similarity matrix. Selecting a measure to determine how similar or dissimilar two data points is an important step in any clustering process. Proximity measures can affect the shape of clusters as some data points may be relatively close to one another according to one measure and relatively far from each other according to another.

In addition to the clustering task, the similarity computation task uses Euclidean distance as the proximity measure between clustering results. All index values (e.g. multidimensional points in Euclidean space) of each clustering result are used in the distance computations. The pair-wise similarity comparisons (e.g. the similarity matrix) are then persisted in a database for down-stream results exploration via a RESTful API.

The similarity matrix is stored in the database using two tables. The first table summarizes clustering results with rows consisting of a unique clustering result ID (*result_id*) and meta-data about running the algorithm (e.g. input file name, clustering execution time, all validity index values, etc.). The second table, which is linked to the first table, contains rows consisting of a source result ID (*from_result_id*), a target result ID (*to_result_id*) and a Euclidean distance. Links between result IDs are not duplicated as directionality is not considered.

4.3   Clustering and Results Exploration

The proposed analytical workflow enables the basic identification and interactive querying of potentially interesting clustering results. Additionally, the resulting assembly enables drilling down into relative rankings of comparable results for diagnostic and downstream analytical tasks. This process leverages the aforementioned RESTful API in order to facilitate this capability. The workflow facilitates the comparison of clustering results by practitioners with different priorities and preferences.

Selecting the appropriate algorithm and hyperparameters in clustering is critical. However, interpreting the level of "success" achieved once modeling results are available can be cognitively demanding. Their may exist several viable combinations of algorithms and hyperparameters that result in plausible clusters. Comparing and contrasting multiple clustering results can help uncover interesting structure in data. Nevertheless, this comes at a cost since practitioners will have to expend effort to cognitively encode and interpret these results. Additionally, in data with a temporal component such as EV charging events for example, assessing the structure consistency of discovered clusters over different temporal granularities adds additional demands. Supporting the practitioner in analytical results exploration helps reduce mental demand in comparing and contrasting results.

The traditional usage of CVI has been for validation purposes. However, utilizing multiple CVI together in combination with a proximity measure such as Euclidean distance has a strong potential to offer a new pairwise similarity measure that can enhance the comparison of clustering results. Supporting the practitioner by automating clustering workflows and presenting meaningful analytical results in a way that increases the opportunity to understand and compare similar groupings can assist in recognizing patterns and identifying meaningful results for downstream analysis.

5   Implementation

This work makes use of real operational data from public EV charging stations provided by the New Brunswick Power Corporation. 9,505 EV charging events that occurred between the dates of April 2019 and April 2020 at Level-2 (L2) and Level-3 (L3) public charging stations were included in the analysis. Table 1 describes the raw EV charging dataset features. Our practitioners are utility company managers and planners that are responsible for coordinating various projects including EV charging station condition assessments, operating and capital budget forecasting, and maintenance and operation practices development. Figure 3 describes the overall end-to-end implementation of our EV case study.

Table 1. Raw data [25].

Column name	Description
Connection ID	Unique identifier for a connection
Recharge start time (local)	Timestamp denoting start of charging event
Recharge end time (local)	Timestamp denoting end of charging event
Account name	Unused (all null)
Card identifier	Unique identifier for a charging plan member
Recharge duration (hours:minutes)	Duration of charge event
Connector used	Connection used during charge event
Start state of charge (%)	State of charge % at beginning of charging event
End state of charge (%)	State of charge % after charging event is complete
End reason	Charge event end reason
Total amount	Unused (all null)
Currency	Unused (all null)
Total kWh	Energy transferred to vehicle during charging event
Station	Unique identifier for charging station

Custom-written Python code and a scientific Python stack were leveraged to implement the proposed clustering process. Task elements were executed in sequence from a centralized management script. The software programs used in this work were packaged using a Docker [6] container in order to ensure a reproducible and consistent computational environment.

Figure 4 highlights noteworthy aspects of the implementation. The numbered boxes represent individual parameterized Python scripts. The data flow is such that the output of one script is the input for the next script. Input and output file names contain

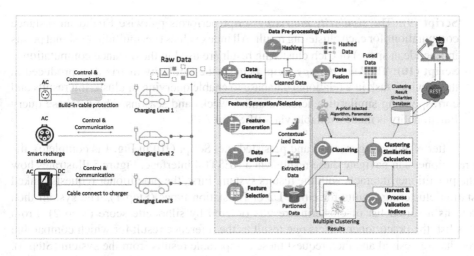

Fig. 3. Overview of our implemented EV case study [25].

parameter values that were used when calling the workflow's scripts. The grey elements represent a job's input file(s). The blue elements represent a job's output file(s). The detailed implementation of each script is described as follows:

- **Script (1):** The *one_way_hash.py* script imports raw event data and casts column elements to appropriate types. Additionally, a one-way hash function is applied to the *Card identifier* column.
- **Script (2):** The *locations_to_parquet.py* script imports raw station location data and integrates multiple input files into one.
- **Script (3):** The *fuse_location_w_events.py* script fuses event data with charging station location information.
- **Script (4):** This work focuses on recharge report event data in the downstream analysis. The *feat_eng_rech_report.py* script creates new features (contextualized) based on calculations involving existing data attributes and removes events with a duration of 5 min or less (eliminating 11% of the raw records).
- **Script (5):** The *create_batch_ranges.py* script creates temporal partitions of the data. These partitions facilitate the cluster analysis based on charging events occurring during a particular week, month or season of the year.
- **Script (6):** The *generate_ev_station_features.py* prepares the input data for clustering by calculating, for each charging station, station type and temporal granularity, the proportion of total charging events and the proportion of total power used to charge vehicles relative to all stations.
- **Script (7):** The *cluster_data.py* script applies the agglomerative clustering algorithm to all temporal slices of the data produced in the previous task. This is done for a cluster count hyperparameter that varies from 2 to 7. Other hyperparameter settings are kept constant to simplify the experimental setup. Internal cluster validity indices are recorded during each application of the clustering algorithm (See Table 2 for the list of indices).
- **Script (8):** The *scale_indices.py* script normalizes the internal cluster validity indices in preparation for the downstream Euclidean distance computations.

– **Script (9):** The *similarity_matrix.py* script performs pairwise Euclidean distance computations for each clustering result. All index values (i.e. multidimensional points in Euclidean space) of each clustering result are used in the distance computations.
– **Script (10):** The *load_data.py* script persists the similarity matrix data produced in the previous task in a relational database to enable querying of clustering results and corresponding similarities across months, weeks and seasons. The database query functionality is made available via a RESTful API.

After results are generated and persisted (i.e. Script (10) in Fig. 4 is complete), the practitioner can navigate these results via a RESTful interface. Figure 5 illustrates how the practitioner interacts with the results system. First, the practitioner requests ranked station clustering results for either L2 or L3 station types (Step 1). The system then returns a sorted list of clustering results ordered by silhouette score (Step 2). From this list, the practitioner selects one result as the reference result for which comparable results are desired and then request these comparable results from the system (Step 3). Finally, the system returns a sorted list of comparable clustering results that is ordered by Euclidean distance (Step 4). This sorted list contains result-specific artefacts such as scatter plots, mapped station cluster memberships and silhouette plots.

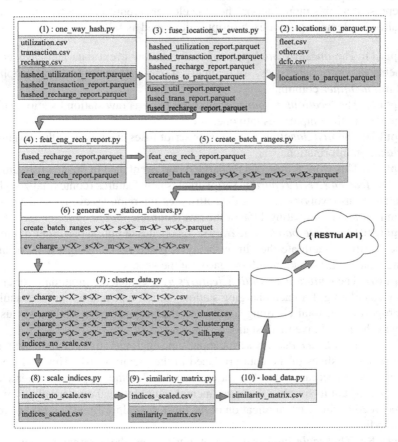

Fig. 4. Implemented clustering process data flow [25]. (Color figure online)

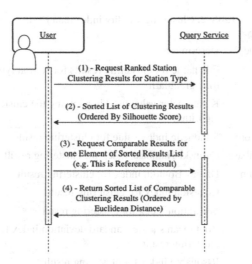

Fig. 5. Results query sequence [25].

The clustering process implementation and RESTful API facilitate the comparison of clustering result similarities across various temporal granularities. This process is useful in identifying avenues for further analysis. One Level 3 station clustering result for the week of May 27th, 2019 has been selected as a case study to demonstrate our approach. The case study is presented in the next section.

6   Discussion of the Results

This section highlights the results of our proposed approach in identifying similar station clusterings over multiple weeks with a case study. Table 3 highlights similar clustering results relative to station clusterings for a target week starting on May 27th, 2019. In all results, the number of clusters is 2 and the station type is L3. The table is sorted in ascending order by Euclidean distance relative to the target week. According to the multi-dimensional pairwise distance calculations obtained using the indices described in Table 2, the most similar clustering result to the week starting on May 27th, 2019 is the result for the week starting on February the 17th 2020. The least similar clustering result is the result for the week starting on December 2nd, 2019.

A corresponding visual presentation of the clustering results found in Table 3 can be seen in Figs. 6 through 10. Each figure contains a silhouette plot, scatter plot and a map describing the clustered data. In the silhouette plots, an observation with a silhouette width near 1, means that the data point is well placed in its cluster; an observation with a silhouette width closer to negative 1 indicates the likelihood that this observation might really belong in some other cluster.

6.1   Week of May 27th, 2019 - (Reference Week)

We can see from Fig. 6 that a reasonable structure in the data has been found for our reference week, which starts on May 27th, 2019. In this clustering, stations are grouped

Table 2. Clustering validity index data [25].

Column name	Description
file_name	File name for clustering results for station type and time granularity
n_cluster	K parameter value used in applying the clustering algorithm
silhouette_score	Silhouette index value for clustering result
calinski_harabasz	Caliński-Harabasz index for clustering result
davies_bouldin	Davies-Bouldin index for clustering result
cohesion	Cohesion index for clustering result
separation	Separation index for clustering result
RMSSTD	Root mean square standard deviation index for clustering result
RS	R-squared index for clustering result
XB	Xie-Beni index for clustering results

Table 3. Clustering similarities - L3 - May 27th, 2019 [25].

WEEK	Sil	CH	DB	C	S	RMS	RS	XB	*Dist*
MAY-27-2019	**0.60**	**51.37**	**0.51**	**1.12**	**2.40**	**0.15**	**0.68**	**0.09**	*N/A*
FEB-17-2020	0.60	49.35	0.57	0.19	2.44	0.16	0.67	0.10	*0.081*
MAR-02-2020	0.65	55.51	0.52	1.14	2.63	0.15	0.70	0.07	*0.101*
JUL-29-2019	0.60	55.82	0.53	0.99	2.30	0.14	0.70	0.11	*0.105*
...	...	...	...	...	...	...	...	...	...
DEC-02-2019	0.63	56.55	0.58	1.26	2.97	0.16	0.70	0.09	*0.177*

Column Name Abbreviations:
Sil: Silhouette index
CH: Caliński-Harabasz index
DB: Davies-Bouldin index
C: Cohesion
S: Separation
RMS: Root mean square standard deviation
RS: R-squared
XB: Xie-Beni index
Dist: Euclidean distance between current and previous row

in terms of relatively higher and lower utilization rates. The average silhouette score is 0.600 in this clustering result (See Fig. 6a).

In Fig. 6b, cluster 0, the cluster with relatively lower utilization rates, has more station members than cluster 1. Cluster 1 is the grouping of stations with relatively higher utilization rates. In the scatter plot, crisp clusters identified by the HAC algorithm can be observed. However, cluster 1 has an observation that is comparatively far from its other station members. The map in Fig. 6c, indicates that cluster 1 member stations are mostly located in the lower half of the province.

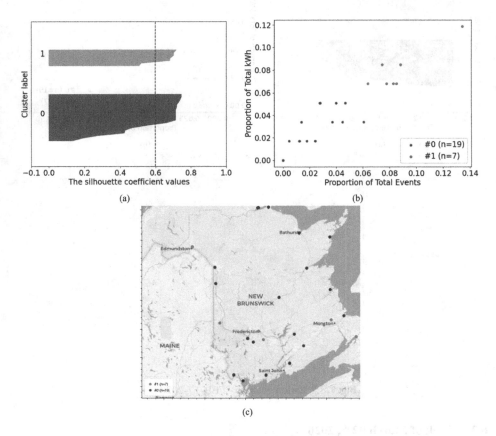

Fig. 6. L3 station clusters - MAY-27-2019.

6.2   Week of February 17ᵗʰ, 2020

We now focus on the closest clustering result relative to our reference week. This grouping is for the week starting on the 27ᵗʰ of February, 2020. The average silhouette score for this result is also 0.60 (See Fig. 7a). The scatter plot of Fig. 7b denotes relatively well separated clusters similar to our reference week. The clusters can also be thought of as groupings of high vs. low station utilization rates with this result. Additionally, the number of observations in each cluster is the same as the reference week. Results for the week of May 27ᵗʰ, 2019 are slightly better when considering all cluster validation indices. This can also be observed visually. Data points seem to be closer together in the scatter plot of Fig. 6b than in Fig. 7b. The in-between cluster separation in both results are similar.

The map in Fig. 7c reveals that cluster 1 - the higher utilization stations cluster - member stations are mostly located in the right half of the province with this clustering result.

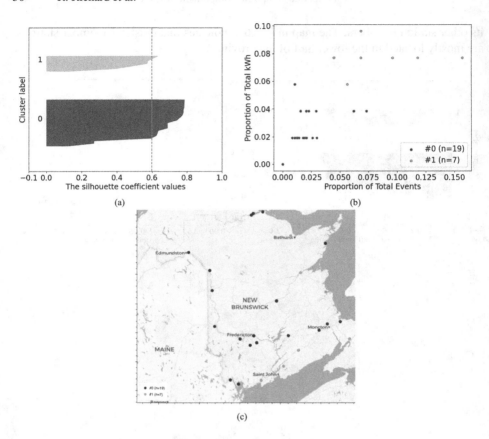

Fig. 7. L3 station clusters - FEB-17-2020.

6.3   Week of March 02nd, 2020

The next closest clustering result relative to our reference week is the grouping for the week starting on March 02nd, 2020. The average silhouette score for this result is 0.65. The silhouette plot in Fig. 8a suggests a less optimal clustering. This plot indicates that some observations would seemingly belong to clusters other than the one they are in; these observations have a negative silhouette width value. A less than optimal clustering is confirmed by observing the scatter plot of Fig. 8b. Some observations in cluster 1 could be outliers. Additionally, the cluster's cohesion is not as prevalent as cluster 0's. Perhaps a cluster count of 3 would be more appropriate with this result.

Figure 8c, indicates that cluster 1 - the higher utilization stations cluster - member stations are mostly located in the lower-right half of the province with this clustering result.

6.4   Week of July 29th, 2019

The silhouette plot in Fig. 9a and the average silhouette score of 0.60 suggest a reasonable structure in the data has also been found in this week. Figure 9b denotes relatively

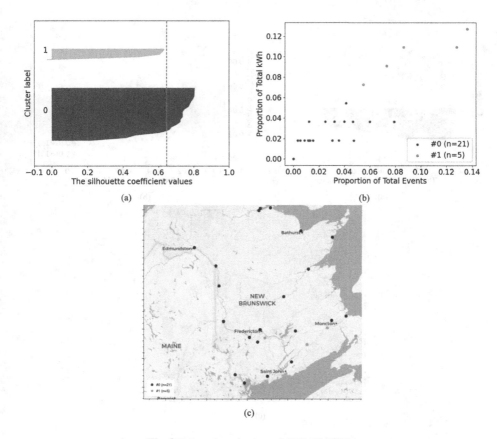

Fig. 8. L3 station clusters - MAR-02-2020.

well separated clusters. Cluster 1 has an observation that is comparatively far from its other station members. The number of observations in each cluster for both the reference clustering result and this result are different. Based on the various indices, clustering results for July 29th, 2020 are better in some aspects and inferior in others to results for the week of May 27th, 2019. This result was identified as being the 3rd most similar result for our target week.

Figure 9c, indicates that cluster 1 - the higher utilization stations cluster - member stations are mostly located along a major freeway in the province, mostly covering the left and the bottom sections of the province.

6.5 Week of December 02nd, 2019

The decreasing relative similarity of results is especially visible when comparing the results for the week of May 27th, 2019 with results having the least similarity (i.e., results for the week of December 2nd, 2019). In Fig. 10a we can see that all cluster 1's members have below average silhouette scores and the clustering of stations is much

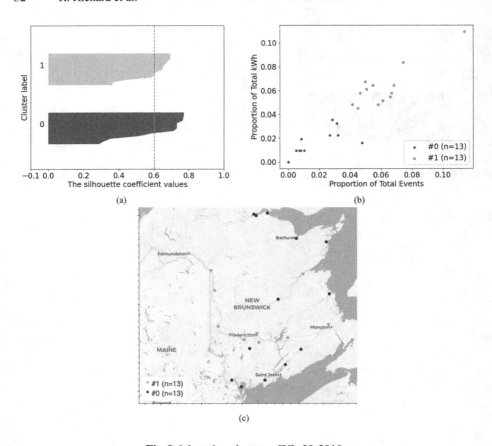

(a)   (b)

(c)

Fig. 9. L3 station clusters - JUL-29-2019.

less similar than the other clusterings. Additionally, as can be observed in Fig. 10b, perhaps a cluster count of 3 would be more appropriate with this result.

Figure 10c, indicates that cluster 1 - the higher utilization stations cluster - member stations are mostly located in the lower-right half of the province with this clustering result.

6.6 Overall Results

As can be observed in Figs. 6, 7, 8, 9 and 10 of the previous sections, the decreasing relative similarity of clustering results is especially noticeable when visually comparing the silhouette and scatter plots for the week of May 27th with the same visualizations in other weeks and doing so in a step-wise fashion down the ranked list of results.

Individual index calculations embed implicit trade-offs on what is prioritized when expressing inter-cluster separation, inter-cluster homogeneity, density, and compactness as one numeric value. One can view the various indices as averages where a certain precision is lost in the summary. This can lead to situations where one index will suggest a better clustering relative to another grouping and another index will inverse this

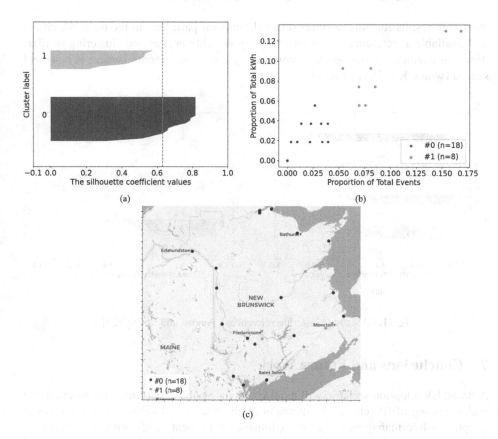

Fig. 10. L3 station clusters - DEC-02-2019.

assessment. This is illustrated in Table 3 where for example, the silhouette, Caliński-Harabasz, separation and R-squared index values for December 02nd suggest a better clustering than on the week starting on May 27th. However, the Davies-Bouldin, cohesion and RMS index values inverse this assessment.

Capital investments in public charging infrastructure involves the use of public funds and necessitates robust informed decision making. Identifying similar station utilization patterns over multiple weeks can be useful planning information for station operators. The cluster analysis presented in our case study provides useful insights by identifying similar groupings of EV charging stations according to their usage patterns in time.

The results highlighted in the case study provided in this section demonstrate that given a clustering result of interest, a process of objectively highlighting and recommending similar clustering results can indeed be automated in order to support the practitioner in evaluating how structure in data persists over multiple time slices in a dataset with temporal properties. The relative ranking of similar clustering results that our approach affords makes it easy to objectively identify similar station groupings over multiple weeks based on a reference week. Not highlighted in the case study, are the clustering results for other a-priori selected temporal partitions in the data, which are also available as reference points for exploring monthly or seasonal clustering similarities. For example silhouette plots representing a reference month (where K = 4) and season (where K = 3), see Fig. 11.

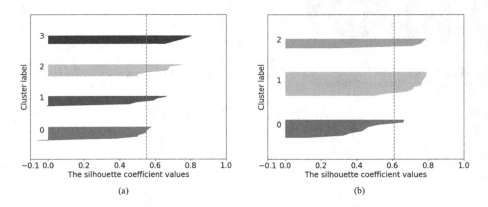

(a)   (b)

Fig. 11. L3 station clustering references - August and Spring [25].

7   Conclusions and Future Work

A broad EV adoption scenario will require adequate public charging infrastructure. An understanding of EV charging patterns at public charging stations is crucial to foster adoption while managing costs and optimizing placement of charging infrastructure. The outcomes of this research is believed to provide useful insights in planning and expanding infrastructure allocation. To optimize operations, EV station operators often seek market-related insights. EV charging station clustering can reveal useful segmentations in service consumption patterns.

   Although clustering has become a routine analytical task in many research domains, it remains arduous for practitioners to select a good algorithm with adequate hyperparameters and to assess the quality of clustering and the consistency of identified structures over various temporal slices of data. The process of clustering data is often an iterative, lengthy, manual and cognitively demanding task. The subjectivity in determining the level of "success" that unsupervised learning approaches are able to achieve and the required expert knowledge during the modeling phase suggest that a human-in-the-loop process of supporting the practitioner during this activity would be beneficial. Ascertaining whether a particular clustering of data is meaningful or not requires expertise and effort. Doing this for multiple results on data that has been sliced by weekly, monthly or seasonal partitions prior to applying the clustering algorithm would be very time consuming. Manually identifying one meaningful result of interest and then having an automated mechanism to select similar results is extremely useful in reducing the amount of effort required to identify avenues that merit further analysis and assist in downstream analytical tasks such as improving regression or classification model performance.

The contributions of this work include an end-to-end analytical workflow that enables the analysis of energy utilization patterns at public charging infrastructure using real charging data from station operators in Atlantic Canada. This workflow facilitates the comparison of clustering results by practitioners with different priorities and preferences. Utilizing the combination of eight internal cluster validity indices to compute a proximity measure of clustering results in a priori selected temporal partitions of the data reduces the cognitive demand on users in identifying, understanding and comparing of similar clustering results over time. A case study demonstrates that given a clustering result of interest, the process of objectively highlighting and recommending similar clustering results can be automated in order to support the practitioner in evaluating how structure in data persists over multiple time slices and reduce effort in identifying multiple meaningful clustering results from a large number of modeling artifacts.

Currently, the initial ranked list of clustering results described in Step 1 of Fig. 5 is created using silhouette scores only. Framing the creation of the initial ranked list of results as a Multiple Criteria Decision Making (MCDM) problem may improve the initial results exploration experience. This will be included in future work. EV charging patterns can be more effectively analyzed by referencing the social and economic contexts in which they occur. Once clusters are obtained, it may be useful to explain the clusters with features other than the original features used to obtain the clusters. The use of real-world EV charging event data combined with nearby traffic volumes and nearby amenities may help to further contextualize the clustering results. This will also be included in future work. Lastly, other avenues will explore if utilizing the Euclidean distances and clusters obtained in this work can improve predictive performance of a baseline classifier such as improving the predictive performance of classifiers for predicting peak day of week kWh.

Acknowledgements. The authors of this paper like to thank the New Brunswick Power Corporation for providing access to station operator users and the EV charging data referenced in this research. This work was partially supported by the NSERC/Cisco Industrial Research Chair, Grant IRCPJ 488403-1.

References

1. Aggarwal, C.C., Hinneburg, A., Keim, D.A.: On the surprising behavior of distance metrics in high dimensional space. In: Van den Bussche, J., Vianu, V. (eds.) ICDT 2001. LNCS, vol. 1973, pp. 420–434. Springer, Heidelberg (2001). https://doi.org/10.1007/3-540-44503-X_27
2. Ahmed, S.T., Sreedhar Kumar, S., Anusha, B., Bhumika, P., Gunashree, M., Ishwarya, B.: A generalized study on data mining and clustering algorithms. In: Smys, S., Iliyasu, A.M., Bestak, R., Shi, F. (eds.) ICCVBIC 2018, pp. 1121–1129. Springer, Cham (2020). https://doi.org/10.1007/978-3-030-41862-5_114
3. Al-Ogaili, A.S., et al.: Review on scheduling, clustering, and forecasting strategies for controlling electric vehicle charging: challenges and recommendations. IEEE Access **7**, 128353–128371 (2019)
4. Arbelaitz, O., Gurrutxaga, I., Muguerza, J., PéRez, J.M., Perona, I.: An extensive comparative study of cluster validity indices. Pattern Recogn. **46**(1), 243–256 (2013)

5. Bae, J., Helldin, T., Riveiro, M., Nowaczyk, S., Bouguelia, M.R., Falkman, G.: Interactive clustering: a comprehensive review. ACM Comput. Surv. **53**(1), 1–39 (2020). https://doi.org/10.1145/3340960, https://dl.acm.org/doi/10.1145/3340960

6. Boettiger, C.: An introduction to docker for reproducible research. ACM SIGOPS Oper. Syst. Rev. **49**(1), 71–79 (2015)

7. Chakrabarty, A.: An investigation of clustering algorithms and soft computing approaches for pattern recognition. Ph.D. thesis, Assam University (2010)

8. Desai, R.R., Chen, R.B., Armington, W.: A pattern analysis of daily electric vehicle charging profiles: operational efficiency and environmental impacts. J. Adv. Transp. **2018** (2018)

9. Ekta Meena, B., et al.: Global EV outlook 2021: accelerating ambitions despite the pandemic (2021)

10. Han, J., Pei, J., Kamber, M.: Data Mining: Concepts and Techniques. Elsevier, Amsterdam (2011)

11. Heuberger, C.F., Bains, P.K., Mac Dowell, N.: The EV-olution of the power system: a spatio-temporal optimisation model to investigate the impact of electric vehicle deployment. Appl. Energy **257**, 113715 (2020)

12. Iglesias, F., Kastner, W.: Analysis of similarity measures in times series clustering for the discovery of building energy patterns. Energies **6**(2), 579–597 (2013)

13. Ji, D., et al.: A spatial-temporal model for locating electric vehicle charging stations. In: Bi, Y., Chen, G., Deng, Q., Wang, Y. (eds.) ESTC 2017. CCIS, vol. 857, pp. 89–102. Springer, Singapore (2018). https://doi.org/10.1007/978-981-13-1026-3_7

14. Kang, J., Kan, C., Lin, Z.: Are electric vehicles reshaping the city? An investigation of the clustering of electric vehicle owners' dwellings and their interaction with urban spaces. ISPRS Int. J. Geo Inf. **10**(5), 320 (2021)

15. Kapil, S., Chawla, M.: Performance evaluation of k-means clustering algorithm with various distance metrics. In: 2016 IEEE 1st International Conference on Power Electronics, Intelligent Control and Energy Systems (ICPEICES), pp. 1–4. IEEE (2016)

16. Khedairia, S., Khadir, M.T.: A multiple clustering combination approach based on iterative voting process. J. King Saud Univ.-Comput. Inf. Sci. (2019)

17. Kuwil, F.H., Atila, Ü., Abu-Issa, R., Murtagh, F.: A novel data clustering algorithm based on gravity center methodology. Expert Syst. Appl. **156**, 113435 (2020)

18. Liu, Y., Li, Z., Xiong, H., Gao, X., Wu, J.: Understanding of internal clustering validation measures. In: 2010 IEEE International Conference on Data Mining, pp. 911–916. IEEE (2010)

19. Mann, A.K., Kaur, N.: Review paper on clustering techniques. Glob. J. Comput. Sci. Technol. (2013)

20. Morton, C., Anable, J., Yeboah, G., Cottrill, C.: The spatial pattern of demand in the early market for electric vehicles: Evidence from the united kingdom. J. Transp. Geogr. **72**, 119–130 (2018)

21. Ofetotse, E.L., Essah, E.A., Yao, R.: Evaluating the determinants of household electricity consumption using cluster analysis. J. Build. Eng. **43**, 102487 (2021)

22. Oliveira, M.: 3 reasons why AutoML won't replace data scientists yet (2019). https://www.kdnuggets.com/3-reasons-why-automl-wont-replace-data-scientists-yet.html/. Accessed March 2019

23. Poulakis, G.: Unsupervised AutoML: a study on automated machine learning in the context of clustering. Master's thesis, Πανεπιστήμιο Πειραιώς (2020)

24. Rendón, E., Abundez, I., Arizmendi, A., Quiroz, E.M.: Internal versus external cluster validation indexes. Int. J. Comput. Commun. **5**(1), 27–34 (2011)

25. Richard, R., Cao, H., Wachowicz, M.: An automated clustering process for helping practitioners to identify similar EV charging patterns across multiple temporal granularities.

In: Proceedings of the 10th International Conference on Smart Cities and Green ICT Systems - SMARTGREENS, pp. 67–77. INSTICC, SciTePress (2021). https://doi.org/10.5220/0010485000670077

26. Si, C., Xu, S., Wan, C., Chen, D., Cui, W., Zhao, J.: Electric load clustering in smart grid: methodologies, applications, and future trends. J. Mod. Power Syst. Clean Energy **9**(2), 237–252 (2021)

27. Singh, A., Yadav, A., Rana, A.: K-means with three different distance metrics. Int. J. Comput. Appl. **67**(10) (2013)

28. Sisodia, D., Singh, L., Sisodia, S., Saxena, K.: Clustering techniques: a brief survey of different clustering algorithms. Int. J. Latest Trends Eng. Technol. (IJLTET) **1**(3), 82–87 (2012)

29. Straka, M., Buzna, L.: Clustering algorithms applied to usage related segments of electric vehicle charging stations. Transp. Res. Proc. **40**, 1576–1582 (2019)

30. Sun, C., Li, T., Low, S.H., Li, V.O.: Classification of electric vehicle charging time series with selective clustering. Electr. Power Syst. Res. **189**, 106695 (2020)

31. Xiong, Y., Wang, B., Chu, C.C., Gadh, R.: Electric vehicle driver clustering using statistical model and machine learning. In: 2018 IEEE Power & Energy Society General Meeting (PESGM), pp. 1–5. IEEE (2018)

32. Xydas, E., Marmaras, C., Cipcigan, L.M., Jenkins, N., Carroll, S., Barker, M.: A data-driven approach for characterising the charging demand of electric vehicles: a UK case study. Appl. Energy **162**, 763–771 (2016)

33. Zolhavarieh, S., Aghabozorgi, S., Teh, Y.W.: A review of subsequence time series clustering. Sci. World J. **2014** (2014)

Facade Material Identification for Optimizing Building Energy Consumption Across Various WWRs for ECBC(Code) Compliant Buildings in Warm-Humid Climate, India

Pranav Kishore[1], Sathwik Bysani[1], Stuthi Shetty[1], Pradeep Kini[1(✉)], Anuthama Mahesh[2], and Anupam Raj[3]

[1] Centre of Sustainable Built Environment, Manipal School of Architecture and Planning, Manipal Academy of Higher Education, Manipal, India
`pradeep.kini@manipal.edu`
[2] Manipal School of Architecture and Planning, MSAP, Manipal Academy of Higher Education, Manipal, India
[3] Tech Architect/Team Lead at YourMD.ca, Calgary, AB, Canada

Abstract. Increase in population has led to increase in built up environment around the world. The demand for a better lifestyle has developed a high pressure on the Energy Sector to keep up with the day-to-day needs. Increased demand in jobs have caused an increase in the commercial buildings in India. Even today India depends highly on non-renewable sources of energy to meet the energy demands. To regulate the demand and supply chain, India has various energy policies, some mandatory and some a voluntary schemes. Energy Conservation Building Code 2017 is one such policy which is mandatory in only very few states in the country. The study in this paper demonstrates how the use of this energy policy on the building envelope along with Window-To-Wall Ratios help in reducing building's Energy Performance Index and helps conservation of energy consumption in the long run. The existing building envelope taken from the case example is documented on-site and recorded. The case example considered in this study is situated in the Warm and Humid Climate zone of India. The application of ECBC 2017 and further Design Alternatives to the building envelope, observes a reduction of 32% when compared to the contemporary.

Keywords: Energy conservation building code · Building envelope · Climate change · Warm & humid climate · Building energy simulation · Sustainable development

1 Introduction

1.1 Urbanization in India

Urbanization is closely linked to modernization, industrialization, and the sociological process of rationalization. Urbanization occurs as individual, commercial, and governmental efforts reduce time and expense in commuting and improve opportunities for jobs,

© Springer Nature Switzerland AG 2022
C. Klein et al. (Eds.): SMARTGREENS 2021/ VEHITS 2021, CCIS 1612, pp. 58–86, 2022.
https://doi.org/10.1007/978-3-031-17098-0_4

education, housing, and transportation [1]. This can be well corroborated from the fact that every 12th city dweller of the world and every 7th of the developing countries is from India. It is estimated that 75% of the buildings required in the upcoming decade is yet to be built, and a study conducted in 2010 estimates that 700–900 million square metres of commercial and residential spaces are expected to be built every year in India [2]. The fast Increasing World Energy consumption levels are raising concerns over the depletion of natural resources and the increasing environmental pollution impacts like Ozone depletion, Climate change, global warming etc. In India, as per the National Mission for Enhanced Energy Emissions (NMEEE) document, 2009, from annual consumption of 19200 KWh in 2005 only from Residential & commercial buildings, it is predicted to reach 89,823 KWh in 2030 [3]. Construction industry has a very important role in the Indian economy, contributing on an average 6.5% of the Gross Domestic Product (GDP). At the same time, it has lot of impact on the environment with its consumption of energy both operational energy and embodied energy in the materials that it uses. Commercial Building space accounts for 33% of the total built space and increasing at a rate of 8–10% annually. The average annual electricity consumption for space conditioning and lighting in India is around 80 KWh/m^2 and 160 KWh/m^2 for residential and commercial buildings respectively [3]. Increase in the use of energy consumption from the building sector is contributing negatively towards the environment. Non-renewable resources are still majorly in demand for the production of energy hence contributing towards climate change.

1.2 Sustainable Development Goals

The Sustainable Development Goals (SDGs) a universal call to action which was formulated by the United Nations (UN) in 2015. SDGs aim to terminate poverty, secure the planet and everybody attain peace and prosperity by 2030. Countries have committed to prioritize progress for those who are furthest behind. The SDGs are predominantly designed to end poverty, hunger, AIDS, and discrimination against women and girls [4]. Elimination of poverty, food for everyone, good health and well being for all ages, ensure quality education, achieve gender equality, sustainable management of water and sanitation for all, affordable and clean energy, decent work and economic growth, industry innovation and infrastructure, reduced inequalities, sustainable cities and communities, responsible consumption and production, climate action, life below water, life on land, peace justice and strong institutions and partnerships for the goals, are the seventeen SDGs [5]. The real challenges we stand before as we enter an era of climate breakdown and biodiversity loss, coupled with exponential population growth, accelerated urbanization, escalated social division and inequality are putting unprecedented pressures on the way we live and how we see our future. Among the seventeen SDGs eight goals directly relate to the building sector. As architects play a major role in controlling the eight goals i.e., good health and well being for all ages, sustainable management of water and sanitation for all, affordable and clean energy, decent work and economic growth, industry innovation and infrastructure, sustainable cities and communities, responsible consumption and production, and climate action. The architect's design process and ideas lead to the final product, the building. A 'well built structure' is able to incorporate all eight goals and contribute positively towards a greener future.

India is one of the countries who volunteered to take part in the Voluntary National Reviews (VNRs) at the High Level Political Forum (HLPF) which is the highest international platform for SDGs. In light with the national development agenda and SDGs the country's Parliament has formulated various policies and action perspectives that help deal with eradication of poverty, promoting gender equality and addressing climate change. NITI Aayog is one such organisation with the Prime Minister as its chairperson that looks over the SDGs implementation in the country in the National and Sub-National level. The institution has carried out a detailed mapping of the 17 Goals and 169 targets to Nodal Central Ministries, Centrally Sponsored Schemes and major government initiatives [6]. While reporting about the various facets of the SDGs, this VNR focuses on the progress made towards achieving Goals 1 (end poverty), 2 (end hunger, achieve food security and improved nutrition and promote sustainable agriculture), 3 (ensure healthy lives and good well-being for all ages), 5 (achieve gender equality), 9 (Built resilient infrastructure, promote inclusive and sustainable industrialization and foster innovation), 14 (conserve and sustainably use the oceans, seas and marine resources) and 17 (revitalize the global partnership for sustainable development). These Goals have been agreed upon in the HLPF as focus areas for this year. The nature of SDGs, however, is such that the advancement of one global goal may lead to progress in other goals as well.

The Science Track as shown in Fig. 1 is divided into six panels that together frame the 17 UN SDGs. The panels are developed using Professor Katherine Richardson's model for understanding the overarching strategizing of the goals as an interfacing between the needs of the planet and the needs of humanity. By moving from concerns of the environment, through resources to the needs of humanity, the goals are grouped into topics that engage existing research communities in academia and industry [7].

It can be observed that Panel 1 (climate adaptation), 2 (rethinking resources), 3 (resilient communities), 4 (design for health), and 6 (partnerships of change) all are linked directly or indirectly to architecture practice. Rapid urbanization has caused a ten-fold increase in built up space around the world contributing to the temperature rise every year, this is a concern stating to Panel 1, climate adaptation. It is the role of an architect to be responsible of the harmful emissions and excessive energy consumption taken up by the building sector and should promote more green buildings. Panel 2, rethinking resources also talks about resource consumption and the need for optimised use of resources left on the face of the earth. Even today most of the energy is produced using non-renewable energy sources and buildings also exploit these resources immensely. Panel 3, resilient communities is a goal which emphasises to build a better neighbourhood around the globe that makes the cities safe, clean and sustainably responsible. Panel 4 talks about design for health, a better environment comes with better sanitation, cleaner air through cleansing harmful emissions from vehicles or through commercial and industrial building and their activities. Lastly, panel 6 encourages the architects across the globe to team up to find solutions and keep strengthening the means of implementation of SDGs through built environment which can be a better place through their innovative and sustainable designs.

Energy savings, environmental gains, health and productivity improvement, or return premiums are some of the economic benefits stated promote the adoption of sustainability in buildings everywhere [8]. Increased population resulting in increased built environment in India demands for better liveable standards. The concept of 'sustainability' is saving for the future. It the planning of sustaining our resources and the cities for the future of human kind. It is the role of the architect to design a liveable space flexible enough to accommodate that future. Just like how it is important to save water and electricity, it is also important to save space, because land comes with a price. A responsible planning of a city with green buildings and safe neighbourhood is very important. Green building is a holistic concept that starts with the understanding that the built environment can have profound effects, both positive and negative, on the natural environment, as well as the people who inhabit buildings every day. Green building is an effort to amplify the positive and mitigate the negative of these effects throughout the entire life cycle of a building [9].

Energy performance index (EPI) is total energy consumed in a building over a year divided by total built up area in kWh/sqm/year and is considered as the simplest and most relevant indicator for qualifying a building as energy efficient or not. The EPI of the building is greatly influenced by the materials used for building construction, building envelope designing and planning, orientation of the building, Heating and cooling loads etc. Building envelope plays a major role in impacting the EPI as it covers the major part of a building. The Envelope includes external walls, fenestrations and roof. The materials used for construction of this envelope is crucial in determining the amount of heating and cooling load requirement of the building and hence the EPI of the building. So an architect should be careful in the material selection and envelope designing of a building. Fenestration also plays a key role in letting in or blocking heat into the building. An architect should be aware of the Window-To-Wall Ratios that go by the different facades based on the orientation and typology of the building.

1.3 Energy Consumption Management in India

The Energy Conservation Act authorises the Central Government of India to prescribe the Energy Conservation Building Code (ECBC), 2017. In order to mitigate the harmful effects caused by such large-scale growth, on the environment and to promote energy efficiency in the built environment, the ECBC 2017 was formulated by the Bureau of Energy Efficiency (BEE). Studies have shown that building sector, which contributes about 30% of the total national energy consumption, has the potential to control the effect of energy consumption on climate change through the implementation of energy conservation measures. More than 80% of the electrical energy consumed in buildings is for lighting and cooling [10]. One of the factors that impact the energy consumption of a building is the climate of the place the building is situated. If the designing of the building does not resonate with the climate of the place then the building demands active modes of comfort for better functioning hence the increase in the demand of energy consumption. India is expected to add 40 billion m^2 of new buildings till 2050. A study conducted by Sha Yu et al., by the use of the Global Change Assessment Model, this study assesses growth in the buildings sector and impacts of building energy policies in Gujarat, which would help the state adopt Energy Conservation Building Code (ECBC) and expand building energy efficiency programs. The study in Gujarat confirms that ECBC improves energy efficiency in commercial buildings and could

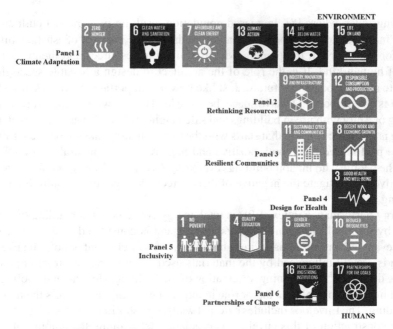

Fig. 1. SDG 17 goals divided into Panels of Six 4.

reduce building electricity use in Gujarat by 20% in 2050, compared to the no policy scenario [11]. Another such example of a case study in Jaipur that shows promising results from the implementation of ECBC on commercial buildings is a study conducted by Tulsyan et al. Percentage energy savings with ECBC compliance in these buildings vary from 17% in the case of institutional building to 42% in the case of Hospital building. Using these estimates and the trend of increase in commercial building energy consumption, the potential of energy saving in the city of Jaipur has been identified as 12,475 MWh/year in the next five years [12]. ECBC also states climate specific design guidelines on aspects like thermal transmittance values, solar heat gain coefficients, etc. to help design a building, appropriate to the five climatic zones of the country. Various studies also reciprocate to this problem and support the strong correlation of a climates' impact on building energy performance. Huang and Gurney in their research identified variation of climate change impact on building energy consumption to building type and spatiotemporal scale. Large increases in building energy consumption are found in the summer (e.g., 39% increase in August for the secondary school building), especially during the daytime (e.g., >100% increase for the warehouse building, 5–6 p.m.), while decreases are found in the winter. At the spatial scale of climate-zones, annual energy consumption changes range from −17% to +21%, while at the local scale, changes range from −20% to +24%. Buildings in the warm-humid (Southeast) climate zones show larger changes than those in other regions [13].

This study is inspired by the research conducted by Dr. Pradeep Kini et al. [14]. The study showed how the energy saving potential of a commercial building can be increased by the application of the Energy Conservation Building Code 2017 and using

Design Alternatives for buildings specific to Warm and Humid Climate in India. The study uses a shopping complex as a case example for the original EPI scenario and a detailed survey of the Building envelope was documented. The EPI of the optimized case was directly obtained from a simulation software called the DesignBuilder to obtain the results. The materials used as inputs to change the building envelope to obtain solutions were a random practical application. The study does not optimize all possible materials available in the market to find out the most optimum solution. The paper also does not alter Window-To-Wall ratio a crucial part of the Envelope that determines the intake of heat through the façade and also the amount of external wall area it covers to run a proper thermal transmittance through the wall and fenestration simulation. Hence this paper will be an extended version of the study conducted by Pradeep Kini et al.

Energy Conservation Building Code 2017 offers initiatives to achieve a green building and help conserve energy consumption of the building. The objective of this paper is to minimise the Energy Performance Index (EPI) of the building following the ECBC 2017, India from the contemporary by changing the Window to Wall Ratio (WWR), material design change of the wall with respect to u-value of the section of the wall and change in the material design of the roof slab section with respect to u-value of the roof slab using filler slab technique.

2   Methodology

The study in this paper is based on a five-storey commercial building located in Manipal, Udupi city in Karnataka, India. As shown in Fig. 2, the building is encased with heavy glazing on two sides. Extensive glazing on majority of the façade captures higher heat thus creating heat gain issues within the building. This study is conducted in a city classified under Warm and Humid climate zone according to the National Building Code of India. The city receives heavy rainfall from June to late September with peak humidity level up to 90% and a mean annual temperature of 29 °C. The temperature peaks up to 37 °C with humidity level of 72% during summers from March to May.

Fig. 2. Exterior of the commercial building.

The objective of the paper is to analyse and demonstrate how much EPI reduction is possible by the implementation of ECBC 2017 on the commercial building from its original EPI and contribute towards the Energy Saving Potential through a change in the Building Envelope. The study focuses on the Design Alternatives to be considered for a building to be constructed in a warm and humid climate zone in India.

An on-site documentation of the building was conducted and recorded. Figure 3, Fig. 4, Fig. 5, Fig. 6, and Fig. 7 depicts the floor plans of the commercial complex documented for the study on site. The data collected includes: building dimensions, annual energy consumption, occupancy, building materials etc.

Building Information Details required for the building simulation:

1. Location: 13°20′48.4″N 74°47′03.1″E
2. Site area: 910 m^2
3. Building size: G + 4
4. Total built-up area: 2595 m^2
5. Ground coverage: 34.3%
6. First floor carpet area: 538 m^2
7. Ground floor area: 312 m^2
8. Mezzanine – third floor area: 570.7 m^2
9. Building entrance facing: North-West
10. Operating schedule: 9:00 AM – 9:00 PM (12 h operation)

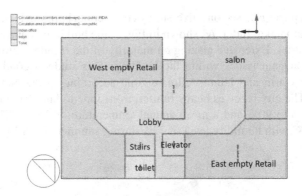

Fig. 3. First floor plan.

2.1 Building Envelope Optimization: WWR, External Wall and Roof Slab Design

A building envelope majorly constitutes of wall, roof and fenestrations. The envelope connects the building to the outside environment and is in contact with heat, light and moisture first. In this study the roof slab, external walls and fenestrations of the existing case scenario is documented. The opaque exterior walls have an overall u-value of 2.03 W/sqmK and the section is made of 150 mm thick concrete masonry with interior and exterior finishing made of plaster of thickness of 10 mm. The building roof and floor are 150 mm thick reinforced concrete slabs with a thermal transmittance of 2.97 W/sqmK.

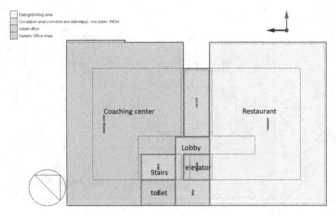

Fig. 4. Mezzanine floor plan.

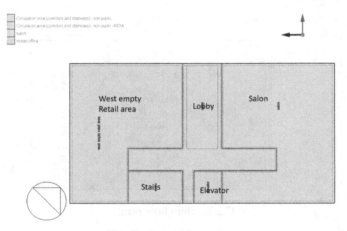

Fig. 5. Ground floor plan.

The facade consisting of glazing curtain wall as vertical fenestration with clear glass of 10 mm thickness and solar heat gain coefficient of 0.76. The building considered for the study is a B1 building typology, i.e., All building types except No star hotel < 10000 sqm AGA, Business < 10000 sqm AGA and School < 10000 sqm AGA, as given in ECBC 2017 [15]. The building lies in the warm and humid climate zone of India, specified as per the National Building Code (NBC), hence u-values considered in the study comply with the climate zone specifications.

2.2 Window to Wall Ratio

The commercial building is a G+4 shopping centre. The building has a ground coverage of 350 sqm, total built up area of 2595 sqm and total carpet area of 1900 sqm. The stores have an operation time up to 12 h from 9:00 AM to 9:00 PM. A 3 m cantilever on all sides is designed from the first floor onwards to increase the floor plate of the upper

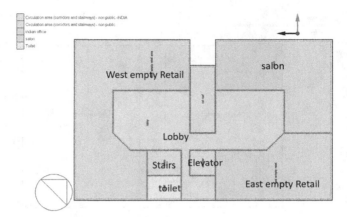

Fig. 6. Second floor plan.

Fig. 7. Third floor plan.

floors. The front façade of the building stands facing the North-West direction with an overall window to wall ratio of 0.62, covered overall with glazing. Daylighting into the building is received through an atrium which runs through the centre of the building from ground to the third floor. Table 1. Provides the current WWR of the building on each façade and on each floor.

The maximum Window to Wall Ratio (WWR) considered for this building typology is 40% [15]. Hence the four facades of the building with their WWR add up maximum to 40%. The four facades lie facing four cardinal directions i.e., NE, NW, SW, and SE. The NE façade receives minimum direct sunlight hence can have the maximum percentage of WWR and is kept at a constant value of 50%. The WWR for the remaining three facades are considered for 27 combinations as shown in Table 3. The averages are considered as 27 cases, taken as an input to the Solver to obtain the optimized result which will reduce the EPI of the building. Table 2 provides the 27 possible combination of WWR ranked in order of logic of obtaining the least EPI of the building, in terms of maximum heat gain through fenestrations.

Table 1. Window to Wall Ratio percentages considered on four facades.

Window to Wall Ratio	NE	NW	SW	SE
Ground floor	83.34	85	71	0
Mezzanine floor	83.34	50.77	0	0
First floor	83.34	50.77	0	0
Second floor	83.34	50.77	24.69	0
Third floor	83.34	50.77	4.23	0

Table 2. Window to Wall Ratio Ranking.

Combination code	NW	SW	SE	Ranking for least EPI value
WR1	0.8	0.8	0.8	1
WR2	0.6	0.8	0.8	2
WR3	0.8	0.8	0.6	3
WR4	0.8	0.6	0.8	4
WR5	0.6	0.8	0.6	5
WR6	0.6	0.6	0.8	6
WR7	0.8	0.6	0.6	7
WR8	0.4	0.8	0.6	8
WR9	0.6	0.4	0.8	9
WR10	0.8	0.6	0.4	10
WR11	0.6	0.8	0.4	11
WR12	0.4	0.6	0.8	12
WR13	0.8	0.4	0.6	13
WR14	0.6	0.6	0.6	14
WR15	0.4	0.8	0.8	15
WR16	0.8	0.8	0.4	16
WR17	0.8	0.4	0.8	17
WR18	0.4	0.8	0.4	18
WR19	0.4	0.4	0.8	19
WR20	0.8	0.4	0.4	20
WR21	0.4	0.6	0.6	21
WR22	0.6	0.6	0.4	22

(continued)

Table 2. (*continued*)

Combination code	NW	SW	SE	Ranking for least EPI value
WR23	0.6	0.4	0.6	23
WR24	0.4	0.6	0.4	24
WR25	0.4	0.4	0.6	25
WR26	0.6	0.4	0.4	26
WR27	0.4	0.4	0.4	27

Table 3. Window to Wall Ratio percentages considered for four facades.

Options	NE	NW	SW	SE	Avg
1	0.50	0.37	0.37	0.37	0.40
2	0.50	0.20	0.20	0.20	0.28
3	0.50	0.20	0.20	0.20	0.28
4	0.50	0.37	0.37	0.20	0.36
5	0.50	0.37	0.20	0.37	0.36
6	0.50	0.20	0.37	0.37	0.36
7	0.50	0.37	0.37	0.20	0.36
8	0.50	0.37	0.20	0.37	0.36
9	0.50	0.20	0.37	0.37	0.36
10	0.50	0.37	0.20	0.20	0.32
11	0.50	0.20	0.37	0.20	0.32
12	0.50	0.20	0.20	0.37	0.32
13	0.50	0.37	0.20	0.20	0.32
14	0.50	0.20	0.37	0.20	0.32
15	0.50	0.20	0.20	0.37	0.32
16	0.50	0.20	0.20	0.20	0.28
17	0.50	0.20	0.20	0.20	0.28
18	0.50	0.20	0.20	0.20	0.28
19	0.50	0.20	0.20	0.20	0.28
20	0.50	0.20	0.20	0.20	0.28
21	0.50	0.20	0.20	0.20	0.28
22	0.50	0.37	0.20	0.20	0.32
23	0.50	0.20	0.20	0.37	0.32

(*continued*)

Table 3. (*continued*)

Options	NE	NW	SW	SE	Avg
24	0.50	0.20	0.37	0.20	0.32
25	0.50	0.20	0.20	0.37	0.32
26	0.50	0.20	0.37	0.20	0.32
27	0.50	0.37	0.20	0.20	0.32

2.3 Material Design of External Walls and Roof Slab

Different combination of materials for walls result in different thermal transmittance values, hence change in the wall section along with the permissible thermal transmittance value is given as per ECBC 2017 is considered as inputs for the optimization. A similar design intervention is carried out for roof slab design. The different combinations of the wall for various possible u-values compliant with ECBC 2017 is a study taken from Pranav Kishore et al. [16]. The warm and humid category results from the paper is applied over this study to understand how much EPI reduction occurs due to its application. For the wall, seven wall thicknesses ranging from 0.15 m to 0.45 m at changing intervals of 0.5 units and four finishing types (F1 = Finished Inside & Finished Outside, F2 = Exposed Inside & Exposed Outside, F3 = Finished Inside & Exposed Outside, F4 = Finished Outside & Exposed Inside) are considered. The material library given in Table 4, Table 5, and Table 6 are an accepted and currently in use compilation of materials used in the industry which is in compliance with the ECBC 2017 and tested by CARBSE, CEPT Ahmedabad and verified by CSBE, MSAP, Manipal. Figure 8 shows a general section of a wall with F1, F2, F3, and F4 scenarios. The number of layers of each material is restricted up to three layers as per practical application of each materials. More than three layers is not supported in current practice unless in special construction cases.

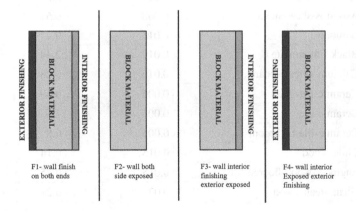

Fig. 8. Wall finishing cases; F1, F2, F3, and F4.

Table 4. Block materials.

S no.	Material-opaque wall	Thickness - (in m)	k-value (W/sqmK)
1	Aerated-autoclaved-concrete(aac) block	0.2032	0.18
2	Armor-rock-boulders	0.2032	0.07
3	Autoclaved-aerated-concrete-block-(aac)	0.1524	0.18
4	Brick – burnt-red-clay	0.1016	1.27
5	Cellular-concrete	0.2032	0.19
6	Cement-stabilized-soil-block-(cseb)	0.0762	1.3
7	Cement-stabilized-soil-block-(cseb)	0.1016	0.84
8	Compressed-mud-blocks	0.09	1.21
9	Fly-ash-brick	0.0762	0.64
10	Foam-cement-block	0.0508	0.16
11	Foam-concrete	0.1016	0.07
12	Perforated-burnt-clay-brick	0.0762	0.63
13	Solid-burnt-clay-brick	0.0762	0.62
14	Solid-concrete-block	0.1016	1.4

Table 5. Interior wall finish materials.

S no.	Material	Thickness (in m)	k-value - (W/m.K)
1	Acrylic-sheet	0.01	0.22
2	Ambaji-marble	0.019	2.81
3	Asbestos-cement-board	0.015	0.47
4	Asbestos-mill-board	0.01	0.25
5	Asbestos-sheet-shera	0.008	0.51
6	Bamboo	0.015	0.2
7	Black-fine-granite	0.019	2.44
8	Calcium-silicate-board	0.016	0.28
9	Ceramic-frit-glass	0.006	0.69
10	Ceramic-tile	0.005	1.6
11	Ceramic-tile-bathroom	0.005	0.8
12	Chile-wood	0.015	0.14
13	Engineer-wood-floored-tile	0.015	0.25
14	Ghana-teak-wood	0.02	0.21

(continued)

Table 5. (*continued*)

S no.	Material	Thickness (in m)	k-value - (W/m.K)
15	Granite-cat-eye	0.019	3.44
16	Granite-green-galaxy	0.019	2.62
17	Granite-ivory-fantasy	0.019	2.55
18	Granite-kashmiri-gold	0.019	2.47
19	Granite-tan-brown	0.019	2.95
20	Green-marble	0.019	2.37
21	Gypsum-board	0.012	0.25
22	Gypsum-plaster	0.002	0.51
23	Hard-board	0.006	0.28
24	Hard-board	0.01	0.28
25	Hard-board	0.012	0.28
26	Hard-board	0.014	0.28
27	Hard-board	0.016	0.28
28	Italian-black-granite	0.019	2.36
29	Italian-marble	0.019	2.78
30	Laminated-particle-board	0.019	0.18
31	Medium-density-fiberboard-(mdf)	0.012	0.2
32	Malamine-fiberboard	0.012	0.25
33	Oak-laminated-floor-tiles	0.012	0.27
34	Plain-particle-board	0.012	0.27
35	Pop-board	0.01	0.5
36	Pumice-square-bronze-tile	0.01	0.99
37	Rajnagar-marble	0.019	5.64
38	Rubber-wood	0.008	0.17
39	Saag-wood	0.02	0.29
40	Sandstone	0.019	3.01
41	Soft-board	0.012	0.09
42	Steam-beech-wood	0.012	0.23
43	Teak-wood	0.075	0.24
44	Udaipur-brown-marble	0.019	2.92
45	V-board	0.018	0.3
46	Veneered-particle-board	0.012	0.24

(continued)

Table 5. (*continued*)

S no.	Material	Thickness (in m)	k-value - (W/m.K)
47	Veneered-particle-board	0.016	0.24
48	Vitrified-tile	0.006	1.48
49	Wall-board	0.006	0.05
50	Wall-board	0.008	0.05
51	Wall-board	0.01	0.05
52	Wall-board	0.012	0.05
53	Wood-plastic-composite	0.012	0.12

The filler slab considered for the roof slab is again a result from a study by Ramya et al. [17]. The thickness of the slab is taken to be 0.3 m. The thermal transmittance value taken for the simulation for the roof slab is 0.15 W/sqmK. Figure 9 show the section of the filler slab with and without external insulation.

2.4 Building Simulation

The building simulation software used for this study is the Design Builder. Figure 10 shows the perspective image of the building modelled within the DesignBuilder. All the inputs where updated within the software and compared from the base case scenario. A step by step procedure of reducing the EPI was seen during the study. Firstly, the WWR was changed from the base model to see how much reduction in EPI was observed, then the various material design for walls were changes and u-value combinations taken as cases for optimization was considered and compared. Finally the roof slab was changed and the final building was obtained. A total of 84 results were obtained within the study. For a given WWR type the cases considered were 7 types of wall thicknesses, 4 types of wall finishing, 3 types of ECBC types which resulted in a total of 84 results. A total of 27 such WWR types were studied in this paper resulting in 2268 results, most of which show solutions to reduce EPI of the building. As shown in Fig. 11 an evolutionary optimization is run along with the simulation software to obtain the best possible results. The material library, block materials and its thickness, inside finish material and its thickness and exterior finish material and its thickness is taken as six variable inputs in this model. Therefore for every WWR case all these variable combinations are checked for optimum solution to obtain the final result.

The permittable thermal transmittance constraint of the wall section for a building of B1 category i.e., All Building Types to be constructed in a Warm and Humid climate zone, is taken as suggested from ECBC 2017 as 0.40 W/sqmK (ECBC Type), 0.35 W/sqmK (ECBC + Type), and 0.22 W/sqmK (ECBC Super Type). The heat transfer through the section of the wall is given as:

$$R_t = R^1 + R^2 + R^3 + R^4 + \ldots = \frac{L_1}{K_1} + \frac{L_2}{K_2} + \frac{L_3}{K_3} + \frac{L_4}{K_4} + . \tag{1}$$

Table 6. Exterior wall finish materials.

S no.	Material	Thickness - (in m)	k-value (W/m.K)
1	Ac-sheet	0.006	0.25
2	Aluminium	0.004	212.2
3	Armor-rock-boulders	0.025	0.07
4	Asbestos-sheet-shera	0.008	0.51
5	Black-coarse-granite	0.025	2.54
6	Black-fine-granite	0.019	2.44
7	Brick-cladding	0.02	1.27
8	Brick-tile	0.015	0.8
9	Cement-board	0.01	0.44
10	Cement-board	0.016	0.44
11	Cement-bonded-particle-board	0.016	0.33
12	Cement-fiber-board	0.016	0.39
13	Cement-mortar	0.012	0.72
14	Cement-mortar	0.015	0.72
15	Cement-plaster	0.015	1.21
16	Clay-roof-tile	0.012	0.63
17	Clay-ceiling-tile	0.012	0.63
18	Composite-marble	0.02	2.44
19	Concrete-paver-tiles	0.06	1.72
20	Dholpuri-stone	0.02	3.08
21	Floor-board	0.015	0.27
22	Granite-lakha-red	0.018	3.57
23	Jaisalmer-yellow-stone	0.02	2.74
24	Kota-stone	0.02	3.02
25	Kota-stone	0.03	3.02
26	Mangalore-roof-tile	0.02	0.61
27	Mild-steel-(ms)	0.004	44.12
28	Paver-tile	0.025	1.48
29	Porcelain-tile	0.025	1.53
30	Pumice-square-bronze-tile	0.01	0.99
31	Sandstone	0.019	3.01
32	Stainless-steel-(ss)	0.002	13.56

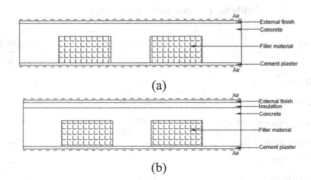

(a)

(b)

Fig. 9. (a) Section of a filler slab and (b) section of filler slab with external insulation.

where, L is the thickness of the material used and K is the thermal conductivity of the said material.

Hence, the thermal transmittance is given by,

$$U = \frac{1}{R_t} \qquad (2)$$

where,

$$R_t = \frac{1}{h_i} + \frac{1}{h_o} + \frac{L_1}{K_1} + \frac{L_2}{K_2} + \frac{L_3}{K_3} + \frac{L_4}{K_4} \qquad (3)$$

R_t is the total thermal resistance and h_i and h_0 are the inside and outside air heat transfer coefficients. Air is a good insulator of heat and thus has a thermal transmittance associated to it. During the wall construction certain amount of air gets embedded within the construction thus helping to resit heat flow in and out of the space. Therefore, the total U-value for inside and outside air gap is given in SP-41 Part-2, heat insulation. The outside air film at a velocity of 8 km/h (h0) is 19.86 W/m²K and the inside air film for still air is 9.36 W/m²K [18].

3   Results and Discussion

3.1   Graph Apprehension

The paper shows all the 2268 results thus obtained after the optimization with the changes made in WWR, External Wall Material Design, and Roof Slab Material Design. All the results have been converted into Pivot Graphs for better apprehension of the study. The results have be categorised based on three Tiers of Building Energy Performance suggested by ECBC 2017 i.e., ECBC, ECBC+ and ECBC Super. Under each tier there are three graphs showing results for all 27 WWR cases split as WWR1-WWR9, WWR10-WWR18, and WWR19-WWR27. The x-axis of the graph captures the cases considered in the study starting from the ECBC typology, the WWR, 7 wall thicknesses under each WWR, and four type of wall finishing under each Thickness of the wall. Table 7

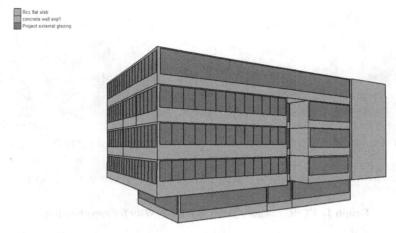

Rcc flat slab
concrete wall exp1
Project external glazing

Fig. 10. Perspective view of the building designed in DesignBuilder.

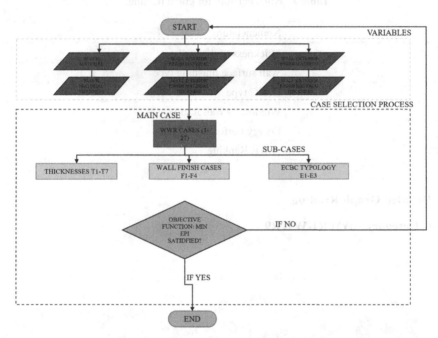

Fig. 11. Optimization process flow chart.

provides the nomenclature for the cases on the x-axis. The EPI of the base case scenario is 235 kWh/m^2/year. The EPI of the optimized scenario is given on the primary y-axis in kWh/m^2/year. The secondary y-axis shows the percentage reduction in EPI after the application of new WWR, external wall materials and roof slab materials (Graph 1).

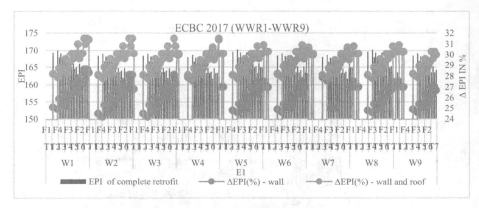

Graph 1. ECBC category graph WWR1-WWR9 for apprehension.

Table 7. Nomenclature for graph reading.

	Nomenclature
T	Thickness of the wall
F	Wall surface finishing type
E	ECBC type
W	Window to Wall Ratio cases
EPI	Energy Performance Index
WR	WWR Ranking

3.2 Detailed Graph Reading

ECBC Category - WWR1-WWR9

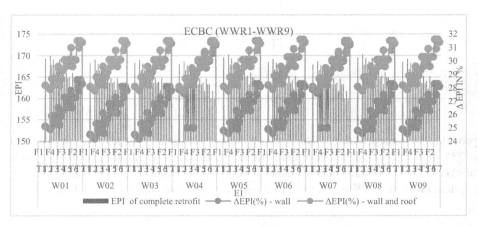

Graph 2. ECBC category; WWR1-WWR9.

The results propound that the least reduction in EPI observed in WWR1-WWR9 is 159.9 kWh/sqm/year i.e., a total of 32% reduction of the EPI from the contemporary case with EPI of 235 kWh/sqm/year. In this solution the suggested material design of the external wall section is an interior finishing comprising of three layers of 12 mm thickness Wall Board, with Armor Rock Boulder as the block material of 8 in. thickness of 2 layers along with the external wall finishing as 1 layer of AC Sheet of 6 mm thickness. All cases from WWR1-WWR9, show that the EPI reduction lies between 159.9 kWh/sqm/year to 170.2 kWh/sqm/year.

Graph 2 results suggests the most recurring solution for interior wall finishing as Wall Board of minimum two layers. The material suggestion for block material include Foam Concrete Block and Armor Rock Boulder. The Foam Concrete Block is the frequent solution when used for a thinner/moderate section of wall construction whereas Armor Rock is suggested for more of a thicker section of wall construction. Exterior wall finish material is recommended to be a cladding of Armor Rock Boulder of 25 mm thickness, minimum of two layers. For a rather thicker section of the wall i.e., T7 thickness, the alternate exterior finish is suggested to be of AC Sheet of 6 mm thickness.

WWR10-WWR18 - ECBC Category

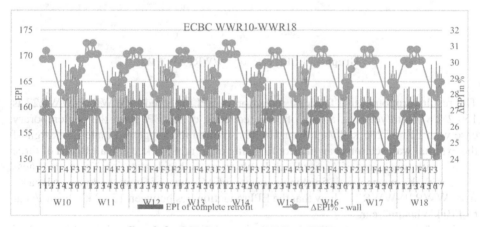

Graph 3. ECBC category; WWR10-WWR18.

The results propound that the least reduction in EPI observed in WWR10-WWR18 is 159.2 kWh/sqm/year i.e., a total of 32% reduction of the EPI from the contemporary case with EPI of 235 kWh/sqm/year. In this solution the suggested material design of the external wall section is an interior finishing of 12 mm thickness Wall Board of three layers, with two layers of Armor Rock Boulders as the block material of 8 in. thickness along with the external wall finishing as one layer of AC Sheet, 6 mm thickness. All cases from WWR10-WWR18, show that the EPI reduction lies between 161.7 kWh/sqm/year to 170 kWh/sqm/year.

Graph 3 results suggests the most recurring solution for interior wall finishing as Wall Board of minimum two layers. The material suggestion for block material include Foam Concrete Block and Armor Rock Boulder. The Foam Concrete Block is the frequent solution when used for a thinner/moderate section of wall construction whereas Armor Rock is suggested for more of a thicker section of wall construction. Exterior wall finish material is recommended to be a cladding of Armor Rock Boulder of 25 mm thickness, minimum of two layers. For a rather thicker section of the wall i.e., T7 thickness, the alternate exterior finish is suggested to be of AC Sheet of 6 mm thickness.

WWR19-WWR27 - ECBC Category

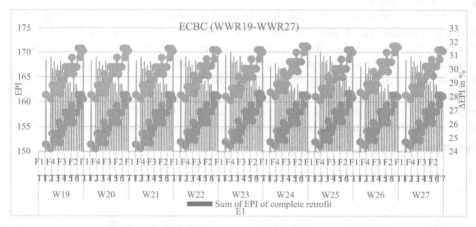

Graph 4. ECBC category; WWR19-WWR27.

The results propound that the least reduction in EPI observed in WWR19-WWR27 is 159.2 kWh/sqm/year i.e., a total of 32% reduction of the EPI from the contemporary case with EPI of 235 kWh/sqm/year. In this solution the suggested material design of the external wall section is an interior finishing of 12 mm thickness Wall Board of three layers, with two layers of Armor Rock Boulders as the block material of 8 in. thickness along with the external wall finishing as a layer of AC Sheet of 6 mm thickness. All cases from WWR19-WWR27, show that the EPI reduction lies between 159.2 kWh/sqm/year to 170 kWh/sqm/year.

Graph 4 results suggests the most recurring solution for interior wall finishing as Wall Board of minimum two layers. The material suggestion for block material include Foam Concrete Block and Armor Rock Boulder. The Foam Concrete Block is the frequent solution when used for a thinner/moderate section of wall construction whereas Armor Rock is suggested for thicker section of wall construction. Exterior wall finish material is recommended to be a cladding of Armor Rock Boulder of 25 mm thickness, minimum of two layers. For a rather thicker section of the wall i.e., T7 thickness, the alternate exterior finish is suggested to be a layer of AC Sheet of 6 mm thickness.

ECBC+ Category - WWR1-WWR9

The results propound that the least reduction in EPI observed in WWR1-WWR9 is 159.9 kWh/sqm/year i.e., a total of 32% reduction in the EPI from the contemporary case with EPI of 235 kWh/sqm/year. In this solution the suggested material design of the external wall section is an interior finishing of Wall Board 12 mm thickness of three

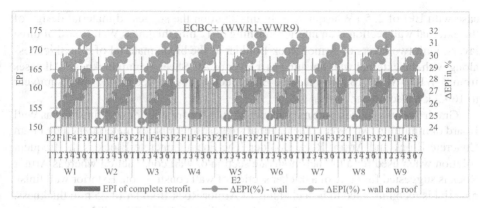

Graph 5. ECBC+ category; WWR1-WWR9

layers, with two layers of Armor Rock Boulder as the block material of 8 in. thickness along with the external wall finishing as a layers AC Sheet, 6 mm thickness. All cases from WWR1-WWR9, show that the EPI reduction lies between 159.9 kWh/sqm/year to 169.6 kWh/sqm/year.

Graph 5 results suggests the most recurring solution for interior wall finishing as Wall Board of minimum two layers. The material suggestion for block material include Foam Concrete Block and Armor Rock Boulder. The Foam Concrete Block is the frequent solution when used for a thinner/moderate section of wall construction whereas Armor Rock is suggested for more of a thicker section of wall construction. Exterior wall finish material is recommended to be a cladding of Armor Rock Boulder of 25 mm thickness, minimum of two layers. For a rather thicker section of the wall i.e., T7 thickness, the alternate exterior finish is suggested to be of AC Sheet of 6 mm thickness.

ECBC+ Category - WWR10-WWR18

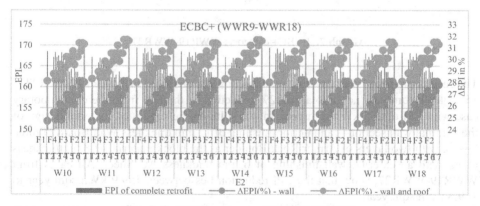

Graph 6. ECBC+ category; WWR10-WWR18.

The results propound that the least reduction in EPI observed in WWR10-WWR18 is 159.2 kWh/sqm/year i.e., a total of 32% reduction in the EPI from the contemporary case with EPI of 235 kWh/sqm/year. In this solution the suggested material design of the external wall section is an interior finishing of 12 mm thickness Wall Board of three layers, with two layers of Armor Rock Boulder as the block material of 8 in. thickness along with the external wall finishing as a layer of AC Sheet, 6 mm thickness. All cases from WWR10-WWR18, show that the EPI reduction lies between 159.2 kWh/sqm/year to 169.3 kWh/sqm/year.

Graph 6 results suggests the most recurring solution for interior wall finishing as Wall Board of minimum two layers. The material suggestion for block material include Foam Concrete Block and Armor Rock Boulder. The Foam Concrete Block is the frequent solution when used for a thinner/moderate section of wall construction whereas Armor Rock is suggested for more of a thicker section of wall construction. Exterior wall finish material is recommended to be a cladding of Armor Rock Boulder of 25 mm thickness, minimum of two layers. For a rather thicker section of the wall i.e., T7 thickness, the alternate exterior finish is suggested to be of AC Sheet of 6 mm thickness.

ECBC+ Category - WWR19-WWR27

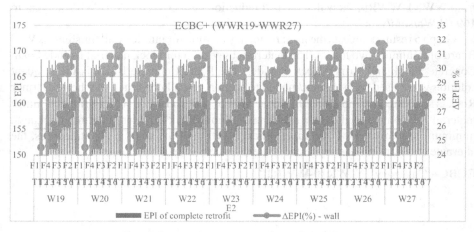

Graph 7. ECBC+ category; WWR19-WWR27.

The results propound that the least reduction in EPI observed in WWR19-WWR27 is 159.2 kWh/sqm/year i.e., a total of 32% reduction of the EPI from the contemporary case with EPI of 235 kWh/sqm/year. In this solution the suggested material design of the external wall section is an interior finishing of 12 mm thickness Wall Board of three layers, with two layers of Armor Rock Boulder as the block material of 8 in. thickness along with an external wall finishing of 6 mm thickness AC Sheet. All cases from WWR19-WWR27, show that the EPI reduction lies between 159.9 kWh/sqm/year to 169.3 kWh/sqm/year.

Graph 7 results suggests the most recurring solution for interior wall finishing as Wall Board of minimum two layers. The material suggestion for block material include Foam Concrete Block and Armor Rock Boulder. The Foam Concrete Block is the frequent solution when used for a thinner/moderate section of wall construction whereas Armor

Rock is suggested for thicker section of wall construction. Exterior wall finish material is recommended to be a cladding of Armor Rock Boulder of 25 mm thickness, minimum of two layers. For a rather thicker section of the wall i.e., T7 thickness, the alternate exterior finish is suggested to be a layer of AC Sheet of 6 mm thickness.

ECBC Super Category - WWR1-WWR9

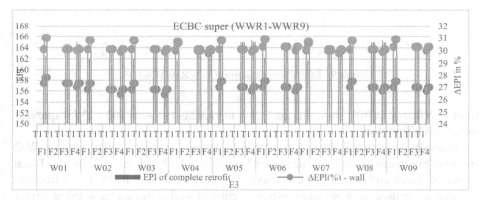

Graph 8. ECBCSuper category; WWR1-WWR9.

The results propound that the least reduction in EPI observed in WWR1-WWR9 is 161.7 kWh/sqm/year i.e., a total of 31% reduction of the EPI from the contemporary case with EPI of 235 kWh/sqm/year. In this solution the suggested material design of the external wall section is an interior finishing of 12 mm thickness Wall Board if three layers, with two layers of Armor Rock Boulder as the block material of 8 in. thickness along with the external wall finishing as a layer of AC Sheet of 6 mm thickness. All cases from WWR01-WWR09, show that the EPI reduction lies between 161.7 kWh/sqm/year to 165.29 kWh/sqm/year.

Graph 8 results suggests the most recurring solution for interior wall finishing as Wall Board of minimum two layers. The material suggestion for block material include Foam Concrete Block and Armor Rock Boulder. The Foam Concrete Block is the frequent solution when used for a thinner/moderate section of wall construction whereas Armor Rock is suggested for more of a thicker section of wall construction. Exterior wall finish material is recommended to be a cladding of Armor Rock Boulder of 25 mm thickness, minimum of two layers. For a rather thicker section of the wall i.e., T7 thickness, the alternate exterior finish is suggested to be of AC Sheet of 6 mm thickness.

ECBC Super Category - WWR10-WWR18

The results propound that the least reduction in EPI observed in WWR10-WWR18 is 160.3 kWh/sqm/year i.e., a total of 31% reduction of the EPI from the contemporary case with EPI of 235 kWh/sqm/year. In this solution the suggested material design of the external wall section is an interior finishing of 12 mm thickness Wall Board if three layers, with two layers of Armor Rock Boulder as the block material of 8 in. thickness along with the external wall finishing as a layer of AC Sheet of 6 mm thickness. All cases

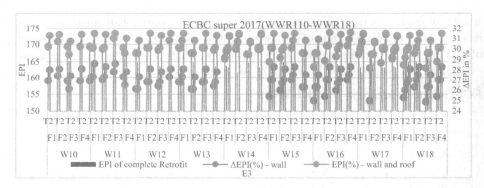

Graph 9. ECBCSuper category; WWR10-WWR18.

from WWR01-WWR09, show that the EPI reduction lies between 160.3 kWh/sqm/year to 165 kWh/sqm/year.

Graph 9 results suggests the most recurring solution for interior wall finishing as Wall Board of minimum two layers. The material suggestion for block material include Foam Concrete Block and Armor Rock Boulder. The Foam Concrete Block is the frequent solution when used for a thinner/moderate section of wall construction whereas Armor Rock is suggested for more of a thicker section of wall construction. Exterior wall finish material is recommended to be a cladding of Armor Rock Boulder of 25 mm thickness, minimum of two layers. For a rather thicker section of the wall i.e., T7 thickness, the alternate exterior finish is suggested to be of AC Sheet of 6 mm thickness.

ECBC Super Category - WWR18-WWR27

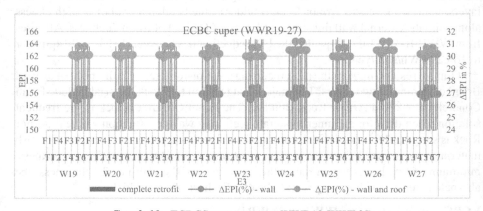

Graph 10. ECBCSuper category; WWR19-WWR27.

The results propound that the least reduction in EPI observed in WWR10-WWR18 is 160.3 kWh/sqm/year i.e., a total of 31% reduction of the EPI from the contemporary case with EPI of 235 kWh/sqm/year. In this solution the suggested material design of the external wall section is an interior finishing of 12 mm thickness Wall Board if three layers, with two layers of Armor Rock Boulder as the block material of 8 in. thickness along with the external wall finishing as a layer of AC Sheet of 6 mm thickness. All cases from WWR01-WWR09, show that the EPI reduction lies between 160.3 kWh/sqm/year to 165 kWh/sqm/year.

Graph 10 results suggests the most recurring solution for interior wall finishing as Wall Board of minimum two layers. The material suggestion for block material include Foam Concrete Block and Armor Rock Boulder. The Foam Concrete Block is the frequent solution when used for a thinner/moderate section of wall construction whereas Armor Rock is suggested for more of a thicker section of wall construction. Exterior wall finish material is recommended to be a cladding of Armor Rock Boulder of 25 mm thickness, minimum of two layers. For a rather thicker section of the wall i.e., T7 thickness, the alternate exterior finish is suggested to be of AC Sheet of 6 mm thickness.

Table 8 summarises all the 9 graphs from the results. The table specifies the results obtained from three ECBC categories and WWR considered from 1–27 in each category. The max reduction in EPI in percentage is specified per WWR in each category along with the wall assembly associated with the max reduction scenario. The table also mentions the range of EPI per category and the most recurring solution of wall assembly suggestion.

Table 8. Result summary

ECBC Category	Window-to-Wall Ratio	Max reduction in EPI in percentage	Wall assembly of max EPI reduction	Range of EPI (kWh/m^2/year)	Recurring solution for wall assembly
ECBC	WWR1-WWR9	32	Interior finish - Wall Board, 12 mm thickness, 3 layers	159.9–170.2	Interior finish - Wall Board, 2 layers
	WWR10-WWR18	31		161.7–170	
	WWR19-WWR27	32		159.2–170	
ECBC+	WWR1-WWR9	32	Block - Armor Rock Boulder, 8 in. thickness, 2 layers	159.9–169.6	Block - Armor Rock Boulder and Foam Concrete Block
	WWR10-WWR18	32		159.2–169.3	
	WWR19-WWR27	32		159.9–169.3	
ECBC Super	WWR1-WWR9	31	Exterior finish - AC sheet, 6 mm thickness, 1 layer	161.7–165.29	Exterior finish - Armor Rock Boulder Cladding, 25 mm thickness, 2 layers
	WWR10-WWR18	31		160.3–165	
	WWR19-WWR27	31		160.3–165	

The results depict that a max reduction of 31%–32% is possible by optimizing the façade with various WWR and in compliance with ECBC 2017. The results suggest a combination of wall assembly of interior finish material, block material and exterior finish material shown in Table 9 to achieve max reduction in EPI for a building.

Table 9. Material recommendation

	Material	Thickness
Interior finish material	Wall Board	10 mm
	Wall Board	12 mm
Block material	Foam Concrete	4 in.
	Foam Concrete	8 in.
	Armor rock boulder	8 in.
Exterior finish material	Armor rock boulder clad	25 mm
	AC Sheet	6 mm

4   Conclusion

India is growing at a rapid pace every year. Every year the energy consumption, resource consumption, etc. increases due to increasing population and better need of lifestyle. Sustainability is no more a concept it will become a necessity for an assurance of a secured future. India has stepped up and is voluntarily participating in the SDGs 2030 Agenda. Energy efficiency policies are becoming mandatory across the country as well. This challenges an architect to keep in mind to design a responsible neighbourhood for everybody. Smart City programs are also envisioned and are being worked out to live in a place that in turn helps out people.

The objective of this study is to enable architects across the country to design using the energy policies and enhance Design Alternatives for buildings, depending on the climate zone they are to be constructed. This paper suggests the Building Envelope optimization strategies using 27 cases of Window-To-Wall Ratios to reduce the EPI of a shopping complex building situated in a warm and humid climate zone.

In all three levels of energy efficiency offered by the ECBC 2017 i.e., ECBC, ECBC+ and ECBC Super, it is observed that the minimum possible EPI that can be obtained is 159.2 kWh/sqm/year, i.e., up to 32% reduction from the contemporary case example having EPI of 235 kWh/sqm/year.

Graph 11 depicts the analysis of variation in the EPI with respect to 27 WWR cases. The linear regression equations enables researchers and architects to solve for cases that lie within these 27 cases and identify the building envelope material design solutions to reduce EPI of a building.

The study suggests a common solution for construction using typical material for wall section comprising of an interior finish material as Wall Board, with block material

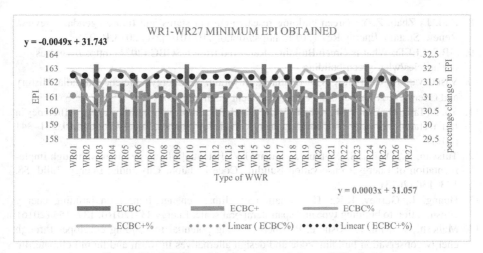

Graph 11. WWR ranking based on minimum EPI values.

either as Foam Concrete for moderate to thinner wall sections or Armor Rock Boulder for a thicker wall section, with exterior finish material as Armor Rock Boulder Cladding or use of AC Sheet of 6 mm thickness for a thicker wall section.

Acknowledgement. Authors would like to acknowledge every member part of this study for supporting throughout the study. We would like to thank our institution Centre for Sustainable Built Environment, Manipal School of Architecture and Planning, MAHE, Manipal for the support and resources.

Fund Disclaimer. The author(s) received no financial support for the research, authorship, and/or pub-lication of this article.

References

1. Jaysawal, N., Saha, S.: Urbanization in India: an impact assessment. Int. J. Appl. Sociol. **4**(2), 60–65 (2014). https://doi.org/10.5923/j.ijas.20140402.04
2. McKinsey: Environmental and Energy Sustainability: An Approach for India. Magnum Custom Publishing, New Delhi (2009)
3. Kaja, N.: An overview of energy sector in India. Int. J. Sci. Res. (2015). ISSN (Online): 2319-7064
4. UNDP. The SDGs in Action. Retrieved from United Nations Development Programme (2021). https://www.undp.org/sustainable-development-goals
5. UN. United Nations. Retrieved from Department of Economic and Social Affair; Sustainable Development (2021). https://sdgs.un.org/goals
6. VNR. On the Implementation on Sustainable Development Goals. United Nations, High Level Political Forum (2017)
7. Thomsen, M.R., Miller, N.M.: Architecture for the UN Sustainable Development Goals: A Map of Global Efforts. CITA: Centre for Information Technology and Architecture (2020)

8. Zuo, J., Zhao, Z.-Y.: Green building research-current status and future agenda: a review. Renew. Sustain. Energy Rev. (2014). https://doi.org/10.1016/j.rser.2013.10.021
9. GBC. LEED; What is Green Building. Retrieved from USGBC (2021). https://www.usgbc.org/articles/what-green-building
10. Vasudevan, R., Cherail, K., Cdr Bhatia, R., Jayaram, N.: Energy Efficiency in India: History and Overview. Alliance for an Energy Efficient Economy (2011)
11. Yu, S., Tang, Q., Evans, M., Kyle, P., Vu, L., Patel, P.L.: Improving building energy efficiency in India: state-level analysis of building energy efficiency policies. Energy Policy **110**, 331–341 (2017)
12. Tulsyan, A., Dhaka, S., Mathur, J., Yadav, J.V.: Potential of energy savings through implementation of Energy Conservation Building Code in Jaipur City India. Energy Build. **58**, 123–130 (2013)
13. Huang, J., Gurney, K.R.: The variation of climate change impact on building energy consumption to building type and spatiotemporal scale. Energy **111**(2016), 137–153 (2016)
14. Mahesh, A., Kini, P., Kishore, P.: Energy saving potential in building envelopes through energy conservation building code and design alternatives in warm and humid climate. In: Proceedings of the 10th International Conference on Smart Cities and Green ICT Systems, SMARTGREENS 2021, pp. 27–34 (2021). https://doi.org/10.5220/0010433900270034
15. ECBC. Energy Conservation Building Code. Bureau of Energy Efficiency (2017)
16. Kishore, P., Kini, P., Raj, A.: Optimizaton based feasibility analysis for energy conservation building code compliance of opaque wall assemblies in different climatic zones of India. Procedia Manuf. **44**, 221–228 (2020)
17. Kishore, P., Acharya, R.R., Raghuprem, M., Kini, P., Shetty, S., Raj, A.: Optimization based feasibility study for filler slabs as a response towards the ECBC roof compliance with respect to thermal transmittance for five climatic zones of India. Procedia Manuf. **44**, 213–220 (2020)
18. SP-41. Handbook on functional requirements of buildings (other than industrial buildings). Bureau of Indian Standards, New Delhi (1987)

Hierarchical Clustering of Complex Energy Systems Using Pretopology

Loup-Noé Lévy[1,2(✉)], Jérémie Bosom[2,3], Guillaume Guerard[4], Soufian Ben Amor[1], Marc Bui[3], and Hai Tran[2]

[1] LI-PARAD Laboratory EA 7432, Versailles University,
55 Avenue de Paris, 78035 Versailles, France
{loup-noe.levy,soufian.amor}@uvsq.fr
[2] Energisme, 88 Avenue du Général Leclerc, 92100 Boulogne-Billancourt, France
{loup-noe.levy,jeremie.bosom,hai.tran}@energisme.com
[3] EPHE, PSL Research University, 4-14 Rue Ferrus, 75014 Paris, France
{jeremie.bosom,marc.bui}@ephe.psl.eu
[4] De Vinci Research Center, Pole Universitaire Léonard de Vinci,
12 Avenue Léonard de Vinci, 92400 Courbevoie, France
guillaume.guerard@devinci.fr

Abstract. This article attempts answering the following problematic: How to model and classify energy consumption profiles over a large distributed territory to optimize the management of buildings' consumption?

Doing case-by-case in depth auditing of thousands of buildings would require a massive amount of time and money as well as a significant number of qualified people.Thus, an automated method must be developed to establish a relevant and effective recommendations system.

To answer this problematic, pretopology is used to model the sites' consumption profiles and a multi-criterion hierarchical classification algorithm, using the properties of pretopological space, has been developed in a Python library.

To evaluate the results, three data sets are used: A generated set of dots of various sizes in a 2D space, a generated set of time series and a set of consumption time series of 400 real consumption sites from a French Energy company.

On the point data set, the algorithm is able to identify the clusters of points using their position in space and their size as parameter. On the generated time series, the algorithm is able to identify the time series clusters using Pearson's correlation with an Adjusted Rand Index (ARI) of 1.

Keywords: Artificial intelligence · Data analysis · Clustering algorithms · Pretopology

1 Introduction

In 2015 was signed the Paris agreement in which government from all over the world undertook to keep global warming behind a 2 °C increase compared to the temperatures of 1990. The year of the Cop21, the worldwide buildings sector was responsible for 30% of global final energy consumption and nearly 28% of total direct and indirect CO_2 emissions. Yet the energy demand from buildings and building's construction

© Springer Nature Switzerland AG 2022
C. Klein et al. (Eds.): SMARTGREENS 2021/ VEHITS 2021, CCIS 1612, pp. 87–106, 2022.
https://doi.org/10.1007/978-3-031-17098-0_5

still rises, driven by improved access to energy in developing countries, greater owner-ship and use of energy-consuming devices and rapid growth in global buildings floor area, at nearly 3% per year[1]. The International Energy Agency's Reference Technol-ogy Scenario (RTS), which accounts for existing building energy policies and climate-related commitments, shows that final energy demand in the global buildings sector will increase by 30% by 2060 without more ambitious efforts to address low-carbon and energy-efficient solutions for buildings and construction. As a result, buildings-related CO_2 emissions would increase by another 10% by 2060, adding as much as 415 $GtCO_2$ to the atmosphere over the next 40 years - the half of the remaining 2°C carbon budget and twice what buildings emitted between 1990 and 2016.[2] Yet there are significant opportunities for improvement, as in the United States where 16% of energy savings could be achieved by reducing performance deficiencies [23]. Energy actors such as Trusted Third-Party for Energy Measurement and Performance can play a role in identifying the most relevant actions to optimize energy consumption by exploiting the massive energy data now available [6].

There are many ways to decrease buildings' energy consumption [9]: social pro-grams, incentive programs, new energies, energy efficiency, dynamic pricing, demand-response programs. But it is challenging to identify precisely what action to take.

Furthermore, the energy systems are not necessarily buildings. They can be a build-ing floor or simply a place inside a building. In consequence, it is more accurate to talk about **sites** [6].

The scales of analysis are various both in time (consumption time series are ana-lyzed on a 24h profile as well as on a yearly profile) and space (the studied system can go from one room to a group of buildings across a country). Because of that, there is no universal performance scale on which to compare a site to another.

Because sites present an important heterogeneity both in intrinsic properties and geographic situation [22] only a comparison between similar sites might be meaningful to understand the performance of a new site. By investigating the works that were effec-tive on a certain site, one can deduce what programs will probably be efficient for sites of similar nature. Hence, clustering sites based on their characteristics and consumption will enhance their evaluation and the recommendations system.

Therefore the topic of our paper is as following: *How to cluster a large number of heterogeneous sites based on their energy consumption profiles to recommend the most relevant energy optimization solution possible?*

In this article, we will consider that the energy consumption profile encompasses all the physical characteristics of a site as well as the external factors and the consumption data (time series, categorical data and numerical data). The latter is considered as a time series.

Our goal is to study a group of sites to optimize their consumption thanks to recom-mendations done on similar sites. This can be assimilated to portfolio analysis. Portfolio analysis represents a domain in which a large group of buildings, often located in the same geographical area or owned or managed by the same entity, are analyzed for the purpose of managing or optimizing the group as a whole [22].

---

[1] http://www.eia.gov/.

[2] https://www.iea.org/topics/energyefficiency/buildings/.

The key contribution of this paper is to provide a clustering method adapted to portfolio analysis based on a pretopological framework. - new definitions, properties, and demonstrations - detailed explanations of the algorithms and their pseudo-codes

Compared to the previous paper [17] this paper gives greater theoretical understanding of pretopology through added definitions, properties, and demonstration. It demonstrates how the pretopological framework used for the algorithms allows for the clustering of any finite set of items. It also explains the algorithms in greater details as well as presenting the pseudo-code of the algorithms. It also discusses the future work to exploit clustering for energy performance.

The paper is structured as follows: the Sect. 2 introduces clustering methods and some relevant examples on energy systems. The Sect. 3 presents the pretopology theory and the different types of pretopological spaces. The Sect. 4 explains in details the algorithms developed in the python library with pseudo-code, demonstrating how all finite set of items can be hierarchically clustered. The Sect. 5 presents the clustering of different types of datasets. We discuss the results and futur work in the Sect. 6. We conclude in the Sect. 7.

2   Literature Review

In this section, we present clustering methods and their application on energy systems. Clustering is a set of unsupervised machine learning methods that group unlabeled items into clusters. The journal paper of Iglesia et al. in Energies [12] presents a deeper analysis of clustering in energy system. To consult an exhaustive list of clustering algorithms, please read Xu et Al. survey [25].

There are four classes of clustering algorithms. Each of them having pros and cons: density-based clustering, centroid-based clustering, hierarchical clustering, distribution-based clustering. Let us present each class and their application to portfolio analysis in energy system.

Centroid-Based Clustering. In these methods, a cluster is a set of items such that an item in a cluster is closer to the center of a cluster than to the center of any other cluster. The center of a cluster is called the centroid, the average of all points in the cluster, or medoid, the most representative point in a cluster. The well-known centroid-based algorithm is the *K-means* algorithm and its extensions. The *K-means* algorithm is a powerful tool for clustering, but it requires to determine in advance the number of clusters that the algorithm should find.

Therefore, centroid-based algorithms are sensitive to initial conditions. Clusters vary in size and density and include outliers (isolated items) from the nearest cluster. Finally, centroid-based algorithms do not scale with the number of items and dimensions. In this case, centroid-based algorithms are combined with principal component analysis or spectral analysis to be more efficient.

Regarding portfolio analysis in energy systems, Gao et al. [8] compare a multidimensional energy consumption dataset using a *k-means* algorithm. Freischhacker et al. [7] design a spatial aggregation method, combined with *k-means*, based on block characteristics to reduce reductions due to energy consumption.

Density-Based Clustering. In density-based clustering, a cluster is a set of features distributed in the data space over a contiguous region of high feature density. Elements located in low density regions are generally considered noise or outliers [13]. The well-known methods in this class are Density-Based Spatial Clustering of Applications with Noise (*DBSCAN*) and its extensions.

Two parameters influence the formation of clusters: density and accessibility. Therefore, clusters are distinct according to these parameters. The main strength of this density-based clustering algorithm is it does not require apriori specification and that it is able to identify noisy data during clustering. It fails in the case of neck type datasets and does not work well for high dimensionality data.

Regarding portfolio analysis in energy systems, Li et al. [18] present a density-based method with particle swarm optimization of building portfolio parameters. Their method predicts the next day's electricity consumption through clustering. Marquant et al. [21] use a density and load-based algorithm to facilitate large-scale modeling and optimization of urban energy systems.

Hierarchical Clustering. Hierarchical clustering is most often a procedure whose goal is to transform a proximity matrix into a sequence of hierarchically structured partitions.

The two methods of hierarchical clustering are the bottom-up method (or agglomeration) or the top-down method (or division). Bottom-up methods start from disjoint classes and place each of the elements in an independent class. From the proximity matrix, the procedure searches at each step for the two closest classes, merges them, then places them in a second partition. The process is repeated to build a sequence of nested partitions in which the number of classes decreases as the sequence progresses until a unique class contains all elements. Top-down methods perform the reverse process.

The key problem of these algorithms is to define the criterion for grouping or aggregating two classes, i.e. a distance measure. Sites are defined as complex systems: [1,5,6,10]. They are defined with numerical and categorical data as well as time series. For this reason calculating a distance between two elements is challenging and does not allow to use every feature of the site in a relevant way. Another drawback is the difficulty of identifying a precise number of clusters, especially in a large data set.

Regarding portfolio analysis in energy systems, Wang et al. [24] analyze the spatial disparity of final energy consumption in China through hierarchical clustering and spatial autocorrelation. Li et al. [19] implement a strategy based on agglomerative hierarchical clustering to identify typical daily electricity usage patterns.

Distribution-Based Clustering. Application to large spatial databases requires from clustering algorithms to have no or minimal input parameters and arbitrarily shaped clusters. Distribution-based clustering produces clusters that assume concisely defined mathematical models underlying the items, a relatively plausible assumption for some item distributions.

Most of the time, the mathematical models are based on the Gaussian, multinomial, or multivariate normal distribution. Clusters are considered fuzzy, which means that an item can be found in several clusters at a defined percentage. The best known algorithm is the Expectation-Maximization (EM) clustering with Gaussian mixture models (GMM). Thus, the GMM algorithm provides two parameters to describe the shape of the clusters: the mean and the standard deviation. The main drawback of these algorithms is that they cannot work on categorical dimensions.

Regarding portfolio analysis in energy systems, Lu et al. [20] use GMM clustering for the identification of heating load patterns. Habib et al. [11] provide EM clustering to detect outliers in the energy building portfolio.

Conclusion About Clustering Methods. None of the methods described above can answer the specificities of the studied system, either because they require the definition of a distance between the items, or because they cannot return the hierarchical clustering necessary to apprehend the different scales of a complex system.

Relevance of Pretopology-Based Clustering. A pretopological space is defined by a relationship between a set of items and a larger set of items. It is therefore suitable for creating a hierarchical structure. It is based on the concept of abstract space. In such a space, the nature of the element is not relevant, it is rather the relations and properties linking the elements together that are important. This allows us to manipulate heterogeneous and complex elements such as our sites. Therefore, pretopology can be considered as a mathematical tool to model the concept of proximity for complex systems [2]. Pretopology is therefore the approach chosen to build our hierarchical clustering.

3 Pretopology

In this section we will explain the key concepts and definition of pretopology, such as pretopological space and pseudo-closure. We won't go into detail on the origins of pretopology but it is important to understand that the concept of pretopological space is obtained by weakening the hypothesis of the topological spaces. It allows the modeling of discrete structures unlike topology [2].

3.1 Pretopological Space

Central Definitions and Propositions

Definition 1. *A pseudoclosure function* $a : \wp(U) \to \wp(U)$ *on a set* U, *is a function such that:*

- $a(\emptyset) = \emptyset$
- $\forall A \mid A \subseteq U : A \subseteq a(A)$

where $\wp(U)$ *is the power set of* U

Definition 2. *A tuple* $(U, a(.))$, *where* U *is a set of elements and* $a(.)$ *is a pseudoclosure function on* U, *constitutes a pretopological space.*

We note that a pretopological space is defined by establishing a relation between any set of elements and a bigger set. This is interesting in the construction of a hierarchy. The previous definition determines the most general pretopological space. By asking the function to fulfill some additional conditions we get more specific pretopological spaces: (Fig. 1).

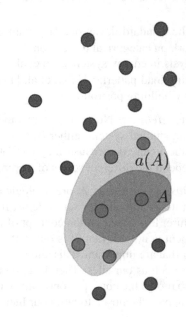

Fig. 1. Example of a pseudoclosure function [14].

Definition 3. *If* $\forall\ A, B \mid A \subseteq U,\ B \subseteq U : A \subseteq B \implies a(A) \subseteq a(B)$, *then we get a pretopological space of type V. This property is called isotony.*

Definition 4. *If* $\forall\ A, B \mid A \subseteq U,\ B \subseteq U : a(A \cup B) = a(A) \cup a(B)$, *then we get a pretopological space of type* V_D.

Definition 5. *If* $\forall\ A \mid A \subseteq U : a(A) = \bigcup_{x \in A} a(x)$ *then we get a pretopological space of type* V_S.

Given any pretopological space $(U, a(.))$, we can ask ourselves the question of what becomes of the concepts of closure classically defined in topology. In fact, the definition remains the same in pretopology [16].

Definition 6. *A part F of U will be a closure of U if and only if* $a(F) = F$

Proposition 1. *In a pretopological space of type V, the intersection of closures is a closure.*

Proposition 2. *In a pretopological* $V - type$ *space, the closure and opening of any part of U still exists.*

Proposition 3. *In a pretopological space of type V, the closure of a part A of U is the smallest closure containing A. Denoted F(A).*

Proposition 4. *In a pretopological space of type V, every set has a closure. The proof can be found in [3].*

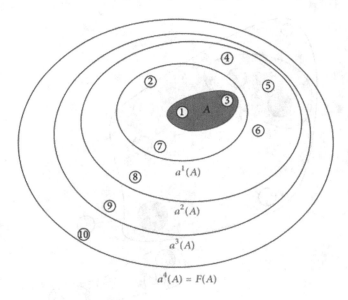

Fig. 2. Closure of set A [14].

In a pretopological space of type V we can find the closure by repeatedly applying the pseudoclosure operator to the set and its subsequent images until it stops expanding. We can see an example of this in Fig. 2 [14].

If we have a pretopological space of type V_D and $\forall A \mid A \subseteq U : a(A) = a(a(A))$, then we get a topology. The pseudoclosure function here is said to be idempotent [14]. It's clear that in a finite space, $V_S = V_D$ [3]. Also, in pretopological spaces of type V_D the pseudoclosure of a set is completely defined by the pseudoclosures of its singletons. So if the space is also finite, we could draw an edge from an element to every element of its pseudoclosure, and the pseudoclosure would be equivalent to a particular graph. Figure 3 shows the relation between the two. This demonstrates that pretopology is also a generalization of graph theory [14].

There is a second way of characterizing pretopologies of type V and V_D. To understand it we need to give a few more definitions first:

Definition 7. *We say that a set $\mathcal{F}$ of $\wp(\wp(U))$ is a prefilter over U, if:*

$$\forall F \in \mathcal{F}, \forall H \in \wp(U), F \subset H \implies H \in \mathcal{F} \tag{1}$$

Definition 8. *We say that a set $\mathcal{F}$ of $\wp(\wp(U))$ is a filter over U, if it is a prefilter stable under finite intersection, i.e.*

$$\forall F \in \mathcal{F}, \forall G \in \mathcal{F}, F \cap G \in \mathcal{F} \tag{2}$$

In other words, and restricting ourselves to a finite space, a filter is the family of all supersets of a set $\mathcal{B}$, while a prefilter is the family of supersets of every member B_i of a family of sets $\mathcal{B}$. The family of sets $\mathcal{B}$ is called the basis of the prefilter. We can see in Fig. 4 an example of a filter and a prefilter with basis $B = 1, 4, 2, 4$ [14].

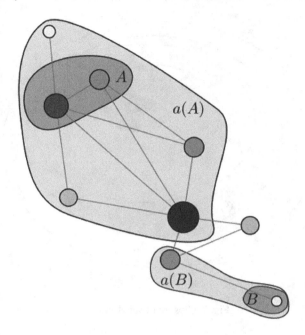

Fig. 3. Pseudoclosure function on a graph [14].

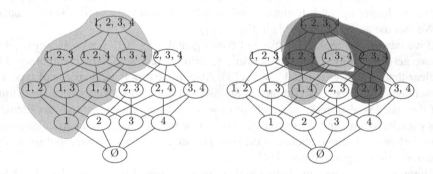

Fig. 4. Filters vs Prefilters [14].

Now, if we have a set U, and for every $x \in U$ we have a prefilter $V(x)$ such that every member of $V(x)$ contains the element x, we can define a pseudoclosure function in the following way:

$$\forall A \subseteq U, a(A) = \{x \in U | \forall V \in V(x), V \cap A, \emptyset\} \tag{3}$$

We call the prefilter $V(x)$ the family of neighborhoods of x, and each set in the family is called a neighborhood of x. Figure 5 shows a graphical representation of this definition of the pseudoclosure. On the other hand, if we have a pseudoclosure function $a(.)$ in a pretopological space of type V, the family of sets given by:

$$V(x) = \{V \subset U | x \in i(V)\} \tag{4}$$

where $i(A) = a(A^c)^c$, is a prefilter. The following proposition shows that we can go from one definition to the other interchangeably [3]:

Proposition 5. *No two families of prefilters $\{V(x_i)|x_i \in U\}$ define the same pseudoclosure function $a(.)$, and no two pseudoclosure functions define the same family of prefilters $\{V(x_i)|x_i \in U\}$.*

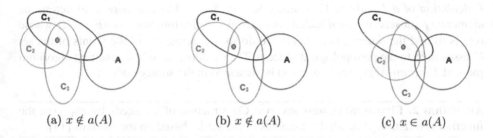

(a) $x \notin a(A)$ (b) $x \notin a(A)$ (c) $x \in a(A)$

Fig. 5. Neighborhood definition of a pretopology [14].

4   Hierarchical Clustering Algorithms

This section describes the algorithms developped in a Python library used for the construction of a closure and to build a hierarchical clustering of sites. This algorithm, whose pseudo-code is given in the source code 1, is organized in four phases:

- Determine a family of elementary subsets called seeds.
- Construct the closures of the seeds by iterative application of the pseudoclosure function.
- Construct the adjacency matrix representing the relations between all the identified subsets (even the intermediate ones).
- Establish the quasi-hierarchy by applying the associated algorithm on the adjacency matrix.

Algorithm 1. QuasistructuralAnalysis: Algorithm for the analysis of the quasi-hierarchy of a pretopological space, based on the work of [14].

Require: $((U, a(.)), d, seedFunc(.), th_{qh})$
Ensure: $QF_{qh}, quasiHierarchy$
   $seedList \leftarrow ElementaryQuasiclosures((U, a), d, seedFunc)$
   $QF_e \leftarrow ElementaryClosedSubsets((U, a), seedList)$
   $Adj_{qh} \leftarrow ExtractAdjencyQuasihierarchy(QF_e)$
   $QF_{qh}, quasiHierarchy \leftarrow ExtractQuasihierarchy(QF_e, Adj_{qh}, th_{qh})$

Several methods are possible to determine the seeds. Therefore, the algorithm is influenced by the following two hyperparameters:

- the $seedFunc(.)$ function which determines, for an element, a set of close elements which will constitute a seed,
- the degree d to specify the size of the seeds.

The algorithm takes an additional hyperparameter, required by the *ExtractQuasi-hierarchy* algorithm in order to establish the quasi-hierarchy: th_{qh}, which corresponds to the threshold beyond which it is estimated that two elements are close. This number is generally between 0 and 1.

We now detail each phase of the algorithm.

Calculation of a Family of Elementary Sets or Seeds. The aim here is to determine elementary subsets of size d called seeds thanks to the function $seedFunc(.)$ whose role is to find the d needed neighbors. To do so, we iterate on all the points of the set U associated to the pretopological space p. The pseudo-code of the resulting algorithm (named $ElementaryQuasiclosures$) is presented in the source code 2.

Algorithm 2. ElementaryQuasiclosures: Construction of the seeds by applying the function $seedFunc(.)$ on all the elements of the set U, based on the work of [14].

Require: $((U, a(.)), degree, seedFunc(.))$
Ensure: $seedList$
  $seedList \leftarrow list()$
  for all $x \in U$ **do**
    $seedList \leftarrow list()$
    $seedList.append(seed)$
  end for

Algorithm 3. FindNeighbors: Determine the d neighbors of $firstNode$ using the $seedFunc(.)$ function, based on the work of [14].

Require: $(firstNode, d, seedFunc(.))$
Ensure: $path$
  $path \leftarrow list()$
  $lastTreatedNode \leftarrow firstNode$
  for all $i \in range(d)$ **do**
    $newNode \leftarrow seedFunc(lastTreatedNode)$
    $path.append(newNode)$
    $lastTreatedNode \leftarrow newNode$
  end for

The algorithm 2 uses the function $FindNeighbors$ whose peudo-code is given in the source code 3. The latter takes as parameters an element of U, the number of neighbors sought d and the function determining the nearest neighbors $seedFunc(.)$. The $seedFunc(.)$ function usually takes as its value one of the following two functions:

- $ClosestNode(node)$ which identifies the closest nodes to an element. It is used in cases where a distance can be calculated, for example in the case where the studied relations are quantifiable.
- $RandomNeighbor(node)$ randomly browses the neighboring nodes. Its use is preferred when the relations are not quantifiable, for example in the case of values describing categories.

Construction of Subsets by Applying Pseudoclosure. To construct the subsets that will then be organized by the pseudo-hierarchy algorithm, *ElementaryClosedSubsets* uses the seed list *seedList* computed previously by *ElementaryQuasiclosures*. For each of the seeds in *seedList*, the membership function is applied iteratively until the pseudo-closure no longer gives bigger sets.

The intermediate and final subsets are stored in a list of unique element lists (*list* of *set*) named QF_{tmp} so that we don't have to reapply the membership later on the same sets. QF_{tmp} indexes the subsets according to the number of elements they contain. Since the membership of a set is always greater than or equal to its size, such indexing ensures that all elements are processed once and only once.

The list QF_e, constructed from the lists in QF_{tmp}, is then returned. The associated pseudo-code is presented in the source code 4.

Algorithm 4. ElementaryClosedSubsets: Computes the set of subsets by iterative application of the pseudo-closure function, algorithm inspired from [14].

Require: $((U, a(.)), seedList)$
Ensure: QF_e
  QF_{tmp} a list of $Size(U)$ sets
  for all $seed \in seedList$ **do**
    $QF_{tmp}[Size(seed)].append(seed)$
  end for
  for all $i \in range(1, Size(U) + 1)$ **do**
    for all $s \in QF_{tmp}[i]$ **do**
      $pseudoclosure \leftarrow a(s)$
      if $lastTreatedNode \leftarrow newNode$ **then**
        $QF_{tmp}[Size(pseudoclosure)].append(pseudoclosure)$
      end if
    end for
  end for
  $QF_e \leftarrow list()$
  for all $i \in range(Size(QF_{tmp}))$ **do**
    $QF_e.extend(QF_{tmp}[i])$
  end for

Construction of the Adjacency Matrix. The objective of this algorithm is to establish the hierarchical relations between the graphs of QF_e identified by *ElementaryClosedSubsets*. These relationships, between all QF_e sets, are represented as an adjacency matrix Adj_{qh}.

In a space of type V, two distinct closed elementary subsets F_x and F_y of QF_e :

- are either disjoint then $F_x \cap F_y = \emptyset$,
- either contain a nonzero intersection such that $\forall; z \in F_x \cap F_y, F_z \subset F_x \cap F_y$, where F_z is the closure of z.

Thus, if two subsets F_x and F_y overlap without one of them being contained in the other ($F_x \cap F_y \neq \emptyset, F_x \not\subset F_y$ and $F_y \not\subset F_x$), we know that a smaller set F_z contained

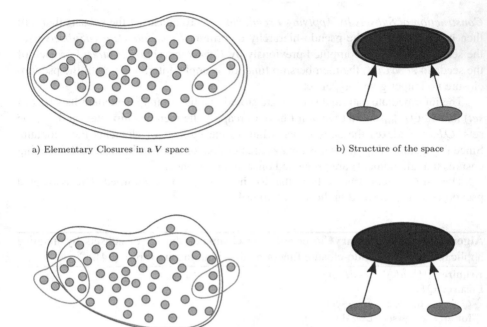

a) Elementary Closures in a V space   b) Structure of the space

c) Elementary "Closures" in a $non - V$ space   d) Structure of the space

Fig. 6. Construction of a quasi-hierarchy in a pretopological space of type V, according to the method of [15], and of type non-V, according to the method of [14], figures by this later author.

in $F_x \cap F_y$ exists. The resulting hierarchical graph must therefore connect F_x and F_y as parents of F_z.

However, as we mentioned, the Laborde's algorithm [14] is intended to be applicable to non-V spaces as well.In such pretopological spaces, there is no guarantee that an element of $F_x \cap F_y$ will not grow beyond this intersection. This is illustrated in Fig. 6. Furthermore, in the case of $d - n$ elementary sets, where n is the cardinality of U and d is the degree applied for creating the seeds, it is possible that none of the seeds are contained in the intersection. Thus, it is possible that no obvious structure emerges from the collection of quasi-closures.

To solve this problem, Laborde et Al. [14] generalizes the type of hierarchy constructed from quasi-closures so as to satisfy the following constraints:

- Two subsets should be connected only if their intersection is nonzero ($F_x \cap F_y$),
- The larger the cardinality of the intersection $F_x \cap F_y$ is compared to that of F_x, the stronger the relation of F_x to F_y is,
- The larger the cardinality of the subset F_y compared to that of F_x, the less necessary it is that $F_x \cap F_y$ is large for the relation from F_x to F_y to be strong. In other words, a very large set will attract smaller sets even if their intersection is not very large.

The algorithm presented in the source code 5 implements this logic. It quantifies the relations between each pair of QF_e whose intersection is not empty and then returns the resulting matrix.

Algorithm 5. ExtractAdjencyQuasihierarchy: Construction of the adjacency matrix for the quasi-hierarchy, algorithm inspired from [14]

Require: (QF_e)
Ensure: Adj_{qh}

$\quad Adj_{qh} \leftarrow SquaredMatrixZeros(size(QF_e))$
$\quad$ **for all** $F, G \in QF_e$ **do**
$\quad\quad FhasG \leftarrow Size(F \cap G)/Size(G)$
$\quad\quad GhasF \leftarrow Size(F \cap G)/Size(F)$
$\quad\quad FbiggerG \leftarrow Size(F)/Size(G)$
$\quad\quad GbiggerF \leftarrow Size(G)/Size(F)$
$\quad\quad Adj_{qh}[Index(G), Index(F)] = GbiggerF * GhasF$
$\quad\quad Adj_{qh}[Index(F), Index(G)] = FbiggerG * FhasG$
$\quad$ **end for**

Construction of the Quasi-Hierarchy. The quasi-hierarchy is built from the adjacency matrix by checking if the relations computed by *ExtractAdjencyQuasihierarchy* exceed the threshold th_{qh}. The new adjacency matrix thus obtained defines the quasihierarchy returned by the algorithm. The algorithm also returns the final list QF_{qh} of identified subsets for the set U. QF_{qh} corresponds to the list QF_e updated following the potential addition of new subsets during the construction of the quasi-hierarchy.

The quasi-hierarchy is established by applying the following rules on the values of Adj_{qh}:

- A link between two subsets is established in the quasi-hierarchy if their relationship exceeds the threshold th_{qh},
- Two subsets that have strong mutual relations (exceeding the threshold th_{qh}) are considered equivalent. They are subject to a subsidiary treatment improving the resulting quasi-hierarchy.
- The resulting quasiclosures with the respective links determine the quasihierarchy.

Laborde et al. [14] treats the case of equivalent sets by keeping the largest set and deleting the other. If the sets are of the same size then one of them is chosen randomly.

5 Model Validation and Visualization of Results

Validation Tool. To evaluate the pretopological hierarchical clustering, we also provide a set of tools to validate the model and show the results.

This program is developed to create a point dataset with the following parameters:

- the number of groups of dense items;
- the number of items of each group;
- the spatial dispersion of each group;
- the position of each group.

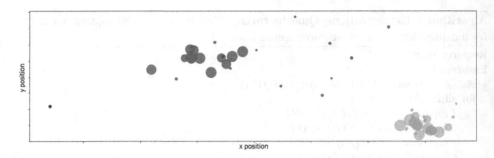

Fig. 7. The four clusters determined by our algorithm using both size and position as parameters, on a 2D disks dataset [17]. (Color figure online)

The size of an item is added as a second parameter, to evaluate multi-criteria clustering. Groups with different item size can be produced with the following parameters:

- the number of groups;
- the number of items of each group;
- the range of sizes of each group.

This program allows us to evaluate our method in different types of situations and to easily make adjustments or corrections.

Visualization Tool. The program colors each of the largest sets determined by our algorithm with a single color to make the clusters apparent. The validation tool is tested with two groups of large and small elements and a two-dimensional position. The elements are shown in Fig. 7. In this example, four clusters were determined: blue, green, orange and red. The black dot at the far left of the Fig. 7 is an element identified as an outlier by the algorithms. For example, the red and orange elements are close to each other but separated into two clusters due to their different sizes, and the orange and green dots are similar in size but divided into two sets due to their different positions.

The program also displays the hierarchical classification consisting of the seeds, intermediate sets and final clusters. The hierarchical classification is displayed as a tree in which each set is identified by a number and is represented by a node.

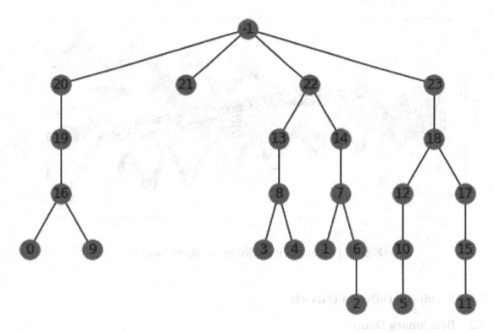

Fig. 8. A tree representing the pseudohierarchy relation between each intermediate set from the seed to the cluster [17].

For example, the hierarchy shown in Fig. 8 shows the relationships between the sets determined by our algorithm applied to the dataset displayed in Fig. 7. Only the sets with more than two elements are shown on this tree. We can recognize the four clusters that have been colored on Fig. 7, they are labeled 20, 21, 22 and 23. Figure 9 displays cluster 14 which is a child of cluster 21 (colored in green) in the hierarchical clustering. This hierarchy identifies large clusters of relatively similar items and provides more detail about small clusters of very similar items.

Fig. 9. The subset 14 in red representing a subgroup of the green clusters (subset 22) in Fig. 7 [17]. (Color figure online)

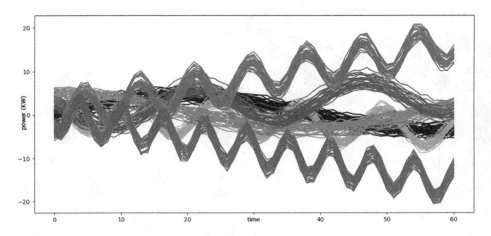

Fig. 10. The clusters identified by our algorithm [17].

5.1 Results on Different Datasets

5.2 Benchmark Dataset

Since the main data we have from the sites are time series of power consumption, we needed to test, visualize, and evaluate the clustering of a time series set. This section presents this test set and the results of our algorithm. The test set created, consisting of six clusters, is shown in Fig. 10. Each cluster is composed of 30 time series of 60 points.

The similarity measure used to establish the value between two items is the Pearson's coefficient. The Pearson correlation coefficient measures the linear relationship between each pair of items, which in this case are time series.

Our program colored the time series based on the clusters it had identified (see Fig. 10).

5.3 Results Analysis on Benchmark Dataset

The program identified exactly the same clusters as the ground truth given by the benchmark. To evaluate the validity of the clusters determined by the algorithm, our metric is the Adjusted Rand score, also called Adjusted Rand Index (ARI).As we have perfectly identified the clusters, the ARI of our clustering is 1.Figure 11 shows the confusion matrix between the cluster found by our method and the ground truth given by the benchmark.

Further experiments will be conducted in a future contribution.

5.4 Real Dataset

This dataset is built from Enedis (the French electricity network manager) consumption time series for 400 sites over one year. It is resampled with a time step of half an hour, a day, a week and a month. The proximity between Enedis delivery points is evaluated on

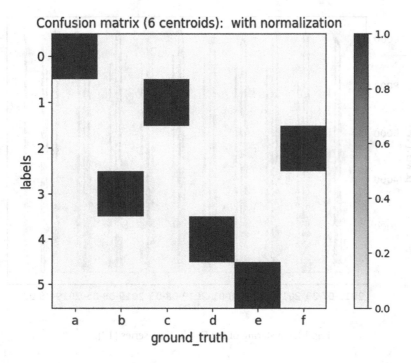

Fig. 11. Confusion matrix of the clusterization [17].

each resampled time series, each resampled time series corresponding to a characteristic of a site. After the Enedis dataset is constructed, the algorithm described in Sect. 3 is applied on the time series.

5.5 Result Analysis on Real Dataset

Figure 12, displays the grouping of 50 Enedis time series representing all the clusters. Three clusters have been identified, in the green cluster there are two peaks per day, one in the morning, one in the evening, in the red clusters there is a single peak per day that lasts half the day, and in the blue cluster the consumption is constant during the day.

The algorithm identified relevant clusters in the sense that each items shares a characteristic with items in its cluster that it does not share with items in a different cluster.

6   Discussion and Future Work

The results we have shown on a real dataset are preliminary. To fully exhibit the potential of this algorithm, the clustering will have to be applied to a richer data set. This data set should include relevant features extracted from the consumption time series as well as physical characteristics of the buildings (such as the site's floor area, the type of heating, the insulation material, etc.). Correlation between the sites consumption and meteorological environment will also be a feature used for future works. By taking

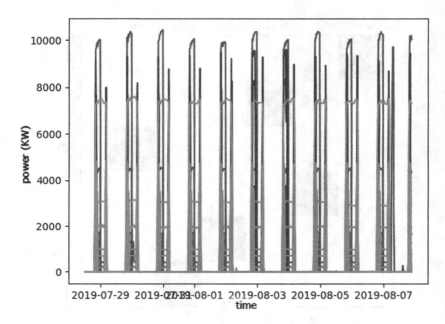

Fig. 12. Clustering of the Enedis time series [17].

all these elements into account, the relevance of the clusters identified will be greatly improved.

There are two possibilities regarding the identified building clusters:

- The clusters correspond to an already defined classification i.e. the clusters can be compared to ground truth. For example, the clusters identified might correspond to the usage of the sites. In this case, we will implement semi-supervised learning and by using Machine Learning to tune the hyper-parameters of the algorithm we will optimize the ARI index of our clustering.
- The clusters do not correspond to any known classification of buildings. In that case, we will have to apply knowledge extraction methods as well as energy experts' insight to give meaning to the newly found taxonomy of buildings.

Because the energy performance key indicators are not the same depending on the type of building [4], the insight given on building types will enhance energy performance evaluation and recommendation.

7 Conclusion

Building energy performance is a major challenge of the 21st century because of its important impact on climate change. Allowed by the growth of energy data, clustering of building based on consumption profile is a promising solution to efficiently identify the most relevant action to take for such complex energy systems. After a presentation of the state of art of the clustering methods, we propose a novel approach based on pretopology. The presented framework using pretopology allows for the multi-criteria hierarchical clustering of any finite set of items. Having a hierarchical structure gives insight into the similarities between building at different scales and therefore should provides a more refined understanding of the families and subfamilies of consumption profiles. The algorithm developed in Python for the construction of a Hierarchical Clustering of sites exploits this framework. The validation and visualization tools developed to test our algorithm allowed us to demonstrate visually and through ARI the relevance of the method on generated datasets as well as on real consumption time series dataset. The results demonstrate the potential of this solution for hierarchical clustering of heterogeneous systems.

Acknowledgements. This paper is the result of research conducted at the energy data management company *Energisme*. We thank *Energisme* for the resources that have been made available to us and Julio Laborde for his assistance with the conception of our pretopological hierarchical algorithm library.

References

1. Ahat, M., Amor, S.B., Bui, M., Bui, A., Guérard, G., Petermann, C.: Smart grid and optimization. Am. J. Oper. Res. **03**(01), 196–206 (2013). https://doi.org/10.4236/ajor.2013.31A019, http://www.scirp.org/journal/doi.aspx?DOI=10.4236/ajor.2013.31A019
2. Auray, J.P., Bonnevay, S., Bui, M., Duru, G., Lamure, M.: Prétopologie et applications : un état de l'art. Studia Informatica Universalis (Hermann), **7**, 27–44 (2009)
3. Belmandt, Z.: Manuel de prétopologie et ses Applications. Hermès science publications (1993)
4. Boemi, S.-N., Tziogas, C.: Indicators for buildings' energy performance. In: Boemi, S.-N., Irulegi, O., Santamouris, M. (eds.) Energy Performance of Buildings, pp. 79–93. Springer, Cham (2016). https://doi.org/10.1007/978-3-319-20831-2_5
5. Bosom, J., Scius-Bertrand, A., Tran, H., Bui, M.: Multi-agent architecture of a MIBES for smart energy management. In: Hodoň, M., Eichler, G., Erfurth, C., Fahrnberger, G. (eds.) I4CS 2018. CCIS, vol. 863, pp. 18–32. Springer, Cham (2018). https://doi.org/10.1007/978-3-319-93408-2_2
6. Bosom, J.: Conception de microservices intelligents pour la supervision de systèmes sociotechniques: application aux systèmes énergétiques. Ph.D. thesis, Université Paris sciences et lettres (2020)
7. Fleischhacker, A., Lettner, G., Schwabeneder, D., Auer, H.: Portfolio optimization of energy communities to meet reductions in costs and emissions. Energy 173, 1092–1105 (2019). https://doi.org/10.1016/j.energy.2019.02.104,http://www.sciencedirect.com/science/article/pii/S0360544219303032
8. Gao, X., Malkawi, A.: A new methodology for building energy performance benchmarking: an approach based on intelligent clustering algorithm. Energy Build. **84**, 607–616 (2014). https://doi.org/10.1016/j.enbuild.2014.08.030, http://www.sciencedirect.com/science/article/pii/S0378778814006720
9. Guerard, G., Pichon, B., Nehai, Z.: Demand-response: let the devices take our decisions. In: SMARTGREENS, pp. 119–126 (2017)
10. Guérard, G., Ben Amor, S., Bui, A.: A context-free smart grid model using pretopologic structure. In: 2015 International Conference on Smart Cities and Green ICT Systems (SMARTGREENS), pp. 1–7 (2015)

11. Habib, U., Zucker, G., Blochle, M., Judex, F., Haase, J.: Outliers detection method using clustering in buildings data. In: IECON 2015–41st Annual Conference of the IEEE Industrial Electronics Society, IEEE, pp. 000694–000700 (2015)
12. Iglesias, F., Kastner, W.: Analysis of similarity measures in times series clustering for the discovery of building energy patterns. Energies 6(2), 579–597 (2013)
13. Kriegel, H.P., Kröger, P., Sander, J., Zimek, A.: Density-based clustering. Wiley Interdisc. Rev.: Data Min. Knowl. Discovery 1(3), 231–240 (2011)
14. Laborde, J.: Pretopology, a mathematical tool for structuring complex systems: methods, algorithms and applications. Ph.D. thesis, EPHE (2019)
15. Largeron, C., Bonnevay, S.: A pretopological approach for structural analysis. Inf. Sci. 144(1–4), 169–185 (2002)
16. Le, T.V.: Classification prétopologique des données: application à l'analyse des trajectoires patients. Ph.D. thesis, Lyon 1 (2007)
17. Levy, L.N., Bosom, J., Guérard, G., Amor, S.B., Bui, M., Tran, H.: Application of pretopological hierarchical clustering for buildings portfolio. In: SMARTGREENS, pp. 228–235 (2021)
18. Li, K., Ma, Z., Robinson, D., Lin, W., Li, Z.: A data-driven strategy to forecast next-day electricity usage and peak electricity demand of a building portfolio using cluster analysis, cubist regression models and particle swarm optimization. J. Cleaner Prod. 273, 123115 (2020). https://doi.org/10.1016/j.jclepro.2020.123115, http://www.sciencedirect.com/science/article/pii/S0959652620331607
19. Li, K., Yang, R.J., Robinson, D., Ma, J., Ma, Z.: An agglomerative hierarchical clustering-based strategy using shared nearest neighbours and multiple dissimilarity measures to identify typical daily electricity usage profiles of university library buildings. Energy 174, 735–748 (2019). https://doi.org/10.1016/j.energy.2019.03.003, http://www.sciencedirect.com/science/article/pii/S0360544219304074
20. Lu, Y., Tian, Z., Peng, P., Niu, J., Li, W., Zhang, H.: GMM clustering for heating load patterns in-depth identification and prediction model accuracy improvement of district heating system. Energy Build. 190, 49–60 (2019). https://doi.org/10.1016/j.enbuild.2019.02.014, http://www.sciencedirect.com/science/article/pii/S0378778818308326
21. Marquant, J.F., Bollinger, L.A., Evins, R., Carmeliet, J.: A new combined clustering method to analyse the potential of district heating networks at large-scale. Energy 156, 73–83 (2018). https://doi.org/10.1016/j.energy.2018.05.027, http://www.sciencedirect.com/science/article/pii/S0360544218308478
22. Miller, C.: Screening meter data: characterization of temporal energy data from large groups of non-residential buildings. Ph.D. thesis, ETH Zurich (2016)
23. Mills, E.: Building commissioning: a golden opportunity for reducing energy costs and greenhouse gas emissions in the United States. Energy Effi. 4(2), 145–173 (2011). https://doi.org/10.1007/s12053-011-9116-8
24. Wang, S., Liu, H., Pu, H., Yang, H.: Spatial disparity and hierarchical cluster analysis of final energy consumption in china. Energy 197, 117195 (2020). https://doi.org/10.1016/j.energy.2020.117195
25. Xu, D., Tian, Y.: A comprehensive survey of clustering algorithms. Ann. Data Sci. 2(2), 165–193 (2015)

Analysis of Citizen's Feedback from the Lens of Smart City Framework: A Case Study Based Approach

Priyanka Singh[1]([✉]) [iD], Fiona Lynch[2] [iD], and Markus Helfert[1] [iD]

[1] Innovation Value Institute, Lero, Maynooth University, Maynooth, Kildare, Ireland
priyanka.singh.2020@mumail.ie

[2] School of Science and Computing, Waterford Institute of Technology (WIT), Waterford, Ireland

Abstract. There have been many initiatives to involve citizens in the development of smart cities. The aim is to enhance the quality of life for the citizens of these cities by providing better services to them. There are various concepts and platforms discussed in the literature to support citizen's feedback in smart city development. However, there is a lack of studies that guide how to utilize citizens' feedbacks to improve the quality of life for the citizens of the city. This paper provides an overview of existing platforms and concepts which are associated with the involvement of the citizens in the smart city domain. The smart city framework has been adapted to classify the existing literature from different architectural layer's perspectives. Moreover, this study proposes key concepts for service and context layers for an adapted smart city framework based on the conducted case study and a literature review. These key concepts can assist city authorities in better decision-making of designing effective services that meet citizen's requirements based upon their feedback.

Keyword: Smart city framework · e-parking service · Service layer · Context layer · Citizens · Smart service

1 Introduction

Currently, the interests and concerns of citizens are forthcoming to a leading edge with the awareness that smart cities do not only offer nice infrastructure and sustainable services but also value the citizen's feedback [40]. Smart cities should be implemented by taking into consideration of local constraints, opportunities, requirements, diverse cultures, and features of cities in different geographical areas and countries [17]. Smart cities should not be solely dependent on the utilization of ICT if it aims to empower social, economic, cultural, and environmental development [25]. Citizen's requirements are critical for the development of successful smart cities, which are often ignored over the technological and strategic development [24]. Urban issues should be considered beyond technological innovation and focus should be given to non-technical problems including policy, management, and citizens and thus providing opportunities to fill the void in

© Springer Nature Switzerland AG 2022
C. Klein et al. (Eds.): SMARTGREENS 2021/ VEHITS 2021, CCIS 1612, pp. 107–124, 2022.
https://doi.org/10.1007/978-3-031-17098-0_6

the field [23, 42, 62]. Social objectives formed in response to the citizen's needs and originating in societal challenges can play a significant role in driving smart innovation [58].

There has been a gradual shift from the concept of sustainable cities over the last few decades to emerging citizen-centered cities with many initiatives taken in that direction [35]. However, public sector organizations use such initiatives to change citizen's behavior rather than involving them in the design of public sector processes [45]. [13] argue that Many 'citizen-centric' initiatives seem distraction around smart cities which are highly visible as compared to their effective participation and actual impact. Exploratory innovation methods such as participatory workshops are being replaced by exploitative methods, whereby, the vision of the project, specifically citizen's needs fail to transfer from planning to the implementation phase [44]. Citizen participation provides meaningful remarks that can inform the decision-making process even if their participation rate is low [24]. It is imperative to consider a socio-technical viewpoint while embarking on smart initiatives [11, 19]. Therefore, a sense of community should be integrated into policymaking while considering citizen's evaluation of public services, facilities, and smart sustainable cities [37]. Citizen engagement also plays a fundamental role in accomplishing smart sustainable urban development and there is a requirement for more suitable tools and protocols to support greater public participation [16]. However, citizen-led or citizen-engaged smart city development does not necessarily converse notions of citizenship to the digital city [13]. Moreover, citizen participation and engagement within Living Labs initiatives are often very limited, structured, and run under a technocratic model of governance (ibid). [46] proposed the Smart City Enterprise Architecture Framework to capture concerns of various smart city stakeholders including city authorities, service providers, and citizens. Therefore, this study adopted the framework to identify how their concerns can be addressed at an architecture level. Thus, this study firstly classifies the existing literature from the lens of an adapted framework [46]. Additionally, this research proposes key concepts which can assist decision-makers in designing effective services for the citizens while considering their valuable feedback. This paper is an extended version of the previous paper, [54] published in the SMARTGREENS2021 proceedings. In this paper, additional detail about the existing platforms and concepts have been provided that are associated with the citizen's involvement in the smart city domain and can be found in Table 4. Furthermore, this study proposes key concepts for service and context layers in an adapted smart city framework. The detail of these concepts is provided in Sect. 3. The remaining sections of the paper are structured as follows: Sect. 2 provides an overview of the conducted case study. Section 3 provides a detailed overview of the literature findings and proposed concepts. In Sect. 4, a discussion on findings has been laid out. Lastly, Sect. 5 provides the conclusion of this study with future guidelines of the remaining work.

2   e-Parking Service (Case Study)

A deductive and an exploratory case study approach was used for investigating the research problem from the real environment. A case study approach explores and investigates the contemporary phenomenon within its real-life context when the boundaries between context and phenomenon are not clear [63]. This case study has been designed as per the template and guidelines provided by [10, 21].

Table 1. Case study design on smart service design [54].

Context: According to the literature citizens play a vital role in the design and development of smart city services to provide effective services to them. Therefore, this study investigates their role in the design of the smart city services in the Irish context and highlights existing issues from the citizen' end based on the feedback they provided for one of the smart services in Ireland

---

The Case: E-parking service in City/Counties of Ireland

Objective:
- To understand the experience of citizens towards this service
- To understand how requirements are provided to design such smart city services

---

Study design: Exploratory deductive approach

Data collection: Interviews, online review comments from end-users

---

Analysis: Qualitative data were analysed to identify the challenges from the citizen's viewpoint and Council's perspective. Based on this analysis, feedback was classified against the associated requirements for other layers of the architecture

---

Key findings:
1. The feedback obtained from the citizen's end can be useful in identifying a set of requirements for the services
2. Citizens have no formal role in the design of the services that lead to lower quality of the service in the end
3. There is a lack of understanding of how to incorporate citizen's feedback for designing effective services
4. There is a challenge in mapping citizen's requirements with existing resources

---

An e-parking service was chosen for the case study which is offered by many of the City/County Councils in the Republic of Ireland. The motive behind selecting this case study was to first understand the experience of citizens towards this service. Secondly, to understand how requirements provided for designing such services. This study also tried to understand if Councils have any other engagement activities with citizens. For conducting this case study, two sources of data (Online review comments, Interviews) were used. Firstly, interviews were carried out with City Council to understand the design process of the service. Secondly, the textual data (review comments) were analyzed to identify the performance of the services based upon the citizen's feedback. The result of the analysis can be found in Table 2 that shows how review comments were classified against different quality factors. Then based upon this classification, the service requirements have been identified. The results of this case study showed that there are engagement programs and projects that focus on involving citizens at different levels. However, after observing the poor citizen's satisfaction level towards the e-parking service, it remains questionable if citizen's feedback had any role either in the actual implementations of the services or for further improving the quality of the services. That is in line with what [13] found in Smart Dublin projects (Ireland) and highlighted that administrators claim they involve citizens in planning and decisions, though, it remains a question, how proposed changes are implemented and who has the command of real decision making. The summary of this case study can be found in Table 1 and a detailed discussion has been provided in a previous publication [54]. Section 3 will provide an overview of the adapted framework and also propose new concepts for context and service layers based upon the literature findings and case study.

Table 2. Sample of impacted quality factors, corresponding themes, and their links to identified requirements [54].

Sample of online reviews *(Source: https://play.google.com/store)*	Codes	Identified impacted quality factors from service layer (Themes)	Associated requirements adopted from [9]	Link to other layers for associated requirements
"App will not load so cannot access my account, nor can I park my car. It's not an internet issue as my other apps work fine. I uninstalled and then reinstalled it and now it won't let me log in as it says there's no available host… I rely on this almost every day and cannot believe that this has happened"	Application issue	Effectiveness	Availability/Software engineering tools	Technology
"10% top-up fee without warning. Total scam"	No information on additional charged Fees	Transparency	Trust	Context
"Charged a processing fee for adding cash to account. It's the last time I'll be using this"	No information on additional charged Fees/Usage	Transparency/Usefulness	Trust/City Oriented	Context/Information

(continued)

Table 2. (*continued*)

Sample of online reviews (*Source:* https://play.goo gle.com/store)	Codes	Identified impacted quality factors from service layer (Themes)	Associated requirements adopted from [9]	Link to other layers for associated requirements
"Appallingly bad. Only used it a few times and some of the roads don't have a code applicable. Also if you move to another street within the time you've to pay again, whereas with the disk you can use it for the 2 h (or whatever the limit is in the area)"	Application issue	Personalisation	Flexibility	Context/Information
"It won't even accept my car registration. There's no guidance provided or feedback the city council haven't responded to emails either"	Application issue	Usability	Extensibility	Information

3   Smart City Framework

This study adapted the smart city framework proposed by [46] to understand the role of citizens at the different levels of architecture and how scientific literature supports the role of citizens in creating effective smart cities which meet their requirements. A brief overview of the architectural specification has been provided in Table 3. Additionally, it has been elaborated in the table how individual layer's specification has been used as a lens to understand the current literature around the involvement of citizens in smart city development. Moreover, based on this literature review, different concepts and platforms have been summarized in Table 4. The motive behind selecting this framework was to firstly analyze literature that supports citizens in smart city development. Secondly, to classify it based upon the architectural layers would provide a holistic viewpoint of the overall literature on this topic. Additionally, a case study was conducted on a smart service (e-parking), and based on the observed results and extensive literature review, new key concepts are proposed for service and context layers in this section. In a former publication, a conceptual model was proposed as shown in Fig. 1 to understand citizen's requirements based upon their feedback that has been further linked back to other layers. This proposed model aimed to show how their feedback can be utilized to map various requirements that have been originated from the citizen's end. The feedback was collected based on the review comments that citizens provided for the e-parking service. In this model, it was highlighted how feedback at the service layer can further assist in understanding citizen's requirements at context, information, and technology layers. In this paper, new concepts have been proposed for the model that provides more detail of utilizing citizen's feedback at two different levels (service and context). Furthermore, other concepts have been proposed for measuring the performance of the services based upon their feedback. In the following sections, the detail of the newly proposed concepts has been discussed for context and service layers.

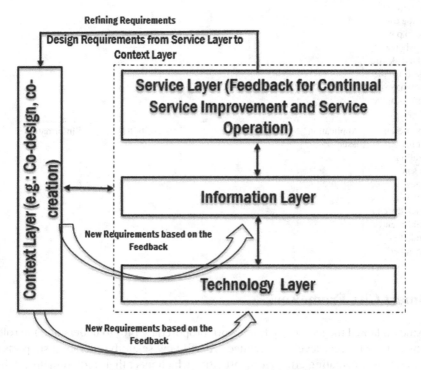

Fig. 1. Proposed conceptual model [54].

3.1 Context Layer

There are four governance paradigms to classify the citizen and administration relationships, named as bureaucratic, consumerist, participatory, and platform facilitating a better understanding of governance arrangements that could lead to better sustainable development [28]. Online communication platforms and social media have changed the way citizens engage in different aspects of their lives, thus governments need innovative methods to listen to the citizens [4]. Although public meetings with citizens in

Table 3. Architectural layers and their specification adapted from [46].

Layer name	Layer specification	Description in the context of this study
Context layer	This layer captures contextual information about strategies, priorities, and other critical aspects such as stakeholders and their concerns including citizens	This study provides an overview of the literature which encapsulates citizen's concerns and supports their inputs into strategies and priorities for smart city projects
Service layer	It defines appropriate goals, scope, and other factors associated with services concerning smart city requirements, concerns, and priorities. It is also associated with an experience and value proposition that the service intends to provide	From this layer viewpoint, the focus is to understand the literature that considers citizen's feedback for understanding smart city requirements, concerns, and priorities from the citizen's perspective. Moreover, those studies have been discussed which emphasize on experiences of citizens and where the aim is providing a better quality of services to the citizens based upon their feedback at the service level
Technology layer	This layer supports the system/application and information function	In this layer, those studies have been included that discuss technological platforms associated with system/application or information function to support citizen's input/feedback for delivering effective services to them
Information layer	This layer identifies data elements/flows and the data interrelations for supporting service function	Studies, which deliberate about data originating from the citizen's side have been included within this layer. Additionally, it has been highlighted how this data is associated with any function of the service

participation workshops do not ensure their participation in a project, the co-design and information sharing processes should be seen as an isolated measure [44]. It is not a matter of how design ideas are being collected from co-creators (e.g. Citizens) but also how this information will be converted into valuable inputs for the designer of the service [40]. Even though so many smart city initiatives have been taken for citizen engagement through e-government technologies, citizen's understanding remains elusive and dispersed [59]. Therefore, there is a need to change service delivery models for e-government systems from a pull to push down approach through which government can provide services to the citizens designed based upon their explicit needs, preferences, location, and circumstances [33]. Strategic drivers such as Collaboration (CO),

Transparency (TRANS), Accountability (ACC), Participation and Partnership (PP), and Communication (COM) can benefit smart city rulers in improving QoL and in the development of public policies [22]. Prioritization of the citizen's requirement for a long-term city transformation can accelerate smart city development [32]. However, present guidance, specifications, and standards do not have enough focus on the requirements of the citizens [24]. Therefore, this study proposes the below concepts for the context layer that support citizens in the design process of the services and can assist in understanding their requirements effectively.

Feedback at Context Level. As this layer encapsulates context-related information about smart cities covering stakeholders and their concerns, strategies, priorities for delivering effective services to the citizens [46]. Therefore, those examples from the literature have been discussed that focus on citizens and their concerns, prioritize strategies that are aligned with the citizen's feedback. For example, [7] presented a reference model in which design proposals were co-created by sharing a common design path with the local community and they provided feedback to those proposals. Similarly, [61] introduced a set of design templates during the co-design process for converting citizen's ideas into technology applications. The key application functionalities can also be co-designed with interested citizens and can result in more substantial impacts on urban governance practices [14]. Today, citizen's opinions, challenges, and responses to policies have become interpretable, noticeable, and sharable [12]. Platform administrators can also consider incrementing the private value as perceived by citizens that have a better effect on continuous e-participation over public value [30]. The research initiatives such as involving both public institutions and the private sector in the design process and analysis, and community feedback to the design proposals have affected the relationship between citizens and urban technologies and turned into a motivation for numerous smart city projects [7]. Therefore, it is important to include non-traditional stakeholders such as citizen groups and informal sector representatives for obtaining their feedback in urban planning processes [51]. It was also discovered during the interviews with practitioners that they engage with citizens to understand their concerns, however, citizens do not have any influence in the actual design of the services or during the later stages of the service design process. Therefore, this study does not only suggest including citizen's feedback at the context level for understanding their concerns but also after the implementation phase to have a better understanding of their experience and to improve the performance of the services further.

Citizens Satisfaction. Citizen satisfaction is an important parameter for evaluating city performance, therefore, sustainable city development should be evaluated based on citizen's life satisfaction and subjective city evaluation rather than only based on municipal service evaluations and objective performance data [41]. Satisfaction surveys can also be used as an evaluation for assessing the strategy's success and as feedback to strategic planning that is vital for public policy planning [31]. Additionally, a service's usefulness can be assessed based on the user satisfaction level [8]. Even though, as highlighted in the literature that service performance should be measured based upon the user satisfaction level, it is still not clear if existing smart city initiatives have taken any major actions in this direction. Lower satisfaction level for e-parking service is a perfect example to highlight this issue which can be improved by considering citizen's satisfaction levels.

Assessing Quality of Service (QoS)

The quality of service can be referred to as the Quality of Experience (QoE) observed by citizens that also includes how the quality is being represented, delivered, and perceived by the users (citizens) and ultimately it can refer to the quality of life [43]. QoE can also be defined from the end user's perspective that includes factors such as Usability, Personalization, Usefulness, Transparency, Effectiveness [8]. This would ensure if users can accomplish desired goals with satisfaction, efficiency, and effectiveness in a specified context [8]. Moreover, [47] defined quality factors for the services as Interoperability, Usability, Availability, Security, Recoverability, Maintainability, Confidentially within the context layer. Therefore, this study suggests having some measures at the context level to assess whether services meet the pre-defined quality factors that are not only associated with application or service but also with Quality of Experience as perceived by the citizens from the service layer.

3.2 Service Layer

The translation of smart city visions into real urban implementations often fails to position citizen's experience in the name of the optimization and efficiency of the urban processes and systems [7]. Although providing service feedback via E-participation platforms has a positive impact on the performance of delivered services, it is still not convincing whether the innovative government-citizen interface has accomplished the fundamental goal of smart cities which is to provide improved quality of the services to the citizens [5]. Soft assets such as social, organizational, information, and knowledge-related capitals are interconnected with the cycle of improving the quality of services and also a prime foundation for smart city development [60]. The quality of services should be accounted for, and assessed to exploit and develop tactics for improving the offered services and can lead to increased satisfaction levels [49]. However, there is a lack of studies that guide how to evaluate these systems based on Quality of Experience (QoE) [8]. Therefore, this study proposes the below concepts to capture their experience at the service level.

Feedback at Service Level. Feedback is captured at two different levels, firstly at the context level where City authorities tend to support citizen's ideas and concerns in policy-making and design of the services that have been discussed within the context layer [7, 12, 14, 61]. And secondly at the service level where citizens provide their feedback after consuming the service, therefore, the concept of feedback has been proposed at both levels. This concept has already been elaborated from a context layer perspective, in this section a brief overview of the existing literature has been provided that proposes the utilization of the feedback after the implementation and delivery of the services at the service layer.

[5] highlighted that service feedback via the E-participation platform has a positive impact on service performance. For instance, the citizens of London are fortified to provide feedback and rate on their experiences which can be used to shape services as per their requirements [53]. Moreover, various online platforms have been discussed for obtaining citizen's feedback once services have been delivered, for instance, citizens converse their concerns on urban projects and often leave meaningful observations on

social media (Twitter) that can inform the decision-making process [4]. Similarly, for reporting any damages or any other infrastructure-associated issues, citizens can also use mobile applications that can lead to a better quality of the services [3]. Likewise, a dashboard has been designed based upon the analysis of citizen's experience and on the identified indicators that would enable public administrators to anticipate the real expectation of citizens for optimizing the investment or for predicting the potential impact on citizens while redesigning the services [2]. Nevertheless, if citizens are not satisfied with the services, then it does not matter whether we have fantastic performance indicators or not as it will ultimately disappoint the citizens in the end [56]. Thus, monitoring should be carried out after the implementation of the actions to compare the actual and expected impact of the services from the citizen's standpoint [1]. Systems such as e-government platforms are most likely to be re-used by citizens if their experience with these systems is better than the traditional ones and thus such systems should be assessed based upon citizen's prior experience and the level of expectations [6]. Additionally, citizen's behavioral data can also be used for the optimization of the services [57]. Thus, this study proposes the concept of feedback at the service level based upon citizen's experience to confirm that their requirements have been met as per their feedback or concerns raised at the context level. For example, citizens may demand e-parking services for their cities to have better parking facilities. However, the council may provide such smart services in the cities, but if these services do not meet the ultimate requirements of the citizens, then smart cities would not achieve their goals.

Contract. From an architectural perspective, a Contract has been defined as an entity that validates the functional and non-functional features of service interaction with external applications, users, or other services [65]. It has also been observed during the interviews with practitioners from the Councils that the service providers have a contract with Councils. Additionally, if Council needs to add any functionality to the services, they describe it to the service providers, and accordingly, service is designed and delivered by them. E-parking service is an example of such service which has been selected as a case study for this research. Furthermore, one of the Councils confirms that for the evaluation of the service performance, KPIs are being used by Council. The service provider submits KPI reports monthly and based on the submitted report, Council evaluates the service performance of the providers. If Council finds that the service providers are not working effectively as promised at the initial of the project, then their contract could be canceled further. However, as highlighted in Sect. 2 that the user satisfaction level for e-parking service was quite low. Therefore, it is questionable if the community had any role in evaluating service provider's performance for e-parking service or any other similar services in the County/City. As the overall objective of smart city services is to improve the quality of life for the citizens of the city [55]. Therefore, it is important to assess service performance based on the citizen's experience and satisfaction level [41]. This would provide more clarity to the Council or city authorities in terms of taking measures and actions against the defined contracts with service providers. Moreover, it would also allow the Council to trace back the objective of the services against defined contracts and quality factors. Thus, this study suggests that the contract should have some KPIs directly related to the citizen's feedback and their satisfaction so that better quality of services can be provided to them. In Sects. 3.1 and 3.2, literature findings have been discussed that support citizen's feedback at context and service level based upon which new concepts have been suggested for the existing framework. In the following sections, a detailed discussion of the existing literature regarding technological platforms and information/data applications has been provided that assist in obtaining citizen's feedback and show how their data can be useful for improving the quality or performance of the services.

3.3 Technology Layer

Digital urban services are not limited to e-government systems rather it covers a wide range of services that citizens utilize on daily basis such as Google Maps, smart parking apps, E-governance portals, and share-economy (e.g.UBER) [52]. Platform technologies such as data analytics, IoT, and social media also can change the role of transparency in policymaking [12]. Furthermore, IoT offers an exceptional opportunity to government as well as citizens to work together to improve the current performance of the services [20]. Government considers technology acceptance by citizens as an important factor and essential element for the development of successful smart cities [52]. Technology provides cheap and effective techniques for citizen engagement, however offline face-to-face engagement cannot be replaced by online engagement platforms [26]. Additionally, greater access to public information can also overwhelm citizens while improving transparency and facilitating citizen engagement [27]. Therefore, a hybrid form of interaction can play a vital role while reaching out to citizens [50]. In the domain of mobility-related applications, smartphone technologies and platforms were found to be an effective tool for including citizens for environmental cognizant mobility behaviors, and it is possible to influence social trends and behaviors in different mobility directions using information communication technology (ICT) technologies [18]. Initially, ICT integrated with city operations and promoted concepts such as digital city, information city, telicity, and later on, the concept of IoT established the term smart cities that support city operations with minimum interaction of humans [53]. There are numerous approaches utilizing ICT and data to full fill citizen's needs and their livelihoods while widely sharing the smart city benefits [58]. However, the advancement and usage of participative smart city software interfaces try to produce an idyllic citizen who can keenly subscribe to the ideas of technological solutions promoted by SC discourses [13]. Therefore, we still need technologies that can fulfill the specific need of citizens, for instance, senior citizens may need urban environments which are elderly-friendly [29]. In this context, Quick Response codes (QR codes) on mobile platforms offer an innovative way for effectively allocating various types of information to the public [34]. Authors propose this system for park navigation and to provide incentives for using parks through gaming applications that would provide improved safety, more effective distribution of the information, and improved feedback. Likewise, Graph-based technology has been designed using Apache Spark and GraphX to assist citizens in making mobility associated decisions and to assist traffic authorities in traffic regulations by applying graph algorithms [48]. Moreover, there are many data analytics techniques and algorithms for identifying solutions to the smart city problems, such as text analytic technique can be used for channeling citizen's inputs [15]. Similarly, Living Labs (LL) use Lo-Fi technologies to advance digital invention and engage with local citizens for co-creating digital interferences and apps that are aimed to solve local issues [13].

3.4 Information Layer

Inventions in mobile, cloud, and data are offering new visions to enhance the quality of governance and can accomplish citizen's expectations [33]. For instance, data from Twitter (social media) can also be analyzed to understand citizen's concerns on urban projects as they often leave meaningful observations that can be utilized in a better decision-making process [4]. Moreover, geospatial data can be utilized for secondary usage such as for application development or for producing public services, etc., and to support service delivery, decision making, and government operations as well [64]. Similarly, the dashboard's associated data can enable users to visualize what actions to take, and can also be used by governments for various purposes including decision making, policy processes, communication, and interaction with citizens [38]. Additionally, data produced from user-generated content as a part of the co-design/co-production process or while co-creating services with citizens, can be used to create predictive models that foresee services and thus enabling local government to shift from reactive responses to proactive one and at the end to citizen's need [15]. Citizen-generated open data can provide an information basis for cooperative governance wherein significant information is produced about issues such as air quality, the maintenance of public space, and many more [39]. Open data aims to motivate citizen's participation, improve government transparency, and unlock commercial inventions, however, there are many barriers to achieve it including the absence of public participation mechanism, unsatisfied citizens and not knowing the real requirements of citizens [36]. Co-creation with citizens in living labs using open data impact the creation of smart city services and ideas, and citizen's life can be improved if cities optimize and nurture the ecosystems by reusing their data for creating innovative services [2]. As citizens communicate with smart city services using different platforms such as smartphones, computers, and other smart devices, therefore it is also important to manage data privacy or security-related issues [53].

4 Discussion

This study aimed to discuss the literature around the involvement of citizens in the design of the services from the lens of the adapted smart city framework [46]. Based upon the case study and the literature findings new key concepts have been proposed within this framework. The concept of 'Feedback' has been deliberated from two different perspectives and why it is important to include this concept at the service and context level. Moreover, other concepts such as citizen's satisfaction, assessment of QoS, and contract have also been introduced. These concepts have been introduced for two layers of the framework. Firstly, at the service layer, wherein the aim is to capture citizen's feedback about their experience towards the service that has been utilized by them. Secondly, at context kevel, where citizen's ideas are supported during the co-design/co-production process for designing the new services. This study emphasizes closing the

Table 4. Identified concepts and platforms supporting citizens in smart city development.

References	Concepts	Associated platforms
[14]	Co-design	Mobile applications
[59]	Citizen's Social Value	e-government System
[22]	Strategic Drivers/Smart governance	ICT
[32]	Smart Planning	Crowdsourcing Platforms
[6]	Citizen's experience	e-government systems
[50]	Hybrid forms of interaction	Online/offline engagement platforms
[14, 61]	Co-design	Smart apps
[5]	Co-production	e-participation/Mobile platform
[8, 31, 41]	Citizen's satisfaction	Survey/online platforms (Apps)
[27]	Citizen engagement	e-government systems/Websites
[20]	Co-creation	IoT
[29]	Citizens requirements	PPGIS (Public Participation GIS) system
[31]	Citizen's need	Electronic voting systems/Crowdsourcing Tools
[58]	Citizen's need	ICT
[12]	Citizens participation	Social media, IoT and data analytics
[4]	Smart participatory	Online platforms (Social media)
[24]	Citizen's requirement	IoT
[30]	Citizen's participation	e-governance
[51]	Citizen engagement	Framework
[7]	Co-creation	Reference Model
[60]	Soft assets	Framework
[52]	E-governance	Google Maps, smart parking apps, E-governance portals
[1]	Citizen's experience	Service Design Methodology
[64]	Geo-participation data	Mobile Applications
[4]	Communication Channels	Social Media (Twitter)
[26]	Citizen's participation	Framework
[36]	Citizens participation	Open data
[48]	Mobility associated decisions	Graph-based technology
[15]	Co-design/co-production	Text analytic technique
[13]	Co-creation	Lo-Fi technologies

(*continued*)

Table 4. (*continued*)

References	Concepts	Associated platforms
[39]	Cooperative governance	Open data platforms
[18]	Citizen's involvement	ICT, smartphone technologies, and platforms
[38]	Communication and interaction platform	Dashboard
[3]	Citizen Reporting Engagement	Mobile applications
[2]	Citizen's experience /Co-creation	Dashboard
[57]	Citizen's Behavioral Data	Framework
[34]	Citizen's specific information	Quick Response codes (QR codes)

feedback loop from the service layer to the context layer to ensure that the services have been implemented as per citizen's requirements gathered as a part of the co-design process at the context level. Additionally, these services should be assessed based on the defined quality criteria considering citizen's satisfaction towards the service at the service level. Based upon this analysis, further requirements can be understood for other layers (Information/technology) while redesigning the services or during the next phases of the implementations. Lastly, it was discovered during the interviews that service providers are bounded with a Contract. However, it was not known if these contracts also consider factors from a citizen's perspective to validate the functional and non-functional features of a service or to measure the performance of these services based on their feedback. Therefore, this study suggests including this factor while proposing contracts to the service providers. These concepts have been proposed for service and context layers in the adapted framework that would assist city authorities to design effective services in the future.

5   Conclusion and Future Work

The paper is an extension of our earlier publication [54]. In this paper, a detailed discussion has been provided about the existing concepts and platforms proposed in the literature regarding the involvement of citizens in the design and development of smart cities. Moreover, based upon the conducted case study and literature findings this study proposed new concepts for context and service layers within the adapted framework. In the previous publication, it was highlighted that there is a lack of studies guiding the utilization of the citizen's feedbacks into more structured requirements for designing effective services for them. To solve this problem, a conceptual model was proposed that linked the different architectural layers for understanding the citizen's requirements. In this paper, this notion has been further extended and new key concepts have been proposed. These concepts provide more detail on how architectural layers (Context, Service, Technology, Information) have been linked logically to complete the feedback loop from the citizen's end. This can guide city authorities in better decision-making of designing effective services that meet citizen's requirements based upon their feedback. As a part of future work, this study aims to identify other concepts associated with these layers and continue to complete the evaluation of the proposed concepts.

Acknowledgment. This work was supported with the financial support of IVI (Home - Innovation Value Institute (ivi.ie)) and the Science Foundation Ireland grant 13/ RC/2094_P2 and co-funded under the European Regional Development Fund through the Southern & Eastern Regional Operational Programme to Lero - the Science Foundation Ireland Research Centre for Software (www. lero.ie).

References

1. Abella, A., et al.: A methodology to design and redesign services in smart cities based on the citizen experience. Inf. Polity. **24**(2), 183–197 (2019). https://doi.org/ 0.3233/IP-180116
2. Abella, A., et al.: A model for the analysis of data-driven innovation and value generation in smart cities' ecosystems. Cities **64**, 47–53 (2017). https://doi.org/10.1016/j.cities.2017. 01.011
3. Abu-Tayeh, G., Neumann, O., Stuermer, M.: Exploring the motives of citizen reporting engagement: self-concern and other-orientation. Bus. Inf. Syst. Eng. **60**(3), 215–226 (2018). https://doi.org/10.1007/s12599-018-0530-8
4. Alizadeh, T., et al.: Capturing citizen voice online: Enabling smart participatory local government. Cities. **95**, 102400 (2019). https://doi.org/10.1016/j.cities.2019.102400
5. Allen, B., et al.: Does citizen coproduction lead to better urban services in smart cities projects? An empirical study on e-participation in a mobile big data platform. Gov. Inf. Q. **37**(1), 101412 (2020). https://doi.org/10.1016/j.giq.2019.101412
6. Alruwaie, M., et al.: Citizens' continuous use of eGovernment services: the role of self-efficacy, outcome expectations and satisfaction. Gov. Inf. Q. **37**(3), 101485 (2020). https:// doi.org/10.1016/j.giq.2020.101485
7. Andreani, S., et al.: Reframing technologically enhanced urban scenarios: a design research model towards human centered smart cities. Technol. Forecast. Soc. Change. **142**(September 2018), 15–25 (2019). https://doi.org/10.1016/j.techfore.2018.09.028
8. Ballesteros, L.G.M., et al.: Quality of Experience (QoE) in the smart cties context: an initial analysis. In: 2015 IEEE 1st International Smart Cities Conference, ISC2 2015 (2015). https:// doi.org/10.1109/ISC2.2015.7366222
9. Bastidas, V., et al.: A requirements framework for the design of smart city reference architectures. In: Proceedings of 51st Hawaii International Conference on System. Sciences, p. 9 (2018). https://doi.org/10.24251/hicss.2018.317
10. Baxter, P., et al.: Qualitative case study methodology: study design and implementation for novice researchers. Qual. Rep. **13**(4), 544–559 (2008). https://doi.org/10.2174/187443460 0802010058
11. Bednar, P.M., Welch, C.: Socio-technical perspectives on smart working: creating meaningful and sustainable systems. Inf. Syst. Front. **22**(2), 281–298 (2019). https://doi.org/10.1007/s10 796-019-09921-1
12. Brunswicker, S., et al.: Transparency in policy making: a complexity view. Gov. Inf. Q. **36**(3), 571–591 (2019). https://doi.org/10.1016/j.giq.2019.05.005
13. Cardullo, P., et al.: Living labs and vacancy in the neoliberal city. Cities **73**, 44–50 (2018). https://doi.org/10.1016/j.cities.2017.10.008

14. Cellina, F., et al.: Co-creating app-based policy measures for mobility behavior change: A trigger for novel governance practices at the urban level. Sustain. Cities Soc. 53, 101911 (2020). https://doi.org/10.1016/j.scs.2019.101911

15. Chong, M., et al.: Dynamic capabilities of a smart city: an innovative approach to discovering urban problems and solutions. Gov. Inf. Q. 35(4), 682–692 (2018). https://doi.org/10.1016/j.giq.2018.07.005

16. Corsini, F., et al.: Participatory energy: research, imaginaries and practices on people' contribute to energy systems in the smart city. Technol. Forecast. Soc. Change. 142(July 2018), 322–332 (2019). https://doi.org/10.1016/j.techfore.2018.07.028

17. Dameri, R.P., et al.: Understanding smart cities as a glocal strategy: a comparison between Italy and China. Technol. Forecast. Soc. Change 142, 26–41 (2019). https://doi.org/10.1016/j.techfore.2018.07.025

18. Di Dio, S., et al.: Involving people in the building up of smart and sustainable cities: How to influence commuters' behaviors through a mobile app game. Sustain. Cities Soc. 42(May), 325–336 (2018). https://doi.org/10.1016/j.scs.2018.07.021

19. Ekman, P., et al.: Exploring smart cities and market transformations from a service-dominant logic perspective. Sustain. Cities Soc. 51(February), 101731 (2019). https://doi.org/10.1016/j.scs.2019.101731

20. El-Haddadeh, R., et al.: Examining citizens' perceived value of internet of things technologies in facilitating public sector services engagement. Gov. Inf. Q. 36(2), 310–320 (2019). https://doi.org/10.1016/j.giq.2018.09.009

21. Greenwood, R.E.: The case study approach. Bus. Commun. Q. 56(4), 46–48 (2011). https://doi.org/10.1177/108056999305600409

22. De Guimarães, J.C.F., et al.: Governance and quality of life in smart cities: towards sustainable development goals. J. Clean. Prod. 253 (2020). https://doi.org/10.1016/j.jclepro.2019.119926

23. Habibzadeh, H., et al.: A survey on cybersecurity, data privacy, and policy issues in cyber-physical system deployments in smart cities. Sustain. Cities Soc. 50(August 2018), 101660 (2019). https://doi.org/10.1016/j.scs.2019.101660

24. Heaton, J., Parlikad, A.K.: A conceptual framework for the alignment of infrastructure assets to citizen requirements within a smart cities framework. Cities 90(January), 32–41 (2019). https://doi.org/10.1016/j.cities.2019.01.041

25. Hollands, R.G.: Will the real smart city please stand up? City 4813 (2008). https://doi.org/10.1080/13604810802479126

26. Horgan, D., Dimitrijević, B.: Frameworks for citizens participation in planning: from conversational to smart tools. Sustain. Cities Soc. 48, 101550 (2019). https://doi.org/10.1016/j.scs.2019.101550

27. Jae, H., Viswanathan, M.: Effects of pictorial product-warnings on low-literate consumers. J. Bus. Res. 65(12), 1674–1682 (2012). https://doi.org/10.1016/j.jbusres.2012.02.008

28. Janowski, T., et al.: Platform governance for sustainable development: reshaping citizen-administration relationships in the digital age. Gov. Inf. Q. 35(4, Supplement), S1–S16 (2018). https://doi.org/10.1016/j.giq.2018.09.002

29. Jelokhani-Niaraki, M., et al.: A web-based public participation GIS for assessing the age-friendliness of cities: a case study in Tehran, Iran. Cities 95, 102471 (2019). https://doi.org/10.1016/j.cities.2019.102471

30. Ju, J., et al.: Public and private value in citizen participation in E-governance: evidence from a government-sponsored green commuting platform. Gov. Inf. Q. 36(4), 101400 (2019). https://doi.org/10.1016/j.giq.2019.101400

31. Kopackova, H.: Reflexion of citizens' needs in city strategies: the case study of selected cities of Visegrad group countries. Cities 84(August 2018), 159–171 (2019). https://doi.org/10.1016/j.cities.2018.08.004

32. Kumar, H., et al.: Moving towards smart cities: Solutions that lead to the smart city transformation framework. Technol. Forecast. Soc. Change. **153**, 119281 (2020). https://doi.org/10.1016/j.techfore.2018.04.024
33. Linders, D., et al.: Proactive e-governance: flipping the service delivery model from pull to push in Taiwan. Gov. Inf. Q. **35**(4, Supplement), S68–S76 (2018). https://doi.org/10.1016/j.giq.2015.08.004
34. Lorenzi, D., et al.: Enhancing the government service experience through QR codes on mobile platforms. Gov. Inf. Q. **31**(1), 6–16 (2014). https://doi.org/10.1016/j.giq.2013.05.025
35. Lorquet, A., Pauwels, L.: Interrogating urban projections in audio-visual 'smart city' narratives. Cities **100**, 102660 (2020). https://doi.org/10.1016/j.cities.2020.102660
36. Ma, R., Lam, P.T.I.: Investigating the barriers faced by stakeholders in open data development: a study on Hong Kong as a "smart city". Cities **92**, 36–46 (2019). https://doi.org/10.1016/j.cities.2019.03.009
37. Macke, J., et al.: Smart sustainable cities evaluation and sense of community. J. Clean. Prod. **239**, 118103 (2019). https://doi.org/10.1016/j.jclepro.2019.118103
38. Matheus, R., et al.: Data science empowering the public: Data-driven dashboards for transparent and accountable decision-making in smart cities. Gov. Inf. Q. 101284 (2018). https://doi.org/10.1016/j.giq.2018.01.006
39. Meijer, A., Potjer, S.: Citizen-generated open data: an explorative analysis of 25 cases. Gov. Inf. Q. **35**(4), 613–621 (2018). https://doi.org/10.1016/j.giq.2018.10.004
40. Mueller, J., et al.: Citizen design science: a strategy for crowd-creative urban design. Cities. **72**, 181–188 (2018). https://doi.org/10.1016/j.cities.2017.08.018
41. Nakamura, H., Managi, S.: Effects of subjective and objective city evaluation on life satisfaction in Japan. J. Clean. Prod. **256**, 120523 (2020). https://doi.org/10.1016/j.jclepro.2020.120523
42. Nam, T., Pardo, T.A.: Smart city as urban innovation. In: Proceedings of the 5th International Conference on Theory and Practice of Electronic Governance - ICEGOV 2011, p. 185 (2011). https://doi.org/10.1145/2072069.2072100
43. Nepal, S., et al.: A note on quality of service issues in smart cities. J. Parallel Distrib. Comput. **127**, 116–117 (2019). https://doi.org/10.1016/j.jpdc.2019.02.001
44. Nielsen, B.F., et al.: Identifying and supporting exploratory and exploitative models of innovation in municipal urban planning; key challenges from seven Norwegian energy ambitious neighborhood pilots. Technol. Forecast. Soc. Change. **142**(December 2017), 142–153 (2019). https://doi.org/10.1016/j.techfore.2018.11.007
45. Pedersen, K.: What can open innovation be used for and how does it create value? Gov. Inf. Q. **37**(2), 101459 (2020). https://doi.org/10.1016/j.giq.2020.101459
46. Pourzolfaghar, Z., Bastidas, V., Helfert, M.: Standardisation of enterprise architecture development for smart cities. J. Knowl. Econ. **11**(4), 1336–1357 (2019). https://doi.org/10.1007/s13132-019-00601-8
47. Pourzolfaghar, Z., Helfert, M.: Taxonomy of smart elements for designing effective services. In: Proceedings of 23rd Americas Conference on Information Systems, pp. 1–10 (2017). https://doi.org/10.1037/rmh0000009
48. Rathore, M.M., et al.: Exploiting IoT and big data analytics: defining smart digital city using real-time urban data. Sustain. Cities Soc. **40**(December 2017), 600–610 (2018). https://doi.org/10.1016/j.scs.2017.12.022
49. Sá, F., et al.: From the quality of traditional services to the quality of local e-Government online services: a literature review. Gov. Inf. Q. **33**(1), 149–160 (2016). https://doi.org/10.1016/j.giq.2015.07.004
50. Salvia, G., Morello, E.: Sharing cities and citizens sharing: perceptions and practices in Milan. Cities. **98**, 102592 (2020). https://doi.org/10.1016/j.cities.2019.102592

51. Schröder, P., et al.: Advancing sustainable consumption and production in cities - a transdisciplinary research and stakeholder engagement framework to address consumption-based emissions and impacts. J. Clean. Prod. **213**, 114–125 (2019). https://doi.org/10.1016/j.jclepro.2018.12.050

52. Sepasgozar, S.M.E., et al.: Implementing citizen centric technology in developing smart cities: a model for predicting the acceptance of urban technologies. Technol. Forecast. Soc. Change **142**, 105–116 (2019). https://doi.org/10.1016/j.techfore.2018.09.012

53. Silva, B.N., et al.: Towards sustainable smart cities: a review of trends, architectures, components, and open challenges in smart cities. Sustain. Cities Soc. **38**(August 2017), 697–713 (2018). https://doi.org/10.1016/j.scs.2018.01.053

54. Singh, P., et al.: Role of citizens in the development of smart cities: benefit of citizen's feedback for improving quality of service. Smartgreens 35–44 (2021). https://doi.org/10.5220/0010442000350044

55. Singh, P., Helfert, M.: Smart cities and associated risks: technical v/s non-technical perspective. In: CHIRA 2019 - Proceedings of the 3rd International Conference on Computer-Human Interaction Research and Applications, pp. 221–228 (2019). https://doi.org/10.5220/0008494402210228

56. Sofiyabadi, J., et al.: Key performance indicators measurement in service business: a fuzzy VIKOR approach. Total Qual. Manag. Bus. Excell. **27**(9–10), 1028–1042 (2016). https://doi.org/10.1080/14783363.2015.1059272

57. Solaimani, S., Bouwman, H., Itälä, T.: Networked enterprise business model alignment: a case study on smart living. Inf. Syst. Front. **17**(4), 871–887 (2013). https://doi.org/10.1007/s10796-013-9474-1

58. Trencher, G.: Towards the smart city 2.0: empirical evidence of using smartness as a tool for tackling social challenges. Technol. Forecast. Soc. Change. **142**(October 2017), 117–128 (2019). https://doi.org/10.1016/j.techfore.2018.07.033

59. Vidiasova, L., Cronemberger, F.: Discrepancies in perceptions of smart city initiatives in Saint Petersburg, Russia. Sustain. Cities Soc. 102158 (2020). https://doi.org/10.1016/j.scs.2020.102158

60. Wataya, E., Shaw, R.: Measuring the value and the role of soft assets in smart city development. Cities **94**, 106–115 (2019). https://doi.org/10.1016/j.cities.2019.04.019

61. Wolff, A., et al.: Supporting smart citizens: design templates for co-designing data-intensive technologies. Cities. 101, 102695 (2020). https://doi.org/10.1016/j.cities.2020.102695

62. Yigitcanlar, T., et al.: Can cities become smart without being sustainable ? A systematic review of the literature. Sustain. Cities Soc. **45**(June 2018), 348–365 (2019). https://doi.org/10.1016/j.scs.2018.11.033

63. Yin, R.K.: Validity and generalization in future case study evaluations. Evaluation **19**(3), 321–332 (2013). https://doi.org/10.1177/1356389013497081

64. Zhang, S.: Public participation in the Geoweb era: defining a typology for geo-participation in local governments. Cities **85**, 38–50 (2019). https://doi.org/10.1016/j.cities.2018.12.004

65. The Open Group Standard (2018)

A Decision Support System Based on Rainfall Nowcasting and Artificial Neural Networks to Mitigate Wastewater Treatment Plant Downstream Floods

Loris Francesco Termite[1,4](✉), Emanuele Bonamente[2], Alberto Garinei[3,4],
Daniele Bolpagni[5], Lorenzo Menculini[4], Marcello Marconi[3,4], Lorenzo Biondi[3,4],
Andrea Chini[6], and Massimo Crespi[6]

[1] K-Digitale S.R.L., Perugia, Italy
ltermite@idea-re.eu, loris.termite@k-digitale.com
[2] Department of Engineering, University of Perugia, Perugia, Italy
[3] Department of Engineering Sciences, Guglielmo Marconi University, Rome, Italy
[4] Idea-Re S.R.L., Perugia, Italy
[5] A2A Ciclo Idrico S.P.A., Brescia, Italy
[6] Radarmeteo S.R.L., Due Carrare, PD, Italy

Abstract. This contribution presents a Decision Support System for operators working in a wastewater treatment plant, aimed at helping them in taking appropriate mitigation strategies in case of extreme rainfall events. The Decision Support System is based on the real-time monitoring of several variables within the area of interest and on the forecasting of specific variables in key points. The forecasting relies on Artificial Neural Networks, predicting water levels and flows from rainfall inputs. The use of very-short-term Quantitative Precipitation Estimates – nowcasting – allows for an extension of the forecasting horizon with respect of using measured rainfall only. Different Artificial Neural Networks architectures are tested. The Decision Support System was developed and tested on a real setting, specifically a wastewater treatment plant collecting the sewage from the city of Brescia, Italy. The quickness of the computation is compliant with the real-time needs and makes the developed platform an efficient tool to be used in a Smart City.

Keyword: Decision support systems · Artificial neural networks · Flood mitigation

1 Introduction

In many urban areas, sewer systems are threatened by intense rainfall events, which can make discharge pass the pipe capacity. Resulting floods endanger buildings, infrastructures, and human lives. In separate sewer systems, storm drains are affected by flooding risk. In combined sewers, which collect both stormwater and gray/blackwater, the potential combined sewer overflow (CSO) is also connected to pollution issues [1].

© Springer Nature Switzerland AG 2022
C. Klein et al. (Eds.): SMARTGREENS 2021/ VEHITS 2021, CCIS 1612, pp. 125–150, 2022.
https://doi.org/10.1007/978-3-031-17098-0_7

After sewage has been processed in a wastewater treatment plant (WWTP), clean water is committed to receiving water bodies. However, if the stage of the receiving bodies is already high due to rainfall, additional inflows may result in floods after the WWTP.

Even if specific structures – spillway gates, buffer tanks, pumps, etc. – are designed to mitigate such occurrences, an accurate knowledge of the system status (water flows, levels, gate openings) and, possibly, the weather conditions (observations and forecasts) would greatly help in applying a proper intervention strategy during a critical event. In the lack of such a comprehensive monitoring, operators should choose the intervention strategy by relying mostly on their experience. In this context, a decision support system (DSS) may represent a fundamental aid [2].

DSSs are platforms that provide support to the human operator in deciding which operations to perform. Examples from scientific literature for sewerage systems-related applications [3, 4] mainly focus on the design, renovation, and upgrade of the physical system or on the offline reanalysis of past events aimed at the optimization of future intervention strategies. Conversely, real-time data have been used primarily to monitor pollution emissions and concentrations [5]. In recent years, the smart network monitoring theme has emerged and begun to find practical applications. Municipalities, utilities, and related organizations can benefit from technological advances and implement smart data infrastructure for wet weather control. Real-time or near real-time decision making is supported by advanced data monitoring. These advances lead to the development of smart infrastructures, which the United States Environmental Protection Agency defines as "the integration of emerging and advanced technology to enhance the collection, storage, and/or reanalysis of water-related data", making use of "hardware, communication and management analytics to provide real and tangible benefits to utilities", as "maximizing existing infrastructure and optimizing operations and responses to be proactive, not reactive" [6]. Smart infrastructures are generally implemented in connection with a supervisory control and data acquisition (SCADA) system. Their main objective is usually the real-time monitoring of CSO's flow rates and effluent level, to assess potential flooding and pollution incidents and to support decision making [7].

To the best of our knowledge, however, the diffusion of smart infrastructures is still quite limited, with specific reference to the Italian territory. Few existing studies have the objective of reducing CSO through Real-Time Control of gates and sluices [8, 9]. In our opinion, some issues are still not addressed properly, among which the potential risk of flooding related to excessive discharge from the WWTP to the receiving body. Most of real-world DSS that aim at flood mitigation still rely on traditional hydraulic models. These are often characterized by a high computational demand and are therefore unsuitable for real-time usage. Moreover, these models are not resilient to climate change or to changes in boundary conditions, becoming outdated in these occurrences. Another feature that is generally missing is the use of very-short-term precipitation forecasts, which are crucial in case of high-intense and short-lasting rainfall events.

In this contribution, as an extended version of our previous paper [10], we present a case study about the design of a DSS dedicated to WWTP management. The developed DSS allows for real-time monitoring of the system status through a network of ground-based meters and weather radars and includes a forecasting tool which provides additional information to help operators in planning maneuvers. Water levels and flows inside the network are forecasted by means of Artificial Neural Networks (ANNs) [11], artificial intelligence tools that are suitable for the purposes of this study. Indeed, they allow both to reduce input data variety – and thus to select only the most statistically significant in the input-output relation – and to neglect parameters needed by traditional models, as for example the soil properties in rainfall-runoff modelling. Moreover, their execution is immediate and perfectly matches the real-time requirements. In fact, once calibrated, the ANNs algorithms consist in linear algebra operations on matrices which require negligible computational times, unlike more traditional hydraulic models that as of today require large computational times and computing resources [12]. ANNs models can also be easily updated, well facing possible changes in the real environment. In [10] we used a basic ANN architecture, the Multilayer Perceptron (MLP). Here, we also show the results obtained with a different architecture, the Long Short-Term Memory (LSTM) [13].

The DSS has the final aim of providing useful insights about the current system status and the estimated evolution of the strategic variables, by collecting all data and showing them in a single User Interface. The deriving information will hopefully guide operators to apply a proper risk mitigation strategy.

As said above, the knowledge of the upcoming rainfall in the very-short term (next couple of hours) can play a fundamental role to predict the further evolution of the hydraulic variables of interest, allowing to manage the potential emergencies with a reasonable advance. This is particularly true in case of urban watersheds characterized by rainfall-runoff lags comparable with the "very-short term" range. Naively, if the use of measured rainfall inputs allows to estimate the hydraulic variables behavior within a forecasting horizon equal to the watershed lag, the addition of predicted rainfall inputs allows to further extend the forecasting horizon up to the time of the last rainfall prediction plus the lag time. The developed DSS achieves this goal thanks to the integration of high resolution very-short-term quantitative precipitation forecasts (QPF), also known as "nowcasting" [14].

The rest of the paper is organized as follows. Sect. 2 provides a description of the study area and of the system layout. In Sect. 3 the methodology is explained. With respect to [10], additional information about nowcasting is given and the LSTM approach is illustrated. Section 4 shows the results of the ANNs models, for both MLP and LSTM. In Sect. 5 the User Interface of the DSS is displayed. A discussion on the study is given in Sect. 6. Conclusions are reported in Sect. 7.

2 Study Area and System Layout

The WWTP for which the DSS was developed is located in the city of Brescia (Italy), specifically in the Verziano district (southern area). It collects the sewage and urban runoff of the city and its surrounding area, serving a total of 296 000 inhabitants over a 146 km^2 surface (Fig. 1).

A view of the downstream area is given in Fig. 2, while a not to scale representation of the system layout, comprising flow directions and measuring points, is shown in Fig. 3.

An urban drainage canal named Vaso Fiume (VF) runs parallel to the final sewer collector, upstream the WWTP. When the sewer flow raises above a critical level, the

Fig. 1. Wastewater treatment plant location and watershed.

excess is directed into the VF trough two lateral spillways, one located just before the WWTP and one a few km upstream. The VF also receives the treated wastewater. A bigger urban drainage canal, named Vaso Garzetta (VG), collects water from the VF approximately 2.4 km downstream and eventually flows into the Mella river after a 3.4 km path. The whole network of receiving water bodies is characterized by potential hydraulic risk in case of extreme rainfall events: over the last years urban flooding has occurred several times along the VG canal, in a critical location corresponding to the *gz_lt01* measuring point (approximately 1.7 km after the confluence with VF), affecting the red area on the left in Fig. 2.

In such dangerous circumstances, the water flowing from VF into VG should be constrained and the WWTP technicians must pay close attention in order to minimize the risk of flooding. To this aim, the VF canal is equipped with a series of inline or lateral gates, which can be used effectively for flood prevention. Two lateral gates (*g10* and *g15*), which are closed in standard conditions, can be gradually opened to direct the flow in the surrounding rural area, still respecting environmental law limitations and avoiding excessive discharges which could put in danger the red area on the right in Fig. 2. A couple of paired inline gates (*g14a* and *g14b*), which are kept open in standard conditions, can be progressively closed to reduce, and in certain cases completely arrest, the VF flow into the VG. A storage area is also present next to the WWTP and is used to reduce the peak discharge into the VF: an inline gate (*g2*) can be partially closed to increase the upstream water level and activate a lateral spillway into the storage area.

Fig. 2. Wastewater treatment plant downstream area.

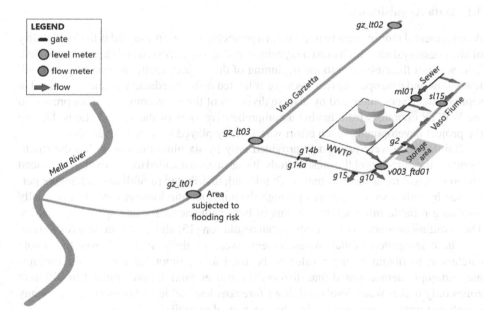

Fig. 3. System layout (from [10]).

The WWTP and the sewage network are managed by a leading multiutility company which has been playing much effort in Smart City projects over the last years. The wish of the WWTP managers was to have a tool able to assist them in taking proper decision especially when dealing with severe rainfall events. Indeed, prior to the development of the present DSS platform, the gate-opening strategy relied only on operator experience – based on information from the upstream gz_lt02 meter – to foresee impending flood waves. Operators decided whether to use the storage area and to open lateral spillways to reduce the outflow towards the VG canal and prevent downstream overflows. However, the users lacked an interface allowing a thorough monitoring of the system status. In particular, information about forthcoming rainfall amounts, water levels and sewer flows was completely missing. In case of severe events, such an approach was not able to completely avoid risks.

In addition to the VG level at gz_lt02, particular attention is also devoted to the WWTP inlet ($ml01$), as treatment cycles can be optimized thanks to the presence of an internal buffer tank. Since during extreme events the flow at $ml01$ may exceed the WWTP processing capacity, knowing this flow in advance can help to properly manage the internal operation of the plant. Therefore, the VG level at gz_lt02 and the flow at $ml01$ are key parameters to be monitored. Their expected values are forecasted by the ANNs developed for the DSS.

3   Methodology

3.1   Data Acquisition

A fundamental requirement to implement a project as the one presented is the availability of all necessary data, which must be synchronized, easily accessed and clearly visualized. This was not the case prior to the beginning of the project. Quite the contrary, rainfall, level, flow and gate opening records were collected in diverse databases and visualized in separate interfaces, managed by diverse divisions of the main company. This prevented the WWTP operators from having a comprehensive view of the system status. During the project development, much effort was actually played to set up the database.

Rainfall data were previously provided only by six pluviometers within the catchment; for the purposes of the present study, it was instead decided to also exploit advanced meteorological radar measurements. To this end, distributed rainfall measurements performed by radars were calibrated through the punctual pluviometer records, eventually obtaining reliable information in terms of both value accuracy and spatial variability. The resulting product has 1×1 km spatial resolution [15] and a 10-min time resolution.

These integrated rainfall measurements were spatially averaged over the whole catchment to obtain a single value to be used as an input for the ANNs. Preliminary attempts demonstrated that distinguishing over rainfalls precipitated in different zones only makes water levels and flows forecasts less stable and does not produce any significant improvement over using the mean areal rainfall.

The readout of each sensor was synchronized, the time step was fixed to 10 min, and a dedicated server was realized to host the system database containing all the records of measured data, computed quantities and final parameters.

3.2 Nowcasting

In meteorology, nowcasting refers to very-short-term quantitative precipitation forecasts (QPF): the time horizon is of the order of few hours, on a spatial resolution of a few kilometers. QPF for nowcasting is performed by means of algorithms working on atmospheric condition measures provided by weather radars [16, 17] and, to a lesser extent, by satellites [18]. While numerical weather prediction (NWP) produces more reliable forecasts on longer time ranges, it has been proved that radar-based nowcasting can give more reliable results than NWP within a time horizon of 3–8 h [19], being therefore a valuable tool for real-time decision-making. Nowcasting systems use radar images as immediate snapshots of the state of the atmosphere and, by combining multiple of such images, estimate where precipitation systems are likely to move soon [18]. The computational complexity of this approach is much lower than NWP at small temporal and spatial scales.

Nowcasting algorithms are generally based on advection models, which estimate the movement of a precipitation system via its velocity field. The simplest models, as the Lagrangian persistence method (or extrapolation), consist in moving forward the current radar echoes along the advection path. This approach is acceptable for large scale stratiform systems but is not suitable for convective ones. More sophisticated approaches take into consideration also growth or decay factors of precipitation fields.

At the time of project development nowcasting was performed via a proprietary algorithm, consisting in an extrapolation-based method that extracts local maxima from the input reflectivity field and other random points. The sub-sampled field is then moved in the direction of the wind as forecasted by the global forecast system (GFS) model. An interpolation is then performed to reconstruct the final reflectivity field. This approach is used in the first implementation of the DSS. However, in addition to its intrinsic limitations, it is quite time expensive and consequently the predictions are calculated on a 20-min basis. Therefore, with the aim of improving the forecasting accuracy and reducing the computational demand, a survey of the more recent techniques was performed [18].

As a result, the ANVIL (Autoregressive Nowcasting Vertically Integrated Liquid) model [20] was found as a suitable candidate to replace the current nowcasting algorithm. ANVIL combines two previous methods, namely RadVil [21] and S-PROG [22]. Like RadVil, ANVIL takes in consideration growth and decay phenomena by estimating the variation of the vertically integrated liquid water content (VIL) in an atmosphere column as:

$$\frac{dVIL}{dt} = \frac{\partial VIL}{\partial t} + v_x \frac{\partial VIL}{\partial x} + v_y \frac{\partial VIL}{\partial y} = S(t) - P(t) \tag{1}$$

where VIL is expressed in $kg \cdot m^{-2}$, v_x and v_y are the horizontal components of the advection velocity, S is the input term of the rainwater column and P is the output term, i.e. the ground rainfall rate. Moreover, like S-PROG, ANVIL follows the basic idea that the predictability of growth and decay is scale-dependent and thus the VIL is decomposed into multiple spatial scales and a separate autoregressive integrated model is applied to each scale.

As all advection-based nowcasting approaches, ANVIL must be used in conjunction with a model describing the movement of the rainfall system via its velocity field. To this aim, the optical flow technique by Lucas and Kanade [23] can be adopted.

The use of the ANVIL model is foreseen in the next future. In addition to its accuracy, its limited computational demand will allow to perform nowcasting on a 10-min basis, aligning its updating frequency with all other data.

3.3 Artificial Neural Networks

Dataset and ANNs Common Features. Rainfall, gz_lt02 level and $ml01$ discharge data were made available for a period spanning from October 2016 to August 2018. All the implemented models that predict VG level were trained and validated using 18 suitably trimmed rainfall events in the analyzed period, corresponding to a total 1714 datapoints; the models that predict sewer flow used 17 events, with 12057 datapoints. Due to the available data, the two samples refer to different sets of events. The higher number of datapoints used to train sewer-related ANNs depends on the fact that events were trimmed in larger chunks, because flows at $ml01$ take longer to return to the unperturbed value after rainfalls with respect to levels at gz_lt02. It is customary in Machine Learning to use three different sets of data, namely the calibration, validation and testing set: the calibration and validation set are used to train the networks, with the first used to fix weights and biases and the latter to adjust the hyperparameters; the testing set is used to test the ANNs performance on unseen data. However, due to some uncertainties in the available data, and since our aim was not to explore ANNs' theory but instead it was necessary to exploit as much data as possible to build a ready-to-use product, we decided to disregard the testing set. Therefore, the available datasets were split using the last four events (380 datapoints, i.e. 22.17% for level forecast; 2274 datapoints, i.e. 18.86% for flow forecast) for the validation set and the previous ones for the calibration set.

The effect produced on target variables by rainfall is visible with a lag time that was found to vary between 30 min and 2 h. Thus, we decided to predict them up to 60 min beyond the last known rainfall information, whether measured or predicted. For all the implemented ANNs, the targets are the level/flow variations induced by rainfall, with respect to the current value. The expected levels at gz_lt02 are obtained by the algebraic sum of current values and predicted variations. The expected flows calculation needs an additional term to be considered in the sum, i.e. the characteristic daily modulation of sewer discharge. Thus, the average flow profile at $ml01$ was obtained disregarding rainy days and was found to lie in the range 0.5–1.2 m^3/s (Fig. 4), then the corresponding 144 average flow variations – on a 10-min basis from 0:00 to 23:50 – were computed. These values were subtracted during the dataset preparation, to obtain the flow variation induced by rainfall, and then added again to obtain the actual predicted flows.

In [10] we developed four MLP ANNs, two predicting VG level variation and the other two predicting sewer flow variation. More specifically, the MLP hereinafter called MLP_{LS} (level/short-term) makes use of measured rainfalls only and provides gz_lt02 level forecast up to 60 min; MLP_{LL} (level/long-term) uses also nowcasting up to +80 min, thus extending the forecast horizon to 140 min. Similarly, MLP_{FS} (flow/short-term) and MLP_{FL} (flow/long-term) forecast sewer discharge at $ml01$.

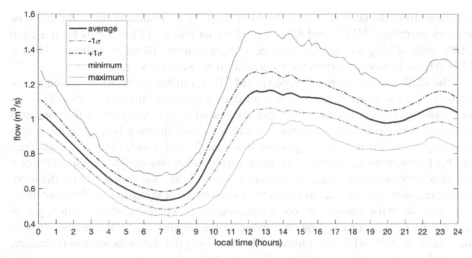

Fig. 4. Average *ml01* profile during dry days (from [10]).

In this paper, we also test the LSTM architecture to predict the same target variables. LSTM networks are in general particularly suited in modelling time series and could give better results than the MLP [24]. At this stage we just focused on short-term predictions using only measured rainfall. The LSTM architecture belongs to the class of Recurrent Neural Networks, having feedback connections that allow information to persist over the data sequence. In a standard LSTM, the extension of the past data over which the algorithm should work must be defined by the user and must be the same for all input data. Using forecasted in the identical way we did in [10] for the MLP would appears quite pointless. One possible way to use forecasted inputs is the preparation of specific datasets in such a way that at time t the LSTM would scan backward the predicted inputs from $t + p$ to t and then the measured inputs from t to t-m, with p being the time horizon of predicted inputs and m the extension of past timesteps to analyze. Another way could be the creation of a hybrid model such that only measured inputs are passed to LSTM units, while predicted ones are directed to non-recurrent units. Both these approaches go beyond our immediate intention of performing preliminary tests with an alternative architecture. Thus, we only developed short-term models which, according to the same nomenclature used for MLP, are hereinafter called $LSTM_{LS}$ and $LSTM_{FS}$.

MLP Setup. Measured rainfall inputs for MLP_{LS} and MLP_{LL} cover the antecedent 2-h interval. This extension was considered appropriate, covering the whole range of observed lags. A longer period (six hours) was required for *ml01* forecast, due to the longer-lasting observed perturbation induced on the sewer collector by precipitation.

Rainfall measurements are updated every 10 min, while nowcasting is updated every 20 min due to the described computing limitations. This results in two different updating frequencies for short-term and long-term predictions, consistent with rainfall input updates. For convenience, the rainfall measurements provided to the ANNs are also aggregated in 20-min bins, although updated every 10 min. Moreover, to keep track of the initial conditions, the current level/flow is also used as input. The targets (level/flow variations from the current value induced by rainfall) are evaluated on a 10-min basis: at every execution, MLP_{LS} and MLP_{FS} produce six outputs (10-min bins from $+10$ to $+60$), while MLP_{LL} and MLP_{FL} produce fourteen outputs (10-min bins from $+10$ to $+140$). All the inputs and targets were normalized between 0 and 1.

The MLP networks were developed in a MATLAB environment. After trial-and-error attempts, the layout was chosen so that all share a common structure, with a 20-nodes single hidden layer connecting the input and output layers. A logistic activation function is used in the hidden layer, and a linear activation function is used in the output layer to produce the results. Weights and biases in the nodes were randomly initialized, and the Levenberg-Marquardt backpropagation algorithm was used to minimize the cost function, specifically the mean square error between the target/output pairs; the algorithm execution was imposed to stop if the validation error increased for 20 consecutive iterations. Since the training procedure outcome varies depending on the randomly generated initial parameters and on the chance of the training algorithm getting stuck in local minima, each MLP was trained 2000 times using the above-mentioned procedure, and the best-performing network was then selected.

LSTM Setup. For the LSTM implementation, the number of past timesteps to be analyzed by the algorithm was set, in accordance with the choice we made for the MLP inputs, to 11 for $LSTM_{LS}$ and to 35 for $LSTM_{FS}$, covering the previous 2 and 6 h, respectively. The LSTM models scan backward the timeseries – which are composed of 10-min records – within the defined horizons and use those values as inputs. Therefore, the rainfall inputs are on a 10-min basis rather than being cumulated in 20-min bins as we did for the MLP models. The time series of observed levels/flows was also provided as input. Given the LSTM functioning, in this case both the current and all the past values within the defined timesteps are used, rather than just the current value as for the MLP.

Our original will was to train LSTM models to forecast the target values for all the prediction timesteps at once, as we did for the MLP. However, after a number of attempts, the results were not good enough and we decided to predict the targets separately for the diverse timesteps. Therefore, both $LSTM_{LS}$ and $LSTM_{FS}$ are ensembles of six LSTM networks each predicting one specific output from $+10$ to $+60$ min.

As for the MLP approach, the inputs and targets were normalized between 0 and 1.

The LSTM models were developed in a Python environment using the TensorFlow library. A structure with a single LSTM layer was tested. To select some of the hyperparameters, we performed a grid search. The considerered hyperparameters are the number of neurons in the LSTM layers (5, 10, 20, 30 or 40), the learning rate (0.001, 0.005 or 0.01) and the batch size (32, 64 or 128 for $LSTM_{LS}$; 320, 640 or 1280 for $LSTM_{FS}$). For each combination, ten training iterations were performed. The combinations giving the lower loss value were selected: 40 neurons, learning rate $= 0.01$ and batch size $= 32$ for $LSTM_{LS}$; 40 neurons, learning rate $= 0.005$ and batch size $= 320$ for $LSTM_{FS}$. All the parameters in the nodes were randomly initialized and the ADAM optimizer [25] was used, with 1000 training epochs and the condition of stopping the training and restoring the best weights after ten consecutive epochs of non-decreasing loss.

Selection of the Best Performing Networks. Rather than considering the cost function, a more detailed multi-objective optimization was implemented to select the best performing MLP networks, keeping in mind their final purpose, i.e. a correct and prompt forecast of the most severe events. Thus, for both level and flow, three threshold values were defined, i.e. 70, 100 and 140 cm at *gz_lt02* and 2.5, 3.5 and 4.5 m^3/s at *ml01*. Four objectives were defined to select the best performing models.

1. The Nash-Sutcliffe Efficiency index (*NSE*) computed on actual network targets and outputs (normalized values). The optimization variable to be minimized is the subtracted ratio in the *NSE* definition:

$$NSE = 1 - \frac{\sum_{i=1}^{n}(O_i - S_i)^2}{\sum_{i=1}^{n}(O_i - \overline{O})^2} \tag{2}$$

   where O_i are the observed values, $\overline{O}$ is their mean value and S_i are the simulated values. *NSE* is computed for each prediction horizon (10 min, 20 min, ... etc.) and the objective is found from the mean of the computed values.
2. Maximum number of correct predictions of threshold values crossing. The optimization variable, to be minimized, is the ratio of missed predictions to observed crossings. It is computed for each alert level and the objective is set to the mean of the three computed values.
3. Minimum number of false alerts (threshold crossing prediction not corresponding to observed crossing). The optimization variable, to be minimized, is the ratio of false alerts to total predictions, either true or false. It is computed for each alert level and the objective is set to the mean of the three computed values.
4. Optimal prediction timing. Every time there is an observed threshold level crossing in the forecast time horizon after current timestamp and there is also a predicted crossing, the delay between the observed and predicted time of crossing is computed. The objective to minimize is the mean squared delay for all alert levels.

Objectives n.2 and n.3 vary between 0 and 1. In order to give objective n.1 the same range of variability, the upper boundary of the subtracted ratio was set to 1, as values greater than 1 would imply a non-acceptable performance and the related solution should be discarded. Objective n.4 was normalized between 0 and 1 with respect to its possible minimum and maximum values (i.e. 0 and 50 min for short-term predictions and 0 and 130 min for long-term predictions). In looking for the Pareto front of undominated solutions, the second and fourth objectives were given a weight triple than the others. This was mainly due to sewer management reasons. Among these points in the 4-D resulting spaces, the best performing combinations were selected as those with the minimum Euclidean norm and the corresponding sets of weights and biases matrices were used in the algorithms running in the DSS.

Since objectives n.2, n.3 and n.4 can be computed only on threshold crossings – and therefore on a small amount of data – the above-mentioned optimization procedure was performed on the whole available dataset, comprising both training and validation datapoints.

This selection procedure was not repeated for the LSTM networks. As a preliminary investigation of the new architecture, we decided to follow the more basic approach of selecting the networks giving the minimum value of the cost function.

4 ANNs Performance

4.1 Multilayer Perceptron

The multi-objective optimization led to the selection of the best performing models. A first evaluation of their performance was made according to the objectives described in Sect. 3. The obtained values are shown in Table 1.

Table 1. Results of the multi-objective optimization: values for the selected ANNs (from [10]).

	OBJ 1	OBJ 2	OBJ 3	OBJ 4
MLP_{LS}	0.241	0.150	0.106	0.061
MLP_{LL}	0.128	0.137	0.039	0.037
MLP_{FS}	0.531	0.175	0.117	0.100
MLP_{FL}	0.412	0.201	0.069	0.083

A better general performance of level prediction with respect to sewer discharge prediction can be noticed. Moreover, better predictions are obtained from ANNs exploiting nowcasting information.

Statistical analyses were performed on the results. For all the selected MLP models, the *NSE* index was calculated for each forecasting horizon (+10 to +60 min or +10 to +140 min). Calibration values for MLP_{LS} range between 0.484 and 0.888, with higher values corresponding to shorter forecasting horizons. Similarly, average validation values are comprised between 0.294 and 0.906. MLP_{LL} gave *NSE* average values ranging between 0.301 and 0.601 for calibration events and between 0.103 and 0.903 for validation ones. The ranges of average *NSE* values are 0.987 ÷ 0.909 and 0.904 ÷ 0.989 for MLP_{FS} calibration and validation events, respectively. Finally, *NSE* average ranges for MLP_{FL} are 0.843 ÷ 0.986 (calibration) and 0.789 ÷ 0.988 (validation). As a term of comparison, in [26] $NSE = 0.74$ is obtained for calibration data and $NSE = 0.63$ for validation data when modelling stream flows in a small watershed using the SWAT tool.

However, this kind of analysis does not give useful insights on the ANNs effectiveness in the DSS and may even be misleading. Indeed, the main goal of a real-time DSS like as the one presented in this case study is to guarantee that accurate alerts are sent sufficiently in advance, allowing operators to act promptly. Therefore, the performances of the selected ANNs were also evaluated according to the metrics defined in Table 2 (please note that values outside brackets refer to the whole datasets, while first and second values in brackets refer to calibration and validation sets, respectively). For each MLP model, the total number of observed crossings of the defined threshold values (70, 100 and 140 cm *at gz_lt02*; 2.5, 3.5 and 4.5 m³/s at *ml01*) is displayed (*obs*), along with the number of corresponding predictions (*pred*) and related percentages (%) of correctly predicted crossings. Given the DSS updating frequency, observed crossings can be forecasted with an anticipation varying (with a 10-min resolution) from 60 to 10 min for MLP_{LS} and MLP_{FS} and from 140 to 10 min for MLP_{LL} and MLP_{FL}. A crossing is considered predicted if it is signaled to occur at least once in the available forecasting horizon. Two other parameters that were evaluated are the average warning time (*awt*), i.e. the mean anticipation corresponding to the first alert of impending crossing, and the average prediction delay indicating the accuracy of the prediction timing. As an example, if the DSS first signals an impending crossing by warning that it will happen after 40 min, but the actual crossing is observed after 30 min, then the warning time is 30 min and the prediction delay is 10 min. The average prediction delay is calculated for both the absolute values (| *apd* |), giving a hint on the mean magnitude, and the actual positive or negative values (*apd*) indicating the alert tendency to be early or delayed. Finally, the number of false alerts (*f.a.*) is shown. In contrast to correct crossing predictions, an alert is considered false if there is no actual crossing at any time step of the forecasting horizon.

From Table 2 it is possible to see that all the MLP models can predict the majority of the most severe *gz_lt02* level occurrences: Threshold 3 crossings are predicted three times on four occurrences, with the missed prediction referring to a validation event. The validation set comprises only two crossings of the higher threshold and the prediction percentage is 50%, but more data would be necessary to better assess the performance. All the lower threshold crossings are predicted, while some are missed for the intermediate one, and for both the performances on the calibration and validation sets are comparable.

The average warning time ranges between approximately 25 and 40 min for short-term predictions, while the use of nowcasting information allows to increase the forecast anticipation to approximately 2 h. The absolute value of the average prediction delay is generally lower than 20 min, with only one exception for MLP_{LL} with respect to the five predicted Threshold 1 crossings in the validation set. The analysis of the positive or negative delays suggests a slight tendency for alerts to be delayed if only rainfall data are used and to be early when nowcasting is used, for the first two thresholds, while the opposite seems to happen for Threshold 3. As regards sewer flow predictions, they are again slightly outperformed by level forecasts. This may be due to observed *ml01* flows during rainfall events being less regular with respect to those of the VG level. The highest flow threshold crossings are always predicted, even if they occur just once in the calibration events and once in the validation events. The average warning times are comparable to the ones obtained for level forecasts, while prediction delays are slightly higher and show a general tendency for late predictions. All models generate some false alerts, especially for the lowest threshold, while never for the highest one.

Some examples of the prediction performance on a severe event in the validation set (event #16), during which all the thresholds are crossed, are shown in the figures below. Fig, 5 and Fig. 6 show, for all the short-term prediction horizons, the envelop of the forecasted level vs the observed one. Figure 7 shows, for the same event, a sort of "snap-shot" of the User Interface (UI) at some specific times prior to the first crossing of the L3 threshold. As in the actual UI described Sect. 5, the time axis spans from 120 min prior to the current time to 180 min after. Measured and forecasted rainfalls and levels are shown. The observed future level is also shown for comparison purpose. The first alert is given 110 min before the actual crossing, thanks to the long-term predicting MLP (red line), even if the crossing is signaled to occur within 120 min. 80 min before the crossing, the amount of expected level becomes more reliable. At this time the short-term prediction (blue line) is still quite flat, and it raises above L3 only 30 min

Table 2. Performance of the selected MLP networks in predicting threshold crossings. Values outside brackets refer to the whole dataset; values in brackets refer to calibration and validation sets, respectively (table updated from [10]).

		Threshold 1	Threshold 2	Threshold 3
MLP_{LS}	obs	22 (17/5)	9 (6/3)	4 (2/2)
	pred	22 (17/5)	6 (4/2)	3 (2/1)
	%	100.0 (100.0/ 100.0)	66.7 (66.67/66.7)	75.0 (100.0/50.0)
	awt	36.8 (35.2/42.0)	25.0 (27.5/20.0)	33.3 (35.0/30.0)
	| apd |	12.3 (10.6/18.0)	5.0 (0.0/15.0)	3.3 (0.0/10.0)
	apd	3.2 (3.6/2.0)	1.7 (0.0/5.0)	−3.3 (0.0/-10.0)
	f.a	10 (7/3)	1 (1/0)	0 (0/0)
MLP_{LL}	obs	22 (17/5)	9 (6/3)	4 (2/2)
	pred	22 (17/5)	5 (3/2)	3 (2/1)
	%	100.0 (100.0/100.0)	55.6 (50.0/66.7)	75.0 (100.0/50.0)
	awt	97.7 (91.8/118.0)	116.0 (110.0/125.0)	113.3 (115.0/110.0)
	| apd |	17.3 (15.3/24.0)	10.0 (3.3/20.0)	10.0 (10.0/10.0)
	apd	−7.3 (−5.9/−12.0)	−10.0 (−3.3/−20.0)	3.3 (0.0/10.0)
	f.a	9 (6/3)	4 (2/2)	0 (0/0)
MLP_{FS}	obs	56 (45/11)	11 (7/4)	2 (1/1)
	pred	34 (31/3)	7 (4/3)	2 (1/1)
	%	60.7 (68.9/27.3)	64.7 (57.1/75.0)	100.0 (100.0/100.0)
	awt	35.9 (36.4/30.0)	22.9 (22.5/23.3)	45.0 (30.0/60.0)
	| apd |	12.4 (13.2/3.3)	14.3 (20.0/6.7)	15.0 (20.0/10.0)
	apd	0.0 (0.3/−3.3)	5.7 (15.0/−6.7)	5.0 (20.0/−10.0)
	f.a	16 (10/6)	2 (1/1)	0 (0/0)
MLP_{FL}	obs	56 (45/11)	11 (7/4)	2 (1/1)
	pred	36 (32/4)	9 (5/4)	2 (1/1)
	%	64.3 (71.1/36.4)	81.8 (71.4/100.0)	100.0 (100.0/100.0)
	awt	71.4 (69.7/85.0)	73.3 (98.0/42.5)	100.0 (70.0/130.0)
	| apd |	32.2 (32.8/27.5)	16.7 (18.0/15.0)	15.0 (30.0/0.0)
	apd	8.9 (8.4/12.5)	5.6 (2.0/5.0)	15.0 (30.0/0.0)
	f.a	15 (5/10)	2 (2/0)	0 (0/0)

before the crossing. Indeed, up to the previous timestamp (40 min before the crossing), the amount of measured rainfall is still low, and consequently MLP_{LS} predicts just a small level raise. The considerable rainfall intensity increase that is measured 30 min before the crossing is finally allowing MLP_{LS} to predict a steep raise of gz_lt02 level.

This example underlines the importance of nowcasting information, that permits to have alerts of incoming critical events with a reasonable advance.

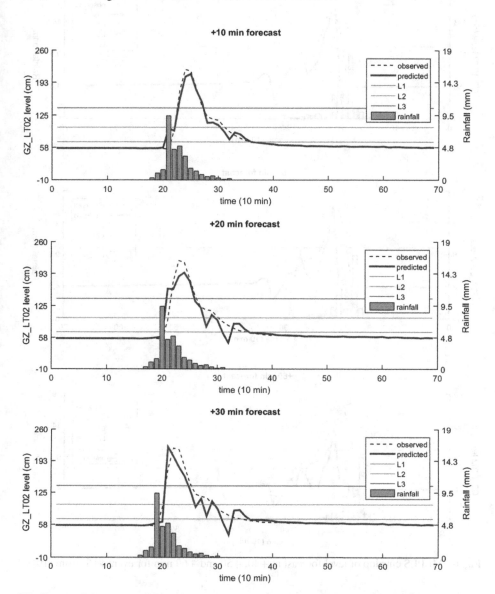

Fig. 5. MLPLS envelop of level forecast at +10, +20 and +30 min for event #16 (from [10]).

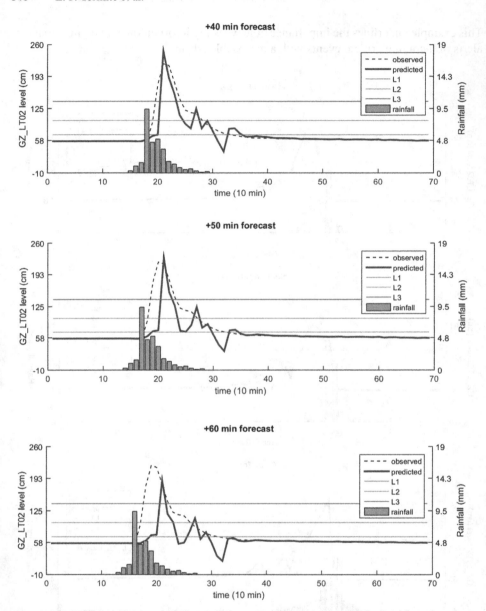

Fig. 6. MLPLS envelop of level forecast at +40, +50 and +60 min for event #16 (from [10]).

4.2 Long Short-Term Memory

The results were analyzed according to the same metrics we used for the MLP models. As said above, both $LSTM_{LS}$ and $LSTM_{FS}$ are ensembles of six LSTM networks each predicting one specific output from +10 to +60 min.

For MLP_{LS}, NSE ranges between 0.233 and 0.951 for the calibration set, and between 0.402 and 0.966 for validation events. Again, NSE values tend to decrease for longer

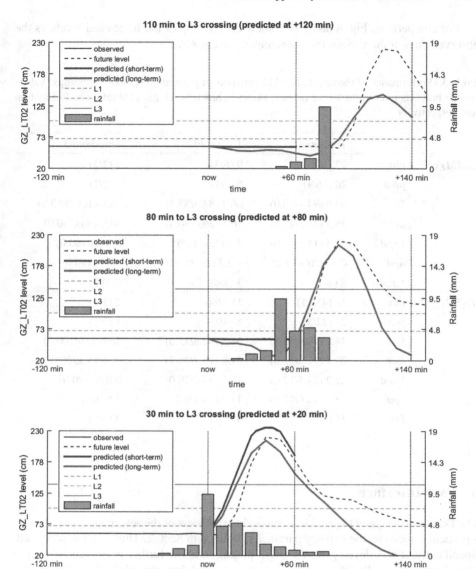

Fig. 7. Effectiveness of MLP_{LS} in predicting the crossing of the third level threshold, for event #16, 110, 80 and 30 min before the first occurrence (from [10]).

forecasting horizons. For MLP_{FS}, calibration *NSE* spans between 0.844 and 0.985, while validation values span between 0.905 and 0.991.

The analysis of the effectiveness in threshold crossing prediction is summarized in Table 3. From comparison with Table 2, a lower percentage of predicted crossings can be observed especially for Threshold 1. In contrast, on several occasions the average warning time is greater. The prediction delays appear generally smaller for level predictions, but slightly higher for flow predictions.

For comparison, Fig. 8 and Fig. 9 show the envelop of the forecasted levels vs the observed ones at the various time horizons for event #16.

Table 3. Performance of the selected LSTM networks in predicting threshold crossings. Values outside brackets refer to the whole dataset; values in brackets refer to calibration and validation sets, respectively.

		Threshold 1	Threshold 2	Threshold 3
$LSTM_{LS}$	*obs*	22 (17/5)	9 (6/3)	4 (2/2)
	pred	20 (16/4)	6 (5/1)	3 (2/1)
	%	90.9 (94.1/80.0)	66.7 (83.3/33.3)	75.0 (100.0/50.0)
	awt	36.5 (33.8/47.5)	26.7 (26.0/30.0)	30.0 (30.0/30.0)
	| *apd* |	12.5 (11.8/15.0)	3.3 (2.0/10.0)	6.7 (10.0/0.0)
	apd	0.5 (3.1/−10.0)	−3.3 (−2.0/−10.0)	0.0 (0.0/0.0)
	f.a	8 (4/4)	3 (3/0)	0 (0/0)
$LSTM_{FS}$	*obs*	56 (45/11)	11 (7/4)	2 (1/1)
	pred	27 (22/5)	6 (3/3)	1 (0/1)
	%	48.2 (48.9/45.5)	54.5 (42.9/75.0)	50.0 (0.0/100.0)
	awt	20.4 (22.3/12.0)	21.6 (16.7/26.7)	30.0 (n.a./30.0)
	| *apd* |	22.2 (24.5/12.0)	18.0 (16.7/20.0)	0.0 (n.a./0.0)
	apd	13.3 (13.6/12.0)	11.7 (16.7/6.7)	0.0 (n.a./0.0)
	f.a	15 (10/5)	4 (3/1)	3 (3/0)

5 User Interface

The DSS was designed to provide a comprehensive view of the sewerage network, with a particular focus on the two key parameters defined in Sect. 2. Thus, a UI was created. Specifically, it was developed as a QGIS plugin, to allow further improvements using georeferenced data. Weights and biases were extracted from the selected MLP networks allowing to write real-time running forecast algorithms consisting in in linear algebra operations on matrices. These algorithms, together with all the other necessary scripts running behind the DSS, were developed through the Python language. All measured and processed data are stored in the DSS database. From there, data are picked to be shown in the User Interface. In particular, the UI (Fig. 10) shows directly measured quantities (e.g., current values of levels along the VG canal, VF gate openings, flows) together with derived quantities (as for example the estimated CSO after *ml01* that, given the difficulty in placing a meter due to morphological issues, was estimated by means of water mass balance between the collector flow and the internal WWTP flow during rainfall events). The UI also can display the results of simulations of the VF canal behavior using different mitigation strategies, as explained later on. The main

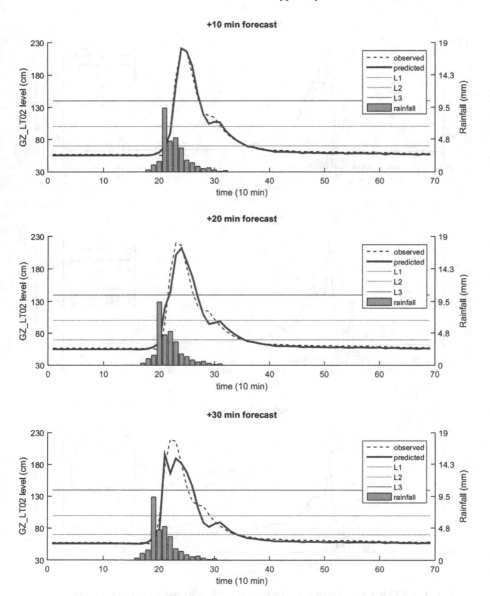

Fig. 8. LSTMLS envelop of level forecast at +10, +20 and +30 min for event #16.

section is dedicated to the visualization of the VG levels at *gz_lt02* (blue lines) and *ml01* discharge (orange lines) as recorded for the past 6 h (continuous lines) and predicted for the next 60 min (dashed lines) or 140 min (dotted lines). Above the main plot, the current and suggested openings for the 5 operable gates (labelled as Nr.2, Nr.10, Nr.14A, Nr.14B, and Nr.15 in the UI) is also shown. The gate-opening strategy is driven by the measured VG level at *gz_lt02*. The three threshold values defined for the VG level (L1 = 70 cm, L2 = 100 cm, L3 = 140 cm) trigger four different combinations of suggested

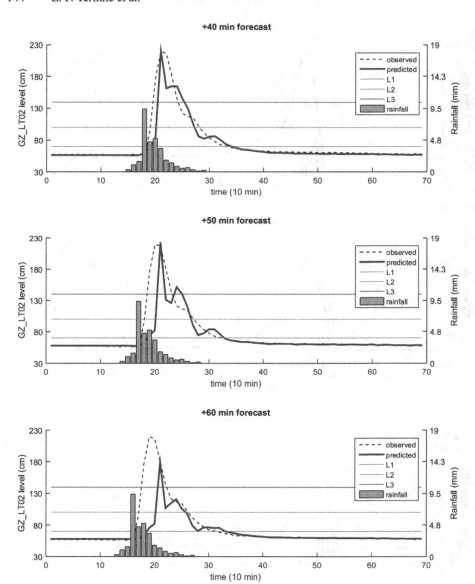

Fig. 9. LSTMLS envelop of level forecast at +40, +50 and +60 min for event #16.

gate openings (namely "A", "B", "C" and "D" in the UI) that are characterized by an increasing quantity of spilled water and storage area usage, resulting in a decreasing discharge into the VG canal until it is completely blocked for the most severe events. The suggested strategy is highlighted in yellow, and the current openings are highlighted in green or red, depending on whether they are in accordance or not with the proposed ones, with a 5 cm tolerance. At this first stage, the suggested strategies are based on the long-time experience of the WWTP technicians. However, the "Simulation" section of the UI, below the main plots, embeds a physically-based HEC-RAS hydraulic model of the VF (not discussed here for the sake of brevity) that can be executed between two selected timestamps using past boundary conditions. Thus, by changing the threshold values of the VG level or the suggested gate openings, ex-post analyses can be performed with the final aim of assessing the goodness of the adopted strategies or detecting more efficient parameter combinations.

The described UI, allowing to change the DSS parameters, is thought to be used by expert operators. In addition, for all other operators, a visualization-only UI was developed through the Grafana platform. It allows data visualization on desktop and mobile devices and is composed of three dashboards, the main one showing the current system status (Fig. 11), another showing past data in a selected time interval and the last showing on top a snap-shot of the main dashboard plots at a selected past timestamp and below a comparison between the observed level and the envelop of the predicted one for a selected forecast horizon (Fig. 12).

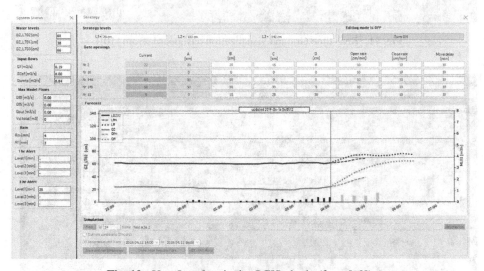

Fig. 10. User Interface in the QGIS plugin (from [10]).

6 Discussion

The obtained results indicate that the developed DSS is already able to give useful insights to the WWTP operators and to help them in managing potentially critical events.

The real-time monitoring of measured quantities gives useful advice to the operator: when the crossing of a threshold level happens, the flood wave takes some time (approx. 30 to 90 min) to reach the overflow point, allowing for a timely intervention to mitigate the risk of overflows. Furthermore, the system status forecast provides operators with additional information, guiding them in taking the proper decision. As an example, if an alert in the UI suggests a specific strategy related to measured *gz_lt02* threshold

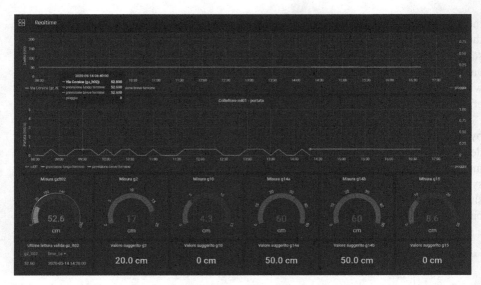

Fig. 11. Real-time Grafana visualization dashboard (from [10]).

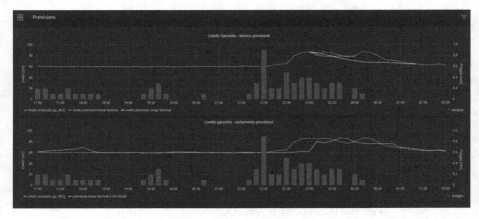

Fig. 12. Grafana visualization dashboard for the analysis of the predictions.

crossing, but the forecast is showing that level is going to decrease soon after, the operator may decide not to adopt any mitigation strategy. On the contrary, forecasts of incoming critical conditions allow to be ready and possibly anticipate the mitigation maneuvers. The average warning time is in fact sufficient for operators to be ready to adopt proper risk mitigation strategies. In particular, the most critical events are predicted with an average warning time of approximately 30 min based on observed rainfall only, while nowcasting allows for an alert anticipation greater than 100 min. The prediction timing is fairly accurate, in particular for VG level variation, with an average delay almost always lower than 20 min. Based on these considerations, the currently integrated MLP networks can be considered helpful tools in the developed DSS.

However, this is a first stage project, and several improvements may be foreseen. First, the ANNs performance may be enhanced in several ways. The current MLP networks may be updated as long as more data become available, being all collected in the DSS database. Also, different ANN structures may be implemented. In this paper we have presented a first attempt in this direction, trying a different architecture based on LSTM. The results so far don't suggest changing the ANNs that are currently working in the DSS, however we think that it is worthy to perform additional research. Several structures can still be tested, even combining different architectures, as for example Convolutional Neural Networks and LSTM units [27, 28].

Given the DSS structure, changing the operating ANN would not be complicated. New ANNs can be trained offline, then if better performances are gained the scripts may be easily adjusted. Moreover, at the current stage we decided not to use a testing set to evaluate the ANNs performance. The future availability of more records will allow to perform analyses on unseen data.

Another aspect that should be investigated is related to rainfall forecasts. As already said, nowcasting allows to generate alerts with a reasonable advance. Currently, a proprietary nowcasting algorithm is working to provide rainfall forecasts to the DSS. The ANVIL algorithm, in conjunction with the Lucas-Kanade advection model, is a valid candidate to replace the current algorithm, to obtain faster performances. However, in the present study measured rainfalls were used also as predicted ones, in a perfect forecast hypothesis. Obviously the actual nowcasting information could be less accurate and the effects on level and flow predictions should be evaluated. This is why we chose to keep also the short-term ANNs in the DSS, as they rely only on measured data which are not affected by uncertainties.

As regards the risk mitigation strategies, they are currently suggested in the UI based on the level of the receiving canal. The four different gate openings combinations, associated to three VG thresholds levels, have been discussed with the WWTP technicians and at this stage are still based on their long-time experience. However, the hydraulic model integrated in the DSS allows operators to perform ex-post simulations, assessing the effectiveness of the adopted strategy or evaluating the effects of different gate openings or different threshold levels. On this basis, the predefined suggested strategies may be easily changed by expert operators directly in the UI.

Future developments will include the integration of multi-objective optimization functionalities in the system, benefitting from the detailed information that will become available in the database, in order to face conflicting objectives as the need of sending as much water as possible to the receiving body while minimizing the chance of overflows, eventually obtaining case-specific threshold levels and gate openings combinations. For example, the premature filling of the storage area may produce negative effects during successive intense rainfalls, and unnecessary lateral spills may result in exceeding the allowed discharge in surrounding rural canals. Such improvements could be achieved by integrating real-time execution of the hydraulic model, performing simulations based on forecasted variables and different sets of threshold levels and gate openings: optimization algorithms will eventually determine the best combination to face the incoming events. Finally, when a considerable amount of available data will allow to accurately understand

and model all the hydraulic processes, the VF gates could be provided with automated actuators in order to implement a Real Time Control System.

7 Conclusions

In this paper we presented the design of a DSS platform which has the purpose of providing help in managing a wastewater treatment plant. The goal is achieved through real-time monitoring of the system status – sewer flows, internal flows, hydraulic stage of urban canals, gate openings – and forecasts on strategic variables as rainfalls, incoming sewer flows and expected level of the receiving water body. Rainfall forecasts are based on nowcasting techniques, while flow and lever forecasts are performed by Artificial Neural Networks. All the monitored and forecasted data are visualized in a User Interface which gives a comprehensive knowledge to the operators and can guide them in reducing the chance of overflow during severe rainfall events. The updating DSS frequency is equal to ten minutes and all data are stored in a single database.

The proposed approach is characterized by some advantages, among which the negligible time demand for model running and the possibility of easily updating the algorithms. Indeed, the current ANNs were trained using past data, but they can be updated as long as more data become available. Different algorithms can also be tested, as shown in this paper, and can replace the current ones without any substantial revision of the software architecture. The whole updating procedure can be performed "offline", this being an important feature of the developed project. Thus, it can also be automated, by writing a script which would read the database with a given frequency, add the new data to the training dataset after having suitably processed them and perform again the training procedure; in case of estimated better performances, the algoritms parameters could be automatically replaced.

The DSS was developed in the context of a smart infrastructure project. In such cases, several challenges arise. The design and operational costs should be lowered to increase the probability of implementation. In addition, the handling of heterogeneous data from multiple sources, the analysis of Big Data and security-related issues must be considered [29]. The proposed approach fulfills these requirements and may represent a valuable step in guaranteeing safety in case of severe rainfall events. Moreover, it can in principle be used in all those settings where sensor measurements over large areas, meteorological data, and other quantitative information should be processed to provide synthetic outputs for the final user.

Acknowledgments. The study we developed in [10] is part of the INNOVA EFD3 research project financed by A2A Ciclo Idrico S.p.A. The additional research on the LSTM networks presented in this paper is part of the REACT project financed by Regione Veneto (IT) POR FESR 2014–2020 Asse I Azione 1.1.4.

References

1. Dittmer, U., Bachmann-Machnik, A., Launay, M.A.: Impact of combined sewer systems on the quality of urban streams: frequency and duration of elevated micropollutant concentrations. Water **12**, 850 (2020)

2. Pereira, A., Pinho, J.L.S., Vieira, J.M.P., Faria, R., Costa, C.: Improving operational management of wastewater systems. A case study. Water Sci. Technol. **80**(1), 173–183 (2019)
3. Park, T., Kim, H.A.: A data warehouse-based decision support system for sewer infrastructure management. Autom. Constr. **30**, 37–49 (2013)
4. Rao, M.: A performance measurement application for a wastewater treatment plant. Int. J. Serv. Stan. **10**(3), 134–147 (2015)
5. Rechdaoui-Guérin, S., et al.: Monitoring the quality of effluents in a unitary sanitation network. Tech.-Sci.-Methodes **113**, 77–90 (2018)
6. US EPA.: Smart data infrastructure for wet weather control and decision support. EPA 830-B-17–004 (2018)
7. Botturi, A., et al.: Combined sewer overflows: a critical review on best practice and innovative solutions to mitigate impacts on environment and human health. Crit. Rev. Environ. Sci. Technol. **51**(15), 1585–1618 (2020)
8. Carbone, M., Garofalo, G., Piro, P.: Decentralized real time control in combined sewer system by using smart objects. Procedia Eng. **89**, 473–478 (2014)
9. Campisano, A., Creaco, E., Modica, C.: Application of real-time control techniques to reduce water volume discharges from quality-oriented CSO devices. J. Environ. Eng. **142**(1), 1–8 (2016)
10. Termite, L.F., et al.: An artificial neural network-based real time DSS to manage the discharges of a wastewater treatment plant and reduce the flooding risk. In: Proceedings of the 10th International Conference on Smart Cities and Green ICT Systems (SMARTGREENS 2021) SCITEPRESS – Science and Technology Publications, pp. 15–26 (2021)
11. Maier, H.R., Jain, A., Dandy, G.C., Sudheer, K.P.: Methods used for the development of neural networks for the prediction of water resource variables in river systems: current status and future directions. Environ. Model. Softw. **25**(8), 891–909 (2010)
12. Clark, M.P., et al.: The evolution of process-based hydrologic models: historical challenges and the collective quest for physical realism. Hydrol. Earth Syst. Sci. **21**, 3427–3440 (2017)
13. Hochreiter, S., Schmidhuber, J.: Long short-term memory. Neural Comput. **9**(8), 1735–1780 (1997)
14. Wilson, J.W., Crook, N.A., Mueller, C.K., Sun, J., Dixon, M.: Nowcasting thunderstorms: a status report. Bull. Am. Meteor. Soc. **79**(10), 2079–2100 (1998)
15. Panziera, L., Germann, U., Gabella, M., Mandapaka, P.V.: NORA –Nowcasting of orographic rainfall by means of analogues. Quart. J. Roy. Meteorol. Soc. **137**(661), 2106–2123 (2011)
16. Bellon, A., Zawadzki, I., Kilambi, A., Lee, H.C., Lee, Y.H., Lee, G.: McGill algorithm for precipitation nocasting by Lagrangian extrapolation (MAPLE) applied to the South Korean radar network. Part I: sensitiity studies of the variational echo tracking (VET) technique. Asia-Pac. J. Atmos. Sci. **46**(3), 369–381 (2010)
17. Lee, H.C., et al.: McGill algorithm for precipitation nowcasting by Lagrangian extrapolation (MAPLE) applied to the South Korean radar network. Part II: real-time verification for the summer season. Asia-Pac. J. Atmos. Sci. **46**(3), 383–391 (2010)
18. Gregori, V., De Tomasi, F., Ferrari, G. Chini, A.: A comparison of nowcasting methods on the Italian radar mosaic. 2nd level master degree thesis, University of Salento. http://master.meteorologiaeoceanografiafisica.unisalento.it/images/students/1920_v gregori/tesi_vgregori_en.pdf, Accessed 04/08/2021
19. Mandapaka, P.V., Germann, U., Panziera, L., Hering, A.: Can Lagrangian extrapolation of radar fields be used for precipitation nowcasting over complex Alpine orography? Weather Forecast. **27**(1), 28–49 (2012)
20. Pulkkinen, S., Chandrasekar, V., von Lerber, A., Harri, A.M.: Nowcasting of convective rainfall using volumetric radar observations. IEEE Trans. Geosci. Remote Sens. **58**(11), 7845–7859 (2020)

21. Boudevillain, B., Andrieu, H., Chaumerliac, N.: Evaluation of RadVil, a radar-based very short-term rainfall forecasting model. J. Hydrometeorol. **7**(1), 178–189 (2006)
22. Seed, A.W.: A dynamic and spatial scaling approach to advection forecasting. J. Appl. Meteorol. **42**(3), 381–388 (2003)
23. Lucas, B. D. and Kanade, T.: An iterative image registration technique with an application to stereo vision. In: Proceedings of the 7th International Joint Conference on Artificial intelligence, vol. 2, pp. 674–679 (1981)
24. Marini, A., Termite, L.F., Garinei, A., Marconi, M., Biondi, L.: Neural network models for soil moisture forecasting from remotely sensed measurements. Acta Imeko **9**(2), 59–65 (2020)
25. Kingma, D. P. and Ba, J.: Adam: A method for stochastic optimization. In: Proceedings of the 3rd International Conference on Learning Representations (2015)
26. Jeong, J., Kannan, N., Arnold, J., Glick, R., Gosselink, L., Srinivasan, R.: Development and integration of sub-hourly rainfall–runoff modeling capability within a watershed model. Water Resour. Manage **24**(15), 4505–4527 (2010)
27. Proietti, M., et al.: Edge Intelligence with Deep Learning in Greenhouse Management. In: Proceedings of the 10th International Conference on Smart Cities and Green ICT Systems (SMARTGREENS 2021), pp. 180–187. SCITEPRESS – Science and Technology Publications (2021)
28. Menculini, L., et al.: Comparing prophet and deep learning to ARIMA in forecasting wholesale food prices. arXiv:2107.12770 (2021)
29. Silva, B.N., Khan, M., Han, K.: Towards sustainable smart cities: A review of trends, architectures, components, and open challenges in smart cities. Sustain. Cities Soc. **38**, 697–713 (2018)

Impact of BIPV Panels Across Various Window-to-Wall Ratios in Commercial Buildings, to Reduce its Energy Performance Index in Warm and Humid Climate Zone of India

Stuthi Shetty[1], Vatsala Bajpai[1], Sathwik Bysani[1], Pranav Kishore[1(✉)], Pradeep Kini[1], Achinta N. Shetty[2], and Anupam Raj[3]

[1] Centre of Sustainable Built Environment (CSBE), Manipal School of Architecture and Planning (MSAP), Manipal Academy of Higher Education (MAHE), Manipal, India
pranav.kishore@manipal.edu
[2] Manipal School of Architecture and Planning (MSAP), Manipal Academy of Higher Education (MAHE), Manipal, India
[3] YourMD.ca, Calgary, AB, Canada

Abstract. People and technology have to keep up with this ever-moving fast-growing world. Building sectors are not only increasing in floor area but also demand more energy and builds up pressure over at the supply end. In such an era renewable energy becomes the key to meet the demand over at the supply end. The building has to be made self-sufficient to sustain even when the supply end experiences a delay. Therefore this study is one such Design Alternative approach that will help the building be more self-sufficient. The integration of the BIPV over the building façade will not only help generate energy within the building premise but also help reduce the EPI of the building resulting in savings both in time and cost. The results of the study propound For low-rise buildings, WWR02 (north façade WWR-50%, east façade WWR-25%, south façade WWR-25% and west façade-25%) gives the minimum EPI values because this combination minimizes the heat gain inside the building through windows. For high rise buildings, WWR01 (north façade WWR-50%, east façade WWR-35%, south façade WWR-35% and west façade-35%) gives the minimum EPI values due to the increase in interior lighting and ventilation requirements which require larger window area percentages.

Keywords: Building integration photovoltaic system · Design Alternative · ECBC 2017 · Energy Performance Index

1 Introduction

1.1 Energy Consumption in Building Sector

Population growth has increased tremendously over the past few decades. Increased health-care benefits have helped prolong the lifespan of human lives. This increases

© Springer Nature Switzerland AG 2022

C. Klein et al. (Eds.): SMARTGREENS 2021/ VEHITS 2021, CCIS 1612, pp. 151–172, 2022.
https://doi.org/10.1007/978-3-031-17098-0_8

demand for a better lifestyle, infrastructure, and comfort in everyday activities. Many villages and small towns have been converted into bigger towns and cities to meet all the demands of people. This process called urbanization has increased the built-up volume all over the world. More the built-up area, the more the contribution it has over the greenhouse gas (GHG) emissions and energy utilization. According to the reports from the United Nations, Global Status Report 2020, the trend in 2019 has reported the highest ever CO_2 emissions i.e., 38% of total global energy-related CO_2 emissions from the building sector alone [1]. Figure 1 shows the percentage contribution of the building sector in consuming energy and percentage emission of harmful gases. The building sector alone consumes 35% of global energy consumption and contributes 38% to emitting harmful gases concerning other sectors.

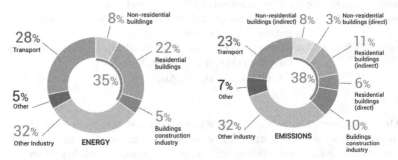

Fig. 1. Energy and emission contribution percentage of the global building and construction sector 1.

In India, the building sector continues to use coal, oil, and natural gas which lead to harmful emissions. Heating and cooking in carbon-intensive regions due to the unavailability of electricity result in a constant level of direct emissions. Over the past decade from 2010 to 2019, there is an increase in percentage built-up floor area, population, emissions, and energy demand as plotted in Fig. 2. It is observed in the graph that the built-up floor area has increased to almost 21% in the past ten years. Comparatively, the growth in energy demand and emissions is lesser but significant and in a similar percentage growth as the population trend.

Currently, in India, buildings contribute for 35% of total energy utilization and annually growing at an 8% consumption rate. Increased economic growth, rising income, growing population, and urbanization are some of the factors responsible for growth in India's buildings' energy utilization. Rural and urban populations have varying energy use patterns. Among the International Energy Outlook (IEO) 2017 regions, India has the world's highest projected gross domestic product (GDP) growth rate averaging 5% annually from 2015 to 2040 [3]. Environmental Impact Assessment (EIA) estimates that total dispatched commercial division energy utilization in India will rise by an average of 3.4% annually. EIA also estimates that India's share of electricity consumption of the total commercial energy consumption will gradually increase from 59% in 2015 to 65% in 2040, eliminating coal usage to a certain extent [3].

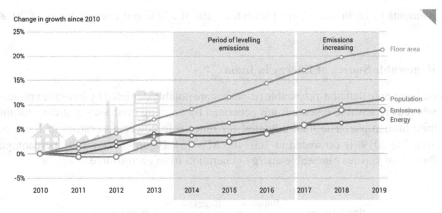

Source: IEA (2020b). All rights reserved. Adapted from "Energy Technology Perspectives 2020"

Fig. 2. Population growth, floor area, energy need, and emissions trend [2].

1.2 Energy Efficiency in India

Initiatives such as World Green Building Council's Net-Zero Carbon Buildings Commitment discuss various approaches to transform buildings into net-zero energy and zero-carbon to promote global de-carbonization strategy and hope to make it the only form of building construction across all economies to achieve net-zero emissions by 2050 [1]. Such Global goals along with the influence of Sustainable Development Goals (SDGs) influenced several countries to take up the challenge and evolve towards a greener built environment.

In India, the Oil Crisis in the 1970s marked the beginning of policy initiatives and research catering to end-use efficiency. In October 2001, Energy Conservation Act (EC) was the first major policy initiative sanctioned in India associated with the methodical use of energy and its conservation. The EC Act lead to the undertaking of the Bureau of Energy Efficiency (BEE) in March 2002. Under the leadership of the Ministry of Power, BEE is responsible for being the forefront organization to see over the improvement of energy efficiency in the current economy by using promotional and bureaucratic instruments. Planning, management, and execution of appliance standards and labeling (S&L), along with Energy Conservation Building Codes are some of the responsibilities of the BEE. The Indian electricity division is governed by the Electricity Act of 2003, under the supposition of which the Government of India (GOI) notified the National Electricity Policy (NEP) in 2005. The initiative directed the BEE to set standards on energy conservation and carefully implemented them in the country with a voluntary and self-regulating approach in the beginning. As the framework strengthened over time they formulated a more regulatory approach. The Integrated Energy Policy Report (IEPR) released in August 2006 entrusted distribution utilities to undertake Energy Efficiency (EE) and demand-side management (DSM) programs.

Due to the growing issues of climate change, the National Action Plan on Climate Change (NAPCC) was introduced in 2008. The plan recognizes EE as essential for addressing climate change problems. One of the eight missions of the NAPCC is the National Mission for Enhanced Energy Efficiency (NMEEE). Energy-efficiency improvements in India since 2010 prevented 12% of additional energy use as of 2018 [4].

1.3   Renewable Source of Energy in India

It is crucial to note that non-renewable resources are notably depleted by human exploitation, whereas renewable resources are generated by ongoing processes that can sustain indefinite human use. The total potential for renewable power generation in India as of March 31, 2019, is estimated at 1097465 MW [5]. Figure 3 shows the percentage contribution of various renewable energy generation from each source.

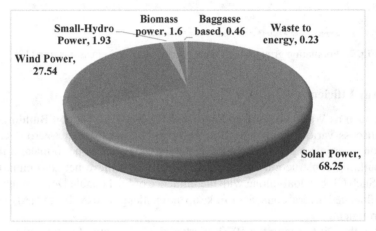

Fig. 3. Contribution of each renewable energy source in India [5].

Developing countries extensively face problems related to energy production. Sources of energy and technologies obtained through renewable resources are promising sources of energy generation that are capable of providing solutions to these energy supply and demand-side crises everywhere. Renewable energy sources like wind energy, solar energy, geothermal energy, ocean energy, biomass energy, and fuel cell technology can be used to overcome energy shortages in India. India is increasingly adopting responsible renewable energy techniques and taking positive steps towards reducing carbon emissions, aiming to have cleaner air and ensuring a more sustainable future. By 2022 India has set itself a target of generating 175 gigawatts (GW) of electricity through renewable sources of energy. Out of 175 GW, around 21 GW of renewable capacity was installed between 2012 and 2016, of which 68% was added in the last two and a half years of that period [6].

Global coal consumption rose by 1%, out of which India consuming 4.8%, recording the fastest growth, as demand both inside and outside of the power sector increased [7]. A study states that solar penetration in India is highly cost-sensitive. It is possible to decrease solar cost by 50% by analyzing alternative Renewable Energy (RE) technology cost developments in the future. This also helps increase solar penetration by eight folds compared to the baseline scenario. Such results prove that popularizing renewable energy is highly cost elastic in the Indian market and further policy support to promote RE will enable the country to meet its target [8]. A constant rise in such research, tests, and application will help make it easier to switch to green energy generation for the entire country.

Rising challenges of energy consumption and supply in India and its impact on climate change have made the Government of India take crucial steps towards enabling clean energy and also taking responsibility to overlook the policies and orders. The Copenhagen Accord in 2009 gave way to the United Nations Framework Convention on Climate Change (UNFCCC) officially decided in 2012 to stream actions under a goal to hold global temperature rise to less than 2 °C above pre-industrial levels [9]. India has put forward eight Nationally Determined Contributions (NDCs) as a part of its international adherence, under the Paris Agreement of UNFCCC. Among the eight NDCs, three of the quantifiable targets to be met by 2030 are Goal 3: focuses to reduce the emissions' severity of its GDP by 33%–35% compared to the 2005 level, Goal 4: To be able to achieve a collective electric power installed capacity of 40% from a non-fossil energy source, and Goal 5: Increase the carbon sink of 2.5–3 billion tonnes of CO_2 equivalent [8].

The solar installation capacity of India has come to 28.18 GW as of March 3, 2019, as compared to 21.65 GW on March 31, 2018 [5]. A downward trend in the renewable source electricity generation cost is observed in India due to an electricity generation expansion of 12.23% over a year and hence has increased usage. It is perceptible that to achieve the Nation's benchmark on the take of Sustainable Development Goals (SDGs) proper integration of policy interventions and regulations is mandatory [5]. India is moving forward with the goals in mind and so by December 2019, India had stationed a total of 84 GW of grid-connected renewable electricity capacity and aiming for further renewable production. India's total renewable electricity generating capacity reached 366 GW in 2019 [4].

2 Literature Review

Sustainability is about savings made now for a better future. This concept applies in every field today especially the building sector. The global initiative of Sustainable Development Goals also talks about the need for greener methods of energy consumption i.e., to be able to use resources that do not exhaust over time. Hence renewable sources of energy are being popularized in the architecture field. Due to exponential population growth in India, the demand for electricity across the country has increased and the electricity department has not been able to keep up with the supply side of electricity to all. Table 1 shows the deficit from the supply side of the country. Depleting resources such as coal, oil, natural gas, etc. have not only created supply-end issues but also have increased cost, which makes it hard for everybody in the country to afford a basic amenity such as electricity. Hence use of renewable resources that do not exhaust will not only bring down the price but also be able to meet the demand of the country.

Life-cycle cost analysis of a building projects how much consumption of energy is required to provide comfort conditions within the building such as for cooling and heating of spaces, electricity for lights, etc. Reducing the consumption of energy as

Table 1. Power supply status in India from 2009–2010 to 2017–2018 [10].

Year	Energy				Peak			
	Requirement	Availability	Surplus(+)/Deficits(−)		Peak Demand	Peak Met	Surplus(+)/Deficits(−)	
	(GWh)	GWh)	(GWh)	(%)	(MW)	(MW)	(MW)	(%)
2009–2010	830,594	746,644	− 83,950	− 10.11	119,166	104009	− 15,157	− 12.72
2010–2011	861,591	788,355	− 73,236	− 8.50	122,287	110256	− 12,031	− 9.84
2011–2012	937,199	857,886	− 79,313	− 8.46	130,006	116,191	− 13,815	− 10.63
2012–2013	998,114	911,209	− 86,905	− 8.71	135,453	123,294	− 12,159	− 8.98
2013–2014	1,002,257	959,829	− 42,428	− 4.23	135,918	129,815	− 6103	− 4.49
2014–2015	1,067,085	1,028,955	− 38,130	− 3.60	148,166	141,160	− 7006	− 4.70
2015–2016	1,114,408	1,090,850	− 23,558	− 2.10	153,366	148,463	− 4903	− 3.20
2016–2017	1,142,928	1,135,332	− 7596	− 0.66	159,542	156,934	− 2608	− 1.63
2017–2018	1,212,134	1,203,567	− 8,567	− 0.7	164,066	160,752	− 3314	− 2.0
2018–2019 (31.10.2018)	769,399	764,627	− 4773	− 0.6	177,022	175,528	− 1494	− 0.8

much as possible or rather obtaining it from renewable sources is one of the effective and sustainable methods that make the buildings self-efficient and makes way to de-carbonize for ecological benefits. Solar energy a non-fossil source of energy can be utilized for active and passive methods for heating, cooling, ventilation, natural lighting, and even to obtain hot water [11]. Wind energy can also be exploited for ventilation and cooling with active and passive systems for an entire building [12]. Another less explored energy source the geothermal energy can be also be used for heating and cooling purposes [13].

RE is a captivating option to provide green energy to the built environment. A drawback of RE is that there is a slight incompatibility when it comes to generating energy from these sources and when the buildings require it. To redeem such problems a study suggests an inventive solution where they create a balance for local energy collection and demand in microgrid by exchanging energy between neighboring homes. The results of the study propose that the system (a) without the use of large batteries, it is possible to reduce the energy loss on the AC line by 64%, (b) performance magnifies with bigger battery storage, and (c) is rugged to different patterns of energy consumption and energy prediction accuracy in the microgrid [14].

Electricity is generated, transmitted, and then distributed within the country. During these processes, it is certain that there will be transmission losses. Even with places having good technical efficiency and low theft, Transmission and Distribution losses generally range between 6%–8% [15]. Therefore, by using technologies such as BIPV, the generation happens at the building hence reduced transmission losses and low theft, and more profitable.

2.1 Use of BIPV Technology in Buildings

India is ranked fifth for having the highest solar installed capacity worldwide [16]. Ministry of New and Renewable Energy (MNRE) under the National Solar Mission, has reconditioned the objective of grid-connected solar power projects from 20 GW by the year 2021–2022 to 100 GW by the year 2021–2022. Domestic manufacturing with support of the 'Made in India' initiative has helped achieve greater height in promoting solar installation capacity.

At present, in the BIPV market, 80% contributes to rooftop-mounted technologies and only 20% of it is façade-mounted [17]. India is the seventh-largest country in the world and lies between 68°7' to 97°25' east longitude and 8°4' to 37°6' north latitude. It covers a total of 2.9 million Km^2 of landmass. The country on average experiences 300 sunny clear days in a year as it is located in the tropical region and receives maximum solar radiation in summer. Climate zones include warm and humid, hot and dry, composite, temperate, and cold zones with ambient conditions varying from 45 °C in summer while 4 °C in winter [18]. Due to its location solar energy has the maximum potential to be exploited for energy production and used all over India.

Kale, et al. (2016) conducted the Life Cycle Cost (LCC) analysis for two commercial buildings of similar parameters, at first without the installation of solar panels and then at the second stage integrating the solar panel system with the building system. In the second stage, one of the buildings considered for the case study had solar panels of minimum capacity installed in it while the other building had solar panels which were of the desired capacity according to the requirements of the building. The LCC analysis showed a 4% cost reduction when minimum capacity solar panels were used while a cost reduction of 54% was observed in case the desired capacity solar panel system [19]. The study conducted by Tripathy, et al. (2017) conducted Life Cycle Cost analysis (LCCA) and Energy Payback Time (EPBT) for BIPV – Building Integrated Photovoltaic thermal performance in Indian weather conditions. The study provides support for the use of BIPV thermal systems providing its economic and environmental viability. 7.5 to 16 years is found to be the EPBT using the BIPV system which is much lower than the expected service life (30 years) of the modules [20]. Bano, et al. (2020) in their study to prepare early-stage design guidelines for Net Zero Energy Buildings (nZEBs) found that BIPV panels were the most suitable type of renewable energy source that can be implemented to meet low energy generation requirements hence reducing the EPI value for the building [21].

This paper is an extended version of the paper "Assessment of Building Integrated Photovoltaic Panels on Facades of Commercial Buildings concerning Energy Conservation Building Code" by Pradeep Kini et.al. [22] which assesses the BIPV integration on the building façade and its contribution to a building energy production. The study compares the results with modeled building and PVGIS systems to analyze the panel costing and payback period. This paper tries to propound the optimum location of BIPV on the building façade and also concerning WWR considerations taken from ECBC 2017 and comparison with the RBM model from Mayank Bhatnagar et al. [23].

3   Methodology

The study aims to encourage the development of the use of Photovoltaic cells' (PV) application on the building façade in the current practice of architecture to maximize energy efficiency in the commercial building sector by on-site energy generation. The Objective of the study is to reduce the Energy Performance Index (EPI) of the commercial building using Building Integrated Photovoltaic cell (BIPV) technology.

This study uses a base case model of a 'Reference Building Model' (RBM) developed by Bhatnagar et.al., in the Indian scenario to compare the EPI results of this study with the EPI model output of the RBM case example [23]. This research is based only in the Warm and Humid climate zone of India and the results of only Warm and Humid climate zone is taken into consideration from the RBM study. An epw file contains weather data that is used for running energy usage simulations are used to extract hourly data for the study.

The RBM research is based on four building typologies i.e., an 8-h operation low rise building, 8-h operation high rise building, 24-h operation low rise building, and 24-h operation high rise building. The Energy Conservation Building Code (ECBC) 2017 specifies that for a commercial building the maximum average permissible Window-To-Wall Ratio (WWR) should be 40% [24]. Hence for this research, the 27 cases of WWR is considered as shown in Table 2, which averages maximum in each case to 40% [25]. The North façade of the building receives the least amount of direct sunlight hence a constant WWR of 50% is considered. The WWR for the other three facades is taken to be 35%, 30%, and 25% as all 27 combinations of this WWR case results in an average of less than 40% as stated in ECBC 2017. The commercial building is analyzed concerning all eight cardinal directions i.e., north, west, east, south, northeast, northwest, southeast, and southwest. There are a total of 11 variables in this study, 3 variables are 3 different PV tilt angles (30, 45, and 60) and 6 PV technologies available in India [26].

The assumptions stated regarding the building set-up are:

- The aspect ratio of the commercial building is 1: 2.8
- There are no obstructions around the commercial building considered within the study that blocks the PV Panels.
- The commercial building does not have any overhangs
- The sill level of the window is taken as 0.92 m as per the RBM reference with window height as 1.2 m and lintel height to be 2.1 m as per practical application experience in the architecture field.

3.1 Building Data Modelling

The commercial building model considered in this study is a rectangular volume with an aspect ratio of 1:2.8. The PV panels are to be placed in four facades of the building with respective resulted tilt values. The PV panels start from the ground floor of the building from 0 levels to 0.92 m sill level, then again it continues from 2.1 m to the sill level of the window on the first floor. This pattern continues throughout the height and width of the building. There are 6 types of PV Panels used in this study available in the Indian Market. These six types and their generation capacities are mentioned in Table 3 below. The size of the panels is taken as 1 m × 2 m [26]. The calculation of EPI is done using the Energy Performance Calculator (EPC) created at the Georgia Institute of Technology [27].

The building considered in this paper is optimized for all possible orientations i.e., for all eight cardinal directions: North (N), West (W), East (E), South (S), NorthEast (NE), NorthWest (NW), SouthEast (SE), SouthWest (SW). For the convenience of understanding the orientations within the study, the nomenclature for the directions is given in Table 4.

Table 2. 27 cases of WWR.

WWR	North	East	West	South
1	50	35	35	35
2	50	25	25	25
3	50	30	30	30
4	50	35	35	25
5	50	35	25	35
6	50	25	35	35
7	50	35	25	25
8	50	25	35	25
9	50	25	25	35
10	50	35	35	30
11	50	35	30	35
12	50	30	35	35
13	50	35	30	30
14	50	30	35	30
15	50	30	30	35
16	50	25	30	30
17	50	30	25	30
18	50	30	30	25
19	50	25	25	30
20	50	25	30	25
21	50	30	25	25
22	50	30	25	35
23	50	30	35	25
24	50	25	30	35
25	50	25	35	30
26	50	35	25	30
27	50	35	30	25

Insertion of PV panels on the facades as overhangs will cast a shadow. The positioning of the panels should be such that the shadow of one panel does not fall over the other. To consider the longest shadow cast in a Warm and Humid climate zone city, Kolkata is taken as the reference. In Kolkata the altitude at 10:00 am is considered the maximum value of all days at 10 m of altitude is taken out and used for the calculation of distance between two panels. The panels are installed in various combinations only on three facades of the building. The North façade/Northeast facing facade irrespective of building entrance

Table 3. PV panel technologies.

Sl. no.	Type of photovoltaic module	Kpk (KW/m^2)
1	Mono crystalline silicona	0.15
2	Multi crystalline silicona	0.13
3	Thin-film amorphous silicon	0.06
4	Other thin-film layers	0.035
5	Thin-film copper-indium-gallium-diselenide	0.105
6	Thin-film cadmium-telluride	0.095

Table 4. Building entrance façade orientation nomenclature.

Nomenclature	Orientation
O1	North (N)
O2	Northeast (NE)
O3	East (E)
O4	Southeast (SE)
O5	South (S)
O6	Southwest (SW)
O7	West (W)
O8	Northwest (NW)

orientation will not have any solar panels installed and will have a constant WWR of 50%. The panels are distanced from each other in such a way that one panel's shadow does not fall over the other as shown in Fig. 4 and calculated using the equation given below.

$$\theta = 55° \tag{1}$$

$$\alpha = 90° - 55° = 35° \tag{2}$$

Depth of the solar panel $= 1$ m,

$$Tan35 = \frac{1}{x}$$

Hence the distance between solar panels is given by,

$$x = \frac{1}{Tan35} = 1.5\,\text{m}$$

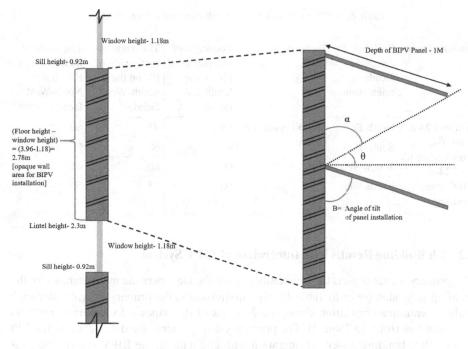

Fig. 4. Distance between solar panels and installation.

4   Results and Discussion

4.1   Optimum BIPV System Details According to Building Entrance Façade Orientation

Table 5 and Table 6 show the details of the BIPV system that should be adopted according to the orientation of the entrance façade of an 8-h and 24-h building.

Table 5. BIPV system details for cardinal orientations.

Building type	Building entrance facade orientation	Technology	The angle of inclination of PV on the East facade	The angle of inclination of PV on the South facade	The angle of inclination of PV on the West facade
8-h and 24-h Low-rise buildings/8-h and 24-h High-rise buildings	North, East, South, and West	Mono-crystalline silicona	60	60	60

Table 6. BIPV system details for sub-cardinal orientations.

Building type	Building entrance facade orientation	Technology	The angle of inclination of PV on the South-East facade	The angle of inclination of PV on the South-West facade	The angle of inclination of PV on the North-West facade
8-h and 24-h Low-rise buildings/8-h and 24-h High-rise buildings	North-East	Mono-crystalline silicona	60	45	60
	South-East		45	60	60
	South-West		60	60	45
	North-West		60	45	60

4.2 8-h Building Results with Integration of BIPV System

The primary x-axis depicts the orientations of the façade where the main entrance of the building is located (refer to Table 4). The subdivision in the primary x-axis under each building entrance orientation shows the 27 cases of the window to wall ratio (WWR) combinations (refer to Table 2). The primary y-axis presents the data denoting the EPI of the office building under consideration with and without the BIPV system that was depicted using bar graphs. The secondary y-axis shows results in the form of an x-y scatter plot depicting the reduction percentage of EPI i.e., the percentage reduction from the base-case scenario of the RBM modeled in EPC.

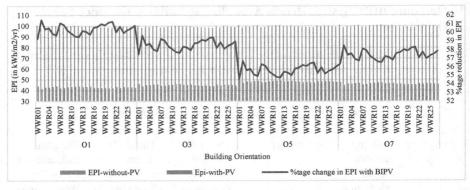

Fig. 5. EPI assessment of 8-h low-rise building with entrance façade oriented towards cardinal directions.

Figure 5 shows percentage change/reduction in EPI values when BIPV panels are integrated with the building system for an 8-h low-rise office building located in the Warm and Humid climate zone in India which has all 4 of its facades oriented towards the 4 cardinal directions (North, East, South, and West), for the 27 predefined window-to-wall ratios (WWR). For a building that has North oriented (O1) entrance façade, the percentage reduction in EPI with the integration of the BIPV system varied from 59.3–61.46%. For an East-oriented (O3) entrance façade, the percentage reduction in EPI varied from 57.49–59.64%. In the case of the South-oriented (O5) entrance façade, the percentage reduction in EPI varied from 54.53–56.69%. For a West-oriented (O7) entrance façade, the percentage reduction in EPI varied from 56.34–58.51%. Hence, the range with the highest EPI reduction percentage was observed to be for the North orientation of the entrance façade of the building.

The minimum EPI value i.e. 41.7 kWh/m²/yr was achieved for a building which has North oriented entrance façade with the WWR02 combination (north façade WWR-50%, east façade WWR-25%, south façade WWR-25% and west façade-25%) where the EPI reduction percentage was 61.46%. The optimum BIPV system technology suggested was Mono-crystalline silicon with an angle of inclination as 60° for the three remaining facades i.e., East, South, and West.

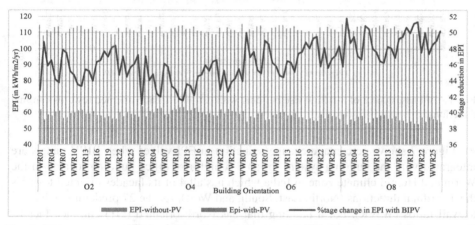

Fig. 6. EPI assessment of 8-h low-rise building with entrance façade oriented towards sub-cardinal directions.

Figure 6 shows percentage change/reduction in EPI values when BIPV panels are integrated with the building system for an 8-h low-rise office building located in the Warm and Humid climate zone in India which has all 4 of its facades oriented towards the 4 sub-cardinal directions (North-East, South-East, South-West and North-West), for the 27 predefined window-to-wall ratios (WWR). For a building that has a North-East oriented (O2) entrance façade, the percentage reduction in EPI with the integration of the BIPV system varied from 42.85–48.87%. For a South-East oriented (O4) entrance façade, the percentage reduction in EPI varied from 41.05–47.07%. In the case of the South-West oriented (O6) entrance façade, the percentage reduction in EPI varied from 43.94–49.97%. For a North-West oriented (O8) entrance façade, the percentage reduction in EPI varied from 45.75–51.77%. Hence, the range with the highest EPI reduction percentage was observed to be for the North-West orientation of the entrance façade of the building.

The minimum EPI value i.e. 52.18 kWh/m^2/yr was achieved for a building which has North oriented entrance façade with the WWR02 combination (north façade WWR-50%, east façade WWR-25%, south façade WWR-25% and west façade-25%) where the EPI reduction percentage was 51.77%. The optimum BIPV system technology suggested was Mono-crystalline silicona with the angle of inclination as 60, 45, and 60° for the South-East, South-West, and North-West facades respectively.

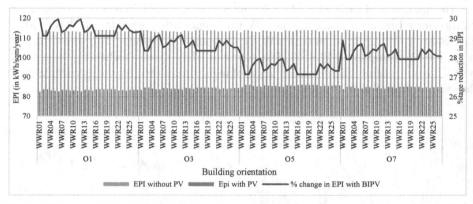

Fig. 7. EPI assessment of 8-h high-rise building with entrance façade oriented towards cardinal directions.

Figure 7 shows percentage change/reduction in EPI values when BIPV panels are integrated with the building system for an 8-h high-rise office building located in the Warm and Humid climate zone in India which has all 4 of its facades oriented towards the 4 cardinal directions (North, East, South, and West), for the 27 predefined window-to-wall ratios (WWR). For a building that has North oriented (O1) entrance façade, the percentage reduction in EPI with the integration of the BIPV system varied from 29.13–30.12%. For an East-oriented (O3) entrance façade, the percentage reduction in EPI varied from 28.37–29.36%. In the case of the South-oriented (O5) entrance façade, the percentage reduction in EPI varied from 27.16–28.15%. For a West-oriented (O7) entrance façade, the percentage reduction in EPI varied from 27.93–28.91%. Hence, the range with the highest EPI reduction percentage was observed to be for the North orientation of the entrance façade of the building.

The minimum EPI value i.e. 82.62 kWh/m^2/yr was achieved for a building which has North oriented entrance façade with the WWR01 combination (north façade WWR-50%, east façade WWR-35%, south façade WWR-35% and west façade-35%) where the EPI reduction percentage was 30.12%. The optimum BIPV system technology suggested was Mono-crystalline silicona with the angle of inclination as 60° for the three remaining facades i.e., East, South, and West.

Figure 8 shows percentage change/reduction in EPI values when BIPV panels are integrated with the building system for an 8-h high-rise office building located in the Warm and Humid climate zone in India which has all 4 of its facades oriented towards the 4 sub-cardinal directions (North, East, South, and West), for the 27 predefined window-to-wall ratios (WWR). For a building that has a North-East oriented (O2) entrance

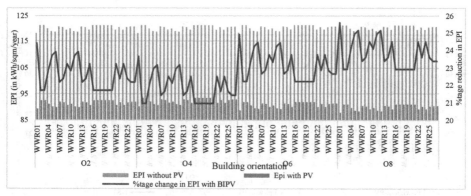

Fig. 8. EPI assessment of 8-h high-rise building with entrance façade oriented towards sub-cardinal directions.

façade, the percentage reduction in EPI with the integration of the BIPV system varied from 21.69–24.37%. For a South-East oriented (O4) entrance façade, the percentage reduction in EPI varied from 20.96–23.64%. In the case of the South-West oriented (O6) entrance façade, the percentage reduction in EPI varied from 22.2–24.88%. For a North-West oriented (O8) entrance façade, the percentage reduction in EPI varied from 22.93–25.61%. Hence, the range with the highest EPI reduction percentage was observed to be for the North-West orientation of the entrance façade of the building.

The minimum EPI value i.e. 87.95 kWh/m²/yr was achieved for a building which has North oriented entrance façade with the WWR01 combination (north façade WWR-50%, east façade WWR-35%, south façade WWR-35% and west façade-35%) where the EPI reduction percentage was 25.61%. The optimum BIPV system technology suggested was Mono-crystalline silicona with the angle of inclination as 60, 45, and 60° for the South-East, South-West, and North-West facades respectively.

4.3 24-h Building Results with Integration of BIPV System

The primary x-axis depicts the orientations of the façade where the main entrance of the building is located (refer to Table 4). The subdivision in the primary x-axis under each building entrance orientation shows the 27 cases of the window to wall ratio (WWR) combinations (refer to Table 2). The primary y-axis presents the data denoting the EPI of the office building under consideration with and without the BIPV system that was depicted using bar graphs and compared to BEE star rating benchmarks of EPI for office buildings i.e. 1-Star (200 – 175 kWh/m²/yr), 2-Star (175 – 150 kWh/m²/yr), 3-Star (150 – 125 kWh/m²/yr), 4-Star (125 – 100 kWh/m²/yr) and 5-Star (Below 100 kWh/m²/yr) [28]. The secondary y-axis shows results in the form of an x-y scatter plot depicting the reduction percentage of EPI i.e., the percentage reduction from the base-case scenario of the RBM modeled in EPC.

Figure 9 shows percentage change/reduction in EPI values when BIPV panels are integrated with the building system for a 24-h low-rise office building located in the Warm and Humid climate zone in India which has all 4 of its facades oriented towards

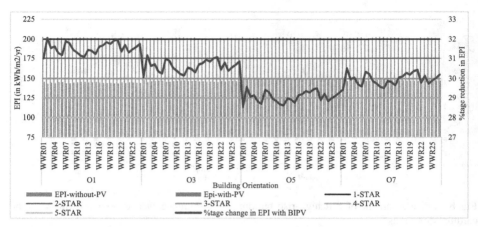

Fig. 9. EPI assessment of 24-h low-rise building with entrance façade oriented towards cardinal directions.

the 4 cardinal directions (North, East, South, and West), for the 27 predefined window-to-wall ratios (WWR). For a building that has North oriented (O1) entrance façade, the percentage reduction in EPI with the integration of the BIPV system varied from 30.99–32.06%. For an East-oriented (O3) entrance façade, the percentage reduction in EPI varied from 30.07–31.15%. In the case of the South-oriented (O5) entrance façade, the percentage reduction in EPI varied from 28.52–29.59%. For a West-oriented (O7) entrance façade, the percentage reduction in EPI varied from 29.44–30.51%. Hence, the range with the highest EPI reduction percentage was observed to be for the North orientation of the entrance façade of the building.

The minimum EPI value i.e. 143.57 kWh/m^2/yr was achieved for a building which has North oriented entrance façade with the WWR02 combination (north façade WWR-50%, east façade WWR-25%, south façade WWR-25% and west façade-25%) where the EPI reduction percentage was 32.06%. The optimum BIPV system technology suggested was Mono-crystalline silicona with the angle of inclination as 60° for the three remaining facades i.e., East, South and West.

Integration of the BIPV system with the building, aided to reach the 3-Star rating benchmark (150 – 125 kWh/m^2/yr) from the initial 1-Star rating benchmark (200 – 175 kWh/m^2/yr) as defined by BEE, for all 4 cardinal orientations and 27 WWR combinations.

Figure 10 shows percentage change/reduction in EPI values when BIPV panels are integrated with the building system for a 24-h low-rise office building located in the Warm and Humid climate zone in India which has all 4 of its facades oriented towards the 4 sub-cardinal directions (North-East, South-East, South-West and North-West), for the 27 predefined window-to-wall ratios (WWR). For a building that has a North-East oriented (O2) entrance façade, the percentage reduction in EPI with the integration of the BIPV system varied from 22.05–25.16%. For a South-East oriented (O4) entrance façade, the percentage reduction in EPI varied from 21.12–24.23%. In the case of the South-West oriented (O6) entrance façade, the percentage reduction in EPI varied from 26.89–28.37%. For a North-West oriented (O8) entrance façade, the percentage reduction

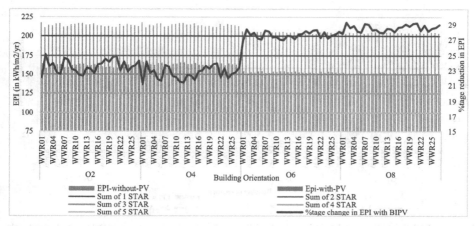

Fig. 10. EPI assessment of 24-h low-rise building with entrance façade oriented towards sub-cardinal directions.

in EPI varied from 27.81–29.29%. Hence, the range with the highest EPI reduction percentage was observed to be for the North-West orientation of the entrance façade of the building.

The minimum EPI value i.e. 149.44 kWh/m^2/yr was achieved for a building which has North-West oriented entrance façade with the WWR02 combination (north façade WWR-50%, east façade WWR-25%, south façade WWR-25% and west façade-25%) where the EPI reduction percentage was 29.29%. The optimum BIPV system technology suggested was Mono-crystalline silicona with the angle of inclination as 60, 45 and 60° for the South-East, South-West and North-West facades respectively.

Integration of the BIPV system with the building, aided to reach the 2-Star rating benchmark (175 – 150 kWh/m^2/yr) as defined by BEE for all 4 sub-cardinal orientations and 27 WWR combinations. For the case where the entrance façade orientation was taken as North-West (O8), the WWR combinations – WWR02, WWR07, WWR18, WWR20 and WWR21 aided in reaching the BEE 3-Star rating benchmark (150 – 125 kWh/m^2/yr).

Figure 11 shows percentage change/reduction in EPI values when BIPV panels are integrated with the building system for a 24-h high-rise office building located in the Warm and Humid climate zone in India which has all 4 of its facades oriented towards the 4 cardinal directions (North, East, South and West), for the 27 predefined window-to-wall ratios (WWR). For a building that has North oriented (O1) entrance façade, the percentage reduction in EPI with the integration of the BIPV system varied from 13.16–13.55%. For an East-oriented (O3) entrance façade, the percentage reduction in EPI varied from 12.81–13.21%. In the case of the South-oriented (O5) entrance façade, the percentage reduction in EPI varied from 12.27–12.67%. For a West-oriented (O7) entrance façade, the percentage reduction in EPI varied from 12.61–13.01%. Hence, the range with the highest EPI reduction percentage was observed to be for the North orientation of the entrance façade of the building.

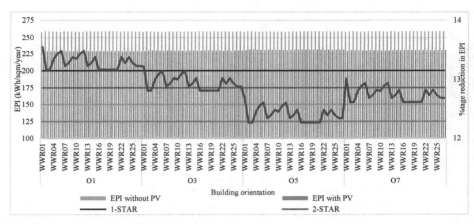

Fig. 11. EPI assessment of 24-h high-rise building with entrance façade oriented towards cardinal directions.

The minimum EPI value i.e. 227.98 kWh/m²/yr was achieved for a building which has North oriented entrance façade with the WWR01 combination (north façade WWR-50%, east façade WWR-35%, south façade WWR-35% and west façade-35%) where the EPI reduction percentage was 13.55%. The optimum BIPV system technology suggested was Mono-crystalline silicona with the angle of inclination as 60° for the three remaining facades i.e., East, South and West.

Integration of the BIPV system with the building reduced the EPI of the building under consideration by a range varying from 12.27–13.55% when different entrance façade orientations and WWR combinations were taken yet the BEE star rating benchmarks were not achieved in any case.

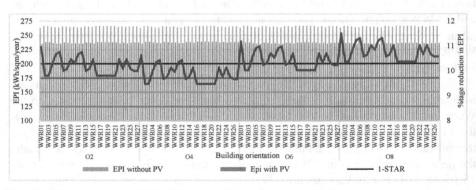

Fig. 12. EPI assessment of 24-h high-rise building with entrance façade oriented towards sub-cardinal directions.

Figure 12 shows percentage change/reduction in EPI values when BIPV panels are integrated with the building system for a 24-h high-rise office building located in the Warm and Humid climate zone in India which has all 4 of its facades oriented towards the 4 sub-cardinal directions (North-East, South-East, South-West and North-West), for the 27 predefined window-to-wall ratios (WWR). For a building that has a North-East oriented (O2) entrance façade, the percentage reduction in EPI with the integration of the BIPV system varied from 9.81–10.96%. For a South-East oriented (O4) entrance façade, the percentage reduction in EPI varied from 9.48–10.63%. In the case of the South-West oriented (O6) entrance façade, the percentage reduction in EPI varied from 10.03–11.19%. For a North-West oriented (O8) entrance façade, the percentage reduction in EPI varied from 10.36–11.51%. Hence, the range with the highest EPI reduction percentage was observed to be for the North-West orientation of the entrance façade of the building.

The minimum EPI value i.e. 233.35 kWh/m^2/yr was achieved for a building which has North-West oriented entrance façade with the WWR01 combination (north façade WWR-50%, east façade WWR-35%, south façade WWR-35% and west façade-35%) where the EPI reduction percentage was 11.51%. The optimum BIPV system technology suggested was Mono-crystalline silicona with the angle of inclination as 60, 45, and 60° for the South-East, South-West, and North-West facades respectively.

Integration of the BIPV system with the building reduced the EPI of the building under consideration by a range varying from 9.48–11.51% when different entrance façade orientations and WWR combinations were taken yet the BEE star rating benchmarks were not achieved in any case.

5 Analysis

The results show that the optimum orientation of the entrance façade of a building was found to be North for which the EPI percentage reduction range values were maximum. Table 1 presents the details of the optimum BIPV system that should be opted when the building entrance façade was North oriented. The angle of inclination of PV panels for the East and West facades was found to be 60° because these facades would mostly receive direct sunlight at lower altitudes during the morning and evening hours hence the BIPV panel's angle of inclination from the normal of the façade surface of should be steep. For the South façade, the BIPV panel's angle of inclination was 60° because the panels serve the purpose of overhangs also. For low-rise buildings, WWR02 (north façade WWR-50%, east façade WWR-25%, south façade WWR-25% and west façade-25%) gives the minimum EPI values because this combination minimizes the heat gain inside the building through windows. For high rise buildings, WWR01 (north façade WWR-50%, east façade WWR-35%, south façade WWR-35% and west façade-35%) gives the minimum EPI values due to the increase in interior lighting and ventilation requirements which require larger window area percentages.

In the case of 8-h and 24-h buildings, the integration of BIPV panels had a lesser impact on the 24-h buildings because of the increase in the occupancy hours of the building and the increased requirement of interior lighting and equipment energy of the buildings 23.

Table 7 denotes the potential of installing additional BIPV panels for the 27 WWR combinations on the three façade areas i.e. East, South and West facades in the case of a building that has all its 4 facades oriented towards cardinal directions and South-East, South-West and North-West façades in the case of a building that has all its 4 facades

Table 7. Ranking of WWR combinations according to availability of area to install BIPV panels.

Ranking	WWR combinations	Percentage area remaining (in %)	Additional opaque area for installation (in sqm)
1	WWR2	9.44	47.95
2	WWR19	8.33	42.31
3	WWR20, WWR21	8.06	40.94
4	WWR9	7.22	36.67
5	WWR16, WWR17	6.94	35.25
6	WWR7, WWR8, WWR18	6.67	33.88
7	WWR22, WWR24	5.83	29.61
8	WWR3, WWR25, WWR26	5.56	28.24
9	WWR23, WWR27	5.28	26.82
10	WWR5, WWR6, WWR15	4.44	22.55
11	WWR13, WWR14	4.17	21.18
12	WWR4	3.89	19.76
13	WWR11, WWR12	3.06	15.54
14	WWR10	2.78	14.12
15	WWR1	1.67	8.48

oriented towards sub-cardinal directions. WWR2 (north façade WWR-50%, east façade WWR-25%, south façade WWR-25% and west façade-25%) has the maximum potential for the addition of BIPV panels on opaque areas as the WWR percentage on each of the 3 facades is minimum hence there is higher availability of the additional opaque area. WWR1 (north façade WWR-50%, east façade WWR-35%, south façade WWR-35% and west façade-35%) has minimum potential because the availability of area is lesser. Few combinations have the same potential as the opposite façade faces are of the same area.

6 Conclusion

As the built-up area increases with increased population and trend of urbanization, more the contribution it has over the greenhouse gas (GHG) emissions and energy utilization across the globe. India is no such exception to this growth and contributes its share of energy utilization and harmful emissions thereafter. Keeping sustainability in consideration and raising awareness for same India has regulated and mandated several policies and programs to promote and keep a check on emissions and maintain a balance between the demand and supply of energy required in the building sector. This study is one such step to make way for the application of BIPV on the building façade in compliance with ECBC 2017.

The paper takes into consideration 27 cases of WWR for which the maximum reduction of EPI is obtained using the EPC. The percentage reduction of EPI is concerning the Reference Building Model taken from Bhatnagar et al. The results also show the results with the BIPV system and without the BIPV system showing how effective are the WWR on the reduction of EPI of the building. In the case of 8-h and 24-h buildings, the integration of BIPV panels had a lesser impact on the 24-h buildings because of the increase in the occupancy hours of the building and the increased requirement of interior lighting and equipment energy of the buildings. The angle of inclination of PV panels for the East and West facades was found to be 60° because these facades would mostly receive direct sunlight at lower altitudes during the morning and evening hours hence the BIPV panel's angle of inclination from the normal of the façade surface of should be steep. For the South façade, the BIPV panel's angle of inclination was 60° because the panels serve the purpose of overhangs also. For low-rise buildings, WWR02 (north façade WWR-50%, east façade WWR-25%, south façade WWR-25% and west façade-25%) gives the minimum EPI values because this combination minimizes the heat gain inside the building through windows. For high rise buildings, WWR01 (north façade WWR-50%, east façade WWR-35%, south façade WWR-35% and west façade-35%) gives the minimum EPI values due to the increase in interior lighting and ventilation requirements which require larger window area percentages.

References

1. GlobalABC, G.A.: 2020 global status report for buildings and construction. UN Environment Programme (2020)
2. IEA, I.E.: Energy Technology Perspective 2020. International Energy Agency(2020)
3. Hojjati, B.: Today in energy. U.S. Energy Information Administration, 10 October 2017. https://www.eia.gov/todayinenergy/detail.php?id=33252
4. IEA, I.E.: E4 country profile: energy efficiency in India, IEA. International Energy Agency (2021). https://www.iea.org/articles/e4-country-profile-energy-efficiency-in-india
5. NSO, N.S.: Energy Statistics 2020. New Delhi: National Statistical Office, Ministry of Statistics and Programme Implementation, GOI, April 2020
6. Teddy, T.E.: India's renewable energy growth. The Energy and Research Institute (2017). https://www.teriin.org/infographics/indias-renewable-energy-growth
7. British Petroleum: BP Statistical Review of World Energy. British Petroleum (2018)
8. Thambi, S., Bhatacharya, A., Fricko, O.: India's energy and emissions outlook: results from india energy model. Energy Clim. change Overseas Engag. Dept. NITI Aayog **2019**, 1–26 (2019)
9. Graham, P., Rawal, R.: The role of the Indian building sector in achieving the 2 °C goals of the COP21 Paris accord. Building Research and Information (2018)
10. GOI, M.O.: Ministry of Power Government of India. Power Sector At a Glance All India (2020). https://powermin.gov.in/en/content/power-sector-glance-all-india
11. Sahoo, S.K.: Renewable and sustainable energy reviews solar photovoltaic energy progress in India: a review. Renew. Sustain. Energy Rev. **59**, 927–939 (2016)
12. Karthick, A., Chinnaiyan, V.K., Karpagam, J., Chandrika, V.S., Kumar, P.R.: Optimization of PV-wind hybrid renewable energy system for health care buildings in smart city. In: Hybrid Renewable Energy Systems, pp. 183–198. Scrivener Publishing LLC (2021)

13. Aggarwal, V., et al.: Potential and future prospects of geothermal energy in space conditioning of buildings: India and worldwide review. Solar energy materials for advanced window and building envelope for less energy hungry building. Sustainability **12**(20), 8428 (2020). https://doi.org/10.3390/su12208428

14. Huang, Z., Zhu, T., Irwin, D., Mishra, A., Menasche, D., Shenoy, P.: Minimising transmission loss in smart microgrids by sharing renewable energy. ACM Trans. Cyber Phys. Syst. **1**(2), Article 5 (2016). http://dx.doi.org/10.1145/2823355

15. Aniti, L.: Today in energy. U.S. Energy Information Administration, 22 October 2015. https://www.eia.gov/todayinenergy/detail.php?id=23452

16. Kumar, C.J., Majid, M.J.: Renewable energy for sustainable development in India: current status, future prospects, challenges, employment, and investment opportunities. Energy Sustain. Soc. **10**(1), 1–36 (2019). https://doi.org/10.1186/s13705-019-0232-1

17. Shukla, A.K., Sudhakar, K., Baredar, P.: Recent advancement in BIPV product technologies: a review. Energy and Build. **140**, 188–195 (2017). https://doi.org/10.1016/j.enbuild.2017.02.015

18. Reddy, P., Gupta, M., Nundy, S., Karthick, A., Ghosh, A.: Status of BIPV and BAPV system for less energy-hungry buildings in India: a review. Appl. Sci. MDPI Appl. Sci. **10**, 2337 (2020). https://doi.org/10.3390/app10072337

19. Kale, N.N., Joshi, D., Radhika, M.: Life cycle cost analysis of commercial buildings with energy efficient approach. Eng. Mater. Sci. **8**, 452–454 (2016)

20. Tripathy, M., Joshi, H., Panda, S.: Energy payback time and life-cycle cost analysis of building integrated photovoltaic thermal system influenced by adverse effect of shadow. Appl. Energy **208**, 1–14 (2017)

21. Bano, F., Sehgal, V., Tahseen, M.: Early-stage design guidelines for net-zero-energy office buildings in tropical climate. In: 2020 International Conference on Contemporary Computing and Applications (IC3A), pp. 143–149. IEEE, Lucknow (2020)

22. Kini, P.G., Shetty, A.N., Kishore, P., Tandon, V.: Assessment of building integrated photovoltaic panels on facades of commercial buildings with respect to energy conservation building code. In: Proceedings of the 10th International Conference on Smart Cities and Green ICT Systems (SMARTGREENS 2021), pp. 148–155 (2021)

23. Bhatnagar, M., Mathur, J., Garg, V.: Development of reference building models for India. J. Build. Eng. **21**, 267–277 (2019)

24. ECBC, E.C.: Energy Conservation Building Code. Bureau of Energy Efficiency; Government of India, New Delhi (2017)

25. Kishore, P.: The use of building integrated photovoltaics (BIPV) towards ultra energy efficient buildings. Georgia Institute of Technology, Atlanta (2016)

26. Luminous: Luminous India. Luminous Solar PV Panels (2017). https://www.luminousindia.com/solar-products/solar-pv-panel.html

27. Quan, S.J., Li, Q., Augenbroe, G., Brown, J., Ju Yang, P.: Urban data and building energy modeling: a GIS-based urban building energy modeling system using the urban EPC engine. In: Geertman, S., Ferreira Jr., J., Goodspeed, R., Stillwell, J. (eds.) Planning Support Systems and Smart Cities. Lecture Notes in Geoinformation and Cartography, pp. 447–469. Springer, Cham (2015). https://doi.org/10.1007/978-3-319-18368-8_24

28. BEE: ECBC Commercial. Bureau of Energy Efficiency (2020). https://beeindia.gov.in/content/ecbc-commercial

Building Rich Interior Hazard Maps for Public Safety

Mazharul Hossain[1(✉)], Tianxing Ma[1], Thomas Watson[2], Brandon Simmers[2], Junaid Ahmed Khan[3], Eddie Jacobs[2], and Lan Wang[1]

[1] Department of Computer Science, University of Memphis, Memphis, USA
{mhssain9,tma1,lanwang}@memphis.edu
[2] Department of Electrical and Computer Engineering, University of Memphis, Memphis, USA
{tpwatson,bsimmers,eljacobs}@memphis.edu
[3] Department of Electrical and Computer Engineering, Western Washington University, Bellingham, USA
khanj@wwu.edu

Abstract. An accurate model of building interiors with detailed annotations is critical to protecting first responders and building occupants during emergencies. First responders and building occupants can use these 3D building models to navigate indoor environments or vacate the building safely. In collaboration with the City of Memphis, we have collected extensive LiDAR and video data from seven buildings in Memphis. We apply machine learning techniques to the video frames to detect and classify objects of interest to first responders. We then utilize data fusion methods on the LiDAR and image data to create a comprehensive colored 3D indoor point cloud dataset with labeled safety-related objects. This paper documents the challenges we encountered in data collection and processing, and it presents a complete 3D mapping and labeling system for the environments inside and adjacent to buildings. Moreover, we used two of the scanned buildings as a case study to illustrate our process and show detailed evaluation results. Our results show that the deep neural network *Mask R-CNN* with transfer learning and hard-negative mining performs well in labeling public-safety objects in our image dataset, especially for large objects.

Keywords: LiDAR point cloud · Indoor 2D image object detection and instance segmentation · Indoor 3D point cloud object detection and instance segmentation · Image dataset · 3D point cloud dataset · 3D indoor map · Public safety objects

1 Introduction

Firefighter casualties and deaths occur every year due to the difficulties of navigation in smoke-filled indoor environments. According to the National Fire Protection Association, local fire departments responded to an estimated 1.3 million fires, 48 firefighters

Supported by the financial assistance award 70NANB18H247 from U.S. Department of Commerce, National Institute of Standards and Technology.

ⓒ Springer Nature Switzerland AG 2022
C. Klein et al. (Eds.): SMARTGREENS 2021/ VEHITS 2021, CCIS 1612, pp. 173–196, 2022.
https://doi.org/10.1007/978-3-031-17098-0_9

and 3,700 people lost their lives, 16,600 people were injured, and 14.8 billion dollars were lost in 2019 [1, 13]. The National Institute for Occupational Safety and Health (NIOSH) provides detailed accounts of firefighter fatalities [7]. One of the most disheartening threads in these stories is how close to an exit the firefighters were found, sometimes less than a mere 10 ft away. A possible technological solution to this problem is to use high-quality 3D maps of the interiors of buildings to train the firefighters before an emergency and guide them during an emergency. In particular, equipping firefighters with VR headsets or helmets that can display these high-quality 3D maps could help them navigate indoor smoky environments more effectively and reduce some of these unfortunate deaths.

We have been working with the City of Memphis, Tennessee, USA to produce high-quality 3D maps of seven Memphis buildings for public safety research. We use Light Detection and Ranging (LiDAR), video cameras, and other sensing technologies to collect the building data. LiDAR is a remote sensing method that uses light (laser) pulses to measure the distance to objects. More specifically, a LiDAR sensor transmits laser pulses which are reflected by objects in a scene. The sensor then measures the time to receive the reflected pulses and determines the precise distance to each surface point on the objects. It is able to measure millions of points distributed across the surfaces in each scan. A Simultaneous Localization and Mapping (SLAM) algorithm then uses the data from multiple LiDAR scans to create a complete 3D point cloud. With additional sensors, one can further determine the color and other attributes of each point. In order to help first responders quickly locate objects of interest during a crisis event, we apply data fusion and machine learning algorithms to identify public-safety related objects in the point clouds.

In this paper, we describe our approach to producing georeferenced labeled RGB building models from raw point cloud and image data. The contributions of our work can be summarized as follows.

First, we document the challenges we encountered in data collection and processing, which may be of interest to researchers in various areas such as building information modeling, LiDAR design, machine learning, and public safety. We have encountered many challenges, such as complex spaces for LiDAR scanning, lack of synchronization among different sensor data sources, and uncommon objects not found in existing labeled datasets. While some of these challenges, e.g., synchronizing data sources, have been (partly) addressed by existing research, the majority require new methodologies, which we focus on in our current and future work.

Second, we have developed a complete 3D mapping and labeling system for the building environments including sensors, data collection processes, and a data processing workflow consisting of data fusion, automatic labeling of hazards and other objects, clustering, cleaning, stitching, and georeferencing.

Finally, we use a case study of two buildings to illustrate our system and evaluate the performance of our automated labeling process, including (a) the precision and recall of the object detection/classification on the 2D image dataset, and (b) the precision and recall of the object labels in the 3D point cloud dataset. Our results show that the deep neural network *Mask R-CNN* with transfer learning from the MS COCO dataset performs well in labeling public-safety objects in our image dataset, especially for large objects. We also observed that, with transfer learning, adding just a few hundred labeled images from a building to the training dataset significantly improves a model's performance. Finally, we investigated hard-negative mining for training the model and observed a considerable performance improvement.

2 Related Work

Generating large-scale labeled 3D datasets is costly and challenging, and not many deep learning methods can process 3D data directly. For these reasons, there are few labeled 3D datasets available currently, especially for indoor environments. Below we describe several public 2D and 3D datasets for indoor environments and relevant deep learning models for object detection and classification in images and point clouds.

2.1 Labeled 2D and 3D Datasets

MCIndoor20000 [6] is a labeled 2D indoor dataset collected from a hospital. It contains more than 20,000 digital images from 3 categories (doors, stairs, and hospital signs). We use some images from this dataset to train our neural network model (see Sect. 5.1). Microsoft Common Objects in Context (MS COCO) dataset [20] is a large-scale labeled 2D dataset containing more than 300,000 images in 81 categories. We use this dataset for transfer learning (see Sect. 7.1). ImageNet [10] includes more than a million labeled images in thousands of categories collected from different Internet sources that can be used for 2D object detection problems. We also tried ImageNet for transfer learning, but its performance is not as good as that of MS COCO (see Sect. 7.1).

Stanford 2D-3D-S [4] is a multi-modal, large-scale indoor spaces dataset extending the Stanford 3D Semantic Parsing work [5]. It contains around 1400 high-definition RGB images with semantic annotations in a variety of registered modalities: 2D (RGB), 2.5D (depth maps and surface normals), and 3D (meshes and point clouds) Gibson Env Dataset [2] also contains 2D, 2.5D, and 3D data. This data is collected from 572 buildings and covers 1447 floors with different indoor areas. The authors provided the 2D-3D information for each space and semantic object labels for a fraction of the spaces. ShapeNet Part [29] is a subset of the ShapeNet [8] repository which focuses on fine-grained 3D object detection. It contains 31,693 meshes sampled from 16 categories of the original dataset, which include some indoor objects. Each shape class is labeled with two to five parts (totaling 50 object parts across the whole dataset).

While the above datasets contain various indoor objects, most of them do not have our needed public-safety objects, e.g., fire extinguishers, fire alarms, standpipe connections, hazmat, and exit signs. Thus, most of the existing labeled images are not immediately helpful to our work, so we produced a new training dataset of our own.

2.2 Object Detection and Classification in 2D RGB Images

Faster R-CNN [25] is an object detection model that belongs to the region-based convolutional neural network (R-CNN) machine learning model family. It produces a rectangular bounding box for each detected object. As we needed to obtain precise per-point labels, a rectangular bounding box was not sufficient. Mask R-CNN [15] is an extension of Faster R-CNN that assigns each pixel to an individual object [15]. It provides polygon masks that tightly bound objects and has a better overall average precision score than Faster R-CNN. Since it generated better per-point labels in our data, we adopted Mask R-CNN in our work.

While the above models solve the object detection problem, the following models classify detected objects. He et al. [16] proposed ResNet, which contains the residual block, a new neural network layer, to solve a network depth problem in traditional CNN models for objection classification. ResNet outperforms other models by a large margin. Szegedy et al. [27] combined their Inception architectures with residual connections and found residual connections accelerate the training of Inception networks significantly. It outperforms similar Inception networks without residual connections by a thin margin.

Huang et al. [18] reported that using either Inception-ResNet-V2 [27] or ResNet-101 [16] as a feature extractor with Faster R-CNN as a meta-architecture showed good detection accuracy with reasonable execution time. Since we prefer Mask R-CNN to Faster R-CNN, we experimented with the Inception-ResNet-v2 model (with 164 layers) and ResNet-101 model as a feature extractor for Mask R-CNN.

2.3   Object Detection and Classification in 3D Point Clouds

PointNet [21] is a deep neural network that takes raw point clouds as input and provides a unified architecture for both detection and classification. The architecture features two subnetworks: one for classification and another for detection. The detection subnetwork concatenates global features with per-point features extracted by the classification network and applies another two Multi-Layer Perceptrons (MLPs) to generate features and produce output scores for each point. As an improvement, the same authors proposed PointNet++ [22] which can capture local features with increasing context scales by using metric space distances.

At the beginning of our work, we experimented with PointNet++ on our point clouds but found that **many public-safety objects, such as fire alarms and fire sprinklers, are too small for the model to segment and classify correctly**. This difficulty motivated us to use images to detect and label the objects first (Sect. 5.1) and then transfer the object labels to the corresponding point clouds to obtain per-point level labels (Sect. 5.2).

2.4   Object Detection and Classification Pipelines in RGB-D Data

Armeni et al. [3] followed the Scene Graph paradigm in 3D. They captured 3D meshes and equirectangular RGB panoramas at several fixed points in each scene. To identify objects, they cropped the panoramas into multiple rectilinear frames, then applied their instance detection algorithm multiple times. They then reprojected the algorithm results to the original equirectangular format, and finally applied various methods to improve accuracy before mapping the labels back to the 3D mesh. In our work, we capture video from a moving camera, and thus have hundreds or thousands of panoramas per scene. This lets us accumulate detection results from many different perspectives for each object, which helps improve final labeling quality and accuracy, even though each individual panorama may be deficient. We also work directly in the equirectangular projection to improve processing speed, and do not generate meshes of our point clouds.

Table 1. List of buildings [17].

Name	Sqft	Use
Pink Palace	170,000	Museum, Theaters, Public Areas, Planetarium, Offices and Storage
Memphis Central Library	330,000	Library, Public Areas, Storage, Offices, Retail Store
Hickory Hill Community Center (HHCC)	55,000	Public Area and Indoor Pool
National Civil Rights Museum	100,000	Museum
Liberty Bowl Stadium	1,000,000	Football Stadium with inside and outside areas
FedEx Institute of Technology (FIT), U. Memphis	88,675	Reconfigurable Facility with Classrooms, Research labs, Offices, Public Areas
Wilder Tower, U. Memphis	112,544	12-Story Building with Offices, Computer Labs, and Public Areas

3   Overview

We have surveyed seven facilities located in Memphis with 1.86 million square feet of indoor space that are of interest to public safety agencies (see Table 1).

Some of the buildings, e.g., the Pink Palace, have undergone many renovations, making it difficult for first responders to obtain accurate drawings. Some buildings, e.g., the Memphis Central Library, have historical artifacts and important documents to protect. Others such as the Liberty Bowl and Wilder Tower have a large number of occupants to evacuate during an emergency.

3.1   Challenges

The buildings in our survey represent a wide variety of structures. They include a museum, library, nature center, store, classroom, office, sports stadium, residence, lab, storage facility, theater, and planetarium (Table 1). They also vary significantly in their age, size, and height.

First, the LiDAR and other equipment we used (Sect. 4.1) are not designed specifically for an indoor survey and therefore present several indoor usage challenges. For instance, it is difficult to scan tight spaces as the field of view of the LiDAR is too small, and the LiDAR operator must be at least 1.5 m away from the walls, which is hard to achieve in tight spaces.

Second, repeatedly scanning the same space while turning corners leads to errors in the Simultaneous Localization And Mapping (SLAM) algorithm. This problem occurs when the algorithm cannot reconcile two views of the same scene, so the points are randomly superimposed on each other. It makes the data unusable and forces us to restart the scan. To avoid this, we pre-plan all the routes. Furthermore, in order to avoid accumulated errors, we divide each building into multiple areas, scan each area separately, and stitch the individual point clouds together later.

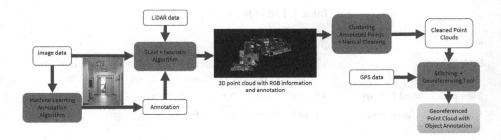

Fig. 1. Data collection and processing workflow [17].

Third, due to scheduling problems, we sometimes surveyed buildings during their business hours when occupants were present in the buildings. As a result, we need to identify and remove humans from the data.

Fourth, we were challenged during the labeling of 2D images. Indoor space does not ensure natural light, and, since artificial lighting does not have a standard, the intensity of light varies a lot. Thus, the ambient light is not always sufficient. There are also not enough labeled images for public-safety objects in existing datasets (Sect. 5.1). Therefore, identifying fire hydrants, hazmat signs, and other public-safety objects requires additional data and training.

Last but not least, we encountered difficulties in fusing LiDAR point clouds and camera images (Sect. 5.2). Compared to RGB-D data, the fusion and synchronization of LiDAR point clouds and camera images are tough as they are independent systems (hardware and software) with different clocks. Further, we found that many points were assigned incorrect labels when we projected a 2D image to a 3D point cloud. For example, an object behind a window can be labeled as a window if it is visible through the window. Section 5.2 describes our solutions to the above problems in data fusion.

3.2 Approaches

Figure 1 shows our overall process. We modified a GVI LiBackpack 50 [14] to mount an Insta360 Pro 2 camera [19]. The Velodyne VLP-16 LiDAR sensor collects point cloud data, and the camera collects 360-degree video data (Sect. 4). We collect both datasets simultaneously to facilitate the association of RGB information from the camera with points from the LiDAR (Sect. 5.2). We sample the 360-degree video frames into equirectangular projection images.

For automated object detection and classification, we use Mask R-CNN with Inception-ResNet-v2 or ResNet 101 on our images (Sect. 5.1). We train this deep learning model using manually labeled images from our buildings and other sources, and leverage transfer learning from the MS COCO dataset [20]. After automatically labeling all our images using this trained model, we fuse the RGB colors and labels from those images with the corresponding point clouds (Sect. 5.2), apply clustering to the labels in the point clouds, and remove the humans and the labels of falsely labeled objects (Sect. 5.3). Finally, we stitch together all the point clouds for a building and georeference the final point cloud (Sect. 5.4).

Fig. 2. Modified GVI LiBackpack [17].

4   Data Collection

In this section, we present our approach to collecting extensive LiDAR and video data in the surveyed facilities. We describe our equipment, data types, data collection workflow, and strategies to overcome the challenges we faced.

4.1   Hardware

We show our LiBackpack setup in Fig. 2. We retrofitted the LiBackpack with the Insta360 Pro 2 camera on the same axis as the LiDAR sensor to allow the sensors to be worn and operated by one person and collect the data simultaneously. The Surface Pro tablet (in the user's hand) connects to the LiBackpack via an Ethernet cable, controls the LiBackpack software, and displays the in-progress scan result for evaluation during scanning.

Video. The camera stores the recorded videos onto seven separate SD cards: six SD cards with the full resolution recordings of each of the six lenses, plus one more SD card with low-resolution replicas, data from the camera's internal IMU (inertial measurement unit), and recording metadata. The video from the six cameras is stitched into a single equirectangular video by the manufacturer's proprietary software. This stitched video has a resolution of 3840×1920 at 30 FPS (frame per second), and we used it for all further video processing. Additionally, this video contains the IMU data, which is used for time alignment during data fusion.

LiDAR. The backpack stores the raw LiDAR and IMU data (from its IMU, separate from the camera) in the open-source ROS [23] bag file format. The manufacturer's proprietary onboard software performs real-time SLAM processing using this data to generate a point cloud in PLY format. Because the bag file contains all the data required for SLAM processing, it can be used to generate an off-board SLAM result later.

Table 2. List of high priority objects [17].

Priority	Label class	Priority	Label class	Priority	Label class
5	Hazmat	4.2	Elevator	3.6	Fire door
4.8	Utility shutoffs - electric	4	Fire alarm	3.6	Extinguisher
4.8	Utility shutoffs - gas	4	Firewall	3.6	Sign exit
4.8	Utility shutoffs - water	4	Mechanical equipment	3.2	Emergency lighting
4.6	Building entrance-exit	3.8	Sprinkler	3.2	Sign stop
4.6	Door	3.8	Sprinkler cover/escutcheon	3.2	Smoke detector
4.6	Fire hydrant	3.8	Interior structural pillar	3	Automated external defibrillators
4.4	Fire escape access	3.8	Standpipe connection	3	Individual First Aid Kit
4.4	Roof access	3.8	Window	2.4	Server equipment
4.4	Stairway	3.6	Fire alarm switch	2	Person

4.2 Data Collection Work Flow

First, the scanning team assembles the hardware, and the operator puts on the backpack. Then, the team plans a route to maximize the distance from the walls and minimize loops and passage through doors. The scanning team opens the doors and ensures there are no other obstacles to the operator. The scanning team uses a map to mark down the area and the start time of the scan. The operator starts the scan from the tablet screen and walks through the designated area, and stops the scan once finished. The scanning team then determines which spaces to scan next and repeats the process.

5 Data Processing

In this section, we present our process of creating the 3D point clouds with RGB color and object labels. First, we automatically label objects in our video frames using a machine learning model. Second, we fuse the labels and RGB data from the video frames with the corresponding point clouds. Next, we apply a clustering algorithm to identify individual objects present in the point clouds, and remove the points labeled as humans and correct the labels of falsely identified objects. As we scan in parts, we finally stitch those point clouds into a complete 3D building structure. We then apply georeferencing to place it on the world map. The first responders can use the final 3D model for planning, training, rescue operations, virtual/augmented reality (VR/AR), and many other applications.

5.1 2D Image Annotation

High Priority Objects. The development of a public-safety object dataset is challenging, as incidents and scope can vary widely. Thus, we met with first responders and collected their needs, requirements, and expectations. Based on their information, we have identified thirty label classes (Table 2) with high priority that pose a significant risk or other importance to first responders.

Table 3. Latest (02/26/2021) labeled image dataset.

Data source	Training	Validation	Testing	Total
Seven facilities	1003	427	441	**1871**
Other sources	903	190	0	**1093**
Total	1906	617	441	**2964**

Image Projection. The Insta360 Pro 2 camera has six fisheye lenses. We stitched the six videos from these lenses into a 360-° panoramic video. These 360-° videos are presented as equirectangular projection with a resolution of 3840×1920 and a field of view (FOV) of 360×180 degrees. Although this projection is stretched and distorted, this 2:1 rectangle is straightforward to visualize. Initially, we explored the cube map projection, which provides six square 960×960 images, each with a 90×90 degrees FOV. The cube map projection avoids the distortion inherent in the equirectangular image. However, with progressions in our manual labeling, we increased the size of our training dataset, which helped the deep learning model handle the distortion in equirectangular projection, leading to better performance than the cube map projection. Compared to the cube map projection, the equirectangular images reduce the processing time significantly as there are six times fewer frames to label.

Manual Annotation. To produce training data for our neural network, we first identified some candidate images with public-safety objects from our video frames. We manually labeled those images using LabelMe [28]. We then trained our Deep Neural Network (DNN) using these images and used the trained model to label new images. Next, we identified the hard to label images where our machine learning model made mistakes (both false positives and false negatives). Then we manually corrected the labels in these images and added them back to our dataset to improve the performance of the DNN. We also labeled images from other sources to enhance and diversify our training dataset.

In our latest image dataset (Table 3), we have 1871 manually labeled images collected from all seven of the buildings. We first divided these images into training, validation, and test datasets. As it is a small dataset, we tried to provide as many images as possible for training. On the other hand, some categories have fewer examples, and we need those categories in the validation and test datasets. Based on those constraints, we set the split ratio of training, validation, and test datasets at 65:17:18. However, we found this dataset was not enough, so we gathered another 1093 images from the MCIndoor 20000 dataset, the Internet (through Google Search), and two open contests we conducted. We first added 903 of these images to the training dataset. We then added 190 images to the validation dataset – the new validation dataset with 617 images is called the *train-dev* dataset.

In Fig. 3, we show the two bars side by side with the least represented classes. The left bars are from the validation dataset, which consist of labeled images from the seven buildings. One can see that some categories have zero or few examples, e.g., fire escape access and utility shutoff (gas). The grey bars on the right represent the labeled images

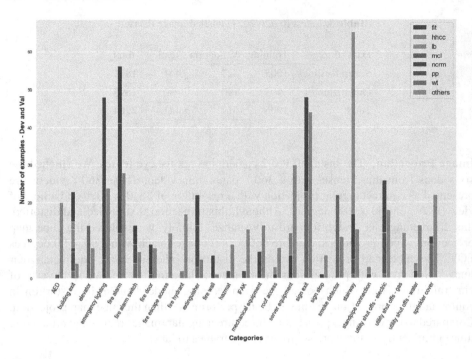

Fig. 3. Distribution of the "Train-Dev" Dataset. Examples from seven buildings and other sources are shown side by side for each category.

from other sources, showing that they add more examples to those categories with fewer examples in the validation dataset. As the train-dev dataset contains both bars, it has a more diverse set of images, which improves the neural network training performance.

Image Annotation Pipeline. As mentioned previously, we encountered multiple challenges in annotating the images, e.g., lack of good ambient lighting and cluttered areas. We leveraged the improvements in object detection/classification algorithms to handle these challenges. For the object detection task, we used Mask R-CNN [15] (from the Python Tensorflow official model repository [18]) to create a bounding box and an accurate mask of each detected object. However, this deep learning model requires a large amount of training data to perform well. To solve this problem, we used transfer learning to detect some basic indoor objects, i.e., we borrowed weights of a Mask R-CNN model already trained on another indoor existing dataset as the initial weights (Sect. 7.1). Figure 4 shows our image annotation pipeline. We apply the trained model on all equirectangular video frames. Then we store the predicted bounding boxes, polygon masks, and class labels in a JavaScript Object Notation (JSON) format file and masks in a Portable Network Graphics (PNG) format file.

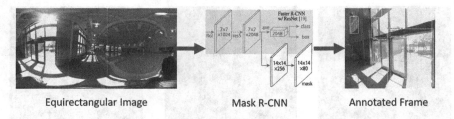

Fig. 4. Image annotation pipeline [17]. Labeled frame is zoomed in for better visualization.

5.2 Data Fusion

Our hardware has two sensors: the video camera, which records color information, and the LiDAR, which records depth information. Data fusion [17] transfers RGB and object labels from the video frames to the LiDAR point clouds.

Coloring LiDAR Point Clouds. The fusion process finds the pixel on the video frame corresponding to each point in the point cloud and applies its color to that point. Calculating this correspondence is straightforward because the transformation between the LiDAR and the camera is known and fixed. This correspondence is only valid if both sensors capture the depth and pixel information simultaneously. If the system moves too much during the capture of the depth point and pixels, it causes the coloring to appear blurry and shift.

We previously found that reducing this time to 0.05 s or less produced good quality coloring. Unfortunately, we could not find a reliable way of enforcing this as the time synchronization methods between the two systems. However, we can perform a coarse synchronization within 20 s window by assuming the clocks within the camera and LiDAR are reasonably accurate to guess the initial clock time. Performing the 0.05 s alignment is then possible using the IMU data recorded by both the camera and LiDAR. As both IMUs experience the same motion, the period of maximum correlation between the IMU streams ends up being the correct alignment around 90% of the time. The other 10% of the time, the alignment ends up wildly incorrect, which is identified during a manual inspection and can then be corrected.

We still had difficulties ensuring the clocks were accurate. The clock in the tablet used to timestamp the LiDAR scans drifted severely, so we had to regularly connect it to the Internet and force a clock synchronization. We could set the clock in the camera through a phone connection, and we could not enforce it. The camera also frequently forgot the time during battery changes. We overcame this problem by ensuring the camera saw the tablet's clock at the start of each recording. We then corrected the timestamp if it was wrong by reading it from the image of it.

Assigning Labels to Points. The annotation process creates label masks for objects in the camera images. A mask contains all pixels of an image that are a part of a particular object, along with the label of that object and the annotation algorithm's confidence in the label. Each pixel is labeled as the label of the mask that contains it. If multiple

Fig. 5. Label filtering demonstration (red is low confidence). (Color figure online)

masks contain the pixel, the label with the highest confidence is used. Some pixels may not be a part of any mask if they are not part of a recognizable object with a known label.

In theory, labels can then be applied to the points in the same way as color. Besides taking the RGB color of a point's corresponding pixel, we also take the label generated from the masks. However, the implicit mapping of 2D image labels to 3D points presents some challenges which must be addressed to improve the final labeling quality.

Objects with holes are problematic because the label masks include the pixels in the object's holes. This is demonstrated in Fig. 5. The left image shows all points labeled "window" in a particular scene, and a window is indeed visible at the top of the image. But because all the pixels in the window panes are labeled "window", objects that are visible through them, like the wall at the bottom, are also labeled "window". To correct this, we find the point in each mask that is closest to the LiDAR and only apply the label to points that are not more than 50cm farther than that one. We determined experimentally that objects visible through other objects, like items visible through windows, almost always exceed this distance, so incorrect labels for them are effectively rejected. The middle image in Fig. 5 demonstrates that the wall is mostly removed after this filter is applied.

After this, we apply a confidence filter to remove low-quality labels. In the right image in Fig. 5, all points with low confidence (illustrated as red) have their labels deleted, though the points still remain. This removes the last remnants of the wall and cleans up the window panes. This threshold is decided independently for each label type based on the algorithm's ground truth IoU predictions.

Objects in the point cloud are a result of many LiDAR captures and camera frames from different times and positions, so some points of an object may not be labeled if the corresponding camera frame was far away or blurry. To ensure such missed points are labeled, we "expand" the point labels to neighboring points. For each unlabeled point in the final labeled cloud, the closest labeled point within 5cm is located. Once all such points have been located, if an unlabeled point has a close labeled point, its label is transferred to the unlabeled point. This effectively ensures all points of an object are labeled, and also extends the labeled border which helps make smaller objects more obvious.

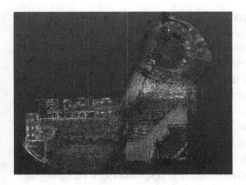

Fig. 6. First floor of the FedEx Institute of Technology (FIT).

Fig. 7. First floor of the FIT in the cleaning tool.

5.3 Label Clustering and Manual Cleaning

We developed an interactive cleaning tool using Open3D [30] to enable a user to remove falsely labeled objects easily from a 3D point cloud. It uses DBSCAN [12] to cluster all the points with the same label into individual clusters. Figure 6 shows the point cloud of the first floor of the FedEx Institute of Technology, and Fig. 7 shows the same area in the cleaning tool. In contrast to the original, the point cloud in the cleaning tool is simplified so the users have to deal with only tens or hundreds of clusters instead of millions of points. After the user selects and removes the labels of falsely labeled clusters or removes the points labeled as humans, the cleaning tool maps the removed clusters to the original point clouds (one for each label class) and exports the corrected point clouds. Finally, it merges all the corrected point clouds into one point cloud.

5.4 LiDAR Data Stitching and Georeferencing

For better data quality, we divided each of the buildings surveyed into sections and scanned each part several times, allowing us to pick the best scan of each part. To generate a complete building, the selected parts must all be stitched together. To do this, we used the "Align by point pair picking" function provided by the open-source CloudCompare software [9]. We choose the larger point cloud as a reference and use this tool to transform the smaller point cloud to match the larger one. The tool calculates the correct transformation once at least 3 pairs of homologous points are picked. We repeat this process for each piece until we have one point cloud which contains all parts of the building.

We measure the GPS coordinates of several points around the building's exterior using the REACH RS+ RTK GPS [24]. With these points, we use the alignment tool again to georeference the building in the Universal Transverse Mercator (UTM) coordinate system as the point cloud data is already in meters. The georeferenced data can then be loaded into ArcGIS Pro [11] and visualized on a map.

6   Application of 3D Building Maps in Public Safety

A 3D building map with annotations can be viewed on a computer, tablet, smartphone, or VR headset, serving a variety of applications in public safety, architecture, computer gaming, and other areas. Below we elaborate on a few of its usages in public safety.

First, these maps can help first responders perform pre-incident planning more effectively, as they provide a much more detailed and accurate representation of indoor space than 2D floor plans. First responders and incident commanders can calculate the best entry/exit points and routes based on the specific type and location of an incident before dispatching and on the way to the incident.

Second, they can be used in 3D simulations to train first responders more safely and with less cost. First responders can put on VR headsets to practice rescue operations in their own stations, instead of physically going into a building under dangerous conditions. Fire, smoke, obstacles, and other digital effects can be overlaid on the map to simulate different emergency situations.

Third, during a real incident, first responders can use the maps for indoor localization and navigation. The maps can be viewed through a 3D display integrated into a first responder's helmet, giving them sight and information in otherwise dark or smoke-filled environments. The first responders would also be outfitted with trackers that show their position on the building map. The 3D display will show them the safest way out of the building or the fastest way to reach a specific location. An incident commander outside the building can also use the map data to locate responders and guide them inside the building.

Finally, a 3D building map can help occupants escape safely in an emergency. It can also help visitors navigate in an unfamiliar building more easily.

7   Evaluation Results

In this section, we present the performance of the deep learning model on the image data and the performance of the data fusion process on the point cloud. We use the Hickory Hill Community Center (HHCC) and the first floor of the FedEx Institute of Technology (FIT) as a case study to show the performance of the final point cloud. We walked through each building and identified all the safety-related objects and their locations to create a complete ground truth.

7.1   Object Annotation

We divided the set of manually labeled images into training, validation, and testing subsets (Table 3) to train and evaluate our machine learning model. We report the average precision (AP) and average recall given ten best detections per image ($AR^{max=10}$) [20] as the performance metrics.

Impact of Transfer Learning in Training the DNN. We first trained our deep learning model without transfer learning. As shown in Fig. 8, we trained a Mask R-CNN with Inception-ResNet-V2 from scratch (green curve) for 117,000 iterations. The $AP^{IoU=.50}$ increases very slowly after 45,000 iterations and never reaches above 0.20.

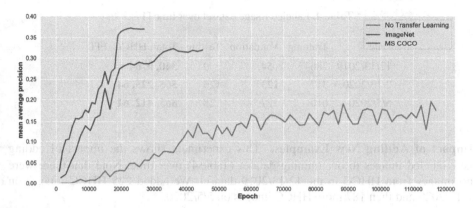

Fig. 8. $AP^{IoU=.50}$ of image annotation with and without transfer learning on "Validation" dataset (Equirectangular Projection, Mask R-CNN with Inception-ResNet-V2).

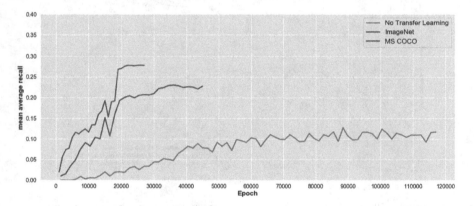

Fig. 9. $AR^{max=10}$ of image annotation with and without transfer learning on "Validation" Dataset (Equirectangular Projection, Mask R-CNN with Inception-ResNet-V2).

We also trained our model with transfer learning. The ImageNet dataset contains object labels and bounding boxes (not masks), we can only apply transfer learning to the classifiers (Inception-ResNet-V2 and ResNet-101). On the other hand, the MS COCO dataset contains object labels and masks, so we can apply transfer learning to the classifiers and Mask R-CNN model. Although both MS COCO and ImageNet's performance curves ($AP^{IoU=.50}$) follow the same pattern, MS COCO (red curve) reaches over 0.35 after training with our dataset for 27,000 iterations the, while ImageNet (blue curve) remains below 0.35 even after 45,000 iterations. Figure 9 shows similar behavior in the AR performance.

As a result, we decided to use the weights from the MS COCO-trained model to retrain and fine-tune our model with our dataset, saving computation time and increasing capacity.

Table 4. Labeled image dataset over time [17].

Date	Training	Validation	Testing	Total, HHCC, FIT
12/13/2019	286	54	0	**340, 0, 64**
2/13/2020	317	123	125	**565, 225, 64**
5/5/2020	610	127	128	**865, 412, 64**

Impact of Adding New Examples. This experiment shows the impact of adding new labeled images to our training dataset (Table 4) over time. Note that there were no images from HHCC in the 12/13/2019 dataset. We added 225 HHCC images on 2/13/2020 and then 187 more HHCC images on 5/5/2020.

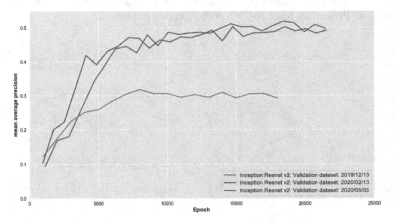

Fig. 10. $AP^{IoU=.50}$ of image annotation on "Validation" datasets (Equirectangular Projection, Mask R-CNN with ResNet-101).

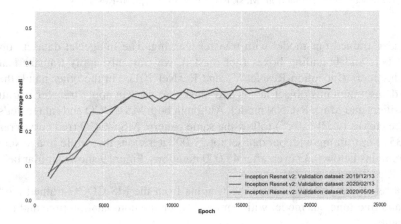

Fig. 11. $AR^{max=10}$ of image annotation on "Validation" datasets (Equirectangular Projection, Mask R-CNN with ResNet-101).

Figure 10 shows that the annotation performance as measured by $AP^{IoU=.50}$ improved significantly from 12/13/19 (green curve) to 2/13/20 (orange curve) This indicates that skewing the distribution of images towards one of the buildings improves that building's performance which also increases the overall performance. However, we can also observe that the 187 additional HHCC images in the 5/5/20 dataset did not lead to significant improvement in the AP and AR (Fig. 11), indicating that the additional images did not contain much new information compared to what was already in the previous training dataset, i.e., the added images lack new instances of the under-performing objects. This suggests that we need to prioritize the selection of images containing under-performing objects which tend to be less common.

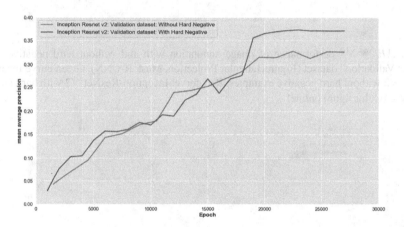

Fig. 12. $AP^{IoU=.50}$ performance of image annotation with and without hard negative examples on "Validation" dataset (Equirectangular Projection, Mask R-CNN). Green curve Inception-ResNet-V2 without hard negative examples. Red curve: Inception-ResNet-V2 with hard negative examples. (Color figure online)

Impact of Hard Negative Mining. We adopted hard negative mining to reduce false positive detections. We manually identified false positive examples, assigned them negative labels, and added them into the training dataset so that our neural network learns to distinguish similar examples from different classes. The ratio of images with only positive examples to images with negative examples for training was 8 to 1. We have tried 2, 4, 6, 8, 10, and found that 8 gives the best results (not shown).

FaceNet [26] is one of the early papers to employ hard-negative training. They proposed a loss function specific for handling the hard-negative examples in training. We have not changed the loss function for training, and we found that manually mining some examples produced better results. As we can see in Fig. 12, the AP for Inception-ResNet-V2 with hard negative mining is 13.55% better compared to a conventional trained Inception-ResNet-V2 model. In Fig. 13, the AR for Inception-ResNet-V2 with hard negative mining is also 16.71% better than without negative mining. Nevertheless, using an offline semi-supervised model for hard-negative mining and applying a modified loss function is part of our future work.

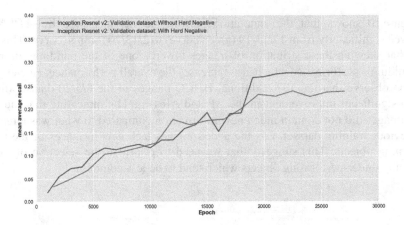

Fig. 13. $AR^{max=10}$ performance of image annotation with and without hard negative examples on "Validation" dataset (Equirectangular Projection, Mask R-CNN). Green curve Inception-ResNet-V2 without hard negative examples. Red curve: Inception-ResNet-V2 with hard negative examples. (Color figure online)

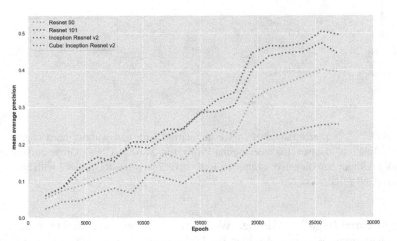

Fig. 14. $AP^{IoU=.50}$ of image annotation with hard negative examples on "Train-Dev" dataset (Mask R-CNN). Yellow curve: Equirectangular Projection, ResNet-50. Magenta curve: Equirectangular Projection, ResNet-101. Red curve: Equirectangular Projection, Inception-ResNet-V2. Green curve: Cubic Projection, Inception-ResNet-V2. (Color figure online)

Performance Comparison Between Neural Network Models and Projections. When we were selecting a neural network for 2D object detection, we found that Faster R-CNN performed slightly better than Mask R-CNN. However, we later chose Mask R-CNN, which provides more precise polygon masks, as we need to transfer our 2D object detection to a 3D point cloud. We then compared different feature extractors, Inception-ResNet-V2, ResNet-50, and ResNet-101, within Mask R-CNN. Figures 14 show that Inception-ResNet-V2 and ResNet-101 have better performance than the others. It also shows that the $AP^{IoU=.50}$ of the equirectangular projection (Red dotted curves) is visibly better than that of the cube map projection (green dotted curves). Therefore, we decided to use the equirectangular image projection for better performance with a much lower processing time (6 time faster).

Performance Measurement on Image Test Dataset. We evaluated our Mask R-CNN with Inception-ResNet-V2 and ResNet-101 model on the image test dataset. The results from individual buildings and overall combined are show in the Table 5 (AP) and Table 6 (AR). We can observe from the tables that Inception-ResNet-V2 performs slightly better than ResNet-101 concerning the AP and AR metrics, especially for the large objects (AP_L). Thus, for our automated annotation task, we used Mask R-CNN with Inception-ResNet-V2.

Table 5. Average precision of object detection on 2/26/21 image test dataset.

Backbone	Data source	AP	AP_{50}	AP_{75}	AP_S	AP_M	AP_L
Inception-ResNet-V2	FIT	0.286	0.472	0.277	0.067	0.228	0.399
ResNet-101		0.246	0.412	0.258	0.040	0.174	0.380
Inception-ResNet-V2	HHCC	0.214	0.357	0.238	0.149	0.193	0.338
ResNet-101		0.207	0.353	0.220	0.123	0.227	0.317
Inception-ResNet-V2	LB	0.23	0.362	0.251	0.034	0.192	0.391
ResNet-101		0.203	0.332	0.224	0.047	0.189	0.369
Inception-ResNet-V2	MCL	0.229	0.365	0.235	0.008	0.18	0.392
ResNet-101		0.222	0.365	0.249	0.036	0.199	0.387
Inception-ResNet-V2	NCRM	0.278	0.437	0.297	0.044	0.327	0.34
ResNet-101		0.273	0.425	0.306	0.056	0.341	0.338
Inception-ResNet-V2	PP	0.27	0.432	0.279	0.036	0.236	0.351
ResNet-101		0.233	0.369	0.258	0.074	0.229	0.298
Inception-ResNet-V2	WT	0.287	0.508	0.293	0.027	0.209	0.5
ResNet-101		0.283	0.514	0.273	0.037	0.238	0.483
Inception-ResNet-V2	All 7 buildings combined	0.196	0.328	0.198	0.03	0.197	0.281
ResNet-101		0.184	0.312	0.198	0.031	0.213	0.273

7.2 Performance Measurement on Point Cloud

The data fusion process (Sect. 5.2) transfers the annotations in our video frames to the corresponding 3D point clouds. The resulting 3D point clouds have multiple error types—some errors carried over from the image annotation and some errors created during the data fusion process. For example, as an object can be visible from different angles, the DNN can generate different labels for the same object in different images (from different angles). Each instance of the object is mapped to a set of points in the point cloud. For each point, the data fusion process simply chooses the label with the highest confidence level above a certain threshold, so different points belonging to

Table 6. Average recall of object detection on 2/26/21 image test dataset.

Backbone	Data source	AR_1	AR_{10}	AR_{100}	AR_S	AR_M	AR_L
Inception-ResNet-V2	FIT	0.224	0.327	0.327	0.096	0.276	0.444
ResNet-101		0.181	0.287	0.287	0.050	0.223	0.418
Inception-ResNet-V2	HHCC	0.19	0.265	0.265	0.173	0.25	0.369
ResNet-101		0.198	0.268	0.268	0.152	0.291	0.347
Inception-ResNet-V2	LB	0.213	0.251	0.254	0.043	0.207	0.421
ResNet-101		0.184	0.228	0.231	0.060	0.213	0.392
Inception-ResNet-V2	MCL	0.151	0.27	0.27	0.015	0.251	0.431
ResNet-101		0.150	0.268	0.269	0.042	0.260	0.430
Inception-ResNet-V2	NCRM	0.23	0.31	0.31	0.053	0.351	0.37
ResNet-101		0.226	0.303	0.303	0.076	0.363	0.365
Inception-ResNet-V2	PP	0.235	0.329	0.329	0.068	0.285	0.41
ResNet-101		0.212	0.263	0.263	0.079	0.280	0.318
Inception-ResNet-V2	WT	0.22	0.325	0.325	0.043	0.276	0.532
ResNet-101		0.211	0.317	0.317	0.080	0.283	0.509
Inception-ResNet-V2	All 7 buildings combined	0.173	0.247	0.248	0.051	0.26	0.315
ResNet-101		0.150	0.222	0.223	0.054	0.268	0.305

the same object may have different labels. Suppose the threshold is 50%. If Point A has labels X and Y with a confidence level of 60% and 40%, respectively, then Point A receives the label X. On the other hand, Point B from the same object may have the label X and Y with a confidence level of 30% and 70%, respectively, so Point B receives the label Y. When we cluster the points into 3D objects, we may find more detected target objects than the ground truth (Tables 9 and 12).

Table 7. Average precision of object detection on 5/5/20 image test dataset.

Backbone	Data source	AP	AP_{50}	AP_{75}	AP_S	AP_M	AP_L
Inception-ResNet-v2	HHCC	0.200	0.338	0.212	0.003	0.110	0.316
ResNet-101		0.220	0.363	0.241	0.006	0.144	0.361
Inception-ResNet-v2	All 7 buildings combined	0.227	0.408	0.229	0.007	0.082	0.359
ResNet-101		0.25	0.451	0.258	0.014	0.104	0.388

HHCC Point Cloud. We used the dataset available on 5/5/2020 to train the DNN, and Tables 7 and 8 show AP and AR performances on the HHCC image test dataset. Table 9 shows the precision and recall for some of the higher priority objects in the HHCC point cloud before the manual cleaning. Note that the table does not include some objects with zero detection (neither true nor false positive), e.g., hazmat, as there were very few instances of them in the training dataset.

We observe that the precision for some of the objects, e.g., door and elevator, in the HHCC point cloud is much lower than that in the HHCC test images. This may be due

Table 8. Average recall of object detection on 5/5/20 image test dataset.

Backbone	Data source	AR_1	AR_{10}	AR_{100}	AR_S	AR_M	AR_L
Inception-ResNet-v2	HHCC	0.168	0.223	0.223	0.004	0.129	0.354
ResNet-101		0.181	0.248	0.248	0.009	0.179	0.405
Inception-ResNet-v2	All 7 buildings combined	0.191	0.265	0.265	0.014	0.101	0.413
ResNet-101		0.208	0.296	0.296	0.024	0.136	0.45

Table 9. Average precision and recall of object detection on HHCC images (5/5/20 Dataset) and point cloud.

Name	HHCC (Image Test Dataset)		HHCC (Point Cloud)		
	Precision	Recall	Precision	Recall	F1-score
Building entrance-exit	0.206	0.248	0.115	0.5	0.187
Door	0.353	0.458	0.235	1	0.381
Elevator	0.900	0.900	0.222	1	0.364
Fire alarm	0.165	0.183	0.663	0.953	0.782
Fire alarm switch	0.050	0.070	0.146	0.5	0.226
Fire suppression systems - extinguisher	0.252	0.229	0.760	0.95	0.844
Sign exit	0.229	0.243	0.493	1	0.661
Utility shutoffs - electric	0.322	0.356	0.778	1	0.875

to two reasons: (a) the performance of the DNN on the entire video of a building may be lower than that on the limited test images; and (b) the fusion process introduced errors that lowered the precision on the point cloud. At the same time, we can also see that some objects. e.g., fire alarm and fire extinguisher, have a higher precision in the point cloud. This is likely due to the fact that the precision on the test images is calculated per image. However, an object missed by the DNN in one image may be detected in another image. Since the point cloud aggregates the labels from many images, as long as one of the images captures the object, the point cloud may have this object labeled. In other words, as we scan an area from multiple angles, the probability of detecting an object is higher than that of using a single image of the area.

Table 10. Average precision of object detection on 11/30/20 image test dataset.

Backbone	Data source	AP	AP_{50}	AP_{75}	AP_S	AP_M	AP_L
Inception-ResNet-v2	FIT	0.274	0.391	0.314	0.034	0.247	0.415
ResNet-101		0.200	0.346	0.185	0.029	0.144	0.329
Inception-ResNet-v2	All 7 buildings combined	0.195	0.303	0.214	0.023	0.135	0.296
ResNet-101		0.191	0.316	0.201	0.03	0.15	0.282

FIT Point Cloud. We trained the DNN with the dataset available on 11/30/2020. This dataset had 16% images from the HHCC and 12.9% from the FIT. We used Mask R-

Table 11. Average recall of object detection on 11/30/20 image test dataset.

Backbone	Data source	AR_1	AR_{10}	AR_{100}	AR_S	AR_M	AR_L
Inception-ResNet-v2	FIT	0.237	0.316	0.316	0.046	0.280	0.473
ResNet-101		0.167	0.233	0.233	0.037	0.174	0.364
Inception-ResNet-v2	All 7 buildings combined	0.159	0.231	0.231	0.029	0.17	0.337
ResNet-101		0.162	0.233	0.233	0.05	0.189	0.324

Table 12. Average precision and recall of object detection in FIT 1st floor images (11/30/20 dataset) and point cloud.

Name	FIT (Image Test Dataset)		FIT (Point Cloud)		
	Precision	Recall	Precision	Recall	F1-score
Building entrance-exit	0.194	0.189	0.118	1	0.211
Door	0.405	0.477	0.356	1	0.525
Elevator	0.314	0.324	0.136	1	0.24
Fire alarm	0.106	0.139	0.284	0.905	0.432
Fire alarm switch	0.125	0.120	0.167	0.667	0.267
Fire suppression systems - extinguisher	0.396	0.415	0.214	1	0.353
Sign exit	0.380	0.465	0.254	1	0.405
Utility shutoffs - electric	0.719	0.725	0.020	0.25	0.037

CNN Inception-ResNet-v2 to label the FIT video data as it got in the best AP 0.274 and AR 0.316 in the FIT image test dataset (Tables 10 and 11). Table 12 shows the precision and recall for some of the higher priority objects in the FIT 1st-floor point cloud before the manual cleaning. Note that this time we had fewer object types with zero detections compared to the previous time when we processed the HHCC data. We found that the precision is lower than the AP of all the objects in the FIT test images except for electric utility shutoffs.

Given our limited training dataset, our results are encouraging, but there is still a large room for improvement in the training of our DNN and the data fusion process.

8   Conclusion

We have developed a system to collect and label indoor scene images and point clouds with thirty types of public-safety objects. While the data collection and processing presented many challenges, we overcame these challenges by leveraging various existing approaches and innovative methods. Our results show that the Inception-ResNet-V2 as backbone architecture for Mask R-CNN performs slightly better than ResNet-101 to label public-safety objects in our test image dataset, especially for large objects. It also shows that the equirectangular projection frame of the panoramic videos works better than cubic projection. Our strategy to use hard-negative mining for training the model showed a considerable improvement. We found that with transfer learning from the MS COCO dataset, adding just a few hundred labeled images from a building to the training dataset can significantly improve the performance of our machine learning model. Our annotation performance is encouraging despite our limited training dataset.

The outcomes show that there exists room for advancements. We will continue to enrich our dataset, find and label more images that contain the under-performing examples. However, it is challenging as these are typically more uncommon objects, and existing public image databases rarely have them. We plan to use artificial data synthesis to increase the number of examples. We are also inspecting a new training strategy to improve the recognition accuracy of small safety objects such as sprinklers and smoke detectors by cropping, zooming, and resampling the training data. Moreover, we will carry out a manual error analysis to identify the differences between the training and validation dataset, reduce discrepancy, and increase the ratio of building images in the training dataset. Finally, we plan to apply machine learning models directly to point clouds as a complementary process to improve the overall accuracy and confidence.

References

1. Ahrens, M., Evarts, B.: NFPA report: fire loss in the United States during 2019 (2020). https://www.nfpa.org/News-and-Research/Data-research-and-tools/US-Fire-Problem/Fire-loss-in-the-United-States
2. Andriluka, M., Uijlings, J.R., Ferrari, V.: Fluid annotation: a human-machine collaboration interface for full image annotation. In: Proceedings of the 26th ACM International Conference on Multimedia, pp. 1957–1966 (2018)
3. Armeni, I., et al.: 3D scene graph: a structure for unified semantics, 3D space, and camera. In: Proceedings of the IEEE International Conference on Computer Vision, pp. 5664–5673 (2019)
4. Armeni, I., Sax, S., Zamir, A.R., Savarese, S.: Joint 2D–3D-semantic data for indoor scene understanding. arXiv preprint arXiv:1702.01105 (2017)
5. Armeni, I., et al.: 3D semantic parsing of large-scale indoor spaces. In: Proceedings of the IEEE Conference on Computer Vision and Pattern Recognition, pp. 1534–1543 (2016)
6. Bashiri, F.S., LaRose, E., Peissig, P., Tafti, A.P.: Mcindoor20000: a fully-labeled image dataset to advance indoor objects detection. Data Brief **17**, 71–75 (2018). https://doi.org/10.1016/j.dib.2017.12.047. https://www.sciencedirect.com/science/article/pii/S2352340917307424
7. CDC/National Institute for Occupational Safety and Health (NIOSH) website: Fire fighter fatality investigation and prevention program (2020). https://www.cdc.gov/niosh/fire/default.html
8. Chang, A., et al.: ShapeNet: an information-rich 3D model repository. arXiv preprint arXiv:1512.03012 (2015)
9. CloudCompare (version 2.10.0) [GPL software] (2019). http://www.cloudcompare.org/
10. Deng, J., Dong, W., Socher, R., Li, L.J., Li, K., Fei-Fei, L.: ImageNet: a large-scale hierarchical image database. In: 2009 IEEE Conference on Computer Vision and Pattern Recognition, pp. 248–255 (2009). https://doi.org/10.1109/CVPR.2009.5206848
11. ESRI: ArcGIS Pro (v2.5.0): Next-generation desktop GIS (2020). https://www.esri.com/en-us/arcgis/products/arcgis-pro/overview
12. Ester, M., Kriegel, H.P., Sander, J., Xu, X., et al.: A density-based algorithm for discovering clusters in large spatial databases with noise. In: KDD, pp. 226–231 (1996)
13. Fahy, R.F., Petrillo, J.T., Molis, J.L.: NFPA report: firefighter fatalities in the US - 2019 (2020). https://www.nfpa.org/News-and-Research/Data-research-and-tools/Emergency-Responders/Firefighter-fatalities-in-the-United-States

14. GVI: GreenValley International LiBackpack 50 (2018). https://greenvalleyintl.com/hardware/libackpack/
15. He, K., Gkioxari, G., Dollár, P., Girshick, R.: Mask R-CNN. In: Proceedings of the IEEE International Conference on Computer Vision, pp. 2961–2969 (2017)
16. He, K., Zhang, X., Ren, S., Sun, J.: Deep residual learning for image recognition. In: 2016 IEEE Conference on Computer Vision and Pattern Recognition (CVPR), pp. 770–778 (2016). https://doi.org/10.1109/CVPR.2016.90
17. Hossain, M., et al.: Building indoor point cloud datasets with object annotation for public safety. In: Proceedings of the 10th International Conference on Smart Cities and Green ICT Systems (SMARTGREENS 2021) (2021)
18. Huang, J., et al.: Speed/accuracy trade-offs for modern convolutional object detectors. In: Proceedings of the IEEE Conference on Computer Vision and Pattern Recognition, pp. 7310–7311 (2017)
19. Insta360 Pro 2 Camera (2018). https://www.insta360.com/product/insta360-pro2
20. Lin, T.-Y., et al.: Microsoft COCO: common objects in context. In: Fleet, D., Pajdla, T., Schiele, B., Tuytelaars, T. (eds.) ECCV 2014. LNCS, vol. 8693, pp. 740–755. Springer, Cham (2014). https://doi.org/10.1007/978-3-319-10602-1_48
21. Qi, C.R., Su, H., Mo, K., Guibas, L.J.: PointNet: deep learning on point sets for 3D classification and segmentation. In: Proceedings of the IEEE Conference on Computer Vision and Pattern Recognition, pp. 652–660 (2017)
22. Qi, C.R., Yi, L., Su, H., Guibas, L.J.: PointNet++: deep hierarchical feature learning on point sets in a metric space. In: Guyon, I., et al. (eds.) Advances in Neural Information Processing Systems, vol. 30. Curran Associates, Inc. (2017). https://proceedings.neurips.cc/paper/2017/file/d8bf84be3800d12f74d8b05e9b89836f-Paper.pdf
23. Quigley, M., et al.: Ros: an open-source robot operating system. In: ICRA Workshop on Open Source Software, p. 5 (2009)
24. REACH RS+: Single-band RTK GNSS receiver with centimeter precision (2018). https://emlid.com/reachrs/
25. Ren, S., He, K., Girshick, R., Sun, J.: Faster R-CNN: towards real-time object detection with region proposal networks. IEEE Trans. Pattern Anal. Mach. Intell. **39**(6), 1137–1149 (2016)
26. Schroff, F., Kalenichenko, D., Philbin, J.: FaceNet: a unified embedding for face recognition and clustering. In: Proceedings of the IEEE Conference on Computer Vision and Pattern Recognition, pp. 815–823 (2015)
27. Szegedy, C., Ioffe, S., Vanhoucke, V., Alemi, A.: Inception-v4, Inception-ResNet and the impact of residual connections on learning. In: Proceedings of the AAAI Conference on Artificial Intelligence (2017)
28. Wada, K.: LabelMe: image polygonal annotation with python (2016). https://github.com/wkentaro/labelme
29. Yi, L., et al.: A scalable active framework for region annotation in 3D shape collections. ACM Trans. Graph. (ToG) **35**(6), 1–12 (2016)
30. Zhou, Q.Y., Park, J., Koltun, V.: Open3D: a modern library for 3D data processing. arXiv preprint arXiv:1801.09847 (2018)

Vehicle Technology and Intelligent Transport Systems

A Scalable Approach to Vocation and Fleet Identification for Heavy-Duty Vehicles

Varun Yadav[1], Andy Byerly[2], Daniel Kobold Jr.[2], and Zina Ben Miled[1(✉)]

[1] Department of Electrical and Computer Engineering (IUPUI), Indianapolis, IN 46202, USA
zmiled@iupui.edu
[2] Allison Transmission Inc., One Allison Way, Indianapolis, IN 46222, USA

Abstract. Understanding the operating profile of different heavy-duty vehicles is needed by parts manufacturers for improved configuration and better future design of the parts. This study investigates the use of a tournament classification approach for both vocation and fleet identification. The proposed approach is implemented using four different classification techniques, namely, K-Means, Expectation Maximization, Particle Swarm Optimization, and Support Vector Machines. Vocations classifiers are developed and tested for six different vocations ranging from coach buses to rail inspection vehicles. Operational field data are obtained from a number of vehicles for each vocation and aggregated over a pre-set distance that varies according to the data collection rate. In addition, fleet classifiers are implemented for five fleets from the coach bus vocation using a similar approach. The results indicate that both vocation and fleet identification are possible with a high level of accuracy. The macro average precision and recall of the SVM vocation classifier are approximately 85%. This result was achieved despite the fact that each vocation consisted of multiple fleets. The macro average precision and recall of the coach bus fleet classifier are approximately 77% even though some fleets had similar operating profiles. These results suggest that the proposed classifier can help support vocation and fleet identification in practice.

Keywords: Classification · Vocation · Fleet · Operating profile · Heavy-duty vehicles

1 Introduction

The ability to understand the behavior of a vehicle or a group of vehicles in the field is of interest to many stakeholders including manufacturers, emission regulators as well as traffic management and planning operators. The aim of this paper is to distinguish between groups of heavy-duty vehicles at the vocation and fleet levels using operational field data collected from the vehicles. As mentioned above, in general this classification is important to several stakeholders. However, the current study is motivated by the desire of parts' manufacturers to gain an insight into the operation of the vehicles that house their parts. As opposed to OEMs, part manufacturers do not have direct access to the vehicle during its assembly. Moreover, their parts can be installed in different vocations (e.g., a school bus versus a coach bus) with varying intended purposes. Even

© Springer Nature Switzerland AG 2022
C. Klein et al. (Eds.): SMARTGREENS 2021/ VEHITS 2021, CCIS 1612, pp. 199–215, 2022.
https://doi.org/10.1007/978-3-031-17098-0_10

within a given vocation, the parts may be installed in different fleets with varying operating conditions. Being able to classify the host vehicle using data collected from the vehicle can help improve both the configuration as well as any future designs of the components.

Vehicles and fleets classification have been primarily addressed in the literature for transportation [2, 4, 9, 12, 14] and emission [1, 11] purposes. For instance, GPS data was used in [14] to distinguish between different types of vehicles. A Long-Short-Term-Memory (LSTM) network is developed in this study to classify the vehicles into different categories for the purpose of facilitating traffic management. Vehicle classification using image data is also investigated in [2]. In this application, the types of vehicle include two-wheelers, cars, and trucks. The classifier is based on a convolution neural network (CNN) architecture. A pipeline consisting of multiple classifiers was proposed in [4] to distinguish between different classes of vehicles including private cars, light trailers, lorries or buses and heavy trailers. Each classifier in the pipeline is based on fuzzy C-Means clustering and uses the dimension of the vehicle and its speed as input variables.

Other studies focus on the identification of fleets using movement patterns. For example, GPS in combination with satellite data were used to identify fleets of vehicles in [12]. First, satellite image data are classified using a CNN network. The output of this first classifier along with GPS data are then presented to a random forest classifier in order to generate the final classification. The importance of fleet identification is not limited to land vehicles. It was also investigated for fishing fleets in [9]. In this latter study, the landing patterns were used to classify the vessels into eight fishing fleets.

The focus of the present paper is on developing vocation and fleet classifiers by using the salient features in the operating profiles of heavy-duty vehicles. All the features of the proposed classifiers are derived from the speed of the vehicle, namely, engine speed, wheel based speed and average speed. These variables can be easily collected and can be processed in a cost effective manner. Moreover, they are less prone to privacy constraints as in the case, for instance, of GPS data. In fact, some of the telematic service providers may be reluctant to share GPS data.

In an initial study by the authors, a one-versus-one tournament classification approach was found to be efficient in distinguishing between different heavy-duty vocations [6]. In the present study, this approach is evaluated in the context of a larger dataset and four classification techniques: K-means (KM) [7], Expected Maximization (EM) [10], Particle Swarm Optimization (PSO) [5] and Support Vector Machines (SVM) [13]. The utility of the proposed tournament classification is investigated for the purpose of vocation identification for several heady-duty vehicles vocations and for the purpose of fleet identification for different coach bus fleets.

2 Related Work

Identifying the vocation of an unknown vehicle is a classification problem. Since there are multiple vocations, this is a multi-class classification with nominal vocation labels. Several general classification techniques are available in the literature. A review of these techniques is provided in [15]. According to the taxonomy in this review, the classification techniques can be organized along the following categories:

- Logic-based (e.g., Decision Trees)
- Perceptron-based (e.g., Neural Networks)
- Statistical learning (e.g., EM)
- SVM
- Instance-based (e.g., KM, PSO)

Some of the above techniques are inherently binary. However, they can be adapted to multi-class problems. For example, a decision tree is typically a binary classifier. It was developed into a multi-class classifier by turning each node of the tree into an SVM classifier which splits a group of target classes into two distinct groups [8]. The tree expansion continues until each class is identified separately. Independently, SVM is also a binary classifier. This classifier uses a kernel to transform the input data into a higher dimensional space where it can be separated by a single hyperplane [13]. A modified SVM using either the one-versus-one or the one-versus-all approach can also be used to develop multi-class classifiers [3].

EM falls under the category of statistical learning and both KM and PSO fall under the category of instance-based techniques. These three techniques are unsupervised clustering techniques. They have been adapted to classification by allowing the centroids of a single or multiple clusters to represent a given class in a multi-class problem.

In the present study, a multi-class classifier that follows multiple rounds of binary one-versus-one classification is proposed. At each round, one class is eliminated [6]. Different one-versus-one classifiers are compared. They utilize either KM, EM, PSO or SVM. The choice of a tournament approach, simple input data and a one-versus-one classifier with a low computational cost is motivated by the large number of classes under consideration in the current application. More complex machine learning models and data have been used for vehicle and fleet classification in previous studies. However, the number of classes was limited to 3 or 4 classes [2,4,9,14] and a large volume of data was needed. These previous models were based on machine learning models such as LSTM [14] and CNN [2,12].

The vocation and fleet identification applications under consideration require a granular classification that may cover a large number of classes. Six and five, respectively, are used in the present study with a potential extension to additional classes. The traditional one-versus-all classification using an LSTM or CNN model is not viable due to the large volume of data needed for training [2,12,14] and the potential confounding between the operating profiles of some of the vocations [6]. This confounding issue was also observed in [4]. In order to mitigate the potential for confounding between several classes in this latter study, a pipeline of classifiers was proposed. The first stage of the pipeline distinguishes between private cars and light trailers, on the one hand, and buses and heavy trailers on the other hand. Subsequently, a classifier is used to distinguish between cars and light trailers and another classifier is used to distinguish between buses and heavy trailers. This pipeline becomes harder to develop with a large number of vocations.

3   Methods

The purpose of the proposed classifier is to identify the vocation of a heavy-duty vehicle using data collected from the vehicle during its daily operation. The classifier is trained using real data collected from the field. This dataset was obtained from two telematic service providers and was collected from a large number of heavy-duty vehicles with varying vocations and operational profiles. The vocations of interest and the number of fleets under each vocation are shown in Table 1.

Table 1. List of vocations and number of fleets for each vocation.

Vocation	Label	Number of fleets
Coach buses	CB	16
Construction trucks	CT	2
Delivery trucks	DT	2
Municipal trucks	MT	3
Rail inspection vehicles	RI	2
School buses	SB	2

A total of 27 fleets from 6 different vocations are considered. The data corresponding to all the coach bus (CB) fleets are obtained from the first telematic provider. The remaining fleets are all non-coach fleets and their corresponding data were obtained from the second telematic provider.

Using this dataset, classifier models are first trained to identify the profile of each vocation using four different techniques: KM, EM, PSO and SVM. For each of these techniques, the one-versus-one tournament assignment approach previously introduced in [6] is used to classify each vehicle. The remainder of this section describes the pre-processing performed on the raw data and the methodology used to develop each type of classifier.

3.1 Data Aggregation

The raw data are collected using an on-board telematic device installed in each vehicle. These data are then transmitted in packets where each packet consists of multiple measurement records. A given packet is uniquely identified with a packet ID, a fleet ID and a Vehicle ID. The measurement record includes multiple measurement-value tuples. Not all measurements are included in all measurement records and the type of measurements can vary from one measurement record to the next. Moreover, a given packet may not include all measurements. The structure of the measurement record consists of the following fields :

- Packet ID: unique identifier of the packet
- Fleet ID: unique identifier of the fleet
- Vehicle ID: unique identifier of the vehicle
- Measurement ID: the type of measurement
- Measurement Value: the value of the above measurement
- Timestamp: the time at which the measurement was collected.

Out of the large number of available types of measurements, three specific measurements are retained for the purpose of the current study: odometer (km), engine speed (rpm) and wheel based vehicle speed (km/hr). Since several different values of these measurements can be collected and transmitted over the operational period of the vehicle, rules are developed to aggregate the measurements into consistent variables that can be used by the proposed classifiers.

The aggregation is anchored around the odometer values. Linear interpolation is used to impute measurement records with missing odometer values from the odomoter values of their predecessor and successor measurement records. The aggregation first establishes dynamic aggregation windows that consists of a varying number of consecutive measurement records depending on the current operating mode of the vehicle.

Two distinct scenarios are considered: vehicle parked and vehicle moving. If the average speed calculated over two consecutive measurement records is less than 3 km/hr the vehicle is considered parked. Otherwise, it is considered moving. For moving vehicles, the aggregation window consists of a maximum of five consecutive measurement records or covers a maximum distance of 100 and 15 km for the first and second telematic providers, respectively. The difference in the aggregation distance between the two providers is the result of the difference in their respective data transmission rates. As mentioned above the first telematic provider is used by the coach buses and the second is used by the non-coach vehicles. The time between two consecutive transmissions is on average 1 h for the first provider and 3 min for the second provider.

For parked vehicles, all the measurement records that satisfy the 3 km average speed criteria are combined into a single aggregation window. However, special considerations are given to records that represent the transition from a moving to a parked vehicle. In order to capture the tail end of a given trip, the constraints of a maximum number of consecutive measurement records or a maximum distance are relaxed. When the vehicle is transitioning from moving to parked, the aggregation window can include two or more records irrespective of the distance covered.

Once the aggregation windows are established, the following five variables are derived for each window:

- MeanEngineSpeed and MaxEngineSpeed: the average and the maximum engine speed across the measurement records in a given aggregation window,
- MeanWheelBasedSpeed and MaxWheelBasedSpeed: the average and the maximum wheel-based speed across the measurement records in a given given aggregation window,
- AverageSpeed: the average speed is calculated from the difference in odometer and timestamp values between the first and last measurement records in the aggregation window.

Since MeanWheelBasedSpeed and AverageSpeed could reflect the same operating behavior, the calculations for MeanWheelBasedSpeed only include non-zero values. In other words, MeanWheelBasedSpeed is the average of wheel speeds when the vehicle is moving. This makes the variables MeanWheelBasedSpeed and AverageSpeed different and introduces another exposure variable that can help capture the operating profile of a given vehicle.

Until now, the label measurement record was used to represent raw data collected from the vehicle. Once the raw data is aggregated, the above five variables are calculated for each aggregation window. As a result, each aggregation window will produce an aggregated record. For simplicity, these aggregation records will be referred to as records in the remainder of the present paper. Moreover, the records associated with the vehicle parked are ignored since they include limited information about the operating profile of the vehicle. It is possible to consider the time a vehicle is parked as a potential class predictor. However, using these records was found to induce more noise in the classifiers.

3.2 Vocation Classifiers

After aggregation, the number of records available to a vehicle varies based on the raw data collected from each vehicle. For any vehicle, 49 records are randomly selected. Vehicles that do not have at least 49 records are excluded from the study. The number of selected records per vehicle is a hyper-parameter that must be tuned for each dataset. In this study, 49 records per vehicle were necessary to provide high classification accuracy. In a previous study [6], 13 records were shown to be sufficient for a more heterogeneous set of vocations. In general, a prime number of records per vehicle can help reduce ties between two vocations. Out of the vehicles that satisfy the minimum number of records criterion, 30 are randomly selected from each vocation to train the classifier and 100 are randomly selected for testing. The number of vehicles used for training is also a hyper-parameter. In this study, the goal was to reduce this number to a minimum while maintaining high classification accuracy.

Two types of vocation classifiers are constructed. The first type is based on clustering techniques and the second type uses a traditional classifier. As mentioned earlier, KM, EM and PSO are clustering techniques that can be modified in order to serve as classifiers. SVM is originally designed as a classifier and follows a supervised learning approach.

For the first type of classifiers, the profile of each vocation is defined during training. This profile consists of five records that are representative of the operating profile of the vocation. These records are often referred to as centroids and are meant to represent the space of all the records of all the vehicles in a given vocation. The number of centroids is a hyper-parameter specific to the first type of classifiers. Five centroids were previously shown to be sufficient for the vocation classification of heavy-duty vehicles [6].

Under KM, the five centroids are initialized to random records selected from the training set of vehicles in the vocation. All the records in the training vehicles are then assigned to the closest centroid using the Euclidean distance. This establishes a cluster of records around each centroid. The element-wise average of all the records in the cluster is then calculated and becomes the new centroid. This step is repeated multiple times during training.

EM uses a similar approach. However, EM is a soft classifier whereas KM is a hard classifier. That is, in EM, a record is assigned to each cluster with a given probability where to sum of all the probabilities across the five clusters is equal to one. In contrast, under KM, a record is assigned to exactly one cluster. After each iteration, the EM centroids are updated according to the new soft record assignment.

PSO is an optimization technique that can be used for clustering. This techniques keeps track of the best position achieved by each centroid from one iteration to the next. It also keeps track of the best overall position among the five centroids. The former is called the local best position for a centroid and the latter is called the global best position across all centroids. The local best position is defined according to a fitness function. In this study, the fitness function is the average of the Euclidean distance between the centroid and all the member records in its cluster. The tighter the cluster, the higher is the fitness. After each iteration, the centroid is encouraged to move towards both its local best position and the global best position according to a weighted velocity in each direction. The weights associated with each direction are hyper-parameters that are referred to as local conscience and global conscience, respectively. While both KM and EM start from a randomly selected set of centroids, PSO is initialized with the centroids that are generated by KM. This biasing technique is typically used to encourage PSO to find globally optimal positions and to reduce the amount of fine tuning needed for the local and global consciences parameters [5].

KM, EM and PSO are clustering algorithms that learn the profiles of the vocations using unsupervised training. SVM uses a supervised classifier that directly assigns the records of each vehicle to a vocation. It accomplishes this classification by first transforming the input record to a higher dimensional space which is easier to separate into two vocations using a hyperplane. Several transformations are possible. In the present paper, the Radial Basis Function (RBF) was used to create one-versus-one classifiers for each pair of vocations.

Once the classifiers are developed, they are tested using a bracket tournament approach among pairs of vocations. This approach was first introduced in [6]. Basically, the set of records belonging to an unknown vehicle are presented to a classifier that discriminates between two specific vocations. The winning vocation (i.e., the one that collects the highest number of records) is retained for the next round. When the tournament is completed, the vehicle is assigned to the vocation that survives the last round. For EM, KM and PSO, the record of each unknown vehicle must select among ten centroids in each round. For SVM, the record is classified using the corresponding one-versus-one classifier for the two vocations being considered in the round.

3.3 Fleet Classifiers

In addition to exploring vocation classification, the potential for fleet classification was also investigated. This latter investigation was motivated by two main reasons: 1) establishing the impact of the service provider and the data rate on the vocation classification and 2) developing an understanding of whether the classification of the operational profile of a heavy-duty vehicle is more appropriate at the fleet level or at the vocation level.

Towards this purpose, the CB vocation was chosen because it has a large number of fleets (Table 1). Out of the 16 available coach fleets, 5 fleets with the most number of vehicles were chosen. The remaining CB fleets did not have sufficient vehicles. Each of the selected coach bus fleet operates in a different region of the country and most likely on different routes. For each fleet, 30 vehicles were randomly selected for training and the remaining vehicles in the fleet were used for testing. For this set of fleet classifiers, there was not enough coach buses to test on 100 vehicles as previously done in the case of the vocation classification.

4   Results

The average and standard deviation of all speed variables are shown in Table 2 for each vocation. These statistics are calculated from the aggregated records of all the vehicles involved in both the training and testing. The last row of the table includes the average distance covered by an aggregation record for each vocation. These results indicate that CB vehicles have higher average distance than the other vocations. This is primarily due to the lower transmission rate of the telematic provider that services the coach buses and the maximum distance constraint for an aggregation window being equal to 100 km. This constraint also affects wheel speed for this vocation by introducing noise.

Mean wheel speed is the average of non-zero wheel speed values within an aggregation window whereas the average speed is computed from the odometer and time stamp difference. For non-CB vocations, the transmission rate of the telematic data is higher than that of the CB vocation. Therefore, for the non-CB vocations the average speed and the mean wheel speed are more in alignment. That said, some of the non-CB vocations still have frequent stops and as a result show a difference between mean wheel speed and average speed (e.g., SB).

Moreover, the engine speed for CB vehicles is on average lower than that of the other vocations. This may be due to the importance of fuel economy as an operating parameter for CB vehicles compared to other vocations. The high standard deviation of engine speed in non-CB vocations is due to the pattern of frequent stops with rapid acceleration and deceleration in the operating profiles of some of vehicles from these vocations.

4.1   Vocation Classification

Table 3 shows the precision and recall for the four vocation classifiers and the six heavy-duty vehicle vocations. For each of the methods used, other than PSO, a high precision and recall is seen for the CB vocation. As mentioned earlier, the service provider for all the CB fleets is different from the provider for all the other vocations. Given that the transmission rates for both providers are different, this can explain the high precision and recall of the CB vocation. This observation is supported by the low average engine speed values and the high average distances (last row) in Table 2 for the CB vocation compared to the other vocations.

The confusion matrices for the EM and KM classifiers (Table 5) indicate that there are three CB vehicles that were misclassified out of the entire set of 100 test CB vehicles. These vehicles belong to two fleets that did not participate in the training of the corresponding classifier. Therefore, these CB fleets were undertrained. However, a review of the results show that there were other fleets that participated in the training and operated in the same geographical region as the misclassified CB vehicles. Therefore, the CB classifier was able to develop a good overall understanding of the collective operational profile of the CB vocation despite the exclusion of some of the CB fleets from the training.

Table 2. Average and *standard deviation* for each speed variable after aggregation for all training and testing vehicles. The last row of the table includes the average and *standard deviation* of the distance covered by each vocation per aggregation window.

	CB	CT	DT	MT	RI	SB
MeanEngineSpeed	857	1299	1205	1265	1436	1453
rpm	*238*	*280*	*391*	*299*	*339*	*266*
MaxEngineSpeed	1286	1796	1828	1904	2085	2135
rpm	*305*	*279*	*403*	*344*	*369*	*277*
MeanWheelSpeed	48	50	36	32	40	35
km/hr	*35*	*24*	*25*	*19*	*31*	*14*
MaxWheelSpeed	71	89	67	64	62	68
km/hr	*40*	*23*	*30*	*27*	*33*	*18*
Average Speed	22	42	31	22	36	27
km/hr	*19*	*34*	*29*	*22*	*36*	*18*
Average Distance	115	21	33	10	19	24
km	*182*	*375*	*333*	*56*	*110*	*532*

Table 3. Precision and Recall of the KM, EM, PSO and SVM classifiers for the 100 heavy-duty test vehicles in each of the six vocations. The last row of the table includes the macro average precision and recall for each classifier.

Vocation	KM		EM		PSO		SVM	
	P(%)	R(%)	P(%)	R(%)	P(%)	R(%)	P(%)	R(%)
CB	100	97	100	97	100	39	99	98
CT	71	84	83	85	36	81	66	98
DT	82	59	84	54	19	15	86	64
MT	61	62	63	78	29	32	88	59
RI	87	82	87	82	37	34	90	91
SB	74	87	81	96	78	42	85	93
Macro Average	79	78	83	82	50	40	86	84

The macro precision and recall averages in Table 3 indicate that across all classifiers and vocations, SVM has the best performance. While every effort was made to reduce confounding among vocations, some of the vocation may still be hard to distinguish since they have similar operating profiles. For example, the CT and MT vehicles often operate over short distances and with frequent stops. Several of the MT vehicles were assigned by the SVM classifier to the CT vocation (Table 6). Moreover, the DT vocation is a large vocation that consists of delivery trucks operating in almost all the regions of the United States. The results indicate that this vocation was not properly trained as shown by the low recall rate for this vocation across all classifiers including the SVM classifier.

The SB vocation benefits from one of the highest precision and recall. This is possibly due to the fact that the two fleets that makeup this vocation are geographically localized. That is, they both operate in a single district, one in New Jersey and the other in South Carolina. In fact, since the training vehicles were selected randomly, a retrospective analysis indicated that only one vehicle from the first SB fleet participated in the training and all the remaining 29 vehicles were from the second SB fleet. However, during testing 16 vehicles were selected from the first fleet and 84 from the second fleet. Out of the 13 misclassified SB vehicles (Table 5) a disproportionate number (i.e., 4) belongs to the undertrained SB fleet. Moreover, most of the misclassified vehicles from the SB vocation were wrongly assigned to the MT vocation. This suggests that vehicles in the SB and MT vocations may have similar operating profiles. Given the potential for confounding among fleets from different vocations, a fleet rather than a vocation classifier may be more appropriate for some of the fleets as discussed in the next section.

In order to better understand the shortcomings of the PSO classifier, the centroids generated by the PSO classifier (Table 11) are compared to those produced by KM and EM (Tables 9 and 10, respectively) in the case of the SB vocation. It should be also noted that the PSO classifier is initialized with the centroids generated by the KM classifier in an effort to boost its performance. The SVM classifier is omitted from this comparison because it does not generate a profile (i.e., centroids) for each vocation. All the PSO centroids are very similar indicating that this classifier is converging to a single local minimum. While this is only shown for the SB vocation, similar trends were observed for other vocations. In contrast, the centroids generated by KM and EM are distinct and reflect different operating profiles. For instance, the mean wheel speed ranges from 12.2 to 56.6 km/hr and the average speed ranges from 11.8 to 61.4 km/hr for the KM centroids. Two alternative implementations of PSO were attempted to help create more diverse centroids. The first PSO variant introduced a third hyper-parameter that encourages the centroids to move away from the global best. The second PSO alternative encouraged the centroids to move away from the other centroids in the same vocation. Unfortunately, neither of these alternatives improved the performance of the PSO vocation classifier.

4.2 Coach Bus Fleet Classification

The same training and testing approach was applied to a subset of the CB fleets that had sufficient vehicles. The precision and recall rates for these five CB fleets with the tournament KM, EM, PSO and SVM classifiers are shown in Table 4. These results were derived from the confusion matrices in Tables 7 and 8. Among the chosen fleets, CB1, CB2, and CB5 operate in different states of the southern region of the US; CB3 operates in the northeast and CB4 operates in the west regions of the US. For each fleet, 30 vehicles were used for training and the remaining vehicles were used for testing. The number of testing vehicles for each CB fleet is shown in the first column of Table 4.

Table 4. Precision and recall of the KM, EM, PSO and SVM classifiers for the test vehicles from each of the five coach fleets. The first column of the table includes the number of test vehicles in each fleet and the last row represent the macro average precision and recall across all the five CB fleets.

Fleet	Num. of Test Vehicles	KM		EM		PSO		SVM	
		P(%)	R(%)	P(%)	R(%)	P(%)	R(%)	P(%)	R(%)
CB1	49	61	45	94	33	68	55	96	51
CB2	45	53	78	58	73	38	18	78	78
CB3	28	64	75	57	89	17	29	69	71
CB4	65	93	75	91	89	47	54	85	97
CB5	19	50	47	71	89	18	21	56	95
Macro Average		64	64	74	75	37	35	77	78

Table 4 shows lower precision and recall for the fleet classifiers compared to the vocation classifiers. However, in terms of comparative performance among the different classifiers, the same trend is observed consistently for both the vocation and fleet classifications. That is, SVM and EM have a better performance than KM with PSO having the worst performance.

Among the fleets, the worst performance is observed for CB1 and CB2. These fleets have the highest misclassification rates. In fact, 14 out of the test vehicles from CB1 were wrongly assigned to CB2 by the KM classifier (Table 7). In the case of SVM, 13 out of the test vehicles from CB1 were assigned to CB5 (Table 8). Upon further investigation and even though the CB fleets operate in different regions of the US, this confounding is possible due to similar operating conditions. The centroids produced by KM for the fleets CB1 (Table 12) and the fleet CB2 (Table 13) are in fact very similar especially for the low average speed centroids. Despite these similarities, the SVM classifier was able to achieve precision and recall rates higher than 75%.

5   Discussion

The present study investigates the potential of a tournament approach with four different classification techniques in accurately classifying heavy-duty vehicles according to their respective vocations and fleets. The proposed classifiers were trained using only five variables, all derived from the speed of the vehicle and are therefore easy to obtain.

The raw data were collected from two different telematic providers with different data transmission rates. The first telematic provider provided the data for all coach buses and the second provided the data for all the remaining vocations. The raw data were aggregated using different distance criterion for each provider according to the data transimission rate. As a result, the standard deviation of the extended aggregation distance for the CB vocation exhibits less variability than the remaining non-CB vocations. For some of these latter vocations, the standard deviation of the average distance across aggregation windows is as high as five times the mean value (Table 2). This high standard deviation is due to gaps in record transmission or collection. While this is a clear indication that raw data for non-CB vehicles includes more noise, it also allowed the classifiers to easily distinguish between the CB vehicles and the non-CB vehicles. A preprocessing step could have eliminated these noisy records. In the present study, these records were retained in order to replicate data processing in the real world as well as to highlight some of the challenges and potential pitfalls of the current application.

The above not withstanding, the classification results still show high precision and recall for the non-CB vocations. In general, the performance of SVM is the best followed by EM and KM. The performance of PSO is the lowest across all vocations. Moreover, some of the vocations are easier to identify than others. For example, with the SVM classifier, the RI vocation achieved a precision and recall of 90% and 91%, respectively (Table 3). Similarly, the SB vocation has precision and recall rates of 85% and 93%, respectively.

The same classification approach was then applied to a set of CB fleets. Both EM and SVM are able to distinguish between the fleets with a high level of precision and recall despite the fact that the fleets in this vocation may have similar operating profiles. As in the case of vocation classification, some of the fleets (e.g., CB4) were more distinguishable than other fleets. While some of the fleets tend to have more similar operating profiles (e.g., CB1 and CB2). These findings suggest that the classification results may not always align with our commercial definition of vocation or operating profiles.

While the SVM tournament classifier delivered the best performance, this approach is not without limitations. This classifier requires a total of 6×5 binary classifiers, one for each distinct pair of vocations. In comparison, the EM classifier requires only 6 vocation profiles and these are developed independently of one another. The tournament is only used for the assignment of a given vehicle to a vocation or a fleet. Thus, EM is computationally more efficient and a strong contender for SVM.

6 Conclusion

In this study, a tournament-based classification approach was proposed and demonstrated for a set of heavy-duty vocations and coach bus fleets. The data used to develop the classifiers are collected in the field from two different telematic service providers for a large number of vehicles belonging to various vocations. These data are collected at different transmission rates and the current study shows that this difference can directly impact the results of the classification. Therefore, different classifier models should be developed for different telematic service providers.

The tournament classification was implemented with four different techniques: KM, EM, PSO and SVM. The results show that PSO is hard to fine tune for the current application and delivered to worst accuracy. Both EM and SVM had precision and recall rates high enough to make the respective models suitable for the practical purpose of vocation and fleet identification.

The input features of the classifiers were derived from the speed of the vehicle and therefore can be easily obtained and shared. Despite the use of simple features and noisy data, the proposed classifiers delivered nearly 80% macro average precision and recall rates.

Several directions for future work are currently being considered. The first is the ability to define the number of clusters needed for each vocation as some of the vocations may have more variations in their profiles than others. The second direction consists of the implementation of an ensemble of classifiers that combine EM and SVM. While SVM had higher precision and recall than EM for most of the vocations, this result was not consistent across all the vocations. For instance the CT vocation was better classified with EM than SVM. The same observation is applicable to the fleet classifiers. Therefore, an ensemble classifier that uses different techniques for each vocation or fleet may lead to an increase in accuracy. Finally, some previous studies show good results with the addition of route patterns using GPS data. These data are harder to share with third parties than vehicle data and may not be widely accessible. However, it may be possible to develop route characteristics using speed and distance data (e.g., city driving versus highway driving).

Acknowledgments. This research was supported in part by Allison Transmission, Inc.

Appendix

Table 5. Confusion matrix using the KM, EM, and PSO vocation classifiers for the 100 heavy-duty test vehicles from each of the six vocations.

Vocation	KM						EM						PSO					
	CB	CT	DT	MT	RI	SB	CB	CT	DT	MT	RI	SB	CB	CT	DT	MT	RI	SB
CB	97	0	0	3	0	0	97	0	0	2	1	0	39	44	0	3	14	0
CT	0	84	2	13	1	0	0	85	1	14	0	0	0	81	19	0	0	0
DT	0	17	59	12	4	8	0	9	54	23	6	8	0	31	15	34	14	6
MT	0	7	4	62	6	21	0	3	1	78	3	15	0	2	36	32	27	3
RI	0	10	4	3	82	1	0	5	7	6	82	0	0	56	6	1	34	3
SB	0	0	3	9	1	87	0	1	1	0	2	96	0	10	4	42	2	42

Table 6. Confusion matrix using the SVM vocation classifier for the 100 heavy-duty test vehicles from each of the six vocations.

Vocation	CB	CT	DT	MT	RI	SB
CB	98	0	1	1	0	0
CT	0	98	1	0	1	0
DT	1	21	64	3	5	6
MT	0	20	7	59	4	10
RI	0	8	0	0	91	1
SB	0	2	1	4	0	93

Table 7. Confusion matrix using the KM, EM, and PSO vocation classifiers for the test vehicles from each of the coach bus fleets.

Fleet	KM					EM					PSO				
	CB1	CB2	CB3	CB4	CB5	CB1	CB2	CB3	CB4	CB5	CB1	CB2	CB3	CB4	CB5
CB1	22	14	4	0	9	16	16	9	1	7	27	1	7	8	6
CB2	1	35	5	4	0	0	33	7	5	0	2	8	12	18	5
CB3	3	4	21	0	0	1	2	25	0	0	5	3	8	9	3
CB4	2	11	3	49	0	0	4	3	58	0	0	8	18	35	4
CB5	8	2	0	0	9	0	2	0	0	17	6	1	3	5	4

Table 8. Confusion matrix using the SVM vocation classifier for the test vehicles from each of the coach bus fleets.

Fleet	SVM				
	CB1	CB2	CB3	CB4	CB5
CB1	25	1	6	4	13
CB2	0	35	3	6	1
CB3	1	7	20	0	0
CB4	0	2	0	63	0
CB5	0	0	0	1	18

Table 9. Average and *standard deviation* for each speed variable and each centroid generated by the KM classifier for the SB vocation.

Centroid	KM				
	1	2	3	4	5
MeanEngineSpeed	1155.5	1488.3	1439.7	1580.0	1664.8
	249.0	*244.0*	*217.5*	*245.7*	*289.6*
MaxEngineSpeed	1780.6	2171.1	2109.2	2197.6	2131.4
	289.2	*272.6*	*235.1*	*278.8*	*331.6*
MeanWheelSpeed	12.2	44.8	28.6	40.0	56.6
	5.9	*10.2*	*6.4*	*8.0*	*9.4*
MaxWheelSpeed	27.0	80.9	60.3	71.9	84.5
	9.7	*9.6*	*8.5*	*10.2*	*12.5*
AverageSpeed	11.8	17.6	17.9	40.0	61.4
	9.1	*8.0*	*8.7*	*8.6*	*11.7*

Table 10. Average and *standard deviation* for each speed variable and each centroid generated by the EM classifier for the SB vocation.

Centroid	EM				
	1	2	3	4	5
MeanEngineSpeed	1343.3	1049.3	1494.5	1572.3	1673.8
	244.3	*363.9*	*171.5*	*157.5*	*188.5*
MaxEngineSpeed	2013.8	1593.2	2173.4	2218.4	2146.0
	248.6	*453.4*	*171.0*	*171.6*	*218.3*
MeanWheelSpeed	27.4	24.5	29.0	41.5	57.3
	10.5	*16.5*	*4.6*	*5.2*	*7.8*
MaxWheelSpeed	56.6	45.1	61.8	75.3	84.2
	14.8	*23.5*	*8.9*	*9.8*	*10.7*
AverageSpeed	8.1	20.1	23.7	34.2	56.0
	3.0	*18.1*	*8.3*	*12.8*	*17.5*

Table 11. Average and *standard deviation* for each speed variable and each centroid generated by the PSO classifier for the SB vocation.

Centroid	PSO				
	1	2	3	4	5
MeanEngineSpeed	1536.0	1534.2	1535.9	1537.9	1535.9
	510.0	*487.5*	*330.7*	*305.7*	*310.0*
MaxEngineSpeed	2148.1	2148.3	2148.3	2145.5	2148.2
	599.4	*559.3*	*348.7*	*371.6*	*361.4*
MeanWheelSpeed	37.9	37.9	37.8	37.9	37.9
	21.2	*12.0*	*13.9*	*9.4*	*29.0*
MaxWheelSpeed	71.0	71.0	71.0	71.1	71.0
	36.4	*21.7*	*14.3*	*22.9*	*24.4*
AverageSpeed	29.6	29.7	29.7	29.7	29.7
	19.0	*14.6*	*13.6*	*13.8*	*37.3*

Table 12. Average and *standard deviation* for each speed variable and each centroid generated by the KM classifier for the CB1 fleet.

Centroid	CB1 fleet				
	1	2	3	4	5
MeanEngineSpeed	719.6	910.3	878.2	952.7	1031.7
	195.7	*165.2*	*182.6*	*176.1*	*175.1*
MaxEngineSpeed	941.0	1345.0	1310.6	1319.8	1362.7
	328.2	*239.3*	*194.9*	*190.7*	*184.3*
MeanWheelSpeed	3.9	34.4	37.3	94.4	97.7
	6.7	*13.6*	*13.8*	*13.2*	*14.7*
MaxWheelSpeed	7.2	54.6	103.6	105.3	109.8
	10.6	*11.3*	*8.7*	*10.3*	*5.0*
AverageSpeed	11.0	11.0	17.2	19.2	66.9
	4.9	*7.9*	*13.6*	*8.4*	*16.3*

Table 13. Average and *standard deviation* for each speed variable and each centroid generated by the KM classifier for the CB2 fleet.

Centroid	CB2 fleet				
	1	2	3	4	5
MeanEngineSpeed	673.6	811.1	906.8	868.3	990.9
	179.3	*176.6*	*162.7*	*155.0*	*200.3*
MaxEngineSpeed	894.4	1247.0	1312.4	1311.5	1368.7
	276.9	*243.7*	*212.9*	*199.4*	*199.7*
MeanWheelSpeed	4.2	27.8	85.1	47.4	79.7
	6.7	*13.0*	*12.2*	*12.4*	*14.2*
MaxWheelSpeed	7.7	45.3	100.4	88.9	102.8
	11.4	*10.8*	*10.3*	*12.2*	*10.4*
AverageSpeed	11.0	12.1	15.5	18.0	52.3
	5.2	*9.0*	*7.5*	*11.0*	*17.8*

References

1. Berkowicz, R., Winther, M., Ketzel, M.: Traffic pollution modelling and emission data. Environ. Model. Softw. **21**(4), 454–460 (2006). https://doi.org/10.1016/j.envsoft.2004.06.013, https://www.sciencedirect.com/science/article/pii/S136481520400307X, urban Air Quality Modelling
2. Chauhan, M.S., Singh, A., Khemka, M., Prateek, A., Sen, R.: Embedded CNN based vehicle classification and counting in non-laned road traffic. In: Proceedings of the Tenth International Conference on Information and Communication Technologies and Development. ICTD 2019, Association for Computing Machinery, New York, NY, USA (2019). https://doi.org/10.1145/3287098.3287118

3. Duan, K.-B., Keerthi, S.S.: Which is the best multiclass SVM method? an empirical study. In: Oza, N.C., Polikar, R., Kittler, J., Roli, F. (eds.) MCS 2005. LNCS, vol. 3541, pp. 278–285. Springer, Heidelberg (2005). https://doi.org/10.1007/11494683_28

4. Javadi, S., Rameez, M., Dahl, M., Pettersson, M.I.: Vehicle classification based on multiple fuzzy c-means clustering using dimensions and speed features. Procedia Comput. Sci. **126**, 1344–1350 (2018). https://doi.org/10.1016/j.procs.2018.08.085, https://www.sciencedirect.com/science/article/pii/S1877050918313632, knowledge-Based and Intelligent Information & Engineering Systems: Proceedings of the 22nd International Conference, KES-2018, Belgrade, Serbia

5. Kennedy, J., Eberhart, R.: Particle swarm optimization. In: Proceedings of ICNN 1995 - International Conference on Neural Networks, vol. 4, pp. 1942–1948 (1995). https://doi.org/10.1109/ICNN.1995.488968

6. Kobold Jr., D., Byerly., A., Bagwe., R., Santos Jr., E., Ben Miled., Z.: Vocation identification for heavy-duty vehicles: a tournament bracket approach. In: Proceedings of the 7th International Conference on Vehicle Technology and Intelligent Transport Systems - VEHITS, pp. 259–266. INSTICC, SciTePress (2021). https://doi.org/10.5220/0010298702590266

7. Krishna, K., Narasimha Murty, M.: Genetic k-means algorithm. IEEE Trans. Syst. Man Cybern. Part B (Cybern.) **29**(3), 433–439 (1999). https://doi.org/10.1109/3477.764879

8. Madzarov, G., Gjorgjevikj, D.: Multi-class classification using support vector machines in decision tree architecture. In: IEEE EUROCON 2009, pp. 288–295 (2009). https://doi.org/10.1109/EURCON.2009.5167645

9. Meyer, S., Krumme, U.: Disentangling complexity of fishing fleets: using sequence analysis to classify distinguishable groups of vessels based on commercial landings. Fish. Manag. Ecol. **28**(3), 268–282 (2021). https://doi.org/10.1111/fme.12472, https://onlinelibrary.wiley.com/doi/abs/10.1111/fme.12472

10. Moon, T.: The expectation-maximization algorithm. IEEE Signal Process. Mag. **13**(6), 47–60 (1996). https://doi.org/10.1109/79.543975

11. Peng, J., Parnell, J., Kessissoglou, N.: A six-category heavy vehicle noise emission model in free-flowing condition. Appl. Acoust. **143**, 211–221 (2019). https://doi.org/10.1016/j.apacoust.2018.08.030, https://www.sciencedirect.com/science/article/pii/S0003682X18303591

12. Sambo, F., Salti, S., Bravi, L., Simoncini, M., Taccari, L., Lori, A.: Integration of GPS and satellite images for detection and classification of fleet hotspots. In: 2017 IEEE 20th International Conference on Intelligent Transportation Systems (ITSC), pp. 1–6 (2017). https://doi.org/10.1109/ITSC.2017.8317636

13. Schölkopf, B., Smola, A.J., Bach, F., et al.: Learning with Kernels: Support Vector Machines, Regularization, Optimization, and Beyond. MIT press (2002)

14. Simoncini, M., Taccari, L., Sambo, F., Bravi, L., Salti, S., Lori, A.: Vehicle classification from low-frequency GPS data with recurrent neural networks. Transp. Res. Part C Emerg. Technol. **91**, 176–191 (2018). https://doi.org/10.1016/j.trc.2018.03.024, https://www.sciencedirect.com/science/article/pii/S0968090X18304017

15. Soofi, A.A., Awan, A.: Classification techniques in machine learning: applications and issues. J. Basic Appl. Sci. **13**, 459–465 (2017). https://doi.org/10.6000/1927-5129.2017.13.76

A New Traffic Sign Detection Technique Using Two-Stage Convolutional Neural Networks

Huei-Yung Lin[1(✉)] and Ying-Chi Chiu[2]

[1] Department of Computer Science and Information Engineering,
National Taipei University of Technology, 1, Sec. 3, Zhongxiao E. Rd., Taipei 10608, Taiwan
`lin@ntut.edu.tw`
[2] Department of Electrical Engineering, National Chung Cheng University,
168 University Rd., Chiayi 621, Taiwan

Abstract. In the past few decades, the advanced driver assistance systems (ADAS) have achieved great advances. Many computer vision based techniques have been proposed for traffic scene understanding using on-board cameras. One important task is detection and recognition of traffic signs to provide the road conditions for drivers. In this paper, a two-stage approach is proposed for traffic sign detection and classification with real scene images. In the first detection network, we adopt Faster R-CNN to detect the locations of traffic signs. The parameter setting is designed to achieve a very low miss rate at the cost of increasing false positives. This is then passed to the classification networks with ResNet, VGG and SVM for traffic sign validation. The public dataset TT100K and the images collected from Taiwan road scenes are used for network training and testing. Our proposed technique is carried out the videos acquired from highway, suburb and urban scenarios. The experimental results obtained using Faster R-CNN for detection combined with VGG for classification have demonstrated its superior performance compared to YOLOv3 and Mask R-CNN.

Keywords: Traffic sign detection · Traffic sign classification · Advanced driver assistance systems (ADAS) · Two-stage network

1 Introduction

In the past few years, advanced driver assistance systems (ADAS) have achieved great advances and provided practical solutions for the real world applications. A number of techniques are proposed for traffic scene understanding using on-board cameras, which is then utilized for high level decision making. Among the existing ADAS modules, the implementation for detection and recognition of traffic signs is specifically important for road safety. The indispensable information extracted from road scene images is provided for drivers or autonomous vehicles to comply with the traffic laws and regulations [11]. Some major traffic accidents occasionally occurred when drivers did not pay enough attention to the road signs. However, the detection of traffic signs in the outdoor environments have many difficulties such as occlusion, distortion and lighting, etc. To deal with these problems, many traditional methods utilizing image features,

© Springer Nature Switzerland AG 2022
C. Klein et al. (Eds.): SMARTGREENS 2021/ VEHITS 2021, CCIS 1612, pp. 216–231, 2022.
https://doi.org/10.1007/978-3-031-17098-0_11

including color, shape and gradient, are proposed to detect and recognize traffic signs [9]. Nevertheless, the approach is still restricted to certain application scenarios.

In the early work, Kiran *et al.* presented a technique for traffic sign detection using color-based segmentation [10]. The product of enhanced hue and saturation components were adopted to achieve better segmentation results. An edge-based approach was then followed to extract feature vectors for traffic pattern classification using support vector machine (SVM). Wahyono *et al.* extracted possible traffic sign locations using MSER (maximally stable extremal regions) on red and color regions [24]. The geometric properties of traffic signs were then used to remove incorrect region candidates. Finally, a cascade support vector machine classifier was adopted for traffic sign classification. In [20], Shao *et al.* presented a real-time traffic sign detection and recognition technique. Their two-stage approach had first the image segmentation carried out by MSER on a Gabor filter feature map, followed by filtering based on the pre-defined rules such as size and aspect ratio of the traffic sign. In the traffic sign detection stage, triangular and circular shapes were classified using HOG features by SVM. A convolutional neural network (CNN) was then adopted for traffic sign classification.

Recently, deep learning based techniques have made significant progress for object detection and classification. Many deep neural network architectures are constructed specifically for vehicle related applications. The techniques for detection and classification of road signs have also been greatly improved using the deep learning approaches. Saha *et al.* presented a method to classify traffic sign images based on existing neural network structures [19]. By using a planted master network followed by the modified architectures of VGG and GoogLeNet, the number of parameters was reduced while maintaining the classification accuracy. In [23], Tabernik and D. Skǒcaj proposed a technique for road sign detection and classification in large scale scenes. Their method was based on Mask R-CNN and Detectron [6,7], with an online hard-example mining (OHEM) module [21]. The datasets collected using digital video recorders (DVRs) for more than 200 types were utilized for training and testing. One major disadvantage of their presented was the computational load. The detection and recognition took 0.5 s per image.

In [16,28], Zhang *et al.* modified the YOLOv2 model [16] with several changes to the network architecture, and then compared the accuracy and recall. In their implementation, the traffic signs were divided into three categories for detection and classification, which included 'mandatory', 'danger' and 'prohibitory' classes. Alternatively, Rajendran *et al.* improved the accuracy of YOLOv3 for traffic sign detection and recognition by changing the size of anchor boxes [15,17]. They have performed the evaluation on German traffic sign detection benchmark (GTSDB) and German traffic sign recognition benchmark (GTSRB) datasets for both the detection and recognition. Arcos-Garcia *et al.* provided the empirical evaluation and experimental comparison of several deep neural network based traffic sign detectors [1]. The network models, including Faster R-CNN, R-FCN, SSD and YOLOv2, were trained on Microsoft COCO dataset and tested on the GTSDB dataset with three categories mandatory, danger and prohibitory. Some performance issues have been addressed along with different feature extraction networks.

In addition to the above literatures, there also exist many works using public datasets for the evaluation of road sign detection and recognition algorithms [12,14,26]. Among the public road scene datasets currently available, most of them were collected in the US and Europe. However, there are still some variations on the traffic signs in many different countries. As shown in Table 1, the number of classes, images, as well as the resolution are very different when collected from Germany, US, Solvenian and China. The available datasets include GTSDB, GTSRB, DFG, LISA and TT100K. Some of them are mainly used for traffic sign detection, and there is also for recognition purpose. The network models developed and trained on different road scene datasets might have different traffic sign recognition results.

Table 1. The comparison of various public datasets for traffic sign detection and recognition. GTSDB [8], GTSRB [22], DFG [23], LISA [13], TT100K [29]. The traffic signs are not all identical for different countries.

	GTSDB	GTSRB	DFG	LISA	TT100K
Resolution	1360 × 800	15 × 15 | 250 × 250	1920 × 1080	640 × 640 | 1024 × 522	2048 × 2048
Number of images	900	over 50,000	7,000	6,610	100,000
Number of classes	3	43	200	47	221
Usage	Detection	Classification	Detection	Detection	Detection
Country	Germany	Germany	Slovenian	USA	China

This paper presents a new convolutional neural network technique for traffic sign detection. It is an extension of our previous work on a two-stage learning approach for traffic sign detection and recognition [2]. First, Faster R-CNN implemented in Detectron is used as the backbone of our traffic sign detection framework [18]. We adopt a fairly loose criterion to detect the possible traffic signs to ensure the lowest miss rate in the first stage. With a low threshold setting for the detection, there might contain a large number of false positives similar to traffic signs from the background regions. This detection result is then passed to the second stage of our proposed system flow to recognize the traffic sign individually. In the recognition stage, two different approaches, SVM and CNN, are adopted for traffic sign classification. The public dataset TT100K is mainly used for our training and testing [29]. In addition, we also collect our own traffic scene datasets since the traffic signs are not identical for many different countries [3]. It is required to increase the number of samples for network training.

In our implementation, the images with resolution of 512×512 in the datasets are used in the first stage for traffic sign detection. As for the second recognition stage, the road sign sub-image region extracted from the first detection stage are used for training and testing. However, due to many problems in general outdoor scenes such as occlusion and image blur, it is a difficult task to classify the small size road sign image regions into specific categories. To cope with this issue, we define a minimum size of 25×25 pixels for traffic sign recognition. In this case, it roughly corresponds to about 50–60 m from the camera we used in the experiments. Currently, there are 22 types of traffic signs considered for detection and recognition based on the frequency of appearance in the road scenes. The number of traffic sign categories will be gradually increased as more images are collected for annotation in the future.

2   The Proposed Approach

In this work, a new two-stage approach is proposed to improve the accuracy of traffic sign detection and recognition built on up of the existing machine learning algorithms and neural network structures. The system flowchart of our proposed technique is illustrated in Fig. 1. Given an input road scene image, the first stage focuses on the detection of traffic signs and their locations. It is then followed by the second stage for the traffic sign classification using the extracted regions of interest. Different from the commonly adopted two-stage object detectors such as R-CNN and Faster R-CNN [5, 18], the idea of our two-stage approach is based on a sophisticated filtering process. The first stage is designated to achieve a very low miss rate while disregarding the number of possible false positives. All of the candidates are then carried out to the second recognition stage for the further validation and classification of traffic signs.

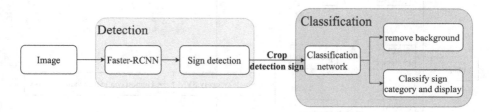

Fig. 1. The system flowchart of the proposed two-stage traffic sign detection and recognition technique. It consists of the first detection stage aims to achieve a low miss rate, followed by the second recognition to classify and validate the detected traffic signs [2].

2.1 Detection Network

Our first stage detection network is constructed based on Detectron, with Faster R-CNN+ResNet50 [6]. It is used to detect the possible traffic signs and calculate the miss rate (or false negative rate, FNR) given by

$$FNR = \frac{FN}{FN + TP} \tag{1}$$

where FN and TP are the numbers of false negatives and true positives, respectively. Compared with the general techniques for traffic sign detection, the most common problem in the proposed approach is the difficulty to tell the difference between the traffic signs and signboards in similar shapes.

In this work, we adopt Faster R-CNN as the detection framework because of its low miss rate and high accuracy on general objects. One of the most important architectures of the network model is the Region Proposal Network (RPN). It utilizes softmax to distinguish the foreground regions from the background, and adopts the bounding box regression to correct the anchor position. There contain two paths and a proposal layer in the RPN to eliminate the smaller and out-of-bounds proposals. Our first stage traffic sign detection network also incorporates Feature Pyramid Network (FPN) by fusing the higher level and low-level features [25]. We combine the semantic features from the high convolutional layers with the features from the low convolutional layers to improve the accuracy of target detection. In addition to the detection of individual traffic signs in the first stage, we also perform the experiments which divide the detection results into three categories, mandatory, danger and prohibitory.

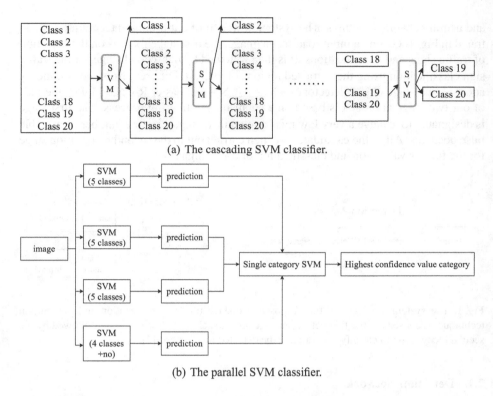

(a) The cascading SVM classifier.

(b) The parallel SVM classifier.

Fig. 2. Two different SVM variations (cascading and parallel) used for the second stage [2]. (a) The implementation with all SVMs connected in series. (b) The parallel SVMs for initial predictions, followed by another SVM to select the one with the highest confidence value.

2.2 Classification Network

For traffic sign recognition, possible candidate regions detected in the first stage are extracted from the input images, and only the classes of interest are used for network training in the second stage. A total number of 22 most common types of traffic signs plus an additional non-sign category are selected for classification. These road sign types are further divided into 1 category for 'danger', 2 categories for 'mandatory' and 19 categories for 'prohibition'.

In our second recognition stage, SVM, VGG16, ResNet and SE-ResNet are adopted for traffic sign classification. For the SVM classifiers, HOG (Histogram of Oriented Gradient) features are used for training [24, 27]. The first approach is setting one category versus the rest categories. Figure 2(a) illustrates the implementation with all SVMs connected in series. A second approach is to utilize the parallel SVMs for initial predictions. It is then followed by another SVM to select the one with the highest confidence value. Figure 2(b) shows the parallel SVM structure for traffic sign classification. One major drawback of these two approaches is the computational speed. Thus, we have further investigated other machine learning techniques.

For the deep neural network based methods, both VGG16 and ResNet have achieved good performance in ImageNet classification competition [4]. VGG16 has a relatively simple network structure. It contains 13 convolutional layers, 5 pooling layers and 3 fully connected layers. The input image size, batch size and learning rate are set as 224×224, 32 and 0.002, respectively, in the implementation. It is noted that the network training will stop due to insufficient memory if the batch size is set as 64. We trained the VGG16 network with roughly 900 epochs and the weights are stored for every 300 epochs. Finally, the model with the highest accuracy is used for testing. The second network adopted for traffic sign classification is ResNet. It is a residual network which is able to deal with the problem of information loss caused by too many convolutional layers. Moreover, we use SE-ResNet with the SE (Squeeze-and-Excitation) module inserted into the residual structure of ResNet. The important and unimportant features can then be enhanced and weakened by controlling the scale size. In our implementation of ResNet and SE-ResNet for traffic sign recognition, the network parameters are given as follows: the input image size for training: 40×40, the batch size: 64, the learning rate: 0.002, the training epoch: 3000. The weights in these models are also stored for every 300 epochs. For all cases, we use cross-entropy for the loss function and stochastic gradient descent (SGD) for the deep learning models.

3 The Dataset

Most of public datasets for traffic sign detection and recognition were collected in the United States and Europe. However, the traffic signs are not all identical for different countries. For example, the complexity of traffic scenes in Taiwan is different from the US, Europe and China. There are many motorcycles on the streets in the urban areas, but it is relatively uncommon in the western countries. In the latest investigation, the public traffic dataset TT100K is by far the most suitable for the network training used to detect the traffic signs in Taiwan's road scenes. All types of traffic signs in TT100K are illustrated in Fig. 3. Since there are still some discrepancies between our application scenario and the images in the dataset (such as no danger signs), we further include self-labeled Taiwan road scene images for network training and testing. In addition to the still images, we also perform video testing. The image sequences are captured by an on-board digital video recorder (DVR) with the original resolution of 1280×800.

There are totally 23 categories (including 1 non-sign category) in the dataset for the first stage detection, with 29,659 images for network training and 15,766 images for testing. To improve the traffic sign detection result in terms of the accuracy and its location, the input images are cropped into multiple 512×512 regions. A sliding window is carried out on the image starting from the upper left corner to detect the traffic signs in the extracted region. The stride of the sliding windows is set as 400, and each movement has an overlap of 112 pixels to minimize the possibility of miss detection. We have ensured that if there is a sign in an ROI (region of interest), it will be cropped into a 512×512 image.

For the second recognition stage, the traffic sign regions are extracted from the images in TT100K and our dataset for classification. There are totally 10,474 (including 711 background) images for training and 4,496 (including 55 background) images for testing in 23 categories. We use the extracted background regions as training samples to reject the false positives (FP) shown in the detection stage. These images are

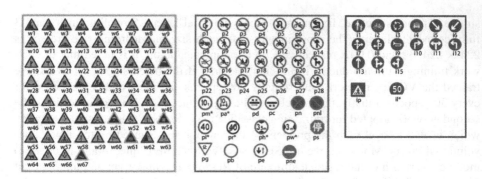

Fig. 3. All types of traffic signs in the public dataset TT100K. It is mainly used in this work for initial network training [2]. Since there are differences between our application scenario and the images in TT100K (such as no danger signs), we further include self-labeled Taiwan road scene images for training and testing.

extracted from the false detection results, and aim to be used for training the classification network. A number of false positives of the traffic signs detected in the first stage and adopted as the training samples in the second stage classification are shown in Fig. 4. The images do contain some features or characteristics, which are prone to be recognized as common traffic signs.

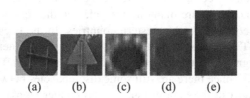

(a)   (b)   (c)   (d)   (e)

Fig. 4. Some false positives of the traffic signed detected in the first stage and used as the training samples in the second stage classification [2].

(a) Some examples of cropped traffic sign images from TT100K.

(b) Some examples of cropped traffic sign images captured by the vehicle on-board camera.

Fig. 5. Examples of cropped traffic sign region from TT100K and vehicle on-board camera. The images captured by the on-board digital video recorder are generally blurry and noisy compared to most TT100K dataset images [2].

In real application scenarios, we are mainly interested in traffic sign detection from the images acquired by on-board digital video recorders. However, TT100K is used to provide about 80% of images for network training. The dataset contains primary the still images. They are generally different from those image sequences recorded when the vehicle is in motion (which might introduce severe blur and noise). As illustrated in Figs. 5(a) and 5(b), the images captured by the on-board digital video recorder are blurry and noisy compared to most TT100K dataset images. Consequently, an image pre-processing step is first carried out to make the dataset images degraded and close to the recorded video data. For traffic sign detection and recognition, Fig. 6 illustrates the two-stage processing flowchart with three-category detection. It is noted that the traffic signs are detected with different categories in the first stage, followed by the classification in the same category.

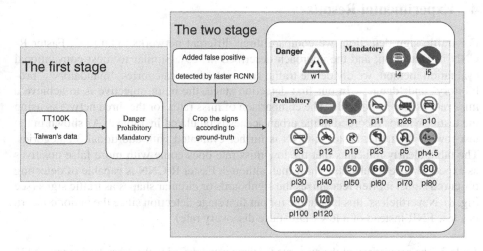

Fig. 6. The two-stage processing flowchart with three-category detection [2]. The network training of the first stage is for all signs or three categories. In the second stage, the background false positives are added for training.

To create a more realistic testing environment for traffic sign detection and recognition algorithms, we generate three types of testing scenarios which consist of the videos acquired in highway, suburb and urban driving. There are totally 6 real scene videos are used for testing, with each scenario containing two image sequences. The videos are also generated with high speed playback for the areas without traffic signs to facilitate the evaluation of detection and recognition algorithms. All testing videos are created with about 3-min long, and contain approximately 5,400 image frames. The input images with resolution of 1280×800 are cropped with a 612×612 ROI for further processing, as illustrated in Fig. 7. With these restricted regions of interest for processing, the detection speed and accuracy can be greatly improved since some unnecessary areas such as sidewalks and opposite lanes are removed [3].

Fig. 7. The input images with resolution of 1280×800 are cropped with a 612×612 ROI for further processing.

4   Experimental Results

For traffic sign detection, we compare three different networks: YOLOv3, Faster R-CNN in Detectron, and the approach described in [29]. Similar to most conventional evaluation method, we divide the traffic signs into three categories, 'mandatory', 'prohibitory' and 'danger'. In our first detection stage, the main objective is to achieve a miss rate as low as possible. The comparison of miss rates for the three networks using the testing videos recorded in the urban scenes is tabulated in Table 2. As shown in the last row of the table, Faster R-CNN is further evaluated with additional 3 categories. The table clearly indicates that the low miss rate does come with more false positives as expected. The results also show that, although Faster R-CNN is capable of detecting obscured signs, it often recognizes the signboards or circular shapes as traffic signs (see Fig. 8). Nevertheless, this is suitable for our first stage detection since the major concern is a low FNR instead of a low FDR (false discovery rate).

Table 2. The comparison of the miss rate for three networks using the urban testing videos [2]. Faster R-CNN is also evaluated with additional 3 categories. It is indicated in the table that the low miss rate usually comes with more false positives. Only the traffic signs larger than 25×25 in the videos are considered.

	Miss rate	# of Signs	# of Missed	False positive
YOLOv3	0.0796	1,257	100	1,766
Mask R-CNN	0.0387	1,257	68	1,995
Faster R-CNN	0.0135	1,257	17	1,985
Faster R-CNN (3 classes)	0.0220	1,257	50	1,436

For the second recognition stage, two different classification approaches are evaluated for comparison. The first approach is to use a still image dataset which contains 80% and 20% of the images from TT100K and our dataset, respectively, for testing. The second evaluation method is taking the 6 video sequences created from highway, suburb and urban road scenes as described in the previous section as inputs. Since the

(a)   (b)

Fig. 8. Although faster R-CNN is capable of detecting obscured signs, it often recognizes the signboards or circular shapes as traffic signs.

Fig. 9. Some traffic signs images captured with unusual viewpoints in the TT100K datasets.

testing sets are the output of the first stage detection results, the accuracy evaluation of this stage is purely for the traffic sign classification and recognition.

There are two approaches adopted for the first stage in the implementation: one is to detect the traffic signs without classification, and the other is to identify and classify the traffic signs into three given categories, mandatory, danger and prohibition. Consequently, there will be four different classification networks to be trained separately. It is important to notice that, if the second approach is providing an incorrect category, the subsequent classification network will always derive wrong traffic sign recognition results. On the other hand, the first approach does not have such issue but at the cost of resulting in a higher false positive rate.

First, we consider the traffic sign classification for the mandatory category. As shown in Fig. 6, there are currently two different traffic signs denoted by 'i4' and 'i5' for evaluation. The experimental results of Image Test and Video Test using two classifiers, ResNet18 and SVM, are tabulated in Table 3. In the table, it shows that the better accuracy was derived for the video inputs compared to the still image inputs. This is caused by some unusual viewpoints of traffic signs appeared in TT100K testing images (see Fig. 9). However, our video testing dataset contains the images all captured with

Table 3. The evaluation of image test and video test using two classifiers, ResNet18 and SVM for the mandatory category [2]. 'i4' and 'i5' are the traffic signs shown in Fig. 6. 'i4' is not available in Video Test because it does not appear in our test video. The input image size to ResNet18 is 40×40.

	Image test		Video test	
Classifier	ResNet18	SVM	ResNet18	SVM
mAP	81.53%	79.387%	95.42%	95.38%
i4	86.06%	93.97%	–	–
i5	86.07%	98.37%	97.35%	99.77%
Non-sign	72.45%	45.79%	93.49%	91.00%

Table 4. The evaluation of Image Test and Video Test using two classifiers, ResNet18 and SVM for the danger category [2]. 'w1' is the traffic signs shown in Fig. 6. The input image size to ResNet18 is 40×40.

	Classifier	mAP	w1	Non-sign
Image test	ResNet18	83.6%	90.01%	77.2%
	SVM	97.46%	98.55%	96.36%
Video test	ResNet18	75.77%	98.33%	53.21%
	SVM	46.23%	72%	20.45%

the camera facing the traffic signs. For the danger category, there is only a single traffic sign and denoted by 'w1', as shown in Fig. 6. Table 4 shows the classification results using ResNet18 and SVM for Image Test and Video Test. As illustrated in the table, the accuracy of SVM is higher in Image Test while the accuracy of ResNet18 is higher in Video Test. It is mainly due to many triangular signs detected in the first stage, as shown in Fig. 10, are considered as 'w1' for training in the second stage.

In our experiments, there are totally 19 types of prohibitory traffic signs for testing, and the recognition is much more challenging than danger and mandatory categories. We have tested several classifiers, including various SVM implementations, VGG16, ResNet18 and SE-ResNet50. The evaluation results and comparison are tabulated in Table 5. As shown in the table, there is a big difference between the accuracy of Image Test and Video Test. This is caused by the low image quality of the video testing data compared to the training images in the TT100K dataset. To deal with the problem, we incorporated Gaussian blur and Gaussian noise to TT100K images for training. Some examples of the processed images are shown in Fig. 11. They can be considered as the transferred version of TT100K dataset images to the on-board camera images.

To evaluate the effectiveness of the proposed pre-processing approach on the dataset images, we perform an additional Image Test and Video Test using only the pre-processed TT100K images (without the use of Taiwan road scene images) for training. The evaluation shows the mAPs of Image Test and Video Test without image pre-processing using ResNet18 are 79.42% and 42.67%, respectively. After the dataset images are incorporated for training, the mAPs are increased to 79.88% and 45.61%,

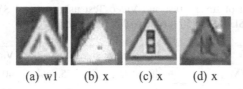

(a) w1   (b) x   (c) x   (d) x

Fig. 10. The correct and incorrect triangular signs detected in the first stage. Many triangular signs detected in the first stage are considered as 'w1' for training in the second stage [2].

Fig. 11. The TT100K images post-processed with Gaussian blur and Gaussian noise to simulate more realistic road scene images captured by the on-board camera for network training [2].

respectively. It shows only a slight improvement on Video Test using ResNet18. Table 6 tabulates the evaluation of the pre-processing approach on the TT100K dataset and Taiwan road scene images using ResNet18. When we examined the resulting images, it was found that some detection results were worse if the pre-processed training data were used. This could be the result of over-filtering from some low quality images in the TT100K dataset. To address this issue, image sharpness and Laplacian edge blur degree are used as thresholds for image filtering. The evaluation and comparison of SE-ResNet50 and VGG16 with various dataset image alteration are tabulated in Table 7.

From the experiments and analysis for the traffic sign detection on the three categories separately, VGG16 has the best detection accuracy for the prohibitory signs. Thus, we use it as the framework for the direct detection for all signs in 23 classes without the initial mandatory, danger and prohibitory classification. The resolution of training images is set as 224×224. The mAPs of Image Test and Video Test are 83.41% and 78.57%, respectively. It is noted that, when compared to the case with the three categories separated in the first stage, the miss rates are lower but the classification mAPs are similar.

For the two-stage network using Faster R-CNN combined with classifiers, we adopt SE-ResNet50 as the basic model. As the evaluation results and comparison tabulated in Table 8, the mAP of 80.86% is achieved for the urban scene videos. Our results using Faster R-CNN+VGG16 without and with setting 3 categories for detection are shown in the first and second rows. The third row in the table illustrates the results using Mask R-CNN [23] with the network training carried out on our dataset. The evaluation results using Faster R-CNN and YOLOv3 are tabulated in the fourth and last rows, respectively.

Table 5. The evaluation of Image Test and Video Test using several SVM implementations, VGG16, ResNet18 and SE-ResNet50 for the prohibitory category [2].

Classifier	Input image size	Image test	Video test
Linear SVM	40 × 40	75.66%	40.16%
RBF SVM	40 × 40	76.66%	47.07%
Cascaded SVM classifier	64 × 64	89.85%	61.77%
Cascaded SVM classifier	40 × 40	85.22%	52.35%
Parallel+Cascaded SVM	64 × 64	89.78%	60.99%
VGG16	224 × 224	80.63%	66.46%
ResNet18	40 × 40	76.25%	56.9%
SE-ResNet50	40 × 40	76.77%	66.9%

Table 6. The evaluation of the pre-processing approach on the dataset images using ResNet18 [2]. The training data are TT100K combined with Taiwan road scene images. The input image size is 40 × 40.

Classifier	Categories for pre-processing	Image test	Video test
ResNet18	–	76.25%	56.9%
ResNet18	all	76.74%	64.13%
ResNet18	pl40, pl50, pl60, p12 (Gaussian Blur)	76.12%	56.74%
ResNet18	pl40, pl50, pl60, p12 (Motion Blur)	74.6%	62.99%

Table 7. The evaluation and comparison of SE-ResNet50 and VGG16 with various dataset image alteration [2].

Classifier	Input image size	Categories for pre-processing	Image test	Video test
SE-ResNet50	40	–	76.77%	64.42%
SE-ResNet50	40	pl40, pl50, pl60, p12	78.63%	75.34%
SE-ResNet50	40	All	79.41%	71.34%
VGG16	224	no	80.63%	66.64%
VGG16	224	all	83.54%	77.9%

In the last experiments, we we re-train the proposed networks using GTSDB and GTSRB and, compare the results with the technique presented by Yang *et al.* [25]. Their approach first extracts the traffic signs using a color probability model and classify them into three categories using an SVM, and then followed by a CNN for the recognition of individual traffic signs. Our classification accuracy using VGG16 in the GTSRB dataset is 97.68% for prohibition and restriction, 86.33% for compliance, and 93.62% for warning categories, respectively. The overall accuracy is 97.43%, compared to 97.75% as presented in [25]. It is mainly due to the low recognition rate for the compliance category. Furthermore, the calculation is different because our algorithm counts all targets but their method is based on the detected signs.

Table 8. The comparison of the proposed two-stage network using Faster R-CNN combined with classifiers evaluated on urban scene videos. The first and second rows show our results using Faster R-CNN+VGG16 without and with setting 3 categories for detection. The third row shows the results using Mask R-CNN and trained on our dataset. The fourth and last rows are the result of using Faster R-CNN and YOLOv3, respectively. The computation time is given per fame [2].

	mAP	P23	p5	i5	p19	pl50	Computation time
Faster R-CNN (1class) with VGG16	80.86%	0.81%	0.74%	0.87%	0.91%	0.71%	0.087 + 0.02 s
Faster R-CNN (3class) with VGG16	72.05%	0.77%	0.77%	0.36%	0.84%	0.87%	0.087 + 0.02 s
Mask R-CNN	54.92%	0.57%	0.6%	0.57%	0.5%	0.5%	0.94 s
Faster R-CNN	61.6%	0.76%	0.28%	0.88%	0.52%	0.28%	0.10 s
YOLOv3	53.55%	0.74%	0.33%	0.6%	0.52%	0.48%	0.03 s

5 Conclusions

Advanced driver assistance systems have achieved great advances and adopted for real world applications in the past few years. Many techniques are proposed for traffic scene understanding using on-board cameras. This paper presents a new traffic sign detection technique using two-stage convolutional neural networks. In the proposed approach, we first utilize Faster R-CNN and set a lower threshold to detect any possible traffic signs with a low miss rate. It is then followed by the subsequently stage to recognize the type of a specific traffic sign using another classifier. In the experiments, the discrepancy between the training dataset and the road scene images recorded by on-board is analyzed. We also perform an image pre-processing stage to make the image quality of the public dataset similar to the testing data. The proposed two-stage traffic sign detection and recognition has achieved the mAP of over 80% on testing videos. It is superior to the mAPs of about 50% obtained from YOLOv3 and Mask R-CNN. The future work will focus on integrating more recent detection networks in our two-stage approach for traffic sign recognition. It is possible to improve the detection rate without altering the system flow and overall structure.

Acknowledgments. The support of this work in part by Create Electronic Optical Co., LTD, Taiwan and the Ministry of Science and Technology of Taiwan under Grant MOST 106-2221-E-194-004, is gratefully acknowledged.

References

1. Arcos-Garcia, A., Alvarez-Garcia, J.A., Soria-Morillo, L.M.: Evaluation of deep neural networks for traffic sign detection systems. Neurocomputing **316**, 332–344 (2018)
2. Chiu, Y.C., Lin, H.Y.: A two-stage learning approach for traffic sign detection and recognition. In: The 7th International Conference on Vehicle Technology and Intelligent Transport Systems. Prague, Czech, (VEHITS) (2021)
3. Chiu, Y.C., Lin, H.Y., Tai, W.L.: Implementation and evaluation of CNN based traffic sign detection with different resolutions. In: 2019 International Symposium on Intelligent Signal Processing and Communication Systems (ISPACS), pp. 1–2 (2019). https://doi.org/10.1109/ISPACS48206.2019.8986319

4. Deng, J., Dong, W., Socher, R., Li, L.J., Li, K., Fei-Fei, L.: Imagenet: a large-scale hierarchical image database. In: 2009 IEEE Conference on Computer Vision and Pattern Recognition, pp. 248–255 (2009). https://doi.org/10.1109/CVPR.2009.5206848
5. Girshick, R., Donahue, J., Darrell, T., Malik, J.: Rich feature hierarchies for accurate object detection and semantic segmentation. In: 2014 IEEE Conference on Computer Vision and Pattern Recognition, pp. 580–587 (2014)
6. Girshick, R., Radosavovic, I., Gkioxari, G., Dollár, P., He, K.: Detectron (2018). https://github.com/facebookresearch/detectron
7. He, K., Gkioxari, G., Dollár, P., Girshick, R.: Mask r-cnn. In: 2017 IEEE International Conference on Computer Vision (ICCV), pp. 2980–2988 (2017)
8. Houben, S., Stallkamp, J., Salmen, J., Schlipsing, M., Igel, C.: Detection of traffic signs in real-world images: the German traffic sign detection benchmark. In: The 2013 International Joint Conference on Neural Networks (IJCNN), pp. 1–8 (2013)
9. Huang, S.C., Lin, H.Y., Chang, C.C.: An in-car camera system for traffic sign detection and recognition. In: 2017 Joint 17th World Congress of International Fuzzy Systems Association and 9th International Conference on Soft Computing and Intelligent Systems (IFSA-SCIS), pp. 1–6 (2017). https://doi.org/10.1109/IFSA-SCIS.2017.8023239
10. Kiran, C., Prabhu, L.V., V., A.R., Rajeev, K.: Traffic sign detection and pattern recognition using support vector machine. In: 2009 Seventh International Conference on Advances in Pattern Recognition, pp. 87–90 (2009). https://doi.org/10.1109/ICAPR.2009.58
11. Lin, H.Y., Chang, C.C., Tran, V.L., Shi, J.H.: Improved traffic sign recognition for in-car cameras. J. Chin. Inst. Eng. **43**(3), 300–307 (2020). https://doi.org/10.1080/02533839.2019.1708801
12. Liu, C., Li, S., Chang, F., Wang, Y.: Machine vision based traffic sign detection methods: review, analyses and perspectives. IEEE Access **7**, 86578–86596 (2019)
13. Mogelmose, A., Trivedi, M.M., Moeslund, T.B.: Vision-based traffic sign detection and analysis for intelligent driver assistance systems: perspectives and survey. IEEE Trans. Intell. Transp. Syst. **13**(4), 1484–1497 (2012)
14. Philipsen, M.P., Jensen, M.B., Møgelmose, A., Moeslund, T.B., Trivedi, M.M.: Traffic light detection: a learning algorithm and evaluations on challenging dataset. In: 2015 IEEE 18th International Conference on Intelligent Transportation Systems, pp. 2341–2345 (2015)
15. Rajendran, S.P., Shine, L., Pradeep, R., Vijayaraghavan, S.: Real-time traffic sign recognition using YOLOv3 based detector. In: 2019 10th International Conference on Computing, Communication and Networking Technologies (ICCCNT). pp. 1–7 (2019)
16. Redmon, J., Farhadi, A.: Yolo9000: better, faster, stronger. In: 2017 IEEE Conference on Computer Vision and Pattern Recognition (CVPR), pp. 6517–6525 (2017). https://doi.org/10.1109/CVPR.2017.690
17. Redmon, J., Farhadi, A.: Yolov3: an incremental improvement (2018)
18. Ren, S., He, K., Girshick, R., Sun, J.: Faster r-cnn: towards real-time object detection with region proposal networks. In: Proceedings of the 28th International Conference on Neural Information Processing Systems - Volume 1, pp. 91–99. NIPS 2015, MIT Press, Cambridge, MA, USA (2015)
19. Saha, S., Islam, M.S., Khaled, M.A.B., Tairin, S.: An efficient traffic sign recognition approach using a novel deep neural network selection architecture. In: Emerging Technologies in Data Mining and Information Security, pp. 849–862. Springer (2019). https://doi.org/10.1007/978-981-13-1501-5_74
20. Shao, F., Wang, X., Meng, F., Rui, T., Wang, D., Tang, J.: Real-time traffic sign detection and recognition method based on simplified Gabor wavelets and CNNs. Sensors, **18**(10), 3192 (2018). https://www.mdpi.com/1424-8220/18/10/3192

21. Shrivastava, A., Gupta, A., Girshick, R.: Training region-based object detectors with online hard example mining. In: 2016 IEEE Conference on Computer Vision and Pattern Recognition (CVPR), pp. 761–769 (2016)
22. Stallkamp, J., Schlipsing, M., Salmen, J., Igel, C.: Man vs. computer: benchmarking machine learning algorithms for traffic sign recognition. Neural Netw. **32**, 323–332 (2012). https://doi.org/10.1016/j.neunet.2012.02.016, http://www.sciencedirect.com/science/article/pii/S0893608012000457, selected Papers from IJCNN 2011
23. Tabernik, D., Skočaj, D.: Deep learning for large-scale traffic-sign detection and recognition. IEEE Trans. Intell. Transp. Syst. **21**(4), 1427–1440 (2020)
24. Wahyono, Kurnianggoro, L., Hariyono, J., Jo, K.H.: Traffic sign recognition system for autonomous vehicle using cascade SVM classifier. In: IECON 2014–40th Annual Conference of the IEEE Industrial Electronics Society, pp. 4081–4086 (2014). https://doi.org/10.1109/IECON.2014.7049114
25. Yang, Y., Luo, H., Xu, H., Wu, F.: Towards real-time traffic sign detection and classification. IEEE Trans. Intell. Transp. Syst. **17**(7), 2022–2031 (2016)
26. Yuan, Y., Xiong, Z., Wang, Q.: Vssa-net: vertical spatial sequence attention network for traffic sign detection. IEEE Trans. Image Process. **28**(7), 3423–3434 (2019)
27. Zaklouta, F., Stanciulescu, B.: Real-time traffic-sign recognition using tree classifiers. IEEE Trans. Intell. Transp. Syst. **13**(4), 1507–1514 (2012)
28. Zhang, J., Huang, M., Jin, X., Li, X.: A real-time chinese traffic sign detection algorithm based on modified YOLOv2. Algorithms, **10**(4), 127 (2017). https://doi.org/10.3390/a10040127, https://www.mdpi.com/1999-4893/10/4/127
29. Zhu, Z., Liang, D., Zhang, S., Huang, X., Li, B., Hu, S.: Traffic-sign detection and classification in the wild. In: 2016 IEEE Conference on Computer Vision and Pattern Recognition (CVPR), pp. 2110–2118 (2016)

Traffic Estimation and MPC-Based Traffic Light System Control in Realistic Real-Time Traffic Environments

Kevin Malena[1]([✉])(iD), Christopher Link[1], Leon Bußemas[1], Sandra Gausemeier[1], and Ansgar Trächtler[1,2]

[1] Heinz Nixdorf Institute, Paderborn University, Fürstenallee 11, 33102 Paderborn, Germany
{kevin.malena,christopher.link,leon.bussemas,sandra.gausemeier,
ansgar.traechtler}@hni.uni-paderborn.de
[2] Fraunhofer Institute for Mechatronic Systems Design IEM, Zukunftsmeile 1,
33102 Paderborn, Germany

Abstract. Modern traffic control systems are key to cope with current and future traffic challenges. In this paper information obtained from a microscopic traffic estimation using various data sources is used to feed a new developed traffic control approach. The presented method can control a traffic area with multiple traffic light systems (TLS) reacting to individual road users and pedestrians. In contrast to widespread green time extension techniques, this control selects the best phase sequence by analyzing the current traffic state reconstructed in SUMO and its predicted progress. To achieve this, the key aspect of the control strategy is to use Model Predictive Control (MPC). In order to maintain realism for real world applications, among other things, the traffic phase transitions are modelled in detail and integrated within the prediction. For the efficiency, the approach incorporates a fuzzy logic preselection of all phases reducing the computational effort. The evaluation itself is able to be easily adjusted to focus on various objectives like low occupancies, reducing waiting times and emissions, few number of phase transitions etc. determining the best switching times for the selected phases. Exemplary traffic simulations demonstrate the functionality of the MPC-based control and, in addition, some aspects under development like the real-world communication network are also discussed.

Keywords: Traffic control · Traffic estimation · Real-time · MPC · Fuzzy · Isolated intersection · Networked intersection · Sensor fusion

1 Introduction

In modern times, the options for assessing and sensing traffic have become more diverse and accurate, allowing outdated approaches for estimating and controlling the traffic to be replaced. In near future, the knowledge of the current traffic state will be even more reliable, e.g., with the inclusion of autonomous vehicles and V2X-communication. This could enable sophisticated control strategies for the traffic system, which are not

© Springer Nature Switzerland AG 2022
C. Klein et al. (Eds.): SMARTGREENS 2021/ VEHITS 2021, CCIS 1612, pp. 232–254, 2022.
https://doi.org/10.1007/978-3-031-17098-0_12

necessarily dependent on TLS [1, 2]. Since this scenario is still several years in the future, this paper addresses the more contemporary exploitation of a known traffic state obtained by a real-time traffic estimator to control the system through its TLS. The overall system, which contains the information processing discussed in this chapter, is sketched in Fig. 1. Multiple sensors gather data of the current traffic situation. These involve induction loops in the vicinity of the TLS, radio telegrams of public busses as well as additionally installed radar sensors at key positions that can also identify the vehicle types and measure their velocities. The traffic estimator uses this data to reconstruct the current traffic situation and to update it periodically. Based on this information the control algorithm presented below calculates the control signals for the TLS which in turn influence the real traffic situation.

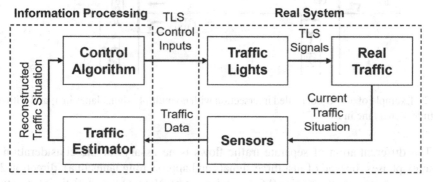

Fig. 1. Overview of the closed control loop of the traffic control system.

The approach of this paper uses a microscopic traffic simulation in SUMO [3] to represent the current traffic state as a multimodal scenario including multiple types of vehicle users and pedestrians. The developed traffic estimator [4] takes advantage of real-time sensor technology to reconstruct the unknown traffic state on a microscopic level in contrast to generating macroscopic statements on origin-destination (OD) flows, which have been determined offline solely based on historical data [5, 6]. By algorithmically linking all available information from different data sources (offline and online), the current state of a selected complex traffic area can be estimated in real-time and additionally predicted on a well-founded basis. E.g., in the Kalman Filter approach of [7] the test area is simple and only consists of highways with their off- and on-ramps and no further routing options. The essential inclusion of pedestrians is realized using the TLS push button information obtained directly from the central traffic computer.

With this detailed traffic state, the control strategy is able to react to individual actions of each vehicle user and pedestrian. In the literature there are already numerous approaches trying to optimize the traffic through the traffic lights of the system. The methods reach from pure fuzzy controllers [8–10] over reinforcement learning techniques [11–13] to MPC controllers [14–16] and others. In addition to the methodology used, a distinction can also be made as to whether the control approaches were developed for isolated [17] and/or networks of traffic intersections [18, 19]. However, these strategies still exhibit some shortcomings, which is the reason why this contribution presents a new technique. There is currently no holistic approach to control a traffic area in a highly adaptive way that covers each of the key criteria reliably. The first criterion is mainly realism. It is expressed, among other things, by the accuracy of the traffic light phases to be switched as well as their phase transitions and the flexibility to ensure an optimal phase selection. This means that there is no predefined phase sequence where only the green times are adjusted. The meaning and importance of realism can be demonstrated by a simple example as shown in Fig. 2.

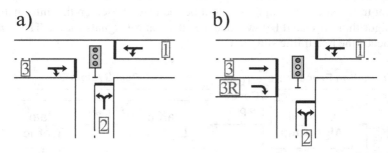

Fig. 2. Example of a TLS-controlled intersection with no multiple signal lanes in a) and with one multiple signal lane in b).

The differentiation of separate traffic flows is necessary for the consideration of complex phases. Instead of just three signals and approaching lanes in a), direction 3 is split into two lanes with one signal for each lane in b). Note, a) is a realistic intersection, but in many approaches an intersection like in b) cannot be represented or treated. Thus, with higher complexity allowed, signal compatibility can be captured in a more differentiated way just like in reality and phase transitions can be modeled accordingly. The second excelling criterion is flexibility in the phase choice. With the integration of a real traffic controller (ECU), the approach in [14] is a rare one paying detailed attention to the complexity of phase transitions, but also does not allow the free phase choice in optimizing the respective green time durations of the upcoming phases. In this research, a control approach which is suitable to achieve the desired TLS optimization goals based on the MPC principle is developed. Being the main principle, MPC is sometimes used synonym to MPC-based strategy, although the whole controller consists of many more aspects. Besides considering the past and current system state to determine the needed control inputs, the presumed future traffic development is also included. Therefore, a prediction model is required to project the current system state into the future depending on the selected control inputs and to assess the estimated outcome. However, including a prediction simulation in an optimization process is considerably costly and requires multiple measures to reduce the computational effort, which are described further below.

To rewind back to the mentioned complex phase transitions, the presented method uses a similar program to the real ECU to include correct phase transitions into the prediction model and remedies the downsides of the fixed phase order (see Sect. 4). The switching times and phases for the upcoming phase sequences are determined by optimization. In terms of the prediction model, this strategy extends the state-space model approaches from [14–16] to a micro- and macroscopic hybrid model (see Sect. 4), which offers plenty of levers to reproduce and predict the real situation. The last criterion to be mentioned is the consideration of different vehicle types and the accuracy of the traffic state which depends highly on the traffic estimation. In terms of consideration within the control approach, this marks another difference compared to the strategies that have been widely discussed in literature. Since the traffic state obtained provides additional and periodically updated information, it can be used in the optimization process of the MPC to react even more specifically to the current traffic situation with its various participants.

2 Online Real-Time Traffic Estimator

Since the concept of the traffic estimation concept has already been published in [4] and its validation in [20], this section focusses on the recap of the most important and basic aspects. Just a brief explanation of the general procedure for integrating and updating of the various data is given, as well as an outline of the basic interactions of the implemented routing concepts.

2.1 General Aspects

The concept of this dynamic traffic assignment (DTA) algorithm is to feed a microscopic simulation model in SUMO with real-time sensor measurements to act as an event-based observer for the current traffic state. Especially the keyword 'real-time' is important in the whole concept because the real-time data also has to be processed efficiently as there must be sufficient computing time remaining for the TLS control, which is described in the following section. Predictive route choices link past and (expected) future measurements to reconstruct the traffic situation between the local detector positions. The structure of the presented simulation-based method is sketched in the block diagram of Fig. 3. It shows how the real-world scenario interacts with the simulation and what kind of data is used for which purpose.

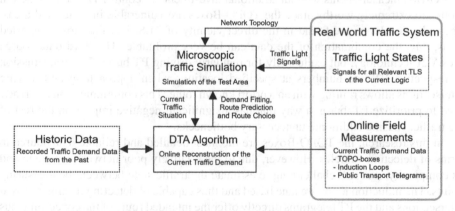

Fig. 3. Structure of the presented DTA concept (inspired by [4]).

A crucial aspect of the implementation is the differentiation between the online and offline processing and calculations, e.g., the computation of average travel times can be performed as an initialization. The update-intervals of other state estimators are often minutes, e.g., in [21]. The adjusting of a running simulation and the outsourcing of calculations to the initialization are reasons why very small update intervals of a few seconds can be used for this online state estimation. Enhanced traffic counts of so-called TOPO-Boxes, i.e., not only a time stamp for crossing the detector, but also the vehicle type and the current speed are provided via radar technology as well as induction loop data and public transport (PT) telegrams (V2I-communication of PT buses and TLS) are used as inputs for this traffic estimation. The vehicle type distinction is important because the developed TLS control is equipped with a vehicle-specific prioritization. The accuracies of the different sensor information result in interdependent levels in the decision-making process of individual vehicle routing. The vehicle types within this whole approach are generally classified according to the '8 + 1 + F' class defined by the German Federal Road Research Institute (BASt) in [22] and the sensor manufacturer [23]. Thus, eight different vehicle types are considered in this approach, i.e., passenger cars together with motorcycles, trucks, trailers, etc., an unclassified group of road users which cannot be identified with certainty and additionally bicycles (the 'F' results from the German translation for bicycles).

As mentioned before, due to the variety of available data sources, the algorithm has multiple routing levels which is briefly touched upon in the following section.

2.2 Routing Levels and Interactions

The more information and data the algorithm is capable of processing, the more precise the traffic estimation can become and the better the control for the TLS can adapt to the current traffic. The most exhaustive routing level is the so-called TOPO-Box Routing. It takes advantage of known vehicle types and speeds, so that the respective measurements at the given positions are considered in detail. Induction loops are used as the second data source. As they are very common nowadays, this information can complement the TOPO-Box measurements without additional investment. To control TLS, the induction loops are extremely worthy since the TOPO-Boxes are vulnerable in congested areas. The induction loops are found in the direct vicinity of TLS, i.e., the most congested areas, thus the combination of the data can be very profitable. The third data source uses V2I-technology, but exclusively for regularly driving PT buses. The transmission of respective PT line numbers at specified locations when approaching and leaving intersections allows routing with an a priori known route. This communication is already used to prioritize PT, but in a way that has a significant negative impact on the rest of the traffic, causing additional unnecessary bottlenecks.

In this research, the TOPO-Boxes are the most detailed and reliable data source in terms of detecting vehicles. However, due to the relatively poor network coverage and its complexity, it is still challenging to estimate the traffic state between the measuring points. The induction loops are lane based and thus capable of detecting turning ratios at intersections and the PT telegrams directly offer the intended route of the concerning bus since it is scheduled. Figure 4 indicates the mutual interaction of the routing concepts according to the drawn arrows as well as the corresponding 'Spawn' and 'Routing' features. These different strategies depend on the particular data quality and can change based on the vehicles' previous assignments by other concepts.

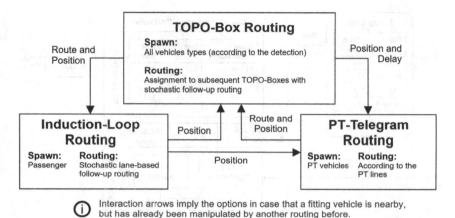

Fig. 4. Methods and interactions of the different routing concepts according to [4].

Basically, the individual routing concepts can therefore influence vehicles based on their current routing status and the consistency of the combined data (previous and current measurements). It is therefore important, e.g., whether a road user is currently being routed to a subsequent TOPO-Box based on the TOPO-Box Routing or has already passed this sensor, i.e., the vehicle is equipped with a stochastic follow-up route. Depending on this, the Induction-Loop Routing can influence the vehicle or not. Such interactions are especially important in the vicinity of TLS, as the information can complement each other beneficial when properly synchronized. Since the influence of the PT-Telegram Routing is limited to PT buses, the concept is very specific and plays a rather minor role in the overall traffic estimation, as it only complements the main traffic.

3 MPC-Based Traffic Controller

Due to safety considerations, federal regulations define a framework TLS have to comply with, i.e., the 'RiLSA' in Germany [24], whose regulations are currently being applied in this research work, but it could also be extended to other regulations like [25] for the USA. These rules define legal phases, minimum split times, transition times between phases, allowed phase sequences etc. Since these restrictions have a considerable impact on the traffic situation, the presented predictive control algorithm takes them into account while enabling a flexible control method including variable phase sequences and switching times.

3.1 Controller Structure

As depicted in Fig. 5, the controller comprises of two main components: A fuzzy logic-based phase preselection and the actual MPC.

The former is a mean to reduce the computational effort posed by the MPC by narrowing down the regarded phases for further consideration. This is done by rating the eligibility of all defined phases for the current traffic situation. A set of simple,

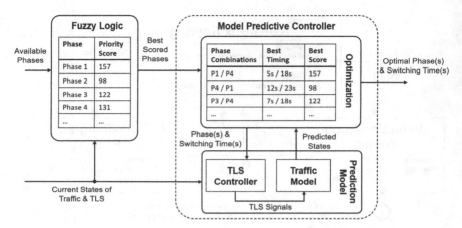

Fig. 5. Scheme of the traffic controller.

generically defined rules is applied to the fuzzified system state and is used to assign a priority score to each phase after defuzzyfication as shown in Fig. 6.

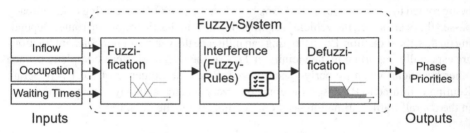

Fig. 6. Structure of the used fuzzy system.

The introductory literature in [26] explains the basics of fuzzy-systems just as various membership functions as well as aggregation and defuzzyfication methods in more detail. In this research, triangular and trapezoidal membership functions are used to define the possible linguistic sets for each input and output variable. The inputs derived from the current traffic state are the inflows, occupations and waiting times for each of the lanes in the vicinity of the TLS. The different rules for the interference are generated depending on all possible phases of the TLS based solely on the respective released signals of the individual phases. Within the defuzzyfication process the centroid method computes a single crisp output value for the priority of each possible phase as output. Based on that, the lowest-scored options of all phases are rejected since they are not suitable for the current situation. An exemplary fuzzy rule for the 'All Red' phase is "If the occupancies of all lanes are LOW, then the priority of phase 'All Red' is HIGH." favoring quick responsiveness to switch to any phase in the near future.

The remaining phases, representing the currently best options for a phase change, are passed to the MPC to make the final decision on which phases to use at which time.

Since the prediction model is capable of simulating the system for an extended prediction horizon (e.g., $t_p > 30\,\text{s}$), n_{splits} consecutively applied phases can be considered. Therefore, for each possible combination of the remaining phases of the length n_{splits}, the MPC is used to find the respective switching times by minimizing a defined target function which is explained in detail in the upcoming subsections. Finally, the phase combination and the corresponding timing that leads to the best target function value (score) is selected for application.

To demonstrate the application of the calculated phases in more detail, an example using $n_{splits} = 2$ calculated phase changes in the prediction horizon is explained. The following Fig. 7 shows a timeline for each of three consecutive calculation steps assuming constant calculation times to simplify the illustration. The calculation processes in the example start at $t_{0,i}$ with $i = 1, 2, 3$ and the prediction horizon t_p is split into the calculation time (red), the application interval for applying the calculated switches (green) and the remaining prediction (yellow). Since switches in the red marked range cannot be applied, a minimum threshold for the calculation $t_{u,min}$ has to be implemented (see also (4)).

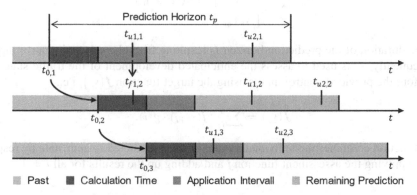

Fig. 7. Exemplary application timeline for two calculated switches within the prediction. (Color figure online)

The green range accordingly results from the calculation time of the upcoming step. In the shown example, the arising control inputs $t_{u1,1}$ and $t_{u2,1}$ are therefore handled differently. The first switch is meant to be at $t_{u1,1}$, thus is fixed (i.e., $t_{f1,2}$) for the next calculation step, meaning it is transferred to the control unit. Because the second switch $t_{u2,1}$ is not in the relevant range, it can be changed in the following step. This phenomenon can be seen in the third step, since $t_{u1,2} \neq t_{u1,3}$. Due to a changed initial situation at $t_{0,3}$ in the meantime, the optimization has rated a different switching time, and possibly a completely new phase, as a better control input.

3.2 MPC Properties and Characteristics

The MPC consists of two components: an optimizer and the prediction model $P(s_k, u, t_u)$ see Fig. 5. Given a set of n_{splits} phases, the preselected phase combination u and the corresponding switching times t_u, the prediction model is able to perform a traffic simulation based on the current system state s_k at all times $k \in \mathbb{N}_0^+$ (step length in analogy to SUMO and the real ECU). The state includes information about the traffic composition with the current TLS state, the regarded lanes, expected incoming vehicles and pedestrians[1]:

$$s_k : \begin{cases} \text{TLS signal state,} \\ \text{Last activation time of each selectable TLS signal state for TLS signals,} \\ \text{Position and type of all vehicles on each lane,} \\ \text{Expected arrival time and type of incoming vehicles for each direction,} \\ \text{Waiting pedestrians at each side of the crosswalks.} \end{cases}$$

To access specific information of the system state, functions can be defined to extract the desired data. E.g., in order to get the number of vehicles x_k on each lane at time step k, the function x is used, i.e., $x_k = x(s_k)$. The simulation being in the k-th time step provides the estimated future system states

$$\underline{s}_k = \begin{bmatrix} s_{k+1} \\ \vdots \\ s_{k+tp} \end{bmatrix} = P(s_k, u, t_u) \tag{1}$$

for the duration of the prediction horizon t_p resulting from the selected control inputs. Subsequently, $\underline{s}_k$ is used to assess the anticipated development of the traffic state and therefore the provided control inputs using the target function $J(\underline{s}_k)$, i.e.,

$$J(\underline{s}_k) = \sum_{i=1}^{t_p} j(s_{k+i}) \cdot g(i). \tag{2}$$

This function combines the individual ratings of each predicted system state by respectively applying the assessment function j and adding up the results for all $i = 1, \ldots, t_p$ as

$$j(s_{k+i}) = g_w^T \cdot t_w(s_{k+i}) + g_x^T \cdot x(s_{k+i}) + g_u \cdot \delta_u + g_{w,max}^T \cdot t_{w,max}(s_{k+i}). \tag{3}$$

Since the simulation results presumably deviate with each further time step from the actual future system behavior, a weighting function g can be used to reduce the influence of later simulation steps (see (2)). The rating for each state is based on several criteria, most of which can be derived from the given state s_{k+i} and for the whole prediction horizon ($i = 1, \ldots, t_p$). An important optimization goal is the reduction of waiting times for vehicles and pedestrians alike. The vector $t_w(s_{k+i})$ includes this data broken down by lane and vehicle type. By defining the weighting factor g_w^T, the influence of selected vehicle types and lanes can be customized e.g., in order to prioritize public transportation or pedestrians over regular vehicles. Besides the waiting times another goal is to decrease the total amount of road users in the vicinity of the TLS and to increase the traffic flow. Therefore, the vector $x(s_{k+i})$, which also distinguishes between lanes and vehicle types,

---

[1] Depending on the used sensor technology, the pedestrian count can be a binary value (push buttons) or a measured number (e.g., radar sensors). The waiting times are applied and calculated respectively.

is read from the system state and weighted by g_x^T. The same procedure is used for the maximum waiting time $t_{w,max}(s_{k+i})$ of individual road users (also separated by vehicle type and lane and weighted by $g_{w,max}^T$). In addition, the number of phase changes δ_u is taken into account with the weighting factor g_u to provoke a steadier phase sequence (i.e., $\delta_u \leq n_{splits}$ due to all possible phase permutations). The assessment function j of (2) serves as an example and thus can be individually manipulated according to special requirements, e.g., to ideas of the respective city administration.

For each given set of phase combination u obtained by the fuzzy logic, the optimizer searches for the switching times t_u that minimize $J(P(s_k, u, t_u))$, as depicted in the following equation:

$$t_u = \underset{t_{u,min} \leq t_u \leq t_p}{\text{argmin}} \ J(P(s_k, u, t_u)). \tag{4}$$

Finally, after solving the optimization problem for each relevant phase combination, the program and its corresponding switching times that lead to the best target function value are selected by the controller.

3.3 Prediction Model

The prediction model has to fulfill two major requirements: 1) It must be sufficiently accurate to enable a meaningful assessment of the control inputs. 2) At the same time, it is executed repeatedly during each MPC optimization interval and therefore must not be computationally demanding. To illustrate that, consider a prediction horizon of 30 s which would require 30 simulation steps using a step size of 1 s. An optimization process (for $n_{splits} = 1$) takes about five prediction model evaluations for each preselected target phase. Depending on the junction an amount of five preselected phases would be realistic. Since the system is designed to control several TLS from a central location, a total amount of approximately 4,500 time steps of the prediction model per MPC execution has to be performed. This imposes high demands on the computational efficiency of the model.

TLS Controller Logic. As shown in Fig. 5, the prediction model is comprised of a representation of the TLS controller logic and a traffic model. The former is used to implement the given control inputs u and t_u and to generate the light signals that control the simulated traffic. As mentioned before, this process is constrained by several regulations that are defined in the RiLSA [24], which can have a significant effect on the TLS behavior and therefore must not be neglected. These include the compliance with following standards:

- Yellow change time,
- Red-yellow signal time (preceding the green signal in Germany),
- Minimum green time,
- Red clearance for conflicting signals,
- Delayed vehicle release for a permissive phase including pedestrians (optional).

The yellow change time depending on the maximum allowed speeds and the red-yellow signal time have a fixed duration and need to be considered each time a green- or red-light signal is changed. However, the latter elements have a dynamic influence on the system behavior, since they delay the implementation of the desired phase depending on the previous signal states. Especially if pedestrians are involved, the minimum green time added to the subsequent red clearance time can exceed 20 s for some lanes, prohibiting a fast reaction for certain phases. By modelling these effects within the prediction model, the MPC considers them while choosing the most suitable target phase. It has to be noted again, that an adaptation of the controller model to comply with other national or regional standards can easily be achieved through modification of configuration parameters.

An efficient implementation of the TLS controller logic frequently employing logical operators ensures sufficient performance to be used in the context of the prediction model. If the current signal state differs from the desired one, for each signal a series of checks is performed to determine whether the signal state must be changed and whether this change should be applied in the current time step. The controller logic is depicted in Fig. 8.

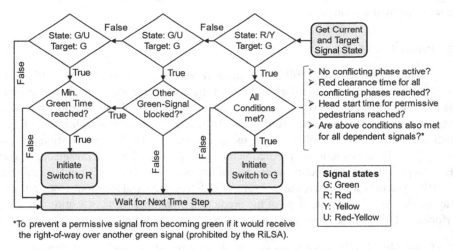

*To prevent a permissive signal from becoming green if it would receive the right-of-way over another green signal (prohibited by the RiLSA).

Fig. 8. Controller logic for each TLS-signal.

Traffic Model. In order to model the traffic flows in the vicinity of the TLS, the incoming lanes are regarded in a macroscopic way. On the one hand, this enables a computational efficient way to simulate traffic since only every lane and not every vehicle (including their interactions) has to be described individually. On the other hand, this is a mean to handle the uncertainty concerning the true system state at the TLS. For example, the system cannot know with certainty whether a vehicle intends to drive straight ahead, turn left, or turn right at an intersection with only one incoming lane. However, the effects of this intent for the system can differentiate considerably. If the driver wants to turn left, he may have to wait for opposing traffic, hindering the following vehicles, while the traffic flow is not affected if the desired route is straight ahead. A macroscopic model enables to mitigate such effects as it is less influenced by decisions of individual drivers and aims to describe the 'average' system behavior.

To describe the system, the vector $x_{i,k}$ represents the vehicle counts of each vehicle type on lane i at time step k and is selected as the system state for each lane. It is influenced by the incoming flow $f_{in,i,k}$ and the outgoing flow $f_{out,i,k}$ which leads to the discrete system dynamics equation

$$x_{i,k+1} = x_{i,k} - m(x_{i,k}) \cdot f_{out,i,k} + f_{in,i,k}. \tag{5}$$

For the inflow, an estimation over the whole prediction horizon based on the current system state s_k is made. Depending on the vehicles' positions and their velocities, an algorithm computes at which time new vehicles of which type presumably are going to enter each lane. The outgoing flow $f_{out,i,k}$ is a scalar value and does not distinguish between vehicle types. Therefore, the function m in (5) is used to allocate the outflow to the available vehicle types depending on their ratio and characteristics (e.g., length, acceleration). For example, a given outflow effects busses differently compared to motorcycles since they occupy different amounts of space and have diverse driving characteristics. A parameter vector μ is introduced that defines how different vehicle types are affected by $f_{out,i,k}$. Given the example of passenger cars being the standard ($\mu_{pass} = 1$) and for motorcycles the value $\mu_{moto} = 1.8$ is used. This would result in an 80% increase of the outflow for a given $f_{out,i,k}$ if only motorcycles were present. Since for this model multimodal traffic is considered, the outflow factor for each vehicle type depends on $x_{i,k}$ and can be determined by

$$m(x_{i,k}) = \frac{\mu^T x_{i,k}}{\left([\, 1 \, \dots \, 1 \,] x_{i,k} \right)^2} \cdot x_{i,k}. \tag{6}$$

To examine $f_{out,i,k}$, simulations of accelerating traffic consisting of passenger cars after a traffic light turns green were carried out. These simulations were performed in SUMO because it is used to model the controlled system. They show that the outflow rate is approximately constant at $f_{out,i,max}$ until the majority of waiting vehicles has dissolved. At this point the outflow approaches the inflow rate, i.e., the final slope of the curves. Multiple simulations of this kind with varying initial queue lengths and inflow rates are depicted in Fig. 9. Note that the initial $f_{out,i,max}$, which corresponds to the slope of the graphs until the first bend, is identical for each case. Various drivers' imperfections are neglected in these simulations to illustrate the general principle. Based on these observations the following equation can be derived:

$$f_{out,i,k} = r_i(s_k) \cdot \min\left(f_{out,i,max}, \varphi_i \cdot [\, 1 \, \dots \, 1 \,] x_{i,k} \right). \tag{7}$$

Here, the outflow $f_{out,i,k}$ is assumed to be proportional to the current vehicle count $x_{i,k}$ on the lane, using the factor φ_i that can be selected individually for each vehicle type. Nevertheless, the outflow must not exceed $f_{out,i,max}$. The initially constant outflow rate can also be understood by picturing the vehicles' velocity and the corresponding gaps between the cars. After the green light is given, the vehicle queue accelerates which would result in an increasing vehicle flow. At the same time, however, the safety gap between the vehicles increases and compensates this effect.

When entering the intersection, several effects can inhibit traffic flows from an incoming road to an outgoing one depending on the current traffic situation, the geometry of the

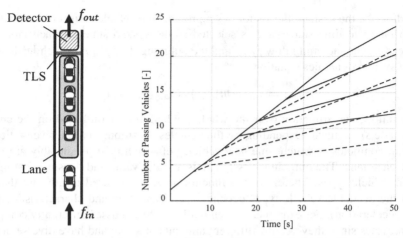

Fig. 9. Left: Initial situation of passenger vehicles waiting at a TLS; Right: Simulation results of the vehicle flow for accelerating passenger vehicles after receiving green in the situation shown on the left.

junction and the state of the TLS. To incorporate them, the outflow factor $r_i(s_k) \in [0, 1]$ is introduced in (7). There are four types of influences that are taken into account in the prediction model and depicted in Fig. 10:

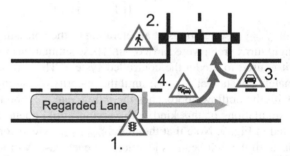

1. TLS signal state,
2. Crossing pedestrians,
3. Higher prioritized permissive traffic flows,
4. Tailback due to the effects above.

Fig. 10. Types of traffic interferences considered in the prediction model.

The outflow of each lane composes of the sum of the partial outflows of the regarded lane to each connected lane leading away from the junction. Thus, the equation

$$r_{i,k} = \sum_j a_{ij} \cdot r_{part,ij,k} \tag{8}$$

can be derived for $r_{i,k}$ in which a_{ij} describes the average proportion of vehicles that travel from lane i to lane k. It can be calculated from historical data for the regarded junction. Consequently, the expression

$$\sum_j a_{ij} = 1 \qquad (9)$$

holds. The partial flows are affected by the four obstruction effects described above which are included in the respective outflow factors $r_{part,ij,k}$ as

$$r_{part,ij,k} = r_{tls,i,k} \cdot r_{ped,ij,k} \cdot r_{veh,ij,k} \cdot r_{tb,ij,k}. \qquad (10)$$

The factor $r_{tls,i,k}$ represents the TLS signal state for the regarded lane i and either allows or denies traffic flow for outgoing traffic from this lane:

$$r_{tls,ij,k} = \begin{cases} 1, & \text{if the signal for lane } i \text{ is green at step } k, \\ 0, & \text{otherwise.} \end{cases} \qquad (11)$$

To model the influence of pedestrians for turning traffic in a permissive green phase another binary factor $r_{ped,ij,k}$ is used and defined analogously as

$$r_{ped,ij,k} = \begin{cases} 0, & \text{if pedestrians are present on lane } j \text{ at step } k, \\ 1, & \text{otherwise.} \end{cases} \qquad (12)$$

In a real-world application pedestrians can be detected using the respective push buttons. It is assumed that they need a certain time to cross the street and that this duration varies depending on the side from which the pedestrians enter. E.g., if they wish to cross the street starting from the outgoing-road side a shorter crossing-time is assumed since the relevant lane is cleared earlier. It would also be possible to include pedestrians based on other sensor data, if available. The third influencing factor for the outflow is oncoming traffic which inhibits the traffic flow of left-turning vehicles. To model this effect, a descending linear function for $r_{veh,ij,k}$ is chosen

$$r_{veh,ij,k} = \min\left(1, \max\left(r_{veh,ij,min}, m_{veh,ij} x_{j,k} + b_{veh,ij}\right)\right), \qquad (13)$$

where

$$b_{veh,ij} > 1; m_{veh,ij} < 0 \text{ and } 0 \leq r_{veh,ij,min} < 1. \qquad (14)$$

The function depends on the vehicle count $x_{j,k}$ of the conflicting lane j and can be adjusted using the parameters $m_{veh,ij}$ and $b_{veh,ij}$. Also $r_{veh,ij,k}$ is limited to the range $r_{veh,ij,min} \leq r_{veh,ij,k} \leq 1$ which allows to set a minimum outflow factor. A simple binary outflow factor would not be suitable for this kind of obstruction because the true target and therefore the intended turning behavior of incoming vehicles is not known with certainty, as mentioned above. Thus, a gradual transition for $r_{veh,ij,k}$ is required.

For presented influencing factors the obstruction of the individual traffic flows from the regarded lane to all possible target lanes are determined independently. However due to tailback which is caused by an inhibited flow the other traffic flows can be affected, too. To model this, $r_{tb,ij,k}$ is introduced which can be calculated from the other flow factors and the parameter vector $p_{tb,ij}$ as

$$r_{tb,ij,k} = r_{tb}\left(r_{tls,i,k}, r_{ped,ij,k}, r_{veh,ij,k}, p_{tb,ij}\right). \qquad (15)$$

3.4   Parameter Selection and Model Tuning

The presented TLS controller relies on multiple parameters which are used in various parts of the system. These must be set adequately to ensure satisfactory control results. In a first step the prediction model is considered. The goal was to match its behavior to measurements obtained from simulations conducted with SUMO using different traffic volumes. For any time step k of the reference simulation in SUMO, $\underline{s}_k$ is predicted using the current traffic situation as initial state. The results are stored and compared to the reference simulation once the test scenario is completed. To rate the prediction results, the mean square error of the vehicle count on all lanes between the prediction and the reference simulation is determined. A parameter set which minimizes this error was selected to be used in the prediction model. Note that some parameters can be estimated a priori based on measurements or historical data (e.g., the average pedestrian crossing times or a_{ij}) and therefore reduce the number of optimization variables. In addition, traffic situations can be defined in a way to analyze specific cases isolated. For example, it is useful to initially optimize the outflow behavior in situations without interactions with other permissive traffic flows to select the corresponding parameters first.

Once the prediction model parameters are tuned, further optimizations of the whole system are conducted. Similar to the MPC, a target function can be formulated which encompasses the subjective optimization goals e.g., the time loss of vehicles and pedestrians, the maximum waiting time including a weighting factor for different vehicle types. In contrast to the optimizer used in the MPC, the source for this data is the SUMO reference simulation. Thus, the actual effect of the controller is used and not the predicted one. By incorporating this, the weighting factors of the target function of the MPC are adjusted to meet the requirements for the closed-loop system.

4   Simulative Application of the Control Strategy

To explain the fundamentals of a new and holistic MPC-based TLS control strategy, the previous section has already addressed many different structural and technical aspects. Therefore, two examples will be used to illustrate the feasibility of the implementation. The first example is fictional just to point out the capabilities of this approach and to introduce the framework. Exemplary phases and transition times to be abided by the controller are presented. The second example is a real-life intersection located in Schloß Neuhaus (Paderborn) in Germany. The applicability of the control strategy to challenging real-world scenarios is demonstrated and preliminary results are shown comparing different parameter settings with the currently applied TLS control of the area for selected test scenarios. It should be noted that the results were obtained without use of the traffic estimator. The necessary data for the control are thus perfect and taken directly from the controlled system (ground truth simulation (GTS), see [20]) to focus on the pure controller performance.

4.1   Simple Fictional Example

To provide a simple and clear example, the intersection already shown in the first section in Fig. 3 b) is picked. Its phases and especially the difference between the scenarios a) and b) are shown in the following Fig. 11.

Phases/Model	a) - 3 Signals (1,2,3)	b) - 4 Signals (1,2,3,3R)	
1	R-R-R	R-R-R-R	
2	G-R-G	G-R-G-R	
3	R-G-R	G-R-R-R	
4	-	R-G-R-G	
5	-	R-G-R-R	
6	-	R-R-G-G	
7	-	R-R-R-G	

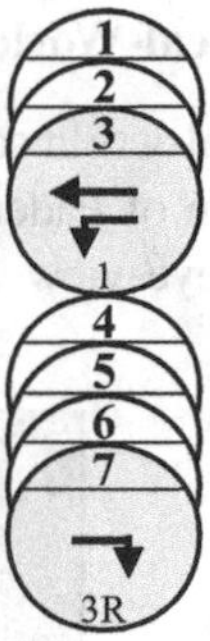

Fig. 11. Phases for the simple examples of Fig. 3

Given only the simplest three phases for a), a larger selection of seven phases is available for model b). These phases are indicated next to the table in Fig. 11. With the additional lane and the corresponding signal an increased number of phases is conceivable which offers a more flexible reaction to the traffic situation and individual vehicles. The transition times that must be met by the TLS and thus by the prediction model are listed in the following Table 1, broken down by the corresponding signals. If the highlighted phases 3 and 7 of Fig. 11 serve as an example of an arbitrary phase transition, i.e., from phase 3 to phase 7, then a transition time of 7 s must be established according to Table 1 (first row and fourth column).

Table 1. Transition Times for the simple example.

		IN			
	SIGNAL	1	2	3	3R
OUT	1	0	6	5	7
	2	7	0	5	0
	3	0	6	0	0
	3R	4	0	0	0

Those transition times influence the traffic and therefore the simulations massively. Their consideration enables a significantly more realistic prediction for the control strategy. The flexibility of the general approach is indicated by the fact that all possible phases were used in a sample randomized traffic simulation of 15 min. The phase sequences and their frequencies were only influenced by the performed optimization as well as the traffic volume and distribution.

To avoid repetition, simulations and first results are discussed in the next section with a more sophisticated and challenging example.

4.2 Real-World Scenario

The real-world scenario presented here is developed in cooperation with the city administration of Paderborn. In Fig. 12 the TLS-controlled intersection is illustrated using a bird's-eye-view with the included SUMO-GUI roads.

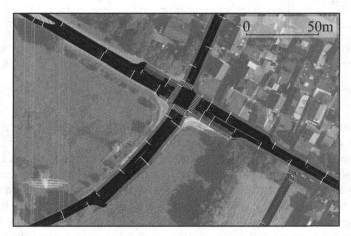

Fig. 12. SUMO-GUI embedded in a bird's-eye view of a real world TLS controlled intersection in Schloß Neuhaus [27].

Due to the four arms and individually signalized turning lanes for two directions, the number of phases for this TLS-controlled intersection increases to 19. The phases incorporate the respective governmental regulations and restrictions. As mentioned in the previous section, the fuzzy interference system is used to reduce the number of eligible phases for the optimization down to the most suitable six for the current traffic situation. In addition to that, in this example the prediction horizon is set to 20 s and just one scheduled switching time ($n_{splits} = 1$) for a phase change is calculated within the optimization process. For the evaluation of the MPC-based control, the strategy is compared with the currently implemented logic of this specific intersection. To incorporate the original control, the additional software LISUM [28] is used, which has the advantage of directly loading TLS configurations developed in LISA[2] compared to e.g., a SUMO-internal replication.

This evaluation acts as a first demonstration for the capabilities of the presented strategy since an intensive and detailed study still has to be performed. The test scenarios consist of randomized, realistic and multimodal[3] traffic situations with different loads. They range from around 3,600 veh/h for the 'high' traffic volume down to 2,400 veh/h for the 'medium' volume and just 1,200 veh/h for the 'low' one. The distribution of road user types is determined based on real sample measurements of this examined road

---

[2] LISA is a comprehensive proprietary software package for traffic engineering, testing control systems and for supplying ECU.

[3] The traffic consists of eight different vehicle types (passenger, delivery, bicycle, bus, trailer, semi-trailer, truck and motorcycle).

section. For each scenario, the vehicle inflow into the traffic system is always limited to a duration of 90 s and the simulations last until each of the corresponding vehicles has finished its route.

As mentioned before, the presented strategy is also pedestrian-capable, which means that the controller reacts to pedestrians and can be tuned to favor of them. Nevertheless, pedestrians are neglected in these exemplary test simulations for comparability reasons, since LISUM cannot handle pedestrians in the same way. In contrast to the MPC-based controller, the original control with LISUM does not recognize pedestrians meaning that selected phases are not chosen with respect to them.

An excerpt of the generated results of the different simulations is provided in Table 2. It shows the three scenarios for four control approaches with the original control realized with LISUM, i.e., a traffic-dependent TLS control with release time adjustment, and three configurations of the MPC-based strategy presented in this contribution. The parameters of the different configurations will not be discussed in detail, but some weightenings will be explained with meaningful data from the table. As mentioned before, the traffic composition is identical for each case, but depending on the applied TLS control, the simulated traffic is managed in a different period of time. The criteria listed in the table, according to which the strategies are preliminarily evaluated, are the maximum (Max.), the average (Ø) and the number (#) of either waiting times (WT), travel times (TT), speeds, time losses (TL) and stops. In order to indicate the special effects on individual road user groups, the average travel time of buses is presented separately. Since the sample measurements for the low traffic volume does not include buses, the average bus travel time is left empty in this scenario for each control strategy.

Before looking deeper into the generated data of Table 2, it should be mentioned that the cumulated computation time of all MPC executions was less than one third of the respective simulated time (<30 s), even though additional debugging queries were made. Of course, further studies on the computation time are under investigation, but the algorithm clearly shows the potential for a real-time implementation.

Starting the analysis of the different control approaches with the waiting times, the table outlines that the MPC configurations show great advantages relative to the original control. If the high traffic loads are compared, the deviations in the maximum and average time are quite small with less than 10% improvement in the best case. However, the lower the load, the better the performance of the MPC becomes, since the strategy reacts much better to individual vehicles. The average wating time for the vehicles is reduced to nearly a third of the times for the original control. The reason for this difference is that in the high load case the intersection is already too heavily loaded or working at capacity. The MPC nevertheless shows an improvement there but cannot react as well to individual vehicles and vehicle flows. It is also noticeable that Config 2 is (in terms of waiting times) inferior to the other MPC setups, which is because this configuration induces a high bus prioritization and thus controls the overall traffic less effectively. Config 1, on the other hand, is designed in such a way that the weighting of the various road users is based on the average number of people within the vehicle as well as its emissions. The last setup (Config 3) provides equal treatment for all road users (vehicle classes).

The next compared criteria shown in Table 2 are the travel times. Regardless of the chosen configuration, the picture is similarly positive in favor of the MPC. All

Table 2. Results of multiple scenarios using the current control as well as various configured versions of the presented approach.

	Volume	Max. WT [s]	Ø WT [s]	Ø TT [s]	Ø Bus TT [s]	Ø Speed [km/h]	Ø TL [s]	Ø #Stops [-]
Original Control	high	147	41.25	80.54	125	12.09	56.82	1.45
	med	114	36.82	72.45	72	13.41	48.68	1.27
	low	68	27.07	58.00	/	17.23	34.51	0.85
MPC Config 1	high	135	37.78	73.39	109	13.27	50.01	0.98
	med	102	25.25	58.91	63	16.50	35.22	0.86
	low	57	9.81	40.48	/	24.68	16.68	0.59
MPC Config 2	high	151	43.08	79.28	67	12.28	55.89	1.09
	med	99	26.07	59.20	59	16.42	35.56	0.89
	low	38	9.33	40.26	/	24.82	16.41	0.67
MPC Config 3	high	144	40.31	77.21	99	12.61	53.79	1.18
	med	89	25.59	59.39	63	16.37	35.79	0.89
	low	57	9.81	40.48	/	24.68	16.68	0.59

illustrated travel times for all traffic loads can be reduced with the use of the MPC strategy. Again, it is noticeable that the lower the volume is, the greater the positive influence of the MPC becomes. As an example, the bus-specific Config 2 influences the travel times in a decreasing manner of approx. 18% for the medium load scenario. For the high traffic volume, the effect on the corresponding bus-specific average travel times is even more striking, as these are cut down to half. In this case, the required number of phase changes most likely explains the underlying cause, as the original controller is not as responsive and tuned to the current traffic as the MPC. The differences within the various configurations themselves clearly show that the operator of the MPC (e.g., the city administration) can deliberately affect and manipulate the results.

To summarize the remaining criteria, the MPC, regardless of the configuration used, improves the results of the original control by increasing the average speeds, reducing time losses and reducing stops (i.e., fewer halts lead to lower emissions and less fuel consumption). The extent of the improvements varies and depends on the focus of the particular setup, i.e., the traffic itself, the configuration as well as the considered criterion.

Because the maximum and average data alone cannot display the distribution of the measurements and both properties are prone to outliers or at least react strongly to them, the following Fig. 13 is attached.

The boxplots of Fig. 13 confirm the impressions created by the data in the table considered so far. Not only the extreme and average values of the travel times, waiting times, average speeds and stops show the great impact of the MPC, but also the statistical distribution of all data points are in favor of the presented approach. The median tends to be 'better' for each of the criteria, e.g., for the average speeds it is 0.7 km/h higher

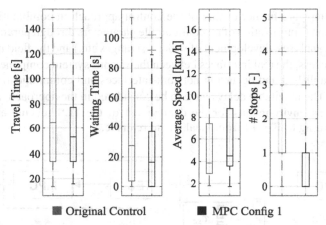

■ Original Control   ■ MPC Config 1

Fig. 13. Boxplots for the 'medium' traffic load scenario controlled with both, the original control and the MPC with Config 1.

compared to the original control. The difference for the third quartile is even bigger with a gap of 1.5 km/h.

Generally, the simulations and their results are very promising. Obviously, the positive effects of the MPC can be manipulated within certain limits by modifying the configurations and therefore offer decision makers individual levers. Since there are configurations that are superior to the current original control in all criteria, the approach can be judged as very positive based on this (small) evaluation.

5 Conclusion and Future Work

The presented MPC-based traffic control approach provides a customizable solution for the fast and flexible control of real traffic systems through their TLS. Special attention has been paid to an efficient and transferable implementation with respect to the basic structure as well as the prediction model of the MPC. In the approach, the required guidelines are met in all necessary components.

The topic of isolated and networked intersections was already briefly addressed in the introduction. As seen in the remarkable results of the real-world example in Sect. 4.2, the concept is applicable for isolated intersections, but not limited to them. The traffic estimator can cover areas with several TLS and via the inflows, among other things, the individual TLS-controlled intersections are linked and influence each other. Obviously, the influence is stronger depending on the road network (spatial proximity and turning options), so that, for example, the alignment of traffic light signals of neighboring intersections can also be integrated into the objectives of the MPC. However, as far as the actual calculation is concerned, individual optimization should be provided for each TLS to keep the already mentioned computational effort as low as possible. In order to scale the overall approach also for large urban areas, a clustering within the traffic estimation has to be applied creating several subareas. The boundaries can be defined, for example, by TOPO-Boxes or other sensors. The traffic of the respective clusters can then be improved with the presented control method.

The next steps are further testing of the control approach in combination with the traffic estimation (optimization of all configurable parameters through parameter studies and sensitivity analyses, development of wider test ranges etc.) and the field implementation. In this process, the real interfaces between the various system components of Fig. 1 have to be established and occurring network interfaces and communications must be implemented. The inevitable delays have to be considered in the approach, analogously to [29]. The test environments for the deployment of the TLS scheme are currently evolving according to Fig. 14 from idealistic to realistic.

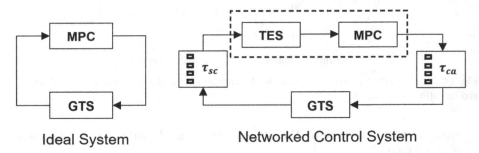

Fig. 14. MPC integrated in an idealistic (left) and realistic control loop (right).

The integration of the traffic estimation simulation (TES) and communications delays τ_{sc} and τ_{ca} (see [30]) will improve the development of the presented TLS control approach (dashed rectangle).

All this research is expected to result in various applicable configurations of the MPC to meet different needs and requirements, such as varying traffic conditions or political decisions (e.g., to prioritize certain road users) and different strategies to handle the network effects, which is becoming apparent during the first analyses.

With these measures in place, the approach should then be able to be tested in real field trials and eventually used for permanent operation.

Another goal is to utilize this control approach in context of a traffic control system for mixed autonomy traffic currently under development which offers additional potential for optimization.

Acknowledgment. The research is funded by the Ministry of Economy, Innovation, Digitalization and Energy of North Rhine-Westphalia, Germany. The authors would like to thank all partners of the Pilot Project Schlosskreuzung for their support and the provided data.

References

1. Henning, S., Biemelt, P., Rüddenklau, N., Gausemeier, S., Trächtler, A.: A simulation framework for testing a conceptual hierarchical autonomous traffic management system including an intelligent external traffic simulation. In: Driving Simulation Association (ed.) Proceedings of the DSC 2018 Europe VR. Driving Simulation & Virtual Reality Conference & Exhibition. New Trends in Human in the Loop Simulation and Testing, Palais des Congrès, Antibes, France, 05–07 September 2018, pp. 91–98. Driving Simulation Association (2018)

2. Mertin, S., Malena, K., Link, C., Gausemeier, S., Trächtler, A.: Macroscopic traffic flow control using consensus algorithms. In: The 23rd IEEE International Conference on Intelligent Transportation Systems. International Conference on Intelligent Transportation Systems (ITSC) (2020). https://www.ieee-itsc2020.org

3. Lopez, P.A., et al.: Microscopic traffic simulation using SUMO. In: 2018 IEEE Intelligent Transportation Systems Conference, Maui, Hawaii, 4–7 November 2018. 2018 21st International Conference on Intelligent Transportation Systems (ITSC), Maui, HI, 11 Apr 2018–11 July 2018, Piscataway, NJ, pp. 2575–2582. IEEE (2018). https://doi.org/10.1109/ITSC.2018. 8569938

4. Malena, K., Link, C., Mertin, S., Gausemeier, S., Trächtler, A.: Online state estimation for microscopic traffic simulations using multiple data sources. In: 7th International Conference on Vehicle Technology and Intelligent Transport Systems, pp. 386–395 (2021)

5. Osorio, C.: Dynamic origin-destination matrix calibration for large-scale network simulators. Transp. Res. Part C Emerging Technol. **98**, 186–206 (2019). https://doi.org/10.1016/j.trc. 2018.09.023

6. Osorio, C.: High-dimensional offline origin-destination (OD) demand calibration for stochastic traffic simulators of large-scale road networks. Transp. Res. Part B Methodol. **124**, 18–43 (2019). https://doi.org/10.1016/j.trb.2019.01.005

7. Antoniou, C., Ben-Akiva, M., Koutsopoulos, H.N.: Kalman filter applications for traffic management. In: Kordic, V. (ed.) Kalman Filter. InTech (2010)

8. Adewoye, O.O., Ajibade, S.M., Akin-Olayemi, T.: Modelling of a fuzzy traffic light controller. Int. J. Res. Mech. Mater. Eng. **1**, 6–14 (2015)

9. Ge, Y.: A two-stage fuzzy logic control method of traffic signal based on traffic urgency degree. Modell. Simul. Eng. (3), 1–6 (2014). https://doi.org/10.1155/2014/694185

10. Collotta, M., Lo Bello, L., Pau, G.: A novel approach for dynamic traffic lights management based on Wireless Sensor Networks and multiple fuzzy logic controllers. Expert Syst. Appl. **42**(13), 5403–5415 (2015). https://doi.org/10.1016/j.eswa.2015.02.011

11. Zheng, G., et al.: Diagnosing reinforcement learning for traffic signal control. http://arxiv. org/pdf/1905.04716v1 (2019)

12. Wei, H., Zheng, G., Yao, H., Li, Z.: IntelliLight: a reinforcement learning approach for intelligent traffic light control. In: Proceedings of the 24th ACM SIGKDD International Conference on Knowledge Discovery and Data Mining, New York, NY, USA, pp. 2496–2505. Association for Computing Machinery (2018)

13. Higuera, C., Lozano, F., Camacho, E.C., Higuera, C.H.: Multiagent reinforcement learning applied to traffic light signal control. In: Demazeau, Y., Matson, E., Corchado, J.M., De la Prieta, F. (eds.) PAAMS 2019. LNCS (LNAI), vol. 11523, pp. 115–126. Springer, Cham (2019). https://doi.org/10.1007/978-3-030-24209-1_10

14. Tettamanti, T., Varga, I., Kulcsar, B., Bokor, J.: Model predictive control in urban traffic network management. In: 16th Mediterranean Conference on Control and Automation, pp. 1538–1543 (2008)

15. Wang, Y., Wang, D., Xu, B., Wongpiromsarn, T.: Junction-based model predictive control for urban traffic light control. In: 2013 International Conference on Connected Vehicles and Expo (ICCVE), Las Vegas, NV, USA, pp. 54–59. IEEE (2013). https://doi.org/10.1109/ICCVE. 2013.6799769

16. Kamal, M.A.S., Imura, J.-I., Hayakawa, T., Ohata, A., Aihara, K.: Traffic signal control of a road network using MILP in the MPC framework. Int. J. Intell. Transp. Syst. Res. **13**(2), 107–118 (2014). https://doi.org/10.1007/s13177-014-0090-3

17. Haddad, J., Mahalel, D., Ioslovich, I., Gutman, P.-O.: Constrained optimal steady-state control for isolated traffic intersections. Control Theory Technol. **12**(1), 84–94 (2014). https://doi. org/10.1007/s11768-014-2247-7

18. Lee, S., Wong, S.C., Varaiya, P.: Group-based hierarchical adaptive traffic-signal control part I: formulation. Transp. Res. Part B Methodol. **105**, 1–18 (2017). https://doi.org/10.1016/j.trb. 2017.08.008

19. Mohajerpoor, R., Saberi, M., Ramezani, M.: Analytical derivation of the optimal traffic signal timing: minimizing delay variability and spillback probability for undersaturated intersections. Transp. Res. Part B Methodol. **119**, 45–68 (2019). https://doi.org/10.1016/j.trb.2018. 11.004

20. Malena, K., Link, C., Mertin, S., Gausemeier, S., Trächtler, A.: Validation of an online state estimation concept for microscopic traffic simulations. In: IEEE Transportation Electrification Conference and Expo (2021)

21. Bierlaire, M., Crittin, F.: An efficient algorithm for real-time estimation and prediction of dynamic OD tables. Oper. Res. **52**(1), 116–127 (2004). https://doi.org/10.1287/opre.1030. 0071

22. Bundesministerium für Verkehr, Bau und Stadtentwicklung: Technische Lieferbedingungen für Streckenstationen. Bundesministerium für Verkehr, Bau und Stadtentwicklung, Berlin (2012)

23. Produktprospekt TOPO. Fahrzeug-klassifizierungssysteme, Deutschland, Bad Lippspringe (2019)

24. Forschungsgesellschaft für Straßen- und Verkehrswesen: Richtlinien für Lichtsignalanlagen. RiLSA: Lichtzeichenanlagen für den Straßenverkehr. FGSV R1 - Regelwerke, FGSV-321, Köln (2015)

25. Urbanik, T., et al.: Signal Timing Manual -, 2nd edn. Transportation Research Board, Washington, D.C. (2015)

26. Schulz, G., Graf, C.: Regelungstechnik 2. Mehrgrößenregelung, Digitale Regelungstechnik, Fuzzy-Regelung, 3rd edn. De Gruyter, München (2013)

27. Land NRW: Karte Schloß Neuhaus. Datenlizenz Deutschland -Namensnennung -Version 2.0 (2019). www.govdata.de/dl-de/by-2-0

28. Bottazzi, M., Tcheumadjeu, L.C.T., Trumpold, J., Erdmann, J., Oertel, R.: LiSuM: design and development of a middleware to couple virtual LISA+ TLS controller and SUMO simulation. In: Proceedings of the SUMO 2017, vol. 31, pp. 179–192 (2017)

29. Liu, G.P.: Predictive controller design of networked systems with communication delays and data loss. IEEE Trans. Circuits Syst. II **57**(6), 481–485 (2010). https://doi.org/10.1109/TCSII. 2010.2048377

30. Hirano, H., Mukai, M., Azuma, T., Fujita, M.: Optimal control of discrete-time linear systems with network-induced varying delay. In: Proceedings of the 2005 American Control Conference, ACC, Hilton Portland & Executive Tower. Portland, OR, USA, 8–10 June 2005, pp. 1419–1424. IEEE Service Center, Piscataway (2005). https://doi.org/10.1109/ACC.2005. 1470164

Solving Complex Intersection Management Problems Using Bi-level MINLPs and Piecewise Linearization Techniques

Matthias Gerdts[1] , Sergejs Rogovs[1(✉)], and Giammarco Valenti[2]

[1] Department of Aerospace Engineering, Institute of Applied Mathematics and Scientific Computing, Universität der Bundeswehr München, Neubiberg, Germany
{matthias.gerdts,sergejs.rogovs}@unibw.de
[2] Department of Industrial Engineering, University of Trento, Trento, Italy
giammarco.valenti@unitn.it

Abstract. We investigate a complex Intersection Management Problem (IMP) for automated vehicles and introduce a method for the automated coordination of vehicles with the aim to minimize total clearance time for the intersection. The method is capable of handling multiple vehicles (per lane or distributed over several lanes), multiple lanes, variable arrival times and velocities, and multiple turn options in non-symmetric intersection scenarios. In order to optimally coordinate the vehicles we employ a bi-level optimization formulation coupling a scheduling problem at the upper level with an optimal control problem at the lower level. The latter takes into account the dynamics of the vehicles and the former aims to find an optimal sequence of arrivals at the intersection. Collision avoidance on the complete driving paths, i.e., at, before and after the intersection, is ensured by the problem formulation. In order to solve the resulting mixed-integer nonlinear bi-level optimization problem we develop suitable piecewise linearization techniques for the value function of the optimal control problems which eventually yields a large-scale mixed-integer linear problem. Numerical examples show the efficiency of the proposed approach.

Keywords: Connected and automated vehicles · Cooperative driving · Intersection management · Piecewise linearization · Mixed integer nonlinear programming

1 Introduction

The emerging development of automated and autonomous vehicles introduces many challenges in view of perception, path planning, and control. The coordination of interacting automated vehicles is among such challenges with high demands regarding collision avoidance. Especially, intersection scenarios are well-suited to develop and to demonstrate useful coordination control methods, since they frequently occur in everyday urban traffic, and many vehicles typically interact in a comparatively small area. Such intersection scenarios have gained a lot of attention in recent years, see the surveys [14, 18, 20] for an overview. The coordination problem can be addressed in a centralized or distributed fashion. Distributed control approaches can be found in [1, 2, 16]. A

© Springer Nature Switzerland AG 2022
C. Klein et al. (Eds.): SMARTGREENS 2021/ VEHITS 2021, CCIS 1612, pp. 255–273, 2022.
https://doi.org/10.1007/978-3-031-17098-0_13

priority-based model-predictive control approach is described in [15], while [2,5] use generalized Nash equilibrium problems for coordination.

In this paper we adopt the centralized viewpoint and assume that there is a central instance which determines the driving schedule and communicates it to the vehicles. Note that vehicle-to-X communication is required in either case, be it centralized or distributed. From a centralized viewpoint traffic efficiency is desirable, that is, the vehicles should be coordinated such that the total time, which is necessary to clear the intersection, is minimized. Nevertheless, other objectives, e.g. energy efficiency or driving comfort, may be considered as well. Of course, collision avoidance is an indispensable requirement throughout. We propose a bi-level optimization problem to coordinate the vehicles. The so-called upper-level problem is a mixed-integer scheduling problem, which aims to find optimal arrival times at the intersection for the vehicles. The upper level-problem depends on the actual trajectories of the vehicles and their velocity profiles. The latter are determined by optimal control problems at the lower-level. Both optimization levels are coupled and we obtain a mixed-integer nonlinear bi-level optimization problem. A related problem was investigated in [11–13], where an SQP-type method was used for its solution. In contrast, we propose a method based on piecewise linearization, compare [19], which results in an MILP formulation. It turns out that the MILP can be solved quickly and robustly even for complex scenarios. Scheduling problems with simplifying assumptions are also considered in [7, 17].

The method developed in this paper builds upon the basic intersection management model derived in [9] and extends it in several directions. An algorithmic improvement is achieved by adding an adaptive linearization method in Sect. 4, which enhances the previous non-adaptive strategy. The adaptive method allows to control the approximation error in the piecewise linearization more effectively. Moreover, the model was improved such that multiple cars per lane can be handled. To this end, additional constraints for collision avoidance became necessary, compare (8)-(10), while the original model contained merely constraints (7). Furthermore, rear-end collision avoidance constraints before the intersection were introduced in (11) and rear-end collision constraints after the intersection are given by (8) and (10). As a result of these modifications even more realistic, and thus more complex scenarios can be handled. The piecewise linearization approach allows to approximate the bi-level MINLP as a single-stage MILP, which can be solved to global optimality in a very reasonable time. Herein, the approximation error introduced by the piecewise linearization can be controlled using the adaptive scheme. We consider this property a great advantage. The proposed approach outperforms as a simple first-come first-serve heuristic (FCFS) by more than 60%. A similar result was obtained in [11], where no turns or rear-end collision avoidance constraints outside the intersection are considered.

The paper is organized as follows. Underlying assumptions and modeling concepts are presented in Sect. 2. The intersection management problem is formulated as a bi-level optimization problem with an optimal control problem at the lower-level and a scheduling problem at the upper-level in Sect. 3. Section 4 is devoted to the adaptive piecewise linearization technique, which is the key to an efficient solution of the intersection management problem. Numerical simulations for complex intersection scenarios are presented in Sect. 5. Finally, Sect. 6 contains conclusions and an outlook with potential extensions.

2   General Considerations and Assumptions

In this section we define the scope of our considerations by introducing main definitions and assumptions on vehicle states and intersection geometry. Most of the following considerations were essentially discussed in [9], and in the underlying work we try to keep the corresponding descriptions as short as possible. The most significant difference lies in [9, Assumption 1], namely in its absence in this paper. Here, in comparison to [9] a general case with an unlimited number of vehicles per lane is considered. Moreover, in this work we consider three (instead of two) phases of vehicle motion.

2.1   Vehicles

Throughout this paper we denote by N the total number of vehicles and the corresponding index set by $\mathcal{V} = \{1, \ldots, N\}$, where two consecutive vehicles in the same lane possess consecutive indices. We assume that the states of each vehicle result from some optimal control problem and are known without any uncertainties.

Assumption 1. *The states of each vehicle are known without any uncertainties.*

Moreover, we assume that we deal only with feasible initial conditions. This is straightforward and essentially means that those initial conditions which eventually lead to an accident are excluded. Note that in the context of CAVs this assumption is either fulfilled or some vehicles have to execute a fail-safe maneuver.

Assumption 2. *Only feasible initial conditions are considered.*

2.2   Intersection Geometry

Lanes: The lanes that enter/exit an intersection are called *entering/exit* lanes. It is not allowed to overtake within the same lane, and no lane change is allowed within the portion of the intersection considered in the problem. This assumption is a very common in the literature, see e.g. [18].

Assumption 3. *No overtake or lane change maneuvers are allowed.*

Paths: There exists some predefined path with explicitly known geometry which connects each entering lane with each exit lane. The number of all paths is denoted by M and the corresponding index set by $\mathcal{P} = \{1, \ldots, M\}$. The corresponding vehicle-to-path mapping reads as

$$P : \mathcal{V} \to \mathcal{P},$$

where for every $i \in \mathcal{V}$ there exists exactly one $k \in \mathcal{P}$ such that $P(i) = k$. We assume that every car follows exactly one path which depends on the car's route.

Assumption 4. *Each vehicle follows exactly one predefined path.*

Conflict Zone: Obviously, a vehicle can not be represented by just a single point on the corresponding path, its planar dimensions also have to be taken into account. We assume that the footprint of each vehicle is represented by a rectangle whose geometrical center coincides with its position. A *conflict zone* (CZ) is the area of an intersection that contains all the overlapping points of all paths enhanced by vehicle footprints. For simplicity it is usually assumed that a CZ is given by some polygon, see Fig. 1 where a canonical intersection which a square CZ is depicted.

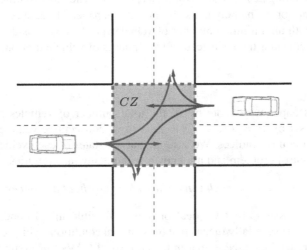

Fig. 1. Example of an intersection geometry. The figure shows a classical road intersection. It consists of 4 entering lanes, 4 exit lanes, and 3 possible paths for each arriving car ($M = 12$ paths in total). The conflict zone (CZ) is the ark area in the center.

Once a conflict zone is defined, the longitudinal motion of each vehicle can be broken down into three phases: the *approaching phase*, the *intersection phase* and the *departure phase*. The approaching phase deals with the vehicle motion from the initial position to the point where the conflict zone begins. The main issue in this phase is rear-end collision avoidance of consecutive vehicles in the same entering lane. We solve this issue by introducing constraints (11). The intersection phase starts where the first phase finishes and ends when a vehicle leaves the conflict zone. In this phase we have different types of possible collisions. Constraints (7)–(10) handle all those conflicts. And, the departure phase begins when the intersection phase ends. The issue related to this phase is rear-end collision avoidance of the vehicles which possess the same exit lane. The remedy for this issue lies in the introduction of some headway time between a pair consecutive vehicles sharing the same exit lane. This appears in constraints (8) and (10). The velocity of each vehicle is assumed to be constant during the intersection phase. This assumption is also widely used in the literature, see e.g. [18].

Assumption 5. *The velocity of each vehicle during the intersection phase is constant.*

Conflict Matrix: A so-called *conflict matrix* captures all possible combinations of pairwise intersecting paths. If there is no conflict between a pair of paths the corresponding entry of the matrix is equal to zero. For all conflicting pairs $k, l \in \mathcal{P}$ we distinguish among four cases depending on the entering and exit lanes of each path. Each of these cases corresponds to some integer entry of the matrix. Consequently, the entry of the conflict matrix corresponding to paths $k, l \in \mathcal{P}$ is given by

$$
c_{kl} = \begin{cases}
0, & \textit{no conflict,} \\
1, & \textit{different entering lanes, different exit lanes,} \\
2, & \textit{different entering lanes, same exit lane,} \\
3, & \textit{same entering lane, different exit lanes,} \\
4, & \textit{same entering lane, same exit lane.}
\end{cases}
$$

We use this matrix for the formulation of collision avoidance constraints (7)–(11). An example of the 10-lane intersection (see Fig. 5) is given in Appendix A.

All the quantities and variables from this paper are collected in Table 1, see Appendix A.

3   Bi-level Problem Formulation

This section is devoted to the formulation of a bi-level optimization problem which we use as a model to solve the intersection management problem. For each vehicle in our consideration the lower-level problem is represented by OCP (4). The objective of such problem is to maximize the velocity of the vehicle at the end of the corresponding approaching phase. Due to its simplicity the OCP (4) can be solved analytically by treating the final times as parameters. As a result we get final velocities (5) as functions of the corresponding final times. The upper-level problem is another optimization problem whose objective is to obtain optimal intersection crossing sequence (with the corresponding intersection entering times) in terms of minimal total time elapsed. For this reason, the series of scheduling and collision avoidance constraints (7)–(11) is defined where final velocities (5) and their reciprocals (6) play an essential role. This results in a mixed-integer nonlinear problem (P).

3.1   Lower-Level Problem: Vehicle Motion

As stated above, the vehicle model we use is the double integrator. This choice is motivated by the fact that for such a model we can find an analytic solution. The states of each vehicle are given by its curvilinear coordinates along a predefined path $s_i(t)$, $i \in \mathcal{V}$, and its derivatives (longitudinal velocities) $v_i(t)$, $i \in \mathcal{V}$. The controls are longitudinal accelerations/decelerations denoted by $a_i(t)$, $i \in \mathcal{V}$. We assume that the coordinates $s_i(t)$ vanish at the end of the corresponding approaching phase, the velocities $v_i(t)$ are non-negative and bounded from above, and the controls $a_i(t)$ are bounded from below and above by some box constraints by $a_{m,i}$ and $a_{M,i}$, $i \in \mathcal{V}$, respectively. The resulting model for each $i \in \mathcal{V}$ reads as

$$
\begin{aligned}
\dot{v}_i(t) &= a_i(t), \\
\dot{s}_i(t) &= v_i(t)
\end{aligned}
\tag{1}
$$

with

$$
\begin{aligned}
a_{m,i} &\le a_i(t) \le a_{M,i}, \\
0 &\le v_i(t) \le v_{M,i},
\end{aligned}
\tag{2}
$$

where $v_{M,i}$ denotes the legal speed limit. The corresponding initial conditions read as

$$s_i(t_0) = -s_{0,i},$$
$$v_i(t_0) = v_{0,i},$$

(3)

where $s_{0,i}$ is the distance to the CZ staring at time, and $v_{0,i}$ is the corresponding initial velocity. Note that we have a minus sign in front of the terms $s_{0,i}$, $i \in \mathcal{V}$, since those have positive values.

For the formulation of an optimal control problem we argue as follows. Taking into account Assumption 5 and the fact that the global objective of the intersection management problem is to minimize the total time it takes for all vehicles to clear a given intersection, we want each vehicle to enter an intersection with the maximum possible velocity. Hence, the underlying OCP for each $i \in \mathcal{V}$ reads as

$$\max_{a_i(t)} \ v_i(t_i)$$

(4a)

$$\text{s.t.} \quad (1), (2), (3),$$

(4b)

$$s_i(t_i) = 0, \quad v_i(t_i) \leq v_{P(i)}, \quad t \in I_{t_0}^{t_i},$$

(4c)

where $I_{t_0}^{t_i}$ denotes the time interval from the starting time t_0 to the time t_i at which the geometrical center of the i-th car enters an intersection, and is treated as a parameter. The upper bound on the final velocity $v_{P(i)}$ depends on the maximum curvature of the corresponding path $P(i) \in \mathcal{P}$. The OCPs from above can be solved analytically, hence we obtain final velocities as continuous functions of final times

$$v_i(t_i), \quad t_i \in I_{t_{i,min}}^{t_{i,max}}, \quad i \in \mathcal{V}.$$

(5)

where $t_{i,min}$ denotes the minimal time when the i-th car can enter the intersection, and $t_{i,max}$ denotes some reasonable time after which we are sure that the i-th car will not enter the intersection. In Sect. 3.2, when we state constraints for the upper level problem, we require reciprocal of these functions, which are given by

$$T_i(t_i) := 1/v_i(t_i), \quad t_i \in I_{t_{i,min}}^{t_{i,max}}, \quad i \in \mathcal{V}.$$

(6)

Obviously, the lower limits $t_{i,min}$, $i \in \mathcal{V}$, can be determined as a minimal time problem, i.e. by substituting (4a) with

$$\min_{a_i(t)} \ t_i$$

in problem (4). The upper limits $t_{i,max}$, $i \in \mathcal{V}$, on the other hand, do not have to be determined precisely, because starting from some $t_{i,\star} \in I_{t_{i,min}}^{t_{i,max}}$, $i \in \mathcal{V}$, which in turn can be found analytically, the corresponding velocities will be constant due to velocity saturation.

As in [9], in the underlying work we also restrict ourselves to the final velocity optimization subject to the double integrator for each vehicle. However, techniques presented in this papers can be also applied to any parametric functions of t_i, and if no analytic solution can be found, one can use instead some interpolation of the corresponding numerical solution.

3.2   Upper-Level Problem: Intersection Management

In this part of the underlying work we formulate the intersection management problem subject to individual vehicle motions from the previous section. In the sequel we define a series of different constraints which ensure not only collision avoidance in the CZ, but also in the approaching and departure phases, and conclude this section with the complete problem formulation.

By means of scheduling constraints, which we discuss first, one can determine an optimal sequence of entering the CZ provided that no collisions occur between any pair of vehicle whose corresponding footprints can possibly overlap. Such overlaps together with some *safety margin* form a so-called *overlapping zone*. Possible overlapping zones are discussed in the sequel of this section. The first set of scheduling constraints, which apply for those pairs of cars which possess **different entering lanes** and **different exit lanes**, reads as

$$t_i + L_{ij}^a T_i(t_i) - t_j - L_{ji}^b T_j(t_j) \leq C_{large}(1 - w_{ij}), \tag{7a}$$

$$t_j + L_{ji}^a T_j(t_j) - t_i - L_{ij}^b T_i(t_i) \leq C_{large} w_{ij},$$

$$w_{ij} \in \{0, 1\},$$

$$\forall i, j \in \mathcal{V} \quad \text{with} \quad c_{P(i)P(j)} = 1, \tag{7b}$$

where C_{large} denotes some large positive constant, at least as large as the time at which the last vehicle clears the intersection. Since this quantity is never known in advance, one can choose instead just some very large constant. So, in case of $c_{P(i),P(j)} = 1$ for some $i, j \in \mathcal{V}$ we want to know which of the corresponding vehicles should go first. For this reason, we introduce the binary variable w_{ij} which actually indicates the priority, i.e. if $w_{ij} = 1$, the i-th vehicle goes before the j-th one and vice versa for $w_{ij} = 0$. That is why constraints (7) are usually called "either-or" constraints [19]. Indeed, assume that $w_{ij} = 1$. In this case (7a) reads as

$$t_i + L_{ij}^a T_i(t_i) \leq t_j + L_{ji}^b T_j(t_j),$$

where L_{ij}^a denotes the length of the path $P(i)$ which i-th vehicle has to travel in a CZ in order to leave the overlapping zone with the path of j-th vehicle. The term L_{ji}^b, in turn, denotes the length of the path $P(j)$ which the j-th vehicle has to travel in a CZ before entering the overlapping zone with the path of i-th vehicle. For a better understanding of the quantities see Fig. 2. Taking into account (6), the inequality from above states exactly what we wanted: the i-th car has to leave the overlapping zone before the j-th car enters it. Inequality (7b) becomes inactive due to the choice of C_{large}. An analogous argument holds for $w_{ij} = 0$.

There are different ways how to define an overlapping zone. Two limiting cases are worth to discuss, namely when an overlapping zone is defined in a way such that vehicle footprints do not overlap, but there is no additional safety margin (vehicles can touch each other at one single point), and when a safety margin is the whole CZ. Obviously, the first case is not appropriate in any real-world situation, hence in a real-world scenario we need to preserve some safety margin for each pair of conflicting paths. In the second case constraints (7) can be simplified to

$$t_i + L_{P(i)}T_i(t_i) - t_j \le C_{large}(1 - w_{ij}),$$
$$t_j + L_{P(j)}T_j(t_j) - t_i \le C_{large}w_{ij},$$
$$w_{ij} \in \{0, 1\},$$
$$\forall i, j \in \mathcal{V} \quad \text{with} \quad c_{P(i)P(j)} = 1,$$

where $L_{P(i)}$ and $L_{P(j)}$ denote the lengths of the $P(i)$'s and $P(j)$'s paths, respectively, see Fig. 2.

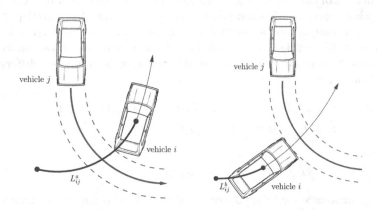

Fig. 2. CZ representation with the quantities L_{ij}^a (left picture) and L_{ij}^b (right picture), respectively.

The other set of scheduling constraints applies for those pairs of vehicles which possess **different entering lanes** and the **same exit lane**. These constraints differ from the first ones by the fact that we have to avoid rear-end collisions in the departure phase. This issue can be solved e.g. with a help of some headway time which is defined as the time it takes for the leading vehicle to reach the maximum velocity in the exit lane. Only after that the following vehicle is allowed to exit the intersection. The corresponding scheduling conditions read as

$$t_i + L_{P(i)}T_i(t_i) + T_i^{headway}(t_i) - t_j - L_{ji}^b T_j(t_j) \le C_{large}(1 - w_{ij}), \qquad (8a)$$
$$t_j + L_{P(j)}T_j(t_j) + T_j^{headway}(t_j) - t_i - L_{ij}^b T_i(t_i) \le C_{large}w_{ij},$$
$$w_{ij} \in \{0, 1\},$$
$$\forall i, j \in \mathcal{V} \quad \text{with} \quad c_{P(i)P(j)} = 2, \qquad (8b)$$

where

$$T_i^{headway}(t_i) := \frac{v_{exit} - v_i(t_i)}{a_{M,i}}, \quad t_i \in I_{t_{i,min}}^{t_{i,max}}, \quad i \in \mathcal{V},$$

and v_{exit} denotes the maximum velocity in the exit lane. We assume that v_{exit} is the same for each exit lane. Moreover, without loss of generality, we assume that $v_{exit} \ge v_{P(i)}$, $i \in \mathcal{V}$.

So far, we successfully defined constraints which ensure both collision avoidance within the intersection (and after in case of same exit lanes) and optimal entering sequence. However, this is not sufficient, and we need to take care of those vehicles which approach the intersection from the same lane. Note that this is not a scheduling case due to Assumption 3. The constraints corresponding to the case with the **same entering lane** and **different exit lanes** read as

$$t_i + L_{ii+1}^a T_i(t_i) - t_{i+1} \leq 0,$$
$$\forall i \in \mathcal{V} \quad \text{with} \quad c_{P(i)P(i+1)} = 3, \tag{9}$$

and the case when a pair of consecutive cars possesses the **same entering lane** and the **same exit lane** is covered by

$$t_i + L_{ii+1}^a T_i(t_i) - t_{i+1} \leq 0, \tag{10a}$$
$$t_i + L_{P(i)} \left(T_i(t_i) - T_{i+1}(t_{i+1}) \right) + T_i^{headway}(t_i) - t_{i+1} \leq 0,$$
$$\forall i \in \mathcal{V} \quad \text{with} \quad c_{P(i)P(i+1)} = 4. \tag{10b}$$

Constraints (9) and (10a) have the same meaning as constraints (7). One can actually derive them from e.g. (7a) by taking into account that no scheduling variables are required in this case, and by setting $L_{ji}^b = 0$. The latter can be explained by the fact that the corresponding overlapping zones are always located at the very beginning of the CZ. However, this is also not sufficient if a pair of consecutive vehicles share the same exit lane, and in this case we additionally exploit the same argument as for (8). We obtain inequality (10) from e.g. (8a) (without scheduling variables) by setting $L_{ji}^b = L_{p(i)}$, since all overlapping zones in this case coincide with the whole CZ.

The last, but arguably, the hardest issue in the intersection management problem is rear-end collision avoidance during the approaching phase. Due to the formulation of the underlying OCPs one can show that each vehicle's motion is subject to a bang-bang control. Moreover, it always has the following structure: decelerate (if needed) - accelerate - constant velocity $v_{P(i)}$, $i \in \mathcal{V}$ (if reached), and the corresponding control *switching point* form deceleration to acceleration can be explicitly determined as a function of final the time t_i. This function reads as

$$T_i^{switch}(t_i) := \frac{v_{0,i} - v_i(t_i) - a_{m,i}t_0 + a_{M,i}t_i}{a_{M,i} - a_{m,i}}, \quad t_i \in I_{t_i,min}^{t_i,max}, \quad i \in \mathcal{V}.$$

The corresponding rear-end collision constraints are motivated by natural driving behavior, namely the following vehicle starts to accelerate only after the leading vehicle has started its acceleration. The constraints are given by

$$T_i^{switch}(t_i) - T_{i+1}^{switch}(t_{i+1}) \leq 0,$$
$$\forall i \in \mathcal{V} \quad \text{with} \quad c_{P(i)P(i+1)} = 4. \tag{11}$$

Now, we are at a position to formulate the upper level optimization problem. As already stated before, the goal of the intersection management problem is to minimize the total time it takes for all vehicles in our consideration to clear an intersection. Note that we do not know in advance which vehicle is going to be the last one. Therefore, the objective function can be chosen as a total sum of individual maneuver durations. The underlying optimization problem results in the mixed integer nonlinear problem given by

$$\min_{t_i, w_{ij}} \sum_{i=1}^{N} \left[t_i + L_{P(i)} T_i(t_i) \right], \tag{P}$$
$$\text{s.t.} \quad (7) - (11).$$

There are two options of how to approach problem (P) numerically. One can either solve the problem with a non-linear solver, e.g. based on some SQP-type algorithm [6], or first transform the problem into a linear one and then solve it with some linear solver. In in this paper we choose the second option, due to two following reasons. First, nonlinear solvers are not robust, and since we deal with a safety critical problem, we want to have a control over the error of the corresponding numerical solution. Second, as we will see in the sequel, modern linear solvers, e.g. GUROBI MILP-solver [10] which we exploit for our simulations, are fast enough to handle problems resulting from a linearization of (P).

4 Piecewise Linearization

In this section we present two linearization techniques – adaptive and non-adaptive – we use to solve problem (P). The non-adaptive one can be found e.g. in [19]. The idea behind such an approach is to use convex combinations of nonlinear function values at discretization points, and to let the solver choose the *optimal* subintervals where the corresponding variables attain their optimal values by introducing some auxiliary (including binary) variables. This approach, however, has one potential drawback. Namely, one has to use sufficiently fine time discretizations in order to guarantee small error between nonlinear functions and their linearized values, which requires two additional variables (continuous and binary) per discretization point in the problem formulation. Instead, one can start with some coarse discretizations of each interval $I_{t_{i,min}}^{t_{i,max}}$, $i \in \mathcal{V}$, and then adaptively refine optimal subintervals until some predefined discretization error tolerance ε is fulfilled. For this sake, we can slightly modify the adaptive linearization technique from [4], see also [3], by exploiting the structure of the underlying problem in order to get better numerical results. Since the non-adaptive technique was already successfully introduced in [9], and it can be easily derived from the more complex (adaptive) algorithm, we devote this section mostly to the introduction of the adaptive technique.

Before we present the iterative algorithm, let us first present problem's (P) linear relaxation. For this reason, we introduce discretizations (not necessarily equidistant) of the time intervals $I_{t_{i,min}}^{t_{i,max}}$, $i \in \mathcal{V}$ which are given by

$$\mathcal{T}_i := \{t_{i,1}, t_{i,2}, \ldots, t_{i,K_i}\},$$

with $t_{i,1} = t_{i,min}$ and $t_{i,K_i} = t_{i,min}$, where K_i denotes the number of discretization points. Moreover, we need to introduce the maximum linearization error in terms of the maximum under- and overestimator of a function. Let $f(t)$ be some nonlinear function over the interval $I_{t_a}^{t_b}$ and $\phi(t)$ its linear approximation with $f(t_a) = \phi(t_a)$ and $f(t_b) = \phi(t_b)$, then we call

$$e_u(f, I_{t_a}^{t_b}) := \max_{t \in I_{t_a}^{t_b}} f(t) - \phi(t)$$

the maximum *underestimator* error and

$$e_o(f, I_{t_a}^{t_b}) := \max_{t \in I_{t_a}^{t_b}} \phi(t) - f(t)$$

the maximum *overestimator* error. For a detailed discussion on the under- and overestimators see [8, Section 4].

In the next steps we present all necessary auxiliary variables and constraints required for the problem discretization. For each $i \in V$ we introduce the binary variables $z_{i,k}$, $k \in \{1, \ldots, K_i - 1\}$ (*pointers*), and the real variables $\lambda_{i,k}$, $k \in \{1, \ldots, K_i\}$ (*lambdas*). The role of the pointers is to indicate the optimal subinterval (where the variable t_i attains its optimal value). Therefore, only one pointer can have a non-zero value. This results in the following constraints

$$\sum_{k=1}^{K_i-1} z_{i,k} = 1,$$
$$z_{i,k} \in \{0, 1\},$$
$$k \in \{1, \ldots, K_i - 1\}. \tag{12}$$

In turn, the role of the lambdas is nothing else but to build a convex combination over the subinterval which the non-zero pointer is pointing at. Therefore, the lambdas shall also sum up to one

$$\sum_{k=1}^{K_i} \lambda_{i,k} = 1, \tag{13}$$
$$k \in \{1, \ldots, K_i\}.$$

Moreover, in order to build a convex combination over the optimal subinterval, only two consecutive lambdas can be unequal to zero. This can be guaranteed by the following relation

$$\lambda_{i,1} \leq z_{i,1},$$
$$\lambda_{i,k} \leq z_{i,k-1} + z_{i,k}, \quad k \in \{2, \ldots, K_i - 1\}, \tag{14}$$
$$\lambda_{i,K_i} \leq z_{i,K_i-1}.$$

To construct a piecewise linear relaxation of (P), one has to make sure that all feasible points of (P) are also feasible for its corresponding relaxation. This can be provided by building the so-called *envelopes* around piecewise linear functions, i.e. by relaxing them with corresponding maximum under- and overestimators. Since nonlinear functions in our consideration are (5) and (6), for each $i \in V$ the corresponding linearizations read as

$$t_i = \sum_{k=1}^{K_i} \lambda_{i,k} \, t_{i,k}, \tag{15a}$$

$$T_{i,pw} = \sum_{k=1}^{K_i} \lambda_{i,k}\, T_i(t_{i,k}) + e_{i,T}, \tag{15b}$$

$$v_{i,pw} = \sum_{k=1}^{K_i} \lambda_{i,k}\, v_i(t_{i,k}) + e_{i,v}, \tag{15c}$$

$$e_{i,T} \geq - \sum_{k=1}^{K_i-1} e_o\left(T_i, I_{t_{i,k}}^{t_{i,k+1}}\right) z_{i,k}, \tag{15d}$$

$$e_{i,T} \leq \sum_{k=1}^{K_i-1} e_u\left(T_i, I_{t_{i,k}}^{t_{i,k+1}}\right) z_{i,k}, \tag{15e}$$

$$e_{i,v} \geq - \sum_{k=1}^{K_i-1} e_o\left(v_i, I_{t_{i,k}}^{t_{i,k+1}}\right) z_{i,k}, \tag{15f}$$

$$e_{i,v} \leq \sum_{k=1}^{K_i-1} e_u\left(v_i, I_{t_{i,k}}^{t_{i,k+1}}\right) z_{i,k}, \tag{15g}$$

where (15a) is the time variable expressed as a linear combination of discretization points, (15b) and (15c) are the linearizations of the nonlinearities $v_i(\cdot)$ and $T_i(\cdot)$ (see Fig. (3)) with the corresponding envelope terms, respectively, which in turn are bounded by the respective maximum under- and overestimators (15d)–(15g) (Fig. 3).

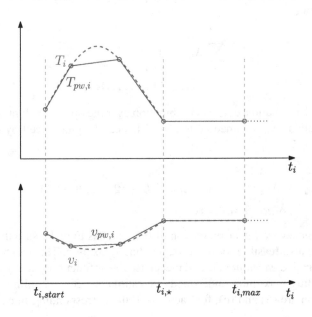

Fig. 3. Example of piecewise linearization of the underlying nonlinear functions.

Finally, the mixed integer linear relaxation of (P) reads as

$$\min_{t_i,w_{ij},T_{i,pw},v_{i,pw},e_{i,T},e_{i,v}} \sum_{i=1}^{N} \left[t_i + L_{P(i)} T_{i,pw} \right], \tag{Π}$$

$$\text{s.t.} \quad (7)-(15)$$

where continuous variables in constraints (7)–(11) have to be replaced by their discrete counterparts. Problem (Π) can be slightly simplified, which actually results in significantly faster runtimes of the corresponding implementation, see Sect. 5. This simplification is given by the following proposition.

Proposition 1. *In problem (Π) conditions* (15d) *and* (15e) *can be replaced by*

$$e_{i,T} = - \sum_{k=1}^{K_i-1} e_o \left(T_i, I_{t_{i,k}}^{t_{i,k+1}} \right) z_{i,k}, \quad i \in \mathcal{V}.$$

Proof. The statement of the proposition follows from the objective function. For each $i \in \mathcal{V}$ consider the second summand in the objective function

$$L_{P(i)} T_{i,pw} = L_{P(i)} \left(\sum_{k=1}^{K_i} \lambda_{i,k} T_i(t_{i,k}) + e_{i,T} \right),$$

where we used condition (15b). Since $L_{P(i)}$ is some positive constant, it is obvious that the minimum is attained when the variable $e_{i,T}$ is equal to the corresponding lower bound. □

The adaptive algorithm works as follows. We start with some coarse discretizations T_i of the corresponding time intervals $I_{t_{i,min}}^{t_{i,max}}$, $i \in \mathcal{V}$. Then, in each iteration step we refine those subintervals where some predefined error bound ε is violated. Note that the nonlinearities $v_i(\cdot)$ and $T_i(\cdot)$, $i \in \mathcal{V}$ share the same argument, hence for each $i \in \mathcal{V}$ we have to consider the maximum of the respective errors. The refined time discretizations are then used in the next iteration step. This procedure is repeated until the error bound is satisfied for all $i \in \mathcal{V}$. A more detailed description is given in Algorithm 1. According to [4, Corollary 3.7], Algorithm 1 terminates after a finite number of steps, if (P) is feasible and all nonlinear functions are at least continuous.

Remark 1. Note that the result in [4, Corollary 3.7] is proven for a midpoint refinement technique. However, by arguing in the same way as in [4, Section 3.1], one can easily show that this result also holds for the refinement strategy with m equidistant discretization points, if all nonlinear functions are one-dimensional.

In contrast, the non-adaptive approach works as follows. Essentially, one has to choose discretizations T, $i \in \mathcal{V}$ such that the error bound ε is preserved for all $t_i \in I_{t_{i,min}}^{t_{i,max}}$, $i \in \mathcal{V}$, and solve problem (Π) without the envelope terms. Note that the corresponding feasible set is not a superset of the feasible set of (P), which is not a big problem in practical applications, if ε is sufficiently small.

For both the non-adaptive approach and each iteration in the adaptive one problem (Π) is solved with the GUROBI MILP-solver [10] whose core is a linear-programming based branch-and-bound algorithm. The next section is devoted to numerical simulations.

Algorithm 1. Global optimization by adaptively refined MIP relaxations.

Require: An MINLP (P), initial tolerance ε_0, the maximal linearization error ε and the number of new discretization points m.

Ensure: If (P) is feasible, the algorithm returns an optimal solution $\bar{t}_i$, $i \in \mathcal{V}$ of an MIP relaxation (Π) of (P) with $|v_i(\bar{t}_i) - v_{i,pw}| \leq \varepsilon$ and $|T_i(\bar{t}_i) - T_{i,pw}| \leq \varepsilon$, $i \in \mathcal{V}$ and the corresponding objective value is minimal for any admissible point of (P).

1: Define initial discretizations $\mathcal{T}_i$, $i \in \mathcal{V}$ such that the corresponding nonlinearities satisfy the initial tolerance.
2: Set $n \leftarrow 0$
3: **repeat**
4:     Construct an MIP relaxation Π^n of (P) from $\mathcal{T}_i^n$, $i \in \mathcal{V}$.
5:     Solve Π^n
6:     **if** Π^n is *feasible* **then**
7:         Set t_i^n, $i \in \mathcal{V} \leftarrow$ optimal solution of Π^n
8:         Set $T_{i,pw}^n$, $v_{i,pw}^n$, $i \in \mathcal{V} \leftarrow$ linear approximation values of the corresponding nonlinear functions
9:     **else**
10:         **return** *infeasible*
11:     **end if**
12:     Set stop $\leftarrow$ true
13:     **for all** $i \in \mathcal{V}$ **do**
14:         Set $err_T^n \leftarrow |T_i(t_i^n) - T_{i,pw}|$
15:         Set $err_v^n \leftarrow |v_i(t_i^n) - v_{i,pw}|$
16:         Set $err^n \leftarrow \max\{err_T^n, err_v^n\}$
17:         **if** $err^n > \varepsilon$ **then**
18:             Set $k \leftarrow$ the index of the corresponding nonzero pointer $z_{i,k}^n$ from the solution of Π^n
19:             Set $\Delta \leftarrow \frac{t_{i,k+1} - t_{i,k}}{m+1}$
20:             Set $\mathcal{T}_{new} \leftarrow \{t_{i,k} + \Delta, t_{i,k} + 2\Delta, \ldots, t_{i,k} + m\Delta\}$
21:             Set $\mathcal{T}_i^{n+1} \leftarrow \mathcal{T}_i^n \cup \mathcal{T}_{new}$
22:             Set stop $\leftarrow$ false
23:         **else**
24:             Set $\mathcal{T}_i^{n+1} \leftarrow \mathcal{T}_i^n$
25:         **end if**
26:     **end for**
27:     Set $n \leftarrow n + 1$
28: **until** stop
29: **return** t_i^{n-1}, $i \in \mathcal{V}$

---

5 Numerical Simulations

We performed numerical simulations for two different intersection geometries: 16-lane intersection and 10-lane irregular intersection as depicted in Fig. 4 and 5, respectively. For both intersection geometries we place 3 identical vehicles with $a_{m,i} = -5 \ m/s^2$, $a_{M,i} = 3 \ m/s^2$, $i \in \mathcal{V}$ in each entering lane. This results in 24 and 12 cars in the 16- and 10-lane intersections, respectively. The minimum distance from the CZ is chosen to be 30 m for the 16-lane intersection and 20 m for the 10-lane intersection. The distance between two consecutive vehicles in the same lane is always 20 m in both cases. This is a reasonable safety distance for the initial velocities which are randomly generated with normal distribution $\mathcal{N}(10, 1)$. For simplicity reasons we assumed that $T^{headway}$ has a constant value of 3 s. For the adaptive approach for all non-linear functions we choose initial linearizations with 4 grid points and the number of refinements in each iteration is $m = 5$. All simulations are performed on an Intel quad-core i7 2, 9 GHz processor.

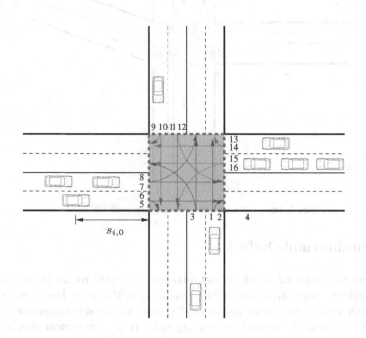

Fig. 4. Intersection geometry with 16 lanes.

Algorithm Performance for the 16-Lane Intersection: In the non-adaptive case a solution is found in 0.63 s, whereas maximum number of grid points for one of the underlying nonlinearities is 84. In the adaptive case a solution is found in 0.61 s.

Algorithm Performance for the 10-Lane Irregular Intersection: In the non-adaptive case a solution is found in 0.24 s. Maximum number of grid points for one of the nonlinearities is 82. In the adaptive case a solution is found in 0.21 s after 3 iterations.

It is worth mentioning that simulation for the adaptive approach are performed with help of Proposition 1 which increased performance of the algorithm by more than 40%. Moreover, in comparison to the FCFS strategy our approach improves the objective function value by 64%.

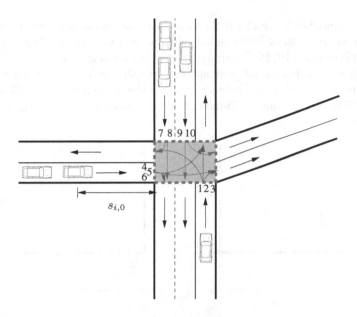

Fig. 5. Irregular intersection geometry with 10 lanes.

6   Conclusions and Outlook

In this paper we proposed a bi-level optimization algorithm for an intersection management problem with turns and multiple vehicles in the same lane. On the lower-level for each vehicle we considered an OCP subject to a double integrator. This OCP provided us maximized intersection entering velocity as a nonlinear function of the corresponding time. On upper-level, in order to solve the underlying IMP, we formulated an MINLP where we exploited those nonliniarities and their reciprocals in the collision avoidance constraints. We solved the MINLP using adaptive and non-adaptive linearization techniques. The numerical experiments demonstrated that both approaches are robust and are indeed applicable to IMPs, however in both cases the adaptive one slightly outperformed its non-adaptive counterpart. Nevertheless, a more detailed numerical investigation is required in order to state the the adaptive algorithm is in general better. Moreover, the experiments showed that our model significantly outperforms the FCFS heuristic. The research presented in the underlying work can by possibly extended by: testing the limits of our model in terms of traffic density; considering vehicle dynamics with uncertainties; performing real-time experiments, i.e. when new cars are randomly generated (without violating feasibility of the problem); performing experiments on real CAVs.

Acknowledgement. This research is funded by dtec.bw – Digitalization and Technology Research Center of the Bundeswehr [projects MissionLab, MORE, EMERGENCY-VRD] and the Air Force Office of Scientific Research, Air Force Materiel Command, USAF, Award No. FA8655-20-1-7026. Any opinions, findings, and conclusions or recommendations expressed in this publication are those of the author(s) and do not necessarily reflect the views of the Air Force Office of Scientific Research, Air Force Materiel Command, USAF.

A   Quantities, Variables, and Conflict Matrix

Conflict matrix for the 10-lane intersection problem:

$$C = \begin{bmatrix} 4 & 3 & 3 & 0 & 2 & 0 & 0 & 0 & 0 & 0 \\ 3 & 4 & 3 & 0 & 1 & 2 & 0 & 0 & 0 & 0 \\ 3 & 3 & 4 & 0 & 1 & 1 & 2 & 0 & 0 & 0 \\ 0 & 0 & 0 & 4 & 3 & 3 & 0 & 2 & 1 & 0 \\ 2 & 1 & 1 & 3 & 4 & 3 & 0 & 0 & 1 & 1 \\ 0 & 2 & 1 & 3 & 3 & 4 & 0 & 0 & 1 & 1 \\ 0 & 0 & 2 & 0 & 0 & 0 & 4 & 3 & 1 & 1 \\ 0 & 0 & 0 & 2 & 0 & 0 & 3 & 4 & 0 & 0 \\ 0 & 0 & 0 & 1 & 1 & 1 & 1 & 0 & 4 & 0 \\ 0 & 0 & 0 & 0 & 1 & 1 & 1 & 0 & 0 & 4 \end{bmatrix}$$

Table 1. Quantities and variables introduced in this paper.

Symbol	Description	Section
$i, j \in \mathcal{V}$	Vehicle and the corresponding index set	2.1
N	Number of vehicles	2.1
$k, l \in \mathcal{P}$	Path indices and corresponding index set	2.2
M	Number of paths	2.2
$P(i)$	Path corresponding to vehicle i	2.2
c_{kl}	k, l entry of a conflict matrix	2.2
$s_i(\cdot)$	Position of vehicle i along its path	3.1
$v_i(\cdot)$	Velocity of vehicle i	3.1
$a_i(\cdot)$	Acceleration (control variable) of vehicle i	3.1
t_i	Arrival time of vehicle i	3.1
$t_{i,min}, t_{i,max}$	Lower and upper bounds of t_i	3.1
$v_i(\cdot)$	Arrival velocity of vehicle i	3.1
$v_{P(i)}$	Maximum allowed velocity on path $P(i)$	3.1
$I_{t_a}^{t_n}$	Time interval $[t_a, t_b]$	3.1
$T_i(\cdot)$	Inverse of the arrival velocity of vehicle i	3.1
$t_{i,\star}$	Velocity saturation starting time of vehicle i	3.1
C_{large}	Some very large constant	3.2
w_{ij}	Binary decision variable (equals to 1 if vehicle i goes first)	3.2
L_{ij}^b	Length to travel before overlapping zone of $P(i)$ and $P(j)$	3.2
L_{ij}^a	Length to travel to clear overlapping zone of $P(i)$ and $P(j)$	3.2
L_k	Length of path k in CZ	3.2
$T_i^{headway}(\cdot)$	Time to reach maximum velocity in exit lane for vehicle i	3.2
v_{exit}	Maximum allowed velocity in exit lanes	3.2
$T_i^{switch}(\cdot)$	Switching time point from deceleration to acceleration	3.2
T_i	Time interval discretization corresponding to vehicle i	4
K_i	Number of discretization points of i-th interval	4
e_u, e_o	Maximum under- and overestimators	4
$z_{i,k}$	Pointer variable corresponding to i-th interval	4
$\lambda_{i,k}$	Lambda variable corresponding to i-th interval	4
$T_{i,pw}, v_{i,pw}$	Linear approximations of $T_i(\cdot)$ and $v_i(\cdot)$	4
$e_{i,T}, e_{i,v}$	Envelope variables corresponding to $T_i(\cdot)$ and $v_i(\cdot)$	4
ε	Linearization error bound	4

References

1. Ahmane, M., et al.: Modeling and controlling an isolated urban intersection based on cooperative vehicles. Transp. Res. Part C Emerg. Technol. **28**, 44–62 (2013)
2. Britzelmeier, A., Dreves, A.: A decomposition algorithm for Nash equilibria in intersection management. Optimization **70**(11), 2441–2478 (2020). https://doi.org/10.1080/02331934.2020.1786088
3. Burlacu, R.: Adaptive mixed-integer refinements for solving nonlinear problems with discrete decisions. doctoralthesis, Friedrich-Alexander-Universität Erlangen-Nürnberg (FAU) (2020)
4. Burlacu, R., Geißler, B., Schewe, L.: Solving mixed-integer nonlinear programmes using adaptively refined mixed-integer linear programmes. Optim. Methods Softw. **35**(1), 37–64 (2020). https://doi.org/10.1080/10556788.2018.1556661
5. Dreves, A., Gerdts, M.: A generalized NASH equilibrium approach for optimal control problems of autonomous cars. Optimal Control Appl. Methods **39**(1), 326–342 (2018). https://doi.org/10.1002/oca.2348
6. Exler, O., Lehmann, T., Schittkowski, K.: A comparative study of SQP-type algorithms for nonlinear and nonconvex mixed-integer optimization. Math. Program. Comput. **4**(4), 383–412 (2012). https://doi.org/10.1007/s12532-012-0045-0
7. Fayazi, S.A., Vahidi, A.: Mixed-integer linear programming for optimal scheduling of autonomous vehicle intersection crossing. IEEE Trans. Intell. Veh. **3**(3), 287–299 (2018). https://doi.org/10.1109/TIV.2018.2843163
8. Geißler, B., Martin, A., Morsi, A., Schewe, L.: Using piecewise linear functions for solving MINLPs. In: Lee, J., Leyffer, S. (eds.) Mixed Integer Nonlinear Programming. The IMA Volumes in Mathematics and its Applications, vol. 154, pp. 287–314. Springer, New York, NY (2012). https://doi.org/10.1007/978-1-4614-1927-3_10
9. Gerdts, M., Rogovs, S., Valenti, G.: A piecewise linearization algorithm for solving MINLP in intersection management. In: Proceedings of the 7th International Conference on Vehicle Technology and Intelligent Transport Systems - Volume 1: VEHITS, pp. 438–445. INSTICC, SciTePress (2021). https://doi.org/10.5220/0010437104380445
10. Gurobi Optimization, L.: Gurobi optimizer reference manual (2020). http://www.gurobi.com
11. Hult, R., Zanon, M., Gras, S., Falcone, P.: An MIQP-based heuristic for optimal coordination of vehicles at intersections. In: 2018 IEEE Conference on Decision and Control (CDC). IEEE (2018). https://doi.org/10.1109/CDC.2018.8618945
12. Hult, R., Zanon, M., Frison, G., Gros, S., Falcone, P.: Experimental validation of a semi-distributed sequential quadratic programming method for optimal coordination of automated vehicles at intersections. Optimal Control Appl. Methods **41**(4), 1068–1096 (2020). https://doi.org/10.1002/oca.2592
13. Hult, R., Zanon, M., Gros, S., Falcone, P.: Optimal coordination of automated vehicles at intersections with turns. In: 2019 18th European Control Conference (ECC). IEEE (2019). https://doi.org/10.23919/ECC.2019.8795770
14. Khayatian, M., et al.: A survey on intersection management of connected autonomous vehicles. ACM Trans. Cyber-Phys. Syst. **4**(4), 1–27 (2020). https://doi.org/10.1145/3407903
15. Kloock, M., Scheffe, P., Marquardt, S., Maczijewski, J., Alrifaee, B., Kowalewski, S.: Distributed model predictive intersection control of multiple vehicles, pp. 1735–1740 (2019). https://doi.org/10.1109/ITSC.2019.8917117
16. Malikopoulos, A.A., Cassandras, C.G., Zhang, Y.J.: A decentralized energy-optimal control framework for connected automated vehicles at signal-free intersections. Automatica **93**, 244–256 (2018). https://doi.org/10.1016/j.automatica.2018.03.056

17. Mohamad Nor, M.H., Namerikawa, T.: Optimal coordination and control of connected and automated vehicles at intersections via mixed integer linear programming. SICE J. Control Meas. Syst. Integr. **12**(6), 215–222 (2019). https://doi.org/10.9746/jcmsi.12.215
18. Namazi, E., Li, J., Lu, C.: Intelligent intersection management systems considering autonomous vehicles: a systematic literature review. IEEE Access **7**, 91946–91965 (2019). https://doi.org/10.1109/ACCESS.2019.2927412
19. Winston, W.L., Goldberg, J.B.: Operations Research: Applications and Algorithms. Thomson/Brooks/Cole, Belmont, CA (2004)
20. Zhong, Z., Nejad, M., Lee, E.: Autonomous and semiautonomous intersection management: a survey. IEEE Intell. Transp. Syst. Mag. **13**(2), 53–70 (2021). https://doi.org/10.1109/MITS.2020.3014074

Interaction-Aware Motion Prediction at Highways: A Comparison of Three Lane Changing Models

Vinicius Trentin$^{(\boxtimes)}$ ⓘ, Antonio Artuñedo ⓘ, Jorge Godoy ⓘ, and Jorge Villagra ⓘ

Centre for Automation and Robotics, Spanish National Research Council, Madrid, Spain
{vinicius.trentin,antonio.artunedo,jorge.godoy,
jorge.villagra}@csic.es

Abstract. The behavior of traffic participants is full of uncertainties in the real world. It depends on their intentions, the road layout, and the interaction between them. Probabilistic intention and motion predictions are unavoidable to safely navigate in complex scenarios. In this work, we propose a framework to compute the motion prediction of the surrounding vehicles taking into account all possible routes obtained from a given map. To that end, a Dynamic Bayesian Network is used to model the problem and a particle filter is applied to infer the probability of being on a specific route and the intention to change lanes. Our framework, based on Markov chains, is generic and can handle various road layouts and any number of vehicles. The framework is evaluated in two scenarios: a two-lane highway and a three-lane merging highway. Finally, the influence of a set of lane-changing methods is evaluated on the predictions of the vehicles present on the scene.

Keywords: Interaction-aware · Motion prediction · Lane change models

1 Introduction

Autonomous vehicles show promise on bringing many benefits to society, such as low accident rates, safety, fuel saving, better life quality, reduce stress, among others. In order to assure the safety aspect, the algorithms implemented need to deal with a large number of possible scenarios, with a varying degree of complexity, and be able to predict the movement of other vehicles present in the scene considering their mutual interactions [1].

The behavior of traffic participants is full of uncertainties in the real world. In order to improve the driving quality, autonomous vehicles should evaluate threats, taking seriously the ones with high probability to happen and not overreacting to the ones with low probability. Probabilistic intention and motion prediction are crucial to accomplish safe and high-quality decision-making and motion planning for autonomous vehicles [2].

This work has been partially funded by the Spanish Ministry of Science and Innovation, the Community of Madrid through SEGVAUTO 4.0-CM (S2018-EMT-4362) Programme, and by the European Commission and ECSEL Joint Undertaking through the Project NEWCONTROL (826653).

© Springer Nature Switzerland AG 2022
C. Klein et al. (Eds.): SMARTGREENS 2021/ VEHITS 2021, CCIS 1612, pp. 274–296, 2022.
https://doi.org/10.1007/978-3-031-17098-0_14

In this paper, an approach to compute the motion prediction of the surrounding vehicles in all their possible routes in a short-term horizon is proposed. Since the focus is on the lateral interaction, three models for the lateral intention are compared. In comparison with a previous work for motion prediction in highways of the same authors sketched in [1], this publication presents modifications in the methods for motion prediction and is evaluated using publicly available datasets.

This paper is divided as follows: Sect. 2 presents a short review of some works similar to the one presented in this article. Section 3 describes the proposed approach with the lateral models evaluated being presented in Sect. 4. Section 5 shows some experimental results and Sect. 6 concludes.

2 Related Work

2.1 Interaction Awareness

Considering that the intention of the other drivers cannot be measured directly, it is necessary to estimate it.

The authors in [3] present a framework for assessing traffic scenes with interaction between traffic participants. The possible behavior patterns of the vehicles involved are transformed into hypotheses and compute the joint probability of each hypothesis by reconstructing the individual probability of each behavior. As a result, the fully interaction-aware joint probability distribution is obtained over all the hypotheses. The approach grows exponentially as the situation complexity and the number of vehicles involved increase.

In [4], the authors implement a Dynamic Bayesian Network to reason about the situations and the risks at intersections on a semantic level. The risk is assessed based on the comparison of the intentions with what is expected from the drivers in a given scenario. The expected vehicle's motions are modeled based on the road network (stop signs, give away lines), distance to the intersections and previous pose and velocity. The intention to stop is computed based on the previous intention and current expectation. With the intention and the maneuver, the future pose and velocity can be estimated. An evolution of this approach considering also lateral expectations has been recently presented [5].

Although these methods take into account the interdependence between vehicles to find the most probable route combination or if the situation offers risk, they do not include the motion prediction of the traffic participants, as all areas they can reach, which is crucial when planning the ego vehicle trajectory.

2.2 Motion Prediction

The authors in [6] propose the use of set-based predictions with reachability analysis to find all possible reachable sets based on a given map and the positions and velocities of the traffic participants. Although this approach ensures safe planning for the ego vehicle, given that all vehicles follow the traffic rules, it is too conservative and, given a complex scenario with many vehicles, the ego vehicle might have to come to a full stop since all paths are occupied.

In another work, [7] abstracted the motion model into Markov chains using reachability analysis. It considers the vehicle's dynamics, their mutual interactions (only based on the road geometry and traffic rules) and also the limitation of driving maneuvers due to road geometry, resulting in crash probabilities for the possible paths of the ego vehicle.

In [8], the authors present an approach to compute the motion predictions of the vehicles, without prior knowledge of the scene, considering separately the lateral and longitudinal movement. The longitudinal over-approximation is based on intervals obtained from real data. The lateral over-approximation is computed with the use of acceptance distributions where it evaluates all considered lateral accelerations for one specific driver influence, such a static or dynamic obstacle. The approach is compared with occupancy predictions computed using SPOT [9] and the comparison showed that the occupancy area size could be reduced up to 70% for a prediction horizon up to 1.3 s without errors.

Although these methods can predict the motion of the surrounding vehicles, they can have low accuracy in complex situations involving many vehicles, such as an intersection, due to their interdependent intentions and resulting actions.

2.3   Motion Prediction with Interaction Awareness

As already mentioned, in order to have a better estimation of the future positions of the vehicles involved in the scene, the motion prediction and the interaction awareness should be jointly considered.

The authors in [10] use a Dynamic Bayesian Network with a particle filter to evaluate the interaction between vehicles and estimate their route and maneuver intentions. From these intentions, an action, represented by an acceleration and yaw rate values, is obtained and the motion prediction is computed. This method considers only the most probable action for the whole time horizon of the prediction, which, in complex scenarios, may negatively influence the motion planning search space.

In [11], the authors expand their work from [6] to include the interaction between drivers in their set-based predictions. They do it by comparing vehicles driving on the same lane and removing the unreachable areas of the following vehicles. As a result, the drivable area of the ego vehicle increases, since some previously occupied areas are removed. This approach, however, considers neither intentions nor traffic rules in the predictions.

3   Architecture

The framework here proposed belongs to the block *Motion prediction* from Fig. 1 and can be mainly divided into 4 blocks: *Find/Reuse corridors*, *Find interactions*, *Compute intentions* and *Motion prediction*, as shown in Fig. 2 where the flowchart and the data entering and leaving each block is presented. The entrance data can be obtained from simulations, exteroceptive sensors, V2X communication or from publicly available datasets. The output of the block goes to the maneuver planner of the ego vehicle.

Below, each of the building blocks appearing in Fig. 2 will be briefly described.

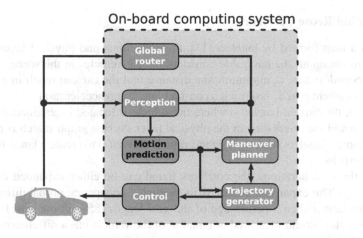

Fig. 1. Architecture overview [12].

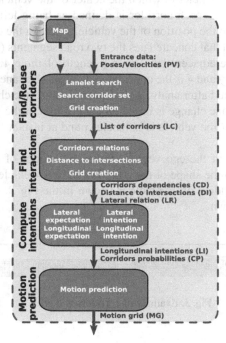

Fig. 2. Intention inference and motion prediction flowchart.

3.1 Map

The maps are loaded at the beginning of the simulation. They are formed by lanelets [13], that are interconnected drivable road segments geometrically represented by a right and left bound. The relation between each pair of lanelets is used to create an adjacency graph.

3.2 Find/Reuse Corridors

Given a map formed by lanelets [13], their relational and physical layers are used in order to obtain all the navigable corridors for the vehicles in the scene. The length of these corridors has, at minimum, the distance that the car can reach in a time interval with its current speed, assuming a constant maximum acceleration.

First, the current lanelet(s) where the vehicle is located is obtained, comparing the position and the orientation in the physical layer. Next, a graph search is performed for surrounding lanelets starting from the vehicle lanelet(s) to create a lanelet-sequence for each corridor.

In the next iterations, the corridors found can be either expanded or removed, if necessary. The expansion occurs if its predicted occupancy probabilities fall in cells that are farther then a percentage of the grid length (85% in our case). The removal occurs if the current measured orientation of the vehicle has a difference bigger than a threshold when compared with the center line of the corridor.

At each iteration, the lanelet in which the center of the vehicle is located is found. Based on this information, each corridor is defined as being left, center, right or not reachable with respect to the position of the vehicle. To reach the corridors at right/left, a Bézier curve is created that concatenates the two road segments (the one in the current lane with the one in the adjacent lane) with a length of $max(4v, 10)$ m, being v the current vehicle's velocity and 4 is the considered duration of a lane change (in seconds). These values were defined after analyzing the patterns of a lane change.

The detection of a lane change is based on the position of the vehicle and occurs in one iteration: at instant t the vehicle is in lanelet x and at instant $t + 1$ the vehicle is in lanelet y.

With the exception of the ego vehicle, for each corridor of the other vehicles, a grid is created based on the shape of the road. For the ego vehicle, a route is assumed. An example of the corridors of a vehicle is shown in the Fig. 3, where for one of the corridors the grid is drawn.

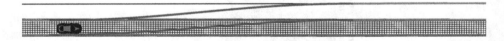

Fig. 3. Example of corridors and grid.

3.3 Find Interactions

A search of surrounding vehicles is performed for all the vehicles in the scene, generating a table that contains their distances and velocities.

In order to restrict the motion probabilities in corridors that have another vehicle or that can collide with the corridors of other vehicles, the collision point between these corridors is obtained as can be seen in Fig. 4. They result from the intersection between the corridors' center lines, where the chosen point is the first one where the distance is less than a given threshold.

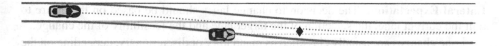

Fig. 4. Example of collision between corridors.

3.4 Compute Intentions

In order to compute the intention of the traffic participants, the Dynamic Bayesian Network (DBN) proposed in [4] and used in [5] is applied. For each of the vehicles present in the scene, with the exception of the ego vehicle, the network represented in Fig. 5 is instantiated, where bold arrows represent the influences of the other vehicles on vehicle n through some key variables ($E_t^n, I_t^n, \Phi_t^n, Z_t^n$) described below.

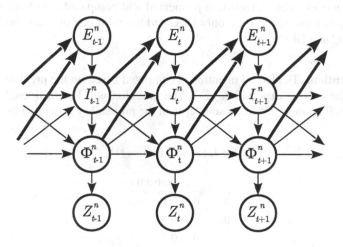

Fig. 5. Bayesian network [1].

$$P(\boldsymbol{E_{0:T}}, \boldsymbol{I_{0:T}}, \boldsymbol{\Phi_{0:T}}, \boldsymbol{Z_{0:T}}) = P(\boldsymbol{E_0}, \boldsymbol{I_0}, \boldsymbol{\Phi_0}, \boldsymbol{Z_0}) \times$$
$$\prod_{t=1}^{T} \times \prod_{n=1}^{N} [P(E_t^n | \boldsymbol{I_{t-1}\Phi_{t-1}}) \times P(I_t^n | \Phi_{t-1}^n I_{t-1}^n E_t^n) \times \tag{1}$$
$$P(\Phi_t^n | \Phi_{t-1}^n I_{t-1}^n I_t^n) \times P(Z_t^n | \Phi_t^n)]$$

- Expected maneuver E_t^n: represents the expected lateral behavior of the vehicle n at instant t according to traffic rules. It models the probability that the vehicle can make a lane change without hindering traffic. It can assume two values: *stay* and *change*.
- Intended maneuver I_t^n: represents the intention of the vehicle and includes the route the vehicle intends to follow.
- Physical vehicle state Φ_t^n: represents the pose and speed of the vehicle. They are calculated at each instant based on the intentions.
- Measurements Z_t^n: represents the real measurements of the physical state of the vehicle, extracted directly from exteroceptive sensors of the ego-vehicle or via V2X communications [14].

Lateral Expectation. The decision to change lanes should be based on the desire to quit the current lane, the selection of the target lane and the feasibility of the change.

Lane changes are usually classified as mandatory or discretionary, depending on the drivers motivation. A Mandatory Lane Change (MLC) is performed when the driver is trying to move his/her vehicle from its current lane into the target lane in anticipation to a left or right exit or a lane closure immediately downstream. A Discretionary Lane Change (DLC) is conducted to improve driving conditions when the driver desires a faster speed, greater following distance, etc. in the target lane [15, 16].

When implementing the aforementioned particle filter, for every vehicle in every particle the vehicle's followers and leaders in all possible lanes are determined. Then, its distances bumper-to-bumper and the velocity differences are found. This information is used to compute the expected lateral motion of the vehicles present at the scene, for which three models were selected, implemented and compared (see Sect. 4 for more details). Two of these models use only DLC and the third one uses a hybrid approach between MLC and DLC.

Lateral Intention. The lateral intention is computed based on the previous intentions (I_{t-1}) and the current expectation (E_t). The intention will be considered equal to 1 (change lane) if a random value is smaller than the probability generated by Table 1.

Table 1. Lateral intention [1].

I_{t-1}	E_t	Probability
0	0	0.1
0	1	0.5
1	0	0.5
1	1	0.9

This step also defines the new corridor of each vehicle in each particle. If the intention is to change, one of the corridors in the target lane chosen in the previous step is selected.

3.5   Motion Prediction

To compute the probabilistic predictions of the vehicles present at the scenarios, the library CORA [17] has been used following the strategy proposed in [7]. The predictions are computed by abstracting the system dynamics into Markov chains, where the state space X and input space U are discretized into intervals. The state space consists of longitudinal position s and velocity v, using intervals with size 0.5 m × 1 m/s, and the input space represents the potential acceleration a ranging from $-3\,\mathrm{m/s^2}$ to $2\,\mathrm{m/s^2}$ normalized into 5 intervals between -1 and 1.

The vehicle's longitudinal dynamics are expressed using the following differential equation:

$$\dot{s} = v$$

$$\dot{v} = \begin{cases} a^{max}u, & 0 < v < v^{max} \cup u \le 0 \\ 0, & v \le 0 \cup v \ge v^{max} \end{cases} \quad (2)$$

where a^{max} and v^{max} are the maximum allowed acceleration and velocity, and u is the input ranging from -1 to 1.

For the lateral dynamics, it is assumed that the vehicle can occupy the entire lane with a deviation centered in the lateral position of the vehicle.

The transition probability matrices of the Markov chains for a time step $\Phi(\tau)$, and for a time interval $\Phi([0, \tau])$, where τ is the time increment, are computed offline with reachability analysis that aims to compute an over-approximation of the potential set of states a system can reach from its initial states. For each state and input, the motion model is applied for a time interval τ resulting in a set covering one or more cells from the state space. The probability of reaching the cell j, starting from cell i under the influence of input β is computed as follows:

$$\Phi_{ji}^{\beta}(\tau) = \frac{V(R_i^{\beta}(\tau) \cap X_j)}{V(R_i^{\beta}(\tau))} \quad (3)$$

where the operator V returns the volume of the set and $R_i^{\beta}(\tau)$ is the reachable set starting from cell i applying input β. The transition probabilities between the input states are represented by the input transition matrix $\Gamma(t_k)$. This matrix is composed by two parts: a transition matrix Ψ, which models the intrinsic behavior of the vehicle when there are no priorities for certain input values, and a priority vector λ, representing the restrictions caused by the road layout and the interaction with other vehicles. This vector also contains two acceleration distributions, $initialInput$ and $freeDriving$: the former representing the initial acceleration of the vehicle and the latter representing the accelerations the vehicle might use in the case of no constrains (caused by the road or other vehicles). A detailed explanation of these variables and how they are joined into the priority vector can be found in [7]. Instead of using the same distributions for every vehicle, the distributions are found for each vehicle following the Algorithm 1. It takes into account the acceleration time series of a given vehicle and the previous initial distribution to generate the distributions applied in the current time step. This way, the future velocities of the vehicle can be better estimated when compared with unique distributions applied to all vehicles.

The input transition matrix and the priority vector are joined as follows

$$\Gamma_i^{\beta\delta} = norm(\hat{\Gamma}_i^{\beta\delta})$$

$$\hat{\Gamma}_i^{\beta\delta} = \lambda_i^{\beta}\Psi^{\beta\delta}, \forall i : \sum_{\beta} \lambda_i^{\beta} = 1, 0 \le \lambda_i^{\beta} \le 1 \quad (4)$$

to form the transition matrix where i is the index of the state space and β and δ are indices of two possible input states. The reason this matrix is not joined into the transition matrix $\Phi(\tau)$, is that the priority vector λ can change at each step.

The probability distributions for future time steps $p(t_{k+1})$ and time intervals $p(t_k, t_{k+1})$ are computed as follows:

$$p(t_{k+1}) = \Gamma(t_k)\Phi(\tau)p(t_k)$$
$$p(t_k, t_{k+1}) = \Phi([0,\tau])p(t_k)$$

(5)

For each corridor from each vehicle a Markov chain is instantiated and its predictions computed for a time interval. To take into account the size of the vehicle a convolution operation is applied between a kernel with the size of the vehicle and the predictions. These predictions are then multiplied with the sum of the weights of the particles that contain the corridors. They are later joined into a single grid based on the ego-vehicle position, whose size is based on the ego-vehicle's velocity and the situation context.

Algorithm 1. Acceleration distributions for a vehicle.

```
   /* current acceleration, acceleration time series, previous
      distribution                                                    */
   Input    : a, aTS, initialInput^{k-1}
   /* current acceleration distributions                             */
   Output   : initialInput^k, freeDriving^k
   /* acceleration's intervals                                       */
 1 accInt = [-3, -2, -1, 0, 1, 2]
   /* global free driving distribution applied for all vehicles
      */
 2 globalFreeDriving = [0.01, 0.04, 0.25, 0.5, 0.2]
 3 Δa = 0.3                                   // acceleration threshold
 4 for i ← 1 to 5 do
 5 │   initialInput^k(i) ← (accInt(i) − Δa) ≤ a < (accInt(i + 1) + Δa)
 6 │   if initialInput^k(i) then
 7 │   │   freeDriving^k(i) ← sum(accInt(i) − Δa ≤ aTS < accInt(i + 1) + Δa)
 8 │   end
 9 end
10 initialInput^k = normalize(initialInput^k)
11 initialInput^k = (initialInput^k + initialInput^{k-1})/2
12 freeDriving^k = normalize(freeDriving^k)
13 freeDriving^k = (freeDriving^k + globalFreeDriving)/2
```

---

4   Lateral Models

The models implemented and compared are presented below. These models were selected based on their simplicity and low computational cost.

4.1   Model 1

The first model implemented is based on [18]. The desire to change lane is computed by the deceleration a provoked by leading vehicles traveling in the current and adjacent lanes:

$$a = \frac{\rho v^m \Delta v}{\Delta x^l} \tag{6}$$

where v is the velocity of the vehicle, Δv is the velocity difference between the leading vehicle and the vehicle, Δx is the distance between vehicles and ρ, m and l are parameter models. With the acceleration values a_i in each of possible lanes, the utility U_i of each lane i is defined as:

$$U_i = \frac{e^{a_i}}{\sum_{j=1}^{N} e^{a_j}} \tag{7}$$

where a_i is the acceleration with respect to the leading vehicle of lane i and N is number of possible target lanes.

If the leading vehicle in the current lane is making the target vehicle brake, the lane with the highest utility is selected, otherwise, a random lane, among the possible lanes, is selected.

Once the lane is selected, it is necessary to verify that the deceleration imposed on the new follower, computed with (6), is below a given threshold b, such that $a > -b$.

If the safety criteria is met, the probability to accept the gap is computed as:

$$P(lead) = 1 - e^{-\lambda(t_{lead} - \tau)}$$
$$P(lag) = 1 - e^{-\lambda(t_{lag} - \tau)} \tag{8}$$

where t_{lead} and t_{lag} are the time gaps with respect to the leading and following vehicle in the target lane.

The probability to change lane is the result of the multiplication of $P(lead)$ and $P(lag)$ and the expected lateral movement will be to change lanes if this probability is bigger than a random value.

4.2   Model 2

The second model implemented is the Minimizing Overall Braking Induced by Lane Changes (MOBIL) [19], used in combination with the Intelligent Driver Model (IDM) [20].

As in the previous model, this one also includes a safety criteria: the deceleration of the new follower a_{nf} in the target lane, after the lane change, cannot exceed a given safety limit b_{safe}

$$a_{nf} > -b_{safe} \tag{9}$$

The authors of MOBIL propose two types of incentive criterion for lane changing: one considering symmetric passing rules and an asymmetric one. The one adopted in this work is the asymmetric model, where the right most lane is the default lane and the lanes on the left should only be used for overtaking purposes.

The incentive criterion for a lane change to a left (L) lane and to a right (R) lane are:

$$L = \tilde{a}_c - a_c + p(\tilde{a}_n - a_n) > \Delta a_{th} + \Delta a_{bias}$$
$$R = \tilde{a}_c - a_c + p(\tilde{a}_o - a_o) > \Delta a_{th} - \Delta a_{bias} \tag{10}$$

where $\tilde{a}_c$, a_c, $\tilde{a}_o$, a_o, $\tilde{a}_n$ and a_n are the accelerations of the target vehicle, old follower and new follower after and before the lane change, p is the politeness factor, Δa_{th} and Δa_{bias} are the acceleration threshold and bias, respectively. It can be noticed that the lane change to a right lane considers only the advantages to the old follower. A lane change to a left lane, on the other hand, takes into account the effects caused to the new follower. The politeness factor p determines how much the other vehicles influence the lane-changing decision of the target vehicle.

The IDM acceleration of each vehicle α depends on the distance s_α and on the velocity difference Δv_α to the leading vehicle. It is composed of two parts: the acceleration $a[1 - (v_\alpha/v_o)^4]$ on a free road and the braking $-a(s^*/s_\alpha)^2$ caused by a leading vehicle.

$$\dot{v}_\alpha = a \left[1 - \left(\frac{v_\alpha}{v_o} \right)^4 - \frac{s^*(v_\alpha, \Delta v_\alpha)^2}{s_\alpha} \right]$$

$$s^*(v, \Delta v) = s_o + vT + \frac{v\Delta v}{2\sqrt{ab}} \tag{11}$$

where a is the maximum acceleration, b is the desired comfortable deceleration, s_o is the minimum distance, v_o is the desired velocity and T is the safe time gap.

4.3 Model 3

The third model implemented is based on [21]. The authors argue that the classification of the lane changes into MLC or DLC does not allow to capture trade-offs between the two types. For this reason, they created a method that includes both types in a single model.

This model penalizes the most right lane, since it considers this lane as being of low speed, caused by the entrances and exits.

At the highest level of the model, the driver chooses a target lane. It is the lane, among all the possible lanes, that the driver recognizes as the best lane to be in after considering a wide range of factors and goals. The utilities of the various lanes are given by:

$$\begin{aligned} U_{int}^{TL} = {} & \beta_i - 0.011 D_{int} + 0.119 S_{int} + 0.022 \Delta X_{int}^{front} \delta_{int}^{adj} \\ & + 0.115 \Delta S_{int}^{front} \delta_{int} - 2.783 \delta_{nt}^{taigate} \delta_{int}^{CL} \\ & + \delta_{int}^{CL} - 2.633 \Delta C L_{int} + \beta_i^{path} [d_{nt}^{exit}]^{-0.371} \\ & - 0.980 \delta_{nt}^{next\ exit} \Delta Exit_i - \alpha_i \nu_n \end{aligned} \tag{12}$$

where U_{int}^{TL} is the utility of lane i as a target lane to the driver n at time t, βi is the lane i constant, D_{int} and S_{int} are the lane-specific densities and speeds, ΔX_{int}^{front} and ΔS_{int}^{front} are the spacing and relative speed of the front vehicle in lane i. δ_{int}^{adj}, δ_{int}^{CL} and $\delta_{nt}^{tailgate}$ are indicators with value 1 if i is the current or an adjacent lane, if i is the current lane, if vehicle n is being tailgated at time t, respectively, lane, 0 otherwise. $\Delta C L_{int}$ is the number of lane changes required to get to lane i from the current lane.

β_i^{path} is the path plan impact coefficient for lane i, $\delta_{nt}^{next\ exit}$ is the distance to the exit driver n intends to use. $\delta_{nt}^{next\ exit}$ indicates with 1 if the driver intends to take the next exit, $\Delta Exit_i$ are the number of lane changes required to get to the exit lane from lane i. α_i is the parameter of the driver specific random term ν_n.

The target lane is chosen as the lane with the highest utility. The probabilities are given by a multinomial logit model:

$$P(TL_{nt} = i|\nu_n) = \frac{exp(V_{int}^{TL})|\nu_n)}{\sum_{j=TL} exp(V_{jnt}^{TL}|\nu_n)} \tag{13}$$

Once the utilities are computed one has to evaluate the lead and lag gaps, which are defined by the bumper-to-bumper distance between the lead and subject vehicles and the bumper-to-bumper distance between the lag distance and the subject vehicles.

The gap is acceptable if it is bigger than the critical gap:

$$P(G_{nt}^{gd} > G_{nt}^{gd,cr}|d_{nt}, \nu_n) = \Phi \left[\frac{ln(G_{nt}^{gd}) - G_{nt}^{gd,cr}}{\sigma_g} \right] \tag{14}$$

where $\Phi[]$ denotes the cumulative standard normal distribution, G_{nt}^{gd} and $G_{nt}^{gd,cr}$ are the gap and the critical gap for vehicle n at time t. Superscript d refers to the direction of change (current, left or right) and g to the type of gap (lead or lag).

The critical lead and lag gaps are given by:

$$
\begin{aligned}
G_{nt}^{lead\ d,cr} &= exp(1.553 - 6.389max(0, \Delta S_{nt}^{lead\ d}) \\
&\quad - 0.14\,min(0, \Delta S_{nt}^{lead\ d} - 0.008\nu_n) \\
G_{nt}^{lag\ d,cr} &= exp(1.429 + 0.471max(0, \Delta S_{nt}^{lag\ d}) \\
&\quad - 0.234\nu_n)
\end{aligned}
\tag{15}
$$

$\Delta S_{nt}^{lead\ d}$ and $\Delta S_{nt}^{lead\ d}$ are the relative speeds of the lead and lag vehicles in the direction of change d.

The probability to accept the gap is computed by multiplying the lead and lag gap acceptance probability and the expected lateral movement will be to change if this probability is bigger than a random value.

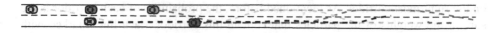

Fig. 6. Paths evolution of each vehicle in the simulated scenario. (Color figure online)

5   Experimental Results

5.1   Scenario 1

The framework proposed in the previous section is evaluated first in a scenario simulated with SCANeR Studio simulator [22]. It is a two-lane highway with the ego vehicle (black) and 4 other vehicles (red, green, yellow and blue), where 4 lane changes are executed. The information about the surrounding vehicles is received by the ego vehicle as a vector of high-level objects containing their estimated pose, velocity, and size. Figure 6 shows the initial position and the path followed by each vehicle and Fig. 7 shows the velocities of each vehicle throughout the simulation.

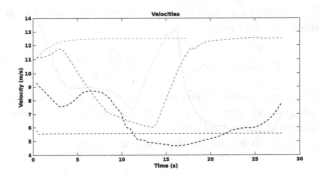

Fig. 7. Velocities throughout the execution of the scenario 1. (Color figure online)

Execution of the Lateral Models. The simulation is executed three times, one for each lateral model. Figure 8 shows the graphs of expectation and intention for each vehicle with the three models in the simulated scenario, where the specificities of each model can be noticed. In the expectation of the green vehicle (Fig. 8b) once it overtakes the blue vehicle, the expectation to change lanes from Model 1 stays around 0.5, since no deceleration is caused, meaning both lanes are possible and feasible. For Model 2, the right most lane has always the priority, which can be seen as the expectation stays around 1 when the vehicle is on the left lane and the right lane is available. For Model 3, in the same situation, the expectation is to stay on the current (left) lane, since it penalizes the right most lane and also penalizes lane changes. The penalization to the right most can be seen in the expectation of the blue vehicle (Fig. 8c) that stays the whole simulation on the right lane and the expectation changes to 1 once the left lane becomes available. Since this vehicle is already on the right lane, the expectation for Model 2 stays around 0 and for Model 1 stays around 0.5 when both lanes are feasible.

Figure 9 shows the evolution of the probabilities for each vehicle and each model. These probabilities are computed as $1 - p_{right}$, where p_{right} is the probability of being on the right most corridor. As mentioned before, the probability of each corridor is the sum of the weights of the particles that contain this corridor. Each line, marked with the color of the vehicle on the top right corner, represents the evolution of this vehicle. The x axis is the time and the y axis is the probability of being on each lane, being 0 the right (bottom) lane and 1 the left (top) lane. The line in black is the ground truth, the lane in which the vehicle is at, at each instant. The three models are represented by the lines in red, green and blue, respectively. The magenta dashed line is the orientation of the vehicle with respect to the orientation of the lane and the numbers mark the lane changes whose leading times for each model are presented in Table 2. The dashed line in blue is the threshold for the detection of a lane change.

Predictions and Evaluation. Figure 10 shows an example of the predictions computed with the model from Sect. 3.5 in the last time interval (2.9–3.0 s) for all three models.

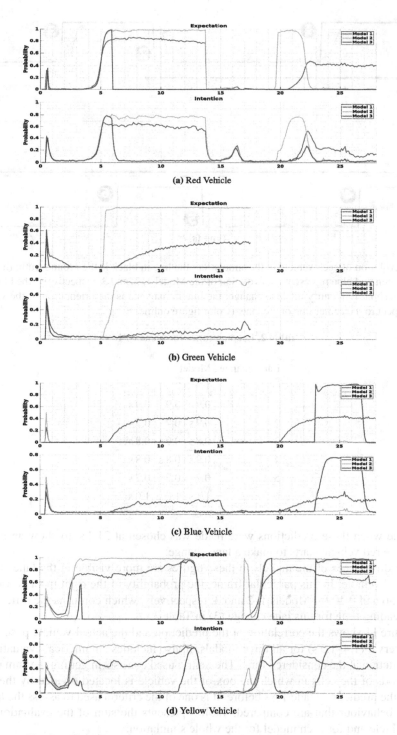

Fig. 8. Expectation and intention for each vehicle. (Color figure online)

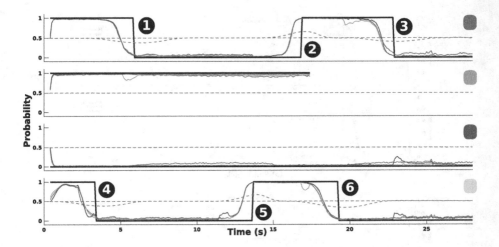

Fig. 9. Evolution of each vehicle in the simulation: the line in black is the ground truth; the lines in red, green and blue represent the evolution of the Model 1, 2, and 3, respectively; the blue line is the threshold to identify the lane change; the line in magenta is the orientation of the vehicle with respect to the center line of the lane. (Color figure online)

Table 2. Leading times for scenario 1.

Lane change	Model		
	1	2	3
1	0.9 s	0.9 s	0.9 s
2	0.7 s	0.7 s	0.7 s
3	0.8 s	0.9 s	0.8 s
4	0.9 s	0.8 s	0.8 s
5	0.7 s	0.7 s	0.7 s
6	1.1 s	1.0 s	1.0 s

The time when these predictions were made was chosen at 21.1 s, to show an instant where the red vehicle starts to make a lane change.

The differences of the models in these figures are more visible in the lane change of the red vehicle. In this particular frame, the probability of the right most corridor is 0.49, 0.56 and 0.40 for Models 1, 2 and 3, respectively, which confirms the differences in the leading time for this lane change (3) in Table 2.

Figure 11 shows the correlation of the prediction and the actual vehicle pose at the time interval (1.4–1.5 s) for all three models. It also includes a numerical evaluation of the prediction at the considered time. The metric used consists in getting the sum of the likelihoods of the cells in which the box of the vehicle is located divided by the total sum of the prediction made 1.5 s before. It is one of the criteria used to assess the lateral models behaviour that are compared. Table 3 presents the sum of the evaluations for each vehicle and for each model for the whole simulation.

The vehicles with the more accurate predictions are the ones that do not change lanes, namely the green and the blue vehicles (the green vehicle leaves the simulation

Table 3. Evaluation of the predictions per model.

Vehicle	Model		
	1	2	3
Red	123.4464	123.8847	124.3137
Green	100.8117	101.1304	102.1097
Blue	160.2665	164.1376	162.1872
Yellow	112.7849	113.3725	113.5978

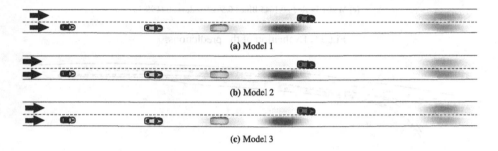

(a) Model 1

(b) Model 2

(c) Model 3

Fig. 10. Predictions at the interval 2.9–3.0 s for each of the models.

10.5 s before its end). Besides the early detection of the lane change, another factor that influences the accuracy of the predictions is the fact that the lane changing corridors do not perfectly match the movement executed by the vehicles.

5.2 Scenario 2

The second scenario is obtained from the publicly available dataset *exiD* [23] recorded from a bird-eye-view perspective. These data contains public traffic data from the participants present at the scene. For each participant, they include their pose, velocity, acceleration, size, and also the frames where they appear.

In order to use this data for the purpose of the work, it has been downsampled and filtered to remove undesired participants, such as static vehicles, vehicles with velocities larger than the maximum velocity from the motion prediction setup and large trucks. After binary tagging each frame as containing or not these participants, the intervals are grouped and the vehicle that stays the longest in each interval is defined as the ego vehicle. The frames in which this vehicle is not present are discarded.

It is a three-lane merging scenario containing 13 vehicles, where 10 lane changes are executed. The evolution of the path followed by each vehicle is shown in Fig. 12 and Fig. 13 shows the velocities of each vehicle throughout the simulation.

Execution of the Lateral Models. The simulation is executed three times, one for each lateral model. Figure 14 shows the evolution of the probabilities for each vehicle and each model. These probabilities are computed as $(1 - 2p_{left} + p_{center})/2$, where p_{left} and p_{center} are the probabilities of being on the left and center corridors, respectively. As mentioned before, the probability of each corridor is the sum of the weights of the particles that contain this corridor. Each line, marked with the color and the number

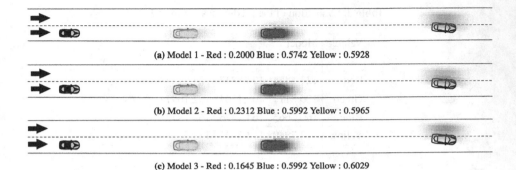

(a) Model 1 - Red : 0.2000 Blue : 0.5742 Yellow : 0.5928

(b) Model 2 - Red : 0.2312 Blue : 0.5992 Yellow : 0.5965

(c) Model 3 - Red : 0.1645 Blue : 0.5992 Yellow : 0.6029

Fig. 11. Evaluation of the predictions.

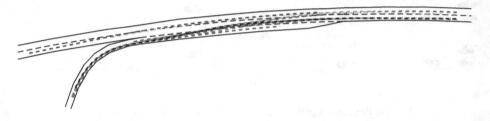

Fig. 12. Paths evolution of each vehicle in the simulated scenario 2. (Color figure online)

of the vehicle on the top right corner, represents the evolution of this vehicle. The x axis is the time and the y axis is the probability of being on each lane, being 0 the right (bottom) lane, 0.5 the center lane and 1 the left (top) lane. The line in black is the ground truth, the lane in which the vehicle is at, at each instant. The three models are represented by the lines in red, green and blue, respectively. The magenta dashed line is the orientation of the vehicle with respect to the orientation of the lane and the numbers mark the lane changes whose leading times for each model are presented in Table 4. The dashed line in blue is the threshold for the detection of a lane change.

Table 4. Leading times for scenario 2.

Lane change	Model		
	1	2	3
1	1.7 s	1.6 s	1.6 s
2	2.5 s	2.5 s	2.6 s
3	1.9 s	1.7 s	1.6 s
4	1.3 s	1.3 s	1.4 s
5	1.5 s	1.8 s	1.5 s
6	1.8 s	1.7 s	1.4 s
7	1.7 s	1.9 s	1.6 s
8	1.9 s	1.9 s	1.7 s
9	2.2 s	2.2 s	1.4 s
10	1.6 s	1.5 s	1.1 s

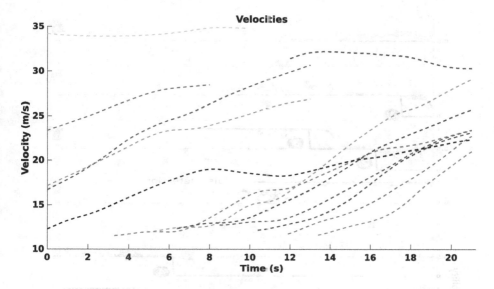

Fig. 13. Velocities throughout the execution of the scenario 2. (Color figure online)

Predictions and Evaluation. Figure 15 shows the correlation of the prediction and the actual vehicle pose at the time interval (1.4–1.5 s) for all three models. It also includes a numerical evaluation of the prediction at the considered time. The metric used consists in getting the sum of the likelihoods of the cells in which the box of the vehicle is located divided by the total sum of the prediction made 1.5 s before. The predictions are evaluated at the time 14.5 s when 4 lane changes are occurring for vehicles 7, 8, 9 and 13. Table 5 presents the sum of the evaluations for each vehicle and for each model for the whole simulation.

Table 5. Evaluation of the predictions per model.

Vehicle	Model		
	1	2	3
V2	29.9947	33.0504	32.5913
V3	63.7473	63.7014	62.3174
V4	51.6042	52.0531	50.7858
V5	46.5430	46.7282	46.6516
V7	80.4974	78.9401	78.9217
V8	46.6093	45.3853	44.5390
V9	55.4693	56.4780	55.5548
V10	49.7602	48.7178	49.6738
V11	39.1920	38.8220	40.1804
V12	27.8884	26.9556	28.6192
V13	31.5722	33.0101	32.2521
V14	22.1231	23.0291	21.0353

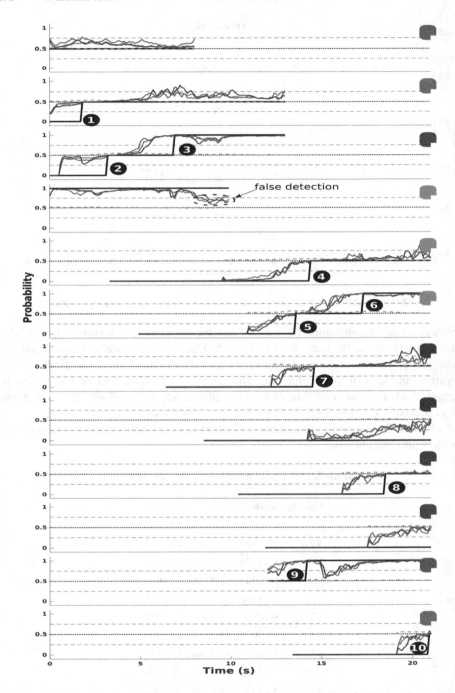

Fig. 14. Evolution of each vehicle in the simulation: the line in black is the ground truth; the lines in red, green and blue represent the evolution of the Model 1, 2, and 3, respectively; the blue line is the threshold to identify the lane change; the line in magenta is the orientation of the vehicle with respect to the center line of the lane. (Color figure online)

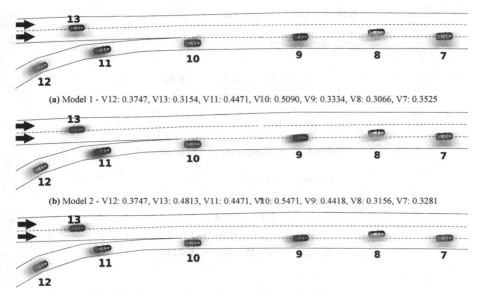

(a) Model 1 - V12: 0.3747, V13: 0.3154, V11: 0.4471, V10: 0.5090, V9: 0.3334, V8: 0.3066, V7: 0.3525

(b) Model 2 - V12: 0.3747, V13: 0.4813, V11: 0.4471, V10: 0.5471, V9: 0.4418, V8: 0.3156, V7: 0.3281

(c) Model 3 - V12: 0.3747, V13: 0.4669, V11: 0.4471, V10: 0.5088, V9: 0.4122, V8: 0.3069, V7: 0.4306

Fig. 15. Evaluation of the predictions. V_X is the evaluated prediction of vehicle X.

Table 6. Metrics of each model for scenario 1.

Parameter	Model		
	1	2	3
l	5.1 s	5.0 s	4.9 s
p	497.3096	502.5252	502.2084
f	0	0	0

5.3 Evaluation Metrics

To evaluate the quality of the results, three metrics were defined: lead time of the detection l, probability p of the current pose based on the predictions from a previous time step, and false lane change detection f.

- Lead time of the detection l is defined as the time where the corridor that is changing lanes has the biggest priority and maintains the dominance until the lane change is detected.
- Probability p of the current pose is a sum of the evaluation's probabilities for the whole simulation.
- False lane change detection f is the sum of intervals where the probability is bigger on a corridor that is not the correct one or a noise in the lane change. The intervals between the lead time and the detection of a lane change are not included. One example of a false detection is marked in Fig. 14.

Table 7. Metrics of each model for scenario 2.

Parameter	Model		
	1	2	3
l	18.5 s	18.5 s	16.4 s
p	545.011	546.8711	543.1223
f	36	40	48

Table 8. Normalized sum of the results.

Parameter	Model		
	1	2	3
l_{norm}	2.66	2.64	2.41
p_{norm}	0.9585	0.9672	0.9641
f_{norm}	0.0325	0.0375	0.0419

Each metric is computed as follows:

$$l_k = \sum_{v=1}^{N}\sum_{c=1}^{Nc_v} l_v^{c^k}, \quad p_k = \sum_{i=1}^{M}\sum_{v=1}^{N} p_v^{i^k}, \quad f_k = \sum_{i=1}^{M}\sum_{v=1}^{N} f_v^{i^k}$$

where $l_v^{c^k}$ is the leading time of the lane change c of the vehicle v for the model k, $p_v^{i^k}$ is the accuracy of a previous prediction at time interval i for the vehicle v for the model k, $f_v^{i^k}$ is the false detection for the vehicle v at the time interval i for the model k, N is the number of vehicles, Nc_v is the number of lane changes for the vehicle v and M is the number of simulated intervals.

Table 6 presents the values of each metric for the three models for the scenario 1. For this scenario, model 1 yield better leading times, although the predictions from model 2 and 3 are slightly more accurate. The reason for this is mostly due to the fact that the lane changing corridors do not perfectly match the movement executed by the vehicles. The number of false detection are the same for the three models.

The results from the scenario 2 are presented in Table 7. In this case, model 1 and 2 yield better leading time and the lowest number of false detections. The predictions from model 2 are better when compared with the other two models.

To combine both experiments, the values of l are normalized by the number of lane changes, and the values of p and f are normalized by the number of simulated intervals each vehicle is present at the simulation and the total number of vehicles. Table 8 presents the sum of the normalized results of both simulations for each model.

Based on the results from Table 8, for the scenarios evaluated, model 1 and model 2 produced, in general, better results, being model 1 slightly better since its normalized leading time and normalized false detection are the best among all models.

6 Conclusion and Future Work

In this work, the current framework that is being used by the AUTOPIA Group for the computation and evaluation of the predictions of vehicles considering their mutual interaction at highways is presented. It is a generic approach that can handle almost any layout and number of vehicles. Three models for the lane change were implemented and compared. With the metrics used in this work and in the scenarios evaluated, the model from [18] yields slightly better results.

As future work, the framework presented and the models compared will be applied in more complex scenarios, such as highways with a larger number of lanes and vehicles.

References

1. Trentin, V., Artuñedo, A., Godoy, J., Villagra, J.: A comparison of lateral intention models for interaction-aware motion prediction at highways. In: Proceedings of the 7th International Conference on Vehicle Technology and Intelligent Transport Systems (VEHITS), Prague, Czech Republic, 28–30 April 2021 (2021)
2. Zhan, W., de La Fortelle, A., Chen, Y., Chan C., Tomizuka, M.: Probabilistic prediction from planning perspective: problem formulation, representation simplification and evaluation metric. IEEE Intell. Veh. Symp. (IV) **2018**, 1150–1156 (2018). https://doi.org/10.1109/IVS.2018.8500697
3. Klingelschmitt, S., Damerow, F., Willert, V., Eggert, J.: Probabilistic situation assessment framework for multiple, interacting traffic participants in generic traffic scenes. IEEE Intell. Veh. Symp. (IV) **2016**, 1141–1148 (2016). https://doi.org/10.1109/IVS.2016.7535533
4. Lefevre, S., Laugier, C., Ibanez-Guzman, J.: Intention-aware risk estimation for general traffic situations, and application to intersection safety. Inria research report. RR-8379 (2013)
5. Villagra, J., Artuñedo, A., Trentin, V., Godoy, J : Interaction-aware risk assessment: focus on the lateral intention, pp. 1–6 (2020). https://doi.org/10.1109/CAVS51000.2020.9334597
6. Althoff, M., Magdici, S.: Set-based prediction of traffic participants on arbitrary road networks. IEEE Trans. Intell. Veh. **1**(2), 187–202 (2016). https://doi.org/10.1109/TIV.2016.2622920
7. Althoff, M.: Reachability analysis and its application to the safety assessment of autonomous cars (2010)
8. Zechel, P., Streiter, R., Bogenberger, K., Göhner, U.: Over-approximation of the driver behavior as occupancy prediction. In: 2019 IEEE 14th International Conference on Intelligent Systems and Knowledge Engineering (ISKE), pp. 735–742 (2019). https://doi.org/10.1109/ISKE47853.2019.9170398
9. Koschi, M., Althoff, M.: SPOT: a tool for set-based prediction of traffic participants. IEEE Intell. Veh. Symp. (IV) **2017**, 1686–1693 (2017). https://doi.org/10.1109/IVS.2017.7995951
10. Schulz, J., Hubmann, C., Löchner, J., Burschka, D.: Interaction-aware probabilistic behavior prediction in urban environments (2018)
11. Koschi, M., Althoff, M.: Interaction-aware occupancy prediction of road vehicles, pp. 1–8 (2017). https://doi.org/10.1109/ITSC.2017.8317852
12. Trentin, V., Artuñedo, A., Godoy, J., Villagra, J.: Interaction-aware intention estimation at roundabouts. IEEE Access **9**, 123088–123102 (2021). https://doi.org/10.1109/ACCESS.2021.3109350

13. Bender, P., Ziegler, J., Stiller, C.: Lanelets: efficient map representation for autonomous driving. IEEE Intell. Veh. Symp. Proc. **2014**, 420–425 (2014). https://doi.org/10.1109/IVS.2014. 6856487

14. Godoy, J., Jiménez, V., Artuñedo, A., Villagra, J.: A grid-based framework for collective perception in autonomous vehicles. Sensors **21**(3), 744 (2021)

15. Vechione, M., Balal, E., Cheu, R.: Comparisons of mandatory and discretionary lane changing behavior on freeways. Int. J. Transp. Sci. Technol. **7**(2), 124–136 (2018). https://doi.org/ 10.1016/j.ijtst.2018.02.002

16. Toledo, T., Koutsopoulos, H., Ben-Akiva, M.: Modeling integrated lane-changing behavior. Transp. Res. Rec. **1857**(1), 30–38 (2003). https://doi.org/10.3141/1857-04

17. Althoff, M.: An Introduction to CORA 2015 (2015). https://doi.org/10.29007/zbkv

18. Mathew, T.V.: Lane changing models (2019). https://www.civil.iitb.ac.in/tvm/nptel/534_ LaneChange/web/web.html. Accessed 19 Nov 2020

19. Kesting, A., Treiber, M., Helbing, D.: General lane-changing model MOBIL for car-following models. Transp. Res. Rec. **1999**, 86–94 (2007). https://doi.org/10.3141/1999-10

20. Treiber, M., Hennecke, A., Helbing, D.: Congested traffic states in empirical observations and microscopic simulations. Phys. Rev. E **62**, 1805–1824 (2000). https://doi.org/10.1103/ PhysRevE.62.1805

21. Toledo, T., Choudhury, C., Ben-Akiva, M.: Lane-changing model with explicit target lane choice. Transp. Res. Rec. **1934**(1), 157–165 (2005). https://doi.org/10.3141/1934-17

22. AVSimulation: SCANeR studio User Manual (2019)

23. Moers, T., Vater, L., Krajewski, R., Bock, J., Zlocki, A., Eckstein, L.: The exiD dataset: a real-world trajectory dataset of highly interactive highway scenarios in germany. In: 2022 IEEE Intell. Veh. Symp. (IV), 958–964 (2022). https://doi.org/10.1109/IV51971.2022. 9827305

A Hierarchical Dependency-Driven Scenario-Based Testing for Autonomous Vehicles

Kaushik Madala[1](✉) and Hyunsook Do[2]

[1] UL LLC, 920 SW 4th Ave, Portland, OR 97204, USA
kaushik.madala@ul.com
[2] University of North Texas, 3490 N Elm St, Denton 76205, USA

Abstract. To assure safety of an autonomous vehicle, it is essential to perform a thorough analysis of vehicle behavior with respect to its operational design domain (ODD). This requires engineers and experts to have a systematic procedure to identify different operational environments/settings that can occur within an ODD and to consider various scenarios that can occur within those environments/settings. While automotive safety standards such as ISO 26262 and ISO 21448 require analysts and engineers to use scenario-based analysis, they do not offer a systematic guidance for scenario-based testing and analysis. Moreover existing scenario-based methods and simulation tools only offer support for few operating environments within an ODD and perform exhaustive or random testing, there by resulting in potentially overlooking ODD factors and dependencies. To address this limitation, in our previous work, we proposed a dependency-based combinatorial approach that reduces the testing effort without compromising the ability to expose safety issues. In this paper, we propose a hierarchical dependency-driven scenario-based testing approach, which is built upon our previous work. Our proposed work uses hierarchy among ODD factors, dependencies among ODD factors and components in the system, and combinatorial testing algorithm, IPOG, to reduce the number of test cases and systematically derive scenarios. The results of our study has shown that our approach reduces the number of test case without missing dependencies and that our hierarchical approach is helpful in ensuring the dependencies among ODD factors and components in vehicle are not overlooked.

Keywords: Dependency-driven · Scenario-based testing · SOTIF · Safety · Autonomous vehicles

1 Introduction

To assure safety of an autonomous vehicle with respect to various known and unknown scenarios that might occur within the operational design domain (ODD) of a vehicle, a scenario-based testing is necessary. The industry safety standards for automotive vehicles such as the functional safety (FuSa) standard, ISO 26262 [10], and the safety of the intended functionality (SOTIF) standard, ISO 21448 [11], despite mentioning the importance of scenarios, do not provide a systematic guidance on how to generate and assess scenarios to assure both FuSa and SOTIF. The standards also do not provide any guidance on how many scenarios will ensure a vehicle is safe and how many times each scenario will need to be tested.

© Springer Nature Switzerland AG 2022
C. Klein et al. (Eds.): SMARTGREENS 2021/ VEHITS 2021, CCIS 1612, pp. 297–312, 2022.
https://doi.org/10.1007/978-3-031-17098-0_15

While there are some approaches [1,2,12] that currently assure safety of autonomous vehicle, they inculcate the usage of amount of miles driven by an autonomous vehicle or the verification of safety-critical driving scenarios with assurance that the vehicle meets a target set by engineers and experts based on data sets such as accident based data [20] or naturalistic driving data [24,25]. For example, Altoff and Lutz [2] proposed a test case generation approach that uses drivable areas to generate potential safety critical scenarios for a vehicle. Despite their ability to expose potential situations that could compromise safety, these existing approaches still pertain the following limitations:

– Although both ISO 26262 and ISO 21448 rely on scenarios as a part of their hazard analysis, both standards do not offer a guidance on systematic identification of scenarios. Rather, the task is conducted through a brainstorming by engineers and experts. During the brainstorming, if any scenarios or ODD factors are missed/overlooked, their corresponding tests would be overlooked or ignored.
– Only if diverse and representative scenarios that could occur within the defined operational design domain (ODD) are covered sufficiently, the amount of miles driven would become an effective metric. If a fleet of vehicles is tested on the same road and operational setting, it is not sufficient enough to ensure safety of the autonomous vehicle as some scenarios could be overlooked or some ODD factors could be ignored.
– Current approaches for scenario generation often fix the operational setting, i.e., these approaches have a fixed set of ODD factors and their attributes. However, a vehicle's ODD can have different operational settings. Hence, relying only on one operational setting will not be sufficient to assure safety of the autonomous vehicle. For an autonomous vehicle, to identify a scenario, as mentioned in ISO 21448, we should consider the combination of driving scenarios (e.g., vehicle cut-in, overtaking), environmental factors (e.g., fog, hail), on road entities (e.g., pedestrians, trucks), road geometry (e.g., straight road), road infrastructure (e.g., traffic signs). Further, in simulation, we need to define goals/objectives of the scenario, i.e., the list of tasks we aim to accomplish in the scenario (e.g., an ego vehicle should stop if there is a vehicle in front of it).
– Current simulation tools (e.g., CARLA [5], Fortellix [8]) have in-built operating environments created based on needs of the customers [7]. However, these built-in operating environments do not necessarily cover different possible operational settings that could occur within the defined operational design domain (ODD) of an autonomous vehicle. Moreover, most of these current simulation tools generate test cases exhaustively, i.e., generate all possible test cases for a given scenario by taking into account different parameters and their respective values defined by the engineers. A few tools such as Fortellix [8] offer support for combining scenarios and operating conditions. However, the scenario description is restricted to Open M-SDL [8] specification, which may not necessarily cover all the required ODD factors and attributes we considered as a part of our ODD. When we perform analysis using such tools, it might result in overlooking ODD factors or attributes, which may increase the number of unknowns. For example, if a pedestrian's gender or race cannot be set in a simulation tool despite a wide presence of pedestrians in

ODD such as city streets, testing may be restricted to only specific types of pedestrians. Further, exhaustive testing is not feasible given the complexity of ODD for autonomous vehicles. This is because as the complexity of the ODD increases, the need for resources, time, and effort also increases.

To overcome these limitations, in our recent work, we proposed a dependency-based combinatorial approach (DBCA) for generating scenarios and test instances within a scenario. The approach used a combinatorial testing algorithm called IPOG [14, 15] to not only reduce the number of test cases but also to use dependencies among ODD factors when assigning 't' value to IPOG to generate t-way combinations. Our analyses have shown that our previous work reduces effort and time without compromising the number of safety issues found. However, one drawback of the approach is there is no systematic derivation from scenarios and corresponding test cases. To address this limitation, in this paper, we propose a hierarchical dependency-driven scenario-based testing (HDST) approach. Our approach is built upon DBCA and utilizes hierarchy among operational design domain (ODD) factors to offer a systematic approach for deriving scenarios and to further reduce the number of test cases, and there by potentially reducing testing effort. We also use component-level information in our technique to identify dependencies and to identify the ':' value to generate t-way combinations using IPOG [14, 15].

Our novel contributions are summarized as follows:

1. *The Use of Hierarchical Relations:* Operational design domain (ODD) can be represented as a hierarchy of scenario factors, and every scenario factor can have associated properties. For example, weather can be classified into rain, snow, sunny and cloudy. But we can further classify rain into light rain, medium rain, and heavy rain. The amount of rainfall can be a property we can consider for rain. In our approach, we exploit this hierarchy by moving to the lower level of hierarchies only if the upper level has an effect on the behavior of the system or component in a system.
2. *Dependency Analysis:* There exist dependencies among environmental properties and properties of components in the system. For example, ambient light luminosity can affect the pixel values captured by a camera. By identifying the properties of ODD factors and components in a system, we aim to explore which ODD factors and components must be tested together to ensure we did not miss any dependency that could potentially affect safety.

To analyze effectiveness of our approach, we conducted an empirical study with a pedestrian detection system by taking into account the scenario factors listed in Table B.4 in ISO 21448 [11], and compared with exhaustive testing and combinatorial testing with no hierarchy. Our results showed that the proposed approach reduces the number of test cases when compared to the control techniques and helps in systematically deriving scenarios.

The rest of the paper is organized as follows. Section 2 discusses basic terminology used in the paper and related work. Section 3 describes our proposed methodology in detail and Sect. 4 presents the empirical study conducted to evaluate our approach and its results. Section 5 discusses the insights we gathered from our analysis as well as limitations of the proposed approach. Finally, we conclude in Sect. 6.

2 Terminology and Related Work

In this section, we discuss some technical terms we use throughout the paper and the related literature to our proposed method.

2.1 Terminology and Definition

1. *Ego Vehicle:* The vehicle for which we perform analysis.
2. *Operational Design Domain (ODD):* A set of conditions that includes but is not limited to environmental factors, static and dynamic entities around vehicles, various driving maneuvers for which a system or a feature of the system is designed, and road infrastructural elements [3, 11].
3. *Scenario*: A scenario can be defined as a temporal sequence of situations that includes actions and events in the surrounding operating environment of a vehicle, where the vehicle aims to achieve the objectives defined by the stakeholders [11]. For a given environmental setting, multiple scenarios can occur.
4. *IPOG Algorithm* [14, 15]: It is a combinatorial testing algorithm that reduces the number of test cases by generating t-way combinations of parameter values. Usually, the value of 't' is smaller than the total number of parameters. When we use the term "t-way combinations" between elements, it implies that between any 't' elements, all the combinations are considered. For example, let us assume four parameters x1, x2, x3 and x4 with two values each. Then, 2-way combinations of these parameters represent that all possible pairs of values between the 4 parameters are identified. In this paper, we use IPOG algorithm to generate hierarchical combinations.
5. *Exhaustive Testing:* The testing strategy in which all possible combinations of the values of parameters are used to generate test cases. It consumes a significant amount of effort and resources.

2.2 Related Work

Scenario-based testing is one of the challenging tasks. Koopman and Wagner [13] have indicated the infeasible nature of testing for autonomous vehicles. Hence, to work on this problem, to date, many researchers [1, 16, 19, 21] have proposed techniques for scenario generation or scenario-based testing.

Some researchers [6, 9, 16, 22] adopted combinatorial strategies to generate scenario-based tests. For example, Rocklage et al. [22] proposed a static and hybrid scenario generation approach that takes a given scenario and identifies feasible trajectories to plan motion by checking feasibility of the trajectory using constraint solving with a backtracking algorithm. Another example is the ontology-based approach proposed by Li et al. [16] in which parameters and values are identified using ontology and are used to generate n-way combinations. The authors then identify critical scenarios by refining these combinations with the help of a machine learning model.

Other researchers [4, 19] have proposed scenario generation using search-based software engineering techniques. For example, Mullins et al. [19] proposed a scenario generation framework which uses adaptive sampling with surrogate optimization as a search strategy. The generated scenarios are then grouped by ranking their effectiveness using a density-based clustering technique.

A few researchers [2,21] have proposed scenario generation approaches that rely on formal methods. For example, Nonnengart et al. [21] proposed CriSGen, a formal-method based scenario generation approach that formalizes abstract scenarios as well as maneuvers to generate critical scenarios. The scenarios are then subjected to for-ward reachability analysis to verify if an unsafe state can be resulted because of any maneuver.

In addition to the prior mentioned methodologies, a few researchers [1,13] have generated scenarios using naturalistic driving data [23–25]. For example, Akagi et al. [1] proposed a scenario generation framework, which uses a probabilistic model built using naturalistic driving data (e.g., SHRP2 [25]) to generate scenarios by sam-pling traffic risk index values and vehicle kinetic information.

While these techniques aid in identifying critical scenarios, they do not consider if their scenarios cover all the ODD factors. Also, the techniques either rely on random generation or exhaustive generation of scenarios for testing. Random testing makes it difficult to guarantee if dependencies among ODD factors and components in a vehicle are sufficiently covered whereas exhaustive generation of scenarios will require a sig-nificant amount of resources, effort and time. In our previous work, we aimed to address these limitations by using a dependency-based combinatorial approach (DBCA) [18]. However, we found that to establish an environment in a simulation environment, we will need to go through different levels of hierarchy among ODD factors so that we can offer more flexibility and insights for testing. The different levels of hierarchy pro-vide a systematic approach for identifying overlooked aspects and in assessing required tools and effort time. Hence, to address these issues, we proposed our hierarchical dependency-driven scenario-based testing (HDST) process.

3   Approach

Figure 1 shows the overview of our hierarchical dependency-driven scenario-based test-ing process. The ovals in the figure refer to the steps in the approach and the rectangles indicate an input to a step or an output from a step. The numbers in the ovals represent the step numbers.

As shown in the figure, we (the stakeholders) start with identifying the ODD factors (Step 1 in Fig. 3). We then identify the different attributes and parameters of the ODD factors (Step 2). We also define a hierarchy among the ODD factors and their parameters (Step 3). We then identify the components in a system (Step 4) and their properties (Step 5). To construct scenarios for testing that are within the scope of the defined ODD, we then find the dependencies between ODD factors and components by taking a hierarchy into consideration (Step 6). We then generate hierarchical combinations by using these dependencies (Step 7) and IPOG algorithm [14 15]. Finally, we generate test cases from these combinations to verify the behavior of the system. We now describe each of these steps in detail as follows.

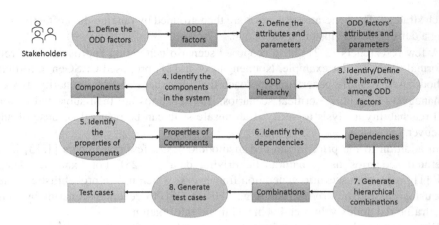

Fig. 1. Overview of the proposed hierarchical dependency-driven scenario-based testing process.

Step 1. Define the ODD Factors

The first step in our approach is to define the ODD factors relevant for the system under development. Standards such as BSI 1883 [3] and ISO 21448 [11] (in Annexes) offer insights on the factors that can be considered as a part of ODD. ODD factors include aspects such as weather conditions, road conditions, road infrastructure conditions, environmental conditions, behaviors of ego vehicle, and behaviors of static and dynamic agents and vehicles around the ego vehicle. Let us consider the case of pedestrian crossing in front of the ego-vehicle. Some of the ODD factors that can be considered are as follows: weather, snow, ice, glare, road type, city street, freeway, vehicles, trucks, cars, road users, pedestrians, and bicyclists.

Step 2. Define the Attributes and Parameters

Once the ODD factors are defined, their attributes and parameters should be identified. An attribute is an aspect possessed by an ODD factor. For example, gender is an attribute of a pedestrian. On other hand, a parameter is a property of an ODD factor. For example, walking speed is a parameter of a pedestrian. Note that an attribute of an ODD factor can also have its own parameters. For example, an elderly pedestrian may have a walking support, and weight of the support is one of the parameters we can consider for the walking support.

Step 3. Identify/Define the Hierarchy among ODD Factors

After defining ODD factors and their respective attributes and parameters, we identify the hierarchy among the ODD factors. A hierarchy can be formed between two ODD factors when one of the factors is a sub-type of the other ODD factor. The ODD factor that contains the sub-type can be referred as a child factor, and the one that contains the main type is referred as a parent factor. For the example, for ODD factors discussed for the pedestrian crossing example in Step 1, we can create a hierarchy as shown in Table 1. Note that sometimes attributes of an ODD factor can be used as a child factor. For example, we can use gender of pedestrians as a sub-type and create a new ODD factors such as male, female, and other.

Table 1. Hierarchy of ODD factors generated from the pedestrian detection example.

Level 0	Level 1
Weather	Ice
	Snow
	Glare
Road type	City streets
	Freeway
Vehicles	Trucks
	Cars
Road users	Pedestrians
	Bicyclists

Step 4. Identify the Components in the System

Once the hierarchical relationships among ODD factors are found, we identify the components in a system. These components typically include the sensors, actuators, any intermediate algorithms, and controllers. For example, if the ego vehicle that is detecting pedestrians uses LIDAR point cloud as input, LIDAR-based pedestrian detection as an intermediate algorithm to detect pedestrians a braking algorithm that applies brakes upon detection, and actual hydraulic brakes that apply braking, then the components of this system are: LIDAR, LIDAR-based pedestrian detection algorithm, braking algorithm, and hydraulic brakes.

Step 5. Identify the Properties of Components

Similar to ODD factors, we identify attributes and properties of components once we identify components. Note that attributes of components often include information such as supplier/manufacturer name and version. Every component has respective properties. These properties can be behavioral properties (e.g., the number of times a button is pressed), user-defined properties (e.g., the number of times a pedestrian misprediction resulted in a collision), physical properties (e.g., weight), chemical properties (e.g., composition, decay rate), mechanical properties (e.g., tensile strength), electrical properties (e.g., voltage) or any other properties (e.g., mathematical, statistical). For the hydraulic braking component we discussed earlier, a property is the braking torque.

Step 6. Identify the Dependencies

After the properties of components are identified, dependencies among components and ODD factors are found. A dependency is said to be exist between two components, a component and ODD factor, or two ODD factors if one of them can affect the behavior of the other. These dependencies include property-based dependencies, where a property of a component or an ODD factor can affect a property of another component or an ODD factor. For example, LIDAR's behavior can be affected because of reflective clothing. Hence, we consider that there is a dependency between LIDAR and reflective clothing or material.

Step 7. Generate Hierarchical Combinations

Once the dependencies are finalized, we generate hierarchical combinations. To do so, we exploit the hierarchy we defined for ODD factors in Step 3 and the dependencies we found in Step 6. To generate the combinations, we use the following procedure.

1. Assign numbers to each level of a hierarchy of the ODD factors, starting 0 from the topmost level.
2. Once the numbers are assigned, from the top level (level 0), identify the maximum number (represented as 't') of ODD factors and components of the system that are dependent on each other at level 0.
3. Using IPOG algorithm [14,15], generate t-way combinations of level 0 of ODD factors taking into account their properties and attributes. These combinations represent the most abstract level of scenarios.
4. Increment the level number. Considering each combination generated in the previous level, repeat steps 2 and 3 for identifying 't' value and generating the t-way combinations for the current level.
5. Repeat the process until the last level of ODD factors is reached. The last level represents the most concrete level of scenarios that can be generated and that needs to be analyzed.

Step 8. Generate Test Cases

The combinations generated in the previous step are converted into a test case format in order to run and evaluate test cases. To do so, we need to define the pass and fail criteria for each combination and also understand the required or allowable test case format by the tool or test environment. Note that test cases can also be generated manually and can be converted to the format required by the target simulation or testing tool.

4   Study

In our previous work [18], we demonstrated how using dependency-based combinatorial approaches reduce effort without compromising the number of issues found. To understand if the proposed approach that exploits a hierarchy among ODD factors is beneficial in terms of reducing effort and time, we conducted a study focusing on the following research questions:

RQ1: Can we exploit a hierarchy among ODD factors to reduce the number of scenarios and test cases?

RQ2: Does exploiting dependencies among ODD factors and components in a system aid to reduce testing effort further when we consider hierarchy among ODD factors?

4.1 Object of Analysis

To conduct our study we utilize the scenario factors mentioned in Table B.4 in ISO 21448 [11], which is illustrated in Tables 2 and 3. The numbers in the parentheses next to the ODD factors represent the number of children a factor has for the next level. For example, Road Geometry and Topology factor has 6 child factors. For the system under analysis, let us consider a pedestrian detection system that has the components and properties defined in Table 4. The values in the parentheses represent the property values that can be used and the number of values that are being planned to be used in testing. Note that the list of properties detailed in the table is not exhaustive, rather we focused only on few properties in our study. To simplify the complexity of the problem, we focused on defining attributes and properties only for the object of interest in the system, which is pedestrian. The attributes and parameters we considered for 'Pedestrian' are shown in Table 5. The numbers in parentheses represent the number of values of attributes or parameters.

4.2 Variables

Independent Variable: The independent variable for the research questions is the technique used to generate test cases. We have one heuristic technique and two control techniques. Our proposed approach is our heuristic technique. The first control technique is the exhaustive testing technique in which all possible combinations among parameters are used to generate test cases. The second control technique is the combinatorial technique without using a hierarchy. In this technique, we remove any hierarchical relationships and flatten out all the ODD factors to a single level (similar to state flattening [17]).

Dependent Variable: The dependent variable for RQ1 and RQ2 is the number of test cases generated. We use this variable to represent the reduction in effort and time for testing and its respective analyses.

4.3 Experimental Procedure

Our experiment is conducted in a collaborative setting of industrial and academic researchers. To generate t-way combinations using IPOG algorithm [14, 15], we utilize ACTS tool [26]. The analysis corresponding to test cases is done manually. This is to ensure a thorough review of quality of test cases and to adhere to guidance offered in standards such as ISO 26262 [10], which mentions the need for verification reviews even for artifacts including test cases.

The procedure we followed for our heuristic technique is similar to the one described in Sect. 3. We started with ODD factors described in Table B.4 of ISO 21448.

Table 2. Scenario factors from Table B.4 in ISO 21448 [11] –1.

Level 0	Level 1	Level 2	Level 3
Road geometry and topology (6)	Road type (3)	Highway Rural Urban	
	Road geometry (2)	Straight Curve	
	Road elevation (3)	Level Uphill Downhill	
	Road cross section (2)	Number of lanes Lane marking	
	Road surface (2)	Roughness (4)	Asphalt Concrete Pavement Gravel
		Damage (2)	Crack Pothole
	Road intersections (4)	Diverging Merging Weaving Crossing	
Road furniture and limitations (2)	Boundary (6)	Pole Guardrail Concrete barrier Noise barrier Tunnel Bridge	
	Traffic signs (3)	Traffic lights Warnings Limits	
Temporary physical limitations (4)	Lane reassignment Lane markings Road work signs Road work barricades		
Movable entities (3)	Entity types (4)	Vehicles (7)	Cars Trucks Buses Motorcycles Emergency vehicles Agricultural vehicles Pedal cycles
		Pedestrians Animals Objects	
	Maneuvers (9)	Cruising (2)	High speed Low speed

Table 3. Scenario factors from Table B.4 in ISO 21448 [11] –2.

Level 0	Level 1	Level 2	Level 3
Movable entities	Maneuvers	Speed change (2)	Deceleration
			Acceleration
		Follow	
		Approach	
		Pass	
		Lane change (2)	Left
			Right
		Turn (2)	Left
			Right
		Turn back	
		Safe stop	
	Relative positions (4)	Left	
		Right	
		In front of	
		Behind	
Environmental conditions (4)	Time of day (4)	Early morning	
		Daytime	
		Evening	
		Night time	
	Atmospheric conditions (5)	Temperature	
		Visibility	
		Wind	
		Clouds	
		Precipitation (4)	Rain
			Hail
			Sleet
			Snow
	Lighting conditions (2)	Sunlight	
		Moonlight	
	Road surface conditions (4)	Dry	
		Wet	
		Snow covered	
		Icy	

Since the list of ODD factors in this table is large, we only defined attributes and parameters for the main object of analysis of our pedestrian detection system: "pedestrian" (shown in Table 5). We did not define any additional hierarchy as Table B.4 has a built-

Table 4. Components and properties of a pedestrian detection system.

Component Name	Properties
LIDAR	Field of view (120 to 360°, 24 values with 10° increment), range (1 m to 20 m, 20 values)
Camera	Resolution (3 mega pixel (MP) –8 MP, 6 values), frame rate (10 frames per second (fps) –30 fps, 3 values with 10 fps increment)
Camera-based pedestrian detection algorithm	Prediction rate (1 Hz, 1 value), precision (0.95, 1 value), recall (0.95, 1 value)
LIDAR-based pedestrian detection algorithm	Point cloud processing time (1 s, 1 value)
Braking system	Braking torque (2700 Nm–4200 Nm, 15 values with 100 value increment)

Table 5. Attributes and parameters of a pedestrian.

Name	Type	Values (# of values)
Gender	Attribute	Male, Female (2)
Race	Attribute	White, Black or African American, Asian, Native Hawaiian or Other Pacific Islander, and American Indian or Alaskan Native (5)
Age group	Attribute	Children, Adolescents, Adults, Elderly (4)
Mobility support	Attribute	None, Walking stick, White cane, Stroller, Walker, Wheel chair, Scooter (6)
Speed	Parameter	0–2 m/s (5 with 0.5 increment)

in hierarchy. The difference however is that we did not consider environmental conditions as an additional fifth layer, rather we combined it with hierarchies of other ODD factors. We then identified the components and their properties for the pedestrian detection system as shown in Table 4. Once the components and their properties are defined, we identified the dependencies among ODD factors and components of the system. For example, one of the dependencies we found is the dependency between camera and weather conditions. For each level in the hierarchy, we first analyzed the number of ODD factors and components that are mutually dependent on each other to choose the 't' value for generating t-way combinations. We then generated combinations for each level of hierarchy of ODD factors. The resultant combinations are used to generate test cases and analyze them.

4.4 Results

RQ1 Results: RQ1 focuses on verifying if the proposed technique is able to reduce testing effort by exploiting the hierarchy among ODD factors. To analyze RQ1, we generated combinations for the factors shown in Tables 2 and 3. To show scenarios only, we did not use parameters or properties for this research question. The results of RQ1 are shown in the Table 6. From the table, we can observe that the proposed technique produces the smallest number of combinations compared to the control techniques. The combinations produced by the proposed approach are resultant of sums of combinations generated across different levels of ODD factors unlike the control techniques. In total, 24 combinations are produced for Level 0 and its values, 56 combinations are produced for Level 1, and 60 combinations for Level 2. For Level 3, we did not generate any combinations as we did not have parameters defined for all of them.

Table 6. RQ1 results. Number of scenarios and test cases generated.

Heuristic (Proposed technique)	Exhaustive testing	Non-hierarchical Combinatorial
140	95,846,400	541

RQ2 Results: To address RQ2, in which we study whether dependencies can reduce the testing effort further, we utilized the information in Tables 4 and 5. We first identified dependencies across the ODD factors, components and their properties, as well as attributes and parameters considered for pedestrians. The results (the number of test cases) are shown in Table 7. After dependency analysis, we found t = 2, hence we generated 2-way combinations. It can be observed that while the number of test cases drastically increased for the exhaustive testing approach, the number of test cases generated using combinatorial approaches remain low. However, the proposed approach produced a higher number of test cases (989) (it is the cumulative count of test cases at different levels) when compared to the combinatorial approach that does not consider hierarchical relationships (686). We further analyzed if there are any dependencies that are lost by comparing the result produced by of our approach which considers dependencies as well as hierarchies and the result produced by the control technique where hierarchical relationships are disregarded. We found that due to lack of considering hierarchical relationships and systematic analysis, certain dependencies covered by test cases generated using our approach are not covered by the control technique. For example, we cannot cover combinations where there is rain at night time using the controlled technique as it considers both rain and night time to be values of the same parameter.

Table 7. RQ2 results. Number of scenarios and test cases generated.

Heuristic (Proposed technique)	Exhaustive testing	Non-hierarchical Combinatorial
989	1.16×10^{23}	686

5   Discussion

From the results of our study, we found that our proposed technique is effective in reducing the testing effort when compared to control techniques. We found that using a hierarchy can reduce the number of test cases further without missing dependencies. We also found that applying the proposed technique helps practitioners to systematically develop test cases.

The proposed technique also fits well into standards such as ISO 21448 [11] and ISO 26262 [10]. It takes into account the functional dependencies which play a vital role in assuring functional safety and it also provides ways to expose functional inefficiencies, making it suitable to verify vehicle's safety of the intended functionality.

Limitations: Despite the advantages offered by our approach, it still suffers from some limitations. First, the determination of dependencies is currently manual and not automatic. We plan to address it by proposing natural language processing based approaches, which can help apply semi-automated or automated processes. Another limitation is that the current approach does not discuss how to deal with conflicting opinions between stakeholders. We aim to address this by proposing guidelines on how to conduct manual steps involved in this approach.

6   Conclusion and Future Work

In this paper, we discussed a hierarchical dependency-driven scenario-based testing process to reduce the amount of testing effort. Our approach exploits the concepts of a hierarchy and dependencies to reduce the number of test cases drastically when compared to exhaustive testing. To evaluate our approach, we conducted an empirical study focusing on two research questions. Our results showed that our approach outperforms the exhaustive technique and non-hierarchical combinatorial testing approach.

As a part of future work, we plan to address the limitations discussed in the Sect. 5. In this paper, we conducted an empirical study only considering a pedestrian. We intend to perform a comprehensive empirical study using a large number of components and scenarios as a part of future work. We also plan to explore how we can apply our proposed technique to various application domains.

References

1. Akagi, Y., Kato, R., Kitajima, S., Antona-Makoshi, J., Uchida, N.: A risk-index based sampling method to generate scenarios for the evaluation of automated driving vehicle safety*. In: 2019 IEEE Intelligent Transportation Systems Conference (ITSC), pp. 667–672 (2019)

2. Althoff, M., Lutz, S.: Automatic generation of safety-critical test scenarios for collision avoidance of road vehicles. In: 2018 IEEE Intelligent Vehicles Symposium (IV), pp. 1326–1333 (2018)
3. BSI/PAS: 1883:2020. Operational Design Domain (ODD) taxonomy for an automated driving system (ADS)–Specification (2020)
4. Caló, A., Arcaini, P., Ali, S., Hauer, F., Ishikawa, F.: Generating avoidable collision scenarios for testing autonomous driving systems. In: 2020 IEEE 13th International Conference on Software Testing, Validation and Verification (ICST), pp. 375–386 (2020)
5. Dosovitskiy, A., Ros, G., Codevilla, F., Lopez, A., Koltun, V.: Carla: an open urban driving simulator. In: Conference on Robot Learning, pp. 1–16 (2017)
6. Duan, J., Gao, F., He, Y.: Test scenario generation and optimization technology for intelligent driving systems. IEEE Intelligent Transportation Systems Magazine (2020)
7. Fadaie, J.: The state of modeling, simulation, and data utilization within industry: an autonomous vehicles perspective (2019). CoRR abs/1910.06075, http://arxiv.org/abs/1910.06075
8. Fortellix: Open M-SDL, Measurable Scenario Description Language (2020)
9. Gannous, A., Andrews, A.: Integrating safety certification into model-based testing of safety-critical systems. In: 2019 IEEE 30th International Symposium on Software Reliability Engineering (ISSRE), pp. 250–260. IEEE (2019)
10. ISO: 26262. Road Vehicles - Functional Safety (2018)
11. ISO/DIS: 21448. Road vehicles - Safety of the intended functionality (2020)
12. Kalra, N., Paddock, S.M.: Driving to safety: how many miles of driving would it take to demonstrate autonomous vehicle reliability? Transp. Res. Part A Policy Pract. **94**, 182–193 (2016). https://doi.org/10.1016/j.tra.2016.09.010, http://www.sciencedirect.com/science/article/pii/S0965856416302129
13. Koopman, P., Wagner, M.: Challenges in autonomous vehicle testing and validation (2016). https://doi.org/10.4271/2016-01-0128, https://doi.org/10.4271/2016-01-0128
14. Lei, Y., Kacker, R., Kuhn, D.R., Okun, V., Lawrence, J.: Ipog: a general strategy for t-way software testing. In: 14th Annual IEEE International Conference and Workshops on the Engineering of Computer-Based Systems (ECBS 2007), pp. 549–556. IEEE (2007)
15. Lei, Y., Kacker, R., Kuhn, D.R., Okun, V., Lawrence, J.: IPOG/IPOG-D: efficient test generation for multi-way combinatorial testing. Softw. Test. Verification Reliab. **18**(3), 125–148 (2008)
16. Li, Y., Tao, J., Wotawa, F.: Ontology-based test generation for automated and autonomous driving functions. Inf. Softw. Technol. **117**, 106200 (2020). https://doi.org/10.1016/j.infsof.2019.106200, http://www.sciencedirect.com/science/article/pii/S0950584918302271
17. Madala, K., Do, H., Aceituna, D.: Hierarchical model exploration for exposing off-nominal behaviors. In: MODELS (Satellite Events), pp. 329–335 (2017)
18. Madala, K., Do, H., Avalos-Gonzalez, C.: A dependency-based combinatorial approach for reducing effort for scenario-based safety analysis of autonomous vehicles. In: VEHITS, pp. 235–246 (2021)
19. Mullins, G.E., Stankiewicz, P.G., Hawthorne, R.C., Gupta, S.K.: Adaptive generation of challenging scenarios for testing and evaluation of autonomous vehicles. J. Syst. Softw. **137**, 197–215 (2018). https://doi.org/10.1016/j.jss.2017.10.031, http://www.sciencedirect.com/science/article/pii/S0164121217302546
20. NHTSA: Fatality Analysis and Reporting System (FARS) Data Tables (2018). https://www-fars.nhtsa.dot.gov/Main/index.aspx
21. Nonnengart, A., Klusch, M., Müller, C.: CriSGen: constraint-based generation of critical scenarios for autonomous vehicles. In: Sekerinski, E., et al. (eds.) FM 2019. LNCS, vol. 12232, pp. 233–248. Springer, Cham (2020). https://doi.org/10.1007/978-3-030-54994-7_17

22. Rocklage, E., Kraft, H., Karatas, A., Seewig, J.: Automated scenario generation for regression testing of autonomous vehicles. In: 2017 IEEE 20th International Conference on Intelligent Transportation Systems (ITSC), pp. 476–483 (2017)
23. van Nes, N., Bärgman, J., Christoph, M., van Schagen, I.: The potential of naturalistic driving for in-depth understanding of driver behavior: UDRIVE results and beyond. Safety Sci. **119**, 11–20 (2019). https://doi.org/10.1016/j.ssci.2018.12.029, http://www.sciencedirect.com/science/article/pii/S0925753517320945
24. VTTI: Canadian NDS Data (2020). https://insight.canada-nds.net/
25. VTTI: SHRP2 NDS Data (2020). https://insight.shrp2nds.us/
26. Yu, L., Lei, Y., Kacker, R.N., Kuhn, D.R.: Acts: a combinatorial test generation tool. In: 2013 IEEE Sixth International Conference on Software Testing, Verification and Validation, pp. 370–375. IEEE (2013)

Optimal Control of Traffic Flow Based on Reinforcement Learning

Urs Baumgart$^{(\boxtimes)}$ and Michael Burger

Fraunhofer Institute for Industrial Mathematics ITWM,
Fraunhofer-Platz 1, 67663 Kaiserslautern, Germany
{urs.baumgart,michael.burger}@itwm.fraunhofer.de

Abstract. We study approaches to use (real-time) data, communicated between cars and infrastructure, to improve and to optimize traffic flow in the future and, thereby, to support holistic, efficient and sustainable mobility solutions. To set up virtual traffic environments ranging from artificial scenarios up to complex real world road networks, we use microscopic traffic models and traffic simulation software SUMO. In particular, we apply a reinforcement learning approach, in order to teach controllers (agents) to guide certain vehicles or to control infrastructural guidance systems, such as traffic lights. With real-time information obtained from other vehicles, the agent iteratively learns to improve the traffic flow by repetitive observation and algorithmic optimization. For the RL approach, we consider different control policies including widely used neural nets but also Linear Models and Radial Basis Function Networks. Finally, we compare our RL controller with other control approaches and analyse the robustness of the RL traffic light controller, especially under extreme scenarios.

Keywords: Reinforcement learning · Optimal traffic control · Microscopic traffic models · Autonomous vehicle control · Traffic light control

1 Introduction

Currently, the amount of traffic increases strongly nearly all over the world - this results in more accidents, traffic jams and emissions as well as a high demand for sustainable, efficient and safe mobility solutions.

At the same time, today's vehicle technology and mobility infrastructure allow to collect and to transmit large and comprehensive data, especially in the light of emerging and maturing communication technologies, such as 5G. This data may be used by complex driver assistance systems or (semi-) autonomous vehicles. Also, intelligent traffic control systems may use this data to enable communication and cooperation between road users and infrastructure.

To develop and implement such solutions, we need intelligent approaches to control traffic flows. These approaches should take into account established modelling as well as available data, with the goal to improve traffic control constantly.

A technique that may be able to combine all of these characteristics is *reinforcement learning (RL)*. In recent years, RL achieved impressive successes, especially in playing games [25] or in robotics [12,24]. Despite the usually huge computational training

© Springer Nature Switzerland AG 2022
C. Klein et al. (Eds.): SMARTGREENS 2021/ VEHITS 2021, CCIS 1612, pp. 313–329, 2022.
https://doi.org/10.1007/978-3-031-17098-0_16

effort, the goal of these controllers is not to simulate every single outcome or position but to determine iteratively which control is most likely leading to a good result. So the central idea of RL is to repeat a certain task several times and then to evaluate it to encourage or *reinforce* controls that lead to good or at least acceptable outputs. This can be applied to traffic control by simulating realistic traffic networks in which RL agents are learning to control a system iteratively.

In [2], we have presented a reinforcement learning approach for traffic control to either increase traffic flow by guiding certain vehicles intelligently or by steering traffic light systems. In this work, the main contribution is twofold. For the first application, we compare our RL approach with other control methods at the ring road experiment, cf. [26, 27]. Then, for the latter one, we analyse certain extreme scenarios, the RL traffic light controller may be confronted with.

Accordingly, the remaining part of the paper is organized as follows. First, in Sect. 2 we give a brief introduction to traffic modelling, especially microscopic car-following models, and a summary over different approaches to control traffic flows. As one approach to control traffic flows, in Sect. 3, we recapitulate the general concepts of model-free reinforcement learning and policy update algorithms. The goal, in these algorithms, is to iteratively find an optimal policy. In Sect. 3, we therefore compare different policy representations in RL with a control approach that has been applied in a real-world experiment of the ring road [26]. Then, in Sect. 5 the RL traffic light controller is tested in scenarios like rush hours and lack of data-availability. Finally, we close the contribution in Sect. 6 with a short summary and conclusion as well as a sketch of open problems and future work.

2   Optimal Control of Traffic Flows

Analysing traffic flows has been subject of research since the last century. This has led to a high variety of traffic models that are capable to represent different aspects of traffic flows [22, 30].

2.1   Traffic Modelling

The first well-known model class are the so-called macroscopic traffic models. They are based on ideas developed in the field of fluid dynamics, starting e.g. with the Lighthill-Whitham-Richards model [14]. While they are capable of explaining a lot of traffic phenomena like the evolution of congested regions on highways realistically, they tend to model traffic flows overly smooth and do not offer any insights on individual vehicle's driving behaviour.

Therefore, in the last couple of years, more microscopic models haven been presented that take every vehicle's specific actions, like acceleration and deceleration, into account and a common modelling approach in this class are car-following models. For a more detailed description of the connection between macroscopic and microscopic models, we refer to [6].

Car-Following Models. In car-following (or follow-the-leader) models, traffic is described by individual driver-vehicle units that form a traffic flow and each vehicle's driving behaviour is determined by observations of other vehicles surrounding them. In our case-studies, we focus on longitudinal dynamics of vehicles on single-lane scenarios. Then, the dynamics of each following vehicle can be described by a system of ordinary differential equations (ODEs)

$$\dot{s}_i(t) = v_i(t),$$
$$\dot{v}_i(t) = f(s_i(t), s_{i+1}(t), v_i(t), v_{i+1}(t)) \tag{1}$$

where $s_i(t), s_{i+1}(t), v_i(t), v_{i+1}(t)$ are the front-bumper positions and speeds at time t of the following car i and leading car $i+1$, respectively. Further, we define the headway between the two vehicles in terms of the bumper-to-bumper distance as follows

$$h_i = s_{i+1} - s_i - l_{i+1} \tag{2}$$

with l_{i+1} being the length of the leading vehicle. Then, the dynamical system is given by

$$\dot{h}_i(t) = v_{i+1}(t) - v_i(t),$$
$$\dot{v}_i(t) = f(h_i(t), v_i(t), v_{i+1}(t)). \tag{3}$$

The right hand side f, that determines the acceleration of the following vehicle, depends on the car-following model [11, 13]. One of them is the Intelligent Driver Model (IDM) [30] that we will use for modelling of human-driven vehicles. In the IDM, the equation for the acceleration of the following vehicle i is given by

$$f(h_i, v_i, v_{i+1}) = a_{\max}\left[1 - \left(\frac{v_i}{v_{\text{des}}}\right)^\delta - \left(\frac{h^*(v_i, \Delta v)}{h_i}\right)^2\right],$$
$$h^*(v_i, \Delta v) = h_{\min} + \max\left(0, v_i T + \frac{v_i \Delta v}{2\sqrt{a_{\max} b}}\right), \tag{4}$$

with $\Delta v = v_i - v_{i+1}$. The input parameters h_i, v_i and v_{i+1} are chosen to reflect human decision making in traffic flows as human drivers usually take into account the headway and both the own and the leader's speed to set their accelerations. Further, different aspects of driving behaviour can be represented by the set of parameters

$$\beta_{\text{IDM}} = [v_{\text{des}}, T, h_{\min}, \delta, a_{\max}, b]. \tag{5}$$

They can be fitted to real-world traffic data or set to model different driver types, e.g. a more or less aggressive driver. The parameter fitting as well as a detailed explanation of the parameters are given in [30].

2.2 Traffic Control

In the real-world, traffic flows are controlled by, e.g., speed limits or traffic light programs with several different goals including efficiency, safety, sustainability, and comfort. In a lot of situations, these limits or programs are determined heuristically as the outcome of time-consuming observations, experience or part of legal requirements.

But since the analysis and modelling of traffic flows have been studied, optimal solutions to control traffic flows have been presented as well, e.g. by setting speed limits and ramp metering [16] or switching through phases of traffic lights [7,18]. For most of these solution approaches, traffic dynamics are defined beforehand, e.g. with one of the models presented in Sect. 2.1, and then a certain traffic situation is optimized. But as traffic dynamics can be very complex and driving behaviour is highly variable and heterogeneous, it is hard to guarantee that such optimal solutions work in real-world situations.

In the last years, an increasing amount of traffic data is being collected by not only vehicles but also infrastructure systems. In view of faster communication technologies (e.g. 5G-communication), these data can be transmitted almost in real-time between vehicles and also between vehicles and infrastructure. Therefore, the use of such data and communication may be crucial to apply optimal traffic solutions to real-world traffic systems. We can use the data to estimate traffic model parameters more precisely to single vehicles that we observe [4] or, from a more macroscopic point of view, take into account phenomena like morning and evening rush hours. Accordingly, more data-driven techniques, like RL, have been applied to control, e.g. ramp metering [3] or traffic light systems [1,31,33].

Further, with the emerge of (semi-) autonomous vehicles, new ways to control traffic flows arise. If we assume that we can control these vehicles directly (e.g. setting their acceleration behaviour) we can affect the driving behaviour of other drivers more easily and increase traffic flow more directly, e.g. with cruise control systems [21].

One specific traffic situation in which the impact of controlling certain vehicles has been studied in recent years, is based on the ring road experiment presented in [27]. In a closed traffic situation, it has been shown that human-driving behaviour can be inefficient and traffic flow may be increased by an intelligently controlled vehicle, either in real-world experiments [26] or in simulation with a RL controller [34]. The controllability and stability of such a control approach have been studied as well [32,35].

In our work, we therefore focus on either controlling traffic flows by intelligently controlled vehicles (we will call them autonomous vehicles (AVs)) or by traffic guidance systems, such as traffic lights. That means, in general, there is a traffic situation in which we can either observe single vehicles or entire lanes by obtaining real-time data. The dynamical system is then represented by discrete-time states x_t. Further, there is a controller, the AV or a traffic light system, that applies controls u_t that directly change or affect the dynamical system. The controller's goal is to find such controls that optimize the traffic flow for all vehicles in the system.

3   Model-Free Reinforcement Learning

In this section, we introduce reinforcement learning (RL) as intelligent and data-driven approach to control and to optimize traffic flow. We recapitulate the general concepts of model-free RL as presented in [2]. RL is based on the idea that an agent (controller) interacts with its environment (dynamical system) and aims at controlling the system optimally. In the general model-free RL framework the dynamics of the system are unknown. The agent, however, is allowed to apply different actions (controls) in different states of the dynamical system such that controls leading to desirable outputs are encouraged or *reinforced* and disadvantageous outputs are discouraged [28].

The mathematical framework for this agent-environment interaction is given by a Markov Decision Process (MDP) [9,23,28]. Such a MDP is given by a tuple $(\mathcal{X}, \mathcal{U}, P, r, \rho_0, \gamma, t_f)$ with state space $\mathcal{X}$, action (or control) space $\mathcal{U}$, transition probability function $P\colon \mathcal{X} \times \mathcal{U} \times \mathcal{X} \to [0,1]$, reward function $r\colon \mathcal{X} \times \mathcal{U} \to \mathbb{R}$, initial state distribution $\rho_0\colon \mathcal{X} \to [0,1]$, discount factor $\gamma \in (0,1]$ and time horizon $t_f \in \mathbb{R}_{>0}$ [8].

At the beginning of each MDP episode, that consists of discrete time steps, the initial state of the environment is drawn from a initial distribution $x_0 \sim \rho_0$. Then, at each time step, the agent determines an action u_t and the environment is described by a new set of states following the transition probability function $P(x_{t+1}|x_t, u_t)$. The reward function r evaluates the combination of state x_t and action u_t such that the agent's goal is to take actions that lead to high rewards. At the end of each episode (often called *rollout*) the trajectory data is summarized by $\tau = (x_0, u_0, x_1, u_1, \ldots, x_{t_f})$. As in [2], the interaction between agent and environment is visualized in Fig. 1.

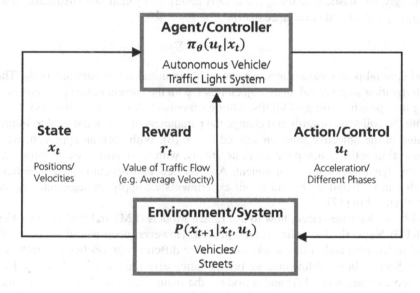

Fig. 1. MDP interaction between agent and environment for traffic control scenarios [2].

3.1 Policy Optimization

In RL, we generally assume that the dynamics of the environment, which are described by the transition probability function $P(x_{t+1}|x_t, u_t)$, are unknown. At the same time, we wish to find optimal actions for each state and a solution approach are so-called policy update methods, cf. [28]. Here, the agent typically determines its actions by a deterministic policy $u_t = \mu_\theta(u_t, x_t)$ or by sampling from a stochastic policy

$u_t \sim \pi_\theta(u_t|x_t)$. The policy depends on a set of parameters θ and the goal is to find such parameters that optimize the following maximization problem

$$\max_\theta \mathbb{E}\left[\sum_{t=0}^{t_f-1} \gamma^t r(x_t, u_t)\right].$$ (6)

That is, we derive parameters such that the expected value of the discounted sum of rewards is maximized for a given time period.

Policies. In general, the policy represents a feedback law from the state space $\mathcal{X}$ to the action space $\mathcal{U}$, which we both assume to be real-valued ($\mathcal{X} = \mathbb{R}^n$ and $\mathcal{U} = \mathbb{R}^p$). First, we define a function $f_\theta: \mathcal{X} \to \mathcal{U}$, that depends on parameters θ. With this function f_θ, the deterministic policy is given by

$$\mu_\theta = f_\theta(x).$$ (7)

Accordingly, stochastic policies π_θ are usually described by Gaussian distributions with mean $f_\theta(x)$ and a fixed covariance matrix $\Sigma \in \mathbb{R}^p \times \mathbb{R}^p$,

$$\pi_\theta \sim \mathcal{N}(f_\theta(x), \Sigma).$$ (8)

To find optimal policy parameters, we start with an initial set of parameters θ_0. Then, at each iteration step, we calculate trajectories τ with the current policy parameters following the episodic setting of MDPs. After each episode (or several episodes), we can evaluate the collected rewards and change the parameters of θ with the goal to improve the value of the objective function defined in Eq. (6). With such an approach, we are able to optimize the policy parameters iteratively, without requiring exact information about the dynamics of the environment. An overview and benchmarking of different methods can be found in [8] and in our experiments we apply an augmented random search as stated in [17].

In [2], we have described, how to use Linear Models (LM) and Radial Basis Function (RBF) Networks for policy representation. However, deep neural nets are often applied in RL [10] and in this work, we compare different approaches for traffic control, see Sect. 4. In the following, we briefly summarize the use of RBF networks for policy representation (cf. [2]) and introduce the main concepts of neural nets, based on [5].

RBF Networks. RBF networks are well known for function approximation and have been used in machine learning [5, 19]. They can be described by a set of parameters consisting of centres $c_i \in \mathbb{R}^n$ and radii $r_i \in \mathbb{R}$ ($i = 1, \ldots, m$), bias vector $b \in \mathbb{R}^p$ and weighting matrix $W \in \mathbb{R}^{p \times m}$. The hyperparameter m determines the number of centres and the Gaussian radius function is defined as

$$h_i(x) = \exp\left(-\frac{\|x - c_i\|_2^2}{2r_i^2}\right).$$ (9)

Then, to obtain a RBF network, these Gaussian radius functions are combined to a weighted sum

$$f_\theta(x) = Wh(x) + b \tag{10}$$

with $h(x) = [h_1(x), \ldots, h_m(x)]^T$.

To include prior knowledge and to reduce the number of optimization parameters, we use an approach to fix the centres and radii such that the parameter vector θ only consists of W and b. We therefore generate a dataset $\{x_1, \ldots, x_N\}$ of observed states that includes different parts of the state space. Then, we apply a k-means clustering algorithm [5] to determine the m centres c_i and set the radii r_i to fixed values.

Neural Nets. A feed-forward neural net can be described by a composition of K layers, $k = 1, \ldots K$. Each layer k consists of M_k neurons and each neuron l obtains an input z_m^k from the neuron m of the previous layer k and feed-forwards an output z_l^{k+1}. The first layer's input is the current state $z_i^1 = x_i$, $i = 1, .., n$, and the last layer's output is the control output for the policy $f_\theta = z^{K+1}$.

Moreover, to each neuron l of layer k, there are assigned weights $w_{l,m}^k \in \mathbb{R}$, $m = 1, \ldots, M_{k-1}$, and biases $b_l^k \in \mathbb{R}$. Additionally, an activation function $\sigma^k : \mathbb{R} \to \mathbb{R}$ for each layer is defined and the output of each neuron l, $l = 1, \ldots, M_k$, is given by

$$z_l^{k+1} = \sigma^k \Big(\sum_{m=1}^{M_{k-1}} w_{l,m}^k z_m^k + b_l^k \Big). \tag{11}$$

To take into account the entire layer, consisting of the M_k neurons, often the following notation is used

$$z^{k+1} = \sigma^k (W^k z^k + b^k) \tag{12}$$

such that all the weights are stored in matrix $W^k \in \mathbb{R}^{M_k} \times \mathbb{R}^{M_{k-1}}$ and all the biases in vector $b^k \in \mathbb{R}^{M_k}$. Also, the activation function is applied component-wise on each entry of the computed vector $W^k z^k + b^k$.

While the number of layers K, the number of neurons for each layer M_k and the activation functions σ^k are hyperparameters that are defined preliminary, the weights and biases have to be optimized. That means, in RL applications, the policy parameters θ consist of the weight matrices and bias vectors $W^1, b^1, \ldots, W^K, b^K$ of the neural net. We visualize both policy representations in Fig. 2.

4   Ring Road Control

The experiment of Sugiyama et al. [27] has shown that human driving behaviour alone can lead to undesirable outcomes like stop-and-go waves and congestions. Since then, it has been studied, how connected autonomous vehicles (AVs) can be used to improve traffic flow in the ring road scenario (Fig. 3). In this work, we compare a RL controller with RBF network policy [2] with an RL approach based on deep learning, e.g. in [34], and an approach that has been studied in a real-world experiment [26].

As the experiment is based on a single-lane scenario, we can represent the dynamics of all vehicles in terms of their speeds and headways. We set-up the ring road with

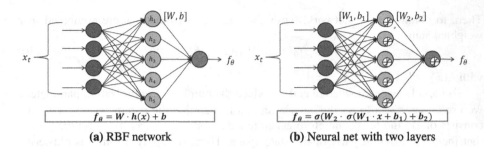

(a) RBF network   (b) Neural net with two layers

Fig. 2. Exemplary visualization of a RBF network and a two-layer neural net with state space dimension $n = 4$ and action space dimension $p = 1$.

radius 50 m and $N = 22$ vehicles in which the human drivers (HDs) are described with the IDM car-following model (cf. Eq. 3 and Eq. 4). In RL, we consider time-discrete systems, so we update the dynamics of each HD following a mixed first-order-second-order scheme [30]:

$$
h_i(t + \Delta t) = \frac{v_{i+1}(t + \Delta t) - v_i(t + \Delta t)}{2} \Delta t,
$$
$$
v_i(t + \Delta t) = v_i(t) + f(h_i(t), v_i(t), v_{i+1}(t)) \Delta t,
$$
(13)

for vehicles $i = 1, \ldots, 21$. In contrast, the acceleration behaviour of the AV ($i = 22$) is described by its control inputs u_t:

$$
h_{22}(t + \Delta t) = \frac{v_1(t + \Delta t) - v_{22}(t + \Delta t)}{2} \Delta t,
$$
$$
v_{22}(t + \Delta t) = v_{22}(t) + u_t \Delta t.
$$
(14)

At each time step t, the RL agent observes a state input $x_t = [h_{22}(t), v_{22}(t), v_1(t)]$ consisting of its own headway and speed, as well as the speed of the leading vehicle. Then, the agent computes the controls u_t with a parametrized policy π_θ and the current state x_t. The parameters θ are optimized with a RL algorithm as described in Sect. 3 and the reward function used here is given by the average speed over all vehicles,

$$
r(x, u) = \frac{1}{N} \sum_{i=1}^{N} v_i.
$$
(15)

4.1 Experimental Set-Up

As in the real-word experiment of [27], we let all vehicles start with equal headways. To observe the emerging stop-and-go wave, we slightly vary each HD's driving behaviour.

This is achieved by first introducing a nominal IDM parameter set $\beta_{\text{IDM}} = [16, 1, 2, 4, 1, 1.5]$ as described in Eq. 5. Then, at the beginning of each episode, we draw samples from a Gaussian distribution with mean β_{IDM} and standard deviation $\sigma = 0.1$. Thus, for one rollout and each vehicle i, we realize each driver's current characteristics in terms of the corresponding IDM parameter set β_{IDM}^i as

$$
\beta_{\text{IDM}}^i \sim \mathcal{N}(\beta_{\text{IDM}}, \sigma).
$$
(16)

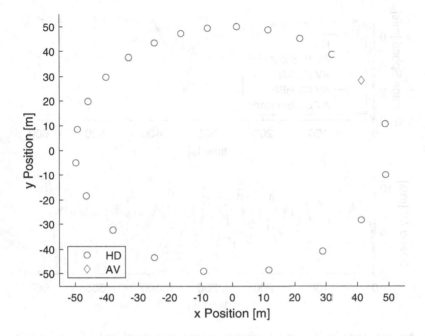

Fig. 3. Visualization of the ring road in *Matlab*.

The deviation of the parameters reflects the heterogeneity of human drivers which, in this experiment, leads to inefficient driving behaviour.

For each simulation, we let the stop-and-go wave evolve for the first 300 s and then one of the following controllers is switched on:

- **HD Control:** First, the AV keeps its human driving behaviour simulated by the car-following model.
- **PI with Saturation Controller:** This control approach has been applied in a real-world experiment of the ring road and we choose the same set of parameters as presented in [26].
- **RL with NN Policy:** In [34] a RL approach with deep learning has been presented. To recreate this controller, we trained an agent with the *Matlab Reinforcement Learning Toolbox* [29]. Here, the policy is presented by a Neural Net with two hidden layers, 32 neurons for each layer and the *tanh* activation function.
- **RL with RBF Policy:** Instead of a neural net, we use a RBF network policy with fixed centres. Here, we generated a dataset of 20 trajectories showing different situations ranging from fluent to congested traffic situations. Then, we determined 50 centres with a k-means clustering approach and fixed the radii such that only the weights and biases of the RBF network had to be optimized.

4.2 Results

For the training of both RL agents mentioned above, the IDM parameters have been chosen randomly before each rollout to simulate different driving styles and, accord-

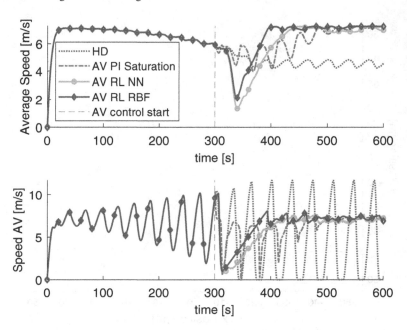

Fig. 4. Average speed [m/s] over all vehicles and the AV's speed [m/s] for different control approaches and time horizon $t_f = 600$ s. The stop-and-go wave evolves and then at $t = 300$ s the different controllers are switched on.

ingly, different traffic situations. Then, after the training of the RL controllers, we apply all controllers to the same randomly chosen (and then fixed) parameters such that all of them are confronted with the same stop-and-go situation at the AV control start.

In Fig. 4, the results are shown in terms of the average speed over all vehicles and the speed of the controlled AV. For the first 300 s, the stop-and-go wave evolves for all scenarios leading to higher variation of speed for each vehicle and a decrease of the average speed. Without AV control, the impact of the stop-and-go wave increases until a certain level and does not vanish over time.

In contrast, for each of the AV controllers, the average speed is increased at the end and all vehicles travel more fluently, indicated by the AV's lower deviation of speed. While it is already remarkable that the traffic flow of 22 vehicles is increased by a single intelligently controlled vehicle, the AV controllers differ in their characteristics and performance. Both RL controllers decelerate strongly at the beginning and then slowly increase their speed to lead the traffic flow back to a stable situation. In contrast, for the PI with saturation controller, it takes some speed oscillations, i.e., phases of acceleration and deceleration, until a stable solution is reached.

We point out that, in this scenario, our RL control approach with RBF policy performs at least as good as the other presented approaches, partially even superior to them. The clustering of the centres, however, increases the performance and drastically decreases the computing time, in particular, in comparison to the approach with deep neural nets, cf. Table 1. This is reasonable, since prior knowledge is included and the number of optimization parameters is reduced.

Table 1. Comparison of different controllers at the ring road scenario. The average speed and standard deviation (SD) are taken over all vehicles and time steps after the AV control start at t =300 s. For the average required computing time in the training of the RL agents, we compare, for each optimization, the time until a certain value of the objective function (cf. Eq. 6) is reached.

Controller	Average speed [m/s]	SD speed [m/s]	Average computing time training [s]
HD	4.71	4.16	
PI saturation	6.17	2.21	
RL NN	5.93	2.07	1198
RL RBF	6.38	1.83	114

5   Traffic Light Control

Optimal control of traffic light systems can have a huge impact on certain traffic situations because the static behaviour of currently used traffic light programs, that are switching through different phases with fixed durations, leaves a big potential for improvement. Especially, if we consider the availability of real-time data, either obtained by vehicles sending data or infrastructure systems observing them. Accordingly, data-driven approaches, like RL, have been applied to find optimal solution for traffic light control [1,31,33].

Most of these RL approaches consider single junctions or road networks of grids that are not always representative for typically very complex real-world situations. We have shown in [2] that a RL agent can outperform a static traffic light program at a real-world traffic situation when it obtains data in real-time.

In this work, we study the robustness of such an approach, especially under extreme traffic situations. First, we analyse the controller's performance in rush hour scenarios in which traffic flows from and towards lanes may differ a lot from usual situations that are observed during training. Then, we study the impact of data-availability. This is highly relevant, since, in the near future, typical traffic will be heterogeneous: some vehicles may be able and willing to provide information, others may not.

5.1   Experimental Set-Up

We briefly summarize the design of the RL controller presented in [2]. First, we set-up the traffic situation in SUMO [15] by importing a digital map based on OpenStreetMap data [20] of the Opel-roundabout. We define realistic frequencies f_{ij} of vehicles entering the system on lane i and leaving it on lane j based on realistic considerations and observations. With these frequencies, the inflow of vehicles from each lane is realized by stochastic processes, to obtain appropriate and varying traffic flows in each simulation.

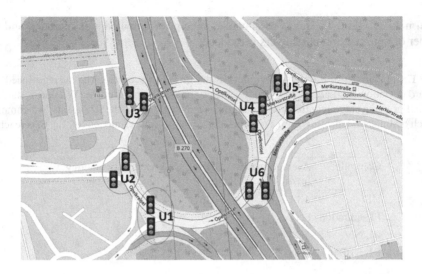

Fig. 5. Opel-roundabout in Kaiserslautern, Germany [2,20].

The RL agent observes aggregated values over all vehicles for each incoming lane. In particular, the traffic density, the minimum distance of the closest vehicle to the next traffic light unit, the number of waiting vehicles in front of the traffic light, the time since the last change has occurred, and a binary variable indicating whether the upcoming traffic light is green or not, is observed. The RL agent controls each of the six traffic light units simultaneously by deciding at every time step whether to stay at the current phase or to switch to the next phase.

By observing the environment and interacting with it during training, the RL agent aims to find an optimal control policy (cf. Sect. 3) with the goal to increase the traffic flow for all vehicles in the system. Then, we compare the RL agent to a realistic traffic light program based on a fixed cycle time of 90 s. We have shown that a RL control approach can increase traffic flow, not only in scenarios that have been observed during training, but also if we evenly scale up and down the number of vehicles entering the traffic situation, cf. [2].

5.2 Rush Hour Scenario

Since the traffic dynamics may not only change evenly, in this section, we analyse certain rush hour scenarios as well. The lane in front of unit $U2$ in Fig. 5 leads to a factory. Thus, the number of vehicles coming from that lane and leaving the system on it can vary a lot depending on the day time.

To make the scenarios comparable and to have a similar number of vehicles in the system, we fix the sum over all frequencies of incoming vehicles

$$Z = \sum_{i=1}^{6} \sum_{j=1}^{6} f_{ij}. \tag{17}$$

Then, we introduce a scalar value r_1 indicating the increase of vehicles leaving the system at lane $j = 4$. To keep the sum over all frequencies fixed, a second scalar value r_2 is computed as follows

$$r_2 = \frac{Z - r_1 \sum_{i=1}^{6} f_{i4}}{\sum_{i=1}^{6} \sum_{j=1, j \neq 4}^{6} f_{ij}}. \tag{18}$$

Finally, we compute new frequencies $r_1 \cdot f_{ij}$ for $j = 4$ and $r_2 \cdot f_{ij}$ for $j \neq 4$. For each of the scaling steps $r_1 \in \{1, 1.1, 1.2, \ldots, 2.9, 3\}$, we simulate 20 scenarios of the RL controller and the 90 s-program. In Fig. 6, we compare the average speed over all of these scenarios. The increased number of vehicles entering from one lane makes it for both controllers harder to optimally guide all vehicles through the traffic situation. However, it is remarkable that the RL controller outperforms the 90 s-program, because the scenarios for high scaling steps differ a lot from the ones that have been observed during training.

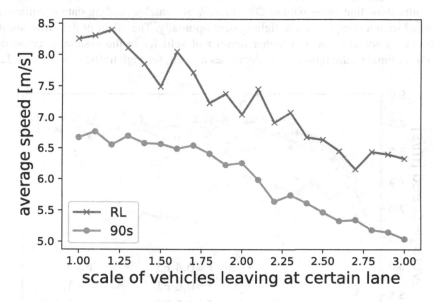

Fig. 6. Rush hour scenario for the Opel-roundabout. The number of vehicles leaving at a certain lane is scaled up while the total number of vehicles in the system is kept fixed. For both controllers, RL and 90 s, and each scaling step, 20 simulation are computed and we compare the average speed [m/s] over all vehicles and simulations at each scaling step.

5.3 Data-Availability

A crucial point in the application of data-driven traffic control approaches is the availability of data. In all our experiments so far, we assumed that traffic data is available in real-time and from all vehicles. However, as already said earlier, it needs to be expected that in the near future, we will be faced with a very heterogeneous situation: only a certain amount of vehicles will be able and willing to communicate and to send information. Consequently, we analyse here the impact of such a heterogeneity and the data-availability, respectively, on the performance of the RL controller.

We define a value p such that for each vehicle that enters the system, a uniformly distributed random variable $z \sim \mathcal{U}([0, 1])$ is drawn. If $z < p$, the RL controller obtains information from the vehicle and if not, the vehicle does not send any data. Again, we scale up $p \in \{0.05, 0.1, 0.15, \ldots, 0.95, 1\}$ and compute 20 different simulations for each scaling step. We repeat this for different frequencies of incoming vehicles and the average speed over 20 simulations for each frequency and scaling step is shown in Fig. 7.

For all frequencies, the controller's performance at $p = 0.2$ is already almost as good as for scenarios with full data-availability and does not increase significantly for higher values than $p = 0.4$. This is plausible, since the controller does not take into account the driving behaviour of individual vehicles but only observes aggregated values (cf. Sect. 5.1). Thus, the controller does not need exact information about these values and our results show that an amount of 20% to 40% of vehicles sending data is sufficient, to control such a complex traffic light system optimally. The effect of data-availability decreases for scenarios with a higher number of vehicles in the system, because the effect of optimal traffic light control decreases as well, for high traffic densities, cf. [2].

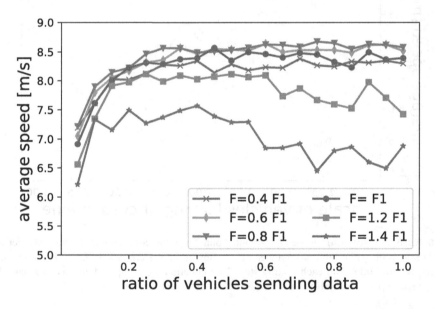

Fig. 7. Impact of data-availability at the Opel-roundabout in terms of the average speed [m/s] over all vehicles in the system and 20 simulations at each scaling step. We increase the ratio of vehicles sending data from 0.05 to 1 and compare different frequencies that determine the number of vehicles in the system.

6   Summary and Conclusion

After an introduction to traffic modelling and control, we have presented model-free RL as an approach to optimally control traffic flows. We have shown that an autonomous vehicle, controlled by a RL agent, can improve traffic flow for all vehicles in the system at the artificial ring road scenario. Our RL agent uses a RBF network policy with fixed centres in comparison to widely used policies based on deep neural nets. We stress that the RBF policy can outperform neural nets, while prior knowledge can be included with a clustering approach and the number of optimization parameters can be reduced.

In addition, we have analysed the robustness of the RL traffic light controller. For rush hour situations, that may differ a lot from the training scenarios, the RL agent is still superior to a static traffic light program. Another remarkable result is that the RL agent only needs between 20% to 40% of vehicles sending data to optimally control the traffic light system. That means, the application of data-driven techniques, like this proposed RL controller, is a quite robust approach concerning the information needed from other actors and, even in mixed traffic scenarios, in which certain amounts of vehicles are not providing any data, its application is promising.

Indeed, real-time data sent from the vehicles, as we have assumed it in our approach, is usually not at all available these days. However, current developments in the vehicle and network technology are promising to enable such real-time communication, which make the experiments of this work realizable in real-world traffic situations.

It is remarkable that the RL agents can outperform other control approaches, without prior knowledge about the environment but with observations they have made during several simulations. However, it is important to point out that a stable and safe transfer and application of RL controllers to real world scenarios is still an open task that has not been fully solved yet. Especially, in safety-relevant situation that involve humans, the typical training, that requires the possibility to run the controller with poor performance up to error and failure, is almost impossible.

In our experiments, we train the controller in a virtual environment. Transferring the controller based on virtual training scenarios would therefore require a good match between reality and virtual environment. Moreover, the controller's performance in different situations can vary a lot, depending on the scenarios that have been observed during training. While the RL traffic light agent showed to be robust under extreme scenarios, guaranteed accuracy and stability of RL are, at least partially, an open task as well.

In future work, we plan to further evaluate RL in traffic control. We aim to compare our RL approach with different control approaches ranging from more physics-based optimal control approaches to other data-driven and AI-based techniques. By studying different approaches, we target to improve both, the performance and interpretability, of traffic control agents.

References

1. Arel, I., Liu, C., Urbanik, T., Kohls, A.: Reinforcement learning-based multi-agent system for network traffic signal control. IET Intel. Transp. Syst. **4**, 128–135 (2010). https://doi.org/10.1049/iet-its.2009.0070

2. Baumgart, U., Burger, M.: A reinforcement learning approach for traffic control. In: Proceedings of the 7th International Conference on Vehicle Technology and Intelligent Transport Systems - VEHITS, pp. 133–141. INSTICC, SciTePress (2021). https://doi.org/10.5220/0010448501330141

3. Belletti, F., Haziza, D., Gomes, G., Bayen, A.: Expert level control of ramp metering based on multi-task deep reinforcement learning. IEEE Trans. Intell. Transp. Syst. **19**(4), 1198–1207 (2017). https://doi.org/10.1109/TITS.2017.2725912

4. Bhattacharyya, R.P., Senanayake, R., Brown, K., Kochenderfer, M.J.: Online parameter estimation for human driver behavior prediction. In: 2020 American Control Conference (ACC), pp. 301–306 (2020). https://doi.org/10.23919/ACC45564.2020.9147924

5. Bishop, C.M.: Pattern Recognition and Machine Learning. Springer-Verlag, New York (2006). https://doi.org/10.1108/03684920710743466

6. Burger, M., Goettlich, S., Jung, T.: Derivation of second order traffic flow models with time delays. Netw. Heterogen. Media **14**, 265–288 (2019). https://doi.org/10.3934/nhm.2019011

7. De Schutter, B., De Moor, B.: Optimal traffic light control for a single intersection. Eur. J. Control. **4**(3), 260–276 (1998). https://doi.org/10.1016/S0947-3580(98)70119-0

8. Duan, Y., Chen, X., Houthooft, R., Schulman, J., Abbeel, P.: Benchmarking deep reinforcement learning for continuous control. In: Proceedings of The 33rd International Conference on Machine Learning. Proceedings of Machine Learning Research, vol. 48, pp. 1329–1338 (2016). https://doi.org/10.5555/3045390.3045531

9. Feinberg, E., Shwartz, A.: Handbook of Markov Decision Processes: Methods and Applications. Springer, US (2002). https://doi.org/10.1007/978-1-4615-0805-2

10. François-Lavet, V., Henderson, P., Islam, R., Bellemare, M.G., Pineau, J.: An introduction to deep reinforcement learning. Found. Trends® Mach. Learn. **11**(3–4), 219–354 (2018). https://doi.org/10.1561/2200000071

11. Helbing, D.: Verkehrsdynamik. Springer-Verlag Berlin Heidelberg (1997). https://doi.org/10.1007/978-3-319-78695-7

12. Kalashnikov, D., et al.: QT-Opt: scalable deep reinforcement learning for vision-based robotic manipulation. In: Proceedings of The 2nd Conference on Robot Learning. Proceedings of Machine Learning Research, vol. 87, pp. 651–673 (2018)

13. Kessels, F.: Traffic Flow Modelling. Springer International Publishing (2019). https://doi.org/10.1007/978-3-642-59063-4

14. Lighthill, M.J., Whitham, G.B.: On kinematic waves II. A theory of traffic flow on long crowded roads. Proc. R. Soc. Lond. A. **229**, 317–345 (1955). https://doi.org/10.1098/rspa.1955.0089

15. Lopez, P.A., et al.: Microscopic traffic simulation using SUMO. In: The 21st IEEE International Conference on Intelligent Transportation Systems (2018). https://doi.org/10.1109/ITSC.2018.8569938

16. Lu, X.Y., Varaiya, P., Horowitz, R., Su, D., Shladover, S.E.: Novel freeway traffic control with variable speed limit and coordinated ramp metering. Transp. Res. Rec. J. Transp. Res. Board **2229**(1), 55–65 (2011). https://doi.org/10.3141/2229-07

17. Mania, H., Guy, A., Recht, B.: Simple random search provides a competitive approach to reinforcement learning. arXiv: 1803.07055 (2018)

18. McNeil, D.R.: A solution to the fixed-cycle traffic light problem for compound poisson arrivals. J. Appl. Probab. **5**(3), 624–635 (1968). https://doi.org/10.2307/3211926

19. Murphy, K.P.: Machine Learning: A Probabilistic Perspective. The MIT Press (2012)

20. OpenStreetMap (2021). https://www.openstreetmap.org. Accessed 22 Oct 2021

21. Orosz, G.: Connected cruise control: modelling, delay effects, and nonlinear behaviour. Veh. Syst. Dyn. **54**(8), 1147–1176 (2016). https://doi.org/10.1080/00423114.2016.1193209

22. Orosz, G., Wilson, R.E., Stépán, G.: Traffic jams: dynamics and control. Philos. Trans. R. Soc. A Math. Phys. Eng. Sci. **368**(1928), 4455–4479 (2010). https://doi.org/10.1098/rsta. 2010.0205
23. Puterman, M.L.: Markov Decision Processes: Discrete Stochastic Dynamic Programming. Wiley, 1st (edn) (1994). https://doi.org/10.1002/9780470316887
24. Rajeswaran, A., et al.: Learning complex dexterous manipulation with deep reinforcement learning and demonstrations. In: Proceedings of Robotics: Science and Systems (RSS) (2018). https://doi.org/10.15607/RSS.2018.XIV.049
25. Silver, D., et al.: A general reinforcement learning algorithm that masters chess, shogi, and go through self-play. Science **362**(6419), 1140–1144 (2018). https://doi.org/10.1126/science. aar6404
26. Stern, R.E., et al.: Dissipation of stop-and-go waves via control of autonomous vehicles: field experiments. Transp. Res. Part C Emerg. Technol. **89**, 205–221 (2018). https://doi.org/ 10.1016/j.trc.2018.02.005
27. Sugiyama, Y., et al.: Traffic jams without bottlenecks—experimental evidence for the physical mechanism of the formation of a jam. New J. Phys. **10**(3), 033001 (2008). https://doi. org/10.1088/1367-2630/10/3/033001
28. Sutton, R.S., Barto, A.G.: Reinforcement Learning: An Introduction, 2nd edn. Adaptive Computation and Machine Learning, MIT Press (2018)
29. The MathWorks Inc: Reinforcement Learning Toolbox. Matlab R2020b. Natick, Massachusetts, United State (2021). https://www.mathworks.com/help/reinforcement-learning/
30. Treiber, M., Kesting, A.: Traffic Flow Dynamics. Springer-Verlag, Berlin Heidelberg (2013). https://doi.org/10.1007/978-3-642-32460-4
31. Vinitsky, E., et al.: Benchmarks for reinforcement learning in mixed-autonomy traffic. In: Proceedings of The 2nd Conference on Robot Learning. Proceedings of Machine Learning Research, vol. 87, pp. 399–409 (2018)
32. Wang, J., Zheng, Y., Xu, Q., Wang, J., Li, K.: Controllability analysis and optimal control of mixed traffic flow with human-driven and autonomous vehicles. IEEE Trans. Intell. Transp. Syst. **22**(12), 1–15 (2020). https://doi.org/10.1109/TITS.2020.3002965
33. Wiering, M.: Multi-agent reinforcement leraning for traffic light control. In: Proceedings of the Seventeenth International Conference on Machine Learning, pp. 1151–1158. ICML 2000 (2000)
34. Wu, C., Kreidieh, A., Parvate, K., Vinitsky, E., Bayen, A.M.: Flow: Architecture and Benchmarking for Reinforcement Learning in Traffic Control. arXiv: 1710.05465 (2017)
35. Zheng, Y., Wang, J., Li, K.: Smoothing traffic flow via control of autonomous vehicles. IEEE Internet Things J. **7**(5), 3882–3896 (2020). https://doi.org/10.1109/JIOT.2020.2966506

Detecting Extended Incidents in Urban Road Networks for Organic Traffic Control Using Density-Based Clustering of Traffic Flows

Ingo Thomsen[✉][iD] and Sven Tomforde[iD]

Intelligent Systems, Christian-Albrechts-Universität zu Kiel, 24118 Kiel, Germany
{int, st}@informatik.uni-kiel.de
http://www.ins.informatik.uni-kiel.de/en

Abstract. The control of urban traffic signals typically works on the basis of predefined plans or as a centralised planning system. At least in research work, a locally organised, self-adaptive approach has been established as a more robust, scalable and efficient alternative. In all three cases, the best case scenario is that the system reacts to observed current situations - but no incidents such as accidents, construction work or road blockages of varying duration and extents are detected and considered as a basis for control decisions. In this article, we present an approach for cluster-based detection of such disturbances without the need to extend the existing infrastructure. Based on our previous approach, additional urban road networks are evaluated, all comprised of intersections equipped with programmable traffic signals. An additional incident type, where not all lanes of a road are blocked, is assessed. The underlying traffic flow data is generated in simulations of varying traffic volumes.

Keywords: Organic traffic control · Traffic flow analysis · Traffic incident detection · Traffic management

1 Introduction

Growing traffic demands and rising mobility cause higher vehicle densities and increased associated travel times, particularly in urban areas with limited space for the necessary infrastructure. The resulting traffic conditions are characterised by strong dynamics as the overall number of vehicles entering the network change during the course of the day as well as the week, and in response to larger events, such as football matches. Especially these hardly foreseeable events call for automated and adaptive control concepts for the traffic light signalisation strategies.

One such approach is the Organic Traffic Control (OTC) system [16], which works in a self-organised, decentralised manner: Within a road network intersections equipped with traffic lights each are controlled by OTC instances which alter the signalisation based on local observations and locally learned decision rules. The effects of these decisions are observed, leading to adapted and improved rule sets and, subsequently, to a resilient traffic management. However, such an approach reacts to the current conditions and is not proactive in circumventing the negative impact of disturbances such as incidents.

© Springer Nature Switzerland AG 2022
C. Klein et al. (Eds.): SMARTGREENS 2021/ VEHITS 2021, CCIS 1612, pp. 330–347, 2022.
https://doi.org/10.1007/978-3-031-17098-0_17

Traffic incidents such as slow moving vehicles, roadblocks due to accidents, defect traffic lights, construction work or unloading of lorries affect the flow of traffic, which in turn leads to a suboptimal signalling strategy of the individual intersection controllers. For this reason, the ability to detect such incidents can enhance the adaptive capabilities of the OTC system, as it can either proactively change its signalisation strategy or even guide the traffic participants to avoid disturbed regions using, e.g., variable message signs. To identify incidents automatically in urban areas, we developed a clustering-based approach for traffic patterns in previous work [20] which uses the well-known DBSCAN (Density-Based Spatial Clustering of Applications with Noise) technique [6] applied to traffic flows based induction loop data.

This article extends the previous work in three directions: How does this approach perform when confronted with flow data from a network consisting of roads with more lanes? How does the detection change in such a network when, as a new incident type, closed lanes instead of full road closures occur? And are there misleading results due to boundary effects generated by the simulation?

The remaining article is organised as follows: The next section Sect. 2 presents current work on traffic light control and traffic incident detection, followed by Sect. 3 with a description of preliminary work in this context and the results of the evaluation of our previous detection approach. Section 4 then expands on core techniques of this approach, while Sect. 5 explains how these are applied in the context of the extended experiments. This includes the results as well, which are discussed in the final Sect. 6, paired with a summary and an outlook on possible future work.

2 Background

2.1 Adaptive Traffic Light Control

Traffic lights in urban areas are usually operated by a traffic control centre. The most prominent systems are SCOOT [14], SCATS [15], MOVA [22], and UTOPIA/-SPOT [9]. These systems typically rely on a centralised control loop that adapts the behaviour of distributed intersection controllers, based on a given cost function. This cost function may include different aspects: Travel times, emissions, or public transport priority, for instance. Despite being centralised, these systems come with at least some self-adaptive and self-organising (SASO) capabilities, i.e., being adaptive and policy-driven. The adaptation mechanism works on-top of a parametrisable system configuration. For a classification and comparison of approaches, see [17]. In addition to these popular approaches, several systems focusing on SASO and learning capabilities have been proposed: A multi-agent approach based on fuzzy control was presented in [7], distributed W-learning was used to optimise a phase-oriented signal control in [5], and [11] used a model with predictive control. As an alternative to phase-based systems, a fluid-dynamic model has been discussed in [8] that uses waiting vehicles as pressure and counter-pressure for switching policies of traffic lights. In contrast to the scope of this proposal, these traffic control systems do not autonomously identify and classify incidents in the traffic networks and adapt their signalisation according to detected incidents subsequently.

2.2 Detection of Traffic Incidents

The continuous assessment of the current road situation as part of intelligent traffic control was addressed as early as 1978 when the California Algorithm [13] was introduced. It uses various traffic states combined with a state-based decision tree to identify incidents on highways. In [12] an exhaustive list of approaches in the context of arterial roads and highways is given. Many approaches focus on accidents and use various data sources, such as video data from first-person videos (dash cams) in [23] or short-range communications between vehicles on motorways as in [18]. Various techniques from machine learning are applied to make use of this kind of radio data. For instance, [4] uses Random Forest classifier for accident detection. But most concepts focus on simpler road network models, such as highways. Our own approach [20], which this works builds upon, is aimed at urban road networks. See Sect. 3.2 for further details and results.

3 Preliminary Work

3.1 Organic Traffic Control

The incident detection approach based on clustering is embedded in the context of potentially improving the Organic Traffic Control (OTC). This traffic management system follows the observer/controller paradigm from Organic Computing (OC) [10]. It is a SASO system and exhibits self-optimising, self-configuring behaviour and self-healing. For instance, the decision-making takes place locally at each traffic light controlled intersection. In the case of a "failing intersection" others can compensate and adapt. As intersection controllers can communicate with direct neighbours, global goals can be achieved without a central control instance. OTC is organised in multiple layers as visualised in Fig. 1.

Layer 0. represents the System under Observation and Control (SuOC). This is the actual (simulated) traffic environment which is equipped with detectors and TLCs. The respective signal configuration can be changed by the layer above.

Layer 1. adapts dynamically to the state of the environment (assessed using the sensors) and its controller which uses a Learning Classifier System. This LCS chooses rules from a rule set to change the traffic signalisation appropriately at runtime.

Layer 2. is activated when layer 1 is confronted with an environment for which it has no suitable rule for. In this case, a traffic simulation software is used to validate new rules which are generated using an evolutionary algorithm.

3.2 Urban Road Networks

In the context of OTC and especially our previous clustering-based approach [20], models describing urban road networks were considered, of which major model assumptions are described here.

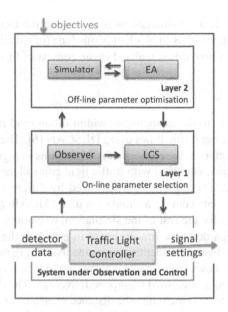

Fig. 1. Overview from [10] that depicts the multilevel OTC architecture with the SuOC at layer 0 as well as the "online layer" and "offline layer" on top.

Infrastructure. Unlike motorways, urban road networks lack highly privileged "main roads" around which all other infrastructure is organised. Instead, single or multi-lane road sections with speed limits considerably lower than on highways form a grid via intersections. These are often equipped with traffic light controllers (TLC) positioned at each incoming section. The control cycle as a basis for the signalisation is coordinated with other intersections. But the network may also contain junctions without a TLC.

An additional assumption is that outgoing and incoming road sections are equipped with sensors to count vehicles. These detectors could represent real-life induction loops. Also, incoming sections of an intersection can be equipped with variable message signs (VMS) that are readable by drivers and enable dynamic route guidance.

Traffic Demand. The edges of such a network under consideration are connected to traffic origins and destination that simulate the incoming and outgoing traffic from the surrounding road network. These traffic volumes can be specified using an origin-destination matrix (O/D matrix): For each possible combination the arising vehicle count for a given time period (e.g. veh/h) is defined. These demands may even change during the observation period to model, for instance, rush hours or reversal commuter traffic.

Incidents. Accidents are common traffic incidents that have an impact on the usability of road sections and their lanes. Also, impairments due to unloading vehicles are possible. An informal description of these and other incident types is given in [19]. A coarse way to model these incidents in simulations is to prohibit the usage of the whole road. A more differentiated approach is to block only one lane (of a dual-lane road). Section 5 provides more details on how this is realised in the context of this work.

3.3 Preliminary Work

Our approach [20] so far to detect incidents within urban road networks applies time series analysis by clustering traffic flows using DBSCAN [6]. These flows are collected from vehicle count detectors at the endings of road sections in regular single-lane 2×2 and 3×3 Manhattan grids equipped with traffic light controllers which use a synchronized 90s control cycle. These sections are affected by different traffic volumes (primary, secondary, and tertiary) during a simulation of 1:15 h. After 45 min access to one of the sections is denied for the rest of the simulation, to emulate a fully blocked road. The first 15 min are regarded as warm-up phase to establish the traffic situation after which the flows are considered for identifying incidents. During preprocessing, the general development of the flows over time was taken into account using flattening where earlier flows are included as weighted (dampened) average. The detection is a two part process: First, a parameter set (including the distance measure) of clustering parameters is used to *indicate* an incident. To then *validate* this a second clustering (parameter set) is applied in combination with certain filters that represent domain knowledge regarding the traffic flows in the network. For example, while the flow should decrease in affected sections, it is expected to rise in "detour routes" at a later time. Also, a higher number of false positives occurring at the fringe of the simulated network were filtered out. Section 4 provides more details on the applied techniques described above. The best parameter sets and filters are the result of a manual and iterative selection process. The authors of DBSCAN recommend to use $minPts = 4$ as the minimal number of points necessary for forming a dense region. This turns out to be adequate, while the neighbouring distance ϵ varies with the applied distance measure. Table 1 gives an overview of these findings.

The application of incident filters results in a significant reduction of false alarms for all cluster distance measures in both Manhattan networks. In the case of the 2×2 grid, several parameter sets yielded good results. For instance, using the average distance for validation and the preceding indication (relative to the mean flow) resulted in an optimal detection and false alarm rate. This distance measure works also best for the 3 $\times$ 3 grid with a fixed $\epsilon = 95$ for the indication. While all incident are detected, false alarms cannot be prevented. Still, the Euclidean and the Cubic approximation distance work marginally better. Finally, an important consequence of this detection approach is the delay between the occurrence of an incident and the indication due to the flattening which for the above results was at least two control cycles.

4   Approach

The general detection procedure as described in Sect. 3 uses density-based clustering and includes additional prepossessing and filtering as a result of the original evaluation process from [20]. This section expands on some of its elements.

Table 1. This table is based on the results as presented in [20]. It summarises the best DBSCAN parameters for detection in combination with incident filters for the 2 × 2 and the 3 × 3 Manhattan networks. In both settings all incidents are detected, but in the second case also false positives occurred.

Validation		Indication		Detection rate	False alarms
Distance measure	ϵ	Relative distance measure	ϵ		
2 × 2 Manhattan Grid					
Euclidean	200	Average	0.8	1	0
DTW	12	Average	0.8	1	0
Linear	20	Average	0.8	1	0
Cubic	24	Average	0.8	1	0
Average	8	Average	1	1	0
3 × 3 Manhattan Grid					
Euclidean	150	Average	0.95	1	4
DTW	9	Average	0.95	1	7
Linear	10	Average	0.95	1	7
Cubic	9	Average	0.95	1	5
Average	8	Average	0.95	1	7

4.1 Preprocessing

Due to traffic light control at intersections there are always time periods when the vehicles cannot freely move through a section: The red phases. But as these are significantly shorter than an hour, this is compensated when calculating the flow in veh/h which is based on the number of incoming and outgoing per section reported every second. The resulting time series of these flow values is further preprocessed to account for preceding control cycles. This *flattening* is achieved by applying a weighted average where older traffic flows are more dampened than recent ones. The flattening factor $w \in [0, 1]$ indicates the ratio of past flows in the weighted average. To determine the flatting f of a flow valued x_t within a section of a network with a control cycle length t_c, this recursive calculation is performed (see Fig. 2 for illustration):

$$f(x_t) = \begin{cases} x_t & \text{at } t = 0 \\ wx_t + (1 - w)f(x_{t-t_c}) & \text{otherwise} \end{cases} \tag{1}$$

4.2 DBSCAN

To detect changing traffic flows, each times series of flattened flow values per section is treated as one data point used for clustering. Based on the characteristics of the learning problem, we decided to apply the *Density Based Spatial Clustering of Applications with Noise* [6], a widely used and commonly accepted sophisticated standard clustering algorithm. The particular reason for the choice is that DBSCAN is powerful, comes

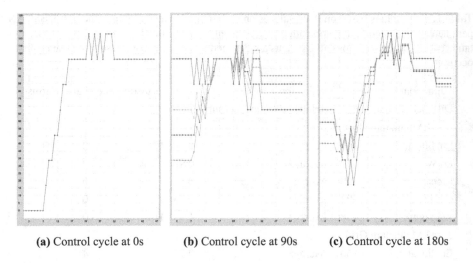

(a) Control cycle at 0s   (b) Control cycle at 90s   (c) Control cycle at 180s

Fig. 2. These charts taken from [20] show an example of preprocessed traffic flows at section BL > TL in the 2 × 2 network at the beginning of the simulation (after warm-up). For the second 45s of each of the first 3 cycles, the flattened and unflattened (blue) flow data is shown. (a) First all graphs align as no weighting can be applied. Different flattening weights are denoted by the colours green (0.33), purple (0.5) and yellow (0.66). Lower numbers indicate less impact of the latest value, which leads to the intended flattening with fewer and smaller spikes in (b) and (c). (Color figure online)

with only a few hyper-parameters, does not need the expected number of clusters as input, and scales with the number of available data. DBSCAN considers the density of data points with regard to a distance measure and works well for clusters of similar density and any shape. It can detect multiple clusters, identifies noise data points, and does not require prior knowledge about the expected number of clusters.

DBSCAN is built around the concept of density-reachability. To determine reachability three parameters are required: ϵ denotes the necessary neighbouring distance so that one point is reachable from the other, making them connected. To determine the distance between two points, another parameter for DBSCAN is required: The distance measure. This can be also non-geometric similarity measure or distance function. Its choice is important for the performance of DBSCAN. Section 5.4 describes the measure considered in this and the previous work.

Based on the distance, the ϵ-neighbourhood N_p of a point p specifies all points p' within the radius ϵ. If such a neighbourhood has a minimal number of points, defined by the parameter $minPts$, the p' points are considered directly density-reachable. With this, all data points fall into three groups:

- *Core points* are directly density-reachable.
- *Density-reachable points* are not core points but are reachable from a core point. They lie at the edge of a cluster.
- All other points are considered *noise* or *outliers*.

Finally, a cluster consists of at least one core point and all other points the are density-reachable or directly density-reachable from that core point. This implies that a cluster has at least $minPts$ points and its non-core points form the edge of the cluster. Also, noise points do not belong to any cluster.

4.3 Domain Knowledge

As mentioned in Sect. 3 the usage of knowledge regarding the general occurrence of incidents or the model in the form of filters can increase the detection rate during the indication phase or reduce the number of false positive findings during the subsequent validation. These strategies of our previous work are reused:

Border Filter. sieves all incidents at the edge of the traffic network.

Blacklist Filter. filters out a previous set of incidents. This is used to exclude incidents that were already used as validators.

Downstream Validation. to check if the demands in the downstream sections decreases as expected.

Upstream and Detour Validation. to verify that demands in the upstream and the detour sections increase.

5 Evaluation

To analyse the behaviour of our clustering-based incident technique, we performed close-to-reality simulations with a professional traffic simulation toolkit. In the following, we briefly describe the simulation environment and the considered scenarios, including the road network topology, the traffic volumes, the applied distance measures, and the definition of different incidents in the simulation. This is followed by an in-depth explanation of the achieved results.

5.1 Traffic Simulator

To simulate the demand-based vehicle traffic, the road networks, and the incidents, the commercial software AIMSUN Next [1] for traffic modelling and simulation is used, as it was for our previous approach and in the context of OTC. A plug-in was written using the Aimsun Next API that collects for every simulation step (of 1s) all detector counts for all sections. These are then used by the analysis server to calculate the means (see Sect. 4.1) as a basis for the further analysis.

5.2   Extended Road Networks

The original fully connected 2 × 2 and 3 × 3 Manhattan networks from previous work featured mainly single lane road sections of 150 m with sides lanes for turning left. After determining appropriate algorithm parameters for the first grid, the larger one was used to revise these parameters. In accordance with possible future work indicated in the original approach, new road networks are introduced to further validate the detection algorithm: Double-lane grids and a 5 × 5 grid. Figure 3 shows the 2 × 2-DL network where the 4 interconnecting sections gain a second main lane. Other aspects, such as the geometry or TLCs, stay consistent in the same way they do in the respective 3 × 3-DL grid in Fig. 4. Finally, the "enclosing" 5 × 5-EC network in Fig. 5 is used to assess the border effects of a 3 × 3 grid, as further described in Sect. 5.6.

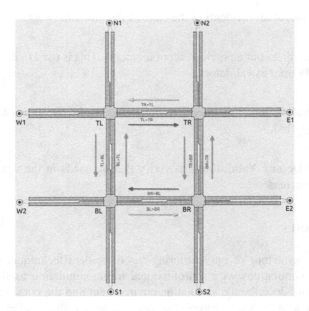

Fig. 3. The connecting sections in the 2 × 2-DL network have two main roads, one doubling also as the turn-off lane to the right, with an additional side lane for left turning vehicles. The general directions of the simulated traffic volumes as described in Sect. 5.3 are indicated by the red ("primary"), red ("secondary"), and red ("tertiary") arrows. (Color figure online)

5.3   Traffic Volumes

The traffic demands utilised here were the same as in our previous work and are based upon [21]: The primary, secondary, and tertiary demands correspond to higher, medium, and lower traffic volumes. They are oriented along the north-south and west-east orientations of the various Manhattan networks, as visualised in Fig. 3 and 4 above. Due to the symmetric nature of the demands, not all combinations of incidents and demand sections were taken into consideration. Again, one representative per demand intensity was evaluated as listed in Table 2 and 3.

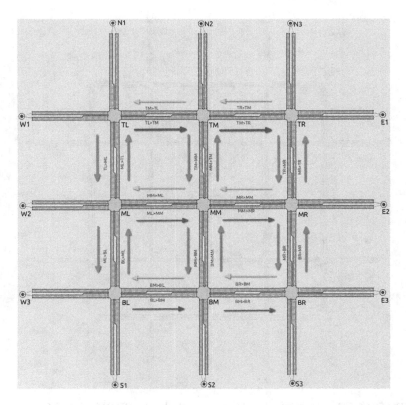

Fig. 4. Analogously to the 2 × 2-DL this 3 × 3-DL grid has double-lane roads plus a side-lane for turning left. Again, the red ("primary"), red ("secondary"), and red ("tertiary") arrows indicate the traffic demands from Sect. 5.3. (Color figure online)

5.4   Distance Measures

As described in Sect. 4, a distance measure has to be specified which enables DBSCAN to compare two time series. These are the flow values of one section for every second of a control cycle.

Average Distance. is the most basic of these measures as simply the absolute difference of the two mean flow values is calculated.

Polynomial Approximation. fits a polynomial function to the data points of the two time series. In this work the linear and cubic variants were evaluated. The distance between the resulting coefficients is computed, again, using the Euclidean distance.

Euclidean Distance. is the distance between two points in Euclidean space. Due to constant sampling resolution in this case, the exact same time points are compared (see Fig. 6).

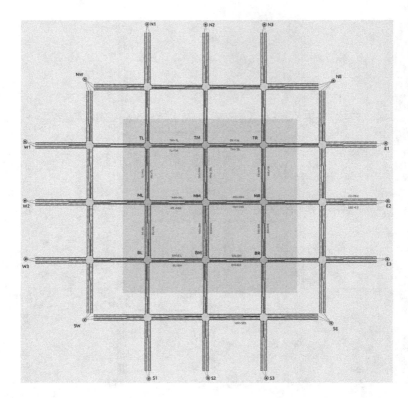

Fig. 5. The 5×5-EC network introduced to examine the border effects in Sect. 5.6 consists of the original 3×3 single-lane grid (the coloured area). This then surrounded by an additional ring of regularly connected junctions. (Color figure online)

DTW. stands for "Dynamic Time Warping" by [2]: Points from two time series are continuously paired, forming a monotonous and continuous "warping path" as visualised in Fig. 6. Points can be chosen multiple times and all start and stop points have to be included. Then an additional distance measure (Euclidean in this case) is employed to calculate the cumulative distance between the points which is then normalised using the length of the whole monotonous and continuous path.

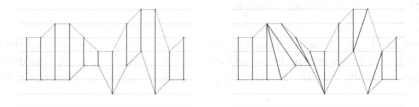

Fig. 6. Illustration taken from [20], showing an artificial example for applying the Euclidean distance (left) and Dynamic Time Warping (right) on a time series.

Table 2. The primary, secondary, and tertiary traffic demands (veh/h) in the 2×2 and 2×2-DL networks. Due to the symmetry (see Fig. 3) one representative sections per demand is chosen for evaluation: TR > TR (primary), the opposite direction TR > TL (secondary), and BR > TR (tertiary).

O/D	Demand	Opposite direction
W1 – E1	400	200
W2 – E2	200	400
N1 – S1	150	150
N2 – S2	150	150
Others	10	10

Table 3. The primary, secondary, and tertiary traffic demands (veh/h) in the 3×3 and 3×3-DL networks (see Fig. 4). The representative sections for occurrence of demands are selected similarly: TR > TR (primary), TR > TL (secondary), and on the bottom right BM > BR (tertiary). These demands are also used for the 5×5 network.

O/D	Demand	Opposite direction
W1 – E1	400	200
W2 – E2	300	150
W3 – E3	300	150
N1 – S1	150	150
N2 – N2	150	150
N3 – N3	150	150
Other	10	10

Relative Distance. is a measure that uses any of these measures and puts it into relation with the traffic flow: The two time series means are calculated and the higher of these is used to normalise the previously calculated distance measure.

5.5 Section and Lane Closures

The introduction of dual-lane networks allows for further expansion of our network model. In addition to section closure incidents, which can be used to replicate heavy traffic accidents, an incident with potential impact on the traffic flows is considered: lane closures, where not all main lanes are closed. Figure 7 illustrates how in the context of this work always the "middle" lane is blocked, as well as the need to use turn closures when applying section closures due to a certain behaviour of the simulator.

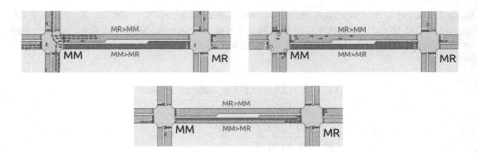

Fig. 7. The top-left screenshot demonstrates an unintended situation created by Aimsun Next: Vehicles that have already entered the intersection when a section closure occurs stay immobile as the simulator is not able to resolve this deadlock. The adjacent screenshot shows how adding 3 fitting turn closures prevents cars from entering the junction. Below this, a closure of the "middle" lane is shown. Note that this does not prevent left turns, as vehicles are allowed to cross this lane *at the end* of a section.

5.6 Experiments

To further evaluate our previous detection approach under the circumstances described in Sect. 3, the following extended experiments were conducted under comparable conditions, like network geometry, traffic demands, and sections selected to exhibit incidents.

Dual-Lane Experiments. In the two dual-lane networks the full section closures at the sections described in Table 2 and 3 were simulated at 45 min; they lasted until the end of the 1:15 simulation time. Furthermore, these simulations were conducted with lane closures (see Fig. 7) instead full section closures.

Simulation Border Effect. The border filter mentioned in Sect. 4.3 was introduced in [20] when the algorithm parameters found for the 2×2 setting were evaluated in the 3×3 grid: A significant number of falsely identified incidents occurred in sections leading towards junctions that are situated at edge of the network and are connected to the simulated centroids. During simulation, these nodes randomly, but independently from the control cycle cars, let vehicles enter the network. To assess this effect, the 3×3 grid is embedded in 5×5-EC network that emulates at least part of an enclosing regular road network.

5.7 Evaluation Criteria

The three criteria to evaluate the algorithm parameters in our previous approach are taken into account again:

1. Detection Rate: As in this experimental setup each simulation scenario has at the most one incident; this corresponds to the true positive rate in binary classification. A true detection implies also a correct estimate as to which section the incident occurs in. This is the primary criterion for the evaluation.

2. False Alarms: The secondary criterion is the number falsely identified incident which should be minimal. This includes locating it in the wrong section.
3. Detection Delay: The time between the start of an incident and its detection and validation becomes especially relevant when flattening during preprocessing is used because incident-induced flow changes have to be pronounced for more than one control cycle.

5.8   Results

Section Closures. As the traffic demands and the road layout are the same as in the original experiment, the impact of the additional lanes is expected to be low. For the 2 × 2-DL grid this was mostly confirmed, while the larger network exhibited an increased number of false alarms as show in Table 4.

Table 4. Results of the 2 × 2-DL and 3 × 3-DL simulation of section closures. For the smaller network the incident indication and validation was as perfect as with the original setup. However, for the 3 × 3-DL the number of false alarms increased slightly, with the combination of Euclidean and the Average distance measure still coming out on top. The detection itself is comparable to the 3 × 3 setting. An interesting exception occurred when Cubic distance measure was used for validation, as it failed to detect the section closure exposed to the tertiary traffic demand. The maximal detection delay for all correctly detected incidents was 3 control cycles (270s).

Validation		Indication		Detection rate	False alarms
Distance measure	ϵ	Relative distance measure	ϵ		
2 × 2-DL Manhattan Grid					
Euclidean	200	Average	0.8	1	0
DTW	12	Average	0.8	1	0
Linear	20	Average	0.8	1	0
Cubic	24	Average	0.8	1	0
Average	8	Average	1	1	0
3 × 3-DL Manhattan Grid					
Euclidean	150	Average	0.95	1	7
DTW	9	Average	0.95	1	9
Linear	10	Average	0.95	1	10
Cubic	9	Average	0.95	0.66	12
Average	8	Average	0.95	1	8

Lane Closures. The detection of lane closures in the double-lane grids following the previous detection approach proved to be flawed, as detection rate dropped significantly. In particular, the incidents in sections with low demand could not be detected. One possible explanation is that the remaining open lane offered enough capacity to compensate. Table 5 and 6 list the respective results. Additionally, the relative DTW distance measure was calculated, as it was the second best in terms of detection rate in the original approach. This proved not to increase the detection rate in general, however, while the number of false alarms even increased.

Table 5. Results of the 2 × 2-DL simulation of lane closures.

Validation		Indication		Detection rate	False alarms
Distance measure	ϵ	Relative distance measure	ϵ		
Euclidean	200	Average	0.8	0.66	1
DTW	12	Average	0.8	0.66	4
Linear	20	Average	0.8	0.66	2
Cubic	24	Average	0.8	0.33	2
Average	8	Average	1	0.66	3
Euclidean	150	Relative(DTW)	0.95	0.66	6
DTW	9	Relative(DTW)	0.95	0.33	8
Linear	10	Relative(DTW)	0.95	0.66	7
Cubic	9	Relative(DTW)	0.95	0.66	9
Average	8	Relative(DTW)	0.95	0.33	5

Table 6. Results of the 3 × 3-DL simulation of lane closures.

Validation		Indication		Detection rate	False alarms
Distance measure	ϵ	Relative distance measure	ϵ		
Euclidean	150	Average	0.8	0.66	6
DTW	9	Average	0.8	0.33	7
Linear	10	Average	0.8	0.66	4
Cubic	9	Average	0.8	0.33	6
Average	8	Average	1	0.66	11
Euclidean	150	Relative(DTW)	0.95	0.33	23
DTW	9	Relative(DTW)	0.95	0.0	21
Linear	10	Relative(DTW)	0.95	0.33	25
Cubic	9	Relative(DTW)	0.95	0.66	31
Average	8	Relative(DTW)	0.95	0.33	20

Border Effects. During the validation of the 5 × 5 simulation, all flows values from the additional lanes (compared to the 3 × 3 network) were ignored and not included in the following analysis. Additionally, the border incident filter was deactivated. Table 7 show the results that are similar to the previous 3 × 3 simulation. This confirms the need for the special treatment of incidents at the fringe of the simulated network.

Table 7. Results of the 5 × 5-EC simulation, with the deactivated border filter and flows from enclosing roads being ignored. Compared to the previous 3 × 3 results in Table 1 with an active filter, the number of false alarms is slightly higher but comparable. The combination of the Euclidean and the Average distance measure still proved to be best.

Validation		Indication		Detection rate	False alarms
Distance measure	ϵ	Relative distance measure	ϵ		
5 × 5-DL Manhattan Grid					
Euclidean	150	Average	0.95	1	4
DTW	9	Average	0.95	1	8
Linear	10	Average	0.95	1	7
Cubic	9	Average	0.95	1	6
Average	8	Average	0.95	1	7

6   Summary

The findings in Sect. 5.8 depict a mixed outcome. The extended experiments confirm that in principle, this clustering detection approach can also work in more complex traffic settings. However, a good performance in terms of detection rate as well as of number of false positives is only achieved in certain situations when the incidents are more pronounced as this is the case with full section closures, ideally combined with higher traffic demands, which induces more distinctive flow changes. This is not the case for lane closures or the lower demands. Also, specific situations (e.g. the simulator fringe effect) have to be recognised and provided for. This, as well as the choice of the clustering parameters, are the result of a laborious manual process, even under the rather basic traffic assumptions so far. An exhaustive simulation of situations with, e.g., less pronounced, dynamic incident types or more complex, real-word traffic network settings is demanding and not cannot be conducted without automation. Even then, previously unforeseen situations might occur. For this reason this clustering-based incident can be enhanced in at least two directions:

On the one hand, the simulations can be extended significantly, featuring more complex, real-life road networks, highly dynamic traffic demands, and diverse road users (e.g., public transport or heavy traffic). Also, the incident model can be more differentiated (see [19]), with larger incidents that also affect intersections, speed restrictions or disturbances that move through the networks, as well as combinations of incidents.

On the other hand, the detection approach itself can be improved: Alternative clustering algorithms, such as Local Outlier Factor (LOF) by [3], can be evaluated and combined with automatic hyperparameter optimisation techniques from Machine Learning. Also, additional distance measures and feature representations are worth exploring.

This all calls for automatised execution and analysis of experiments. The further development must focus on a decentralised detection approach, with the aim of integrating it into the Organic Traffic Control to enhance its self-adaptive and self-organising capabilities.

References

1. Aimsun SLU: Aimsun Next Professional, Version 22. Barcelona, Spain (2021). http://www. aimsun.com/
2. Berndt, D.J., Clifford, J. (eds.): Using dynamic time warping to find patterns in time series, vol. 10. Seattle, WA, USA (1994)
3. Breunig, M.M., Kriegel, H.P., Ng, R.T., Sander, J.: LOF. In: Dunham, M., Naughton, J.F., Chen, W., Koudas, N. (eds.) Proceedings of the 2000 ACM SIGMOD international conference on Management of data - SIGMOD 2000, pp. 93–104. ACM Press, New York (2000). https://doi.org/10.1145/342009.335388
4. Dogru, N., Subasi, A.: Traffic accident detection using random forest classifier. In: 2018 15th Learning and Technology Conference (L T), pp. 40–45 (2018). https://doi.org/10.1109/LT. 2018.8368509
5. Dusparic, I., Cahill, V.: Using distributed w-learning for multi-policy optimization in decentralized autonomic systems. In: Proceedings of 6th International Conference on Autonomic Computing, pp. 63–64. ACM (2009)
6. Ester, M., Kriegel, H.P., Sander, J., Xu, X.: A density-based algorithm for discovering clusters in large spatial databases with noise, pp. 226–231. AAAI Press (1996)
7. Gokulan, B., Srinivasan, D.: Distributed geometric fuzzy multiagent urban traffic signal control. IEEE Trans. Int. Transp. Syst. **11**(3), 714–727 (2010)
8. Helbing, D., Lämmer, S., Lebacque, J.: Self-organized control of irregular or perturbed network traffic. Optimal control and dynamic games, pp. 239–274 (2005)
9. Mauro, V., Taranto, C.D.: Utopia. Control, computers, communications in transportation (1990)
10. Müller-Schloer, C., Tomforde, S.: Organic Computing – Technical Systems for Survival in the Real World. AS, Springer, Cham (2017). https://doi.org/10.1007/978-3-319-68477-2
11. Oliveira, L.D., Camponogara, E.: Multi-agent model predictive control of signaling split in urban traffic networks. Transp. Res. Part C: Emerg. Tech. **18**(1), 120–139 (2010)
12. Parkany, E., Xie, C.: A complete review of incident detection algorithms & their deployment: what works and what doesn't (2005). https://www.dot.ny.gov/gisapps/roadway-inventory-system-viewer
13. Payne, H.J., Tignor, S.C.: Freeway incident-detection algorithms based on decision trees with states. In: Urban system operation and freeways. Transportation research record, National Academy of Sciences, Washington, DC (1978)
14. Robertson, D., Bretherton, D.: Optimizing networks of traffic signals in real time - the SCOOT method. IEEE Trans. Veh. Tech. **40**(1), 11–15 (1991)
15. Sims, A., Dobinson, K.: The Sydney coordinated adaptive traffic (SCAT) system - philosophy and benefits. IEEE Trans. Veh. Tech. **29**(2), 130–137 (1980)
16. Sommer, M., Tomforde, S., Hähner, J.: An organic computing approach to resilient traffic management. In: McCluskey, T.L., Kotsialos, A., Müller, J.P., Klügl, F., Rana, O., Schumann, R. (eds.) Autonomic Road Transport Support Systems, pp. 113–130. Birkhäuser, Basel (2016)
17. Studer, L., Ketabdari, M., Marchionni, G.: Analysis of adaptive traffic control systems design of a decision support system for better choices. J. Civil Environ. Eng. **5**(195), 2 (2015)
18. Sun, L., Lin, Z., Li, W., Xiang, Y.: Freeway incident detection based on set theory and short-range communication. Transp. Lett. **11**(10), 558–569 (2019). https://doi.org/10.1080/19427867.2018.1453273. https://doi.org/10.1080/19427867.2018.1453273
19. Thomsen, I.: Incident-aware resilient traffic management for urban road networks. In: Organic Computing: Doctoral Dissertation Colloquium 2020, pp. 125–138. kassel University Press GmbH (2011)

20. Thomsen., I., Zapfe., Y., Tomforde., S.: Urban traffic incident detection for organic traffic control: a density-based clustering approach. In: Proceedings of the 7th International Conference on Vehicle Technology and Intelligent Transport Systems - VEHITS, pp. 152–160. INSTICC, SciTePress (2021). https://doi.org/10.5220/0010454101520160
21. Tomforde, S., et al.: Decentralised progressive signal systems for organic traffic control. In: 2008 Second IEEE International Conference on Self-Adaptive and Self-Organizing Systems, pp. 413–422. IEEE (2008). https://doi.org/10.1109/SASO.2008.31
22. Vincent, R., Peirce, J., Webb, P.: MOVA traffic control manual (1990)
23. Yao, Y., Xu, M., Wang, Y., Crandall, D.J., Atkins, E.M.: Unsupervised traffic accident detection in first-person videos. CoRR abs/1903.00618 (2019). http://arxiv.org/abs/1903.00618

Cooperative Driving: Research on Generic Decentralized Maneuver Coordination for Connected and Automated Vehicles

Daniel Maksimovski[1]([⊠]) ⓘ, Christian Facchi[1] ⓘ, and Andreas Festag[1,2] ⓘ

[1] Technische Hochschule Ingolstadt, CARISSMA Institute for Electric,
COnnected, and Secure Mobility (C-ECOS), Esplande 10, Ingolstadt, Germany
{daniel.maksimovski,christian.facchi,andreas.festag}@carissma.eu
[2] Fraunhofer Institute for Transportation and Infrastructure Systems IVI, Ingolstadt, Germany

Abstract. Maneuver coordination for *Connected and Automated Vehicles* (CAVs) can be enhanced by *vehicle-to-everything* (V2X) communication. In order to disseminate planned maneuver intentions or requests, *Maneuver Coordination Messages* (MCMs) are exchanged between the CAVs that enable them to negotiate and perform cooperative maneuvers. In this way, V2X communication can extend the perception range of the sensors, enhance the decision making and maneuver planning of the CAVs, as well as allow complex interactions between the vehicles. Various maneuver coordination schemes exist for specific traffic use cases. Recently, several maneuver coordination approaches have been proposed that target at generic decentralized solutions which can be applied for a wide range of use cases relying on direct *vehicle-to-vehicle* (V2V) communication. This paper presents such use cases and existing generic approaches for decentralized maneuver coordination. The approaches are systematically described, compared and classified considering explicit and implicit trajectory broadcast, space-time reservation, cost values, priority maneuvers and complex interactions among vehicles. Furthermore, this paper outlines open research gaps in the field and discusses future research directions.

Keywords: V2X communication · Cooperative maneuver coordination · Connected vehicles

1 Introduction

Advanced Driver Assistance Systems (ADAS) and automated vehicles are becoming one of the biggest trends in the automotive industry. The automated vehicles will reshape the mobility by increasing the safety and efficiency on the road. However, the on-board sensors that allow the automated driving have certain limitations in the sensing of the environment and decision making.

Vehicle-to-everything (V2X) communication with *vehicle-to-vehicle* (V2V) and *vehicle-to-infrastructure* (V2I) communication will allow automated vehicles to strengthen their perception of the environment and enhance the decision making and maneuver planning processes by further enabling cooperative driving between the *Connected and Automated Vehicles* (CAVs). The V2X communication is facilitated by two

© Springer Nature Switzerland AG 2022
C. Klein et al. (Eds.): SMARTGREENS 2021/ VEHITS 2021, CCIS 1612, pp. 348–370, 2022.
https://doi.org/10.1007/978-3-031-17098-0_18

access technologies: WLAN-V2X and Cellular-V2X [22,27]. These access technologies operate in the 5.9 GHz frequency band allocated for traffic efficiency and road safety applications. The data dissemination relies on direct communication among vehicles and with the roadside infrastructure.

For perception and maneuver coordination, three development phases of V2X communication applications are commonly identified based on their time of introduction: *(i) Cooperative Awareness (CA)* for the exchange of vehicle state information (position, heading, speed, acceleration) and *Decentralized Environmental Notification (DEN)* for the dissemination of dangerous events (Day-1); *(ii) Collective Perception (CP)* for the exchange of vehicle sensor data as detected and classified objects in the vehicles' vicinity (Day-2); and *(iii) Maneuver Coordination (MC)* for the exchange of intention and coordination data among vehicles (Day-3). Additional V2X communication services include *Signal Phase and Time (SPAT)* that provides the status of the traffic lights at signalized intersections and *Map (MAP)* that disseminates the road and lane topology with an option to add lane attributes such as emergency or bus lanes.

For the European system, a dedicated message type, i.e., CAM, DENM, CPM, MCM, SPATEM, MAPEM, has been specified for each V2X communication service by the *European Telecommunications Standards Institute* (ETSI).[1] While the standardization of CA, DEN, SPAT and MAP services for Day 1 is completed [7–9], for the CP service [10] a study item (Technical Report) has been published. The MC service is mostly in a research phase and still very early in the standardization process [11].

Cooperative maneuver coordination comprises the exchange of intentions and coordination information among CAVs with the goal of achieving safer and more efficient driving. This process allows the CAVs to exchange their planned maneuvers and intentions, request a certain desired maneuver and jointly cooperate with a group of other vehicles. There are two main ways for maneuver coordination: centralized and decentralized. In a centralized coordination, there is a central unit that receives all the information, calculates coordinated routes and exchanges the planned maneuvers with the involved vehicles. In a decentralized coordination, the vehicles mostly exchange messages and negotiate cooperative maneuvers through V2V communication. A hybrid coordination can consider both, the coordination among the vehicles and also using a centralized system, typically a roadside unit - RSU, to plan certain maneuvers for the involved CAVs.

Another way to differentiate the cooperation between the CAVs is by explicit and implicit coordination. In an implicit coordination, the vehicles share their intentions, but have to observe from the changed intentions of the other CAVs in their vicinity whether their request has been accepted or not. Explicit coordination involves explicit negotiation and agreement between the vehicles to perform a certain acknowledged cooperative maneuver in an event-based manner. Furthermore, the coordination can be divided into use case-specific and generic approaches. Use case-specific coordination approach can be used only for specific traffic situations, while generic coordination can be utilized to solve different cooperative use cases such as cooperative lane change, merging, overtaking as well as cooperative driving in certain junctions, roundabouts and intersections.

---

[1] Published ETSI standards are available at https://www.etsi.org/standards.

Fig. 1. Classification of approaches for generic decentralized cooperative maneuver coordination [20].

The present paper analyzes state-of-the-art approaches for decentralized maneuver coordination considering communication among the vehicles. The existing generic approaches are applicable to various coordination scenarios and are classified into six categories as presented in Fig. 1: *Explicit Trajectory Broadcast* (ETB), *Extended Explicit Trajectory Broadcast* (EETB), *Implicit Trajectory Broadcast with Cost Values* (ITB-CV), *Space-Time Reservation* (STR), *Priority Maneuver Coordination* (PriMa) and *Complex Vehicular Interactions Protocol* (CVIP). For each category, the respective publication is presented and analyzed, followed by a comparison of the characteristics as well as the benefits and disadvantages of the presented approaches. Furthermore, after the review of the existing approaches, open research topics in the field of maneuver coordination are discussed. This systematic review is regarded as a contribution for further development, standardization and research of maneuver coordination for connected and automated driving utilizing V2X communication.[2]

The main research question can be phrased as: *How to enable safe, efficient, fast and comfortable maneuver coordination process among the CAVs that is independent of the use case and satisfies the V2X communication requirements?*

Main contributions of the paper are as follows:

- Selection of use cases for maneuver coordination;
- Description and comparison of the existing decentralized coordination approaches using a similar abstraction level that shows their commonalities and differences;
- Analysis of the novelties and benefits, as well as shortcomings of each approach in relation to the coordination protocol and communication pattern;

---

[2] This paper is an extended version of [20] that describes and compares four approaches for generic decentralized maneuver coordination with CAVs. The present paper covers two additional approaches, PriMa and CVIP that were not available at the publication of [20], as well as two updated versions of the previously published approaches ETB and STR. We have used the same type of figures as in [20] that demonstrate the use cases and extended them for the new approaches. In addition, the comparison and research gaps as well as the references are extended and updated accordingly.

Fig. 2. Cooperative ACC [20].   **Fig. 3.** Driving in a convoy [20].

– Identification and discussion of research questions divided into three main research gaps: detection and decision logic, maneuver coordination protocol and V2X communication;
– Proposal of possible research directions for each research question.

The remainder of this paper is structured as follows. Cooperative driving use cases for maneuver coordination are presented in Sect. 2. Section 3 presents the generic decentralized approaches followed by their comparison in Sect. 4. Discussion of open research gaps is given in Sect. 5 and finally the paper is concluded in Sect. 6.

2 Use Cases for Cooperative Maneuver Coordination

Utilizing V2X communication enabled cooperative driving, the traffic flow can be optimized and the CAVs can achieve safer, more efficient and more comfortable driving. Furthermore, the CAVs can jointly coordinate their maneuvers in some specific traffic scenarios that can cause conflicted situations for the conventional, as well as automated vehicles. The R&D projects AutoNet2030 and IMAGinE [15, 18] identified several cooperative use cases, where utilizing V2X communication based maneuver coordination can bring benefits for the CAVs, summarizing them in the following way:

Cooperative-ACC (C-ACC), Platoon and Convoy. Cooperative Adaptive Cruise Control (C-ACC) as presented by Fig. 2 extends the standard ACC by using V2X communication to allow exchange of additional information between the vehicles to achieve synchronization of the velocities and avoid more frequent acceleration or deceleration, preventing potentially critical situations. Furthermore, C-ACC can enable platooning: A group of vehicles driving on the same lane on a highway, typically trucks, represents a platoon that allows the vehicles to keep small distances between each other and drive in a stable formation. The main goal is to increase the road capacity, as well as the traffic comfort and efficiency. A master vehicle leads the platoon and manages and coordinates the maneuvers with the other following platoon members. Another way for grouping vehicles on highways is driving in a single or multi-lane convoy shown in Fig. 3, where the control is distributed over all convoy participants in longitudinal and lateral direction. Only the information regarding the dynamics of the adjacent vehicles is needed in a convoy to create a stable formation. Driving in a platoon or convoy is considered as vehicles cooperatively driving in a formation.

Fig. 4. Cooperative lane changing [20].   **Fig. 5.** Cooperative lane merging [20].

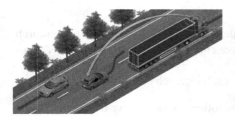

Fig. 6. Cooperative overtaking [20].   **Fig. 7.** Cooperative driving at junction [20].

Cooperative Lane Changing, Lane Merging and Overtaking. Lane change is a very common situation on roads where V2X communication can bring benefits to enable two or more vehicles to cooperatively change lanes in a safe and efficient way. Some of the vehicles will have to decelerate or accelerate in order to create the needed gap for a lane change as shown in Fig. 4 where the red vehicle slows down. Another common maneuver on highways is lane merging as presented in Fig. 5 that can also be performed in a similar safe and efficient fashion by exchanging the planned and desired maneuvers of the vehicles. Also such a maneuver can occur due to construction sites on the roads. Cooperative overtaking is another important maneuver that especially occurs on rural roads, as shown in Fig. 6. Such a cooperative maneuver can also be exploited by heavily loaded trucks on the highway where they can exchange their planned overtaking speed and weight for optimal coordination. The current overtaking assisting systems, which can also be based on periodic vehicle status messages, provide the drivers with a warning if vehicles are detected going in opposite direction on the adjacent lane, but does not actively support the driver. By exchanging the future planned trajectories in the overtaking scenario as well as the other presented traffic scenarios, the connected vehicles in an automated mode can avoid conflicting situations and execute such maneuvers in a safe and efficient way without the need of a driver.

Cooperative Driving at Intersections, Roundabouts or Junctions without Signalization. CAVs can coordinate each other more effectively by exchanging their planned intentions in non-signalized intersections, junctions or roundabouts that can often cause conflicted situations. Such a non-signalized junction where the CAVs exchange their planned maneuvers is illustrated in Fig. 7. In such manner, the CAVs can negotiate and adapt their future trajectories to safely execute the turning maneuvers in a cooperative way.

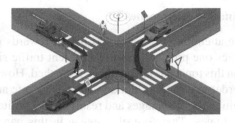

Fig. 8. Cooperative intersection [20].

Infrastructure-Controlled or Assisted Cooperative Driving. V2I communication can be used to plan and optimize the traffic flow with the CAVs in a centralized manner, by creating and exchanging the global plan with the involved vehicles. Such an intersection management can be realized in both, signalized and non-signalized intersections or junctions in order to optimize the traffic lights as well as manage each vehicle's passing through the cooperative intersection as shown in Fig. 8. The cooperative lane merging scenario can also be managed or assisted by the infrastructure.

3 Decentralized Maneuver Coordination

In this context, the decentralized maneuver coordination depends solely on the communication among the CAVs to negotiate cooperative maneuvers. In addition, the decentralized coordination can be categorized into use case-specific and generic. In a use case-specific coordination, a coordination application is required that focuses only on one specific traffic situation, such as the ones presented in Sect. 2, and uses a protocol only relevant to the respective use case. Generic coordination aims at using one protocol to solve all of the presented cooperative driving use cases.

3.1 Use Case-Specific Coordination Approaches

A large number of research contributions exists on the topic of use case-specific coordination to solve separate traffic situations. Typical examples represent the platooning [28] and C-ACC [5] applications that have been widely investigated and numerous approaches exist on their characteristics and control. These applications utilize the communication among the vehicles and are mostly based on a longitudinal coordination. In a decentralized convoy formation, the members of the convoy can keep a stable formation by adjusting their lateral and longitudinal dynamics [21]. Applications designed for cooperative lane change and merging require both, lateral and longitudinal coordination, as the vehicles also accelerate and decelerate to create the required gap. In [15], a cooperative lane change service is proposed consisting of a search, preparation and execution phase. This service supports maneuver negotiations and space reservations using dedicated broadcast lane change messages in each of the three separate phases. An overview of C-ACC that can also be used for lane change and merging coordination is presented in [1]. Distributed resource reservation protocols utilizing various message sets are discussed in [3], where distributed intersection and roundabouts management without the need for infrastructure support is analyzed.

3.2   Generic Coordination Approaches

From recent years, the attention in research has turned towards generic decentralized coordination that utilizes one protocol to solve different traffic situations between the CAVs. A lot of work on this topic has already been published. However, a lot of research gaps remain open in order to design a solution that enables safe and efficient coordination protocol by exploiting the advantages and resolving the limitations of the available communication technologies. Therefore, the review in this paper is also focused on generic approaches that utilize trajectory broadcast, maneuver request or reservation in space and time. A similar lane merging scenario consisting of four CAVs is used to describe the characteristics of each of the reviewed decentralized approaches. The V2X communication messages, that are broadcast by the cooperative vehicles, consist of planned (PT), desired (DT), requested (RT) and alternative (AT) trajectories, as well as space-time reservation (STR). The details of the trajectory planning process and decision making logic of the CAVs are not discussed in the respective publications. The main emphasis is put on the negotiation process that includes the communication patterns required to complete a coordination. Since some of the reviewed approaches do not have a name, in order to differentiate them, a name is assigned to each approach and the appropriate abbreviation is used as a reference, presented in Fig. 1.

Explicit Trajectory Broadcast (ETB). The first generic decentralized approach was proposed by [16] that also defined a new V2X message type based on trajectory related data, named Maneuver Coordination Message (MCM). In order to complete the coordination, three phases were identified that are typical for each maneuver coordination: detection, negotiation and execution. Initially the approach was proposed as an implicit coordination in [16], but was later upgraded into explicit coordination with the inclusion of the IDs of the CAVs in the MCM, followed by an additional safety analysis in [17].

The approach is explained in the following lane merging scenario demonstrated in Fig. 9. The scenario includes four CAVs that exchange MCMs including their PTs. It includes periodic broadcast of planned trajectories (PT) and optionally a desired trajectory (DT) that represents an alternative, more preferred trajectory that is currently hindered by another vehicle's right-of-way.

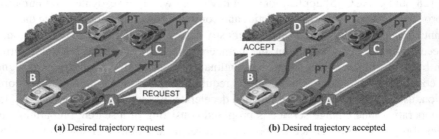

(a) Desired trajectory request   (b) Desired trajectory accepted

Fig. 9. Maneuver coordination process in ETB [20].

After vehicle A detects a need for coordination to merge in the lane, it sends a MCM including its PT and DT that intersects with the PT of vehicle B, in this way starting the negotiation process (Fig. 9a). Vehicle B performs assessment of the received DT and decides whether to accept or reject such a message. Although vehicles C and D also receive the message, the included DT does not interfere with their PTs, therefore they do not react on the message. In this situation, vehicle B accepts the request by broadcasting a new MCM with its adapted PT that allows vehicle A to perform its DT that is now adapted into a new PT (Fig. 9b).

Theoretical safety analysis was performed showing that this simple approach that requires two messages is safe for a coordination between two CAVs impacted by different communication errors such as message losses, as it could only lead to an inefficient but not safety critical coordination. If the *accept* message with the adapted PT is not delivered, vehicle B will perform an inefficient maneuver changing its PT, resulting into vehicle A not executing its accepted DT. An explicit communication pattern with a *request* and *accept* or *reject* message seems to be a promising safe and fast solution with only one initiating requesting vehicle. A safety analysis in a coordination with three vehicles was also demonstrated, however the same approach could lead to inefficient and divergent situation if one of the cooperating vehicles accept the request and changes its PT, while the other vehicle rejects the request as the plan of all included vehicles is not confirmed to be conflict-free.

Extended Explicit Trajectory Broadcast (EETB). EETB extends ETB with a more concrete explicit coordination protocol that puts the emphasis on the negotiation phase, especially in a situation involving three or more vehicles. The approach is also based on the broadcast of trajectories. An additional set of three MCM subtypes is included: *request*, *promise* and *confirm*. Furthermore, the MCM can carry multiple trajectories in parallel, in comparison with the serial ETB approach that considers only one trajectory at a time. Figure 10 explains the protocol including numbers on the messages to indicate their temporal order in the negotiation phase.

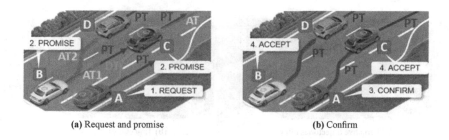

(a) Request and promise   (b) Confirm

Fig. 10. Maneuver coordination process in EETB [20].

In this situation, vehicle A requires a gap between vehicles B and C. A *request* message that can include multiple DTs is sent in order to perform the desired maneuver that is hindered by vehicles B and C. If the receiving vehicles can plan conflict-free trajectories, they can include these alternative trajectories (AT) in a *promise* message (Fig. 10a). Multiple ATs are possible too. After receiving all required messages, the requesting vehicle performs collision checking of all received trajectories, creates and sends the plan with the promised trajectories for each vehicle via a *confirm* message.

However, an additional message is required to complete the coordination. After both of the vehicles, B and C, following the received *confirm* update their PTs and accordingly broadcast a new MCM, the coordination is successful and vehicle A can perform its request after a minimum of four message intervals, given that each message is sent at a first try (Fig. 10b). There is also a certain timeout in which the requesting vehicle can abort the coordination if some of the vehicles is not able to adapt their trajectories as in the *promise* message. Different *promise* and *confirm* messages are forbidden for a certain period of time in order to prevent ambiguities with other vehicles and divergent situations that can result in contradictory trajectories between the vehicles.

Communication failures are discussed in this protocol as well. The only conflicting situation can arise if the *confirm* message is delivered to a subset of the accepting vehicles, otherwise none of the vehicles will change their maneuvers if any communication errors occur before this message. In this case, e.g. vehicle B can change its promised trajectory while vehicle C will not change its PT because it did not receive the *confirm* message. Consequently, the requesting vehicle A will not execute its request. In some situations, this can cause overhead between the movement of the accepting vehicles, but a safety critical situation will be prevented because the *promise* and *confirm* messages ensure that the vehicles can offer and take conflict-free trajectories.

Implicit Trajectory Broadcast with Cost Values (ITB-CV). An implicit coordination approach that also utilizes the trajectory based MCM is proposed in [18]. It differs from the other explicit approaches because it does not include the IDs of the vehicles. Otherwise, similarly to the other approaches, the MCM includes the basic message information, the current position and the trajectory related data. Additional cost values are added to each trajectory that express the necessity and willingness of the involved CAVs to cooperate, which contributes to the decision making system of the vehicles. The following scenario explains the characteristics of the cooperation protocol (Fig. 11).

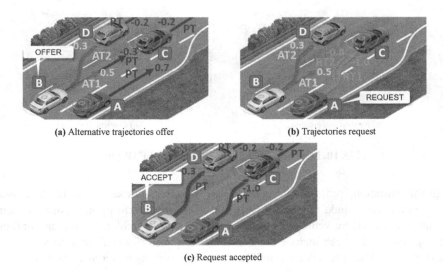

(a) Alternative trajectories offer

(b) Trajectories request

(c) Request accepted

Fig. 11. Maneuver coordination process in ITB-CV [20].

Three different types of trajectories are included: reference (PT), alternative (AT) and requested (RT) trajectory. Each CAV periodically broadcasts a PT with a cost value that represents the future planned trajectory of the vehicle and the willingness or necessity to cooperate. In the presented scenario, vehicle A shares a PT with a cost value $C = 0.7$, showing it has a necessity to cooperate because $C > 0$. Vehicle B broadcasts a PT with a cost value of -0.2, which means $C < 0$ indicating its willingness to cooperate with other vehicles. A vehicle is not interested in a cooperation when $C = 0$. In this scenario, vehicle B recognizes the need of vehicle A and broadcasts a MCM with ATs including cost values on both trajectories which represents an offer for vehicle A (Fig. 11a). These cost values are by definition higher than the reference costs because they can only be executed through a coordination between the vehicles. After receiving this message, vehicle A broadcasts a new MCM including two RTs with high willingness cost values: -1.0 and -0.8 (Fig. 11b). RT1 has the higher willingness cost value of -1.0 which is also the maximum cost value, meaning it is the most preferred trajectory of A. The accepting vehicle B can then decide on the most suitable trajectory that gives lowest total cost and accordingly adapt its new PT in a new MCM. Finally, vehicle A will be able to execute its request to successfully complete the cooperation (Fig. 11c). How the cost values can be generated is not discussed in [18].

Space-Time Reservation (STR). The space-time reservation approach [13,14,24,25] is a continuously developed and upgraded explicit coordination protocol based on a reservation of position and time constraints among the communicating vehicles. It represents a different solution that does not use the concept of periodically broadcast MCM based trajectory exchange. A reservation request is broadcast through an extended CAM message that includes an additional container with required time and position parameters. Furthermore, the aforementioned constraints are exchanged once a need for cooperation is detected in an event based manner, hence requires less message exchange with simple reservation encoding.

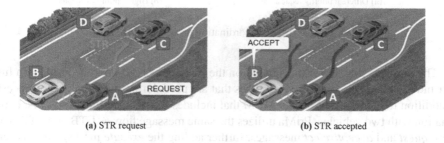

(a) STR request   (b) STR accepted

Fig. 12. Maneuver coordination process in STR [20].

In the lane merging scenario in Fig. 12, a *request* message consisting of time and position constraints is broadcast by vehicle A with the following parameters: starting position of the reservation, time interval, overall length of the area, velocity, ID of the requesting vehicle as well as a reference to the corresponding request (Fig. 12a). After receiving the request, vehicle B evaluates the constraints and sends a *commit* message (Fig. 12b) if the requested reservation area can be avoided for the defined boundaries. A *reject* message can also be broadcast to reject the request. The request can also be canceled by vehicle A. For better visibility, Fig. 12 shows the trajectories of the vehicles. However, the trajectories are not broadcast among the vehicles, only the position and time constraints.

Priority Maneuver Coordination (PriMa).   Priority Maneuver Coordination (PriMa) [19] is a trajectory broadcast approach that additionally introduces three levels of priority requests: low, medium and high. In this way, PriMa contributes to the decision making process to request and accept a maneuver coordination. Low priority request is used in common situations when the CAV wants to perform a desired maneuver in order to improve time efficiency or perform a certain maneuver earlier. Medium priority request is sent in a situation when the vehicle needs to perform a necessary maneuver which is not critical, while high priority maneuvers are requested in order to avoid a safety critical situation.

The accepting vehicles use the priority information to make a decision whether to accept or reject a request. The vehicle accepts low priority requests when a small change of its original plan is required, while the threshold for acceptance is increased for medium priority maneuvers. High priority request is accepted whenever the vehicle can plan a conflict-free trajectory.

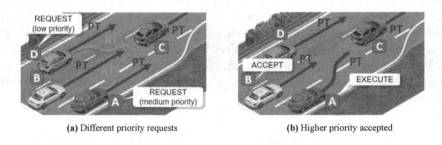

(a) Different priority requests   **(b)** Higher priority accepted

Fig. 13. Maneuver coordination process in PriMa.

The message flow in PriMa is based on the ETB and EETB approaches. PriMa further introduces additional MCM subtypes that are used during the negotiation process, in addition to the regular periodic MCM that includes the planned trajectory. In a coordination with two vehicles, PriMa utilizes the same message flow as ETB and STR with the *request* and *accept/reject* messages, further adding the *execute* message that is sent while the vehicle is performing the maneuver. Such an *execute* message is not required for the accepting vehicle, it only shows that the CAV is performing a requested maneuver. The PriMa approach and its advantage are shown in the lane merging scenario in Fig. 13. The ego vehicle A sends a medium priority *request* including its requested trajectory (RT) to vehicle B to perform the necessary lane merging maneuver. In the same moment, vehicle D sends a low priority *request* to perform lane change in the middle lane too (Fig. 13a). In such a situation without priority, vehicle B might accept the request from vehicle D, which will require vehicle A to decelerate. With the additional priority information, the requesting vehicle will always accept a higher priority request whenever it is possible to plan a conflict free trajectory. If the priority is the same, additional metrics will be used to decide which request is more suitable for the accepting vehicle. Such metrics are not discussed in [19]. After the maneuver was accepted, the requesting vehicle A performs the lane merge while broadcasting an *execute* message (Fig. 13b). After the maneuver is executed, the ego vehicle broadcasts a regular MCM.

In a coordination with three or more vehicles, PriMa uses similar message flow as EETB: *request, offer, confirm, accept/reject, execute.* In such a way PriMa uses safe and effective communication pattern in a coordination with only two vehicles as well as in a coordination involving three or more cooperating vehicles.

Furthermore, PriMa proposes a maneuver cascading approach shown in Fig. 14, that can be used in an initial coordination between two vehicles. For visualization, the temporal order of the messages is numbered. After vehicle B receives the request, it sends a further *cascading request* message to vehicle D including its RT (Fig. 14a). Vehicle B can accept the request only if vehicle D accepts the cascading request. After minimum four message exchange intervals, same as in a regular coordination with more than two vehicles, the requesting vehicle A can execute its RT by broadcasting an *execute* message (Fig. 14b). In order to prevent longer and more complicated process, the cascading maneuver is limited to one additional vehicle, e.g. vehicle D in this scenario.

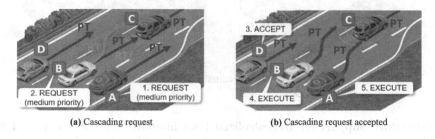

(a) Cascading request   (b) Cascading request accepted

Fig. 14. Maneuver cascading in PriMa.

Complex Vehicular Interactions Protocol (CVIP). The Complex Vehicular Interactions Protocol (CVIP) [12] is a generic explicit maneuver coordination approach consisting of complex maneuvers between arbitrary number of vehicles. Complex interactions between vehicles are defined as interactions consisting of minimum three message exchanges between two or more vehicles where at least one of those messages depends on another. CVIP uses four types of messages that are only broadcast in an event-driven manner, not periodically. The protocol is demonstrated in the following scenario shown in Fig. 15. For visualization, the figures also include the trajectories, however they are not explicitly specified in the protocol. The message containers in CVIP consist of maneuvers that can be described with functions, standardized names or trajectories.

Vehicle A broadcasts a *Cooperative Request Message* (CQM) similar to the MCM which can also have additional information depending on the scenario. After receiving the message and evaluating the information, the accepting vehicles B and C send

Cooperative Response Message (CRM) which shows their willingness to cooperate (Fig. 15a). The CRM is also similar to the MCM that includes the planned maneuver and optionally can include proposed changes. Such an iteration of CPM and CRM can be repeated until there are no changes proposed. This ensures the vehicles that all involved participants have agreed to a maneuver. Also the vehicles can send a negative response. After receiving all of the required responses, vehicle A will update the proposal accordingly and send a new CQM stating which vehicles are willing, necessary or capable to cooperate. In this situation, vehicles B and C are necessary vehicles that also showed willingness to cooperate with the CRMs, therefore vehicle A broadcasts a *Maneuver Status Message* (MSM) with the agreed maneuvers that also shows the state of the maneuver whether it is in progress, finished or cancelled. The accepting vehicles then finally perform the maneuvers broadcasting a *Maneuver Feedback Message* (MFM) as an acknowledgement that the MSM from the requesting vehicle was received, which also prevents divergent situation (Fig. 15b). Certain message timeouts and re-sending of the message can be adjusted accordingly.

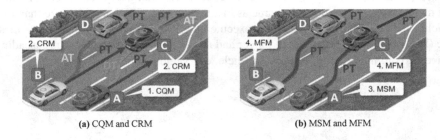

(a) CQM and CRM   (b) MSM and MFM

Fig. 15. Maneuver coordination process in CVIP.

Infrastructure Support for Decentralized Coordination. An enhancement of the MCM to consider infrastructure support is proposed in [4]. Alongside the maneuver container that includes the trajectory related data exchanged through V2V communication, an additional suggested maneuver container is proposed to be included in the MCM broadcast through V2I communication that includes advice on proposed gap between the vehicles, speed, lane and transition of control between the driver and the automated system. In specific traffic situations and transition areas, roadside unit (RSU) information can lead to a more neutral coordination between multiple vehicles in a centralized way as well as an enhanced perception, demonstrated through experiments in [26].

4   Comparison of Approaches

A comparison of the presented generic decentralized approaches for maneuver coordination using different criteria is shown in Table 1. Due to the lack of performance evaluation or incomparable results, the comparison of the approaches is rather based on their conceptual designs, as well as on an analysis of their advantages and shortcomings.

Table 1. Comparison of generic approaches for decentralized maneuver coordination.

	ETB [16,17]	EETB [29]	ITB-CV [18]	STR [13,25]	PriMa [19]	CVIP [12]
Coordination type	Explicit	Explicit	Implicit	Explicit	Explicit	Explicit
Communication type	Periodic	Periodic	Periodic	Non-periodic	Periodic	Non-periodic
Message type	MCM	MCM	MCM	CAM	MCM	(MCM)
Number of messages	2	4	4	2	2/4	4
Request method	DT[a]	DT	RT[b]	space-time	PRT[c]	RM[d]
Type of approach	Serial	Parallel	Parallel	Parallel	Parallel	Serial
Protocol ambiguities	Limited	No	Yes	Limited	No	No
Comm. errors impact	Limited	Limited	Yes	Limited	Limited	Limited
Simulation study	No	Yes	No	Yes	Yes	Yes
Experimental study	No	No	No	Yes	No	No

[a] DT = Desired Trajectory
[b] RT = Requested Trajectory
[c] PRT = Priority Requested Trajectory
[d] RM = Requested Maneuver

Coordination Type. Implicit coordination can result into protocol and communication failure ambiguities as the requesting vehicle does not have a guarantee whether the accepting vehicle is adapting its trajectory because of the given request or because of a request from another vehicle, which can especially be conflicting in a coordination with three or more vehicles. Therefore, most of the approaches are proposing explicit coordination that includes the IDs of the included vehicles and allows safer cooperation that can eliminate the protocol ambiguities and limit the impact of the communication errors.

Communication Type. Four of the presented approaches utilize the periodic broadcast of planned trajectories which can improve the prediction system of the CAVs and reduce the uncertainty in many conflicting situations, as the exchanged planned trajectories represent the best prediction about the movement of the other adjacent vehicles. However, periodic broadcast brings disadvantages with high data rate and increased possibility of channel congestion. On the other side, non-periodic broadcast in an event based manner only when there is a need for cooperation is used in the STR and CVIP approaches which significantly improves the bandwidth usage.

Message Type. Most of the approaches utilize the MCM which is also in the early standardization phase as part of a separate Maneuver Coordination Service (MCS) considering planned and desired trajectories as proposed by [16]. Such a message is shown in Fig. 16. Every MCM consists of the ITS PDU header which describes the protocol, message type and IDs; the timestamp which shows when the message was sent; and the basic container which includes the reference position and station type whether it is a vehicle or a roadside unit. For a coordination between the vehicles using V2V communication, a vehicle maneuver container is proposed that includes the dynamics of the vehicle, the planned and requested trajectories as well as some further information. Additional suggested maneuver container proposed by [4] can be sent by the infrastruc-

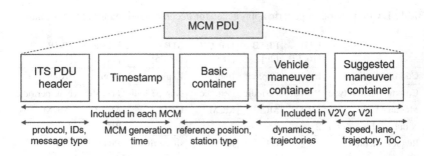

Fig. 16. Format of the Maneuver Coordination Message proposed in [16] and [4].

ture and can include various advice for the vehicles on the lane, speed, gap or transition of control (ToC). CVIP does not mention the MCS or MCM, but proposes a message with a similar content. STR is the only approach that uses an extended CAM only when a coordination is required, hence needs the lowest bandwidth in comparison with the other approaches and can be used on the already standardized Cooperative Awareness Service (CAS).

Number of Messages. Number of messages refers to the minimum number of messages that are required to complete a maneuver negotiation given that each message is successfully sent and received at a first try, without the need to be repeated. The request message is counted as a first message while the response accepting message is the final one. ETB and STR utilize two messages: *request* and *accept/reject*, which is sufficient in a situation with two vehicles. EETB requires four messages to complete a coordination which is advantageous in a situation with three or more vehicles with the additional *confirm* message. However, such a communication pattern is less efficient in a situation with two vehicles and requires longer time. PriMa uses the two message communication pattern in a coordination with two vehicles, same as ETB and STR, while utilizes similar communication pattern as proposed in EETB for a coordination with three or more vehicles, therefore using the more effective and safer way for each coordination. ITB-CV and CVIP also require at least four message intervals regardless of the number of the included vehicles, which is also less efficient in comparison with the other approaches.

Request Method. Most of the approaches use the method of a desired or requested trajectory which clearly describes the maneuvers that the requesting vehicles are willing to take. CVIP also consists of a maneuver request which can be described as a parametrized function or trajectory. A space-time reservation with position and time constraints, proposed by the STR approach, differs from the trajectory related approaches by also offering certain flexibility that the requesting vehicle can modify its planned maneuver within the reserved area. In such a way, the trajectory control errors, that can appear in the trajectory request approaches where the executed trajectory can differ from the requested one, can be considered and eliminated within the reserved area.

Type of Approach. In this context, type of approach refers to whether an approach is serial or parallel. Serial coordination approaches are the ones that can negotiate one request at a time, e.g. one trajectory at a time, while parallel approaches can send more requests with multiple requested trajectories or maneuvers. Negotiation of multiple trajectories at a time increases the probability of performing a successful and faster coordination, however the complexity of the motion planning system increases too.

Protocol Ambiguities. An implicit approach can especially cause protocol ambiguities in a coordination with three or more vehicles, or in a situation when a vehicle receives multiple requests at once. Since the implicit approach does not include the IDs of the involved vehicles in comparison with the explicit coordination, a requesting vehicle can not know whether the accepting vehicle is adapting its planned trajectory due to the given request or because of another vehicle's request. All of the explicit approaches avoid protocol ambiguities in a coordination with two vehicles, however ambiguities can arise in the ETB and STR approaches in a situation with three or more vehicles. A divergent situation can appear if one of the accepting vehicles accept the request and consequently adapts its trajectory, while the other vehicle rejects the request. In such situation, the accepting vehicles can have contradictory trajectories. EETB and PriMa include additional *promise* (*offer*) and *confirm* messages which ensure conflict-free trajectories between the included CAVs. CVIP also includes response messages from each vehicle to confirm the conflict-free plan.

Communication Errors Impact. The impact of the communication errors, in the form of communication delays or message losses, is inevitable. Due to similar reasons as the protocol ambiguities, the communication failures will have bigger effect on the implicit approach, as well as on the explicit approaches in a situation with three or more vehicles. If some communication errors occur in an explicit coordination between two vehicles, a consequence can be an inefficient maneuver for the accepting vehicle when it accepts the requested maneuver, but the *accept* message is not delivered to the requesting vehicle which consequently does not execute its request. In a coordination with three or more vehicles, the impact of the communication errors is limited in the EETB and PriMa approaches through the *promise* (*offer*) and *confirm* messages that ensure that only conflict free trajectories can be offered and taken. Similar response and status messages limit the consequences in CVIP too.

Simulation Study. Several approaches performed simulation studies. In EETB, the vehicular networking simulation framework Artery[3] was used to evaluate the loss of time by driving below the ideal speed in a highway lane merging scenario. The study showed that with the EETB approach the total time loss for the CAVs can be reduced up to 50% compared to non-communicating vehicles. PriMa also presented a proof of concept that shows the benefits of the priority maneuvers in different lane change scenarios. The STR approach is continuously further developed and is validated through simulation in diverse conflict lane change and intersections scenarios [25]. Using the space-time reservation method, the conducted tests show that this approach can effectively resolve different conflicted scenarios. In CVIP, the success rate of successfully

---

[3] https://github.com/riebl/artery.

performed maneuvers was analyzed with different packet loss probability that showed the applicability of the approach for ITS-G5 or LTE-V2X technologies.

Experiments Study. STR is the only approach that performed experiments in different lane change and intersection scenarios using connected and automated test vehicles [24, 25].

5   Research Gaps in Cooperative Maneuver Coordination

The review and analysis from the previous sections show that there are several approaches with different characteristics. In general, a V2X based maneuver coordination between CAVs consists of three phases: detection of the maneuver need, negotiation between the vehicles and execution of the agreed maneuver. Therefore, this section presents maneuver coordination related research questions (RQs) divided into three subsections that represent the following research gaps: detection and decision logic, maneuver coordination protocol and V2X communication. The detection and decision logic research gap discusses RQs related to the logic how CAVs can decide when to send a maneuver request, and accordingly when to accept or reject such a request. The maneuver coordination protocol subsection mainly discusses RQs in relation to the design of the protocol with the required communication pattern, the information included in the messages as well as the security, implementation and required metrics to evaluate the protocol. In the final subsection, the V2X communication requirements for maneuver coordination are discussed alongside advanced features of the access technologies, communication type and multi-channel operation.

5.1   Detection and Decision Logic

RQ 1: How to Decide When to Send a Maneuver Coordination Request? The analysed approaches discuss only what happens after the need for cooperation has been recognized without describing the detection process. Cooperating vehicles equipped with maneuver coordination protocol that hinder the desired maneuver need to be clearly identified in mixed traffic scenarios with connected and non-connected vehicles as scenarios with only CAVs on the road is not likely to happen in the near future. An additional information needs to be included in the request that describes why the vehicle is requesting a certain maneuver. Such a priority maneuver coordination is presented in PriMa that differentiates between desired, necessary and critical maneuvers with low, medium and high priority requests, respectively. ITB-CV proposes cost values on each trajectory that express the necessity or willingness to cooperate. However, the logic how to differentiate between the three levels of priority or cost values is still not exactly defined and will vary in different traffic situations. To make a decision, different metrics are required in relation to time efficiency and safety critical situations.

RQ 2: How to Decide When to Accept a Maneuver Coordination Request? A received maneuver request needs to be correctly assessed by the potential accepting vehicles. This mostly represents a subjective decision when the receiving vehicle needs an evaluation of the request whether it is feasible to accept it and at what cost. The best solution for maneuver coordination is the one that is beneficial for all of the involved vehicles. However, in most of the situations the potential accepting vehicles will be disadvantaged, e.g. to decelerate for a certain period of time or to drive below the desired speed. Different types of cooperative and uncooperative behaviors are defined in [6] based on a total utility function. Different metrics and cost functions considering loss of time, required speed, deceleration or safety critical consequences can be utilized to make such a decision. In PriMa, based on the priority of the request, different thresholds are proposed for different priority requests. However, a high priority request which represents a critical maneuver should be accepted whenever the accepting vehicles can plan a conflict-free trajectory with the surrounding vehicles. Different incentives could also be used that could benefit the accepting vehicles in future coordination situations.

5.2 Maneuver Coordination Protocol

RQ 3: What Kind of Message Type and Format Will Be Used? A new dedicated Maneuver Coordination Message (MCM) for the exchange of trajectory-related data using V2V communication is proposed in most of the existing approaches (Fig. 16), which is also in the early stage of a standardization as a part of a new Maneuver Coordination Service [11]. A suggested maneuver container from the infrastructure is also considered to be part of the MCM format to include V2I communication in order to enhance the coordination process. Different MCM subtypes need to be defined for different situations. The data carried by the maneuver container will be defined by the required standardized format of trajectory representation which has to be application-independent. A cooperation process including in-accurate trajectory related data can lead to conflicted negotiation outcome and potentially a safety-critical situation for the involved vehicles. Therefore, the trajectory and vehicle dynamics data have to be correctly interpreted at both, the requesting and accepting vehicles.

RQ 4: How to Include Additional Use Case-specific Information? Additional information might be required for a specific use case in order to start or complete a maneuver coordination. A generic protocol needs to consider an addition of use-case specific information in the MCM or special use-case specific MCM subtypes. Such type of a specific message can include additional information about the vehicles required for e.g. the management of a platoon or convoy, or to perform any of the presented use cases.

RQ 5: What Kind of Message Generation Rules Can Be Applied? The message generation rules play important role on the data traffic to prevent congestion on the communication channel as they define the rules when and which vehicle should send a message. Periodic broadcast is proposed in most of the approaches, but the exact interval is not defined. Dynamic generation rules that depend on the vehicle dynamics, i.e., speed, heading or acceleration, are applied for CAM and CPM and could also be considered for the MCMs.

RQ 6: How Many Messages Are Required to Complete a Coordination? In order to perform a fast, safe, unambiguous and efficient coordination, certain amount of negotiation messages are required for different coordination situations between two and more than two vehicles. Request and acceptance messages are required for each coordination, while additional final message such as the *confirm* message ensures that the coordination will be executed as planned in a coordination involving three or more CAVs. Specific situations require additional messages that describe the status of the coordination whether a maneuver was canceled, aborted or executed.

RQ 7: How Many Vehicles Can Be Involved in a Coordination? Coordination among two vehicles appears to be the most promising way for an implicit or explicit coordination considering the communication errors, complexity and reduced probability of successful cooperation involving a group of three or more vehicles. The current approaches do not define an upper bound on the cooperating vehicles. Further research is required to analyze the scalability of the coordination and the impact on the number of included vehicles.

RQ 8: Is Maneuver Cascading Feasible? Maneuver cascading represents a situation where a vehicle, in order to accept an incoming request, needs to send a request itself to another vehicle. Most of the approaches avoid such a complex maneuver that can lead to a successful maneuver coordination process in many situations that initially involve two vehicles, however the negotiation process can be significantly prolonged as well. PriMa presents a cascading approach that limits the coordination to one additional vehicle and requires minimum four message intervals to complete the coordination. Further research is required to show the safety and effectiveness of such maneuver.

RQ 9: Are Data Security and Privacy Guaranteed? Safety-critical application such as maneuver coordination needs to guarantee a data security by applying digital signatures and certificates that provide integrity, authentication and non-repudation of the exchanged V2X messages. A guarantee for privacy is expected to rely on short-living and changing pseudonyms. However for a safety-critical application, such pseudonyms must not be changed during the negotiated maneuver.

RQ 10: How to Implement, Test and Evaluate the Maneuver Coordination Protocol? The maneuver coordination protocol that relies on MCMs needs to be implemented with the motion planning and control system of a CAV in order to exchange accurate trajectory related data. The test framework needs to include the V2X communication, the dynamics and the decision making system of the vehicle. Global metrics related to the safety and efficiency of the protocol need to be defined in different traffic scenarios in order to create and validate a safe and efficient protocol that eliminates any additional safety risks. The communication errors impact on the coordination need to be further investigated too. An analysis on the impact of the coordination on the global traffic is required to show whether the coordination can only provide benefits to the requesting vehicle or can improve the traffic flow globally too.

5.3   V2X Communication

RQ 11: What Are the Communication Requirements for a Maneuver Coordination Application? The maneuver coordination represents a safety-critical application that requires very high reliability ($>99\%$) and very low latency (~ 10 ms). The maximum expected data rate per vehicle for an emergency collision avoidance situation is

1.3 Mb/s for a trajectory that is periodically transmitted every 10 ms, e.g. for a trajectory of 5 s length with 12 B per coordinate and 10 ms resolution [2]. These requirements need to be considered when developing such a protocol. The V2X communication applications that are developed so far have relaxed requirements as they do not represent safety-critical applications in comparison with maneuver coordination.

RQ 12: Which Advanced Features of the Underlying Access Technology Can Be Further Exploited? Both access technologies, WLAN-V2X and Cellular-V2X, have been widely studied and are continuously developed to provide more benefits for the potential safety applications [23]. Specific advanced features from the respective access technologies can improve the maneuver coordination performance. An example of such advanced Cellular V2X features is the bounded latency of Sensing-based Semi-Persistent Scheduling (SB-SPS) in network scenarios with high load. Further research is required to investigate whether the evolution of the access technologies, including 802.11bd and 5G NR V2X, can bring additional benefits for the latency or reliability of the V2X message exchange.

RQ 13: What Kind of Communication Type Should Be Used? So far all approaches propose a broadcast communication between the CAVs. Single-hop broadcast or multi-hop broadcast within a defined geographical area are primarily used for V2X communication. The feedback implosion in broadcast communication prevents applying acknowledgements and re-transmissions and therefore does not provide reliable message exchange. Since maneuver coordination mainly involves only a small amount of vehicles located in direct neighborhood, other communication types such as small group multicast with explicit acknowledgement that increases the reliability could be analyzed too.

RQ 14: Will Multi-channel Operation Be Necessary? With the increase of the traffic density, the higher number of exchanged V2X messages between the vehicles can lead to increased channel load that can cause consequences such as channel congestion, higher packet error rates, lower reliability and longer latency. In order to avoid these consequences, an evaluation is required to determine whether in some traffic situations the MCM could be integrated on the same channel with the CAM and CPM messages or a multi-channel operation, where each service is operated on a separate channel, would be a better solution.

6 Conclusion

Cooperative maneuver coordination can be enabled by V2X communication to achieve a safer, more comfortable and efficient driving for CAVs. Many publications have been presented that consider coordination for a specific use case. The most recent state-of-the art research trend introduces generic coordination proposals that offer the possibility to solve different traffic situations using a scenario-independent solution. Such approaches are presented and compared in this paper. The paper also presented use cases where maneuver coordination is expected to bring benefits such as C-ACC, cooperative lane changing, lane merging, overtaking, cooperative intersection as well as infrastructure-controlled cooperative driving.

This paper classifies the existing generic approaches into six categories: Explicit Trajectory Broadcast (ETB), Extended Explicit Trajectory Broadcast (EETB), Implicit Trajectory Broadcast with Cost Values (ITB-CV), Space-Time Reservation (STR), Priority Maneuver Coordination (PriMa) and Complex Vehicular Interactions Protocol (CVIP). Each approach is analyzed and described for a similar lane merging scenario that shows their commonalities and differences. A comparison of the concept designs of each approach is given that opens further discussion regarding their characteristics, as well as benefits of each coordination proposal. The performed analysis shows that mainly explicit maneuver negotiation is proposed based on a periodic broadcast of Maneuver Coordination Messages (MCMs). Main part of the MCM is the trajectory related data in the form of planned and requested trajectories. Additionally, requests with time and position constraints that significantly differ from the trajectory broadcast approaches, are proposed and successfully implemented in the STR approach. The comparison of the approaches shows that two messages in the form of request and accept messages can be sufficient for a coordination between two vehicles. However, in order to avoid protocol ambiguities and divergent situation, coordination with more than two involved CAVs will require additional confirm messages that ensure each vehicle will take a conflict-free trajectory. Additional message information might also be required for specific use case situations. The analysis also shows that explicit maneuver negotiation and broadcast of maneuver intentions and requests using V2X communication can facilitate maneuver coordination that has the potential to be safe and efficient. However, further research is needed to evaluate the impact of the presented approaches on the traffic safety and efficiency, as well as the impact of the communication errors.

In the paper, challenges in the form of research questions were highlighted and future research directions discussed, divided into three research gaps: detection and decision logic, maneuver coordination protocol and V2X communication. The discussion in the first research gap is related to the logic how the CAVs can decide when to request and when to accept or reject a maneuver coordination. An additional information will be required that shows the necessity of each coordination request. Such information that contributes to the decision making process of the vehicles is proposed in the form of cost values in ITB-CV or priority maneuvers in PriMa. In the maneuver coordination protocol subsection, the designs of the protocols are discussed mainly related to the communication pattern in a coordination situation with two or more vehicles, the information included in the messages, as well as research questions related to the security, implementation and evaluation of the protocols. Well-defined metrics for traffic safety and efficiency should be considered to assess the protocol performance as well as the impact on the global traffic flow. The introduction of additional safety risks needs to be eliminated. In the final research gap related to the V2X communication, a discussion is introduced in relation to the V2X communication requirements, advanced features of the access technologies, the required communication type as well as a potential multi-channel operation with the CAM and CPM messages that can help to avoid congestion of the communication channel. A safety-critical application such as maneuver coordination requires very high reliability and very low latency that need to be taken in consideration in the design of the protocol.

The key research question remains: *How to design a use case-independent, reliable and low-latency protocol for safe, fast, unambiguous and efficient maneuver coordination?*

Acknowledgements. This work was gratefully supported by the German Science Foundation (DFG) by project KOALA 2 under number 273374642 within the priority program Cooperatively Interacting Automobiles (CoIn-Car, SPP 1835). The scenario figures in the paper were created with the illustration toolkit from the C2C-CC (URL: https://www.car-2-car.org).

References

1. Bevly, D., et al.: Lane change and merge maneuvers for connected and automated vehicles: a survey. IEEE Trans. Intell. Veh. **1**(1), 105–120 (2016). https://doi.org/10.1109/TIV.2015.2503342
2. Boban, M., Kousaridas, A., Manolakis, K., Eichinger, J., Xu, W.: Connected roads of the future: use cases, requirements, and design considerations for vehicle-to-everything communications. IEEE Veh. Technol. Mag. **13**(3), 110–123 (2018)
3. Chen, L., Englund, C.: Cooperative intersection management: a survey. IEEE Trans. Intell. Transp. Syst. **17**(2), 570–586 (2016). https://doi.org/10.1109/TITS.2015.2471812
4. Correa, A., et al.: Infrastructure support for cooperative maneuvers in connected and automated driving. In: IEEE Intelligent Vehicles Symposium (IV), pp. 20–25 (2019). https://doi.org/10.1109/IVS.2019.8814044
5. Dey, K.C., et al.: A review of communication, driver characteristics, and controls aspects of Cooperative Adaptive Cruise Control (CACC). IEEE Trans. Intell. Transp. Syst. **17**(2), 491–509 (2016). https://doi.org/10.1109/TITS.2015.2483063
6. Düring, M., Pascheka, P.: Cooperative decentralized decision making for conflict resolution among autonomous agents. In: IEEE International Symposium on Innovations in Intelligent Systems and Applications (INISTA), pp. 154–161 (2014). https://doi.org/10.1109/INISTA.2014.6873612
7. ETSI EN 302 637-2 V1.4.1: Intelligent Transport Systems (ITS); Vehicular Communications; Basic Set of Applications; Part 2: Specification of Cooperative Awareness Basic Service (2019)
8. ETSI EN 302 637-3 V1.3.1: ITS; Vehicular Communications; Basic Set of Applications; Part 3: Specifications of Decentralized Environmental Notification Basic Service (2019)
9. ETSI TR 103 301 V1.3.1: ITS; Vehicular Communications; Basic Set of Applications; Facilities layer protocols and communication requirements for infrastructure services (2020)
10. ETSI TR 103 562 V2.1.1: ITS; Vehicular Communications; Basic Set of Applications; Analysis of the Collective Perception Service (CPS); Release 2 (2019)
11. ETSI TR 103 578 V0.0.6 (Draft): Intelligent Transport Systems (ITS); Vehicular Communication; Informative Report for the Maneuver Coordination Service (2021)
12. Häfner, B., et al.: CVIP: a protocol for complex interactions among connected vehicles. In: IEEE Intelligent Vehicles Symposium, pp. 510–515 (2020). https://doi.org/10.1109/IV47402.2020.9304556
13. Heß, D., et al.: Fast maneuver planning for cooperative automated vehicles. In: IEEE International Conference on Intelligent Transportation Systems (ITSC), pp. 1625–1632 (2018). https://doi.org/10.1109/ITSC.2018.8569791
14. Heß, D., Lattarulo, R., Pérez, J., Hesse, T., Köster, F.: Negotiation of cooperative maneuvers for automated vehicles: experimental results. In: IEEE Intelligent Transportation Systems Conference (ITSC), pp. 1545–1551 (2019). https://doi.org/10.1109/ITSC.2019.8917464

15. Hobert, L., et al.: Enhancements of V2X communication in support of cooperative autonomous driving. IEEE Commun. Mag. **53**(12), 64–70 (2015). https://doi.org/10.1109/MCOM.2015.7355568
16. Lehmann, B., Günther, H., Wolf, L.: A generic approach towards maneuver coordination for automated vehicles. In: IEEE International Conference on Intelligent Transportation Systems (ITSC), pp. 3333–3339 (2018). https://doi.org/10.1109/ITSC.2018.8569442
17. Lehmann, B., Wolf, L.: Safety analysis of a maneuver coordination protocol. In: IEEE Vehicular Networking Conference (VNC), p. 8 (2020). https://doi.org/10.1109/VNC51378.2020.9318359
18. Llatser, I., Michalke, T., Dolgov, M., Wildschütte, F., Fuchs, H.: Cooperative automated driving use cases for 5G V2X communication. In: IEEE 2nd 5G World Forum, pp. 120–125 (2019). https://doi.org/10.1109/5GWF.2019.8911628
19. Maksimovski, D., Facchi, C., Festag, A.: Priority maneuver (PriMa) coordination for connected and automated vehicles. In: 2021 IEEE International Intelligent Transportation Systems Conference (ITSC), pp. 1083–1089 (2021). https://doi.org/10.1109/ITSC48978.2021.9564923
20. Maksimovski, D., Festag, A., Facchi, C.: A survey on decentralized cooperative maneuver coordination for connected and automated vehicles. In: Conference on Vehicle Technology and Intelligent Transport Systems (VEHITS), pp. 100–111. SciTePress (2021). https://doi.org/10.5220/0010442501000111
21. Marjovi, A., Vasic, M., Lemaitre, J., Martinoli, A.: Distributed graph-based convoy control for networked intelligent vehicles. In: IEEE Intelligent Vehicles Symposium (IV), pp. 138–143 (2015). https://doi.org/10.1109/IVS.2015.7225676
22. Molina-Masegosa, R., Gozalvez, J.: LTE-V for sidelink 5G V2X vehicular communications: a new 5G technology for short-range vehicle-to-everything communications. In: IEEE Vehicular Technology Magazine, pp. 30–39 (2017). https://doi.org/10.1109/MVT.2017.2752798
23. Naik, G., Choudhury, B., Park, J.M.: IEEE 802.11bd & 5G NR V2X: evolution of radio access technologies for V2X communications. IEEE Access **7**, 70169–70184 (2019). https://doi.org/10.1109/ACCESS.2019.2919489
24. Nichting, M., Heß, D., Schindler, J., Hesse, T., Köster, F.: Explicit negotiation method for cooperative automated vehicles. In: IEEE International Conference on Vehicular Electronics and Safety (ICVES), p. 7 (2019). https://doi.org/10.1109/ICVES.2019.8906401
25. Nichting, M., Heß, D., Schindler, J., Hesse, T., Köster, F.: Space time reservation procedure (STRP) for V2X-based maneuver coordination of cooperative automated vehicles in diverse conflict scenarios. In: 2020 IEEE Intelligent Vehicles Symposium (IV), pp. 502–509 (2020). https://doi.org/10.1109/IV47402.2020.9304769
26. Schindler, J., Coll-Perales, B., Zhang, X., Rondinone, M., Thandavarayan, G.: Infrastructure-supported cooperative automated driving in transition areas. In: IEEE Vehicular Networking Conference (VNC), p. 8 (2020). https://doi.org/10.1109/VNC51378.2020.9318392
27. Sjöberg, K., Andres, P., Buburuzan, T., Brakemeier, A.: Cooperative intelligent transport systems in Europe: current deployment status and outlook. IEEE Veh. Technol. Mag. **12**(2), 89–97 (2017). https://doi.org/10.1109/MVT.2017.2670018
28. Vukadinovic, V., et al.: 3GPP C-V2X and IEEE 802.11p for vehicle-to-vehicle communications in highway platooning scenarios. Ad Hoc Netw. **74**, 17–29 (2018). https://doi.org/10.1016/j.adhoc.2018.03.004
29. Xu, W., Willecke, A., Wegner, M., Wolf, L., Kapitza, R.: Autonomous maneuver coordination via vehicular communication. In: IEEE/IFIP International Conference on Dependable Systems and Networks Workshops (DSN-W), pp. 70–77 (2019). https://doi.org/10.1109/DSN-W.2019.00022

Free-Flow Speed Profile Prediction for Tangent Segments on Urban Roads

Yasmany García-Ramírez[(✉)] [iD], Luis Paladines [iD], Christian Verdesoto [iD],
and Patricio Torres [iD]

Universidad Técnica Particular de Loja, San Cayetano Alto, Loja, Ecuador
ydgarcia1@utpl.edu.ec

Abstract. The free-flow speed profile is one of the essential elements in the design
and operation of the roads. The speed profile is employed to improve road design,
traffic emissions models, fuel consumptions models, evaluate the consistency,
among others. Speed profiles are built with speed, acceleration, and deceleration
models. Therefore, understanding how different factors affect speed, acceleration,
and deceleration is a critical research question. Many studies have focused on
rural roads and only a few on urban roads. In urban environments, studies did
not yet reach conclusive results. This research attempted to address these limitations by developing speed, acceleration, and deceleration models in urban tangents
under free-flow conditions in the city of Loja, Ecuador. Three different tangents
were selected: before stop-controlled intersections, before signal-controlled intersections, and before roundabout intersections. Speeds of light vehicles, equipped
with GPS, were collected in 13 tangents with 45 drivers. Geometric and operation characteristics were also collected: geometric elements of the street, street
environment, driver, and vehicle-related. Forty-five speed, acceleration, and deceleration regression models were calibrated and validated. This research expands
the knowledge of the most influential variables on speed in various urban settings,
offering useful information for city planners and designers.

Keywords: Free-flow speed profile · Speed models · Acceleration and
deceleration models · Urban tangents

1 Introduction

The free-flow, operating, or 85th percentile speed profile is one of the elements that
improve the design and operation of streets and highways. This profile allows determining traffic emissions [1], fuel consumption [2], evaluating consistency [3], among
others. The speed profile can be used during the highway project or in its operation.
When the road is already in operation, speed is collected on-site, and in projects, it
must be calculated indirectly using prediction models. These models must find the relationship between speed, acceleration, and deceleration with the characteristics related
to the driving. This relationship is a critical research question and is complicated to
answer, so the studies have not yet reached conclusive results. Answering this question

© Springer Nature Switzerland AG 2022
C. Klein et al. (Eds.): SMARTGREENS 2021/ VEHITS 2021, CCIS 1612, pp. 371–391, 2022.
https://doi.org/10.1007/978-3-031-17098-0_19

also would help controlling vehicle speed [4–7]. In general, five parameters influencing speed, acceleration, and deceleration in free-flow conditions: driver, vehicle, roadway, environment, traffic operation and control [8].

Driver characteristics impact their vehicle speed choice, such as personality [7, 9, 10], age [11–14], gender [14], driving experience [14], speeding intention [15], among others [16–19]. Speed choice also is influenced by the vehicle characteristics, such as the age of the vehicle [7], vehicle class [7, 16, 20, 21], or vehicle length [22]. Also, roadway impacts on the speed choice, such as number of lanes [16, 23, 24], roadway width [23, 25], lane width [14, 25, 26], length of the street [16, 23], road grade [27], road surface condition [8, 16, 24], or pavement markings [27, 28]. Environment also plays an important role on the driver speed choice, specially, access density [16], roadside objects density [16, 23, 29], parking presence [7, 16, 24], crash barriers [29], bus stop presence [29], adjacent land uses [7, 16, 22], lighting conditions [30–32] weather conditions [33, 34], day of the week [24, 33]. On the other hand, traffic operation and control could also affect speed choice, for instance, the speed limits [14, 35] or the posted speed [36], speed enforcement system [37], speed cameras [36], photo-radar presence [38]. Despite the effort to build prediction models with these parameters, the results have been mixed. Furthermore, little research focused on urban streets that are complex to study.

Therefore, the present study aims to analyze the relationship between various parameters that affect the choice of speed, acceleration, and deceleration in free-flow conditions. Urban tangents were analyzed in three types of intersections: stop-controlled, signal-controlled, and roundabouts. Preliminary results of this study on signalized intersections can explore it in [39] and free-flow speeds [40]. The article is organized as follows: materials y methods, pattern analysis, results, and conclusions. The materials and methods sections describe the sample size, measurement site, equipment, and driver selection. Also, it details the data collection and processing. Then the pattern analysis is shown, which evaluates the parameters and their influence on the variables of speed, acceleration, and deceleration. Subsequently, in the result section, the calibration of the prediction models and their respective validation are shown. And finally, the principal conclusions are presented.

2 Materials and Methods

2.1 Sample Size

Equation 1 [41] allowed to calculate the study sample size. A standard deviation of 13 km/h [42] and an error of 5 km/h were assumed. With a confidence level of 95% (K = 1.96) and a value of U = 1.04 (for operating speed), the minimum number of observations in every tangent was 40. Then, 45 observations were collected in this study, thereby reducing the error or the confidence level of the results is increased.

$$n = \frac{K^2 \times \sigma^2 \times \left(2 + U^2\right)}{2 \times el^2} \tag{1}$$

where: n = sample size, K = constant based on the chosen confidence level, σ = standard deviation, U = normal deviation corresponding to the desired speed percentile, el = precision or maximum permissible error.

2.2 Road Test Section

The road test sections had to have grades less than 3%, have pavement in good condition, and a maximum speed limit of 60 km/h. Thus, thirty-four urban streets were selected in the city of Loja (Ecuador). Of these 34 sections, 13 were tangents before stop-controlled intersections, 12 were tangents before signal-controlled intersections, and 9 were tangents before roundabout intersections. Figure 1. Shows the typical configuration of these intersections. In the first intersections, the tangent lengths were between 47–226 m, up to 2 traffic lanes, and the roadway width was between 7 to 9 m, and one-way or two-way direction. In signal-controlled intersections, the length of the tangents had 94 to 121 m, up to 3 lanes, the roadway width between 7 to 10 m, and both directions. In the roundabouts, the tangent lengths were between 63–830 m, up to 3 traffic lanes, the roadway width had seven up to 13 m. Additionally, the length traveled within the circle was between 17–118 m, the internal diameter was between 11.5 to 25 m, the external diameter was between 26–61 m, the width of entrance and exit of the roundabout was between 7–11 m, and the width of the road within the roundabout was between 9 to 14 m.

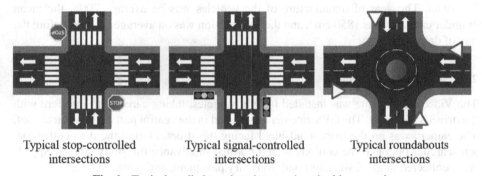

| Typical stop-controlled intersections | Typical signal-controlled intersections | Typical roundabouts intersections |

Fig. 1. Typical studied two-lane intersections in this research.

2.3 Research Instruments

Two types of instruments were used for data collection: traditional and GPS-based. The traditional tools (such as tape measure, paper, pencil) were used to measure the width of the lane, distance to fixed objects, among others. The GPS-based instrument was employed to measure the speed, acceleration, and deceleration of the vehicle. However, it was also used to estimate the length of the tangent. In addition, the GPS equipment has an integrated camera helping to count the number of trees, number of power poles, and others. The GPS equipment, called Video VBOX Lite, was installed inside each driver's vehicle. It has an accuracy of 0.02 km/h in speed and 0.05% in the traveled distance. This equipment has previously been used for speed studies.

2.4 Driver Selection

The participants were drivers who have a valid driver's license, have a light vehicle, and have driven regularly in the last two months. Forty-five drivers participated in this study, of which twenty-three were men. The main requirement was that drivers had to have their light vehicles, to eliminate the effect of out of habit.

2.5 Driver and Car Data Collection

After driving the circuit, the drivers answered two principal surveys: MDSI-S [43] to estimate their personality traits and ZKPQ-50-cc [44] to estimate their driving style. The ZQPK-50-cc survey has 50 questions related to the five traits of personality: aggression - hostility, impulsive sensation seeking, neuroticism - anxiety, sociability, and activity. MDSI-S survey (41 questions) estimates the driving style that prevails in the driver: risky and high-velocity style, dissociative style, angry style, careful and patient style, anxious style, or distress reduction style.

Additionally, drivers answered another survey about their characteristics and their vehicles. Thus, drivers had an average age of 30.5 years and a driving experience of 9.3 years. The year of manufacture of the vehicles was on average 2008, the mean cylinder capacity was 1850 cm^3, and the last revision was on average 52 days before the day of data collection.

2.6 Speed Data Collection

The Video VBOX Lite was installed in light vehicles, taking care not to interfere with the driver's visibility. The GPS antenna was placed in the central part of the vehicle roof. The camera was on the front windshield facing the street. During the data collection, a researcher operated the equipment and notified in advance the study streets. Speeds were collected in good weather conditions, dry pavement, and during daylight.

2.7 Data Processing

The position, distance traveled, and speed were exported every second from the data collected by the Video VBOX Lite. The profiles that were not in free-flow were eliminated, as shown in Fig. 2. In tangents before stop-controlled intersections, there were 21 free-flow profiles for each section and 423 speed profiles in total. In the signal-controlled intersections, 67 profiles in free-flow condition were in a green light, 45 in red, and 13 in amber. On the other hand, the free-flow speed profiles in tangents before roundabout intersections were 90, while inside the roundabout were 125.

It calculated in each street the operating speed, mean free-flow speed, and the standard deviation of free-flow speed in the middle of the tangent. Acceleration and deceleration were estimated based on the recorded speeds data by Eq. (2). The 85th percentile of the acceleration and deceleration, their mean values, and their standard deviations were estimated by using the individual results from Eq. (2).

$$a = \frac{V_f^2 - V_i^2}{25.92 \times d_{i,i-1}} \tag{2}$$

where: a = acceleration or deceleration in m/s², V_f = final speed in km/h, V_i = initial speed in km/h, $d_{i, i-1}$ = distance between points "i" and "i-1" in m.

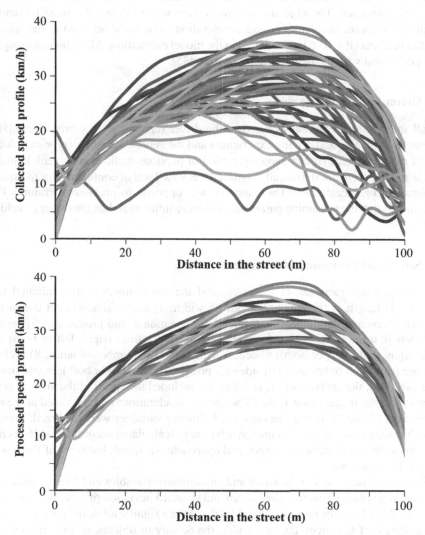

Fig. 2. Example of speed profiles recorded and processed for a street on free-flow condition.

Regarding the results of the ZQPK-50-cc and MDSI-S surveys, most participants had predominant traits such as impulsive sensation-seeking (44.4%) and activity (42.2%). Most drivers were careful and patient style (53.3%) or risky and high-velocity style (26.7%).

3 Pattern Analysis

In this section, a correlation analysis was performed using the independent and the dependent variables. The objective of this section was to detect the most influential variables on speed, acceleration, and deceleration. The variables with a statistically significant effect ($P < 0.05$) will be used in the model calibration. All statistical analyzes were performed with the help of the R program [45].

3.1 Driver and Car Variables

For all intersections, variables related to the driver (driving style scores, personality trait scores, sex, age, and driving experience) and the vehicle variables (type of vehicle, year of manufacture, cylinder capacity, period of previous maintenance, vehicle make, vehicle model) were not statistically significant at 95% level of confidence for the speed, acceleration, or deceleration. This outcome was opposite to previous literature. This result means that the remaining parameters are more influential than the driver or vehicle itself.

3.2 Street and Environmental Variables

Nine independent variables of the street and the environment were evaluated (see Table 1): 1) length of the street, 2) roadway width, 3) lane width, 4) land use in five categories: commercial, industrial, residential, recreational, and productive; 5) density of objects in three categories: poles (right, left or both), trees (right, left or both) and traffic signs (right, left or both); 6) access density; 7) the number of lanes; 8) parking presence (right, left or both) and 9) sidewalk presence (right, left or both). In addition to those variables, the analysis of the acceleration included the speed of the vehicle at the beginning of the tangent (see Table 2), while the decelerations had the speed at the end of the street (Table 3). In roundabouts, the following variables were analyzed: internal circle diameter, external circle diameter, drive curve (calculated according to [46]), entry roadway width, entry deviation angle, and approach/exit speed, but none of them were statistically significant.

Regarding the results of the street and environment variables and their influence on the operating speed, mean free-flow speed and standard deviation of free-flow speed are shown in Table 1. In this table, the variables that have a significant statistical relationship are the length of the street, the lane width, the density of objects, and the presence of parking. The analyzed categories of land use were not statistically significant. A similar outcome in previous investigations [7, 23]. In the case of no predictor variables, for example, mean free-flow speed in a green light, the models or equations will be constant or fixed values.

Table 1. Results of the statistically significant relationship between street and environment variables with operating speed, mean free-flow speed, and standard deviation of free-flow speed.

Tangents before		Independent variables*									
		Vehicle Speed	Length of the street (m)	Roadway width (m)	Lane width (m)	Land use	Objects density (n°/100 m)	Access density (n°/100 m)	Number of lanes	Parking presence	Sidewalk presence
Stop-controlled intersections		V_{85} ■								■	
		V_{AVG}									
		V_{SD}									
Signal-controlled intersections	Green light	V_{85}			■						
		V_{AVG}									
		V_{SD}									
	Red light	V_{85}						■			
		V_{AVG}									
		V_{SD}									
	Amber light	V_{85}									
		V_{AVG}									
		V_{SD}									
Roundabouts intersections		V_{85} ■									
		V_{AVG}									
		V_{SD}									

*the highlighted box means the statistical relationship between the variables at 95% of the confidence level.

v_{85}: operating speed, v_{AVG}: mean free-flow speed, v_{SD}: free-flow speed standard deviation.

The statistical relationships between the 85th percentile of the acceleration, the mean acceleration in free-flow, and the standard deviation of the acceleration in free-flow with the variables of the street and the environment are shown in Table 2. Most independent variables were statistically significant with at least one or more dependent variables, except the number of lanes. Table 2 also shows that the standard deviation of the acceleration in free-flow, the accelerations in amber light, and the standard deviation in tangents before roundabouts intersections did not have any statistically significant relationship.

Table 2. Results of the statistical relationship between the street and environment variables with the 85th percentile of acceleration, mean acceleration in free-flow, and standard deviation of acceleration in free-flow.

Tangents before			Vehicle Speed	Independent variables*									
				Length of the street (m)	Roadway width (m)	Lane width (m)	Land use	Access density (n°/100 m)	Objects density (n°/100 m)	Number of lanes	Parking presence	Sidewalk presence	Initial speed (km/h)
Stop-controlled intersections		a_{85}		▓			▓				▓		
		a_{AVG}											
		a_{SD}											
Signal-controlled intersections	Green light	a_{85}				▓			▓				
		a_{AVG}											▓
		a_{SD}											
	Red light	a_{85}											▓
		a_{AVG}											
		a_{SD}											
	Amber light	a_{85}											
		a_{AVG}											
		a_{SD}											
Roundabouts intersections		a_{85}											▓
		a_{AVG}											
		a_{SD}											

*the highlighted box means the statistical relationship between the variables at 95% of the confidence level.

a_{85}: 85th percentile acceleration, a_{AVG}: mean free-flow acceleration, a_{SD}: free-flow acceleration standard deviation.

The statistical relationships between the 85th percentile of the deceleration, the mean deceleration of free-flow, and the standard deviation of the deceleration in free-flow with the variables of the street and the environment are shown in Table 3. The independent variables that were not predictors of any deceleration values were: roadway width, land use, access density, and parking presence. It is possible that object density close to the street only affects the drivers 'choice of' lateral position [29]. Likewise, other researchers also found no statistical relationship between the parking presence and speed [25].

Table 3. Results of the statistical relationship of the street and environment variables with the 85th percentile of the deceleration, mean deceleration in free-flow, and standard deviation of the deceleration in free-flow.

Tangents before		Vehicle Speed	Length of the street (m)	Roadway width (m)	Lane width (m)	Land use	Objects density (n°/100 m)	Access density (n°/100 m)	Number of lanes	Parking presence	Sidewalk presence	Final speed (km/h)
Stop-controlled intersections	d_{85}	■							■			■
	d_{AVG}				■							■
	d_{SD}											■
Signal-controlled intersections — Green light	d_{85}											
	d_{AVG}								■			
	d_{SD}											
Signal-controlled intersections — Red light	d_{85}										■	
	d_{AVG}											
	d_{SD}		■									
Signal-controlled intersections — Amber light	d_{85}											
	d_{AVG}											
	d_{SD}											
Roundabouts intersections	d_{85}						■					
	d_{AVG}											
	d_{SD}											

**the highlighted box means the statistical relationship between the variables at 95% of the confidence level.

d_{85}: 85th percentile deceleration, d_{AVG}: mean free-flow deceleration, d_{SD}: free-flow deceleration standard deviation.

4   Results

Then it calibrated the speed, acceleration, and deceleration models based on the most influential variables detected in Tables 1, 2, 3. For the calibration, a linear regression analysis was performed with a level of confidence of 95%. When there was no statistically significant variable, fixed values were calculated. After calibration, the models were validated with collected data in other streets with similar characteristics to the initial ones. This validation was carried out by analyzing the prediction errors.

4.1 Calibration Models

Tangents before Stop-Controlled Intersections. The speed, acceleration, and deceleration models were calibrated based on the variables detected in Tables 1, 2, 3. Not all the variables were statistically significant in the global model, despite being individually significant. So, the most influential variables were the length of the street, the initial, and the final speed (See Eqs. 3–11). These equations are coherent with what happens in actual driving. For example, in long tangents, drivers have more freedom to choose their speed, and possibly they decide to speed up; and occur the opposite in short tangents. With high initial speeds, drivers have low accelerations since they are approaching the desired speed or a high velocity for the tangent. Likewise, it is coherent that the deceleration is related to the final speed of the maneuver since it is the speed at which drivers wish to reach when they arrive at the intersection.

Proposed Models for Tangents Before Stop-Controlled Intersections.

- Speed in the center of the tangent. Application range: 47–226 m. R^2 adjusted: 0.94, 0.95, 0.79, respectively.

$$v_{85} = 22.4 + 0.114\,L \tag{3}$$

$$v_{AVG} = 20.1 + 0.105\,L \tag{4}$$

$$v_{SD} = 1.99 + 0.0146\,L \tag{5}$$

where: v_{85} = operating speed in km/h, v_{AVG} = mean free-flow speed in km/h, v_{SD} = free-flow speed standard deviation in km/h, L = length of the street in m, R^2 adjusted = adjusted coefficient of determination.
- Acceleration at the start of the tangent. Application range: 0–45 km/h. R^2 adjusted: 0.86, 0.93, 0.65, respectively.

$$a_{85} = 0.975 - 0.0151\,v_i \tag{6}$$

$$a_{AVG} = 0.807 - 0.0136\,v_i \tag{7}$$

$$a_{SD} = 0.181 - 0.0018\,v_i \tag{8}$$

where: a_{85} = 85th percentile acceleration in m/s^2, a_{AVG} = mean free-flow acceleration in m/s^2, a_{SD} = free-flow acceleration standard deviation in m/s^2, v_i = entry speed in km/h, R^2 adjusted = adjusted coefficient of determination.
- Deceleration at the end of the tangent. Application range: 0–45 km/h. R^2 adjusted: 0.83, 0.94, 0.57, respectively.

$$d_{85} = -1.84 + 0.0314\,v_f \tag{9}$$

$$d_{AVG} = -1.50 + 0.0301\,v_f \tag{10}$$

$$d_{SD} = 0.310 + 0.010\,v_f - 0.00033\,v_f^2 \tag{11}$$

where: d_{85} = 85th percentile deceleration m/s^2, d_{AVG} = mean free-flow deceleration in m/s^2, d_{SD} = free-flow deceleration standard deviation in m/s^2, v_f = exit speed in km/h, R^2 adjusted = adjusted coefficient of determination.

Tangents Before Signal-Controlled Intersections. The tangents before signal-controlled intersections are more complex than in the previous case. In the proposed models (Eqs. 12–38) for the green, amber and red lights they only have two predictors: a) the initial speed at the 85th percentile of the acceleration and the standard deviation of the free-flow acceleration for the green light, and b) density of objects (trees, traffic signs, and poles) for the speed of operation when the light is red. For the rest of the conditions, constant values were calculated. Based on this, it can be said that the choice of speed, acceleration, and deceleration is conditioned mainly by the presence of the traffic light, and not by the characteristics of the street, environment, vehicle or driver.

Proposed Models for Tangents Before Signal-Controlled Intersections and Green Light. When the light is green, the speeds are slower than when the light is amber, since many drivers tend to accelerate to pass the traffic light in amber light, when they are in the zone dilemma [47].

- Speed in the center of the tangent. Application range: 94–122 m. R^2 adjusted: not available.

$$v_{85} = 52.72 \text{ km/h} \tag{12}$$

$$v_{AVG} = 43.55 \text{ km/h} \tag{13}$$

$$v_{SD} = 4.34 \text{ km/h} \tag{14}$$

where: v_{85} = operating speed in km/h, v_{AVG} = mean free-flow speed in km/h, v_{SD} = free-flow speed standard deviation in km/h, R^2 adjusted = adjusted coefficient of determination.

- Acceleration at the start of the tangent. Application range: 0–45 km/h. R^2 adjusted: 0.86, 0.93, not available, respectively.

$$a_{85} = 1.06 - 0.015 \, v_i \tag{15}$$

$$a_{AVG} = 1.13 - 0.021 \, v_i \tag{16}$$

$$a_{SD} = 0.21 \text{ m/s}^2 \tag{17}$$

where: a_{85} = 85th percentile acceleration in m/s^2, a_{AVG} = mean free-flow acceleration in m/s^2, a_{SD} = free-flow acceleration standard deviation in m/s^2, v_i = entry speed in km/h, R^2 adjusted = adjusted coefficient of determination.

- Deceleration at the end of the tangent. Application range: 94–122 m. R^2 adjusted: not available.

$$d_{85} = -0.07 \text{ m/s}^2 \tag{18}$$

$$d_{AVG} = -0.32 \text{ m/s}^2 \tag{19}$$

$$d_{SD} = 0.18 \text{ m/s}^2 \tag{20}$$

where: d_{85} = 85th percentile deceleration m/s^2, d_{AVG} = mean free-flow deceleration in m/s^2, d_{SD} = free-flow deceleration standard deviation in m/s^2, R^2 adjusted = adjusted coefficient of determination.

Proposed Models for Tangents Before Signal-Controlled Intersections and Amber Light. When the traffic light is in amber, the mean deceleration is higher than the high green light, but its dispersion is high, again a characteristic of the zone dilemma. The same happens with the dispersion of the speed in green and amber light. In green lights, drivers would continue crossing the intersection, and low decelerations are expected, which are seen in these models.

- Speed in the center of the tangent. Application range: 94–122 m. R^2 adjusted: not available.

$$v_{85} = 56.28 \text{ km/h} \tag{21}$$

$$v_{AVG} = 43.31 \text{ km/h} \tag{22}$$

$$v_{SD} = 9.82 \text{ km/h} \tag{23}$$

where: v_{85} = operating speed in km/h, v_{AVG} = mean free-flow speed in km/h, v_{SD} = free-flow speed standard deviation in km/h, R^2 adjusted = adjusted coefficient of determination.

- Acceleration at the start of the tangent. Application range: 94–122 m. R^2 adjusted: not available.

$$a_{85} = 0.55 \text{ m/s}^2 \tag{24}$$

$$a_{AVG} = 0.28 \text{ m/s}^2 \tag{25}$$

$$a_{SD} = 0.24 \text{ m/s}^2 \tag{26}$$

where: a_{85} = 85th percentile acceleration in m/s^2, a_{AVG} = mean free-flow acceleration in m/s^2, a_{SD} = free-flow acceleration standard deviation in m/s^2, R^2 adjusted = adjusted coefficient of determination.

- Deceleration at the end of the tangent. Application range: 94–122 m. R^2 adjusted: not available.

$$d_{85} = -0.10 \text{ m/s}^2 \tag{27}$$

$$d_{AVG} = -0.73 \text{ m/s}^2 \tag{28}$$

$$d_{SD} = 0.74 \text{ m/s}^2 \tag{29}$$

where: d_{85} = 85th percentile deceleration m/s^2, d_{AVG} = mean free-flow deceleration in m/s^2, d_{SD} = free-flow deceleration standard deviation in m/s^2, R^2 adjusted = adjusted coefficient of determination.

Proposed Models for Tangents Before Signal-Controlled Intersections and Red Light.
In red light, the speeds are lower than the previous two conditions. This behavior is because drivers already know to stop at a red light, and the high values of decelerations confirm that. However, the acceleration values are higher than the two previous conditions, maybe due to the impulsive sensation-seeking detected in the sample of drivers. Even though the drivers know they must stop at the intersection, they accelerate with a higher value, possibly to cross the intersection.

- Speed in the center of the tangent. Application range: 5.3–29.1 u/100 m. R^2 adjusted: 0.49, not available, and not available, respectively.

$$v_{85} = 33.4 + 0.533 \text{ OD} \tag{30}$$

$$v_{AVG} = 39.71 \text{ km/h} \tag{31}$$

$$v_{SD} = 4.45 \text{ km/h} \tag{32}$$

where: v_{85} = operating speed in km/h, v_{AVG} = mean free-flow speed in km/h, v_{SD} = free-flow speed standard deviation in km/h, OD = Object density in units per each 100 m, R^2 adjusted = adjusted coefficient of determination.

- Acceleration at the start of the tangent. Application range: 0–45 km/h. R^2 adjusted: 0.66, 0,65, and not available, respectively.

$$a_{85} = 1.40 - 0.024 \text{ v}_i \tag{33}$$

$$a_{AVG} = 1.33 - 0.024 \text{ v}_i \tag{34}$$

$$a_{SD} = 0.32 \text{ m/s}^2 \tag{35}$$

where: a_{85} = 85th percentile acceleration in m/s^2, a_{AVG} = mean free-flow acceleration in m/s^2, a_{SD} = free-flow acceleration standard deviation in m/s^2, v_i = entry speed in km/h, R^2 adjusted = adjusted coefficient of determination.

- Deceleration at the end of the tangent. Application range: 94–122 m. R^2 adjusted: not available.

$$d_{85} = -0.75 \text{ m/s}^2 \tag{36}$$

$$d_{AVG} = -1.50 \text{ m/s}^2 \tag{37}$$

$$d_{SD} = 0.54 \text{ m/s}^2 \tag{38}$$

where: d_{85} = 85th percentile deceleration m/s², d_{AVG} = mean free-flow deceleration in m/s², d_{SD} = free-flow deceleration standard deviation in m/s², R^2 adjusted = adjusted coefficient of determination.

Tangents before Roundabouts Intersections. Models 39 to 47 were calibrated based on the variables in Tables 1, 2, 3 The speed values are higher than those recorded in the previous intersections. Also, the acceleration values of the models are slightly higher than the values of the acceleration models at tangents before stop-controlled intersections, since they are tangents with similar starting conditions. Additionally, equation values are closer to the deceleration models in tangents before signal-controlled intersections with amber light. This trend is because there is also a dilemma zone in the circle. The driver may doubt whether to continue or stop the vehicle before the approach of vehicles within the ring. The most statistically significant variables were the length of the tangent, entry or initial speed, and traffic signs density. Speed choice in previous studies were related to entry width [46, 48], internal circle diameter [46, 48], drive curve [46], entry deviation angle [46] and approach/exit speed [48].

Proposed Models for Tangents Before Roundabout.

- Speed in the center of the tangent. Application range: 63–321 m. R^2 adjusted: 0.98, 0,90, and not available, respectively.

$$v_{85} = 28.3 + 0.091 \text{ L} \tag{39}$$

$$v_{AVG} = 20.5 + 0.080 \text{ L} \tag{40}$$

$$v_{SD} = 5.38 \text{ km/h} \tag{41}$$

where: v_{85} = operating speed in km/h, v_{AVG} = mean free-flow speed in km/h, v_{SD} = free-flow speed standard deviation in km/h, L = length of the street in m, R^2 adjusted = adjusted coefficient of determination.

- Acceleration at the start of the tangent. Application range: 10–50 km/h. R^2 adjusted: 0.88, 0,77, and not available, respectively.

$$a_{85} = 1.04 - 0.015 \text{ v}_i \tag{42}$$

$$a_{AVG} = 0.90 - 0.014 \, v_i \tag{43}$$

$$a_{SD} = 0.23 \text{ m/s}^2 \tag{44}$$

where: a_{85} = 85th percentile acceleration in m/s^2, aAVG = mean free-flow acceleration in m/s^2, a_{SD} = free-flow acceleration standard deviation in m/s^2, v_i = entry speed in km/h, R^2 adjusted = adjusted coefficient of determination.

• Deceleration at the end of the tangent. Application range: 94–122 m. R^2 adjusted: 0.66, not available, and not available.

$$d_{85} = 0.002L + 0.07 \text{ TSD} \tag{45}$$

$$d_{AVG} = -0.70 \text{ m/s}^2 \tag{46}$$

$$d_{SD} = 0.55 \text{ m/s}^2 \tag{47}$$

where: d_{85} = 85th percentile deceleration m/s^2, d_{AVG} = mean free-flow deceleration in m/s^2, d_{SD} = free-flow deceleration standard deviation in m/s^2, L = length of the street in m, TSD = traffic signs density in units per each 100 m, R^2 adjusted = adjusted coefficient of determination.

Despite trying to find statistical relationships between geometric and operating elements within the circle and speed, none were found. Therefore, the equations had constant values. The calculated values were: mean speed of 28.60 km/h and standard deviation of 4.66 km/h. These values are valid within roundabouts an internal diameter between 11.5–25 m and an external diameter between 26–61 m. The mean speed found was similar to that recorded in other investigations: 30 km/h [49], 17–26 km/h [48], as well as their standard deviation of 4.13–5.21 km/h [48].

4.2 Validation

The calibrated models were validated using information collected from another circuit in the same city. This circuit had similar geometric and operation characteristics to the initial sections. For the tangents before stop-controlled intersections, there were eight sections between 47 to 112 m. Twelve tangents before signal-controlled intersections were collected to validate the models, with 94 and 120 m long. And for the tangents before the roundabout, six sections, between 66 to 287 m, were used.

Six drivers participated in the validation circuit, of which half were men. Drivers had an average age of 26.3 years and driving experience of 7.2 years. The average year of manufacture was 2007, the mean cylinder capacity was 2000 cm^3, and the last average revision was 53 days. The measuring equipment was the same employed in the collection data, and the same data processing was performed for speed, acceleration, and deceleration data.

For the validation of the speed, acceleration, and deceleration models, forecast errors were calculated: mean squared error (MSE), mean absolute error (MAE), the mean absolute percentage error (MAPE), and the Chi-squared test. Table 4 shows these values. Models with constant values were not included in this table; since it is impossible to calculate forecast errors. However, in those cases, an analysis of variance was performed, to determine if the fixed values do not differ from the values found in the validation, at 95% level of confidence.

Table 4 shows that the highest values of MSE and MAE were obtained by the model of the operating speed and the average speed in free-flow for the tangents before roundabouts, so caution should be taken when using these equations. The prediction error will be around 5 km/h (starting assumption). The highest MAPE values were for the equations of the 85th percentile of acceleration and deceleration for the tangents before roundabouts, so caution is also suggested in their use. However, these equations and others in Table 4, the chi-calculated did not exceed the chi-critical; therefore, the equations are valid. All the fixed models were also valid since in the analysis of variance no significant statistical differences were found (p-value > 0.05).

Table 4. Prediction errors and Chi-square values for the equations of speed, acceleration, and deceleration calibrated models.

Tangents before		Prediction equation	Error estimator				
			MSE	MAE	MAPE (%)	χ^2 calculated	χ^2 critic
Stop-controlled intersections		V_{85}	3.83	1.27	4.04	0.95	14.07
		V_{AVG}	5.85	2.13	7.69	1.68	14.07
		V_{SD}	0.82	0.70	22.84	2.11	14.07
		a_{85}	0.02	0.14	17.52	0.13	9.49
		a_{AVG}	0.02	0.14	22.01	0.16	9.49
		a_{SD}	0.00	0.02	11.36	0.01	9.49
		d_{85}	0.01	0.10	6.85	0.05	9.49
		d_{AVG}	0.01	0.10	8.57	0.05	9.49
		d_{SD}	0.00	0.03	8.52	0.02	9.49
Signal-controlled intersections	Green light	a_{85}	0.04	0.13	22.23	0.68	14.07
		a_{AVG}	0.02	0.08	16.75	0.30	14.07
	Red light	V_{85}	8.77	2.44	5.70	1.41	12.59

(continued)

Table 4. (*continued*)

Tangents before	Prediction equation	Error estimator				
		MSE	MAE	MAPE (%)	χ^2 calculated	χ^2 critic
	a_{85}	0.01	0.09	17.02	0.16	9.49
	a_{AVG}	0.01	0.06	15.56	0.11	9.49
Roundabouts intersections	V_{85}	36.79	5.44	11.60	4.54	11.07
	V_{AVG}	26.60	5.11	14.39	4.44	11.07
	a_{85}	0.04	0.17	34.29	0.54	12.59
	a_{AVG}	0.01	0.10	28.84	0.27	12.59
	d_{85}	0.03	0.16	36.39	0.41	9.49

V_{85} = operating speed in km/h, V_{AVG} = mean free-flow speed in km/h, V_{SD} = free-flow speed standard deviation in km/h, a_{85} = 85th percentile acceleration in m/s^2, a_{AVG} = mean free-flow acceleration in m/s^2, a_{SD} = free-flow acceleration standard deviation in m/s^2, d_{85} = 85th percentile deceleration in m/s^2, d_{AVG} = mean free-flow deceleration in m/s^2, d_{SD} = free-flow deceleration standard deviation in m/s^2, MSE = mean squared error in (km/h)^2 for the speed and (m/s^2)^2 for the acceleration or deceleration, MAE = mean absolute error in km/h for the speed and m/s^2 for the acceleration or deceleration, MAPE = mean absolute percentage error in percentage, χ^2 calculated = Chi-squared calculated, χ^2 critic = Chi-value where if the χ^2 calculated is greater than χ^2 critic the model is not valid.

5 Conclusions

The objective of this article was to investigate the influence of several urban street, driver, and vehicle characteristics on speed, acceleration, and deceleration in free-flow conditions. Three scenarios were analyzed: tangents before stop-controlled intersections, tangents before signal-controlled intersections, and tangents before roundabout intersections. After the presented results, the following conclusions are presented:

In stop-controlled intersections, the length of the tangent, the speed at the start and the end of the maneuver were the most influential variables on speed, acceleration, and deceleration, respectively. In signal-controlled intersections, there were only two sporadic predictors: the initial speed and the object density. Regarding roundabout, the length of the street influenced the operating speed and mean free-flow speed, the initial speed influenced the 85th percentile of the acceleration, and the traffic sign density impacted the 85th percentile of the deceleration. All models were valid, and they can use to get speed profiles on these types of streets. These profiles can be used to analyze the consistency of streets, calculate fuel consumption, calculate polluting gas emissions, or in macroscopic traffic modeling.

In conclusion, the most influential parameters in the driver's speed choice in urban streets are the street characteristics and its environment. Neither the type of vehicle, year of manufacture, cylinder capacity, period of previous maintenance, vehicle brand, vehicle model; or the values of personality traits, values of driving styles, age, or sex of the driver were statistically significant variables. For the drivers, the physical elements of the road scene are more important than their characteristics or their vehicles. This outcome is because an urban environment is limited space, where drivers do not have enough freedom/space to accelerate or decelerate. Thus, on rural roads, drivers should have different behavior; therefore, the prediction models of one type of road cannot be employed in another one different from the calibration data. This issue can be explored in future research.

This study has several limitations. First, the speed in the middle of the tangent was representative; however, the highest speed (for safety reasons) could be found in another spot in the tangent. The models should be used in the range where they were calibrated and validated. The local and geographic characteristics could influence the values of the models. Despite these limitations, the study helps to understand the complex relationship between the knowledge about the speed profile in free-flow conditions. The calibrated models were coherent with the actual driver behavior. Additionally, it covers three types of intersections, that previous research only studies one intersection. Finally, this study would help designers and urban planners.

Acknowledgements. The authors thank the National Secretariat for Higher Education, Science, Technology and Innovation (SENESCYT) of the Republic of Ecuador and the Universidad Técnica Particular de Loja for their support in this research.

References

1. Gunawan, F.E., Chandra, F.Y.: Optimal averaging time for predicting traffic velocity using floating car data technique for advanced traveler information system. In: The 9th International Conference on Traffic & Transportation Studies, pp. 566–575. Procedia Social and Behavioral Sciences (2014). https://doi.org/10.1016/j.sbspro.2014.07.240
2. Ackaah, W.: Exploring the use of advanced traffic information system to manage traffic congestion in developing countries. Sci. African. **4**, e00079 (2019). https://doi.org/10.1016/j.sciaf.2019.e00079
3. Lamm, R., Choueiri, E.M., Hayward, J.C.: Tangent as an independent design element. Transp. Res. Rec. **1195**, 123–131 (1988)
4. Harwood, D.W., Neuman, T.R., Leisch, J.P.: Summary of design speed, operating speed, and design consistency issues. Transp. Res. Rec. J. Transp. Res. Board **1701**(1), 116–120 (2000). https://doi.org/10.3141/1701-15
5. Fitzpatrick, K., Carlson, P., Brewer, M., Wooldridge, M., Miaou, S.: NCHRP report 504: design speed, operating speed, and posted speed practices, Washington D.C (2003)
6. Ray, B., Ferguson, E., Knudsen, J., Porter, R., Mason, J.: NCHRP report 785: performance-based analysis of geometric design of highways and streets of highways and streets, Washington D.C (2014). https://doi.org/10.17226/22285
7. Gargoum, S.A., El-Basyouny, K., Kim, A.: Towards setting credible speed limits: Identifying factors that affect driver compliance on urban roads. Accid. Anal. Prev. **95**, 138–148 (2016). https://doi.org/10.1016/j.aap.2016.07.001
8. Sekhar, C.R., Nataraju, J., Velmurugan, S., Kumar, P., Sitaramanjaneyulu, K.: Free flow speed analysis of two lane inter urban highways. Transp. Res. Procedia **17**, 664–673 (2016). https://doi.org/10.1016/j.trpro.2016.11.121
9. García-Ramírez, Y.: Aceleraciones y desaceleraciones de vehículos livianos en caminos de montaña (Doctoral disertation) (2014). http://repositorio.educacionsuperior.gob.ec/

10. Roidl, E., Frehse, B., Höger, R.: Emotional states of drivers and the impact on speed, acceleration and traffic violations - a simulator study. Accid. Anal. Prev. **70**, 282–292 (2014). https://doi.org/10.1016/j.aap.2014.04.010
11. Keay, L., et al.: Older drivers and rapid deceleration events: salisbury eye evaluation driving study. Accid. Anal. Prev. **58**, 279–285 (2013). https://doi.org/10.1016/j.aap.2012.06.002
12. Chipman, M.L., MacGregor, C.G., Smiley, A.M., Lee-Gosselin, M.: Time vs. distance as measures of exposure in driving surveys. Accid. Anal. Prev. **24**, 679–684 (1992). https://doi.org/10.1016/0001-4575(92)90021-A
13. Thompson, K.R., Johnson, A.M., Emerson, J.L., Dawson, J.D., Boer, E.R., Rizzo, M.: Distracted driving in elderly and middle-aged drivers. Accid. Anal. Prev. **45**, 711–717 (2012). https://doi.org/10.1016/j.aap.2011.09.040
14. Goralzik, A., Vollrath, M.: The effects of road, driver, and passenger presence on drivers' choice of speed: a driving simulator study. Transp. Res. Procedia. **25**, 2061–2075 (2017). https://doi.org/10.1016/j.trpro.2017.05.400
15. Dinh, D.D., Kubota, H.: Speeding behavior on urban residential streets with a 30 km/h speed limit under the framework of the theory of planned behavior. TransportPolicy **29**, 199–208 (2013). https://doi.org/10.1016/j.tranpol.2013.06.003
16. Wang, J.: Operating speed models for low speed urban environments based on in-vehicle GPS data. Ph.D Thesis (2006). https://smartech.gatech.edu/bitstream/handle/1853/10508/wang_jun_200605_phd.pdf
17. Gstaltera, H., Fastenmeier, W.: Reliability of drivers in urban intersections. Accid. Anal. Prev. **42**, 225–234 (2010)
18. Choudhary, P., Velaga, N.R.: Mobile phone use during driving: effects on speed and effectiveness of driver compensatory behaviour. Accid. Anal. Prev. **106**, 370–378 (2017). https://doi.org/10.1016/j.aap.2017.06.021
19. Schmidt-Daffy, M.: Fear and anxiety while driving: differential impact of task demands, speed and motivation. Transp. Res. Part F Traffic Psychol. Behav. **16**, 14–28 (2013). https://doi.org/10.1016/j.trf.2012.07.002
20. Dhamaniya, A., Chandra, S.: Speed prediction models for urban arterials under mixed traffic conditions. Procedia - Soc. Behav. Sci. **104**, 342–351 (2013). https://doi.org/10.1016/j.sbspro.2013.11.127
21. Jevtić, V., Vujanić, M., Lipovac, K., Jovanović, D., Pešić, D.: The relationship between the travelling speed and motorcycle styles in urban settings: a case study in Belgrade. Accid. Anal. Prev. **75**, 77–85 (2015). https://doi.org/10.1016/j.aap.2014.11.011
22. Giles, M.J.: Driver speed compliance in Western Australia: a multivariate analysis. Transp. Policy **11**, 227–235 (2004). https://doi.org/10.1016/j.tranpol.2003.11.002
23. Dinh, D.D., Kubota, H.: Profile-speed data-based models to estimate operating speeds for urban residential streets with a 30 km/h speed limit. IATSS Res. **36**, 115–122 (2013). https://doi.org/10.1016/j.iatssr.2012.06.001
24. Eluru, N., Chakour, V., Chamberlain, M., Miranda-Moreno, L.F.: Modeling vehicle operating speed on urban roads in Montreal: a panel mixed ordered probit fractional split model. Accid. Anal. Prev. **59**, 125–134 (2013). https://doi.org/10.1016/j.aap.2013.05.016
25. Bassani, M., Sacchi, E.: Calibration to local conditions of geometry-based operating speed models for urban arterials and collectors. Procedia - Soc. Behav. Sci. **53**, 821–832 (2012). https://doi.org/10.1016/j.sbspro.2012.09.931
26. Poe, C., Mason, J.: Analyzing influence of geometric design on operating speeds along low-speed urban streets: mixed-model approach. Transp. Res. Rec. **1737**, 18–24 (2000). https://doi.org/10.3141/1737-03
27. Ding, H., Zhao, X., Rong, J., Ma, J.: Experimental research on the effectiveness and adaptability of speed reduction markings in downhill sections on urban roads: a driving simulation study. Accid. Anal. Prev. **75**, 119–127 (2015). https://doi.org/10.1016/j.aap.2014.11.018

28. Guo, Y., Liu, P., Liang, Q., Wang, W.: Effects of parallelogram-shaped pavement markings on vehicle speed and safety of pedestrian crosswalks on urban roads in China. Accid. Anal. Prev. **95**, 438–447 (2016). https://doi.org/10.1016/j.aap.2015.07.001

29. Antonson, H., Ahlström, C., Mårdh, S., Blomqvist, G., Wiklund, M.: Landscape heritage objects' effect on driving: a combined driving simulator and questionnaire study. Accid. Anal. Prev. **62**, 168–177 (2014). https://doi.org/10.1016/j.aap.2013.09.021

30. Bassani, M., Catani, L., Cirillo, C., Mutani, G.: Night-time and daytime operating speed distribution in urban arterials. Transp. Res. Part F Traffic Psychol. Behav. **42**, 56–69 (2016). https://doi.org/10.1016/j.trf.2016.06.020

31. Hjelkrem, O.A., Ryeng, E.O.: Chosen risk level during car-following in adverse weather conditions. Accid. Anal. Prev. **95**, 227–235 (2016). https://doi.org/10.1016/j.aap.2016.07.006

32. Tarko, A., Hall, T., Romero, M., Jiménez, C.G.L.: Evaluating the rollover propensity of trucks - a roundabout example. Accid. Anal. Prev. **91**, 127–134 (2016). https://doi.org/10.1016/j.aap.2016.02.032

33. Giles, M.J.: Correcting for selectivity bias in the estimation of road crash costs. Appl. Econ. **35**, 1291–1301 (2003). https://doi.org/10.1080/0003684032000090717

34. Rahman, A., Lownes, N.E.: Analysis of rainfall impacts on platooned vehicle spacing and speed. Transp. Res. Part F Traffic Psychol. Behav. **15**, 395–403 (2012). https://doi.org/10.1016/j.trf.2012.03.004

35. Gargoum, S.A., El-Basyouny, K.: Exploring the association between speed and safety: a path analysis approach. Accid. Anal. Prev. **93**, 32–40 (2016). https://doi.org/10.1016/j.aap.2016.04.029

36. Schechtman, E., Bar-Gera, H., Musicant, O.: Driver views on speed and enforcement. Accid. Anal. Prev. **89**, 9–21 (2016). https://doi.org/10.1016/j.aap.2015.12.028

37. Montella, A., Imbriani, L.L., Marzano, V., Mauriello, F.: Effects on speed and safety of point-to-point speed enforcement systems: evaluation on the urban motorway A56 Tangenziale di Napoli. Accid. Anal. Prev. **75**, 164–178 (2015). https://doi.org/10.1016/j.aap.2014.11.022

38. Chen, G., Wilson, J., Meckle, W., Cooper, P.: Evaluation of photo radar program in British Columbia. Accid. Anal. Prev. **32**, 517–526 (2000). https://doi.org/10.1016/S0001-4575(99)00071-8

39. García, Y., Paladines, L.: Calibración de modelos de velocidad de operación en calles urbanas no semaforizadas: estudio de caso. Rev. Politécnica. **40**, 41–46 (2018)

40. García-Ramírez, Y., Paladines, L., Verdesoto, C., Torres, P.: Car drivers do not choose their speed in urban environments: speed models in tangent streets. In: SCITEPRESS (ed.) 7th International Conference on Vehicle Technology and Intelligent Transport Systems (VEHITS 2021), pp. 421–428 (2021). https://doi.org/10.5220/0010435904210428

41. Pignataro, L.J.: Traffic Engineering - Theory and Practice. Prentice-Hall Publishing Co., New Jersey (1973)

42. Bennett, C.R.: A speed prediction model for rural two-lane highways. Ph.D Thesis (1994)

43. Taubman-Ben-Ari, O., Mikulincer, M., Gillath, O.: The multidimensional driving style inventory—scale construct and validation. Accid. Anal.Prev. **36**, 323–332 (2004). https://doi.org/10.1016/S0001-4575(03)00010-1

44. Aluja, A., Rossier, J., García, F., Angleitner, A., Kuhlman, M., Zuckerman., M.: A cross cultural shortened form of the ZKPQ (ZKPQ-50-cc) adapted to English, French, German, and Spanish languages. Pers. Individ. Dif. **41**, 619–628 (2006). http://dx.doi.org/10.1016/j.paid.2006.03.001

45. R Core Team: R: A language and environment for statistical computing. R Foundation for Statistical Computing (2013). http://www.r-project.org/

46. Al-Omari, B.H., Ghuzlan, K.A., Al-helo, L.B.: Modeling through traffic speed at roundabouts along urban and suburban street arterials. J. Transp. Res. Forum. **53**, 7–19 (2014)

47. Bar-Gera, H., Musicant, O., Schechtman, E., Ze'evi, T.: Quantifying the yellow signal driver behavior based on naturalistic data from digital enforcement cameras. Accid. Anal. Prev. **96**, 371–381 (2016). https://doi.org/10.1016/j.aap.2015.03.040
48. Gallelli, V., Vaiana, R., Iuele, T.: Comparison between simulated and experimental crossing speed profiles on roundabout with different geometric features. Procedia - Soc. Behav. Sci. **111**, 117–126 (2014). https://doi.org/10.1016/j.sbspro.2014.01.044
49. Bassani, M., Sacchi, E.: Experimental investigation into speed perfomance and consistency of urban roundabouts: an Italian case study. In: Poster Session at the "3rd International Conference on Roundabouts." Transportation Research Board, Carmel, Indiana, USA (2011)

Interpretable Privacy-Preserving Collaborative Deep Learning for Taxi Trip Duration Forecasting

Jelena Fiosina[✉][iD]

Institute of Informatics, Clausthal Technical University,
Julius-Albert Str. 4, 38678 Clausthal-Zellerfeld, Germany
jelena.fiosina@gmail.com

Abstract. Traffic data are obtained from various distributed sources such as infrastructure and vehicle sensors developed by various organisations, and often cannot be processed together because of data privacy regulations. Thus, distributed machine learning methods are required to process the data without sharing them. Federated learning allows the processing of data distributed by transmitting only the parameters without sharing the real data. The federated learning architecture is based mainly on deep learning, which is often more accurate than other machine learning approaches. However, deep-learning-based models are black-box models, and should be explained to increase trust in the system for both users and developers. Despite the fact that various explainability methods have been proposed, the solutions for explainable federated models are insufficient.

In this study, we used a federated deep learning model to predict a taxi trip duration within Brunswick region. We showed situations for which federated learning improves the prediction quality, allowing for an accuracy comparable to that obtained on the complete dataset. Moreover, we investigated how the amount of transmitted information in federated learning can be optimised while maintaining the same accuracy. Finally, we propose how the federated deep learning model can be interpreted using explainability methods without transmitting raw data and compare the results of various explainability approaches.

Keywords: FCD trajectories · Trip duration · Forecasting · Federated learning · Explainability

1 Introduction

Traffic data are geographically scattered across different places, distributed sources, and various organisations, and often cannot be aggregated. These data can be used for various applications, for example, traffic planning, delivery optimisers, and ride-sharing, which require a trip duration forecasting model as a basis for their more complex forecasting and decision-making functionalities. By processing only all available data, it is clearly possible to obtain a more accurate model. However, organisations that possess the data are reluctant to cooperate with each other and have a trade-off between the

© Springer Nature Switzerland AG 2022
C. Klein et al. (Eds.): SMARTGREENS 2021/ VEHITS 2021, CCIS 1612, pp. 392–411, 2022.
https://doi.org/10.1007/978-3-031-17098-0_20

decision to build the model individually without the risk of data sharing and to share the data to get more accurate models.

Distributed machine learning methods can help with this trade-off, providing an alternative to process the distributed data without sharing them. Federated learning [14] allows to organise a privacy-preserving cooperation among the partners. It has three major advantages: 1) no raw data transmission to the server is needed; 2) the computational load is distributed among the participants, and 3) parameter synchronisation of the local models leads to more accurate models. The main assumption is that the federated model should be parametric (e.g., deep learning) because the algorithm synchronises the models by synchronising the parameters.

A known limitation of deep learning is that it is based on "black box" models of neural networks, which should be explained to increase trust in the system for developers and users. Numerous model-agnostic (e.g., LIME, Shapley values) and model-specific (e.g., Integrated gradients (IG), DeepLIFT) methods for explanation of black-box models are available [21]. Distributed versions of these methods exist, which allow them to be executed on various processes on graphics processing units (GPUs) [13]. However studies on the explainability of geographically distributed federated deep learning models are lacking.

Our first research question was to investigate the conditions under which federated learning is profitable for participating companies. This approach was demonstrated using floating car data (FCD) from Brunswick, Germany for a taxi trip duration forecasting. In this study, we extended the research conducted in [10] by providing more evidence regarding which situations federated learning makes sense and how its model synchronisation architecture can be optimised to reduce the data transmission without a significant loss in the forecasting accuracy. We modified the federated learning algorithm proposed in [10].

Focusing on federated deep learning models, we continued to investigate the fact that deep learning is often addressed as a black-box model, in which results and functioning logic are not interpretable. The Intergated Gradients (IG) explanation method was already discussed in [10] and its distributed federated version was provided. Thus, our second research question is to focus on how different explanation methods can be applied to the federated model, how their results differ, and how these results can be aggregated.

The rest of the paper is organised as follows. Section 2 describes the state-of-the-art of trip duration forecast, federated learning and explainability methods. Section 3 introduces our proposed explainable federated learning approach. Section 4 describes the available data, experimental setup and results of the conducted experiments. Section 5 concludes the paper.

2 State of the Art

2.1 Travel Time Forecasting

Accurate travel time or trip duration prediction helps to reduce delays and transport delivery costs in transportation networks. It is an important parameter to improve reliability through better selection of routes and to increases the service quality of commercial delivery by bringing goods within the required time window [5]. In [1] a centralised deep learning based travel-time estimation was discussed as an important stage for ride-sharing problem optimisation. A centralized travel time prediction was considered in-vehicle route guidance and advanced traffic management systems [17]. A decentralized travel time forecasting using neural networks, where travel time is predicted for each link of the network separately was considered in [6].

To build more accurate and specified travel time forecasting models data pre-processing like filtering and aggregation is required. Travel-time aggregation models (non-parametric, semi-parametric) for decentralized data clustering and corresponding coordination and parameter exchange algorithms were proposed in [9]. Decentralised travel-time estimation and forecasting based on multivariate linear and kernel-density regression models with corresponding parameter/data exchange were proposed in [8].

This paper is an extended version of [10], in which various forecasting models on the complete dataset were applied to find the best hypothetical method to have a centralised reference model, to be discussed in the distributed scenarios. Different regression types as linear, Lasso, random forest and XGBoost models were compared with deep-learning. It was discovered that deep learning provides the second best accurate forecast and the only XGBoost and random forest, (which gave the same results) outperform it slightly. However, XGBoost and random forest are non parametric decision-tree based ensemble methods and can not be easily federated. It was also shown that starting with less then 12,5% of the available data, there is no more possible to do accurate forecasts with individual models and a collaboration has sense.

2.2 Federated Learning

Federated learning [14] focuses mainly on development of privacy-preserved machine learning models for physically distributed data and continues the research line of distributed machine learning. When a company cannot create an accurate model with its local dataset only, the mechanism of federated learning enables access to more knowledge and better accuracy of models without sharing local raw data.

Federated learning enables different devices to collaboratively learn a shared prediction model while maintaining all training data on the device and without the need to store the data in the cloud. The main difference between federated learning and distributed learning is attributed to the assumptions on the properties of the local datasets, as distributed learning originally aims to parallelise the computing power, whereas federated learning originally aims to train on heterogeneous datasets [14]. This approach may use a central server that orchestrates the different steps of the algorithm or they may have peer-to-peer architecture.

In this study, we use a central server for this aggregation, while local nodes perform local training [29].

The main procedure consists of training local models on local datasets and exchanging parameters (e.g., the weights or gradients of a deep neural network) between these local models at some frequency to establish a global model [3]. Federated learning relies on an iterative process broken down into learning rounds, which represent a set of client-server interactions [29]. Each round consists of transmitting the current global

model state to participating nodes, training local models on these local nodes to produce a set of potential model updates at each node, and aggregating and processing
these local updates into a single global update and applying it to the global model.

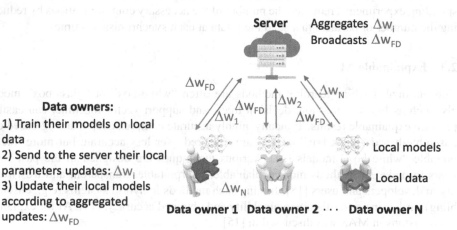

Fig. 1. Federated learning architecture.

We consider N data owners $\{F_i\}_{i=1}^N$, who wish to train a machine learning model
by consolidating their respective data $\{D_i\}_{i=1}^N$. A centralised approach uses all data
together $D = \cup_{i=1}^N D_i$ to train a model M_Σ. A federated system is a learning process
in which the data owners collaboratively train a model M_{FD}, where any data owner F_i
does not expose its data D_i to others. In addition, the accuracy of M_{FD}, denoted as
V_{FD}, should be very close to the performance of M_Σ, V_Σ [29]. Formally, we consider
δ, a non-negative real number; if $|V_{FD} - V_\Sigma| < \delta$, we can state that the federated
learning algorithm has δ-accuracy loss. Each row of the matrix D_i represents a sample,
while each column represents a feature. Some datasets may also contain label data. The
feature X, label Y, and sample Ids I constitute the complete training dataset $(I, X,
Y)$. The feature and sample space of the data parties may not be identical. We classify
federated learning into horizontal, vertical, and federated transfer learning based on
the data distribution among various parties. In horizontal or sample-based federated
learning data sets share the same feature space but different in samples.

In vertical or feature-based federated learning data sets share the same sample ID
space but differ in feature space. In federated transfer learning data sets differ in both
sample and feature space, having small intersections. In this study, we consider a horizontal federated learning case.

In [10] the federated learning algorithm was discussed. We developed a joint
privacy-preserving model of trip duration forecasting of different service providers
based on the horizontal federated learning architecture. The training process of such
a system was independent on specific machine learning algorithms. All participants
share the final model parameters (Fig. 1). We started from the synchronisation at every
batch and reduced the synchronisation frequency watching the obtained accuracy. It

was concluded that with the synchronisation each second batch of data (reducing the number of the transmitted data twice) it is still possible to obtain the results with the same accuracy.

In this study, we aim to extend the federated algorithm and to conduct the corresponding experiments, reducing the number of the necessary communications by reducing the number of partners that send their data at each synchronisation time.

2.3 Explainable AI

Conventional machine learning methods are often "white-box" or "glass-box" models, such as linear regression, decision trees, and support vector machine, can easily produce explainable results. Typically, highly accurate complex deep learning-based or ensemble-based "black box" models are favoured over less accurate but more interpretable "white box" models [21]. Various techniques are designed in the past few years to make AI methods more explainable, interpretable, transparent and trustworthy to developers and users [18]. Joining such methods in hybrid systems (e.g., ensembling) further increases their explainability and obtained accuracy, [12]. AI for explaining decisions in MAS was discussed in [15].

Model-agnostic methods and model-specific explanation methods have been reported in [21]. Model-agnostic methods are implementable for each model and can be local such as LIME [23], Shapley Values [19] or global such as Feature permutation [11]. However, model-agnostic methods often require a large number of computations and often are not applicable for big datasets used in deep learning [21]. Shapley values method was implemented in [28] to interpret a vertical federated learning model. Model-specific methods are focused on only one type of model (e.g., neural networks) and are more computationally effective [21].In this study, we discuss deep learning specific attribution explainability methods: DeepLIFT [24], [2], Saliency [26], Input X Gradient [25], Guided Backpropagation [27], Deconvolution [30] and Layer-wise relevance propagation [16]. These methods have an additive nature, which enables computing them in a distributed manner across processors, machines, or GPUs [13].

DeepLIFT. is a back-propagation based approach that attributes a change to inputs based on the differences between the inputs and corresponding references (or baselines) for non-linear activations. It seeks to explain the difference in the output from reference in terms of the difference in inputs from reference. DeepLIFT uses the concept of multipliers to "blame" specific neurons for the difference in output. The definition of a multiplier is as follows:

$$m_{\Delta x \Delta t} = \frac{C_{\Delta x \Delta t}}{\Delta x},$$

where x is the input neuron with a difference from reference Δx, and t is the target neuron with a difference from reference Δt, and $C_{\Delta x \Delta t}$ is then the contribution of Δx to Δt. Like partial derivatives (gradients) used in back propagation, multipliers obey the Chain Rule. DeepLIFT can be overwritten as the modified partial derivatives of output of non-linear activations with respect to their inputs [2,24].

LIME. [23] provides local model interpretability by means of local surrogate models, which are interpretable models that are trained to explain individual predictions of black box machine learning models. Instead of training a global surrogate model, LIME focuses on training local surrogate models to explain individual predictions. LIME attempts to understand the model by perturbing the input of data samples and understanding how the predictions change. It generates a new dataset consisting of perturbed samples and the corresponding predictions of the black box model. On this new dataset LIME then trains an interpretable model, which is weighted by the proximity of the sampled instances to the instance of interest.

Mathematically, local surrogate models with interpretability constraint can be expressed as follows:

$$explanation(x) = \arg\min_{g \in G} L(f, g, \pi_x) + \Omega(g),$$

The explanation model for instance x is the model g that minimizes loss L, which measures how close the explanation is to the prediction of the original model f, while the model complexity $\Omega(g)$ is kept low. G is the family of possible explanations, for example all possible linear regression models. The proximity measure π_x defines how large the neighborhood around instance x is that we consider for the explanation.

Saliency. (Saliency maps) [26] computes input attribution by returning the gradient of the output with respect to the input. This approach can be explained as taking a first-order Taylor expansion of the network at the input, and the gradients are simply the coefficients of each feature in the linear representation of the model. The absolute value of these coefficients can be taken to represent feature importance.

Input X Gradient. [25] extends the saliency approach, taking the gradients of the output with respect to the input and multiplying by the input feature values. It is like considering a linear model, in which the gradients are simply the coefficients of each input, and the product of the input with a coefficient corresponds to the total contribution of the feature to the output of this linear model.

Guided Backpropagation [27] **and Deconvolution** [30]. Both methods compute the gradient of the target output with respect to the input, but backpropagation of ReLU functions is overridden so that only non-negative gradients are backpropagated. The methods deffer in how they apply the ReLU function: in guided backpropagation this function is applied to the input gradients, and in deconvolution it is applied to the output gradients and directly backpropagated. Both approaches were proposed in the context of a convolutional network and are generally used for convolutional networks, however they can be applied generically.

Feature Permutation. Feature permutation [11,21] is a perturbation based approach which takes each feature individually, randomly permutes the feature values within a batch and computes the change in output (or loss) as a result of this modification. Input features can also be grouped and shuffled together rather than individually.

Shapley Value sampling method is based on the Shapley value attribution method, which is based on a concept from cooperative game theory [21]. This method involves taking each permutation of the input features and adding them one-by-one to a given baseline. The output difference after adding each feature corresponds to its contribution, and these differences are averaged over all permutations to obtain the attribution. To take all permutations as supposed by the Shapley value method is extremely computationally intensive so, Shapley Value Sampling [4] was proposed. It takes only a sample of random permutations and averages the marginal contribution of features based on these permutations.

Kernel SHAP. Kernel SHAP [19] computes Shapley Values based on the LIME framework. Thus setting the loss function, weighting kernel and regularization terms appropriately using LIME approach allows calculating Shapley Values more efficiently.

Layer-wise Relevance Propagation. [16] applies a backward propagation mechanism sequentially to all layers of the model. The model output score represents the initial relevance, which is decomposed into values for each neuron of the underlying layers. The decomposition is defined by rules that are chosen for each layer, involving its weights and activations.

Feature Ablation. [20] is a perturbation based approach to computing attribution, involving replacing each input feature with a given baseline / reference, and computing the difference in output. Given a dataset of n rows and m features, the procedure goes like this: Train the model on your train set and calculate a score on the test set. You can pick whatever scoring metric you like. For each of the m features, remove it from the training data and train the model. Then, calculate the score on the test set. Rank the features by the difference between the original score (from the model with all features) and the score for the model using all features but one.

In this study, we investigate how different explainability methods could be applied to the same model, how they could be distributed, how different are their results and how these results could be aggregated.

3 Explainable Federated Learning

3.1 Federated Deep-learning

In the following we first describe our proposed federated architecture and federated deep learning algorithm for taxi trip duration forecasting. We explain which information and how often should be exchanged and introduce parameters that could be optimised. Moreover, our aim is to describe the application of state-of-the-art explainability methods to federated learning, while maintaining data privacy. However, the application of each explainability method to a concrete task only produces baseline results because the result interpretation is specific to the particular task or application at hand [7].

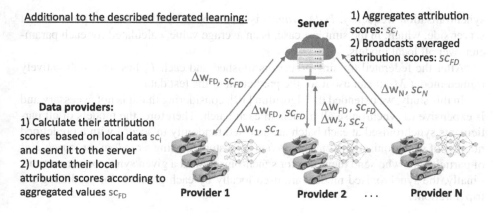

Fig. 2. Explainable federated learning architecture.

Let N participants $\{F_i\}_{i=1}^N$ own datasets $\{D_i\}_{i=1}^N$ as previously defined. For the federated learning process, each participant F_i divides its dataset $D_i = D_i^{TR} \cup D_i^{TE}$ into training set D_i^{TR} and test set D_i^{TE}. We train the models on D_i^{TR} and test the prediction quality on D_i^{TE}. $\{M_i\}_{i=1}^N$ are the local models of each participant, while M_{FD} is the federated model.

Algorithm 1. Federated learning training process.

Result: Collaboratively trained models M_i by each participant F_i

Define initial w_i for M_i, $epoch$=1, N ;

while *The loss function does not converge* **do**

    foreach *batch of data* **do**

        $synch\_list$ =random_ind(N, num_synch);

        foreach F_i *in parallel* **do**

            $Train(M_i^{<epoch,batch>}, D_i^{TR,batch})$;

            if *synchronisation* & F_i *in synch_list* **then**

                F_i sends $\Delta w_i^{<epoch,batch>}$ to the server;

    if *synchronisation* **then**

        Server averages the parameter updates/gradients and broadcasts them:

        $\Delta w_{FD}^{<epoch,batch>} = FedAverage(\Delta w_i^{<epoch,batch>})$;

        foreach F_i *in parallel* **do**

            F_i receives parameter updates from the server and updates its model:

            $w_i^{<epoch,batch>} = w_i^{<epoch,old>} + \Delta w_{FD}^{<epoch,batch>}$;

    $epoch = epoch + 1$

Training process is over. Each participant F_i has its final model M_i;

As we consider learning on batches, $M_i^{<epoch,batch>}$ is the local model of the participant F_i for the current *epoch* and *batch* of data. $w_i^{epoch,batch}$ are the current parameters of the model $M_i^{<epoch,batch>}$: $w_i^{epoch,batch} = w(M_i^{<epoch,batch>})$. The training process is described in Algorithm 1. Note, that the synchronisation should not appear each batch, so a logical variable *synchronisation* supervises this process and defines the synchronisation frequency. *FedAverage()* is a parameter synchronisation procedure at server side, which, in the simplest case, is an average value, calculated for each parameter over all local models.

After the federated training process is finished and each F_i has its collaboratively trained model M_i, it can use it for the prediction of the test data.

In this study, we extended the algorithm [10], considering that it is not necessary and is expensive to synchronise all models in each batch. Therefore, the models of all participants synchronised at each batch are selected randomly in accord with a predefined number of synchronisations num_synch at each step, forming a random set $synch\_list$ of participants, who send their data for synchronisation at a given synchronisation time. Finally, the synchronised models are used locally by each provider for predicting the trip duration.

3.2 Explaining of Federated Models

We start the variable explanation process when the federated training process is finished and each participant F_i has its collaboratively trained model M_i. The mentioned attribution scoring explainability methods have an additive nature, which enables computing them in a distributed manner across processors, machines, or GPUs. For example, the explainability scores can be calculated on the participants' local data, and then accumulated at the server together [13]. This property allowed us to apply those methods to the federated learning case, when each provider does not have enough data to explain the federated model accurately. The cooperation in this case can be organised similar to the federated learning principle, keeping data privacy condition.

The federated attribution scoring is presented in Algorithm 2. The algorithm assumes that no raw data are transferred but only some aggregated information. Thus, each data owner calculates the average attribution scores sc_{i*} based on available local data. The attribution scores are first calculated for each available data instance and then averaged by all locally available data. Note, that $sc_{i,j}$ is a one dimensional vector, in which the number of components is equal to the number of attributes in the model to be explained and the averaging of sc_{i*} is executed for each component. However, the division by $|D_i|$ for the calculation of sc_{i*} and then the multiplying with $|D_i|$ for the calculation of sc_{FD} seems to be redundant, we decided to keep it. This ensures that each local model has its local attribution score properly calculated before it obtains a federated version.

After averaged attribution scores are calculated each participant sends them to the server. Then, the server aggregates the received scores as sc_{FD} and broadcasts the result to all the local participants. Finally, each data owner updates its attribution scores. The scoring function is one of the explainability methods mentioned above (e.g., Integrated gradients, DeepLIFT, LIME).

4 Experiments

4.1 Available Data

We forecast the Brunswick taxi trip duration based on floating car data (FCD) trajectories. The data are obtained from two different taxi service providers of Brunswick and

---

Algorithm 2. Federated attribution score calculation process.

Given: Final synchronised model M_i by each participant F_i;

foreach *participant F_i in parallel* **do**

> **foreach** *instance j of D_i dataset* **do**
>
> > Calculates attribution scores:
> >
> > $sc_{i,j} = ScoringAlgorithm(M_i^{<localFD>}, D_{i,j})$;
>
> F_i calculates its average scores and sends the result to the server: $sc_{i*} = \frac{\sum_j sc_{i,j}}{|D_i|}$;

Server aggregates the participant scores and broadcasts the result: $sc_{FD} = \frac{\sum_i sc_{i*}|D_i|}{|\cup_i D_i|}$;

foreach *participant F_i in parallel* **do**

> Each F_i updates its attribution scores: $sc_{i*} = sc_{FD}$;

---

surrounding for the period of January 2014 - January 2015. We consider only the data inside a coordination box in the latitude range of $51.87° - 52.62°$ and longitude range of $10.07° - 11.05°$ (Fig. 3). The data are available in raw format, so each data item contains: car identifier, time moment, geographical point and status (free, drives to client, drives with client, etc.). The data were received approximately every 40 s.

As the data were not separated into trips, but contained FCD records for longer time periods and multiple trips of one vehicle together, our first task was to split each data record into trips. We developed a multi-step data pre-processing procedure. First, we constructed a script to transform the data into trajectories according to time points, locations, and car identifier. Then, the raw trajectories were analysed to determine their correctness and cleaned accordingly. We split trajectories with long stay periods into shorter trips. Round trips with the same source and destination were separated into two trips. Some noisy unrealistic data with probably incorrect global positioning system (GPS) signals, with incorrect status, or unrealistic average speeds, were also removed. After this cleaning, the number of trajectories was 542066.

The next pre-processing step was to improve the prediction model and filter the noisy data. So, we connected the trajectories with the open street map and obtained a routable graph. Additionally, we divided the map into different size grids (e.g., 200 m × 200 m) to determine whether this aggregation can improve our forecasts. Therefore, we knew to which zone the start and end points of each trip belong. Moreover, we found the nearest road graph node to the source and destination of each trip and calculated the shortest-path distance. We calculated the distance between the start and end points of each trip according to the FCD trajectory. If the distances of the shortest path trajectory and FCD trajectory were considerably different, we analysed the trip more closely and divided it into a couple of more realistic trips, excluding false GPS signal places.

To evaluate whether the trip duration depends on weather conditions, we used corresponding historical data about rains, wind, temperature, atmospheric pressure, etc. However, good-quality weather data for the given region were available only until the end of September 2014, so that we reduced our trajectory dataset accordingly.

For data storage, selection and filtering we used PostgreSQL database with pgRouting and PostGIS extentions, which provided data visualisation and advanced routing algorithms. So the raw data, trip data, weather data, and graph data obtained from open street map (roads and nodes) were available in PostgreSQL. We used QGIS[1] (Fig. 3) for visual presentation of trips, their sources and destinations as well as graph representation of roads network of Brunswick.

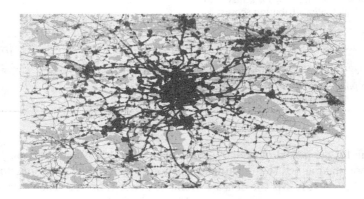

Fig. 3. Road network of Brunswick and surrounding [10].

4.2 Experimental Setup

We predicted the taxi trip duration using different methods (Table 1) and found the corresponding best hyper-parameters by the grid search.

Table 1. Optimal model hyperparameters.

Model	Hyperparameters
XGBoost	$colsample\_bytree = 0.7$; $learning\_rate = 0.12$; $max\_depth = 9$, $\alpha = 15$; $n\_estimators = 570$
Deep learn.	fully conn. percentron with 2 hid. layers, number of neurons: 64–100; Re-Lu act. function; 0.2 dropout between hid. layers; optimiser SGD; MSE loss function; $NN\_batchsize = 128$, $epochs = 800$; $learning\_rate = 0.02$
Federated learn.	synchronisation each 2nd batch, NN_batch_size is proportional to the size of each provider's dataset, the sum of all provider's $NN\_batch\_size = 128$

The best forecasts for trip duration in seconds were based on the following factors: coordinates of the start zone and end zone (200 m × 200 m), FCD distance, transformed (with sine and cosine) weekday and hour, as well as temperature, air pressure, and rain. We divided the dataset into training (80%) and test (20%) sets. The dataset was normalised with MinMax Scaler before the application of the above methods. We used

---

[1] https://www.qgis.org/.

the mean squared error (MSE) as an efficiency criterion and 5-fold cross validation for model comparison. The accuracy with an MSE of .0010 corresponds to 5 min, while that with an MSE of .0018 to 7.5 min. We used Python programming language, PyTorch for deep learning models, and an open-source Python library captum [13], which provides model interpretability for PyTorch, to find the importances of variables for black-box models.

4.3   Alternative Local and Federated Models

Table 2. MSE of travel time prediction with different ML methods.

Model	Number of data providers				
	1	4	8	16	32
XGBoost	.00097	.0011	.0012	.0012	.0013
Deep learning	.0011	.0012	.0013	.0014	.0015
Federated deep learning	—	.0011	**.0011**	**.0011**	**.0011**

Our task was to determine under which conditions federated deep learning was effective. In [10] various alternative local models were investigated like linear and Lasso regression, random forest and XGBoost models were compared with deep-learning. It was discovered that deep learning provides the second best accurate forecast and the only XGBoost and random forest, (which gave the same results) outperform it slightly. Despite the fact that XGBoost method provided the most accurate results for the centralised approach, federated learning could be implemented only on parametric models like deep learning. As it was mentioned above the data were obtained from different taxi providers, however it was unfortunately unknown, which data belonged to which provider. Thus, we randomly distributed the data among the providers and this led to the assumption of identically distributed and equally sized local datasets, which in federated learning is often not true. Our aim was to analyse after which point the distributed non-synchronised local models lose their accuracy and federated learning outperformed them. Thus, we executed various machine learning models locally on each provider without synchronisation.

Each column of Table 2 represents the MSE of trip duration prediction on distributed data increasing the number of providers (decreasing the percentage of data each provider has). The average accuracy of all models except federated deep learning was reduced. The federated approach led to the same result as that of the centralised deep learning. Starting at eight data providers (each provider with 12.5% of data), federated learning became beneficial because it performed better than local machine learning methods. With more data providers, the benefits of federated learning became more evident. The MSE of the federated model's prediction remained constant, 0.0011.

Another important parameter that influenced deep learning models was the batch size. In our centralised deep learning model, the optimal solution was obtained with batch size = 128 or smaller. The experiments showed that with the increase in the batch size, the computing speed increased, but the accuracy of the model decreased. This implied that, to obtain the same accuracy by federated learning, we had to distribute the batches proportionally among the providers. Accordingly, with eight data providers, with equally sized datasets, the batch size will be 128/8 = 16.

Moreover, in [10] the effect of the synchronisation frequency on the accuracy of the federated model was investigated. The accuracy decreased with the step-wise decrease in the synchronisation frequency. It was shown that with the synchronisation every second batch it was still possible to keep the accuracy of 0.0011 for the federated model.

4.4   Further Optimisation of Synchronisation Procedure

We aim to extend the federated algorithm and to conduct the corresponding experiments, reducing the number of the necessary communications by reducing the number of partners, which send their data at each synchronisation round. Therefore, the models of participants that will be synchronised at each batch were selected randomly in accordance with a predefined number of synchronizations num_synch at each step forming random set $synch\_list$ of participants, who send their data for synchronisation at each synchronisation round. As Table 3 shows, when considering an example with eight providers, we reduced the parameter num_synch, in step by step manner, and the prediction accuracy remained high. Figure 4 illustrates the corresponding learning process graphically.

Table 3. MSE of federated models with different number of partners sending their parameter updates.

num_synch	8	5	4	2	1
Federated deep learning, N = 8	.00110	.00110	.00113	.00117	.00131

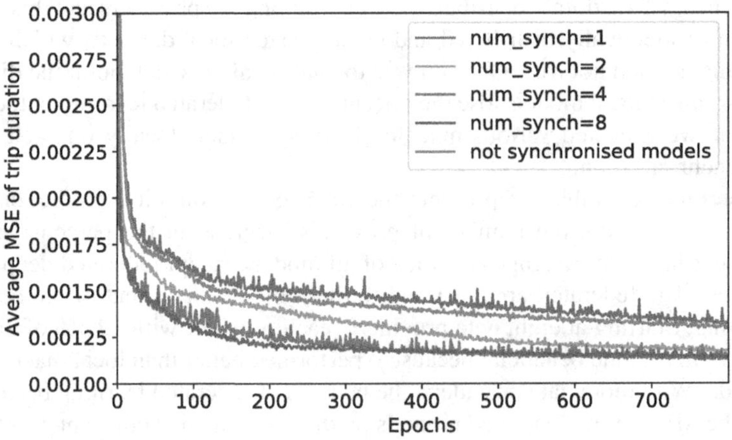

Fig. 4. Learning of federated models.

We can see that reducing num_synch from 8 to 4 did not significantly influence the learning process and led to the same accuracy after 800 epochs. With $num\_synch = 2$, the learning is slower, but after 800 epochs, leads to almost the same accuracy. However, the experiments show that with $num\_synch = 1$ the accuracy within 800 epochs decreases, and the learning process is similar to the learning of the non-synchronised models. This allowed us to conclude that, in the case of eight providers, as a trade-off between accuracy and the amount of information to be transmitted, the number of partners that send their parameters for synchronisation can be reduced to 2. Moreover, this allows the consideration of a peer-to-peer federated learning architecture instead of one with a central server.

4.5   Federated Model Explainability

In this section, we investigate the parameters that have the greatest influence on the results. We show how the size of the dataset influences the accuracy of the feature attribution, which is particularly important for explaining the decisions of local data owners in federated statements. We then compare the results of the variable importance for local predictions and show that federated explanations are comparable with centralised versions. Finally, we apply different explainability methods, i.e. model-agnostic (local and global) and model-specific, and compare their results.

Figure 5 shows the variable importance calculated using the federated model for each of the eight data providers locally when applying DeepLIFT attribution score algorithm for different dataset sizes. Despite the fact that the main tendency in terms of the variable importance by all eight providers remains the same, the locally obtained results differ from the importance scores calculated using all of the data. This may lead to an inaccurate explainability by some local providers, particularly with a small dataset. We can observe that having more data can significantly increase the accuracy of the attribution scores.

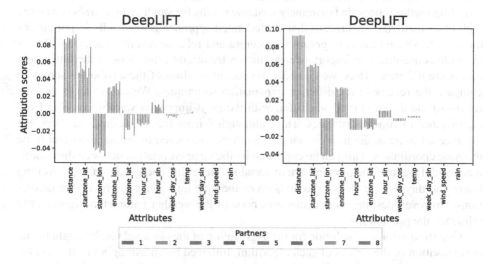

Fig. 5. DeepLIFT explainability of individual models: small dataset of size 2000 (left), big dataset of all locally available data (right).

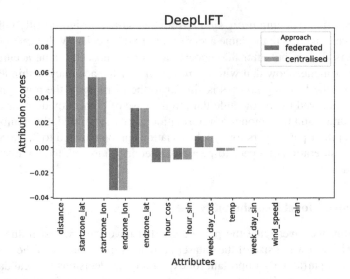

Fig. 6. Explainability of federated vs centralised approach.

The proposed importance score-averaging mechanism (Algorithm 2) avoids this inaccuracy without transmitting the local datasets. Figure 6 shows that the attribution scores obtained by the federated approach are the same as those obtained through the centralised approach using the exemplary DeepLIFT method.

Finally, we investigate which parameters have the greatest influence on the results. We apply various attribution score calculation algorithms, the results of which are provided in Figs. 5, 7, 8.

To compare the attribution score results of the different methods, we used small local datasets with 2000 records. Remarkably, feature permutation and Shapley value sampling methods provided extremely unstable results for small sample sizes compared with other methods. This means that the federated approach is especially important for those methods and helps to get more accurate and reliable results. Because different algorithms use different importance-estimation techniques, the signs of the attribution scores are different. Thus, we consider the absolute values of the attribution scores to compare the results of the different explanation techniques. We can observe that the results of the different methods differ, with the most important variable varying from the distance to zone coordinates. Thus, although 8 from the 11 methods declared the distance attribute as the most important, 3 others considered the most important to be the zone coordinates. This can be explained by the large correlation between the coordinates and distance. The next important variables were sine and cosine of the travelling hours and days of the week. The division of the map into zones improved the predictions. However, despite our expectations, none of the weather parameters significantly influence the predictions.

One straightforward solution for the aggregation of the obtained results might be the normalisation of the results of each algorithm, followed by an averaging of the results. However, simply averaging the attribution scores can be an incorrect technique because

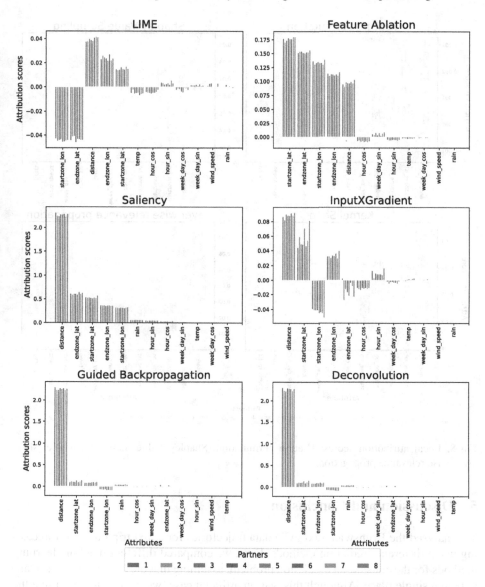

Fig. 7. Local attribution scores: LIME, Feature Ablation, Saliency, InputXGradient, Guided Beckpropagation, Deconvolution.

of the different possible scales and distributions of each attribution algorithm. Therefore, as applied in this study, we propose looking at the results of different methods and trying to find some similarities in the results.

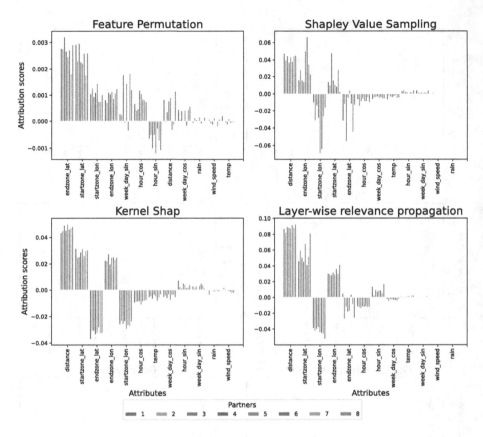

Fig. 8. Local attribution scores: Feature permutation, Shapley Value Sampling, Kernel shap, layer-wise relevance propagation.

5   Discussion and Conclusion

We analysed the Brunswick taxi FCD data trajectories for a taxi trip duration forecasting using different prediction methods. First, we compared different machine learning methods for the considered prediction problem, assuming that the entire dataset is available in a single place. Although this was an artificial case, we wanted to determine the best possible prediction accuracy as well as the best prediction technique. We discovered that XGBoost and random forest slightly outperform deep learning model (with an MSE 0.00097 in comparison to 0.0011, respectively).

Second, we considered a more realistic case in which the data were distributed among various providers. The data owners do not want to share raw data for privacy reasons. However, they agreed to collaborate in a federated way, transferring the model parameters. Because these methods are non-parametric and do not assume sequential learning, there is no known application of federated XGBoost or random forest. The best candidate for the federated approach was deep learning, which showed relatively promising results in the first case with all available data. We divided the data equally among the providers and showed that starting from eight data providers, the federated deep learning approach could outperform the local models without cooperation. This means that for data owners with less than 12% data, the federated approach provides certain benefits. Moreover, we optimised the federated process and showed that upon the synchronisation executed on each second batch, the corresponding federated deep learning model did not decrease in accuracy. Moreover, to reduce the data transmission without significant decreasing the forecasting accuracy, we continued to investigate the possible optimisation of the federated model synchronisation mechanism by reducing the number of data providers sending their data for synchronisation during each round. We discovered that for eight data providers, this number of active providers, can be reduced to 4, mostly without a reduction in accuracy (0.00113), and up to 2 with an accuracy of 0.00117. For a simpler calculation in our experiments, the local datasets of all providers were of the same size, and the data were identically distributed in all datasets, which is often not true in real-world problems. In our future experiments, we plan to consider datasets that are not equally sized and not identically distributed. A particularly beneficial case could be to suppose a confidential and locally processed (self-interested ride providers) datasets of each taxi, as applied in [22].

Third, considering the deep learning approach, we should not forget that this is a black-box model, which should be explained to increase its trustworthiness. We proposed an approach to explaining the horizontal federated learning model using state-of-the-art explainability methods without transferring raw data to the central server. This enables more accurate determination of the most important prediction variables of the federated model as if each provider had access to the data of the other participants. Moreover, the proposed federated explainability approach does not depend on the explainability method. This allowed us to compare different explainability attribution score algorithms, i.e., model-specific and model-agnostic, local and global. Despite the fact that each method shows different results the main tendency remains. Thus, considering the absolute attribution score values, attributes such as the distance and zone geographical coordinates remain the most important for each method. In turn, weather attributes are of little meaning. We believe that this approach could be successfully implemented for more complex prediction and classification tasks with more complex deep learning and federated learning architectures. For example, we aim to implement explainable federated learning for traffic demand forecasting models.

Acknowledgements. The research was funded by the Lower Saxony Ministry of Science and Culture under grant number ZN3493 within the Lower Saxony "Vorab" of the Volkswagen Foundation and supported by the Center for Digital Innovations (ZDIN). The Brunswick taxi FCD data were provided by SocialCars Research Training Group Project of the German Research Foundation.

References

1. Al-Abbasi, A.O., Ghosh, A., Aggarwal, V.: Deeppool: distributed model-free algorithm for ride-sharing using deep reinforcement learning. IEEE Trans. ITSs **20**(12), 4714–4727 (2019). https://doi.org/10.1109/TITS.2019.2931830

2. Ancona, M., Ceolini, E., Öztireli, C., Gross, M.: Towards better understanding of gradient-based attribution methods for deep neural networks. In: Proceedings of 6th International Conference on Learning Representations, ICLR (2018). https://openreview.net/forum?id=Sy21R9JAW

3. Bonawitz, K., et al.: Towards federated learning at scale: system design. CoRR abs/1902.01046 (2019)

4. Castro, J., Gómez, D., Tejada, J.: Polynomial calculation of the Shapley value based on sampling. Comput. Oper. Res. **36**(5), 1726–1730 (2009). https://doi.org/10.1016/j.cor.2008.04.004https://www.sciencedirect.com/science/article/pii/S0305054808000804, selected papers presented at the Tenth International Symposium on Locational Decisions (ISOLDE X)

5. Ciskowski, P., Drzewiński, G., Bazan, M., Janiczek, T.: Estimation of travel time in the city using neural networks trained with simulated urban traffic data. In: Zamojski, W., Mazurkiewicz, J., Sugier, J., Walkowiak, T., Kacprzyk, J. (eds.) DepCoS-RELCOMEX 2018. AISC, vol. 761, pp. 121–134. Springer, Cham (2019). https://doi.org/10.1007/978-3-319-91446-6_13

6. Claes, R., Holvoet, T.: Ad hoc link traversal time prediction. In: IEEE Conference on ITS, pp. 1803–1808 (2011). https://doi.org/10.1109/ITSC.2011.6082970

7. Fiosina, J., Fiosins, M., Bonn, S.: Explainable deep learning for augmentation of sRNA expression profiles. J. Comput. Biol. (2019). (to appear)

8. Fiosina, J., Fiosins, M., Müller, J.: Big data processing and mining for next generation intelligent transportation systems. Jurnal Teknologi **63**(3) (2013)

9. Fiosina, J., Fiosins, M., Müller, J.P.: Decentralised cooperative agent-based clustering in intelligent traffic clouds. In: Klusch, M., Thimm, M., Paprzycki, M. (eds.) MATES 2013. LNCS (LNAI), vol. 8076, pp. 59–72. Springer, Heidelberg (2013). https://doi.org/10.1007/978-3-642-40776-5_8

10. Fiosina, J.: Explainable federated learning for taxi travel time prediction. In: Proceedings of the 7th International Conference on Vehicle Technology and Intelligent Transport Systems: VEHITS2021, pp. 670–677. SciTePress (2021)

11. Fisher, A., Rudin, C., Dominici, F.: All models are wrong, but many are useful: learning a variable's importance by studying an entire class of prediction models simultaneously. J. Mach. Learn. Res. **20**(177), 1–81 (2019)

12. Holzinger, A.: Explainable AI (ex-AI). Informatik-Spektrum **41**(2), 138–143 (2018). https://doi.org/10.1007/s00287-018-1102-5

13. Kokhlikyan, N., et al.: Captum: a unified and generic model interpretability library for pytorch (2020)

14. Konecný, J., McMahan, H.B., Ramage, D., Richtárik, P.: Federated optimization: distributed machine learning for on-device intelligence. CoRR abs/1610.02527 (2016). http://arxiv.org/abs/1610.02527

15. Kraus, S., et al.: AI for explaining decisions in multi-agent environment. In: AAAI-2020. AAAI Press (2020)

16. Lapuschkin, S., Binder, A., Montavon, G., Klauschen, F., Müller, K.R., Samek, W.: On pixel-wise explanations for non-linear classifier decisions by layer-wise relevance propagation. PLoS One **10**, e0130140 (2015). https://doi.org/10.1371/journal.pone.0130140

17. Lin, H., Zito, R., Taylor, M.: A review of travel-time prediction in transport and logistics. In: Proceedings of the Eastern Asia Society for Transportation Studies, vol. 5, pp. 1433–1448. Hamburg (2005)

18. Linardatos, P., Papastefanopoulos, V., Kotsiantis, S.: Explainable ai: a review of machine learning interpretability methods. Entropy **23**(1) (2021). https://doi.org/10.3390/e23010018, https://www.mdpi.com/1099-4300/23/1/18

19. Lundberg, S., Lee, S.: A unified approach to interpreting model predictions. In: Guyon, I., et al. (eds.) Advances in Neural Information Processing Systems, vol. 30, pp. 4765–4774. Curran Associates, Inc. (2017). http://papers.nips.cc/paper/7062-a-unified-approach-to-interpreting-model-predictions.pdf
20. Meyes, R., Lu, M., de Puiseau, C.W., Meisen, T.: Ablation studies in artificial neural networks. CoRR abs/1901.08644 (2019). http://arxiv.org/abs/1901.08644
21. Molnar, C.: Interpretable machine learning. a guide for making black box models explainable. Lulu.com (2020). https://christophm.github.io/interpretable-ml-book/index.html
22. Ramanan, P., Nakayama, K., Sharma, R.: Baffle: blockchain based aggregator free federated learning. CoRR abs/1909.07452 (2020)
23. Ribeiro, M., Singh, S., Guestrin, C.: "why should i trust you?": explaining the predictions of any classifier. In: Proceedings of 22Nd ACM SIGKDD International Conference on Knowledge Discovery and Data Mining, pp. 1135–1144. KDD 2016, ACM, New York, NY, USA (2016). https://doi.org/10.1145/2939672.2939778
24. Shrikumar, A., Greenside, P., Kundaje, A.: Learning important features through propagating activation differences. In: Proceedings of ML Research, vol. 70, pp. 3145–3153. PMLR, Int. Convention Centre, Sydney, Australia, 06–11 August 2017
25. Shrikumar, A., Greenside, P., Shcherbina, A., Kundaje, A.: Not just a black box: learning important features through propagating activation differences. CoRR arXiv:1605.01713 (2017)
26. Simonyan, K., Vedaldi, A., Zisserman, A.: Deep inside convolutional networks: visualising image classification models and saliency maps. In: 2nd International Conference on Learning Representations, ICLR 2014, Banff, AB, Canada, 14–16 April 2014. Workshop Track Proceedings (2014). http://arxiv.org/abs/1312.6034
27. Springenberg, J., Dosovitskiy, A., Brox, T., Riedmiller, M.: Striving for simplicity: the all convolutional net. In: ICLR (Workshop Track) (2015). http://lmb.informatik.uni-freiburg.de/Publications/2015/DB15a
28. Wang, G.: Interpret federated learning with Shapley values. CoRR abs/1905.04519 (2019)
29. Yang, Q., Liu, Y., Chen, T., Tong, Y.: Federated machine learning: concept and applications. ACM Trans. Intell. Syst. Technol. **10**(2) (2019). https://doi.org/10.1145/3298981
30. Zeiler, M.D., Fergus, R.: Visualizing and understanding convolutional networks. In: Fleet, D., Pajdla, T., Schiele, B., Tuytelaars, T. (eds.) ECCV 2014. LNCS, vol. 8689, pp. 818–833. Springer, Cham (2014). https://doi.org/10.1007/978-3-319-10590-1_53

Development of a Safe Charging Infrastructure System: Requirements, Design, Verification and Validation

Tommi Kivelä[1]([⊠])(iD), Marvin Sperling[1](iD), Mohamed Abdelawwad[2](iD),
Malte Drabesch[2], Michael Schwarz[2], Josef Börcsök[2](iD), and Kai Furmans[1](iD)

[1] Institute for Material Handling and Logistics (IFL), Karlsruhe Institute of Technology (KIT),
Karlsruhe, Germany
`tommi.kivelae@kit.edu`
[2] Department of Computer Architecture and System Programming, University of Kassel,
Kassel, Germany
`m.abdelawwad@uni-kassel.de`

Abstract. With the ongoing shift from fossil fuels towards electric mobility, there's an increasing need for charging infrastructure for electric vehicles, both private and public. With this increasing role of charging infrastructure in day-to-day life, safety and security should be guaranteed for these systems. In this work we report on the development of an integrated electronic charging infrastructure system. The development was based on both current functional safety and charging infrastructure standards. The whole development process is presented, including requirements analysis, overall system design, safety hardware and software design, as well as the verification & validation of the safety system against the requirements set in the beginning. The presented work can be used as a basis and reference for the functional safety aspects when developing next generation charging infrastructure systems.

Keywords: Electric vehicle charging · Functional safety · Safety-related systems · System design · Verification & validation

1 Introduction

Climate concerns are driving a significant shift from the use of fossil fuels towards electric vehicles. According to the IEA [3], the amount of electric vehicles (EVs) jumped from 17 000 cars in 2010 to 7.2 million in 2019. To be feasible, this shift requires significant investments in charging infrastructure for EVs. Aside from a network of public

We gratefully acknowledge that this research is funded by the German Federal Ministry of Education and Research (BMBF: Bundesministerium für Bildung und Forschung) under grant numbers 16EMO0329 and 16EMO0330. We would additionally like to thank the partner companies, ProSystems GmbH and kortec Industrieelektronik GmbH & Co. KG, for the collaboration on the project. Finally, we would like to thank the IFL student assistants Nicolas Walter, Sevastiyan Bozhkov and Kerong Xu for their contributions to the simulation model and test setup presented in this work.

© Springer Nature Switzerland AG 2022
C. Klein et al. (Eds.): SMARTGREENS 2021/ VEHITS 2021, CCIS 1612, pp. 412–434, 2022.
https://doi.org/10.1007/978-3-031-17098-0_21

charging stations, charging equipment will be increasingly installed in homes and used on a daily basis to charge electric vehicles overnight. In 2019, 7.3 million chargers worldwide have been installed, majority of them private [3]. With this increasing role of charging infrastructure in day-to-day life, safety and security should be guaranteed for these systems.

In this work we present results from the research project SiLis ("Sicheres Lade-infrastruktursystem für Elektrofahrzeuge": "a safe charging infrastructure system for EVs"). The goal of the project was to develop a compact and cost-effective electronic control system for both private and public 3-phase AC (mode 3) charging stations. The developed system integrates several functions which are currently implemented by separate discrete components (e.g. residual current device, charging controller and contactor, energy meter) into a single electronic system. As this electronic system implements safety-related functions previously handled by discrete electromechanical components, functional safety, i.e. the "part of the overall safety [...] that depends on the correct functioning of the electric/electronic/programmable electronics (E/E/PE) safety-related systems and other risk reduction measures" [9], needs to be considered during the development. The system was therefore developed considering, apart from the requirements from the current EV supply equipment (EVSE) standards, also the current functional safety standards.

The relevant background information about EVSE and functional safety is provided in Sect. 2. Section 3 discusses the performed risk assessment for the charging application, and the derived safety requirements for the system. The system design, alongside the detailed design of the safety hardware and software and performed FMEA are discussed in Sect. 4. Finally, Sect. 5 discusses the verification and validation (V&V) activities performed in the project, including e.g. software- and hardware-in-the-loop (SIL/HIL) tests, fuzzing for the internal communication, and reaction time measurements to validate the fault current protection safety function (SF).

This work is a revised and extended version of the paper presented at the 7th International Conference on Vehicle Technology and Intelligent Transport Systems [17]. The focus in the previous work was on the requirements analysis and the overall system design. In this work the requirements analysis is presented in a summarised form. The focus is shifted towards the system design, presented in more detail, and the V&V, included as a new section.

2 Background

2.1 Electric Vehicle Supply Equipment

The general and safety requirements for EVSE are provided by the IEC 61851 standard series [7]. The complete EV charging system includes the EVSE and the functions within the EV required for charging [7]. The standard sets general safety requirements for EVSE, but does not currently include explicit functional safety requirements. The EV side safety requirements for the charging system are defined in ISO 17409 [16]. IEC 61851-1 [7] defines different configurations of the EV charging system and different charging modes, including AC and DC charging. The presented system targets mode 3 charging, i.e. AC charging with dedicated EVSE permanently connected to the grid [7].

The standard series IEC 62196 [10] defines standardized plugs, socket-outlets, vehicle connectors and vehicle inlets for EV charging. Specifically, IEC 62196-2 [11] defines standardized connectors for use in AC charging, including the Type 2 connector, commonly used in Europe. The standards IEC 62196-1 [10] and IEC 61851-1 [13] define the basic vehicle interface for AC charging and the Control Pilot (CP)-function for basic communication between the EVSE and the EV during charging, allowing for continuous monitoring of the proximity of the EV, basic signalling between the EVSE and EV, and encoding the charging cable current capability. The power supply to the EV shall be energized and de-energized based on the state of the CP signal [13]. For this work, we assumed the use of IEC 62196-2 [11] conforming connectors and the basic interface with CP function. The developed system can optionally support high-level communication e.g. according to ISO 15118 [15], but the safety-related functions are based on the basic interface.

The basic electrical protection requirements [4] and other requirements from IEC 61851-1 [13] were taken into account during the development project, but for the purposes of this paper we focus on the main functions relevant for the development of the safety-related control system.

In addition to the mandatory functions related to mode 3, IEC 61851-1 [13] sets requirements for electrical fault protection. Fault protection (protection against indirect contact) shall be provided with one or more measures according to IEC 60364-4-41 [4]. When using a socket-outlet or connector according to IEC 62196 series [10], in addition to AC, a DC sensitive residual current protection device (RCD) shall be used. Protective earthing conductor shall be provided and for mode 3 it shall not be switched. The developed system shall therefore include fault current protection for both AC and DC faults.

2.2 Safety Engineering and Functional Safety

Since the system to be developed is an infrastructure system and not part of the EV itself, the standard IEC 61508 [7] was chosen as development guidance and certification target. The standard provides generic guidance for the development of safety-related E/E/PE systems. The goal of safety engineering is to assure the safety of a system over its lifecycle. In the concept phase, the system to be developed is analysed: the hazards related to the system are first identified and the associated risk is estimated and evaluated. Based on the risk assessment, risk reduction measures are designed to reduce the risks in the system to an acceptable level. Risk reduction measures can be passive measures, such as basic electrical isolation or active measures, such as fault current protection. A safety integrity level (SIL) is used to specify the integrity requirements for a safety function, which will be allocated to a E/E/PE-system. The standard defines SILs 1–4, with a higher level corresponding to higher risk reduction [7].

2.3 Related Work

Scientific literature regarding charging infrastructure systems seldom include considerations for functional safety, focusing instead on other aspects, such as for example power electronic solutions for high power charging [27] or smart charging strategies and grid integration [29,31].

Schmittner et al. previously studied functional and electrical safety for charging stations [25]. The authors considered a typical implementation of a charging station with the safety-related functions implemented mainly through discrete electromechanical and electronic components, whereas we consider an integrated software controlled system.

A thorough safety assessment for EV charging was presented by Vogt et al. [30]. They considered several hazard types (e.g. electrical, mechanical, ergonomic) based on ISO 12100 [14] and defined safety goals to be fulfilled by the EVSE or through other means and assigned SIL-targets for each. Their work provided a basis for the risk analysis performed in the SiLis-project. However, some safety goals are reached through a combination of risk reduction measures. Thus, a more detailed analysis is required in order to determine the required contribution of each risk reduction measure towards the safety goal.

Several charging systems and in-cable-charging devices are available on the market today. To the author's knowledge, none of them are currently certified with respect to functional safety.

3 Safety Requirements

The project target was to develop a compact and cost-effective electronic charging infrastructure system, which integrates several functions, currently typically implemented with multiple discrete components (e.g. RCD, charging contactor, charging controller, energy meter), required in a charging station. As safety functions, such as fault current protection, will be implemented on a programmable electronic system instead of the traditional electromechanical solution, the functional safety of the system needs to be considered. The charging application and associated risks need to be assessed to determine the required risk reduction and the functional safety requirements for the system.

In this section we briefly present the risk assessment for the charging application and the defined safety requirements for the charging infrastructure system. The charging infrastructure system should provide a common basis for both public and private charging. Mode 3 was the main target, but the risk analysis was held as generic as possible to cover the different charging configurations defined by IEC 61851-1. The focus of the work was on AC-charging, but the developed safety system should also be adaptable to DC-charging in the future.

3.1 Risk Assessment

The goal of the risk assessment was to specify the functional safety requirements for the system. This section presents a summary of the previously reported work [17]. The approach and results of Vogt et al. [30] was taken as a basis for the assessment. The focus of the assessment was on electrical hazards. Basic electrical protection against electrical hazards were considered covered through following the product standardisation.

This includes for example fulfilling the isolation, breaking capacity and IP-classification requirements set for housing and cabling in IEC 61851-1 [13] and using the charging plugs and sockets as defined in e.g. IEC 62196-2 [11]. Other, e.g. mechanical or ergonomic hazards were similarly considered covered through the existing standardisation. The hazards considered are shown in Table 1.

Vogt et al. [30] considered several environmental and operational conditions. For this work, some of the conditions were summarised to focus on the worst case scenarios to derive the functional safety requirements. The considered environmental conditions and process states are shown in Table 2. All combinations were considered, but some non-realistic combinations, e.g. VS2 and A were filtered out, or situations were combined where e.g. the weather conditions made no significant difference. To cover all cases, the worst case location, a public charging station on the side of a public road and no cover or roofing, was taken as the basis for the assessment. The user of the charging station was assumed to be a layperson with limited knowledge regarding electric equipment. Thus in most cases a worst case assumption has to be made about the capability of the user to detect and avoid hazards. Assumed was, that the vehicle fulfils ISO 17409 [16] requirements, which do not allow vehicle movement powered by its own drives while it is connected to external power supply, excluding this as a possible state. Other possible situations where the vehicle is moving are covered by VS2.

For each situation, all the 4 hazards and possible hazard situations were considered. Considered hazard situations included, for example, the user touching live parts or the system short-circuiting, both due to failure of the basic protection as the user is plugging the charging connector into the EV to begin charging. A total of 53 cases were analysed. As the functions related to the basic vehicle interface are part of the risk reduction measures, the analysis assumed that they are not yet present in the system, in order to evaluate their required contribution to risk reduction. The considered risk reduction measures are shown in Table 3. For each case the initial risk was evaluated and risk reduction measures were added until the remaining risk was considered acceptable. For a more detailed discussion of the risk assessment, refer to the previous publication [17].

Table 1. Hazards considered in the risk assessment [17].

ID	Hazards
Hz1	Electric shock through contact with live electric parts
Hz2	Electric shock through contact with live electric parts when considering external misuse (e.g. vandalism)
Hz3	Fire, burnout, projection of molten parts due to arcing or sparking
Hz4	Fire, burnout, projection of molten parts due to short-circuit or overload of the charging system

3.2 Functional Safety Requirements for the Charging Station

Based on the risk assessment, the safety functions required to reduce the risk of the hazards related to the charging application were defined as shown in Table 4. The defined safety functions cover the risk reduction measures RM1-RM3 (SF1-SF3). SF4 is additionally needed to safely activate the power supply to allow charging in the first place.

Table 2. Situation parameters [17].

ID	Weather conditions
W1	Fog or otherwise high humidity
W2	Ice, snow or snowfall
W3	Rain, driving or heavy rain, water splashes from passing vehicles, or flooding
ID	Operating states
A	User insert charging connector, charging process is started
B	Charging connector is plugged in, charging process ongoing
C	User removes charging connector, charging process is stopped
ID	Vehicle states
VS1	Vehicle is standing (velocity = 0)
VS2	Vehicle is moving (velocity > 0) due to external influences

Table 3. Considered risk reduction measures based on IEC 61851-1 [13,17].

ID	Risk reduction measures
RM1	Overload and short circuit protection
RM2	Fault current protection (AC & DC)
RM3	EV Proximity monitoring, energy supply only when present and automatic disconnection by loss of continuity (CP/Basic vehicle interface)
RM4	Charging cable capacity detection and overload protection (CP/Basic vehicle interface)
RM5	Locking mechanism for the charging connector (Optional requirement for modes 2–4)

The measures RM4 & RM5 provide further risk reduction, but were assigned no SIL requirements.

Risk assessments are always subjective [23], the results might vary significantly depending on the assessors. The participants tried to remain conscious of any subjective biases, and to make worst case estimates as objectively as possible. Thus the requirements here are tending towards conservative. Considering that charging station usage is still relatively limited and that as a society we have relatively little experience over longer periods of time in laypersons using such equipment on a daily basis, a conservative approach seems reasonable. Once more information and real-life experiences over the lifecycle is gathered with the currently installed equipment, the risk assessment could be revisited. For low power home charging a lower risk level can possibly be argued. For high power public DC-charging a more detailed analysis should be performed considering the specific characteristics of those systems.

4 Design

4.1 System Design

The designed overall system architecture is shown in Fig. 1. The main subsystems are the main board, safety board (SAB), and the operational board (OPB). The main board

Table 4. Safety requirements for the system [17].

ID	Safety functions	SIL	Related hazards
SF1	EVSE Overload and short circuit protection	SIL3	Hz4
SF2	AC & DC Fault current protection	SIL2	Hz1, Hz2
SF3	Proximity monitoring, disconnection of energy supply upon loss of continuity	SIL2	Hz1–Hz4
SF4	Safe start and stop of charging process. Start only when EV connected and self-test successful. Internal system supervision and stop upon detection of unsafe state or internal faults	SIL2	Hz1–Hz4

includes fuses and the main charging circuit. The main charging circuit includes redundant charging relays, to supply power to the EV, and associated feedback signals, a fault current sensor, current sensors, the basic vehicle interface circuitry, DC power supply and interfaces for SAB and OPB. The SAB is responsible for the safety-related functions (core charging control) and the OPB for non-safety-related functions such as energy monitoring, EV communication, communication with the user over a web- or application-based GUI and with the backend servers required in public charging for e.g. payment processing. The safety and operational board communicate over a serial bus with a Modbus RTU-protocol modified with additional reliability measures. The system architecture allows for separation and freedom from interference between safety- and non-safety-related functions.

The SF1 (Overload protection) is implemented through fuses on the main board. The SAB does not take part in this SIL3-rated SF. The SAB is responsible for implementing the control logic for the remaining SFs, which are all rated SIL2. Thus, the SAB development targets systematic capability SC2 (required for SIL2) according to IEC 61508 [7].

The control loop implementing SF2 (AC & DC Fault current protection) consists of the fault current sensor within the main charging circuit, the SAB and the charging relays. Detected fault current leads to immediate disconnection of the power supply. The chosen 30 mA AC & 6 mA DC fault current sensor (Bender RCMB121) includes a self-test function. Additionally, an independent fault current emulation circuit is implemented as part of the main charging circuit. The self-test and independent test are performed each time before a charging process is started to detect possible faults in the sensor circuit.

The CP driver signal is generated by the OPB. The SAB has a separate measurement of the CP signal to independently detect the EV proximity and that the charging cable is properly plugged in. The IEC 62196-2 [11] charging connectors guarantee that the CP-lines are connected last and disconnected first. The SF3 is implemented with the control loop consisting of the CP voltage measurement circuit, the SAB and the charging relays.

The SF4 is implemented by the control loop including the SAB and the redundant charging relays and their contact feedbacks. For the targeted current rating (32A), force guided relays, were not available. Thus, a redundant set of standard relays (the contacts in two rows in series connection) were used. In order to detect faults in the relay contacts (contact welded shut, contact remains open), a feedback signal was included for each grid phase (L1–L3) contact. The SAB controls each relay row separately, and thus is capable of diagnosing each relay row separately during energization and de-energization, and reliably de-energize the system if any single relay contact is welded shut. Additionally, the SAB and the used safety MCU (Microcontroller unit) include numerous self-diagnostics. Upon detection of internal faults, the system is brought to a safe state (energy supply de-energized).

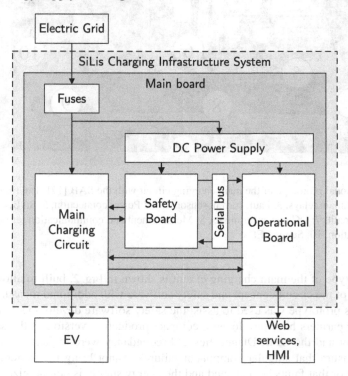

Fig. 1. System architecture [17].

The risk reduction measures RM4 (and the optional RM5) were not allocated any SIL-requirements, and thus these functions were allocated onto the OPB instead of the SAB. For RM4 (Cable capacity detection and overload protection), the OPB detects the capacity through the basic vehicle interface. The OPB utilises the current sensors in the main circuit for charging cable protection as well as for energy monitoring of the charging process. Upon overload the OPB requests the SAB to stop the power supply to the EV.

To initiate or stop the charging process, the OPB can send requests to and get diagnostics from the SAB through the communication interface. The SAB is in control of and continuously monitors the charging process and deactivates the power supply to the EV if any faults are detected. The system design and communication solution provides moderate protection against cybersecurity threats to safety. Since all external communication is implemented on the OPB, the SAB itself is not in direct connection to the internet and uses direct physical digital and analogue IO for the safety-related functions.

Fig. 2. Functional prototype of the main charging circuit with the SAB [17]. 1: Grid connection, 2: Redundant main relays, 3: Fault current sensor, 4: EV Power connection, 5: SAB, 6: FC sensor diagnostic circuit, 7: DC power terminals, 8: Measurement and communication terminals, 9: CP signal generation, 10: Status LEDs.

A prototype of the main charging circuit is shown in Fig. 2, built to allow for easy verification of the circuit concept and safety software with additional measurement terminals. This prototype was used to assist the safety software development. The industrial project partners have developed a compact production version of the same hardware concept and the OPB. Diagnostics and redundancy were included in the system design to ensure that singular component failures cannot bring the system to a hazardous state or that faults are detected and the energy supply is de-energized before an accident can occur. The SAB implements a 1oo1D architecture [2], whereas the main application circuitry is redundant.

4.2 Safety Board Design

The SAB (block diagram and the hardware shown respectively in Figs. 3 and 4) is responsible for carrying out the majority of safety functions. To achieve the safety integrity requirements, the board was designed around a safety-certified MCU (TI Hercules RM48). The MCU has redundant Arithmetic Logic Units (ALUs) in lockstep, error correction code (ECC) memory and built-in self-tests. The SAB includes galvanic isolations for inputs, outputs and the power supply, as well as voltage monitoring and a two-stage hardware watchdog.

The two-stage hardware watchdog consists of two dual retriggerable monostable multivibrator chips (Fig. 5). The output of the first chip is connected to the diagnostic circuit and to the input of the second chip. The second chip is used to verify the operation of the WD by reading its output from the MCU during the periodic test. When the

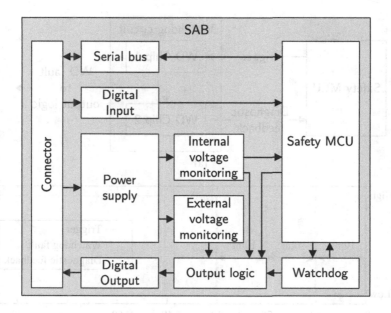

Fig. 3. Block diagram of the safety board.

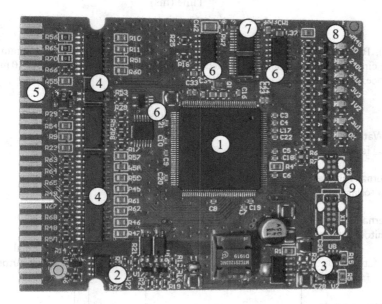

Fig. 4. The safety board [17]. 1: Safety MCU. 2: External voltage monitoring. 3: Internal voltage monitoring. 4: Galvanic isolation. 5: Mainboard connector. 6: Control logic circuitry. 7: Hardware Watchdog. 8: Status LEDs. 9: Programming and diagnostics interface.

WD chips are not triggered, the output is always high. The output is low only when the WD chips are triggered every 10 ms. During the periodic test, the WD is triggered and the WD diagnostic signal is read to test the functionality of the WD.

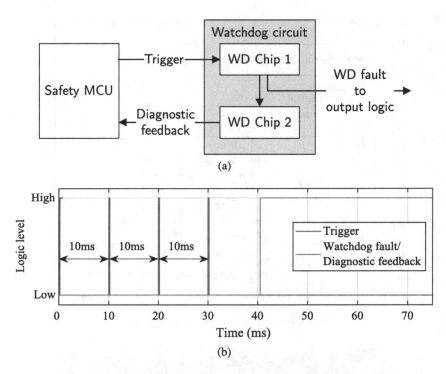

Fig. 5. (a): Block diagram of the two-stage hardware watchdog, (b): Timing diagram for the watchdog circuit: Watchdog fault is activated if the trigger is not repeated within 10 ms of the previous one.

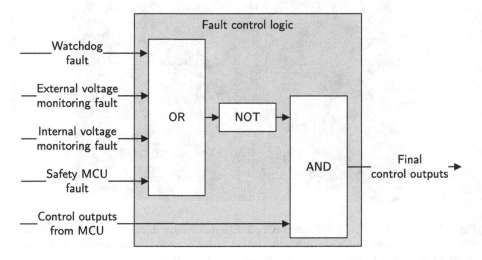

Fig. 6. Fault control logic implemented on the SAB.

A SAB-internal fault control logic was designed as diagnostic system to enforce the charging system to a safe state if faults are detected on the SAB. In the case of a fault, the control signal from the MCU is not passed to the relays. There are four diagnostic signals: Watchdog signal, external and internal voltage monitoring faults signals and a fault signal from the safety MCU. The four signals are coupled through an OR gate, as shown in Fig. 6. The output of the OR gate is inverted and connected to the relay control signal coming from the MCU via an AND gate. The output of the AND gate provides the control signal for the relays. If an error occurs in one of the four signals, the output of the OR gate is "true" and thus the control signal of the relays is always low. This means that the system is in the de-energized mode, which is the safe state.

4.3 Design FMEA

One of the most common techniques used for safety analysis of technical systems is the failure modes and effects analysis (FMEA). There are various types of FMEA, e.g. design FMEA, process FMEA, and system FMEA [24]. During the SiLis-project, FMEAs were performed for both the SAB and the main charging circuit and the designs optimised based on the analysis results. In this section the SAB DFMEA is discussed in more detail.

In DFMEA, after planning and preparation, a structure and function analysis is performed to identify subsystems and components as well as their functions. After this step, the failure analysis is performed. For each component, the possible failure modes, their causes and effects on the system are considered and evaluated [24]. In a functional safety context, the focus of the analysis is on dangerous faults, i.e. faults whose effects could bring the system to a hazardous state. For the SAB DFMEA, a risk priority number (RPN) based evaluation was used. Based on the failure analysis, the quantitative parameters, severity (S), probability of occurrence (O), and detectability (D), are estimated. Each parameter has a value between 1 and 10, where the value of 1 represents the lowest severity, and the probability of occurrence, and the highest detectability of the failure. On the other hand, the value of ten represents the highest severity and probability and the lowest detectability [28]. The three parameters are used to calculate the RPN: $RPN = S \times O \times D$.

If the determined RPN value is higher than 125 ($5 \times 5 \times 5$), the risk is high, and the design has to be optimized in order to reduce this risk. This can be done by reducing the probability of occurrence (e.g. by implementing redundancy in the system) or increasing the detectability of the failure (e.g. by adding further diagnostics). For more information about this methodology, see [28].

The structure of the SAB was previously shown in the SAB block diagram in Fig. 3. All subsystems except the serial bus for communication with the OPB were analysed in the DFMEA. The serial bus subsystem was excluded as it is not a safety-relevant module (functionality not part of directly implementing any SF). All other subsystems were considered in the analysis, their functions identified and the failure analysis was performed accordingly. In the following, examples of the SAB DFMEA for two subsystems are discussed.

Power Supply. The SAB board is supplied with 12 V from the main board. It is used to supply the safety chip with 3.3 V and 1.2 V, while the other chips are supplied with 3.3 V. Therefore, there are two voltage converter modules on the SAB board, namely the

DC-DC converter (converts 12 V to 3.3 V) and the TPS73701DCQR voltage regulator (converts 3.3 V to 1.2 V).

Most failures in this subsystem either have no immediate effects or cause the SAB to have no power, thus effectively bringing the system to a safe state. The maximum RPN of all failures in this module is 60, which is below the critical limit (125). This means that none of the failure modes of the components in this module is critical and therefore no further actions are needed.

External Voltage Monitoring. The task of this module is to monitor the voltages supplied by the main board. The module consists of photocouplers, resistors, bipolar transistors, an analog comparator and a Z-diode. For several resistors used e.g. as part of the comparator circuit as pull-ups or to generate a reference voltage, the failure of the resistor can lead to a loss of the voltage monitoring function, possibly leading to a hazardous failure. The RPN number for the worst cases are 120, close to the critical limit. Thus, further improvements to the system should be considered. Periodical testing of the voltage monitoring can be used for fault detection. High quality MELF resistors, or alternatively two parallel resistors can be used to improve the reliability of the solution.

4.4   Safety Software Design

The modular design of the safety SW running on the SAB was kept as simple as possible for ease of analysis. A time-triggered architecture (single main-loop running at 1 ms with a hardware timer) with a minimum of interrupt routines was implemented. The safety-SW executes the charging supervision functions and handles possible incoming messages each loop. MCU Self-tests are executed at boot time.

A high-level view of the main state machine is shown in Fig. 7. When EV presence is detected, a test sequence for the fault current sensor is first required and performed by the SAB when requested by the OPB. If the test is successfully executed, the system is ready to charge. Upon request from OPB the charging relays are activated row-by-row. Once both rows are on, the power supply to the EV is active. The OPB can request to turn the power off, triggering the row-by-row de-activation sequence. The de-activation sequence is also triggered if the user unplugs the EV during charging. If any faults are detected during the charging sequence, the system transitions to the fault state accompanied by immediate de-energization of both relay rows to bring the charging process to a safe state. For a subset of faults, the OPB can request a fault reset, which moves the system back to the idle state, other faults require cycling power to the SAB to reset.

5   Verification and Validation

The verification and validation of the safety-related subsystem was performed according to the V-model, with the approach including both analysis and testing. Functional tests were performed for the SAB hardware. For the verification of the software and the complete safety-related subsystem (integrated HW and SW), a multistep approach with static analysis, unit tests, software integration tests, and hardware-software integration and system tests was utilised. In this section we report on a selection of the performed V&V work: the verification approach for the safety software and for the integrated

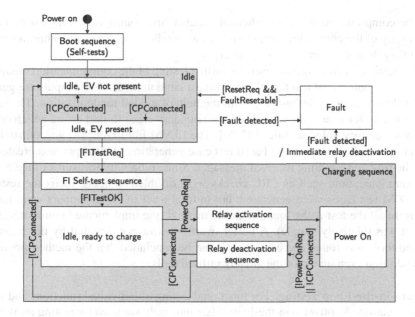

Fig. 7. State machine model for the SAB software [17].

safety system, including e.g. software- and hardware-in-the-loop (SIL and HIL) tests, and finally the functional tests to validate the reaction time of the fault current protection (SF2 in Table 4).

5.1 Software Verification

Software verification was performed in stages according to the V-model [8]. Different approaches were used alongside the progression from verification of software modules to software integration tests.

Unit Testing and Static Analysis. For the software modules, unit testing was performed. In addition to the unit testing, to achieve the safety integrity targets, all the software modules were implemented following the MISRA C:2012 [21] guidelines. The MISRA C rules were checked by both the utilised TI compiler as well as Math-Works Polyspace [20]. Polyspace Bug Finder and Code Prover [20] were additionally used for static analysis of the implemented safety software. Apart from typical issues such as undefined behaviour, the software was analysed for concurrency issues (related to the interrupt handlers) and security issues (focusing on the modules handling the OPB-facing communication), and detected critical issues were handled.

Security. For security, the OPB-facing communication modules are the most critical point in the safety system. The OPB is responsible for most security-measures in the system (such as access control, encrypted communications), but care was taken to further reduce cybersecurity-related risks, which could affect the safety of the charging system. In case of critical bugs in the communication modules, the whole safety system could be compromised if the hypothetical attacker first compromised the OPB. Thus, the integrity of the communication modules was handled equally to the other modules, even if they do not implement safety functions.

Fuzz testing, or fuzzing, was used for further testing of the communication modules. Fuzzing is an automated test technique, where a large number of test inputs are generated for the software under test, e.g. with the help of guided randomization. The technique is useful for exercising a multitude of boundary cases to find errors which could be used as security vulnerabilities [22,26]. The LLVM libFuzzer [18] was utilised for the testing, which uses coverage-based test case generation. A wrapper was created to target the function handling received messages. Some reliability measures of the SAB-OPB-communication, such as CRC-checks were disabled to better focus the testing. Over 100M test cases were generated, but in total a set of 78 test inputs were found to exercise all the test paths found with the method (the implemented communication protocol was relatively simple). A buffer overflow-error not detected by the previous tests and tools was found and corrected. It can be concluded that the method proved a useful addition even on top of the already utilised tools.

Software-in-the-Loop Testing. For functional testing of individual functions and software integration, A software-in-the-loop (SIL) approach was used for testing individual functions and for software integration tests. A simulation model was created in Matlab Simulink [19], see Fig. 8. The model includes the main charging circuit and the EV, with the control pilot circuitry. Interface models for the SAB inputs and outputs (including the SAB-internal circuitry) were created, which allow to manually override each input as well as inject pre-programmed faults. A simplified UART-simulation and OPB-model was implemented to send requests to the safety software. The model was initially implemented based on circuit diagrams and LTSpice [1] simulations of the system design, and later fine-tuned as the design was adjusted and as prototype hardware became available for reference measurements and model validation. The implemented model provides a realistic environment for testing the safety software. A wrapper library was implemented to compile the safety software into a single executable Matlab Executable (MEX) Simulink-model. The wrapper library included a modified implementation for part of the TI-provided HAL (HW Abstraction Layer) to interface calls to TI-libraries with the Simulink-model. This approach allowed testing the safety software with only minor modifications within Simulink.

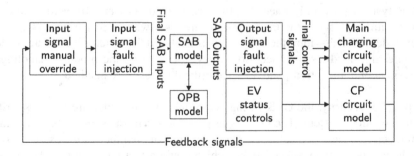

Fig. 8. Structure of the implemented simulation model.

An example performed fault injection SIL test for SF3 is shown in Fig. 9. The charging process has been previously started. Both the relay control outputs are active, energy is provided to the EV. The feedback to the SAB is provided by an analog circuit, which provides a pulsing feedback if the 1kHz CP signal is provided by the OPB and an EV is present to reduce the CP-signal voltage to a correct range according to IEC 61851-1 [13]. This analog signal is shown at the top, with the logical signal provided to the MCU shown below it. The third subplot shows the CP signal frequency estimated by the safety software, which needs to be in the correct range, 980-1020Hz, according to IEC 61851-1 [13]. Additional noise is injected into the analog signal starting from $t = 10$ ms, followed by a stuck-at fault from $t = 20$ ms. The injected fault causes the estimated CP frequency to deviate from the allowed range. This is taken as EV no longer being present, leading to switching off of both the redundant relay rows to de-energize

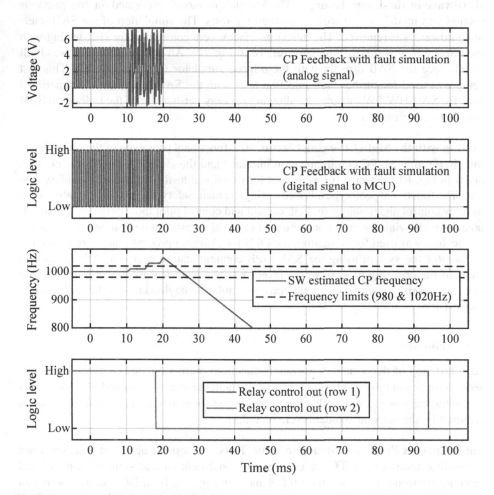

Fig. 9. Example simulation from the SIL-tests for SF3. The analog CP feedback signal is injected with noise (from $t = 10$ ms), followed by a stuck-at fault (from $t = 20$ ms). Charging is stopped as estimated CP frequency is beyond allowed limits.

the system. To maximise the lifetime of the relays, the first row to be opened or closed is alternated to distribute the load cycles (here row 2 was opened first). In the case of a fault current and detected internal faults, both relay rows are opened immediately.

5.2   System Integration Tests

For system integration tests a two-stage approach was used. For integrating the SAB HW with the safety software, hardware-in-the-loop (HIL) testing was used. For system integration tests, a functional prototype of the SiLis main charging circuit was built to test the SAB alongside the safety software. Figure 10 shows the entire experimental setup with all of its hardware components.

Hardware-in-the-Loop Testing. The simulation model presented in the previous section was modified for hardware-in-the-loop-tests. The simulation of the SAB internal hardware was removed. The model interfaces were configured for HIL-testing with the dSpace Scalexio HIL-Simulator (cf. 10 in Fig. 10). An adapter interface was built to interface the SAB directly with the dSpace simulator (cf. 6 in Fig. 10). This test setup was used for further fault injection tests with the SAB hardware and functional tests for SAB HW-SW integration, allowing for easy verification of the individual SAB interfaces and functions.

Testing with the Main Charging Circuit. The functional prototype of the main charging circuit, the test-PC communication interface and the electrical interfaces (cf. 1, 7, and 4 in Fig. 10, respectively) were used for functional testing of the whole safety system. The functional prototype allowed testing the main safety-related functionality, such as relay control and monitoring, fault current and control pilot monitoring, while simultaneously allowing for easy connection of external measuring equipment. The test-PC connection was used for simulating the OPB for charging process control requests and to monitor the system using the SAB-OPB-communication protocol. All the various steps of the charging process were played out. The electrical interfaces were used to connect a normal payload or a fault current-simulating payload to test the fault current supervision.

5.3   Validation

As a last step of the V-model, the safety functions were validated as a whole. In this section we present the validation testing of the fault current protection (SF2). The target of the testing was to validate that the implemented SF achieves the switch-off times as required by the relevant standards (cf. Sect. 2.1).

Fault Current Protection Reaction Time Tests. To test the achieved reaction times for various fault current (FC) values, an additional fault current simulation board and separate controller for it was built (cf. 8 and 9 in Fig. 10). Both DC and AC faults can be simulated, each load can be switched on and off individually. A pulsating half-wave was used for the DC faults.

Figure 11 shows the circuit diagram for the FC experiments. The SiLis Home board includes the redundant relay rows and the FC sensor. The 3 phases and the neutral line

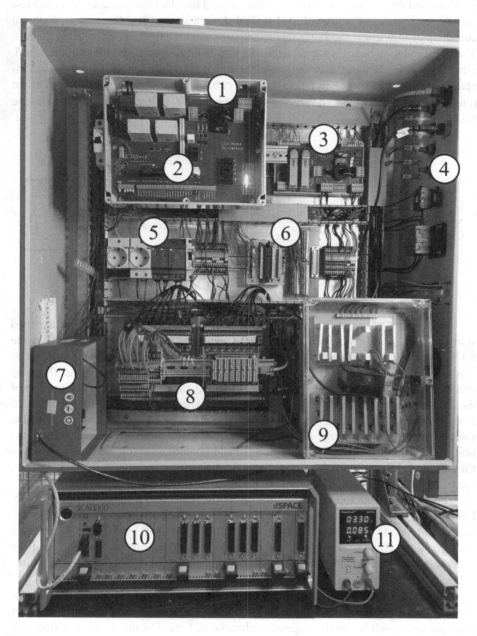

Fig. 10. Test setup for the safety system. 1: SiLis Home functional prototype, 2: SAB, 3: Older functional prototype, 4: Electrical interfaces for e.g. electrical load, 5: Power supply units, 6: SAB-dSpace Interface for HIL-testing, 7: Serial bus to test-PC for OPB-emulation, 8: Controls for fault current simulation, 9: Fault current simulation board, 10: dSpace Scalexio for HIL-tests, 11: 3.3 V power supply.

pass through the sensor. The switch S3 can be used to select the phase used for the test and S2 for connecting a normal load (a 2kW load was used for the testing). External current measurement is used to independently measure the fault current used in the test. The FC simulation board is connected to the grid N-phase before the SiLis home board, allowing for simulation of fault currents. The sum current through the FC sensor is non-zero, as the connected output phase supplies current to the simulated FC load, but the return path of the current bypasses the sensor neutral (N'), flowing directly back to the grid (N).

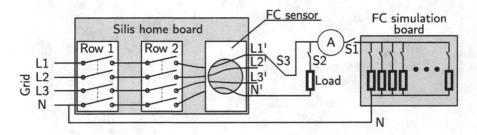

Fig. 11. Circuit diagram for the FC experiments.

An example reaction time measurement is shown in Fig. 12. A fault is activated starting from $t = 20$ ms, is indicated by the FC sensor at $t \approx 59$ ms, switched-off by the SAB at $t \approx 60$ ms, and finally effectively switched off at $t \approx 63$ ms. An oscilloscope was used to measure the fault current, the relevant FC sensor output, as well as the relay control output from, and one of the relay feedbacks to the SAB. The starting time of the fault is detected from the current measurement. The final switch-off time is detected from measured current and the relay feedback, whichever is active last indicates the switch-off time. The difference between the start and switch-off of the fault is the reaction time of the SF. The measurements were additionally used to evaluate the reaction time of the SAB as the time between the activation of the fault current feedback from the FC sensor to the de-activation of the relay control output from the SAB.

The results for the total reaction time of the FC protection SF are shown in Table 5. For each fault current value the measurement was repeated 20 times. For the AC faults, the measurements were performed with and without the 2kW load on the same phase to evaluate the effect of additional load on the fault reaction time. As can be seen from the results, the additional load slightly slows (in the range of 4–5 ms) the reaction time of SF.

In the whole measurement set, for the SAB reaction time the maximum was 1.1 ms, median 0.6 ms and minimum slightly below 0.2 ms. To execute a single tick of the safety software takes well below the targeted cycle time of 1 ms. The maximum reaction time can be explained by the SAB currently executing a single cycle as the signal value changes, causing the full 1 ms delay before the updated signal value is reacted to.

The distributions of the reaction times as function of the tested fault current values are visualised as boxplots in Figs. 13 and 14. The figures additionally illustrate the required reaction time, for AC faults according to IEC 61008 [6] (assumed nominal fault current 30 mA) and for DC faults according to IEC 62423 [5]. Other standards

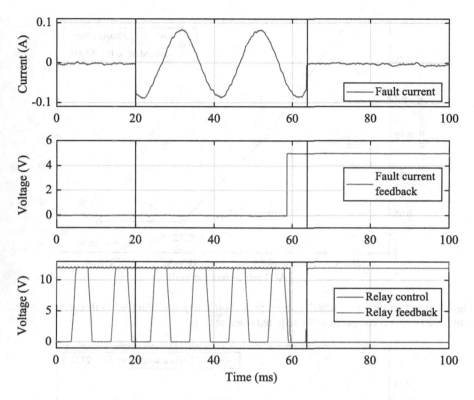

Fig. 12. Example reaction time measurement (60 mA AC fault current). The black vertical lines indicate the start of the fault and when the system reaches a safe state.

Table 5. Results of the reaction time experiments for the fault current protection.

Load current active	Fault current		Total reaction time	
	Type	Value (mA)	Maximum (ms)	Median (ms)
No	AC	30	149.40	141.53
No	AC	60	52.45	47.05
No	AC	150	23.38	19.84
No	AC	250	13.81	12.37
Yes	AC	30	152.54	146.38
Yes	AC	60	56.32	49.15
Yes	AC	150	27.68	22.55
Yes	AC	250	19.03	14.04
No	DC	20	169.82	156.71
No	DC	40	62.15	48.44
No	DC	60	38.90	29.27
No	DC	84	39.17	26.58
No	DC	100	25.24	13.08
No	DC	350	20.93	9.80
No	DC	500	21.31	9.69

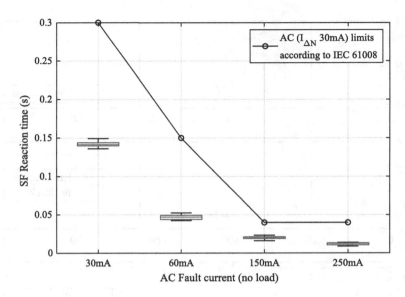

Fig. 13. Reaction time of the fault current protection safety function (AC fault current without active load current) compared to the required reaction time.

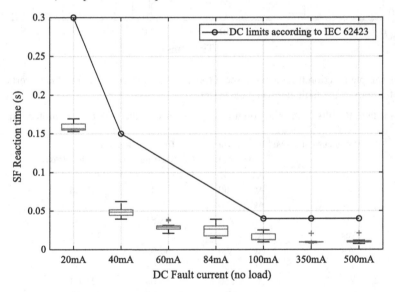

Fig. 14. Reaction time of the fault current protection safety function (DC fault current without active load current) compared to the required reaction time.

were also considered, but the most strict required reaction times were chosen as the validation target. Other AC RCD standards provide the same required reaction time, and for DC faults e.g. IEC 62752 [12] (for mode 2 in-cable charging devices) could be used, but provides less strict reaction times than IEC 62423 [5].

As can be seen from Figs. 13 and 14, the achieved reaction time for the SF is well below the required reaction times for both AC and DC faults. The AC fault reaction times are less spread than reaction times for the DC faults. For the pulsating half-wave, the test might be started towards the beginning or end of the active half-wave, which affects the delay from the start of the test to the FC sensor indicating the fault.

6 Conclusions

In this work we presented the development of a safe electronic charging infrastructure system from requirements to V&V. The developed system fulfils the requirements defined in the initial requirements analysis. The system was developed according to the current functional safety and EVSE standards. The presented results are, however, based on a research prototype. The industrial project partners are developing a commercialised version of the system and a safety certification is planned for the future.

The work presented here can be used as a basis and a reference for the development of safe next generation EVSE. Even with the urgent need for this new critical infrastructure, the proper care should be taken in building it. As more electronics are included in our everyday lives and in charge of controlling critical functions such as charging our vehicles, functional safety considerations should be included directly from the beginning when developing new solutions.

References

1. Analog Devices: LTspice (2021). https://www.analog.com/en/design-center/design-tools-and-calculators/ltspice-simulator.html
2. Börcsök, J.: Electronic Safety Systems: Hardware Concepts, Models, and Calculations. Hüthig, Heidelberg (2004)
3. IEA: Global EV Outlook 2020 - Analysis - IEA (2020). https://www.iea.org/reports/global-ev-outlook-2020
4. IEC: IEC 60364-4-41 - Low voltage electrical installations - Part 4-41: Protection for safety - Protection against electric shock. International Electrotechnical Commission, 5th edn. (2005)
5. IEC: IEC 62423 - Type F and type B residual current operated circuit-breakers with and without integral overcurrent protection for household and similar uses. International Electrotechnical Commission, 2nd edn. (2009)
6. IEC: IEC 61008-1 - Residual current operated circuit-breakers without integral overcurrent protection for household and similar uses (RCCBs) - Part1: General rules. International Electrotechnical Commission, 3rd edn. (2010)
7. IEC: IEC 61508-1 - Functional safety of electrical/electronic/programmable electronic safety-related systems - Part 1: General requirements. International Electrotechnical Commission, 2.0 edn. (2010)
8. IEC: IEC 61508-3 - Functional safety of electrical/electronic/programmable electronic safety-related systems - Part 3: Software requirements. International Electrotechnical Commission, 2.0 edn. (2010)
9. IEC: IEC 61508-4 - Functional safety of electrical/electronic/programmable electronic safety-related systems - Part 4: Definitions and abbreviations. International Electrotechnical Commission, 2.0 edn. (2010)
10. IEC: IEC 62196-1 - Plugs, socket-outlets, vehicle connectors and vehicle inlets - Conductive charging of electric vehicles - Part 1: General requirements. International Electrotechnical Commission, 3.0 edn. (2014)

11. IEC: IEC 62196-2 - Plugs, socket-outlets, vehicle connectors and vehicle inlets - Conductive charging of electric vehicles - Part 2: Part 2: Dimensional compatibility and interchangeability requirements for a.c. pin and contact-tube accessories. International Electrotechnical Commission, 2.0 edn. (2016)

12. IEC: IEC 62752 - In-cable control and protection device for mode 2 charging of electric road vehicles (IC-CPD). International Electrotechnical Commission, 1st edn. (2016)

13. IEC: IEC 61851-1 - Electric vehicle conductive charging system - Part 1: General requirements. International Electrotechnical Commission, 3.0 edn. (2017)

14. ISO: ISO 12100 - Safety of machinery - General principles for design - Risk assessment and risk reduction. International Organization for Standardization (2010)

15. ISO: ISO 15118-1 - Road vehicles – Vehicle to grid communication interface—Part 1: General information and use-case definition. International Organization for Standardization, 2nd edn. (2019)

16. ISO: ISO 17409 - Electrically propelled road vehicles—Conductive power transfer—Safety requirements. International Organization for Standardization, 2nd edn. (2020)

17. Kivelä, T., et al.: Functional safety and electric vehicle charging: requirements analysis and design for a safe charging infrastructure system. In: Proceedings of the 7th International Conference on Vehicle Technology and Intelligent Transport Systems, pp. 317–324. SCITEPRESS - Science and Technology Publications (2021). https://doi.org/10.5220/0010398303170324

18. LLVM: libFuzzer (2021). https://llvm.org/docs/LibFuzzer.html

19. MathWorks: Matlab Simulink (2021). https://se.mathworks.com/products/simulink.html

20. MathWorks: Polyspace (2021). https://www.mathworks.com/products/polyspace.html

21. MIRA Limited: MISRA-C:2012: Guidelines for the use of the C language in critical systems. MIRA Limited, Nuneaton, Warwickshire (2012)

22. Oehlert, P.: Violating assumptions with fuzzing. IEEE Secur. Priv. **3**(2), 58–62 (2005)

23. Redmill, F.: Risk analysis-a subjective process. Eng. Manag. J. **12**(2), 91–96 (2002). https://doi.org/10.1049/em:20020206

24. Romeike, F., Hager, P. (eds.): Erfolgsfaktor Risiko-Management 4.0. Springer Fachmedien Wiesbaden, Wiesbaden (2020). https://doi.org/10.1007/978-3-658-29446-5

25. Schmittner, C., Scharfenberg, G., Mottok, J., Strassmeier, S., Limmer, T., et al.: Analysis of the functional and electrical safety of charging stations

26. Takanen, A., DeMott, J., Miller, C., Kettunen, A.: Fuzzing for Software Security Testing and Quality Assurance. Artech House Information Security and Privacy Series, 2nd edn. Artech House, Norwood (2018)

27. Tu, H., Feng, H., Srdic, S., Lukic, S.: Extreme fast charging of electric vehicles: a technology overview. IEEE Trans. Transp. Electrification **5**(4), 861–878 (2019). https://doi.org/10.1109/TTE.2019.2958709

28. VDA: FMEA-Handbuch. VDA, Verband der Automobilindustrie, Berlin, Germany, 1. ausgabe edn. (2019)

29. Veneri, O. (ed.): Technologies and Applications for Smart Charging of Electric and Plug-in Hybrid Vehicles. Springer, Cham (2017). https://doi.org/10.1007/978-3-319-43651-7

30. Vogt, M., Link, S., Ritzinger, K., Ablingyte, E., Reindl, P.: Sicherheitsaspekte beim Laden von Elektrofahrzeugen, Berichte der Bundesanstalt für Straßenwesen, Unterreihe Fahrzeugsicherheit, vol. Heft F 107. Bundesanstalt für Straßenwesen, Bergisch Gladbach (2016). https://bast.opus.hbz-nrw.de/frontdoor/index/index/docId/1656

31. Wang, Q., Liu, X., Du, J., Kong, F.: Smart charging for electric vehicles: a survey from the algorithmic perspective. IEEE Commun. Surv. Tutor. **18**(2), 1500–1517 (2016). https://doi.org/10.1109/COMST.2016.2518628

Digital Energy: Towards Comprehensive Digital Support for a Renewable-Based Energy Sector

Matthias Jarke[1,2]([✉]), Michael Andres[1], Markus Mirz[1], Dennis van der Velde[1], Julius Zocher[1], Klemens Schumann[1], Christopher Hauk[1], Andreas Ulbig[1], and Antonello Monti[1]

[1] Fraunhofer-Institute of Applied Information Technology FIT, Aachen, Germany
jarke@dbis.rwth-aachen.de
[2] Information Systems, RWTH Aachen University, Ahornstr. 55, 52074 Aachen, Germany

Abstract. To be able to limit the temperature increase to clearly under 2 °C above pre-industrial levels, the European Union and Germany in particular are facing profound change in their energy system in the coming years. The end of coal-fired power generation, the coupling of different sectors (e.g. electricity, heat, mobility…) and the associated digitization are confronting companies with changed market and framework conditions. In order to master this change towards a sustainable and reliable energy supply and to use it as an opportunity, innovative technologies and well-trained specialists and managers are needed. The combination of in-depth knowledge from the fields of energy technology with in-depth knowledge of digitization and its business models as well as IT security offers a unique opportunity to master these challenges in a sustainable and controllable manner. This paper addresses challenges arising from the digitization of the energy system and shows exemplary solutions from projects at the recently established Fraunhofer Center for Digital Energy.

Keywords: Energy systems · Digitization · IT security · Business models

1 Motivation and Concept

For an industrial nation like Germany, production, mobility, communication or trade are the foundation of prosperity, growth and peace. The backbone for this is a reliable, affordable and permanently available energy supply. But this is precisely where a fundamental shift must take place, away from the use of fossil fuels in historically grown infrastructures toward de-carbonization, decentralization and interacting, digitized, and automated energy systems. This is accompanied with the coupling of different sectors (e.g. electricity, heat, gas, mobility,…), communication-technology links among most diverse system participants (e.g. from the areas of energy, industry, transport,…) as well as the development of highly precise digital twins of the energy systems for their planning, monitoring and automation of control.

This paper is an extended version of an invited keynote presentation given by the first author at the SmartGreens 2020 conference.

© Springer Nature Switzerland AG 2022
C. Klein et al. (Eds.): SMARTGREENS 2021/ VEHITS 2021, CCIS 1612, pp. 435–453, 2022.
https://doi.org/10.1007/978-3-031-17098-0_22

1.1 Fundamental Changes in Energy Supply

In order to fulfill the EU commitment in the COP21 agreement [1], to limit the temperature increase to clearly less than 2 °C above pre-industrial levels, the energy system needs to be restructured. Even disruptive structural developments can be necessary. Not only the electricity sector needs to be de-carbonized but also other sectors such as heating, gas, and mobility. Nevertheless, while renewing the energy system, the energy trilemma must be fulfilled, maintaining affordability, sustainability, and safety of supply.

The energy system of the sectors electricity, gas, and heat consists of four central components that can be distinguished with the dimensions asset type and central/decentral level: Transmission infrastructure, distribution infrastructure, centralized technologies, and decentralized technologies (cf. Fig. 1).

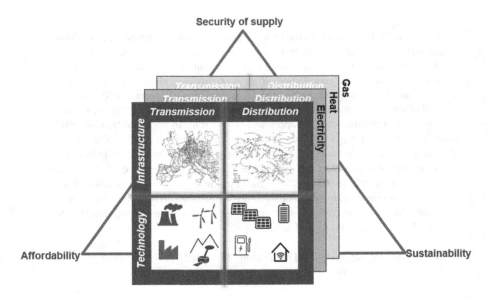

Fig. 1. Components for planning the energy system (based on [2]).

Historically, energy in the electricity and gas sectors has been generated primarily in *centralized technologies*. Centralized large-scale power plants and conveyance systems are the main examples. Heat can also be generated as district heating in large power plants and distributed via distribution infrastructure in district heating networks. However, these centralized technologies need to be re-planned, as renewable energy is often intermittent. High generation from wind energy can be developed mainly in coastal regions, generation from solar energy mainly in southern Europe.

The change in centralized technologies directly impacts the *transmission infrastructure*, which enables the transmission of energy across long distances. In the past, electricity was generated in large power plants close to the load. In the future, generation from renewable energy plants away from load centres, e.g. off-shore wind farms, will increase the amount of electricity, that has to be transported across long distances, thus challenging the transmission system.

A new building block in the energy system is the expansion *of decentralized technologies*. In this field, all sectors can be found, including electricity, heat, and gas. Above all, new generation plants and sector-coupling loads such as heat pumps and electric mobility are being installed as decentralized systems. Local heating networks are also additional building blocks of the decentralized energy system.

The expansion of decentralized technologies influences the *distribution infrastructures* that distribute energy within spatially limited areas. They represent the interface between the transmission infrastructure and the end customers. While in the past unidirectional power flows have been the case at this level (from transmission infrastructure to end customer), bidirectional power flows will also be possible in the future. In addition, new technologies such as renewable generation plants and electrical loads pose challenges due to power peaks.

A look at the electrical energy system shows the impact of these changes particular clearly using the example of residual load. The residual load describes the difference between generated power from volatile, renewable energy sources (e.g. wind, photovoltaics) and the consumption. Based on simulations of an exemplary spring day within the grid development plan of the German Federal Network Agency (Bundesnetzagentur, the residual loads were calculated and the results are shown in Fig. 2 for the "Most Likely" scenarios of the years 2024 (40% renewables) and 2035 (80% renewables).

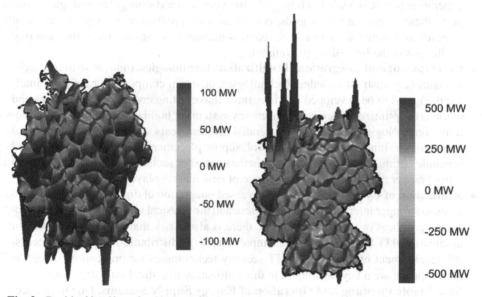

Fig. 2. Residual load based on the most likely scenario of the German power network development plan for 2024 (40% share of renewables) on the left and 2035 + (80% share of renewables) on the right. © RWTH Aachen University, IAEW.

Put simply, generation and consumption must be always in harmony, at each location in the electrical energy system. The residual load thus describes the supply task to be solved. In the past, generation followed consumption. Power plants and power grids were built accordingly to balance the load. Due to the removal of large and fossil power plants as well as the continuous decentral integration of renewable and volatile generation plants, generation and consumption are already no longer in harmony today (Fig. 2, left). Starting from a few thousand power plants, the number of connected generation plants in Germany developed to more than 2 million generation plants in 2020 [3]. In the future, generation is to be considered as decoupled from consumption and a significantly larger dimension is to be expected of connected and controllable equipment in the infrastructures (Fig. 2, right).

This increase is to be expected both on the generation side but also on the flexible consumer and storage side, for example in the areas of mobility or heat supply. Also the grid equipment itself must become more flexible. This leads to a multitude of challenges but also strong opportunities in decarbonized energy supply.

In this paper, we focus on digitalization, cross-sector communication and automation of energy systems as an opportunity to make a significant contribution to build up a sustainable and fully decarbonized energy system. From a research perspective, the following topics, among others, emerge as highly relevant for the success of this transition:

- **Ensuring Reliability of Supply and de-Carbonization.** The development of a sustainable and CO_2-free energy system is based on an increasing number of renewable generation plants, flexible loads (e.g. electric vehicles) and storage technologies. Coupling these assets via power grids, combined with a reduction of large power plant reserves and their rotating masses, requires intensive investigations of the resulting challenges in the field of supply reliability.
- **Development and Integration of Digitization Technologies.** Innovative digital technologies (e.g. distributed ledger technologies, quantum computing or artificial intelligence) need to be developed and integrated into existing energy infrastructures and markets to optimize processes within energy systems or build up verifiable CO_2 reductions. Technological change has accelerated in recent years with numerous new digital technologies. Innovations in grid control, supply placement, demand forecasting and schedule optimization, especially also in the context of sector-coupled microgrids and virtual power plants led to the emergence of new market players.
- **Realization of Cyber Security.** The increased integration of digital technologies also leads to stronger interactions between these and the physical infrastructures (e.g. electricity, gas, heat or water grids). Thus, there is also a risk that intentional attacks or unintentional IT failures can have an impact on energy distribution or trade. A successful development of concepts and IT security technologies for prevention, detection and response are a key instrument in the digitization of critical infrastructures.
- **Sustainable Planning and Operation of Energy Supply Systems.** Due to the necessary investments in the range of several billion euros annually in energy infrastructures, energy systems must continue to be planned and operated in the long term and especially with foresight for sustainability and flexibility.
- **New Business Models in Changing Environments.** The business models of stakeholders in the energy industry are changing dramatically. The success of the introduction of novel digital technologies is based on innovative, digital business models that have had a disruptive impact on the energy industry. It is imperative for companies

to leverage the potential of such disruptive technologies in an economically viable way to enable innovative business models and ensure competitiveness. This creates massive pressure for companies to act.

In summary, this means an enormous need for society, politics, industry and research for deep knowledge of energy systems in combination with deep knowledge of cyber security, digitization and financial management.

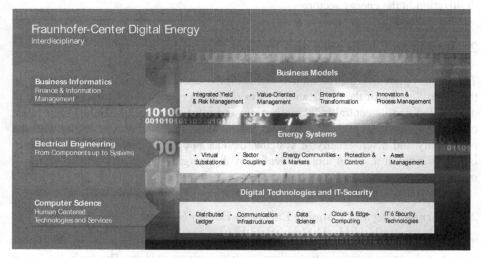

Fig. 3. Fraunhofer-Center digital energy – interdisciplinary research excellence.

1.2 The Fraunhofer-Center Digital Energy

Digitization of critical infrastructures, their operators, users, manufacturers and markets has the potential to cope with central societal challenges (e.g. energy transition, climate change, urbanization or mobility change) while at the same time preserving European business competitiveness. On the other hand, however, this development also involves considerable risks, since erroneous developments, decisions, or even unintentional or intentional criminal external influences can have immediate effects on society (energy costs, jobs, technological leadership, etc.) that threaten its existence.

An application-oriented and responsible design of digitization within the backbone of the society and industry - the energy supply - urgently requires a reorientation of previously specialized research and industry branches, to an interdisciplinary, directly operational and independent research and development as well as education and training. To master this task, the Fraunhofer Society and RWTH Aachen University have founded the "Fraunhofer-Center Digital Energy" in Aachen, as part of the German federal structure renewal program in connection with the plan to end coal-fired power generation within roughly the next decade. The goal is to establish a permanent, cross-domain expertise of leading research institutions in one location. Thus, in-depth knowledge from the energy sector is combined with in-depth knowledge of IT security, digitization as well as finance and information management (Fig. 3).

A successful digitization needs new technologies, qualified personnel and suitable business models. For this reason, the Fraunhofer-Center Digital Energy specifically addresses the pillars "research and development" of new technologies, "education and training" to attract and train qualified personnel, and "testing and verification" to ensure that research results can be integrated into products and services. The cross-domain focus of expertise enables a solid basis for goal-oriented transformation toward successful digitization in the energy sector.

2 Research Challenges and Project Examples

The primary goal in future research of digitization of energy systems has to be to improve the controllability of the digitization process between energy supply, transmission and distribution and its central industrial sectors and infrastructures, as well as their interconnection with current and future market structures. In this context, dealing with the complexity and heterogeneity of systems, devices and communication infrastructures is just as much a research topic as dealing with emerging IT security threats or novel market structures and business strategies.

2.1 Harmonizing and Planning European Energy Systems

The digitization of energy systems describes the next stage in the convergence of information and communications technology with the energy system. The basis for future energy systems and their operational management is the constant exchange of data and the availability of process data between different stakeholders. The transfer of modern data management methods (e.g. platform technologies, cloud-based process data processing, standardized data models, interoperability testing of components) for use in the energy sector is therefore a step towards the digitization of the energy supply and barrier- and discrimination-free networking of the stakeholders. The central goal must to optimize the energy supply structure and the grid infrastructure in line with sustainability, market and operational requirements. To this end, new tools for planning and operating future energy grids (transmission and distribution grid automation, use of market- and grid-side flexibilities, consideration of simultaneity/scale effects, e.g., through the electrification of mobility or heat provision) as well as the necessary IT security tools for the required communication, control, and process technology must be developed, tested, and raised to a technologically usable level. Digital twins could serve to optimize the operating processes of the energy system with regard to energy markets, communication technologies and infrastructures.

Digitization, coupled with modern IT technologies and automation, offers enormous potential to integrate the multitude of sustainable generation and consumption technologies in a technologically and economically sensible way - without affecting the quality of supply or unnecessarily increasing the costs of grid expansion. These partly new tasks require appropriate, scalable and secure solutions. Defining architectures for data management and control (e.g. in the distribution grid) is also a major challenge for industry.

Understanding the right solution in terms of communication and information technology (e.g. 5G networks, integration of cloud & edge computing, blockchain,…) is another key research area.

Project Example: OneNet. The European Commission launched Horizon 2020 project OneNet (One Network for Europe) in October 2020 to tackle the challenges posed to transmission and distribution system operators and consumers in the European electricity market (cf. https://onenet-project.eu/). While the electrical grid is moving from being a fully centralized to a highly decentralized system, grid operators have to adapt to this changing environment and adjust their current business model to accommodate faster reactions and adaptive flexibility. This is an unprecedented challenge requiring an unprecedented solution. For this reason, the two major associations of grid operators in Europe, ENTSO-E and EDSO, have activated their members to put together a unique consortium.

Under the leadership of the Fraunhofer Center Digital Energy, OneNet aims at developing and demonstrating the key instruments for a European approach to energy flexibility. Many projects addressed this issue in the past, but OneNet's scope and size are unparalleled with a total budget of over 28 M€ and more than 70 partners in the consortium. Key elements of the project include:

1. Definition of a common market design for Europe: this means standardized products and key parameters for grid services which aim at the coordination of all actors, from grid operators to customers;
2. definition of a common IT Architecture and common IT Interfaces: this means not trying to create a single IT platform for all the products, but enabling an open architecture of interactions among several platforms so that anybody can join any market across Europe; and
3. large-scale demonstrators implement and showcase the scalable solutions developed throughout the project. These demonstrators are organized in four clusters, aiming to test innovative use cases in each region of Europe.

For example, the Western cluster is developing use cases on cross-system operator grid-prequalification, which checks the capability of a service provider to provide the offered service, considering the grid conditions; and improvements to the information exchange related to short / long-term congestion management.

One focal point of the demos is the improvement of the TSO-DSO information exchange as demanded in the ASM report [4] to coordinate the use of flexibility across voltage levels. Besides, FSPs (Flexibility Service Provider) as well as electricity market operators will participate in the demos. Among the solutions tested in the demos are a local market platform where DSOs and FSPs trade flexibility and a blockchain based distributed ledger to facilitate trusted data exchange between TSOs, DSOs and FSPs (Fig. 4).

Summarizing, OneNet calls for the creation of a unified vision for Europe's electricity market to which operators, consumers and stakeholders across Europe are urged to contribute. To this end, throughout the project duration and afterwards, the project is

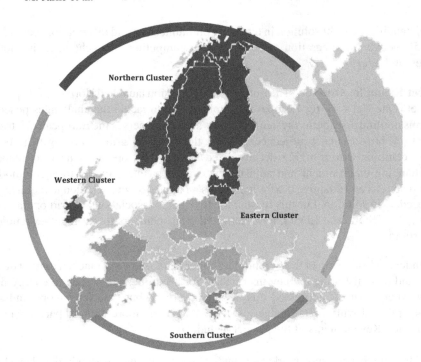

Fig. 4. OneNet – Cluster Overview.

developing the open forum initiative GRIFOn, a platform to freely discuss results with all relevant stakeholders external to the project and collect their feedback.

In addition to energy system operation, the *planning of future energy systems and network infrastructures* and their communication technologies should be a significant component of future research tasks. This complex of topics focuses on aspects of system integration of increasingly decentralized energy systems. Due to the necessity of a cross-sectoral view of future energy systems, approaches that combine the sectors of electricity, heat, gas and mobility are particularly important [5].

Besides the challenges occurring through decentralized technologies, opportunities arise. The new plants can be coordinated to exploit synergy effects and stabilize the distribution grid. In addition, new business models can be developed for municipal utilities and prosumers. In addition to inter-block dependencies, inter-sector dependencies can also be perceived. Through the electrification of mobility and heat generation, new demands in the electric sector arise. The gas sector can in turn relieve the electricity sector by using hydrogen.

Project Example: PlaMES. Against the backdrop of these interdependencies, Horizon 2020 project PlaMES (Integrated Planning of Multimodal Energy Systems) is developing a comprehensive planning tool for optimal transition paths. An operation tool for affordable, sustainable, and secure energy systems shall integrate the sectors and energy system blocks to find the overall optimal system design solution (cf. Fig. 5).

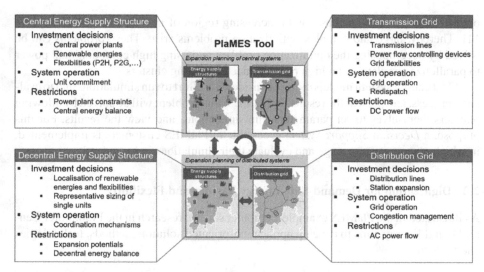

Fig. 5. Conceptual overview of the comprehensive planning tool developed in PlaMES.

Modelling large energy systems and generating such a planning tool address several problems for PlaMES. Four key challenges in the field of digital energy, in which the Fraunhofer-Center Digital Energy is also involved, are: Modelling of the supply structure, data handling, computational complexity, and provision of a decision support system for customers of the energy system modelling.

To be able to model realistic future scenarios, information about the *supply structure* is required. Here, electrical and thermal load, and driving profiles need to be modelled for households, commerce trade and services, and industry. Depending on the modelling target, the granularity needs to be adjusted. To model the central level, the supply structure on transmission grid nodes needs to be determined. Here, models using socio-economic data as a basis can be used [6]. Consideration of the decentral level requires more granular supply structures, e.g., modelling at the building level as in [7]. Other methods include the use of ortho-photography and machine learning.

When energy systems are modeled with high granularity, the resulting large data sets require a well-defined *data handling*. These include the supply task as well as energy grid models, generation plants, and time series. Data formats and storage location need to be clearly defined. Further, scenarios (e.g. for different years) as well as data versions need to be clearly distinguished [8]. To address these issues, a specialized data management system is implemented within PlaMES. To manage different versions of data, a defined data versioning and scenario management has been implemented.

Modeling the energy system can lead to high *computational complexity*. First, many aspects of energy systems such as the transmission of energy (electrical, thermal or chemical) lead to non-linear optimization problems. Second, binary decision variables are often required to model investment decisions, further complicating the optimization. Third, investment decisions can create complicating columns, while time-coupling constraints such as energy storage can create complicating rows. Finally, the size of the optimization problem increases with increasing region of interest and granularity [9–11]. Thereby, large and complex optimization problems arise. These problems can be solved by decomposing the optimization problem and using high computational power to parallelize simulations on high performance computing clusters.

Most energy system models require considerable effort to run simulations and to evaluate, process, and present the results. In PlaMES, this problem will be solved by allowing planners themselves to set parameters, run simulations, and view the results. For this purpose, a *Decision Support System* accessible to PlaMES customers is implemented, in which planners can manage and evaluate their simulations independently.

2.2 Digitization for Demand-Side Energy Savings and Flexibility

As illustrated in the PlaMES example, computer science research in the Fraunhofer Center Digital Energy aims to develop application-oriented solution methods, technologies and tools to.

1. deal with emerging complexity and heterogeneity (reliable software, architectures, middleware, usability, acceptance,…)
2. provide appropriate devices and communication infrastructures (sensor networks, 5G, reliable systems and hardware, energy efficiency/sustainability,…)
3. deal with emerging large, heterogeneous data masses (big data analytics, visualization, machine learning,…)

The volatility of an energy system based on renewable sources requires not just novel solutions from the supplier perspective addressed in the previous section, but also increased demand-side flexibility. This concerns both private households and energy-intensive industries.

Project Examples: SEAM4US and Flex4Grid. Over the past decade, many projects at Fraunhofer FIT have employed Internet of Things (IOT) technologies together with data management and simulation tools for small to medium-scale energy preservation and demand flexibilization applications.

For example, in many major cities, subways are among the largest users of urban electrical energy, e.g. in London equivalent to 250.000 households. In the EU project SEAM4US [12], an energy management system for subway stations was developed and installed in Barcelona's most-frequented subway station. This IoT-based solution combines sensor-based monitoring of visitors, lighting, and air conditioning devices, with dynamic simulation models for their usage planning and control. Based on measurements about an extended period of time, long-term simulations resulted in a savings potential of over 13% without any reduction in comfort for travelers and employees, corresponding to the energy usage of several thousand households (Fig. 6).

Building on early experiments in small segregated energy usage settings such as the Danish island of Fur, the Horizon 2020 EU project Flex4Grid [13] developed a flexibility management system as a low-cost solution for networks of residential consumers wishing to participate in power-grid balancing. The Flex4Grid system continuously forecasts

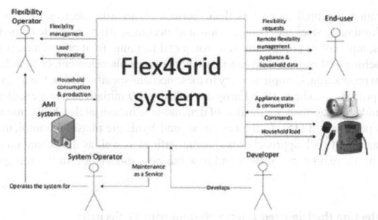

Fig. 6. Digital flexibility management as a key approach to demand-side energy innovation ©
Fraunhofer FIT.

the need for flexibility in a power grid, and informs consumers about the flexibility management periods. Consumers can provide their flexibility to an aggregator in exchange
for a reward which depends on the selected incentive scheme. The automation of the
flexibility-management events is provided by interfacing with devices and the system via
the Z-Wave and open platform communication unified architecture (OPC UA) technologies. The Flex4Grid system was deployed in three pilots in Slovenia and Germany. Two
smaller German pilots with a total of 185 participants were used for testing the technical
capabilities. Whereas a large-scale pilot in Celje, Slovenia, with 1047 participants, was
used to collect statistical data regarding how consumers participate in the flexibility-
management events, using a critical peak-pricing incentive scheme.. On average, the
pilots' participants reduced their load by 10% during a peak event. User-satisfaction
surveys indicate that the proposed approach is appropriate for engaging consumers in
flexibility-management events.

Project Example: SynErgie. In energy-intensive industries, the paradigm shift resulting from the move to renewable energy supplies may be even more disruptive than for
private consumers or suppliers. Here, the traditional approach was that energy usage
demand drives energy production; i.e. a steel or aluminum factory would have a fossil or
nuclear energy plant built close to its site, or would set a new location close to plants with
low-cost energy supply. The foreseen closure of fossil and (at least in Germany) nuclear
power plants will destroy this classical pattern and require new *flexibility in industrial
energy demand patterns* if Europe wants to maintain its industrial base.

Unfortunately, the options for increased industrial demand flexibility are poorly
understood and as diverse as the industries themselves, both in quality and in quantity.
In order to better understand this diversity and to develop associated socio-technical
and business strategies, the German government has set up a 10-year, 100 M€, project
called SynErgie [14] whose industrial partners account over 60% of Germany's industrial energy consumption. In the first three years of SynErgie, detailed analysis of the

flexibilization potential in no less than fourteen (!) industry sectors have been provided: aluminum, steel, air compression and decomposition, graphite, bio-chemical processes, automotive production, non-iron metal forming, food processing, paper, and glass, machine tool engineering, fire-resistant materials management, cement handling, and steam production. Complementary to these domain-specific issues, the usage of IoT-based approaches studied in the European Industry 4.0 initiatives as an enabler for in-domain and cross-domain digitization of demand-side industrial flexibility management has been proposed in [15]. In the current second SynErgie phase, the implementation and evaluation of such approaches is specific settings as well as the debate on required changes in the regulatory systems and new business models are in the foreground of interest.

2.3   Protecting the Digitized Energy System with IT Security

Digitization of the energy system is surely an essential part of the solution. But it also creates severe new problems. Whereas industry-oriented research on threats to energy distribution in the late 2000's focused, e.g., on the safety (e.g., against ice-coverage) and physical security (against attacks with explosives) of high-power transmission lines, the digital transformation requires the additional consideration of new threats and protection opportunities.

Future energy systems will increasingly be confronted with threats (e.g., attacks on ICT, equipment failures, simultaneity effects, conflicts of interest) that can endanger secure grid and system operation, and thus also the critical supply task for industry and the general public. A topic of particular priority is therefore the research of threats and the development of required IT security technologies to enable a reliable energy supply even in the digitalized environment.

Organized IT attacks on industrial and critical infrastructures are often multi-stage and usually have long observation periods for information acquisition in the context of Advanced Persistent Threats (APT). Based on acquisition of information, static networks with deterministic traffic, such as may exist in the context of electricity supply or other industries, allow planning of complex, distributed and synchronized attack vectors. Especially in critical grid situations and operation close to the stability limit, targeted attacks could lead to cascading equipment failures and - in the last instance - supply outages with far-reaching consequences for the physical system.

To prevent such scenarios, the approaches to resilience and reliability of energy systems described above must mesh with the approaches to IT security described below. This building block must address overarching solutions based on the three pillars of prevention, detection and response:

4. In the area of prevention, targeted research must be conducted into measures to prevent IT security incidents. This includes in particular the development of measures for testing, acceptance, and hardening of systems and networks.
5. The goal of *detection* is to identify IT security incidents. The time between an attack and its detection must be minimized by continuous monitoring of the status of systems and networks. Approaches in this area include network monitoring, intrusion

detection systems, security information and event management, decoy systems or threat intelligence.

6. *Response* deals with the actions taken after an IT security incident has been detected. The damage to the victim must be minimized if possible, the attackers' modus operandi must be understood, and knowledge must be gained for attributing the attackers. Important topics in this area include incident response, IT forensics and malware analysis.

The necessary development of technologies, concepts and methods for the detection, prevention and response to energy-system related IT security incidents is carried out within the Fraunhofer Center Digital Energy in close cooperation with authorities, leading industrial companies and infrastructure operators.

Project Example: MEDIT. Monitoring at the IT/OT (information/operation technology) level is not yet fully implemented in practice. Therefore, ICT-caused malfunction sometimes cannot be adequately attributed, leading to a "blind spot", i.e. challenges for the operators to detect early indications of a compromised network that threatens the availability and system security and leads to potentially higher downtimes. In particular, if monitoring and control capabilities of decentralized assets are more closely integrated into operations management, even compromises of decentralized assets can have direct repercussions for the power grid. MEDIT is developing an interoperable, vendor-independent solution for monitoring IT and OT in the process network of grid operators, which can be used analogously to the primary technology control system and enables the differentiation between primary technology, IT, and OT faults [16].

Compared to IT networks, a particular characteristic of OT networks is the comparatively high homogeneity and lower number of different device types. Data traffic within such networks is directly attributable to the configuration of the individual components and can thus be deterministically assigned to fixed endpoints and a specific purpose. In addition, special industrial communication protocols such as the TCP protocol IEC 60870-5-104 are used. These characteristics must be considered when developing an effective approach to intrusion detection for the energy sector.

To detect cyber-attacks on the protocol layer, an approach that extends the classical whitelisting will be the result of MEDIT. Fraunhofer FIT is developing an approach for multi-stage cyber-attack detection, which correlates indicators of compromise from the various domains of primary technology, OT, and IT. On this basis, not only the probability of a cyber-attack is detected, but also a statement is made as to which step of the cyber kill chain an attacker is in, and whether the malicious actor follows a specific attack pattern. This enables situational awareness of the cyber-attack evolution and about the potential threat of a detected cyber-attack [17].

Even the most reliable cyber-attack prevention and detection technologies cannot provide complete protection against security incidents. MEDIT provides stakeholders with actionable incident response guidance, and a simulation environment for security training. The guideline suggest specific actions for non-IT staff who is potentially confronted with observations that could indicate a security incident [16].

In addition to incident response training deployment, simulation and laboratory environments are needed in which cybersecurity technologies can be developed and tested.

In particular, regarding the generation of data traffic for the verification of the intrusion detection system, a co-simulation is being utilized (Fig. 7). It allows to carry out the simulation of the energy grid and the emulation of the OT network as well as the mapping of the dependencies between them in a modular environment. Thus, with the integration of cyber-attack emulation, both data traffic under normal operating conditions and malicious traffic can be generated in a scalable manner.

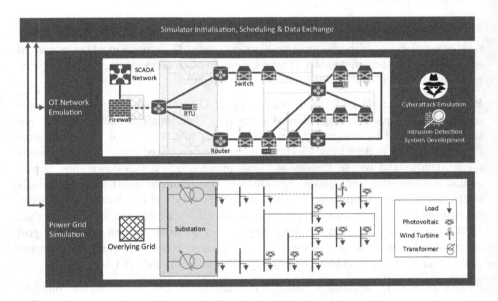

Fig. 7. MEDIT's co-simulation environment for digitized distribution grids to investigate cybersecurity incidents and develop cybersecurity technologies [18].

These technologies are deployed in a laboratory environment, and in a near-field environment at *Schleswig-Holstein Netz AG* in order to provide an improved technology readiness level and evaluate the integrability potential into real power systems.

2.4 Digital Transformation of Energy Business Models

The expansion of decentralized energy conversion systems (DEA) for generation, storage and consumption, which goes hand in hand with the energy transition, requires suitable integration strategies in order to ensure economic and reliable, but also sustainable energy system operation in the future. This creates the opportunity, but also the necessity, of new business models for different stakeholders.

According to a conceptual model of digitalization developed by the Business Informatics department of Fraunhofer FIT (cf. Fig. 8), there are three basic strategies which also apply to the energy sector.

Digital Transformation refers to the derivation of economically sensible and technically as well as organizationally feasible transformation paths towards the digitalization of traditional enterprises. The SynErgie initiative (cf. Sect. 2.2) provides many large-scale examples of industry-specific digital transformations but also a discussion of related market engineering and regulatory aspects, led by Fraunhofer FIT [19].

Genuine *Digital Business* addresses fundamentally new business models in the virtual world, which of course can also influence the physical world. Often, sharing settings are characterized by multi-sided markets in which not only money but also services are exchanged among partners [20]. Typical examples close to the energy sector are Sharing Economy start-ups in the energy and mobility sector which, despite their digital nature, indirectly also influence the physical energy market.

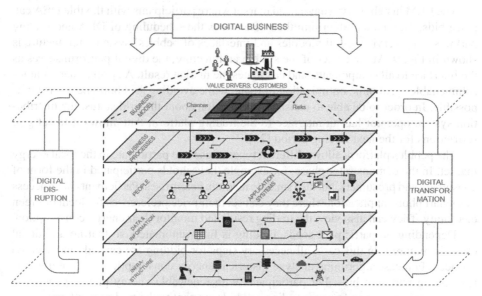

Fig. 8. Different business model strategies for digitization © Fraunhofer FIT.

Digital Disruption leads to the replacement of existing technologies, products, or services by digital innovations, in order to unlock the economic potential of new technologies.

In addition to already established aggregation approaches for the synergetic coordination of increasingly small-scale DEA (e.g. virtual power plants), decentralized approaches such as local energy markets (LEM) and neighborhood concepts are currently designed, simulated and demonstrated in the laboratory or in field trials. They include platforms for trading local energy or flexibility products, as well as alternative sharing or balancing approaches to incentivize the highest possible local resource allocation. Close collaboration with industry partners plays a central role in identifying and evaluating the resulting business models. Simulation models developed at the Fraunhofer Center for Digital Energy contribute to the identification of business models, for example by determining the potential of trading volumes in a LEM [21].

Project Example: Pebbles. The *pebbles* project (peer-to-peer energy trading based on blockchains) was realized by a consortium consisting of Allgäuer Überlandwerk GmbH, AllgäuNetz GmbH & Co. KG, Siemens AG, Hochschule Kempten, and Fraunhofer FIT. The goal of the project was to design, develop and field test a digital platform for peer-to-peer (P2P) trading of electrical energy and flexibility options at a local level. The resulting LEM is intended to reduce grid expansion, and enable citizens and small and medium enterprises to engage in energy and flexibility trading. The background hypothesis is that this would increase the acceptance for the deployment of decentralized energy systems and accelerate the energy transition, and reduce the load on long-distance energy transport [22].

The LEM in pebbles is a day-ahead market where participants with flexible DEA can place bids. The market algorithm then determines the scheduling of DEA and trading partners. An overview of all modules and interfaces of pebbles' system architecture is shown in Fig. 9. At the center of the system architecture, the digital platform serves as the interface to all components, and calculates the market result. A special market algorithm enables economic optimization of trade, while avoiding grid bottlenecks as far as possible. In order to be able to consider information about the grid status, the distribution system operator has an interface to the trading platform that allows it to set grid restrictions for the next trading period [23].

The pebbles platform allows different types of users to participate in the local energy market. In the demonstrator phase, for example, households participated in the form of consumers and prosumers, but also small to medium enterprises. Participants have access to a smart phone application where they can set their price preferences for local or green electricity. They can also view the trading result and monitor their energy consumption.

Depending on participant needs, bidding is fully automated, so that no additional effort is required. In this case, all necessary steps for bidding are carried out by cloud services. Forecast algorithms analyze historical energy consumption and submit corresponding purchase bids. For participants with renewable energy plants, generation forecasts are created and corresponding sell bids are sent to the trading platform.

Another special feature of the pebbles trading platform is that it can coordinate flexible assets by providing general information about them. After the market matching, the trading result is fed back to the controllable assets as a schedule by the energy management system located in the cloud. Participants with their own energy management system have the opportunity to trade their residuals on the local energy market and thus minimize their electricity costs and maximize revenues.

If participants cannot sell their electricity on the LEM or cannot cover their demand through the LEM, they have the possibility to trade with the energy supplier as a backup option. Thus, the power supply for all participants is ensured. After a trading phase is completed, automated billing is performed by smart contracts in a blockchain. If actual consumption or generation deviates from the contracted values, subsequent financial compensation would be required.

Six months of field testing in pebbles have shown that utility sales are reduced by up to 97% in a generation-dominated region. The need for new business models for utilities in the case of a rollout of LEMs becomes thus apparent. One possible business model could be to operate such a LEM platform, with customers paying a fee to participate in

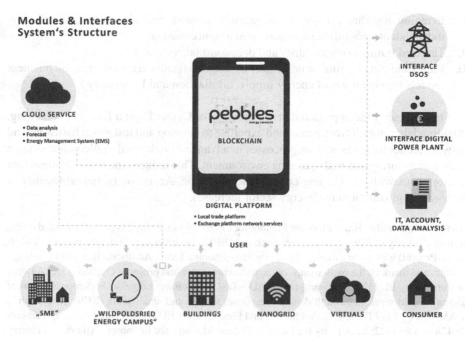

Fig. 9. Modules and Interfaces of pebbles' system architecture.

the LEM. At the same time, the digital platform offers important interfaces for opening up new business models, for example in the form of cloud services.

The field tests have shown that the ongoing digitalization has made LEMs realizable from a technical point of view. This offers added economic value by avoiding grid expansion. However, in order for LEMs to be deployed beyond research projects, the regulatory framework must be adapted by policymakers [24].

3 Impact

Digitization in the area of critical infrastructures calls for new solutions to make the associated risks manageable. By building on existing research infrastructures and the interdisciplinary collaboration of internationally respected research institutions, the interdisciplinary treatment of topics such as IT security, digitization and the financing of a sustainable energy supply can succeed.

Furthermore, the close cooperation of manufacturing and applying companies in cross-thematic future markets must be supported and a targeted and efficient development of products across the entire value chain of the critical energy system infrastructure must be enabled. Only this will enable international top-level research as well as a new type of education and training in the field of digitization of energy systems, which has the following special features:

7. Very short start-up time due to cooperation of respected research institutions ensures short-term realization of relevant results and technologies

8. Bringing together a large, cross-industry network provides access to industry-independent, cross-domain expertise in a future market
9. Targeted training of specialists and decision-makers
10. Rapid and direct diffusion or transfer of research results, technologies and business models into the areas of energy supply, digitization and IT security

This is exactly the approach that the Fraunhofer-Center Digital Energy is pursuing, providing laboratory infrastructure and expertise to develop and test novel hardware and software technologies as well as processes in advance of industrial implementation in a secure, trustworthy and real operating environment. This reduces the risk of undesirable developments with far-reaching consequences later on. Accordingly, the probability of successful digitization in the energy sector increases.

Acknowledgements. Build-up of the Fraunhofer Center Digital Energy is partially funded by the German Ministry of Education and Research (BMBF) as an immediate advance project (Sofort-Sofort-Projekt) within the national "Structure Strengthening Law". Additionally, we acknowledge funding, and thank all the participants, of the following individual projects: OneNet (One Network for Europe) by EU H2020 sub-program "TSO – DSO Consumer: Large-scale demonstrations of innovative grid services through demand response, storage and small-scale (RES) generation" ; SEAM4US by EU FPT (285408); PlaMES and Flex4Grid by EU H2020 under grant agreements 646428 and 863922; MEDIT by the German Federal Ministry for Economic Affairs and Energy (BMWi) reference 0350028. Pebbles by BMWi under Smart Service Welt II grant 01MD18003B; and SynErgie by the BMBF Kopernikus program.

References

1. United Nations: Paris Agreement. Paris (2015)
2. Schumann, K., Schwaeppe, H., Böttcher, L., et al.: Definition of common scenario framework, data/modelling requirements and use cases. PlaMES Deliverable 2.1 (2020). https://doi.org/10.18154/RWTH-2021-09943
3. German Bundesnetzagentur, EEG in numbers 2019, Stand 19.04.2021
4. CEDEC, EDSO, ENTSO-E, Eurelectic, and GEODE: TSO-DSO Report: An Integrated Approach to Active System Management (2019). https://www.entsoe.eu/news/2019/04/16/a-toolbox-for-tsos-and-dsos-to-make-use-of-new-system-and-grid-services/
5. Thie, N., Franken, M., Schwaeppe, M., et al.: Requirements for integrated planning of multi-energy systems. In: Proceedings IEEE ENERGYCON, pp. 696–701 (2020)
6. Müller, C., Hoffrichter, A., Wyrwoll, L., et al.: Modeling framework for planning and operation of multi-modal energy systems in the case of Germany. Appl. Energy **250**, 1132–1146 (2019)
7. Wilhelm, C., Schumann, K., Andres, M., et al.: A simulative framework for a multi-regional assessment of local energy markets – a case of large-scale electric vehicle deployment in Germany. Appl. Energy **299**, 117249 (2021)
8. Schumann, K., Schwaeppe, H., Böttcher, L., Hein, L., Hälsig, P.: Description of workflow coordination, PlaMES Deliverable 3.1 (2021). https://publications.rwth-aachen.de/record/834498
9. Monaci, M., Paronuzzi, P., Punzo, A., Vigo, D.: Analysis of problem structure and first concept of decomposition approach. PlaMES Deliverable 2.3 (2020). https://plames.eu/wp-content/uploads/2020/11/deliverableD2_3_stc.pdf

10. Schwaeppe, H., Moser, A., Paronuzzi, P., Monaci, M.: Generation and transmission expansion planning with respect to global warming potential. In: Proceedings IEEE Powertech (2021)
11. Schwaeppe, H., Böttcher, L., Franken, M., et al.: Mathematical formulation of the model. PlaMES Deliverable 2.2 (2020). https://doi.org/10.18154/RWTH-2021-09942
12. Casals, M., Gangolells, M., Forcada, N., et al.: SEAM4US – an intelligent energy management system for underground stations. Appl. Energy **166**, 150–164 (2016)
13. Kiljander, J., Gabrielcic, D., Werner-Kytölä, O., et al.: Residential flexibility management – a case study in distribution networks. IEEE Acceess **7**, 80902–80915 (2019). https://doi.org/10.1109/ACCESS.2019.2923069
14. Sauer, A., Abele, E., Buh, H-U.l (eds.): Energieflexibilität in der deutschen Industrie (SynErgie). Fraunhofer-Verlag, Stuttgart 2019
15. Bauernhansl, T., Bauer, D., et al.: Industrie 4.0 als befähiger der energieflexibilität. In: Sauer, A., Abele, E., Buhl, H.-U. (eds.) Energieflexibilität in der deutschen Industrie (SynErgie), pp. 245–310. Fraunhofer-Verlag, Stuttgart (2019)
16. Van der Velde, D., Henze, M., et al.: Methods for actors in the electric power system to prevent, detect and react to ICT attacks and failures. In: Proceedings IEEE Energy Conference, pp. 17–22 (2020)
17. Sen, Ö., van der Velde, D., et al.: Towards an approach to contextual detection of multi-stage coordinated cyberattacks in energy information systems. In: IEEE SEST (2021)
18. Van der Velde, D., Sen, Ö., et al.: Towards a scalable and flexible smart grid co-simulation environment to investigate communication infrastructures for resilient distribution grid operation. In: Proceedings IEEE SEST (2021)
19. Buhl, H.-U., Fridgen, G., Dufter, C., et al.: Industrielle energieflexibilität im energiesyystem. In: Sauer, A., Abele, E., Buhl, H.-U. (eds.) Energieflexibilität in der deutschen Industrie (SynErgie), pp. 127–194. Fraunhofer-Verlag, Stuttgart (2019)
20. Pfeiffer, A., Jarke, M.: Digital transformation within the eMobility market – learnings and insights from early market development. SmartER Europe, pp. 23–42 (2016). https://doi.org/10.1007/978-3-319-66553-5_2
21. Cramer, W., Schumann, K., Andres, M., et al.: A simulative framework for a multi-regional assessment of local energy markets – a case of large-scale electric vehicle deployment in Germany. Appl. Energy **299**, 117249 (2021)
22. Vasconcelos, M., Cramer, W., Schmitt, C., et al.: The pebbles project – enabling blockchain-based transactive energy trading of energy & flexibility within a regional market. In: Proceedings 25th International Conference on Electricity Distribution (CIRED), Madrid, paper 1313 (2019). https://cired-repository.org/handle/20.500.12455/36
23. Weinhardt, C., Mengelkamp, E., Cramer, W., et al.: How far along are local markets in the DACH+ region? A comparative market engineering approach. In: Proceeding. 10th International Conference Future Energy Systems (e-Energy 2019). ACM, pp. 544–549 (2019)
24. Klaus, J., Hilpert, J., et al.: Ein Plattform-Konzept für eine kostenoptimierte Energiewende mit Hilfe lokaler Energiemärkte. https://pebbles-projekt.de/wp-content/uploads/2018/05/pebbles_Whitepaper-2.pdf

Author Index

Printed in the United States
by Baker & Taylor Publisher Services.

Printed in the United States
by Baker & Taylor Publisher Services